Fundamentals in Handwriting Recognition

NATO ASI Series

Advanced Science Institutes Series

A series presenting the results of activities sponsored by the NATO Science Committee, which aims at the dissemination of advanced scientific and technological knowledge, with a view to strengthening links between scientific communities.

The Series is published by an international board of publishers in conjunction with the NATO Scientific Affairs Division

A Life Sciences **B Physics**	Plenum Publishing Corporation London and New York
C Mathematical and Physical Sciences **D Behavioural and Social Sciences** **E Applied Sciences**	Kluwer Academic Publishers Dordrecht, Boston and London
F Computer and Systems Sciences **G Ecological Sciences** **H Cell Biology** **I Global Environmental Change**	Springer-Verlag Berlin Heidelberg New York London Paris Tokyo Hong Kong Barcelona Budapest

NATO-PCO DATABASE

The electronic index to the NATO ASI Series provides full bibliographical references (with keywords and/or abstracts) to more than 30000 contributions from international scientists published in all sections of the NATO ASI Series. Access to the NATO-PCO DATABASE compiled by the NATO Publication Coordination Office is possible in two ways:

- via online FILE 128 (NATO-PCO DATABASE) hosted by ESRIN, Via Galileo Galilei, I-00044 Frascati, Italy.
- via CD-ROM "NATO Science & Technology Disk" with user-friendly retrieval software in English, French and German (© WTV GmbH and DATAWARE Technologies Inc. 1992).

The CD-ROM can be ordered through any member of the Board of Publishers or through NATO-PCO, Overijse, Belgium.

Series F: Computer and Systems Sciences Vol. 124

Fundamentals in Handwriting Recognition

Edited by

Sebastiano Impedovo

Dipartimento di Informatica, Università degli Studi di Bari
Via Amendola 173, I-70126 Bari, Italy

Springer-Verlag
Berlin Heidelberg New York London Paris Tokyo
Hong Kong Barcelona Budapest
Published in cooperation with NATO Scientific Affairs Division

Proceedings of the NATO Advanced Study Institute on Fundamentals in Handwriting Recognition, held at Château de Bonas, France, June 21–July 3, 1993

CR Subject Classification (1991): I.5.4, I.5, I.2.7, I.2

ISBN-13:978-3-642-78648-8 e-ISBN-13:978-3-642-78646-4
DOI: 10.1007/978-3-642-78646-4

CIP data applied for.

Softcover reprint of the hardcover 1st edition 1994

Typesetting: Camera ready by authors
SPIN: 10130653 45/3140 - 5 4 3 2 1 0 - Printed on acid-free paper

Preface

For many years researchers in the field of Handwriting Recognition were considered to be working in an area of minor importance in Pattern Recognition. They had only the possibility to present the results of their research at general conferences such as the ICPR or publish their papers in journals such as some of the IEEE series or PR, together with many other papers generally oriented to the more promising areas of Pattern Recognition.

The series of International Workshops on Frontiers in Handwriting Recognition and International Conferences on Document Analysis and Recognition together with some special issues of several journals are now fulfilling the expectations of many researchers who have been attracted to this area and are involving many academic institutions and industrial companies. But in order to facilitate the introduction of young researchers into the field and give them both theoretically and practically powerful tools, it is now time that some high level teaching schools in handwriting recognition be held, also in order to unite the foundations of the field.

Therefore it was my pleasure to organize the NATO Advanced Study Institute on *Fundamentals in Handwriting Recognition* that had its origin in many exchanges among the most important specialists in the field, during the International Workshops on Frontiers in Handwriting Recognition.

This NATO Advanced Study Institute on *Fundamentals in Handwriting Recognition* took place from June 21st to July 3rd, 1993, at Chateau de Bonas, a magnificent place near Toulouse (France), which offered the most comfortable environment for study and friendly discussion, essential for the success of this NATO ASI.

The aim of the Institute was to focus on the fundamental tools and ideas that are generally used in the handwriting recognition field.

The most important algorithms for data acquisition, preprocessing, feature extraction, classification, the most common data base, and devices for on-line and off-line recognition were presented. The role of parallel machines and special networks in solving problems in the field was also discussed during the school.

A total of 78 participants attended the school: 18 lecturers and 60 students. They came from 15 different countries: Austria, Bulgaria, Canada, Czechoslovakia, France, Germany, Italy, Japan, Korea, Portugal, Russia, The Netherlands, Turkey, the United Kingdom, and the United States of America.

The lectures that were presented are included in this book, which consists of nine parts, each one including one or more of the main lectures. A few papers presented by participants in the school, reporting interesting results or original comments on the subject, have also been included in the book.

I am particularly grateful to NATO for supporting this Advanced Study Institute and to the Dipartimento di Informatica - University of Bari, CNR (Consiglio Nazionale delle Ricerche), Tecnopolis CSATA Novus Ortus and Elsag Bailey s.p.a. for their sponsorship.

I also wish to thank Prof. Jean-Claude Simon for his helpful suggestions in organizing the Institute, Prof. Andrew Corin Downton for coordinating the referee committee and his suggestions in arranging this book, Dr. Giovanni Dimauro for his cooperation in the organization of the school, and Mrs. Francoise Simon for her constant, attentive presence during the meeting.

November 1993 S. Impedovo

Contents

Introduction

In the first part, Sebastiano Impedovo introduces the field of handwriting recognition as a whole, outlining all the component areas where research has been undertaken over the last 20-30 years. These include data acquisition and preprocessing of both on-line and off-line handwriting, character and numeral recognition, cursive word recognition, and signature verification. All these areas are then examined in more depth in subsequent parts of the book.

The field of handwritten character recognition, presented in Part 2, is the longest established branch of handwriting recognition, and therefore also the aspect which has been studied in most depth. In his historical review of research in this field, Shunji Mori defines character recognition in terms of four general categories of recognition difficulty. He then presents a taxonomy of key statistical and structural pattern recognition techniques which have been applied to character recognition. It is interesting to note that many of these techniques were first reported in the 1960s, and performance improvements achieved more recently are largely the result of improvements in data quality and attention to detail in implementation.

In his review of developments in the automatic recognition of handwritten characters, Ching Suen pays close attention to human mechanisms of character recognition, since this process provides useful guidance in the choice of features for character recognition which are invariant to common forms of handwriting distortion. He also notes the improvements in performance which have recently been reported by several groups of researchers, investigating combined algorithms based upon the use of several independent 'experts'. It seems possible that such approaches will soon be able to recognise characters better than humans in a context-free situation.

Patrick Wang then broadens the field of character recognition to include artificial intelligence techniques and semantic networks, as well as introducing the particular problem of recognising Chinese characters. Giovanni Dimauro focuses on one particular class of feature space, that provided by orthogonal transforms, and particularly Discrete Fourier Transforms. The application of such transforms is illustrated using a number of examples from the character recognition field. Finally, Bernhard Boser focuses on classification methods which can be applied once features have been extracted from the character, and, after reviewing the field generally, presents a specific approach - the optimal margin classifier, developed as part of his own research.

In Part 3, recognition approaches for complete handwritten words are presented. Jean-Claude Simon starts by comparing some of the characteristics of human word recognition with those of (current) machines, and notes that humans have evolved recognition methods which are much more robust. Some of the context utilised by humans to achieve robustness can be inferred by studying certain perceptual disabilities which occur rarely in humans. Hans-Leo Teulings then introduces a variety of motor models of handwriting production, and shows how the signal to noise ratio for different features can be estimated, so as to identify invariant features useful for recognising cursively written words. N. Gorsky also identifies the differences between the robust word recognition learnt by humans and the more brittle performance achieved by machines, and describes a holographic representation technique for handwritten words which allows word matching even with very degraded input data. He then shows how word recognition performance can be further improved by adding additional features, whose *a priori* probabilities can be easily estimated for a small dictionary of words. He concludes that it may be more worthwhile to approach word recognition by combining information from a number of simple feature extraction techniques than to continue to try to refine a single general approach.

The techniques described in Part 3 are illustrated by three short papers contributed by workshop participants. Torsten Caesar and colleagues from Daimler-Benz describe work on recognition of unconstrained handwriting using statistical methods which has achieved a performance of 80% recognition on a 200 word dictionary and 60% on a 1000 word dictionary. Mohammed Cheriet describes work to segment cursively written words based upon visual features. In contrast, Gilles Houle adopts a hierarchical approach to handwritten word segmentation.

It is now generally accepted that high-performance recognition of handwritten words will only be achieved by the use of context. Therefore Part 4 extends the coverage of handwritten word recognition to explore contextual methods which can be used to augment performance. Eric Lecolinet and Olivier Baret present a comprehensive review of contextual methods, covering both wholistic and analytical strategies. They introduce a wide range of techniques and paradigms, including dynamic programming, Markov models, and linguistic methods. Two of these topics, Markov models and linguistic methods, have been widely applied, and so are explored in more depth in papers by Michel Gilloux and Jonathan Hull respectively. Finally in this part, three papers presented by participants are used to illustrate the techniques described. Hendrawan and Downton's paper describes the use of wholistic feature spotting techniques for verifying handwritten addresses against postcodes; In-Gyu Koh's paper shows how a variety of linguistic techniques have been used to improve recognition rates for Korean handwriting; and finally Dimo T. Dimov presents an approximate string matching method for handwriting recognition post processing using a dictionary.

Neural networks have been widely applied to many pattern recognition problems; Part 5 reviews their application to handwriting recognition. Yoh-Han Pao and Gwang-Hoon Park present a general introduction to neural networks which focuses first upon the development of training algorithms for neural networks which are more efficient than the standard back-propagation method, and then on the application of this approach to recognition of a limited vocabulary of handwritten words. Two participants' papers illustrate the range of current work on neural networks for handwriting recognition. David Price and Stephane Knerr present a neural network for digit recognition, which is based upon 45 single-layer networks trained to distinguish pairs of classes of digits. In contrast, Andrew Senior gives an overview of a complete neural network-based system designed to recognise cursively written words. The network is trained to spot a variety of key features in handwriting, for example: i dots, turning points, descenders and ascenders, and loops.

Computer programs written to implement algorithms within the field of handwriting recognition are computationally intensive. Real applications have to meet demanding real-time performance constraints; and so it is natural that research and development effort is applied not just to algorithms, but also to the design of supporting hardware architectures. In Part 6, Andy Downton presents a review of architectures for handwriting recognition both in the development and application environments. The review focuses particularly upon parallel processing, and presents an approach to generalising parallel processing for embedded applications within the fields of image analysis, pattern recognition and computer vision.

Over the past 30 years, many handwriting databases have been collected, and some have been widely used. Data quality is now very much higher than it used to be, but many papers still report results based upon performance assessment using small laboratory databases, which are not directly comparable with any standard, nor are they representatative of the performance which would be achieved in practical use. In Part 7, Jonathan Hull therefore outlines the requirements for generating realistic databases, and reviews several databases which are widely used and available to researchers.

Part 8 reviews the field of signature recognition/verification, which is often required in OCR forms processing applications, cheque validation, credit card transactions, etc. A wide presentation, ranging from signature generation models to practical systems, is given by Rejean Plamondon. Giuseppe Pirlo presents a general review of algorithms and systems for signature verification. Fathallah Nouboud then presents a participant's paper showing how a variety of independent features may be combined to improve performance of a signature verification system.

In the final part of the book, Kunio Sakai and his colleagues show how OCR algorithms are being applied commercially in Japan, where around $250 million dollars per year is already spent on OCR systems for handwritten forms processing, in areas such as cheque processing, insurance forms, mail orders, tax returns, surveys, etc. The commercial success of OCR in Japan owes much to cultural traditions as well as to the natural Japanese enthusiasm for new technology, but there is no doubt that many of the OCR applications already pioneered in Japan will also soon be introduced in Europe and North America. In the final participant's paper, Annick Leroy describes a novel application for OCR in the future, that of a pen-based music editor.

The simplistic idealised models of OCR and on-line character recognition which were pioneered in the early 1960s have now given way to multi-level systems-oriented approaches, which are beginning to be successfully applied to substantial commercial applications. Handwriting recognition may at last be on the verge of becoming commonplace, after many false dawns over the last 30 years. This book provides an invaluable reference to the techniques being used to achieve this transformation.

Part 1

Introduction and overview of field

Frontiers in Handwriting Recognition

Sebastiano Impedovo

Dipartimento di Informatica, Università degli Studi di Bari
via Amendola 173, 70126 Bari, Italy

1. Introduction

The evolution of computer front panels and punch tapes and punch cards to teletype interfaces and the keyboards of modern personal computers shows that the problem of a faster man-machine interaction has been a great scientific and technological challenge since the origin of computers. During the last decades many efforts have been made in the technological field to design special peripheral devices such as the graphic tablet, the scanner, the mouse, electronic ink and so on. Furthermore, efforts have also been made to study models of writing generation motor and recognition algorithms. But in spite of technological and architectural progress made in the field of computers, the problem of a friendly interaction between man and computer at least at the same friendly level that exists with a sheet of paper and a pencil, still remains unresolved.

Unlike in past times, today the attention of many industrial companies has been captured by these topics. This may be due to the stimulus provoked by the Workshops on Frontiers in Handwriting Recognition and by the International Conferences on Document Analysis and Recognition, and mainly to the fact that pen-based man-machine interaction will easily capture everybody's interest in computers.

This tutorial presents the main problems in handwriting recognition and the new research frontiers in the scientific community, such as the significance of linguistic and contextual information in handwriting recognition also for adaptative preprocessing and for postprocessing, and the problems related to human and computer behaviour in recognition. It consists of four related sections dealing with: Data acquisition and preprocessing, Character and numeral recognition, Cursive word recognition, Signature verification systems.

2. Data Acquisition and Preprocessing

Data acquisition devices for handwriting recognition systems can be divided in two main classes as shown in fig. 1: the class of off-line devices and the class of on-line devices. Generally the off-line devices are scanners. There are three different types: the flatbed scanners, the paper-fed scanners and the handscanners. An extensive presentation of these devices and the discussion of related problems is reported in the paper of ref. [1]. The class of on-line scanners includes both digitizing tablets and tablet-display devices. There are many types of digitizing tablets using various technologies including electromagnetic/electrostatic, pressure sensitive and acoustic sensing in air medium types.

Since in the last few years one of the main goals in computer development has been to make the computer more accessible to non experts, the idea of using handwriting to interface has become extremely attractive. Nowadays, along with the recent advances in packaging technology, a low-priced unified tablet-display device is available for on-line handwriting acquisition. It allows the achievement of a very intelligent "paper and pencil-like" computer interface. The unified tablet-display device, which is roughly the size and the weight of a book, has an electronic stylus which provides electronic ink: an electronic tablet accurately captures the coordinates of pen-tip movements, electronic ink gives the trace of the pen-tip on the screen surface, giving an immediate feedback to the writer.

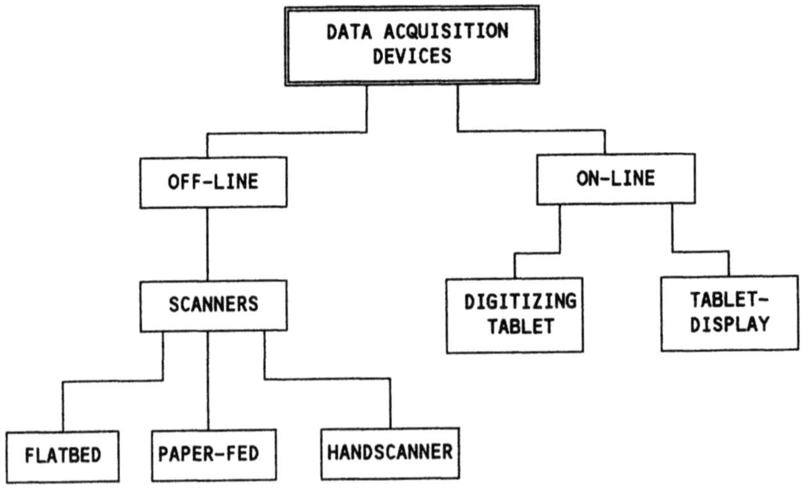

Figure 1. Data Acquisition Devices

The preprocessing algorithms provide the acquired data in a suitable form for further processing. In this phase the input image is generally cleaned from noise and errors caused by the acquisition process. A great number of well-defined algorithms for signal processing are currently used during the preprocessing phase. However, in handwriting recognition, the preprocessing deals with more specific problems than in other fields of pattern recognition.

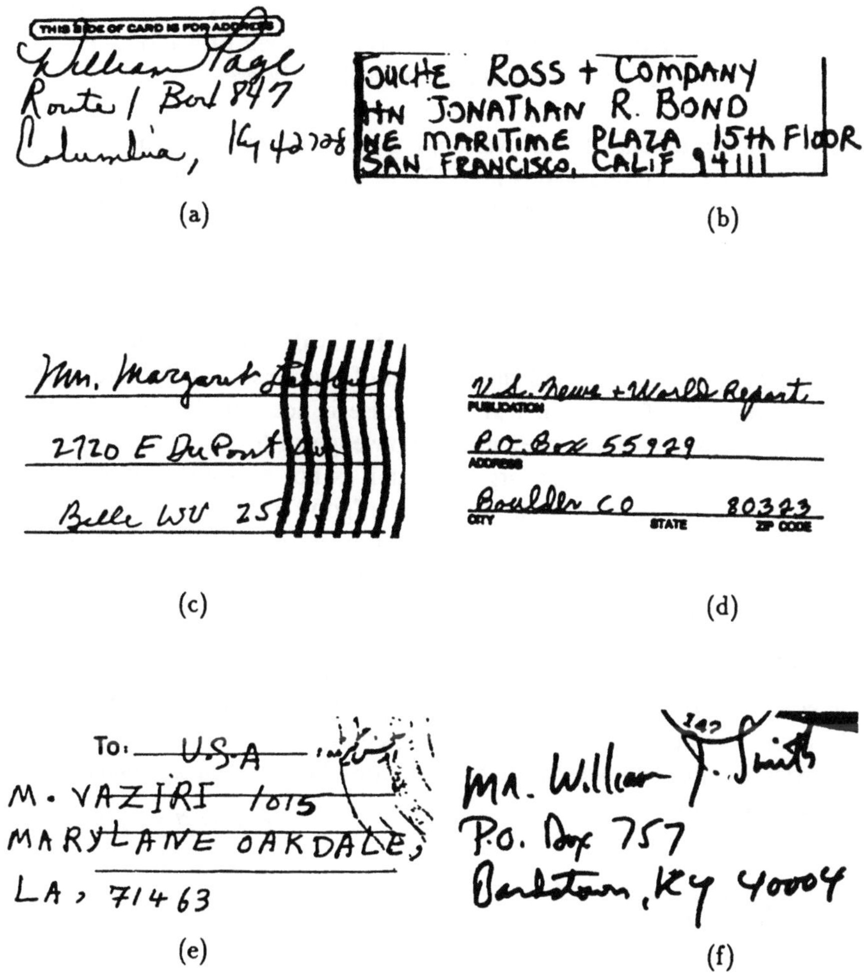

Figure 2. Real examples from mail pieces

The removal of the box in which off-line characters can be included has been faced amongst others by Casey and Takahashi [2] in their work on the data base of the National Institute of Standards and Technology (NIST). The NIST data base contains about one million handprinted alphabetic and numeric characters. The algorithm of Casey and Takahashi first locates the box, using its line characteristics to distinguish it from other image data. Often the characters overlie the box; in this case the algorithm tracks intersections with character patterns and does not erase such intersections to avoid further degradation of character patterns. Further algorithms for cleaning noise are also used: the main body of pixels is located and its envelope is computed. Stray clumps of pixels are erased providing their size is small and their distance from the envelope is sufficiently great.

A more complex problem of text overlapping with non-textual strokes has been encountered by Govindaraju and Srihari [3] in reading handwritten addresses on mail pieces. In this case one encounters underlined words and postal marks running across addresses. Some typical examples are shown in fig. 2.

Govindaraju and Srihari have developed a pre-processor to separate text from extraneous contours. Their preprocessing can be divided into two parts: first the detection of the noise and second the removal of the noise and the return of the text. In fact, the identification of text from noise is not a trivial problem. When humans read a text with noise, they use a knowledge of text in perceiving part of the image. However, it has been argued that it is not necessary to use domain knowledge to perform segmentation. In fact, the "good" continuation principle can be applied to intersect boundaries to arrive at perceptually plausible segmentation. In practice the rule of "good" continuity is applied by following the path of minimal curvature change. In some cases the removal of underlining destroys the lower horizontal strokes of certain characters, creating ambiguity in the interpretation of the remaining part of the character. For example, the following capital letter pairs may get confused: B-P, E-F, I-L, U-II and so on. Figure 3 shows a typical example of ambiguous patching: "TT" could be "II" depending on whether the underline is patched back on the characters. Such cases must be resolved by matching with words in a dictionary.

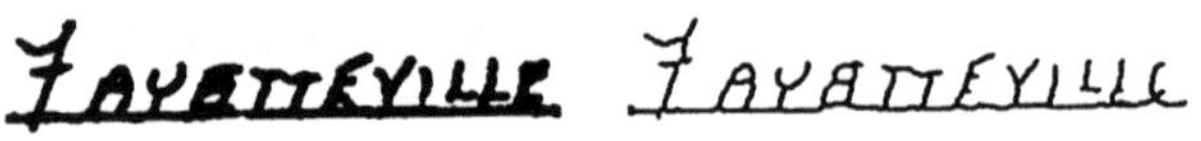

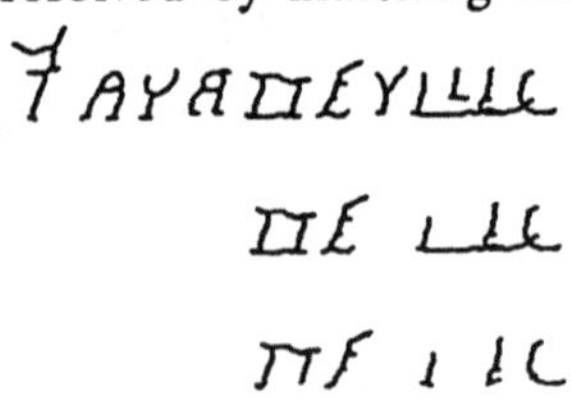

(a) (b) (c)

Figure 3. Patching: (a) FAYETTEVILLE (b) thinned word (c) ambiguous patching.

The thin line representation of the traced line is another preprocessing problem, that arises in several applications of handwriting recognition. Thinning methods can be divided into two categories: pixelwise and non-pixelwise. Pixelwise methods consider the digitized image, representing the plain as a mesh, where each square element is a pixel. Pattern image is locally and iterately processed, so the process is very slow and can lead to problems such as excessive erosion. The new non-pixelwise methodology, presented by Nishida Suzuki and Mori [4], decomposes a line picture into regular regions, singular regions and end-point regions, according to the classification of ordinary points, branch points and end-points. Each region can be represented by a graph node labeled with a number. Thus the nodes are connected to make a region adiancy graph as shown in fig. 4. On the basis of this decomposition, the thinning is treated as an inference problem of singular regions from the adjacent regular regions. In fact, for a regular region, thin line representation can be allowed easily enough from the analysis of its contour.

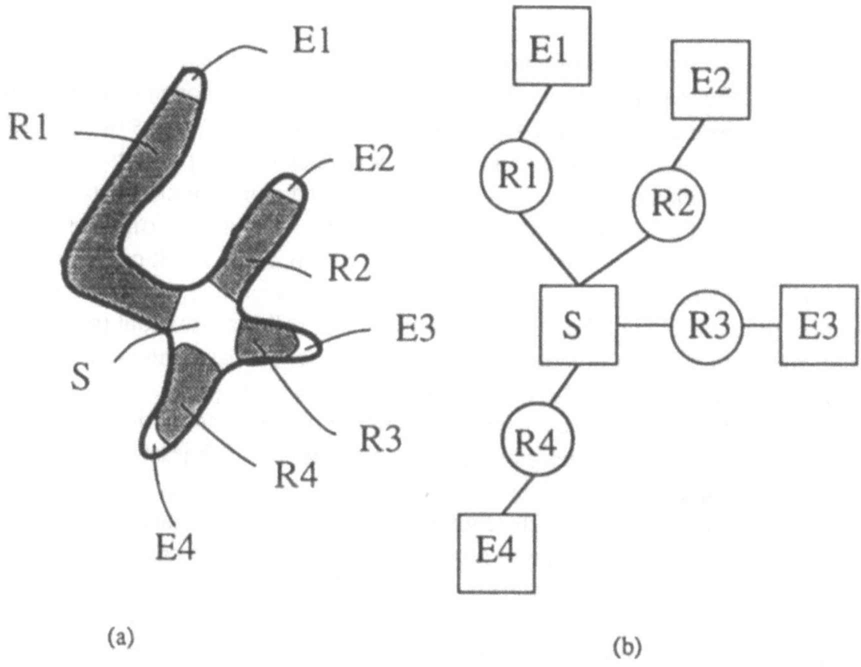

Figure 4. (a) Decomposition of a line picture into regular regions (R1,R2,R3 and R4), end point regions (E1,E2,E3 and E4), and singular Region (S). (b) the region adjacency graph.

However, without any doubt, one of the greatest preprocessing problems in handwriting recognition is the segmentation. The segmentation process consists of the extraction of the writing units from handwriting. The units can be elementary strokes in character and numeral recognition or they can be entire characters in the recognition of entire words in cursive script recognition. The segmentation processes use spatial information for off-line systems, but temporal information can also be used to detect the writing units in on-line handwriting recognition systems.

In handwriting recognition, the performance of the systems in terms of both recognition accuracy and speed are strongly dependent on the correct segmentation of the handwritten trace [5,6,7]. The strategic importance of the segmentation techniques of radicals, characters, words and sentences in Chinese handwriting recognition is also stressed by Liu and Tai [8], Tai, Liu and Zhang [9] and Shiau, Kung, Hsieh, Chen and Kao [10]. In fact Chinese characters are composed of substructures called "radicals". Each radical is composed of strokes and each stroke of line-segments.

In this field, the recent works of Casey-Takahashi [2] and Fenrich [11] suggest new algorithms for the segmentation of off-line characters. The former suggest the following supervised algorithm for segmenting handprinted characters of the NIST database: an initial pattern separation is done by connected components and, in an attempt to mend broken characters, adjacent connected components are combined into single images, if they meet with criteria based on size and location. Most often a connected component is a single complete character pattern, but it can also be an instance of touching characters. The detection of merged characters and the verification that the obtained segmentation is correct follows a manual process. In fact the final stage is interactive. An image editor displays the sequence of segmented patterns in small subsets on a display screen. The operator examines the characters to verify that they are correctly segmented and assigns an identity to each of them. Each time the identities assigned to the sequence of characters previously processed, are displayed above the following segmented patterns with the same sequence. If the characters are well segmented and the identities are correct, then the operator merely enters a carriage return and the patterns are accepted with the suggested identities. If the segmentation is correct, but the characters do not accord with the overhead sequence of identifiers, the operator relabels them by entering new alphabetic symbols at the keyboard. A third possibility is that one or more of the characters is missegmented. In this case the operator enters special symbols that invoke further processing. The kind of processing to be invoked is "join to the left", "join to the right", "delete noise pattern" and "separate touching characters". Results of the editing algorithm are then redisplayed and editing may be repeated iteratively until no more editing symbols are entered.

Conversely to the supervised segmentation approach of Casey, Fenrich [11] proposes an unsupervised system for numeric string segmentation. He points out three basic difficulties in the problem of separating alphanumeric strings: identification of multiple character components, determination of the number of characters in these components, and separation of the identified components into the correct number of characters. For those components with more than one character, four multiple splitting strategies are applied in sequence. They are the histogram method, the upper-lower contour method, the upper-contour method, and the lower-contour method.

- In the histogram method, the vertical density projections provide the features used in histogram splitting. The number of pixels in each column in the neighborhood are summed and the minimal sum is located. The column with the minimal value becomes a candidate for a vertical split through the component.

- The upper-lower contour method utilizes the upper and lower contours of the component as determind by the first and the last foreground pixel in each column. A successful split will be made by connecting the valley to the peak with a dissecting line.If the peak or the valley are not found then this method fails.

- The upper contour method works on valleys in the upper contour. Location of an upper contour valley and a local minimum within this valley start a splitting technique called modified hit-and-deflect. Starting from the point at the pixel in the valley minimum, if the point is foreground, then it is on the cut and the point moves down one row. If the pixels to the left and the right of the point are both background or foreground then the point moves down one row. Otherwise, there is one foreground pixel on one side and one background pixel on the other side. In this case, no cut point is assigned, the point is moved toward the foreground pixel, and the process continues to trace a monotonic sequence toward the bottom of the component.

- The lower contour method performs the same operation as the upper contour splitter, except that the lower contour splitter runs from a maximum in the peak on the lower contour to the top of the image. Thus, the cut is performed from bottom to top.

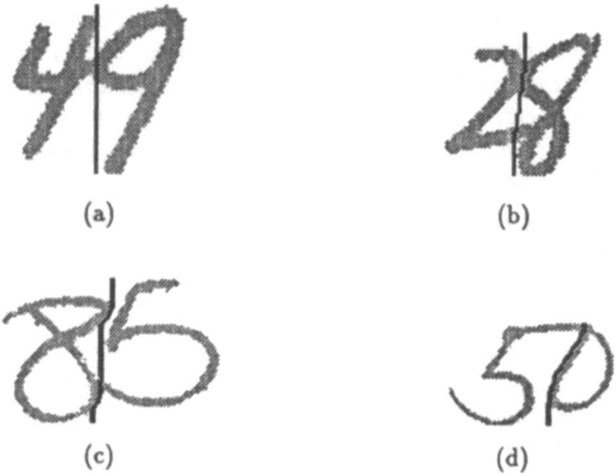

Figure 5. Examples of character splitting: (a) Histogram method, (b) Upper-lower contour method, (c) Upper contour method, (d) Lower contour method.

It should be noted that these approaches are based on the fundamental consideration that the density of pattern pixels in those areas of the image containing significant patterns (characters, numerals etc.) is generally much greater than the density of pixels in areas which contain meaningless patterns (for instance ligatures). Figure 5 shows some examples of character splitting.

A more complex task is, however, the segmentation of handwritten words. Holt, Beglou and Datta [12] point out that traditional approaches based on vertical segmentation in the direction of local minima of the upper profile of the word fail when slanted words are considered. Thus, they propose a new approach based on segmentation boundaries rather than segmentation points. Each segmentation boundary is defined following clockwise the contour of the word from each local maximun to the corresponding local minimum breaking the word at an appropriate splitting point. Some euristics for correct identification of local maximum and minimum points are also given to avoid unsatisfactory segmentation boundaries.

In the same field of word segmentation, many systems use the "divide and conquer" method of chopping the input pattern into segments and attempting to recognize them as components of a word. Some systems try to identify strokes, others try to identify letters or more complex shapes as groups of letters. In the work of Hull,

Ho, Favata, Govindaraju and Srihari [13] for off-line cursive word recognition, the segmentation stage operates by first estimating a number of alternative segmentation points based on the analysis of structural features. The image between two such points is then normalized. Each of them is compared to a database of templates. On the basis of this matching procedure, the most probable segmentation is found. In the work of Fujisaki, Beigi, Tappert, Ukelson and Wolf [14] for on-line recognition, the different segmentation techniques on three different levels of writing have been evaluated. The first level of writing is the spaced-discrete writing while the other two are run-on discrete writing. Compared to the second level, the third level uses script-shaped characters and has more overlapping of strokes. As regards the segmentation methods, the first method corresponds to the segmentation strategy that uses an x-axis projected gap between strokes. Characters are segmented where the gap between shadows of two strokes exceeds a predefined writer-independent threshold. The second method corresponds to the segmentation strategy that uses actual two dimension distances between strokes. The distance between two strokes is defined as the minimum of the distances between constituent points of each stroke. Characters are segmented when the distance between two strokes exceeds a predefined writer independent threshold. The third method corresponds to the proposed "recognition-then-segmentation" strategy based on generation-and-test. In this method the segmentation decision involves the analysis of stroke shapes and verification of the character shape. The result shows that the recognition-then-segmentation strategy performs well in various ranges of writing, whereas the other segmentation methods do not work for writing without sufficient separation between characters. Unfortunately, the verification of each hypothesis needs time-expensive post-processing procedures that make the segmentation process very difficult.

In order to minimize the possible segmentation hypothesis in on-line applications, a new method has been proposed. It aims to produce a list of segments for those input samples that, compared with the number of writing styles, only vary slightly in formation. Therefore a set of criteria, based on the different speed of the pen during the process of a character writing and during the process of the writing of pieces of handwritten trace between two characters, have been proposed. Higgins and Ford [15] point out how the wide variety of handwriting styles has prohibited up to now the possibility of using pen-driven interfaces without training the system. They consider the cusp or sharp corner to be the major features of the script affected by speed of writing. Therefore the basic idea utilized in this research is, as fig. 6 shows, the deformation of the cusp, whereby a cusp becomes a loop or hump and vice-versa, because this deformation represents one of the main features of individuality between writers.

So they propose a new method of consistent segmentation, flexible enough to be incorporated in many on line cursive script recognition systems. The method attempts to create a script sample considering the copy-book style that the writer learnt at school.

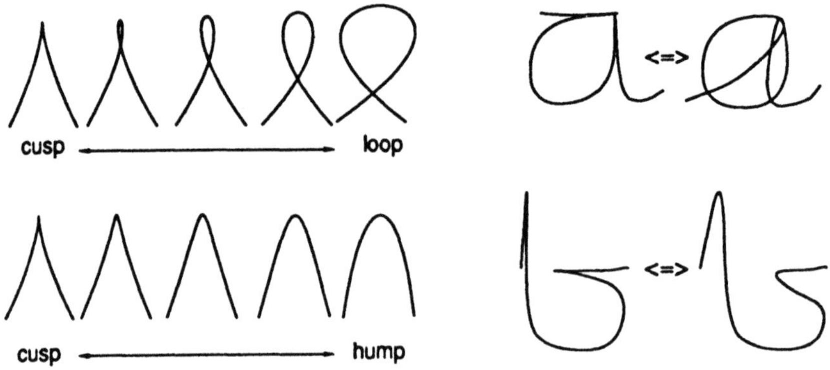

Figure 6. Loop-cusp-hump deformation

Since there are a limited number of copy-book styles, if we can somehow map the graphical representation of the writing which appears on the page to the theoretical representation of the copy-book style, the great variety of personal styles may be considerably reduced. The algorithm detects the possible segmentation points in the case of (see fig. 7):

- *Intersection*: Wherever a stroke crosses its own path to form a closed loop this is defined as an intersection. A possible segmentation point is marked at the digitized point nearest to the intersection at the beginning of the loop and nearest to the intersection at the end of the loop.
- *Cusp*: Wherever there is a discontinuity in the slope of the stroke, i.e. where there is a sharp point, this is defined as a cusp. A cusp is treated as if it were an intersection with an infinitesimally small loop, and so has two superimposed possible segmentation points with a zero length segment in between.
- *Point of Inflection*: Wherever there is a sign change in the angle of curvature, this is defined as a point of inflection. A possible segmentation point is recorded at each point of inflection.
- *End-Point*: Each pen-down or pen-up is replaced by a pseudo-cusp with the corresponding two possible segmentation points and zero-length segment.

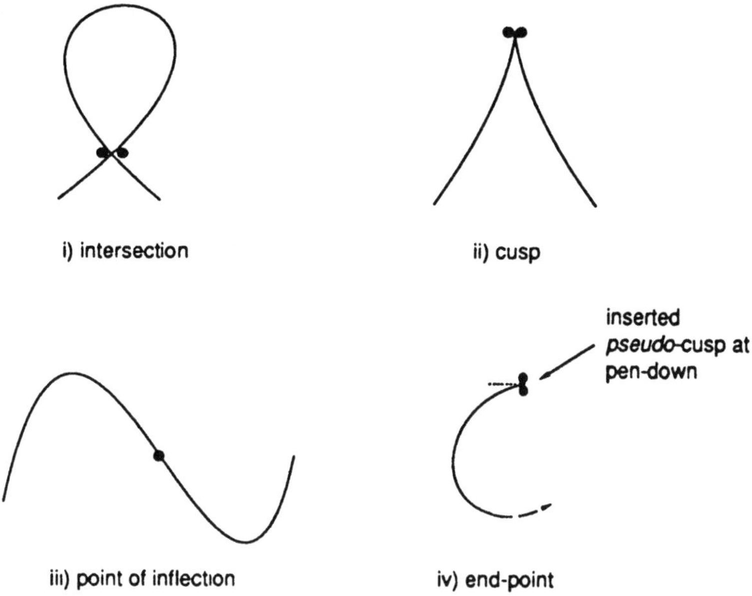

Figure 7. Possible segmentation points.

The segmentation based on these points works well for carefully drawn words, but often it fails in practice, due to two problems. Firstly, it is common that the loops overlap each other within a word. This causes a large number of superfluous intersections and loops to be identified. Secondly, straight lines within the script often wobble by more than the threshold set by the short segments between them. To alleviate the first problem Higgins and Ford consider a simplified model of the motion of the pen during cursive writing. Following this model the fingers move the pen slightly in the horizontal and vertical directions to form the characters, perhaps as they might form separate characters, and the whole hand wrist and arm move slowly from left to right as the writing progresses. Therefore, multiple intersections within a stroke are caused when the horizontal motion of the writing hand is fairly slow, so that the script overlaps itself. If the hand were moving faster in the horizontal direction, or if the paper were moving from right to left, the strokes would not overlap. If we superimpose a time motion in the horizontal direction, we can simulate this increased speed of hand movement. So, if a stroke with multiple intersections is stretched along the horizontal axis with respect to time, by adding an increasing amount to the horizontal coordinate of each plausible segmentation point, the relevant intersections disappear leaving just the important intersections. This allows one to determine the main segmentation points. The second problem, concerning straight line wobbles, can be alleviated by examining the very short segments of the handwriting. If either the segment directly preceding or the segment directly following the short segment is not a loop or a cusp, the segment is considered a wobble and the possible segmentation point of inflection, which define the short segment, are deleted. The segment is then added to the preceding or following segment. This segmentation procedure allows one to split the text into segments which are easy to characterize. Higgins and Ford identify the shapes of a segment as: "closed loop", where the segmentation points occupy the same physical coordinates, but the connecting stroke is non-zero in length; "hump", where the bounding segmentation points are separated; "cusp", where the bounding segmentation points occupy the same physical coordinates, but the connecting stroke is zero in length.

3. Character and Numeral Recognition

Character recognition is the field of handrwiting recognition which has been most investigated up to now for two reasons:

- firstly, because the problem of character recognition is common to both handwritten and printed matter and it is well known that both industry and the scientific community are interested in solving the problem of character reading;
- secondly, because solutions to the character recognition problem can be achieved using a classic pattern recognition approach to feature selection, feature extraction, learning development and classification.

Recently, Sakai, Asami and Tanabe [16] have discussed the aspects of system environment and data flow in handwriting recognition. They point out that, along with the spread of computers, the demand for the prompt and accurate input of a volume of source data is rapidly growing. A high performance OCR system promises to meet this demand. However, only a small part of the source data can be dealt with by current OCR systems, as they still have many restrictions. In this field, current user requirements can be divided into five classes: host computer interface class (the OCR data entry system is a component of the information processing system that the user currently has), operational condition class (the OCR data entry system is usable in an ordinary office work environment in such a way that the user PC/WS can be employed for both daily work and OCR data entry), paper handling capability class (the OCR mechanism is able to handle OCR forms printed on ordinary paper of various sizes), input form flexibility class (removal of individual writing boxes and relaxation of drop-out color restrictions), recognition performance class (omnifont recognition, unconstrained handwritten character recognition and minimum recognition error). The key techniques necessary to cope with the user requirements can be divided into four classes, according to standard OCR system configurations. In the control block class, the most important item is the packaging technique for the OCR control software into DFS (defacto standard) PC/WS. This technique enables the development of an open OCR system, that runs under DFS operating system such as UNIX, OS/2, MS-DOS. In the scanning block class, the transportation mechanism must be reorganized, aiming at reliable handling of thin plane sheets of paper without crumpling them and, in the mixed size case, the real time paper size detection technique and format identification technique are necessary. In the segmentation block class, the free pitch segmentation technique (to cope with the requirement for no writing box), form line detection and the separation technique (to cope with the drop out color free requirement) are to be developed. Finally, two basic problems must be solved: omnifont recognition and free style handwritten character recognition.

	Features			
Methods of feature extraction	Gray level	Stroke density	Stroke direction	Relation between segments
Projection	stroke domain [8]	stroke density multiple features (Fujitsu) [19]	stroke direction	global direction density
Peripheral	peripheral feature [12]	density feature		peripheral direction
Local	mesh pattern [12]	local line density [23]	direction pattern matching (ETL) (IBM-Japan)	structured segment matching (Mitsubishi) [16], [18]
Structure integration	background analysis	stroke density direction	relative structure matching (NEC) [17]	cellular feature (ETL, Sanyo) [14]
Expansion function	complex similarity (Toshiba) [15]			complex structure similarity (Toshiba) [13]

Table 1. Pattern matching method

In the field of character and numeral recognition, Yamamoto, Yamada and Saito point out that two methods are generally adopted [17]: pattern matching and structural analysis. Well-known pattern matching techniques are generally used for printed character recognition and they may be classified, as table 1 shows, depending on the features used (gray level, stroke density, stroke direction, relation between segments) and the method of feature extraction (projections, peripheral, local, structure integration and expansion functions).

An original variation of these methods has been presented by Liu and Tai [8]. However, the recent trend in this field may be expressed as a transition from matching of scalar pattern to that of feature field, which closely resembles the technique of structural analysis in the sense of extracting some features.

In contrast with the pattern recognition methods, structural analysis methods can be classified in accordance with the relative weight of bottom-up or top-down processing and with the techniques for stroke segment extraction. This is shown in Table 2.

Correspondence		Stroke segment extraction		
		Bottom-up ⟷ Top-down		
		Thinning	Contour	Thinning with stroke concept
Bottom-up	Correlation	sub-pattern extraction (Nagoya U.) [23]	direction segment (Osaka U.) [26]	elastic matching (Toyama U.)
↑	Dynamic programming	sub-pattern matching (Nagoya U.)	contour dynamic programming (ETL) [27]	
↓	Relaxation		relaxation method (ETL) [5]	
Top-down	Using knowledge of structure	structural expression (Osaka U.) [21]		structural analysis by on-line information (NTT) [22], [24]

Table 2. Structural analysis method

Some of the most important applications of structural methods concern the recognition of Chinese Characters (Kanji). The recognition of Kanji characters involves several problems in contrast to alphanumeric character recognition:

- P1: Complicated interrelation between line segments and redundancy,
- P2: Occurrence of a great number of categories,
- P3: Existence of mutually resembling categories.

In this field, problem P3 is contradictory to problem P1: while in pattern matching methods it is difficult to overcome problem P3, the structural analysis methods are impeded by problem P1.

The structural decomposition approaches pose other difficult problems: while in off-line character recognition the set of strokes, which compose a character, can be obtained only by taking into account static information, in on-line character recognition systems dynamic information can also be considered. So, in order to identify the strokes, while off-line character recognition systems use control points like end-points, cross-points, bend-points, local extrema in x and y direction and so on, in on-line systems many authors consider as strokes each part of the character between a pen-down and the successive pen-up. The classification is then performed using reference look-up tables or decision tree classifiers. Moreover, in on-line applications, the problem of the number and order of the strokes must be faced for character decomposition. In fact, the current on-line character recognition systems with standard stroke orders and stroke numbers make people feel uncomfortable and frustrated when their accustomed handwritings are different from the standard ones and cannot be correctly recognized. An intuitive solution is to regard different stroke orders or stroke numbers of a character as different categories of characters. But this approach leads to an unlimited expansion of database. A structural decomposition procedure for a stroke-order free, on-line Chinese character recognition system which uses a dynamic matching method has been proposed by Shiau, Kung, Hsieh, Chen and Kao [10]. The "representative point" (starting points, middle points, lowest points, etc.) and the "scanning direction" (horizontal from left to right, horizontal from right to left, vertical from top to bottom, vertical from bottom to top, etc.) are used to describe the geometric configuration of strokes. However, the variation factors of handwritings for different individuals must be taken into consideration when selecting the representative points and scanning directions, because the structural decomposition method is based on the assumption that the spatial relation between strokes can be described very stably by using these concepts. In the system of Shiau, Kung, Hsieh, Chen and Kao, a hierarchical representation of feature strings is used. A radical is the common part of some characters and some structural description procedures for radicals are needed. Therefore, character description procedures include a radical item for indexing the radicals' structural description procedures. This allows one to avoid a complex stroke-by-stroke description of whole characters. In fact, the structural description procedures try to decompose the character into radicals, and then to decompose each radical into strokes. However, if strokes between any two radicals cannot be separated, different procedures for direct character decomposition into stroke domain are used.

An algorithm that combines a characteristic loci method with structural information is described by Downton, Tregidgo, Leedham and Hendrawan [18] for recognizing British postcodes. The British postcode is composed of alphanumeric characters and is of variable length (5,6 and 7 characters). The net result is that valuable postcode recognition rates can be achieved by a high performance character recognition algorithm to be combined with syntactic and contextual knowledge. In the traditional characteristic loci method, for every white point in the background of the character, vertical and horizontal vectors are generated and the number of times the character shape is intersected by these vectors is used as the feature. In the Downton's system the algorithm combines the characteristic loci method with some structural information about the black point in the character (Enhanced Loci Algorithm).

The Enhanced Loci Algorithm can be broken down neatly into three major stages as fig. 8 shows:

- Feature extraction. During this phase each white pixel is characterized by the black pixel regions that surround it in each of the 4 scanning directions (North, South, East and West). Black points are labelled either as being part of a horizontal edge, or a vertical edge, or a slanting edge, or as being completely enclosed by other black pixels.

- Feature unification. In this phase the character is scanned in all 4 directions, and regions of incorrectly labelled pixels are corrected.

- Feature concentration. To reflect both local and non-local region topologies, the feature code of each pixel is combined with the feature codes of surrounding regions of frame. In the case of black pixels, the white regions considered are the nearest ones in each scanning direction. In the case of white pixels, the white point regions considered are those on the outside of the nearest black strokes in the direction of scanning.

One of the problems of the Enhanced Loci Method is the enormous number of possible feature codes. A reduction of the dimensionality of the feature space is necessary. For this purpose, Downton proposes an automated selection procedure and a training procedures which attempts to optimise the position of quadratic order discriminant boundaries between classes.

```
.................11111111.    999999999999999/--------/3    999999999999999/--------/3
............11111111111111    9999999999/----........../    9999999999/----........../
.........11111111111111111    9999999/--.............../    9999999/--.............../
......1111111111111111111.    999999/..---------------/6    999999/..---------------/6
.....1111.................    99999/.-|77777777777777766    99999/.-|77777777777777766
......11..................    99999|..|77777777777777766    99999|..|77777777777777766
.....1111.................    99999|..|77777777777777766    99999|..|77777777777777766
.....11111....1111........    99999|...---------/7777766    99999|...---------/7777766
......11111111111111......    99999/.............-/77766    99999/.............-/77766
......1111111111111111....    99999d/-.....-----.../7766    99999d/-.....-----.../7766
........11111.....11111...    99999ddd/---/fffff/.../766    99999ddd/---/ddddd/.../766
...................1111...    99999dddddddddddddd|..|766    99999dddddddddddddd|..|766
....................1111..    99999dddddddddddddd|.../66    99999dddddddddddddd|.../66
...................11111..    99999dddddddddddddd|...|66    99999dddddddddddddd|...|66
...................1111...    99999dddddddddddddd|.../66    99999dddddddddddddd|.../66
..................11111...    99999ddddddddddddd/.../666    99999ddddddddddddd/.../666
.1...............1111.....    9/bbbffffffffffff/.../6666    9/bbbdddddddddddd/.../6666
111..............1111.....    /.-/bffffffffffff|.-/66666    /.-/bdddddddddddd|.-/66666
11111...........111.......    /...--/ffffffff/-./6666666    /...--/dddddddd/-./6666666
.1111111.......111........    c/-....--------../66666666    c/-....--------../66666666
...11111111111.1..........    ccc/-.........../666666666    ccc/-.........../666666666
.....11111111111..........    ccccc/--......-/6666666666    ccccc/--......-/6666666666
........111111............    cccccccc/----/666666666666    cccccccc/----/666666666666
```

Figure 1(a) Raw Character. (b) Feature Extraction. (c) Feature Unification.

```
999999999999999/--------/3
9999999999/----........../
9999999/--.............../
999999/..---------------/6
99999/.-|77777777777777766
99999|..|77777777777777766
99999|..|77777777777777766
99999|...---------/7777766
99999/.............-/77766
99999d/-.....-----.../7766
99999ddd/---/ddddd/.../766
99999dddddddddddddd|..|766
99999dddddddddddddd|.../66
99999dddddddddddddd|...|66
99999dddddddddddddd|.../66
99999ddddddddddddd/.../666
9/bbbdddddddddddd/.../6666
/.-/bdddddddddddd|.-/66666
/...--/dddddddd/-./6666666
c/-....--------../66666666
ccc/-.........../666666666
ccccc/--......-/6666666666
cccccccc/----/666666666666
```

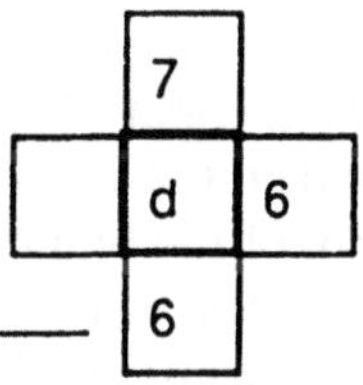

Figure 8. Phases of the Enhanced Loci Algorithm

After the character recognition phase, the syntatic knowledge is used to verify the postcode through the complete postcode tree dictionary. This full dictionary has been constructed as three separated trees: for 5, 6 and 7 character postcodes respectively. This approach has two advantages:

- All postcode words presented to a particular tree are of fixed size; pointers to the postal address corresponding to each postcode are therefore only required at the final node level, and no 'end of word' marker is required (as would be necessary for a variable word length dictionary incorporating 5,6 and 7 character postcodes);

- The average postcode search time is reduced, because each postcode is presented to a sparser tree.

To exploit contextual knowledge several most likely characters must be considered at each postcode character position, so that the overall postcode recognition rate reflects the cumulative probability that the correct character will be found amongst these options, rather than the hard classifier character recognition rate. However, this also increases the probability that an erroneous match for a valid but incorrect postcode will be found.

Often, also hybrid approaches are used for the recognition of characters and numerals. They are usually based on statistical and structural information of the patterns. The hybrid approach for handwritten numeral recognition proposed by Wang, Nagendreprasad, Gupta [19] is based on a specific feature vector called "histogram" and a relaxation matching algorithm for classification. A histogram is a feature vector extracted from the bitmap. It consists of a vector of numbers where each number is obtained as the sum of the number of pixels in a particular direction. The set of histograms for a digit consits of four vectors: vertical histogram, horizontal histogram, right diagonal histogram and left diagonal histogram. Thus the i-th element in the vertical histogram is the sum of the pixels of the pattern in the i-th column of the bitmap. The other histograms are similarly formed. The next stage of this system is based on a neural network that uses the histograms for performing the recognition. The rejects from this stage are fed to a recognition algorithm based on Freeman's octal chain code primitives. From each character, an encoding of a string of primitives is extracted. The relaxed matching is used to compare the elements of this string with the elements of the dictionary strings.

Certain credit is assigned for each comparison between the elements of the two strings, depending on a set of matching criteria. The sum of credits provides the compatibility rating for the string with the elements of the dictionary strings. For example, one set of assignment criteria is:

- If the directions of the two elements are the same, then give a credit of 1.2;

- If the directions differ by one, then give a credit of 1;

- Otherwise, give a credit of 0.

A solution based on stroke analysis is proposed by Chiavetta, DiGesù, Dimauro, Gerardi, Impedovo, Pirlo and Tegolo [20] for an on-line handwritten numeral recognition transputer-based system. They face the problem of on-line numeral recognition by using digital transforms, which is one of the traditional approaches to the problem of handwriting recognition.

A structural supervisor for the recognition of numerals is also used by Moreau [21] in a research dealing with automatic recognition of French postal checks. In this field, some specific characteristics of the check digit amounts make the problem of automated reading particularly difficult:

- digits are very small,
- writers are careless,
- characters are very often joined together,
- digits are intermixed with various non numerical information such as dots, commas, etc.

Thus, a multi-hypotheses segmentation process has been implemented to solve connection ambiguities and a mixed statistical and structural recognition technique takes care of low quality digit recognition. A list of binary images containing black pixels and white pixels is sent in turn to the numeral recognition task. A set of features is first extracted from each binary image based on concavity. Each pattern is thus represented by a measurement vector which is the basic input to the statistical recognition process. This process is divided into two parts: learning and recognition. The output of numeral recognition is a list of possible characters per image. This list is submitted to the structural supervisor. The function of the supervisor is to correct some systematic errors of the recognition process, such as those coming from the recognition of unusual subclasses of characters. Finally, the syntactic analysis module generates all the sentences issued from the combination of all the recognized characters for each segmented component of the amount. This is applied for all the proposed segmentations of the amount and it discards the sentences which are syntactically incorrect.

However, the need to obtain a very high recognition rate has led to the development of sophisticated post-processing systems for error correction. In this field, an expert system for error rectification of handprinted character recognition systems is proposed by Nakano [22]. A set of generic rules is defined on how to select a remedy according to the situation of each error type. When an input pattern is recognized, the result of recognition will be one of C (correct), R (rejection error) or E (substitution error). R can be divided into N (no candidates) and F (conflict by plural candidates). In order to supply a more comprehensive and systematic view, the concept of Result Codes (RC) is introduced. An RC is a diagram of two numbers: the first number represents the existence of a template whose distance is small enough in the correct character class, the second number represents that in the interfering class. The interfering class means the class of the nearest templates except for the correct class. Using this information, the rectification of recognition errors occurs in a supervised session, in fact each pattern must be necessarily displayed and confirmed by a human operator.

A new system for automatic error correction has been proposed by Seino, Tanabe and Sakay [23]. It uses linguistic post-processing based on word occurrence probability, by which mistakes are detected and corrected automatically. In fact, current OCRs are not sufficiently accurate for business use. So, in order to increase the accuracy to a business use level, the Knowledge Processing method has been adopted which detects reading mistakes and corrects them with linguistic information. It consists of a set of methods which can be aggregated into the following four categories:

(1) character level: uses the character occurence probability;
(2) word level: uses the word data base with address, name, etc.;
(3) sentence level: analyzes the morpheme and the costruction;
(4) content level: considers the context and analyzes the semantics.

Assuming that a word X consisting of n characters ($X=x_1...x_n$) is written on a sheet of paper, choosing $R=R_1...R_n$ to represent the series of results obtained in recognizing each character (R_i is the candidate character group, i.e. $R_i=(r_{i1}...r_{in})$ where r_{ij} is the j-th candidate character), when a word dictionary D is given, "word recognition" is defined as finding the word a ($a=a_1...a_n$) or no solution (i.e. rejection) in D. In other words, considering the definition of word recognition, since the character recognition result R is given, word recognition is the process of finding the word in D for which $P(a \mid R)$ has the greatest frequency, where $P(a \mid R)$ is the probability that the correct answer is a, when the recognition result is found to be R. Experimental results show that using this approach, based on word occurrence probability, the correct reading rate increases with the increase of the words in the dictionary and the correct replacement increases too.

The growth in knowledge of character shapes and their recognition during the last twenty years poses new questions today. One of the most important is whether in character recognition, man still remains better than the machine or not. The need to obtain machines capable of matching human performance in character recognition has led to the investigation of human capabilities in recognizing patterns.

Dimauro, Impedovo and Pirlo [24] investigate the behaviour of man in recognizing handwritten characters. For this purpose, from an input mono-stroke numeral, a set of plane curves is obtained which includes a numeral similar to the original one and meaningless curves. In fact, under certain conditions the input numeral can be described through three Fourier descriptors in a three-dimensional discrete space of complex values. In this way, through slight variations of the phase of one of more of the Fourier descriptors describing the original numeral, it is possible to obtain a set of curves very similar to each other, but not always recognizable by man as belonging to the class of the original handwritten numeral. In the experiment, each of the thirteen subjects, (8 men and 5 women), had to recognize each generated plane curve. Every subject was labelled as 'expert' or 'non-expert' and each curve was shown in a random order several times.

The experimental results have shown that each subject needs a short personal learning phase in order to eliminate his uncertainty in recognizing patterns. The duration and development of this learning change depends on the subject. All subjects, after a short learning phase, show a tendency to reject more curves, but "experts" base their decision on a more attentive examination of all the features of curves, while the "non-experts" do this in a more superficial way.

Furthermore, differences between computer and human recognition of handprinted characters have also been investigated by Suen, Guo and Li [25]. They propose a domain decomposition method and a computer algorithm to investigate the recognition rates of patterns based on their distinctive parts, and to find all the potential candidates when there is uncertainty or confusion. Taking into consideration a sample of patterns with 89 most common styles of alphanumeric handprints, the recognition rate of the different parts of a characters is evaluated (see fig. 9).

This research is of great interest where only parts of the pattern are available for recognition due to missing in writing, gambling, poor scanning, noise or various kinds of distorsion. On the other hand, it may also lead to concentrate the efforts of the recognition algorithms on the most distinctive parts of the characters for more effective and efficient recognition.

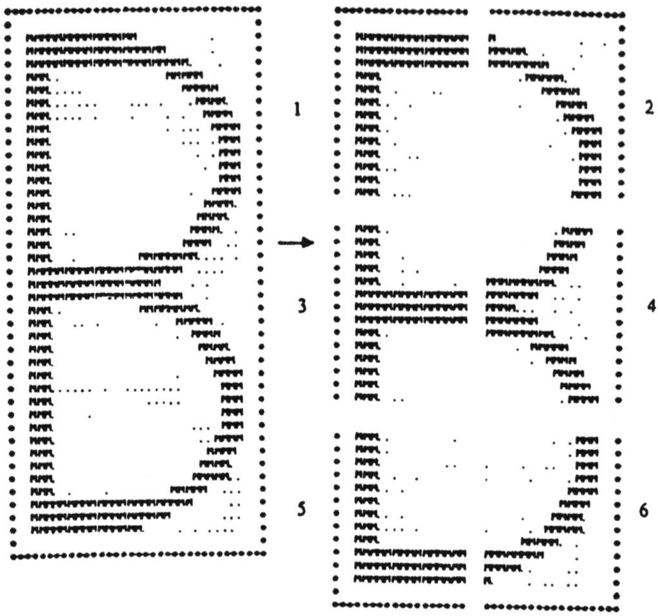

Figure 9. Partition of the letter "B" into six parts.

4. Cursive Words Recognition

Without any doubt, the most interesting and attractive part of handwriting recognition is dealing with entire word recognition. The systems proposed up to now to solve this problem, can be generally divided into off-line and on-line. When the acquisition is made on-line it is easier to get a flexible model, because the temporal or dynamic components of the drawing can be registered. Thus, one of the greatest advantage of on-line devices is that the process itself yields a natural segmentation of the shape into strokes. Off-line recognition appears, and is, more difficult, not only because of the loss of dynamic information, but also because the scripted sheet reading camera process brings additional noise on the remaining information.

One of the major difficulties of the word recognition descends from the great variability observed in different samples of script issued from the same writer over time or from different scriptors. So it is difficult to find a reliable description of a word able to represent all the admitted occurrences of the input shape.

Consequently, in the field of off-line recognition of handwritten words, several works have been devoted up to now to word description techniques using the structural approach. Simon and Baret [26] and Hull, Ho, Favata, Govindaraju and Srihari [13] divide the regular part from the singular part of the trace before performing coding. The concept of regular and singular class of features is spreadly used by many groups in the world: the regular class is made of features, of which the iconic representation is periodic or quasi periodic; the singular class is made of features which are the accidents of the regular features. Examples of regular features are textures and lines. Examples of singular features are edges for textures, extremities, crossing, cusps and forks for line pictures.

Moreover,Simon and Baret's work is based on a dictionary containing a set of codes for the words used in the field of bank cheques.In this approach,after preprocessing, the regular part of the word is extracted. This part, which is also called the axis of the word, is defined as the shortest path from one extremity (left) to the other (right) and that remains in the body of the word. The singularities are then derived by complementation, i.e. by taking off the axis from the word image. Figure 10 shows an example of handwritten word, its regular part (axis) and its singularities (tarsi).

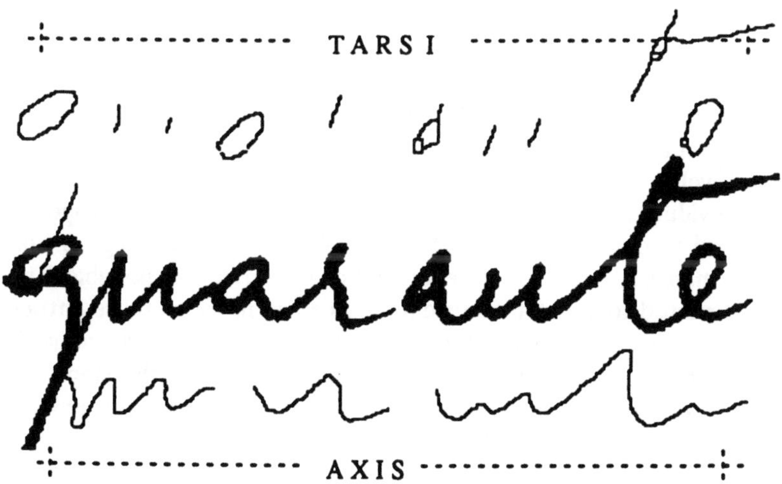

Figure 10. Below:the regular part. Middle:the handwritten word. Above:singularities.

The symbolic description chain reports detailed information about word shape. Among the others it reports the interruptions, points or accent above the word, ascender or descender (with a height value from 0 to 9), extremities, direction of straight segments in the word, direction sector orthogonal to the chord of a curve in the word, loops and so on. The matching procedure is carried out starting from the analysis of anchors in the chain that define robust features and then using a dynamic matching for the other parts of the code.

On the other hand, Hull, Ho, Favata, Govindaraju and Srihari propose a new word recognition technique without explicit segmentation of the word. Specifically this approach, developed for cursive word recognition in postal addresses, extracts a chain code from the contour of the whole word and then uses this code to derive singular features. Furthermore, the algorithm of Hull, Ho, Favata, Govindaraju and Srihari is based on an analysis of writing styles. Each image is assigned to the following categories of writing: discretely printed, fully cursive and broken cursive. Discretely printed is formed by printing nearly every character in the word even if some of those characters touched one another, fully cursive is formed by a single continuous motion of the writing instrument, broken cursive is formed by more than one writing motion and it contains at least one cursively written component spanning more than one character, it can also contain abbreviations. Each category is further categorized into sub-groups. The discretely printed words are classified as well-formed if it is judged that a reasonably straightforward segmentation algorithm can successfully separate any touching character and that also the image is free of extraneous noise such as underline. If any of these conditions are violated, the image is called poorly-formed. A fully cursive word is classified well-formed if it is written relatively neatly and if it is free of any imaging defects. The broken cursive words and abbreviation are also assigned similar quality measures. Both these types of word are called well-formed if all their letters are written so that they do not overlap and the individual letters are completely present. The algorithm proposed for handwritten word recognition works in this way. An input word image is first preprocessed to normalize as many writer dependent characteristics as possible. The word image is then passed to a global feature analysis stage in which those entries from a lexicon that are visually similar to the input word are located. Features such as the estimated number of characters in the input image are used in this step. The reduced lexicon and the original word image are then passed to three recognition techniques, each of which outputs a ranking of the lexicon. The three independent rankings are then combined to generate a single consensus ranking for the word. The algorithm specialized for discrete words first segments an image that is recursively divided in halves vertically until it is determined that individual characters have been isolated. Then the image is passed to a character recognition algorithm using binary template matching, Bayesian classification of structural features, nearest and neighbour matching of moment-based features and polinomial discriminant recognition. At this point a number of top choices of the algorithm are given to a postprocessing routine which matches each dictionary word with the input image using a regular expression matching algorithm. A regular expression looks like "(.?)[B].....(.?!..)" which says that a "B" is detected at a position close to the beginning of the word, with zero or one characters preceding it, and 5, 6, or 7 characters following it. Each regular expression is associated with a score which is assigned to a word when it matches that particular constraint. The words in the dictionary are graded by the scores they accumulate through matching these constraints. After the recognition of the word there is a phase of combination of the decision in which a small number of top decisions are extracted from each ranking. A rank combination function, called Borda count, is then applied and it provides a rank order of choices. The Borda count for each word is computed as the sum of the distance of that word from the bottom of each ranking. The overall result of this system points out that this approach appears to be more stable with respect to variability in writing and it is also supported by the biological behaviour of human beings.

Camillerapp, Lorette, Menier, Oulhadj and Pettier [27] propose a system for off-line handwriting recognition based on a structural approach. Each word is represented by its graph model deduced directly from the grey-level image by detecting specific primitives along the baseline of the word. A horizontal scan of the image detects grey level monotonies and discards those whose contrast is too low. By doing so, the original image is binarized under a relative threshold. It produces a graph of the grey-level valleys, the connectivity being established between adjacent lines. The associated skeleton corresponds to the mid point of each valley. On this skeleton graph, primitive labelling occurs on singular vertices (end-points, crossings, local curvatures). Except for one regular feature: the loop, which is detected by breaking circuits in the graph. In this way, a tree of primitives, the structure of which reflects the drawing of the form is derived. The system performs recognition at the word level: each model in the dictionary is compared to the entity to be recognized. The likelihood is evaluated as the difference between similarity and dissimilarity rates. Tree comparison is based on dynamic programming and may be viewed as a two-dimensional adaptation of the string to string problem. A filter module is used to avoid useless tree comparisons. The final result is a sorted list of the remaining models which are above the final minimum likelihood rate. Up to now, this system has been addressed to a restricted lexicon, that is the vocabulary of the word amount appearing on French bank checks.

A new method based on a syntactic description of the words for automatic recognition of off-line Arabic cursive handwritten words is also proposed by Zahour, Taconet and Faure [28]. They evaluate word geometric characteristics as end-points, nodes, and sometimes sharp point etc. to define a graphical complexity index for off-line drawing. The word complexity index is defined as the double of the difference between the number of branches in the word and the number of nodes in the word. The complexity index is rather stable for one scriptor only, for whom, however, a preliminary vocabulary learning is required. Furthermore it has the advantage of being completely independent from geometrical parameters such as lengths of branches, curvature intensity, position with respect to the basic line etc., and of being a global word index. Unfortunately when a cursive word is written also using discretely printed characters, its complexity index can significantly change. Another measure of complexity is given by the estimated number of main pen-up and pen-down movements. This estimation is usually done by counting the number of transitions between the lower basic line and the upper basic line of the word. This counting can be done practically by counting the number of crossing points with a medium line between the two basic lines. A variation of this technique can be done by counting the number of connected components situated between the medium line and the upper basic line, and having at least one crossing point with it. The existence of word indexes can be useful for fast detection of a reduced list of candidate words on which further, more accurate procedures must be performed.

In the field of on-line recognition of run-on handwriting the results have mainly been obtained using unified tablet-displays such as a paper-like computer interface. Fujisaki, Beigi, Tappert, Ukelson and Wolf [14] developed a system that classifies strokes, generates character hypotheses, by means of a hypothesis generator, and verifies them by means of a hypothesis tester to estimate the most suitable character sequence for each word. Since the strokes in run-on handwriting can touch or overlap one another, the two processes of segmentation, grouping of strokes into character units, and shape identification of characters units, cannot be separated, but should be heavily interrelated. This approach separates the character recognition process into stroke recognition, stroke bundling (character recognition) and character shape validation. After a stroke is acquired, it is matched to stroke prototypes that correspond to strokes of characters, such as 1/2 of A (first stroke of a 2-stroke A). An input stroke produces a list of stroke labels, each of which corresponds to a stroke prototype and to a score that indicates the degree of dissimilarity between the input stroke and the prototype. The score is computed using an elastic shape matcher. For example, a vertical-bar stroke could result in a list of labels such as 1/2 of B, 1/2 of D, 1/4 of E, 1/3 of F. A sequence of input strokes produces a sequence of lists of labels. The system then generates hypothetical character paths, called hypotheses, that is, sequences of stroke labels that are potentially meaningful sequences of character fragments. For example, a sequence of 1/2 of A, 2/2 of A, 1/2 of B, 2/2 of B, 1/1 of C is a valid hypothetical path corresponding to ABC. Since searching for the best solution by the generation-and-test method is a sequential process, it is essential that the hypotheses be generated and sent to the tester in order of plausibility. The standard algorithm ensures the finding of the most plausible hypothesis. For this purpose, different independent filters are cascaded to form a constraint filter. Some filters work for verification, therefore they constitute the test-component in a generated-and-test paradigm, and others work for re-computing the accurate score. The hypothesis is passed through the filters one at a time. If a hypothesis satisfies the constraint, the hypothesis will be passed to the next filter (verified). But, if the hypothesis does conflict with the constraint, the hypothesis will be eliminated (rejected).

Schomaker and Teulings [6] consider the stroke-based approach for cursive script recognition versus the character-based approach. In the first approach, after stroke feature vector quantization by a Kohonen self-organizing network, a symbolic classification procedure is performed on strings of symbolic stroke codes to identify characters. This approach yields a significant, correct classification of neatly written on-line cursive script, but it lacks the generalization capability that is necessary to display invariance in the geometric distortions and variabilities inherent to cursive script. In the second approach the handwritten input word is first segmented into characters on the basis of the minima in the tangential velocity. Feature vectors describing complete characters are used to train a Kohonen network. The character-based recognizer yields a better performance at the cost of a larger amount of computation, due to the high dimensionality of the feature vector.

Moreover, several classification techniques have been tested: models based on nearest neighbour matching, rule-based recognition and the Markov model. For instance Camillerapp, Lorette, Menier, Ouladhj and Pettier [27] use an ergodic Markov model including 8 states to represent a word. The model can be considered a fully connected graph in which each node represents a state corresponding to one direction of chain code, and each arc is associated with a change in the direction of the pen tip trajectory. Markov models of different n orders have also been investigated. In these models the probability of there being a particular change in the direction depends only on the n states which have been encountered previously. In this case a full-word approach is considered to overcome the problem of segmentation.

However, many researchers have pointed out the need for a dictionary and lexical and contextual analysis to improve the performance of the systems for script recognition. In fact, pattern recognition alone is not adequate for recognition of

handwriting, and context is often essential for good performance.
Problems related to the reliable description of a word, keeping only essential information, and to a global method for word classification, using a limited dictionary, have been discussed by Taconet, Zahour and Faure [29]. In their work, characteristic points of the thinned image are detected and used to measure the structural complexity of the word.
Schomaker and Teulings [6] and Evett, Wells, Keenan, Rose and Whitrow [30] emphasize that in the man-machine interaction, based on script recognition, the use of different sources of knowledge (morphological, linguistic and pragmatic) and of a hierarchy of contexts at different levels (for strokes, letters, bigrams, trigrams, words, sentences) will make the recognition much more efficient.
Also the system of Fujisaki, Beigi, Tappert, Ukelson and Wolf [14] for run-on cursive script recognition uses two types of linguistic constraints. A filter based on acceptable character-type transition checks transition of character types over a given hypothesis path, and, if a transition is infrequent or prohibited, a penality score is considered. For instance, a hypothesis path containing a transition from a lower to an uppercase character is penalized. Another filter validates character sequences by character tri-grams. If a sequence of three letter transition is infrequent or prohibited in the character tri-gram data base, a penality score is added to the path.

A system for cursive word recognition based on a closed-loop procedure for on-line handwriting recognition using a prediction-verification strategy is proposed by Camillerapp, Lorette, Menier, Ouladhj and Pettier [27]. This system relies upon generative underlying models, since it is assumed that a large number of literate people share some general models about reading and writing, as a result of education received at primary school. The generative models are hierarchical in the sense that each word is considered as a concatenation of letters and between-letter ligatures and each letter is composed of strokes linked by within-letter ligatures (i.e.cusps,humps,loops). Handwriting is thought to be produced from generative word models, corrupted by distortions and noises due to the writer's personal habits, writing speed and the context of each letter.

Taking into account the aspects related to the use of knowledge in handwriting recognition,Schomaker and Teulings [6] use knowledge of the handwritten script to perform a top-down process for recognizing ambiguous shapes,while they observe that bottom-up information is usually sufficient to recognize unambiguous patterns.

Finally, it must be pointed out that some questions still remain open. They are related to the combination of knowledge from different sources, the discrimination between correct and incorrect recognition, the detection of errors and the automatic acquisition of knowledge.

5. Signature Verification Systems

Another important problem related to handwriting recognition is personal verification by means of signature analysis. In this field the results have mainly been obtained with on-line signature verification systems, where dynamical information from the input process is available.

The signature verification systems proposed up to now can generally be classified according to the type of features that are used for verification. They can be parameters like global length of the signature, local characteristics, or functions like position, velocity, acceleration or pressure of the tip of the pen during the whole writing process. In general, the approaches based on functions show greater efficiency, but they are also time-expensive. Moreover, it is still not clear if it is better to use a local approach, generally requiring a binding preprocessing phase, or a global one, which seems to be more sensitive to the variability in signing. In both cases, the detection of one or more optimal thresholds is still a problem to be solved, that will certainly improve the verification performance of the current systems for signature verification.

Research in the field of high performance signature verification systems has recently been devoted both to the selection of better features conveying more information about the writing process and the integration of many systems in order to produce a final result using the verification response of each system. Yoshimura and Yoshimura [31] propose the use of function features based on the direction of pen movements during signing. They point out the effectiveness of the new features for signature verification. Moreover, they show that by using functions as discriminating features, the elastic matching procedure assures significant advantages in obtaining a similarity measure, but that this is generally not very efficient in terms of computational speed. In order to allow a fast rejection of a very bad imitation or to accept a very good genuine specimen, Plamondon, Yergeau and Brault [32] suggest integrating both the parameter-like and function-like approaches. For their system they consider both parameters and functions and then they compute a weighted sum of three cost factors in order to obtain a verification response.

In order to avoid time-consuming matching procedures, Dimauro, Impedovo and Pirlo [33] use specific Fourier descriptors that contain information on both the shape and dynamics of the writing process of signature strokes. In order to reduce the effect of variability in signing, they propose a knowledge-base oriented to the specific set of components of the signature, as detected in the training phase of the system. Figure 11 shows an example of a signature and of its components obtained from the analysis of the pen-up and pen-down signals of the signature apposition process. The procedure for automatic clustering of the components of each signer, is based on an improved k-means clustering algorithm and uses a simple topological feature vector.

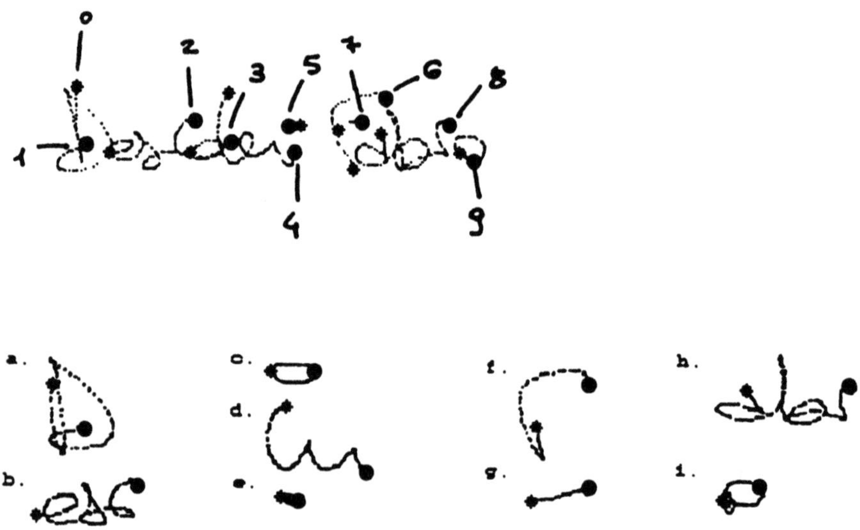

Figure 11. A signature and its components.

For each class of components, some parameters are computed and used in the stroke-verification process. The overall verification of the signature is then performed using the verification responses obtained from each component of the signature.

In the field of signature verification, a conceptual architecture of the image classifier and its matching has been presented by Brittan and Fairhurst [34]. They develop a hierarchically structured, or multi-layer, classifier architecture, where a series of classifiers are cascaded one after the other. By placing a number of contraints on each of the classifiers, a significantly higher level of performance is achieved compared with implementation on a single classifier.

References

1. S. Impedovo, L. Ottaviano, S. Occhinegro, Optical Character Recognition - A Survey, *International Journal of Pattern Recognition and Artificial Intelligence* 5 (1,2), 1-24 (1991).

2. R.G. Casey, H. Takahashi, Experience in segmenting and classifying the NIST data base, in [35].

3. V. Govindaraju, S.N. Srihari, Separating handwritten text from interfering stroke, in [35].

4. H. Nishida, T. Suzuki, S. Mori, Thin line representation from contour representation of handprinted characters, in [35].

5. P. Morasso, A. Pareto, S. Pagliano, Neural models for handwriting recognition, in [35].

6. L.R.B. Schomaker, H.-L. Teulings, Stroke-versus character-based recognition of on-line, connected cursive script, in [35].

7. H.-L Teulings, L.R.B. Schomaker, Unsupervised learning of prototype allographs in cursive script recognition, in [35].

8. Y.-J. Liu, J.-W. Tai, An on-line Chinese character recognition system for handwritten in Chinese calligraphy, in [35].

9. J.-W. Tai, Y.-J. Liu, L.-Q. Zhang, A new approach for feature extraction and feature selection of handwritten Chinese character recognition, in [35].

10. S.L. Shiau, S.J. Kung, A.J. Hsieh, J.W. Chen, M.C.Kao, Stroke-order free on-line Chinese character recognition by structural decomposition method, in [35].

11. R. Fenrich, Segmentation of automatically located handwritten numeric strings, in [35].

12. M.J.J. Holt, M.M. Beglou, S. Datta, Slant-independent letter segmentation for off-line cursive script recognition, in [35].

13. J.J. Hull, T.K. Ho, J. Favata, V. Govindaraju, S.N. Srihari, Combination of segmentation-based and wholistic handwritten word recognition algorithms, in [35].

14. T. Fujisaki, H.S.M. Beigi, C.C. Tappert, M. Ukelson, C.G. Wolf, Online recognition of unconstrained handprinting: a stroke based system and its evaluation, in [35].

15. C.A. Higgins, D.M. Ford, A new segmentation method for cursive script recognition, in [35].

16. K. Sakai, H. Asami, Y. Tanabe, Advanced Application Systems for handwritten Character Recognition, in [35].

17. K. Yamamoto, H. Yamada, T. Saito, Current state of recognition method for Japanese characters and database for research of handprinted character recognition, in [35].

18. A.C. Downton, R.W.S. Tregidgo, C.G. Leedham, Hendrawan, Recognition of handwritten British postal addresses, in [35].

19. P.S.P. Wang, M.V. Nagendraprasad, A.Gupta, A neural net based 'hybrid' approach to handwritten numeral recognition, in [35].

20. F. Chiavetta, V. Di Gesù, G. Dimauro, G. Gerardi, S. Impedovo, G. Pirlo, D. Tegolo, A Transputer-based system for multi-stroke character recognition, in [35].

21. J.V. Moreau, A new system for automatic reading of postal checks, in [35].

22. Y. Nakano, Advanced application systems for handwritten character recognition, in [35].

23. K. Seino, Y. Tanabe, K. Sakai, A linguistic post processing based on word occurrence probability, in [35].

24. G. Dimauro, S. Impedovo, G. Pirlo, Uncertainty in the recognition process: some considerations on human variable behaviour, in [35].

25. C.Y. Suen, J. Guo, Z.C. Li, Computer and human recognition of handprinted characters by parts, in [35].

26. J.C. Simon, O.Baret, Cursive words recognition, in [35].

27. J. Camillerapp, G. Lorette, G. Menier, H. Oulhadj, J.C. Pettier, Off-line and on-line methods for cursive handwriting recognition, in [35].

28. A. Zahour, B. Taconet, A. Faure, Machine recognition of arabic cursive writing, in [35].

29. B. Taconet, A. Zahour, A. Faure, A new global off-line recognition method for handwritten words, in [35].

30. I.J. Evett, C.J. Wells, F.G. Keenan, T. Rose, R.J. Whitrow, Using linguistic information to aid handwriting recognition, in "From Pixels to Features III", S.Impedovo and J.C.Simon eds., Elsevier 1992.

31. I. Yoshimura, M. Yoshimura, On line signature verification incorporating the direction of pen movement - An experimental examination of the effectiveness, in [35].

32. R. Plamondon, P. Yergeau, J.J. Brault, A multi-level signature verification system, in [35].

33. G. Dimauro, S. Impedovo, G. Pirlo, A stroke-oriented approach to signature verification, in [35].

34. P. Brittan, M.C. Fairhurst, An approach to handwritten signature verification using a high performance parallel architecture, in [35].

35. S. Impedovo, J.C. Simon (eds.): *From Pixels to Features III - Frontiers in Handwriting Recognition* Elsevier 1992.

Part 2

Handwritten character recognition

Historical Review of Theory and Practice of Handwritten Character Recognition

Shunji Mori

School of Computer Science and Engineering, The University of Aizu, Ikkimachi, Aizu-Wakamatsu-shi, Fukushima, Japan

Abstract. The problems of optical character recognition are arranged according to their difficulties. This arrangement gives a bird's eye view of the research activities in past, present, and future. The tremendous work to solve these problems is looked at from the angle of "space versus description." The word "space" means a functional analysis approach rather than a statistical one and the word "description" means a structural analysis approach, in each of which some representative work is mentioned historically. Finally, these two approaches are discussed comparatively.

Keywords: historical review, OCR, theory, practice

1 Introduction

This is in some sense a supplement to Mori, Suen, and Yamamoto's paper, "Historical Review of OCR Research and Development" [1]. The paper became too big and I was obliged to omit some important facts and points. Therefore, I have used this opportunity to discharge my discontent. The first thing is to state clearly what is solved and what remains. The second thing is to compare the two approaches with each other, i.e., the statistical and structural approaches, in terms of both theoretical and practical points of view. These things are very educational. Concerning the statistical approach, the mathematical structure of vector space with inner products is taken to make the contrast clear. I hope the reader will see something of the point of the comparison study between them.

2 What is the problem?

History is for predicting the future. In this sense history is not a mere list of facts which were done in the past, but flows or trends of human activities in some specific field, here in character recognition research. Therefore, we consider what the problem of character recognition is. It might be thought very clear, but it is not so obvious. First of all, there are always two views, i.e., the scientific and engineering views. In general, the relation between science and engineer is very complicated, but they complement each other. We would like to make efforts to describe the history from both views although it is a very tough job.

From the engineering point of view, the problems of character recognition changed as the time elapsed. Until the middle of this century, for example, the problem of character recognition was to read printed numerals of one font with a constant size. However, what is the engineering problem now? Shape recognition in general is a very profound problem and has great depths or levels. At first, usually, people are not aware of this fact, because humans recognize shape very easily. As people do research on that, they realize this reality. People can recognize cursive handwriting characters with 100% recognition rate when they are written neatly, but there is no OCR which can read them with a high recognition rate, at present. This is a very good research target of character recognition research.

In this sense, it is educational to define some levels according to the difficulties of character recognition. This is shown in Table 1, which is a list of what the problems were and are. The difficulty is roughly divided into four levels, named 0, 1, 2, and 3, each of which has some sub-levels to define the problems more concretely. Levels 0 through 2 are set in terms of the shape variation and the degree of noise. Level 3 is set by a quite different view of the problem, i.e., the segmentation problem. The segmentation problem is a central one in picture recognition or image understanding, which is so difficult that image understanding is not yet commercialized. Cursive handwriting character recognition can be regarded as a simple instance of image understanding, but is very difficult as mentioned. In other words, we assume that in the levels 0 through 2, a character string can be easily segmented to isolated characters. This assumption is very important and crucial from the engineering point of view, in particular. In fact, a mail numbering system in Japan provides blind color boxes within each of which a digit is to be written. Otherwise, the OCR industry in Japan would not have developed as it has now. Sometimes a compromise between humans and machines is necessary to develop this kind of machine, i.e., that of pattern recognition and artificial intelligence in general. However, the compromise must be reasonable to both humans and machine. This is a reason why setting a problem is difficult and setting it well is very important.

Naturally level 0 is old, primitive and completely solved. Therefore, all OCR which are commercially available now have this capability. However, there is need to define some qualitative words such as little variation and little noise. To be honest with you, this is a big unsolved problem! Therefore, the definitions given in Table 1 are intrinsically ambiguous. The author did it from his intuition and experience. Therefore, the best the author can do may be to give you some typical examples which appeal to your intuition, too. We notice, however, that "variation" includes both geometrical and statistical

Table 1: Level description of character recognition according to its difficulty.

0	Little variation in shape: Small number of characters in the object alphabets: Little noise.	
	0-0	Printed characters of a specific font with a constant size. Roman alphabets, Arabic numerals.
	0-1	Constrained handprinted characters. Arabic numerals.
1	Medium variation in shape: Medium noise.	
	1-0	Printed characters of multi-fonts. Number of characters in the object alphabets is less than 100.
	1-1	Loosely constrained handprinted characters. Number of characters in the object alphabets is less than 100.
	1-2	Chinese characters of little kinds of fonts.
	1-3	Loosely constrained handprinted characters. Number of characters in the object alphabets is nearly 1000.
2	Much variation in shape: Heavy noise.	
	2-0	Printed characters of multi-fonts.
	2-1	Unconstrained handprinted characters.
	2-2	Affine-translated and/or projection-translated characters.
3	Non-segmented string of characters.	
	3-0	Contacted characters.
	3-1	Cursive handwriting characters.

changes in shape, in its broad sense. Here, "variation" means geometrical and topological changes and "noise" means statistical changes. More specifically, geometrical changes include size variation, for example. However, this is excluded under the more specific condition of one font with a constant size in the case of level 0, in which the typical variation is thickness of strokes. Concerning the topological variations, we assume that connectivity of each character is preserved in the level 0. In other words there is no gap which separates strokes into two or more. On the other hand, typical noise is small ruggedness along the boundary of each character stroke. We can allow small number of spots whose size are also small to be added on each character, as the permissible noise. The above mentioned description is not enough to be quantitative, but we face the intrinsic difficulty of pattern recognition itself when proceeding further. Such description will continue and ask your imagination as mentioned before.

What is constrained handprinted characters described as level 0-1? American handprint standard is typical. Canada and Japan have some kinds of standards, also, and they are almost the same [2]. Usually, these standard shapes are printed somewhere on a form and people are asked to fill out the form imitating the standard shapes. Sometimes some instructions are given

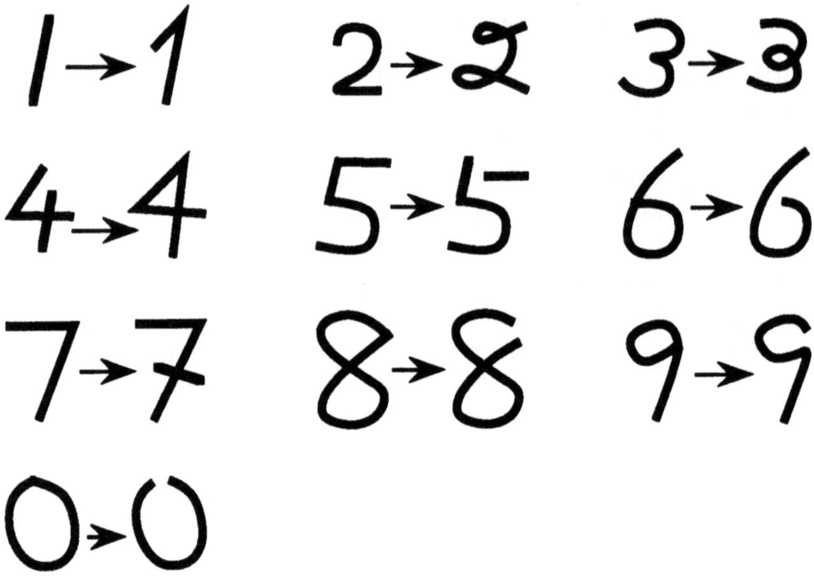

Figure 1: Some examples of loosely constrained handprinted characters.

such as straight and vertical line for "1" and no loop for "4". The first example of the instruction is very important to avoid confusion with "2" and the second one is known as "open four" which is also very important to differentiate it from "9". On the other hand, a box guideline is very useful as mentioned, see also [2].

Moving to level 1, we need to illustrate what "loosely constrained" is. This is shown in Figure 1. In general, topological properties of the shapes are not preserved, but they are still clear for humans. In this sense, it is very important in practice to read such loosely constrained handprinted characters with almost no error. At least, for numerals, this practical request is achieved now. That is, currently commercially available OCR machines can manage handprinted characters of level 1-1. In this connection, level 1-3 means Kanji handprinted character recognition. Some examples of handprinted Kanji/Chinese characters are shown in Figure 2, in which the first two characters from the left mean "character" and the next two characters mean "recognition" and so on. Therefore, a group of Kanji/Chinese characters corresponds to a word in western languages, in general. In Japan, there is strong request for such OCR machine to read Kanji and a few machines are available, but their performance and cost are not enough to be used widely. Kanji was originated from Chinese characters, but it is not exactly the same.

In this context we move to level 2-1, i.e., unconstrained handprinted char-

Figure 2: Some examples of handprinted Kanji/Chinese characters which mean "Character recognition techniques."

acters. At this level people write characters so freely that even humans feel difficulty to read them. Some examples are shown in Figure 3 in which the two digits within the box show two results by the machine (the left side) and by the humans (the right side) who wrote the character image depicted under the box. A serious problem is that sometimes people write characters by own rules which is different from "common rules". Actually note the character images of the right top row of the figure where some careless mistakes of the subjects can be seen. For numerals, no context is used usually. Therefore, recognition of unconstrained characters has an intrinsic problem in practice, although some kinds of character shapes are challenging.

The degrees of noises are illustrated, by quoting Rabinow's paper [3]. A printing in a magazine is a typical example of little noise. It is hard to find "noise" for humans. A newspaper print is also a typical example of medium noise. Figure 4 shows medium noise. Because of the expansion, it looks heavy. Figure 5 is a typical example of heavy noise. It is somewhat hard even for humans to read these characters without context; park.

We have roughly sketched the spectrum of engineering problems of OCR systems. Now, we should mention where we are in terms of the levels. As we alluded, we are at level 2. Problems at level 1 have been almost solved in engineering sense except level 1-3 which is virtually handprinted Kanji recognition.

Considerable number of Kanji characters consist of a few of simply structured ones, which causes a segmentation problem. To avoid this problem the so-called word recognition strategy can be taken, which means that many subclasses are required for a category. In this sense, it might be better to move this problem to the level 3. Here, we assume that "loosely constrained" means "component-wise written", so that such segmentation problem happens rarely. However, such constrain is considerably hard to keep when they are written usually. In any case, good performances for level 1 is commercially available with reasonable cost. However, we must note that there exist still engineering problems in level 1. That is, high performance and low cost are always requested by users. In this sense, some software packages for read-

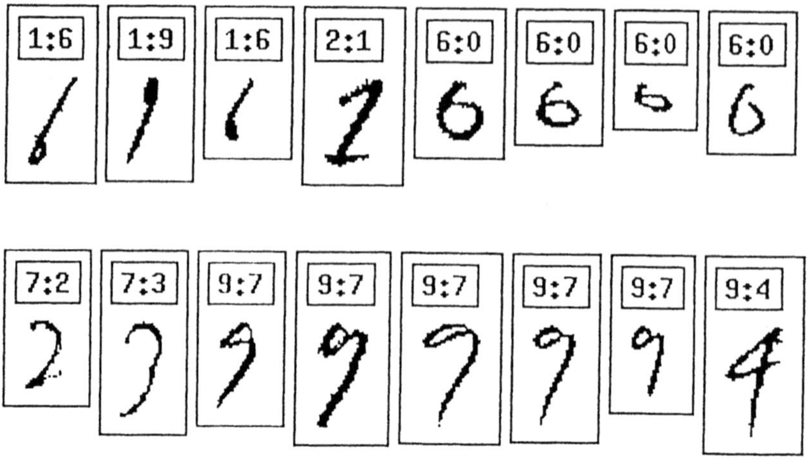

Figure 3: Some examples of unconstrained characters: From Y.Nakajima and S.Mori "A Model-Based Classifier in a Scheme of Recognition Filter," *submitted to ICDAR'93.*

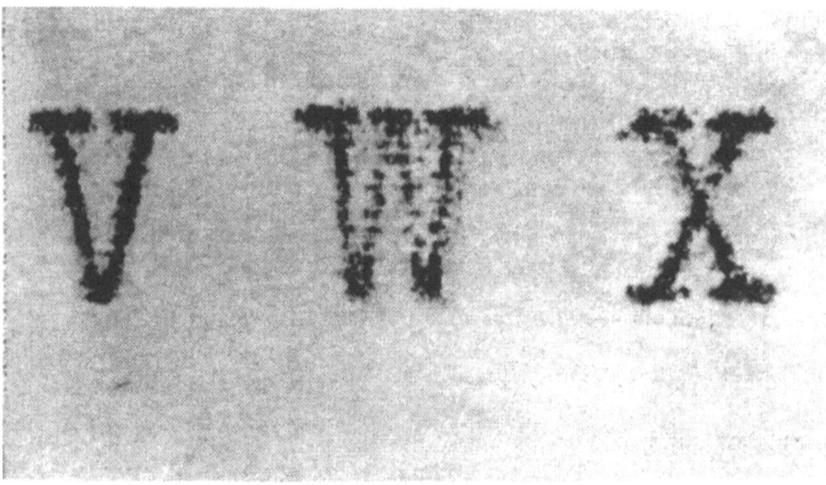

Figure 4: Some examples of medium noise [3].

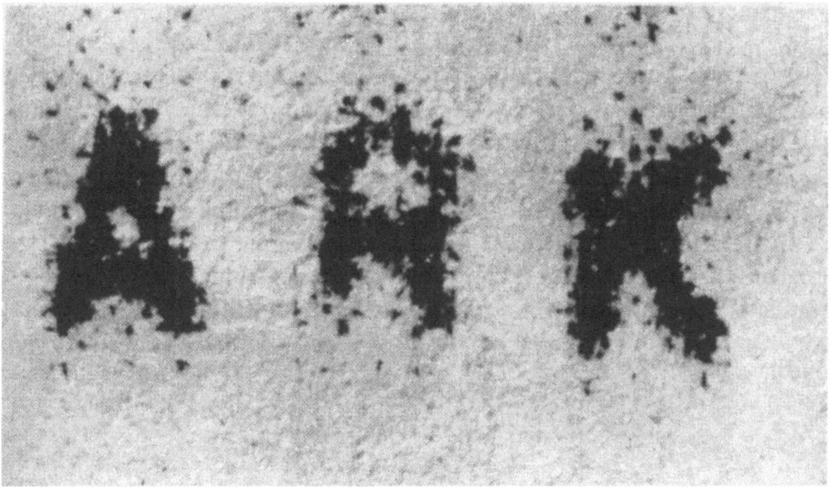

Figure 5: Some examples of heavy noise which can be read using the context of "Takoma Park, Mary-land," [3].

ing printed characters of multi-fonts (western alphabets) and of Kanji (not multi-fonts) are available with low costs.

Now the researchers are investigating level 2 and level 3, but some context information is usually used at these levels. Therefore, it is sometimes difficult to evaluate an intrinsic shape recognition performance. Such knowledge application is not bad, of course, but easy introduction should be avoided, which is the author's opinion. Otherwise, important problems of pattern recognition might be disregarded.

Now we move to describe what scientific problem is. In some sense, it is easy to say it. How do humans recognize characters which have so much variations and heavy noises? Or how can humans learn characters so easily? The latter question attracts many people and they are studying neural networks. However, so far, the way of learning of the neural network invented by humans is totally different from humans' neural network. Essential difference lie in the incremental learning of the artificial neural network. The author has a surprising experience in children's ability of learning. In one evening, the author was walking with his daughter of four years old. She suddenly read a neon sign which was seen from its back. Obviously, she had never seen it before. The structure of learning system of humans is mysterious. Well designed and systematic experiments including comparative studies with contemporary OCR technology should be done. Therefore, tremendous research work still remain for young people, in particular.

3 Space versus "Description"

There are two approaches in pattern recognition, i.e., statistical and structural approaches. However, we can replace these by space and "description", respectively, which reflects more basic differences between them. The quotation marks in the word of description mean that here it is used in the narrow sense as described later. Specifically, template matching is a key technique in OCR technology. Actually, it was a first technique to make OCR system introduced by Tausheck in 1929. The template matching can be formulated in terms of inner product space, more specifically by Hilbert space. Observed signals on x-y plane, denoted as $f(x, y)$'s consist a space, in which a norm is taken as

$$\|f\| = \left(\int_R f(x, y)^2 dxdy \right)^{\frac{1}{2}}. \tag{1}$$

An inner product is defined as

$$< f, g >= \int_R f(x, y) g(x, y) dxdy \tag{2}$$

Thus, it is a metric space, whose completion is a Hilbert space, denoted as L^2. Standard template functions g_i, $i = 1 \sim L$ are selected, where L is a number of the categories in a given alphabet. An input character, f is compared with these g_i, according to the distances, $\|f - g_i\|$. If each g_i is normalized with its norm so that $\|g_i\| = 1$, to seek g_i which gives minimum distances to the input f is equivalent to seek g_i which gives a maximum inner product with the f. There is no doubt that all signals construct a functional space. A key thing, however, is a definition of the metric. First of all, the metric is chosen so as to satisfy the axioms of distance. The above definition of metric satisfies the axioms. However, according to the metric, $f(x + \alpha, y)$ can be totally different from $f(x, y)$, for example. Therefore, the topology of the two dimensional Euclid plain, R^2 is lost, although $f(x, y)$ is given on the domain of the R^2. The $f(x, y)$ is nothing but a point of a functional space (infinite dimension), in which the topology is given by a metric being totally different from that of R^2. Nevertheless, Hilbelt space has so nice properties that people can not abandon this "assumption". These things will be mentioned historically.

On the other hand, it is clear intuitively that a simple template matching has no ability to handle handprinted characters. Therefore, so-called structural analysis method was considered. Its essence is a two dimensional description of shape using symbols. There are so many ways to describe shape that we can not describe them all here. Therefore, we choose some kinds of stands from a theoretical point of view. That is, topological and geometrical descriptions and algebraic representations. For example, a character can be regarded as abstracted lines by so-called thinning pre-processing. Thus, a graph is constructed in which the character is represented by nodes and edges. From the topological point of view, features of nodes are important, i.e., number of outgoing lines. "0" is an isolated point. "One" is an end point. "Two" is a point on a simply connected line at which the point has strong curvature such as corner and cusp. "Three" is a branching point. "Four" is a crossing point and so on. As a first approximation, the "Two" is neglected, which makes the representation very simple. Actually such description was given firstly by Sherman in 1959 [4].On the contrary to the template matching, many kinds of shape is degenerated on a description based on the nodes mentioned above. Therefore, we need to add more detailed features such as length and curvature as geometrical features. We will mention these things comparing with "space" approach.

3.1 Normalization and invariant features

For the approach of Hilbert space, normalization is essentially important. Particularly position normalization is so in practice. There was, however, one hope to deal with characters without it. That was crosscorrelation of autocorrelation functions. However, it disappeared almost from the front of the research after a systematic simulation which gave a very pessimistic results [5] , although both theoretical and experimental work which extended the autocorrelation to the Nth-order one [6], [7]. Therefore, theory of normalization is described. Finally in this section another hope without normalization, i.e., invariant features for some transformations such as shift, size, and rotation will be mentioned.

3.1.1 Normalization

There are two kinds of normalization scheme, i.e., signals are normalized to canonical forms and signals are once transformed feature space on which normalization is performed to obtain features of canonical forms. The first one was investigated by Iijima intensively [8] in 1962 and the second one was done by Amari [9] in 1968.

Firstly, Iijima's is given according to the oldest version which includes the most important point in simple manner. First of all, he made the theory on the observation process in the case of one dimensional pattern, and assumed that an input pattern $f(x)$ is transformed by observation system linearly as

$$\Phi[f(x'); x, \sigma] = \int_{-\infty}^{\infty} \phi\{f(x'); x, x', \sigma\} dx' \tag{3}$$

where σ is a parameter of blurring. Here the problem is how to find a concrete form of ϕ.

He took an axiomatic approach imposing five conditions that strength, shift, and dilatation of an input pattern are preserved after the observation and if an observed pattern with σ_1 is observed further with σ_2, then it is the same as the observation of the original pattern with an appropriate $\sigma_3 = \sigma_3(\sigma_1, \sigma_2)$ and for all the non-negative pattern, the observed pattern is also non-negative. From these conditions he derived the Gaussian kernel for ϕ of Eq.3 as follows:

$$\Phi[f(x'); x, \sigma] = \int_{-\infty}^{\infty} f(x') \frac{1}{2\pi} e^{-\frac{(x-x')^2}{2\sigma^2}} dx' = N(x; 0, \sigma^2) * f(x) \quad (4)$$

This is a blurring transformation. At the time of this research, normalization of a blurring was investigated, but as experience had been accumulated, Iijima was aware that on the contrary a blurring itself is very important. Thus, a blurring has been widely used as an important preprocessing by OCR engineers, in Japan. Marr and Hildreth introduced also this type of blurring as smoothing process, considering uncertainty principle in 1980 [10]. Gaussian type of blurring was derived by Gabor [11], which was based on uncertainty principle.

We could describe the main of the theory, but it is rarely used in practice. For examples, amplitude normalization is done effectively by binarization, dilatation/contraction normalization is done by changing sampling rates. Therefore, it is omitted for the limited space although it is very intersting theoretically.

Normalization in feature space Now the second approach is mentioned. The transformations are linear and represented by kernels. Specifically, such a linear transformation $t : f(x,y) \rightarrow g(x,y)$ is represented by the integral

$$tg(x,y) = \int_R t(x,y;x',y')g(x',y')dx'dy' \quad (5)$$

where t is a kernel corresponding to a transformation. For example, a shift transformation along x-axis is formulated as follows:

$$t_{10} : f(x,y) \rightarrow f(x-\varepsilon, y), \quad (6)$$

$$t_{10}(\varepsilon) = \delta(x - \varepsilon - x')\delta(y - y') \quad (7)$$

and its infinitesimal generator is

$$E_{10} = -\frac{\partial}{\partial x} \quad (8)$$

which is well-known in theoretical physics. The shift transformations constitute a group, denoted as T_1. The dilatation/contraction and rotation transformation including the shift form a group denoted as T_2.

Admissible Feature Space As features, linear features are only considered. Specifically, features ξ^k are derived from the following linear form

$$\xi^k = \int A^k(x,y)f(x,y)dxdy \quad (9)$$

The feature space F is defined by n measuring functions $A^k(x,y)$, $k = 1,2,\ldots,x$. The measuring space is spanned by these functions.

Here we investigate the effect of transformations on F. Let x^i be an original signal represented by an appropriate coordinate on original plane and be transformed to

$$x'^i = t^i_j x^j \tag{10}$$

by t, where t^i_j is a tensor and Einstein's summation convention is applied. Now the question arises on whether it is possible to determine the features ξ'^k of x'^i from the features ξ^k of the original signal x^i. If this is possible, we have

$$\boldsymbol{\xi}' = \tau\boldsymbol{\xi} = (\tau^\lambda_k \xi^k) \tag{11}$$

where τ is a linear transformation represented by a tensor τ^λ_k in the feature space. The transformation t can be carried into effect equivalently by the induced transformation τ in the feature space. This scheme is represented by the following diagram.

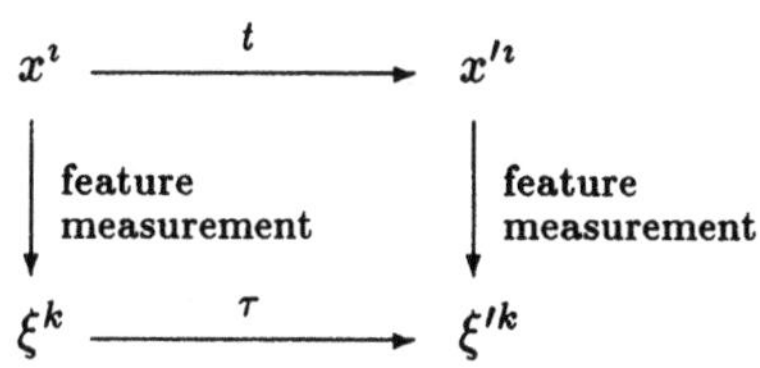

When there exists a transformation τ playing the foregoing role for the given t, we say that the feature space F admits t. Since F is determined by the measuring space M, we may say that M admits t. When M admits all the transformations of a group T, we say that M admits T.

Then the following theorem was proved by Amari.

Theorem. *A necessary and sufficient condition for the measuring space M admitting a transformation t is that M is closed under the conjugate transformation t^*, i.e., for arbitrary $\mathbf{A} \in M$*

$$t^*\mathbf{A} \in M$$

holds.

Based on the theorem, it was proved that the measuring space M which admits the group T_1 is the space which is spanned by the functions $\{x^p y^p e^{\alpha x+\beta y}, x^p y^p e^{\overline{\alpha}x+\overline{\beta}y}\}$, where $0 \le p \le k$ and $0 \le q \le k'$, k and k' are arbitrary integers, and α and β are arbitrary complex numbers. Furthermore, it was proved that the measuring space M_2, which admits the group T_2 is spanned by the functions, $\{x^p y^q\}$, $0 \le p+q \le k$.

Thus the theoretical implication of both Fourier transformation and moment was revealed, both of which are broadly used in character recognition. On the other hand, apart from theoretical point of view, the basic idea of normalizing in features is very useful in practice.

3.1.2 Invariant Features

Normalization process is somewhat cumbersome and there is a problem to choose the criteria. Therefore, theoretical research have moved to finding "Invariant features" for some transformation group, in particular affine transformation group. A pioneer in this field is Hu (1962) [13], who firstly investigated invariant features for the above group theoretically using algebra of invariants, in which moment was used. However, his approach was not in general and poor to have a prospect to find invariant features. On the other hand, for rotation a very systematic method was given by Teague (1980) [14]. As stated before, moment basic function series $\{x^i y^j\}$, $i, j = 1, 2, \ldots$ has a good property to construct invariant features, belongs to $L^2[-1, 1]$ and is complete although it is not an orthogonal function series. In order to find rotation invariant features, polar coordinate is better than x-y coordinate. In this sense, Zernike polygonal is defined as follows:

$$V_{n\ell}(x, y) \quad = \quad R_{n\ell}(r) \exp(i\ell\theta), \tag{12}$$

which is also an orthogonal system. Teague's work was based on Zernike polygonal. A signal $f(x, y)$ is expanded using Zernike polygonal, i.e.,

$$f(x, y) = \sum_n \sum_\ell A_{n\ell} V_{n\ell}(r, \theta) \tag{13}$$

where $n = 0, 1, \ldots$ and ℓ is an integer which satisfies

$$|\ell| \leq n, \;\; n - |\ell| = even$$

The expansion coefficients $A_{n\ell}$ are called complex Zernike moments and given as

$$A_{n\ell} \quad = \quad \frac{n+1}{\pi} \int\int r dr d\theta \; f(r, \theta) R_{n\ell} \; e^{-i\ell\theta} \tag{14}$$

Since $f(x, y)$ is real, $R_{n,\ell} = R_{n,-\ell}$ holds, and

$$A_{n\ell} = (A_{n,-\ell})^*. \tag{15}$$

A signal $f(r, \theta)$ is transformed to $f(r, \theta - \theta_0)$ and complex Zernike moments $A'_{n\ell}$ are given as follows:

$$\begin{aligned} A'_{n\ell} &= \frac{n+1}{\pi} \int\int r dr d\theta f(r, \theta - \theta_0) R_{n\ell}(r) \exp(-i\ell\theta) \\ &= A_{n\ell} \exp(-i\ell\theta_0). \end{aligned} \tag{16}$$

Therefore, A_{20} is an invariant feature and $A_{22} \times A_{2,-2} = |A_{2,2}|^2$ is also an invariant feature, because the phase part is canceled, and so on. Thus, we can find any number of invariant features systematically. These invariant features can be represented by central moments. It is known that moment expansion is not good in terms of convergent [15]. According to an experiment, for Roman alphabet and numerals, it needs 10th-order, which means that $(N+1)(N+2)/2$ Zernike moments are necessary; 66 for $N=10$. Until 1970's it was a serious demerit, but now it is not so a serious problem. For further developments based on moments, see [16], in which useful experimental results are shown.

On the other hand, Otsu pursue Amari's research from the invariant feature extraction point of view and gave a theoretical foundation on that. Now we review his work [17].

Firstly linear invariant feature extraction was investigated. In general the problem of invariant feature extraction is formalized simply as to find functionals such that

$$\psi[T_g f] = \psi[f] \tag{17}$$

where ψ is a functional, f is a signal, and T_g is a transformation. f is usually considered as belonging to Hilbert space L_2. T_g is usually topologically continuous group and has K parameters. However, it is enough to consider one parameter linear continuous operator $T(\lambda)$. In the case of linear, the functionals are represented as

$$\psi = \psi[f] =< g, f >= \int_R g(r)f(r)dr \tag{18}$$

where $f \in P_N$, and $g \in P_N^*$. P_N is a signal space of N dimension and P_N^* is its conjugate space /dual space. In this framework, the following relations hold,

$$\psi =< g, f >, \ \hat{T}(\lambda)\psi =< g, \ T(\lambda)f >=< T^*(\lambda)g, \ f > \tag{19}$$

where $T^*(\lambda)$ and $\hat{T}(\lambda)$ are conjugate operator and generating operator respectively. Here, we relax the condition of the invariant to

$$h(T_\lambda \mathbf{x}) = \eta(\lambda)h(\mathbf{x}), \tag{20}$$

where $\eta(\lambda)$ is a function only depending on λ.

Thus,

$$\psi[T(\lambda)f] = \hat{T}\psi[f] = \eta(\lambda)\psi[f] \tag{21}$$

becomes the condition of the invariant.

The above condition is replaced as

$$\begin{aligned} \psi[T(\lambda)f] - \eta(\lambda)\psi[f] &= < g, T(\lambda)f > -\eta(\lambda) < g, f > \\ &= < T^*(\lambda)g - \eta(\lambda)g, \ f >= 0 \end{aligned} \tag{22}$$

Accordingly the condition of invariant is represented as

$$T^*(\lambda)g = \eta(\lambda)g \ \ for \ \ \forall\lambda, \ g \in P_N^*. \tag{23}$$

However, it is difficult to solve the above function equation, and so infinitesimal transformation is considered, i.e.,

$$\tau^* g = \lim_{\lambda \to u} \frac{T^*(\lambda) - I^*}{\lambda - u} g = \lim_{\lambda \to u} \frac{\eta(\lambda) - \eta(u)}{\lambda - u} g = \eta'(u) g = cg \tag{24}$$

where c is a differential coefficient of $\eta(\lambda)$ at $\lambda = u$.

Thus, the following basic theorem is obtained.

Theorem. *Necessary, and sufficient condition which a linear feature extractor given by the linear functional is invariant under a transformation $T(\lambda)$ is that g is a solution of the following eigen-equation (eigen function),*

$$\tau^* g = cg, \quad c \in C, \ g \in P_N^* \tag{25}$$

Thus, it was proved that for shift, uniform dilation, and rotation the linear feature extractors become Fourier-Laplace transformation and Mellin transformation or moment. This coincides with Amari's results. Furthermore, Otsu extended his theory to nonlinear invariant feature extractor and succeeded in deriving a systematic invariants for affine transformation group, based on function analysis approach.

On the other hand, recently Segman et al [18], took a very elegant approach based on Lie algebra and gave good results for invariant feature extraction scheme in general. The objective is formalized as follows: Given a deformation G, find a kernel such that the associated integral transform

$$T_K[f](k, \ell) = \int_{R^2} K(x, y, k, \ell) f(x, y) dx dy \tag{26}$$

is invariant up to a phase factor under G in the sense that

$$|T_K[f]| = |T_K[f_G]| \tag{27}$$

where f_G represents the deformation of f.

Their essential idea is that original coordinate x,y, is transformed to, so-called canonical coordinate ξ, η, on which the deformation takes a form of simple shift transformation, for which the solution is well known.

At any rate, research on invariant features still continues actively. So far, no direct application to OCR has been known as far as the author knows. However, when considering robotics, it must be very important techniques. Indeed, humans have mysterious ability to this kind of transformation, too. However, for the practical value it must be exposed to more noised and variational character data. In fact the author does not know any systematic experiment which is done on handprinted characters.

3.2 Efficient feature extraction and effective matching

Moments are very attractive as mentioned, but not efficient from the standpoint of practice. In this sense, Fourier and Karhunen-Loève expansions are described. In particular, we focus on the latter and its extension, so-called subspace methods. Then, directional matching method will be mentioned, which is practically very important.

3.2.1 Efficient feature extraction

There is a basic theoretical background in the following mathematical derivations and discussion. That is,

Theorem. (Existence of minimizing vector.) *Let X be an inner product space and $M \neq \phi$, a convex subset which is complete. Then for every given $x \in X$ there exists a unique $y \in M$ such that*

$$\delta = \inf_{\tilde{y} \in M} \|x - \tilde{y}\| = \|x - y\| \tag{28}$$

Furthermore, the following properties hold:

Lemma. (orthogonality.) *Let M be a complete subspace Y and $x \in X$ fixed, Then $z = x - y$ is orthogonal to Y.*

Theorem. (direct sum.) *Let Y be any closed subspace of a Hilbert space H, Then*

$$H = Y \oplus Z \qquad Z = Y^{\perp} \tag{29}$$

Therefore, for every $x \in H$ there is a $y \in Y$ such that

$$x = y + z \qquad z \in Z = Y^{\perp} \tag{30}$$

where y is called the (orthogonal) **projection** of x on Y.

Now let us describe the above general theories more concretely. For this purpose, the following linear mapping is considered;

$$\mathbf{y} = A'\mathbf{x}, \quad A = [\mathbf{a}_1, \ldots, \mathbf{a}_N], \ \mathbf{a}_i \in V^M, \ x \in V^M, \ N < M \tag{31}$$

here some normalized orthogonal base is taken to impose a reasonable structure on A. Then, the above formulation takes the following:

$$\mathbf{y} = U'\mathbf{x}, \ U = [\mathbf{u}_1, \ldots, \mathbf{u}_N], \ \mathbf{u}_i \in V^M, \ U'U = [u_i' u_j] = \delta_{ij} = I_N \tag{32}$$

That is, we look at $\mathbf{x}$ from subspace $R(U)$ spanned by U. Specifically, $\mathbf{x}$ is approximated by projection $\hat{\mathbf{x}}$ as

$$\hat{\mathbf{x}} = \sum_{i=1}^{N} y_i \mathbf{u}_i = U\mathbf{y} \ \ (= UU'\mathbf{x}) \tag{33}$$

where UU' is the projection of $\mathbf{x}$ on $R(U)$. According to the general theory, $\varepsilon^2 = \|\hat{\mathbf{x}} - \mathbf{x}\|^2$ is minimum in this metrics, i.e., the best approximation.

Fourier, Haar, Adamard, and Walsh can be taken as orthogonal bases, but in the field of OCR, only Fourier survives, which is considerably efficient and effective for handprinted characters for feature extraction of contour.

So far, the orthogonal base vectors are given. Now we proceed to choose a system of orthogonal based vectors. Specifically, the orthogonal system is found in such a way that an expected error of a projection to $R(U)$ is minimum, i.e.,

$$\min_{U} \varepsilon^2(U), \quad \text{where}$$

$$\varepsilon^2(U) = \underset{x}{E} \|\hat{\mathbf{x}} - \mathbf{x}\|^2 = \underset{x}{E} \|UU'\mathbf{x} - \mathbf{x}\|^2 \tag{34}$$

This is reduced to solve the following eigen vectors' equation,

$$R_x U = U\Lambda \tag{35}$$

where R is autocorrelation matrix and Λ is a diagonal matrix. If x is normalized so that its averaged value becomes 0, i.e., $\mathbf{x} - \boldsymbol{\mu}$, $\boldsymbol{\mu} \equiv E_x \mathbf{x}$, the above equation is rewritten to

$$\Sigma_x U = U\Lambda \tag{36}$$

where, Σ_x is a covariance matrix, i.e.,

$$\Sigma_x \equiv \underset{x}{E}[(\mathbf{x} - \boldsymbol{\mu})(\mathbf{x} - \boldsymbol{\mu})'] = R_x - \boldsymbol{\mu}\boldsymbol{\mu}' \tag{37}$$

Thus, we obtained basic equations to the best orthogonal system, called Karhunen-Loève transformation. Considerable work has been done on K-L transformation both theoretically and practically. However, conclusion was very pessimistic. People expected K-L transformation too much, which is effective only level 0 problem. That is, it is weak against variations, although it is very efficient for a fixed shape. Thus, the research turned to an original template matching, i.e. inner product, on a functional space.

3.2.2 Effective matching

Template Matching is a very primitive technique and was given intuitively. However, it has a solid mathematical background, as mentioned before. For further development, some formulations are given here, which was given by Otsu [19]. A matching process is formulated simply as

$$\mathbf{s} = F'\mathbf{x}, \; F = [\mathbf{f}_1, \ldots, \mathbf{f}_L] \;\; (N \times L) \tag{38}$$

where $\mathbf{x}$ is a given input pattern vector and $\mathbf{f}_i$ $(i = 1, \ldots, L)$ are some standard pattern or template vectors; $\mathbf{x} \in R^N$, $\mathbf{f}_i \in R^L$ and so the pattern matching is regarded as a linear mapping from R^N to R^K. The problem is how to choose $\mathbf{f}_i$. The simplest one is known as simple matching and $\mathbf{f}_i$ is given by each averaged pattern on each category, i.e., $\mathbf{f}_i \rightarrow \boldsymbol{\mu}_i \equiv \overline{\mathbf{x}_i}$.

Now we construct a matrix M as follows;

$$M \equiv [\boldsymbol{\mu}_1, \ldots, \boldsymbol{\mu}_L], (N \times L), \boldsymbol{\mu}_i = \underset{C_j}{E}\mathbf{x} \text{ and}$$

$$R \equiv M'M \ (K \times K).$$

Thus, the simple matching denoted as s_{SM} is given as follows:

$$s_{SM} = M'\mathbf{x}. \ S_{SM} = M'M = R \tag{39}$$

where S is defined in general as $[\mathbf{s}_1, \ldots, \mathbf{s}_L](L \times L)$. Usually the norms of the templates are normalized, i.e.,

$$F = MD^{-1}, \ D \equiv diag(\|\boldsymbol{\mu}_1\|, \ldots, \|\boldsymbol{\mu}_L\|)$$

which is called normalized matching denoted as s_{NM}

$$s_{NM} = D^{-1}M'\mathbf{x} \quad S_{NM} = D^{-1}R. \tag{40}$$

On the other hand, ideally, it is desirable for S to be I_L; that is, we try to minimize the following error

$$\varepsilon^2 \equiv \frac{1}{L}\sum_{j=1}^{L}\|S_j - e_j\|^2 = \frac{1}{L}\|S - I_L\| = \frac{1}{L}\|F'M - I_L\|. \tag{41}$$

The general solution to minimize the above error is given by

$$F' = M^+ + Q(I_N - MM^+) \tag{42}$$

$$S = M^+M \tag{43}$$

$$\hat{\varepsilon}^2 = 1 - \frac{1}{L}tr(M^+M) = 1 - \frac{1}{L}rank(M) \tag{44}$$

where M^+ is a generalized inverse matrix. Q is an arbitrary matrix with $(K \times N)$. Such matching is called canonical matching, denoted as S_{CM}. In particular, if $M = [\mu_{ij}]$ are linearly independent, then $rank(M) = L$ and $|M'M| \neq 0$. Therefore, the above results are reduced to

$$F' = M^+ = R^{-1}M' \tag{45}$$

$$S_{CM} = M^+M = R^{-1}R = I_L. \tag{46}$$

However, this is a trick of statistics, in some sense. First of all, can we calculate the average patterns in real? This will be discussed later. Here, the question is "Is there an average pattern (vector) in each category?" In other words, can one standard pattern (vector) represent a category? Of course, we can calculate an average for each category using a data-base, which was done based on ETL-8 handprinted Kanji database. This revealed that the averaged pattern is very similar to a blurred pattern for a printed shape. A few much variated pattern can be neglected in a statistical sense, but they cannot be neglected in pattern recognition, because they are very easily recognized by humans in spite of its heavy variations.

Obviously there is two ways. One is to believe it. The other is to give up it. We mention both of them.

Future Matching and subspace methods One person who believed it is Yasuda, who is well-known as man of OCR in Japan. He considered an efficient matching scheme, called feature matching in general. The essential idea is blurring and transforming the the scalar field to vector field, on which the matching is performed. The experimental results for handprinted numerals were surprisingly good considering only one template for each category. However, we must notice that the vector field requires necessarily a plural number of templates. He used four templates for each category virtually corresponding to four quantized directions. He himself admits that the effectiveness for the variations is mainly due to the combination of blurring and directional features, although he used the averaged patterns as the Templates.

The other way to take some plural number of standard templates, to say $m_j (m_j < N)$ to each category, i.e.,

$$\{f_j^i \in R^N\}_{i=1}^{m_j}, \; or \; F_j \equiv [f_j^1, \ldots, f_j^{m_j}](N \times m_j), \; j = 1, \ldots, L. \tag{47}$$

Thus, a given input pattern x is composed with each subspace spanned by F_j denoted as $R(F_j)$ and so this method is called subspace method. The distance between $\mathbf{x}$ and each subspace is easily found employing projection operator to each subspace. That is, the projection operator P_j to subspace F_j is given by

$$P_j \equiv F_j(F_j'F_j)^{-1}F_j', \;\; P_j' = P_j, \; P_j^2 = P_j \tag{48}$$

Thus, the projection component of $\mathbf{x}$ to the subspace F_j is given by

$$\hat{\mathbf{x}}_j = P_j\mathbf{x}, \;\; \|\hat{\mathbf{x}}_j\| = \mathbf{x}'P_j'P_j\mathbf{x} = \mathbf{x}'P_j\mathbf{x} \tag{49}$$

The situation that $\mathbf{x}$ is closest to F_i is equivalent to the situation that $\mathbf{x}$'s projection component to F_j is maximum, which is due to the equation $\|\mathbf{x}\|^2 = \|\mathbf{x} - \hat{\mathbf{x}_j}\| + \|\hat{\mathbf{x}_j}\|^2$, where $\|\mathbf{x}\|$ does not depend n_j.

The problem is how to set each subspace. The most famous one in OCR is so-called complex similarity method, in which three standard templates, $\mathbf{f}_j, \mathbf{f}_j^x, \mathbf{f}_j^y$ are used, where $f_j^x = \frac{\partial}{\partial x} f_j(x,y)$, $f_j^y = \frac{\partial}{\partial y} f_j(x,y)$, and $f_j(x,y)$ is averaged pattern belonging to category C_j. This was chosen to cope with position displacement. See K.Sakai et al's paper on this issue. On the other hand, we can apply K-L expansion to a set of samples which belongs to the same category, say C_j, then higher order eigen vectors are selected to construct the subspace. There are some proposals. At any rate, it is very likely that we can not improve the performance without increasing the complexity of a system. However, the important thing is that the complexity is systematic and not ad-hoc.

3.3 "Description"

A pioneer of a description scheme for pattern recognition is Narashimhan although his main interest was picture recognition. His and related work until 1968 was surveyed by Miller and Shaw [20], among which Shaw's PDL (picture description language) is well-defined from theoretical point of view, i.e., he introduced an algebraic standpoint. Specifically four kinds of operators for connecting primitives was defined. Concerning OCR, Grimsdale et al. [21] gave a geometric description of Roman alphabet characters very systematically. If they had had a present computer power, they would have done considerable work in practice. Pavlidis have pursued this line from both theoretical and practical points of view and have done much work such as polygonal approximation of contours, decomposition of blobs and so on. We discuss the "descriptive" approach comparing with the space approach. From here on we omitt the quotation marks of the word of the description for simplicity.

3.3.1 Primitives

First of all, what is principal difference between them? It is whether "symbol" is used or not. The descriptive approach uses symbols fully. On the contrary, the space approach does not use symbols. In this sense, the former is also called linguistic approach and the latter is called analog/continuous approach. However, in the descriptive approach, the linguistic part was so much emphasized. The most important point to be solved firstly is what are primitives. Shape is described by primitives, and their relations. Shaw used too simplified primitives denoted as h, vp, dp, and dm corresponding to horizontal, vertical, and two diagonal line segments. Contours and thinned lines can be described by such primitive locally. In fact, it is a subset of Freeman's coding scheme. On the contrary, Shaw intended global description by applying his primitives to objects roughly. Primitives correspond to basic vectors in functional space, which are global and the lower order vectors are expected to absorb global variations of a given shape. The detailed parts are represented by the higher order vectors, while it is not so efficient. However, there is mathematical background in the basic vectors. In this sense, the problem of Shaw's primitives is not its small number, but is lack of mathematical background. As noted by Pavlidis, one important criterion for choosing primitives is whether they have mathematical characteristics. In this context, Mori introduced four kinds of primitives, i.e., four monotone functions and constructed an algebraic description scheme of contours [22]. This work has been further developed by Nishida including singular points from both theoretical and practical points of view [23]. The importance to be mathematical is that all lines are decomposed into primitive sequences and singular points uniquely, each of which contains infinite variations (when we consider shape in R^2). Simon also used such scheme in the general framework of "Regularity and singularity" [24]. In other words, the infinite variations are confined into well-defined ranges. This is a very important aspect of the description, because it allows us to describe shape hierarchically in effective manner. For example, curvatures can be an attribute of a primitive sequence. This point is compared with the space approach, in which a high curvature need very high order expansions. See Teh and Chin's experiment of moments on a letter "E". To recover "E" exactly, 20th-order moments (a total of 231 moments) are necessary [16]. Furthermore, a curvature itself is rotation invariant intrinsically and so it is not cost effective to describe them using higher order moments to be invariant for rotation, in particular.

On the other hand, relations between primitives are very important factor of the description. A positional relation is typical such as above/below and right/left. In case of the space, primitives, i.e., basic vectors must be linearly independent. Usually an orthogonal condition is imposed. Although it is well-defined, it is not direct and so a specific relation is represented implicitly by the distribution of strengthes of the expanded basic vectors.

So far, we have discussed the primitives being appropriate for line description, which are usually weak against noise compared with the space approach. There are, however, another kinds of primitive which are two-dimensional, i.e., vector field. The original idea is due to Steinbuch in 1957 [25] and Kazmierczak in 1959 [26]. The problem was how to obtain global features of a given field (gradient of density). Glucksman gave a very efficient way to the global features [27]. This approach was intensively followed by ETL group and later NTT group. The interesting work mainly done by T. Mori was that the globalization was performed by an analog base rather than a symbol base. Therefore it was very strong against noise [28]. However, it took 1 sec for dealing with one character using a computer at that time and so it was abandoned. This was essentially a propagation of stroke density into a white background and was further developed by Oka, in which density gradients along a contour were propagated [29]. A commercial OCR for handwritten Kanji characters was made. This suggests that too early symbolization should be avoided in the description approach and gradient is a key feature. In this connection, so-called topographic primal sketch has been investigated, which is based on differential geometry and functional approximation of density distribution [30][31].

3.3.2 Translation invariant properties

On the other hand, we should mention some translation invariant properties of the descriptive approach. First of all, intrinsically it is shift invariant and for uniform dilatation/contraction it is virtually invariant, because some features can include their lengthes as their attributes, which is easily normalized. For rotation, some specification of the shape description is necessary and so a popular convex/concavity description of a contour is assumed, in which directions of convex/concavity are appropriately defined. One example is shown in Figure 6. Here, the direction list $(\ell_1, \ell_2, \ell_3, \ell_4)$ is not invariant for rotation, but the list of angles between the neighboring directions, $(\theta_1, \theta_2, \theta_3, \theta_4)$ is invariant.

More specifically the above list is circularly equivalent, because of the

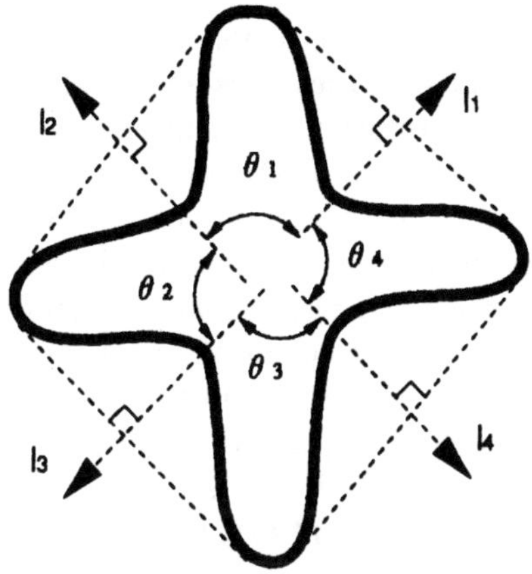

Figure 6: An illustrative example of an appropriate definition of a direction of a concavity around a contour, where × is a position of a center of gravity of a concavity region.

change of the starting point by rotation. The remaining linear transformation is shearing, in which only parallel property is preserved. Therefore a systematic treatment is necessary, one of which was done by Nishida very recently based on the after-feature-extraction normalization [32]. An important point of the descriptive approach in terms of the transformation is that the degree of the transformation can be detected as humans can do. It is important because there are some characters, each of which can be differentiated only by its orientation property such as 6, 9; ∪, ⊃, ∩, ⊂ ; |, /, \, –, and so on. It is interesting to note that the direction is quantized by 45° or 2 × 45°, in which some humans' perceptual nature must be reflected such as a stability of the perception. Another important point is, of course, its high efficiency compared with the space approach.

3.3.3 Flexible matching and non-linear matching

Finally matching processes in the description approach should be mentioned. On the contrary to the space approach, the matching processes are considerably complex, but can be very flexible. As mentioned before, shape are represented by a planer graph, in which features consist nodes and relations between them consist edges of the graph. Formally speaking two graphs are represented as $G_I = (P_i, E_k)$ and $G_S = (P_j, E_\ell)$, where $i, j = 1, \ldots, n$; $k, \ell = 1, \ldots, m$. The matching between them is done taking isomorphism, which was first introduced by Ambler et al, 1973 in the field of computer vision [33]. Imagine a blob like shape and contour which is approximated by a polygon. If the angles of the vertices and the sides connecting the vertices are taken as features and relations respectively, the matching can be invariant to rotation as mentioned above and change of scale (normalization in the features). Therefore, it is very flexible. However, this matching scheme is essentially combinations and NP complete. Hence, a practical method, called relaxation method was invented to prune a association graph which represents correspondence between two graphs. This method is broadly applied in image recognition and a comprehensive illustration is given by Ballard and Brown's book. In the area of OCR, the method was very successfully applied to handprinted Kanji by Yamamoto. Here, we need to note that direction and length of a stroke segment as features was used in the Kanji recognition system and so it is not rotation invariant. Being different from a blob-like shape, characters consist of strokes essentially and so it is hard to rely on only a feature of angles, which is especially true in Kanji. Imagine the difference among "|", "/", "\" and "–". Roughly speaking, Kanji consists of such four kinds of straight line segments. Furthermore in real application of OCR, rotation invariant is not necessary and an allowance of $\pm 10°$ rotation is enough, which can be absorbed by the allowance of the matching of directional features. On the contrary, it is considerable hard to allow such amount of rotation in case of the feature matching in the space approach.

In the field of OCR, however, the relaxation method is not so used, because of mainly time consuming and many parameters to be set appropriately. Instead, so-called rubber string matching is used, which is actually an application of Dynamic Programming (DP). This work was done by Sakoe in 1974 who is a researcher of speech recognition in which he applied it to the numeral speech recognition and succeeded in making the almost commercial base product in NEC [34]. Kovalevsky is also a pioneer in this field (image recognition) [35]. Specifically, a character is represented as a concatenation of vectors. We can easily formalize such a shape as

$$C = \{(c_1, c_2, \ldots, c_k, \ldots, c_K).(i_K, j_K)\},$$

where c_k denotes the kth line segment/vector and is further expressed as $c_k = (d_k, l_k)$, in which d_k and l_k are direction and length of the vector respectively and (i_K, j_K) denotes the coordinates of the terminal point. The above expression is very flexible when changing each c_k and (i_K, j_K). Therefore we need to impose some constraints on it to represent a set of templates. The constraints are described as ranges of direction, length, and the terminal points of a vector. Besides the above constraints, a weight, w_k to each kth vector is set, which is used to connect separated line segments by setting it to zero. Here, a set of the templates is denoted as B.

Now we need to consider how to define "matching" against the template set. Firstly an input image on $I \times J$ matrix is defined simply as follows:

$$A = a(i, j), \quad i = 1, 2, \ldots, I, \; j = 1, 2, \ldots, J,$$

where $a(i,j)$ is multilevel in general. Next the conceptual set of templates has to be transformed to the real pattern set on the matrix. To do so, a template B' is picked from the set B as $B'(b_1, b_2, \ldots, b_K, (i_K, j_K))$. Then a new B' is expressed and defined as follows:

$$B' = \{b(i,j)\}, \quad i = 1, 2, \ldots, I, \; j = 1, 2, \ldots, J,$$

where

$$\begin{aligned} b(i,j) &= w_k, && \text{if } (i,j) \in b_k, \\ b(i,j) &= 0, && \text{else.} \end{aligned}$$

That is, we consider a 2-D template such that it has w_k density level on kth line segment and 0 value elsewhere. Thus, we can perform the matching on the matrix as follows:

$$(A, B') \equiv \sum \sum a(i,j) \cdot b(i,j).$$

One template from the set is picked up, but it is not always the best match among the set. Thus, a similarity between A and B(set) is defined as follows:

$$S(A, B) = \max\{(A, B') | B' \in B\}.$$

The set B consists of many variations of shapes corresponding to a certain category, which corresponds to a subspace in the space approach. In this case, however, we can enumerate the number of the variations concretely. In fact, Sakoe estimated the size of the set of templates of "0", for example, as $4^8 \times 5 \times 5 = 1,640,000$, where K was set to 8, variance of length is 4 pixels, and that of the position of the terminal point is 5×5. Even this simplified model, it gives a considerable number of variations. If we consider negative noise (gap) and positive noise (spot) in addition to that, the number of variations become enormous. In this sense, we can see that incremental learning in neural network approach has basic difficulty considering this big number. Such thing was pointed out by Pintsov [36] recently. On the other hand, we face a big problem on how to search the set to find the best match. In the case of the space, it was easy to find the best matching thanks to the existence of minimizing vector and orthogonality. In this case, however, fortunately there is an efficient technique to solve the problem, which is DP as mentioned above. This is explained below.

Hitachi improved their OCR by applying DP matching along the above line in 1976 [37]. Here, a thinned character is decomposed into branches, each of which has no node whose degree is more than two. So it is linear. In this sense, this is a bud of so-called hierarchical DP matching. Furthermore, each branch is chain coded to be an also feature matching scheme. The matching is non-linear and so many-to-one and one-to-many are allowed. Each branch string of chain codes is denoted as

$$\begin{aligned} A_k &= a_k(0), a_k(1), \ldots, a_k(i), \ldots, a_k(I_k) \\ B_k &= b_k(0), b_k(1), \ldots, b_k(j), \ldots, b_k(J_k) \end{aligned}$$

where A and B mean input and template respectingly, and $k = 1, 2, \ldots, K$ (K: number of branches). The distance between chain codes is defined as

$$\begin{aligned} d(a_k(i), b_k(j)) &= |a_k(i) - b_k(j)| \quad \text{if} \quad |a_k(i) - b_k(j)| < 4 \\ &= 8 - |a_k(i) - b_k(j)| \quad \text{else.} \end{aligned}$$

The distance $d(A_k, B_k)$ is defined according to the recursion as follows:

$$\begin{aligned} g(0,0) &= d(a_k(0), b_k(0)) \\ g(i,j) &= d(a_k(i), b_k(j)) + \min\{\ g(i, j-1),\ g(i-1, j), \\ &\quad g(i-1, j-1)\ \}. \end{aligned} \tag{50}$$

Naturally ranges of i and j are limited to $0 \leq i \leq I_k$, $0 \leq j \leq J_k$ and further constrain is imposed, i.e., a short line can not be a long line in general. The second term of Eq.50 is constructed considering two dimensional matching. Thus, we can calculate $g(i,j)$ for each entry (i,j), and by tracing back $g(i,j)$ from (I_k, J_k) to $g(0,0)$ which gives the minimum value of the $d(A_k, B_k)$, the minimum path, i.e., minimum mapping between A_k and B_k is forward.

However, this matching scheme is still weak compared with the space approach, in terms of noise. Specifically, something must be provided to cope with break of a stroke. This was done by Yamada in which a contour is taken to avoid some distortion caused by thinning process [38]. Contours of a character image are approximated by polygons, and so it is feature matching scheme being more effective than chain coding. To deal with gaps, input features (line segments) are assumed to be unordered, while template features are assumed to be ordered. However, this freedom is a burden to calculation and even dangerous. Therefore to cope with this and to make the freedom effective, the precedable segments with respect to each input segment are defined so that the DP calculation does not increase and it prevents unusual correspondence. Both the difference between a template contour line segment and an input one as well as the distance of a gap in a line are evaluated. Furthermore, DP matching is introduced hierarchically, i.e., one is the matching for a template contour and the other is the matching for the relation between template contours.

The experiments were conducted, in which for handprinted Kanji (881 categories) and Hiragana (71 categories) the correct recognition rate of 98.5% was achieved using only one template per category being mode of the machine printed shapes and so no learning was done. Therefore, in case of the descriptive approach, the ideal object of one template per category seems to be feasible, in the sense that each template set corresponding to a category is constructed easily by one ideal template shape. On the contrary, in the case of the space approach how to select the spanning vectors is a big problem. Very recently Rocha and Pavlidis challenged this object based on graph matching of homeomorphism introducing graph transformations and matching cost [39]. Thus a minimization problem was formalized. For degraded multifont printed characters, the high recognition rate of 97.89% was achieved using less than 2 templates per category on the average. This matching scheme is basically NP complete, but thanks to the semiglobalization of feature extraction, the number of the features are order of 5 and so there is no difficulty of NP complete in practice, which is a key point of this kinds of matching scheme. However, for handprinted Kanji or cursive handwriting characters, the NP complete would be a real big problem. This is an open problem of level 3.

4 Conclusions

Some correspondences between problems and technologies were made clear by defining levels of the engineering problems. The two representative approaches i.e., statistical and structural approaches for character recognition were compared with each other focusing on their inner structures in the historical order.

Acknowledgement

The author thanks Mr. Y. Nakajima of Ricoh Ltd. for his kind help to prepare this paper.

References

1 S. Mori, C. Y. Suen, and K. Yamamoto, "Historical review of OCR research and development," in *Proc. IEEE*, vol. 80, no. 7, pp. 1029–1058, 1992.

2 C. Y. Suen and S. Mori, "Standardization and automatic recognition," in *Computer Analysis and Perception*, C. Y. Suen and R. De Mori, Eds. CRS Press. Inc., pp. 17–40, 1982.

3 J. Robinson, "Developments in character recognition machines at Rabinow engineering company," in *Optical Character Recognition*, G. L. Fisher et al., Eds. Washington DC: McGreger & Werner, pp. 27–50, 1962.

4 H. Sherman, "A quasitopological method for the recognition of line patterns," in *Info. Process., Proc. UNESCO Conf.* paris, 1959.

5 N. Sato, K. Yoneyama, and Y. Ogata, "Printed character recognition," *Bulletin of Radio Wave Laboratory*, vol. 7, no. 33, pp. 489–493, 1961.

6 J. A. Mclaughlin and J. Raviv, "Nth-order autocorrelation in pattern recognition," *Information and Control*, vol. 12, pp. 121–142, 1968.

7 N. Otsu, Shimada, and S. Mori, "An feature extraction method based on Nth-order autocorrelation masks," *Tech. Rep. IECE Japan*, PRL 78–31, 1978.

8 T. Iijima, "Basic theory on normalization of pattern," *Bulltin of Electrotechnical Laboratory*, val.26, no. 5, pp. 368–388, 1962.

9 S. Amari, "Invariant structure of signal and feature space in pattern recognition problems," *PAAG Memoirs*, vol. 4, pp. 553–566, 1968.

10 D. Marr and E. Hildreth, "Theory of edge detection," in *Proc.R.Soc.* Lond. B207, pp. 187–217, 1980.

11 D. Gabor, "Theory of communication," in *Proc. IEEE*, vol. 93, no. 26, pp. 429–441, 1960.

12 T. Iijima, *Theory of Pattern Recognition.* Morishita Publishing, 1989.

13 M. K. Hu, "Visual pattern recognition by moment invariants," *IRE Trans. Info. Theory*, IT-8, pp. 179–187, 1962.

14 M. R. Teague, "Image analysis via the general theory of moments," *J.Opt. Soc. Am.*, vol. 70, no. 8, 1980.

15 Y. S. Abu-Mostafa and D. Psaltis, "Recognition aspects of moment invariants," *IEEE Trans. on Pattern Analysis and Machine Intelligence*, vol. Pami-6, no. 6, pp. 698–706, 1984.

16 C. Teh and R. T. Chin, "On image analysis by the methods of moments," *IEEE Trans. Pattern Anal. Machine Intell.*, vol. PAMI-10, no. 4, pp. 496–513, 1988.

17 N. Otsu, "An invariant theory of linear functionals as linear feature extractor," *Bull. ETL*, vol. 37, no. 10, pp. 893–913, 1973.

18 J. Segman, J. Rubinstein, and Y. Y. Zeevi, "The canonical coordinates method for pattern deformation: Theoretical and computational considerations," *IEEE Trans. Pattern Anal. and Machine Intell.*, vol. PAMI-14, no. 12, pp. 1171–1183, 1992.

19 N. Otsu, "Canonical pattern matching," *Annual Report IECE Japan*, 1146, 1977.

20 W. F. Miller and A. C. Shaw, "Linguistic methods in picture processing — A survey," in *Proc. of FJCC*, pp. 279–290, 1968.

21 R. G. Grimsdale, F. H. Sumner, C. J. Tunis, and T. Kirburn, "A system for the automatic recognition of patterns," in *Proc. Inst. Elec. Eng.*, vol. 106B, pp. 210–221, Dec. 1958.

22 S. Mori, "An algebraic structure representation of shape," *Trans. IECE Japan*, vol. J64-D, no. 8, pp. 705–712, Aug. 1981.

23 H. Nishida and S. Mori, "Algebraic description of curve structure," *IEEE Trans. Patt. Anal. Machine Intell.*, vol. PAMI-14, no. 5, pp. 516–533, 1992.

24 J. C. Simon and K. Zerhouni, "Robust description of line image," in *Proc. ICDAR-91*, pp. 3–14, Sept. 30–Oct. 2, 1991.

25 K. Steinbuch, "Automatische Zeichnerkenung," *SEL Nachrichten*, Heft 3, p.127, 1958.

26 Kazmierczak, "The potential field as an aid to character recognition," in *Proc. Int. Conf. Inf. Processing*, p.244, June 1959.

27 B. A. Glucksman, "Classification of mixed-font alphabetics by characteristic loci," in *Dig. 1st Ann. IEEE Comput. Conf.*, pp. 138–141, Sep. 1967.

28 T. Mori *et al.*, "Hand-printed alphanumerals and special symbols recognition system," *Trans. IECE Japan*, vol. 58-D, no. 8, pp. 442–449, 1975.

29 R. Oka, "Cellular feature extraction from patterns," *Trans. IECE Japan*, vol. J65-D, no. 10, pp. 1219–1226, Oct. 1982.

30 R. M. Haralick, L. T. Watson, and T. J. Lafbey, "The topographic primal sketch," *The International Journal of Robotics Research*, vol. 2, no. 1, pp. 50–72, 1983.

31 L. Wang and T. Pavlidis, "Direct gray scale extraction of features for character recognition," *IEEE Trans. on PAMI.* (to appear).

32 H. Nishida, "A structural approach to character recognition," *Doctorial thesis, the University of Tokyo*, 1992.

33 A. P. Ambler, et al, "A versatile computer controlled assembly system," *Artificial Intelligence*, vol. 6, pp. 129–156, 1975.

34 H. Sakoe, "Hand-printed character recognition based on rubber string matching," *T. R. IECI Japan*, PRL 74-20, pp. 1–10, 1974.

35 V. A. Kovalevsky, "An optimal algorithm for the recognition of some sequences," *Cybernetics*, vol. 3, no. 4, 1967.

36 L. Pintsov, "On view of the methodology in handwriting character recognition," *SPIE/IS&T's Symposium on Electronic Imaging, Science and Technology*, p.115, San Jose, California, Feb. 1992.

37 T. Fujimoto, S. Kadota, S. Hayashi, M. Yamamoto, S. Yajima, and M. Yasuda, "Recognition of handprinted characters by non-linear elastic matching," in *Proc. 3rd IJCPR*, pp. 113–117, Nov. 1976.

38 H. Yamada, "Contour DP matching method and its applications to hand-printed Chinese character recognition," in *Proc. 7th IJCPR*, pp. 389–392, 1984.

39 J. Rocha and T. Pavlidis, "A shape analysis model with applications to a character recognition system," *IEEE Trans. on PAMI.*, (to appear.)

Automatic Recognition of Handwritten Characters

Ching Y. Suen

Centre for Pattern Recognition & Machine Intelligence,
Concordia University, Montreal, Canada H3G 1M8.

Abstract

This tutorial presents the current scene of handwriting recognition, the achievements in the past and the challenges ahead. The performance of various techniques for recognizing totally unconstrained handwritten characters are reviewed and compared. New ideas and promising areas of research are pointed out for discussion. An extensive bibliography is included for reference purposes.

Keywords: handwriting recognition, feature extraction, character recognition

1. Introduction

Recognition technology plays an important role in data processing industry. Many kinds of typewritten and printed data are now being processed by computer using OCR (Optical Character Recognition) techniques. However, the recognition of unconstrained handwriting and cursive scripts, remain far away from practical use even though such capability can be extremely useful in automatic entry of handwritten data. Indeed, many different type of documents exist in our daily life, e.g. bankchecks, payment slips, envelopes, income tax, return forms, etc. All of them have to be processed by the computer and yet this particular technology is lagging behind. The main reason is the high variability of character shapes and handwritten strokes produced by different writers. It is not surprising to find that handwriting recognition is known to be one of the most challenging subjects in the field of pattern recognition.

Machine recognition of both printed and handwritten characters, has been intensively and extensively researched by scientists in different countries around the world. Characters written in many different languages have been recognized, e.g. from numerals to alphaneumerics, and from Roman languages to Oriental languages. See e.g. the proceedings of the international conferences on Pattern Recognition. However, the infinite varieties of qualities and character shapes produced by handwriting and by modern printing machines have posed a major challenge to researchers in the field of pattern recognition. But the urgent need is there, and it has become increasingly evident that satisfactory solutions to this problem would be very useful in applications where it is necessary to process large volumes of printed and handwritten data, e.g. in automatic sorting of mail and cheques, payment slips, utility bills, verification of signatures, and machine recognition and analysis of engineering drawings and maps.

Over the past four decades, many different methods have been explored by a large number of scientists to recognize characters. A variety of approaches have been proposed and tested by researchers in different parts of world, including statistical methods, structural and syntactic methods, model matching, neural networks, and expert systems.

With respect to automatic recognition of handwritten characters, the immense effort spent in this field proves that this is an even more challenging problem due to the geometric diversity of character shapes produced by writers who have different writing styles and habits. The complexity of oriental characters adds another dimension of difficulty to the problem. This is further compounded by our lack of understanding of the ways humans recognize characters. This tutorial will cover subjects related to early efforts of recognizing handwritten characters, the progress made, and new directions in this exciting field.

To probe this problem further, the following questions are posed as a catalyst to generate new ideas. How does the human brain recognize the different characters? Which parts of the characters is it looking for? What kind of features do we get when we see a character? Is there some way we can extract the character recognition knowledge from humans who have become such superb character recognizers? What will be the impact of the new idea of using multiple experts? If we can extract such information from human subjects and experts, what will be the degree of difficulty and complexity in implementing such cues and features on the computer? Answers to these questions will be very enlightening and interesting.

The above indicates that we still have a long way to go before we can build machines that can read and process documents reliably and intelligently. On the other hand, a lot of new activities in this field have emerged. Within the past 10 months, several new international conferences and workshops have been established in handwriting recognition, document analysis and recognition, and advanced technology in mail sorting and recognition. Scientists now realize the shortcomings of current optical reading machines in the market place and the urgent need to conduct more research in this growing area. Hopefully the publication of these efforts will not only shed light to some of the most difficult problems in OCR, but will also bring further growth and progress to this challenging field.

2. Further Efforts and New Directions

During the past 20 years, we have witnessed great progress in this field. Our experience tells us that the following topics should be further investigated:

- Identification and extraction of the salient features
- Discover how human beings recognize characters
- Incorporating human knowledge into the recognition system
- Optimizing the multiple-expert recognition system
- Automating the learning and classification process.

More details will be presented in the tutorial.

3. Concluding Remarks

This tutorial presents the current state-of-the-art of handwriting recognition. It has also pointed out some of the promising directions ahead of us. There is evidence that computers will eventually outperform human beings in these tasks. But until then, we have to reach many milestones. We hope this tutorial will provide some new ideas which will stimulate the growth of this challenging field. In order to help the readers to dig in further, an extensive list of important publications in this area is provided below.

Bibliogrphy

[1] Ahmed, P. and Suen, C.Y., ''Computer recognition of totally unconstrained handwritten zip codes,'' International Journal of Pattern Recognition and Artificial Intelligence, 1(1):1-15, 1987.

[2] Ali, F. and Pavlidis, T., ''Syntactic recognition of handwritten numerals,'' IEEE Trans. Syst. Man and Cybernet., 7:537-541, 1977.

[3] Badie, K. and Shimura, M., ''Machine recognition of roman cursive script,'' Proceedings of 6th ICPR, Munich, 28-30, October 1982.

[4] Baptista, G. and Kulkarni, K.M., ''A high accuracy algorithm for recognition of handwritten numerals,'' Pattern Recognition, 21(4):287-291, 1988.

[5] Beun, M., "A flexible method for automatic reading of handwritten numerals," Philips Tech. Rev., 33:89-101, 1973.

[6] Beun, M., ''A flexible method for automatic reading of handwritten numerals,'' Philips Tech. Rev., 33:130-137, 1973.

[7] Brown, R.M., Fay, T.H., and Walker, C.L., ''Handprinted symbol recognition system,'' Pattern Recognition, 21(2):91-118, 1988.

[8] Casey, R.G., and Takahashi H., ''Experience in Segmenting and Classifying the NIST Data Base'', Proc. 2nd International Workshop on Frontiers in Handwriting Recognition, Bonas, France, 1991, pp. 149-159.

[9] Cheriet, M., and Suen, C.Y., ''Automated entry system for handwritten documents,'' In Proc. Int. Conf. on Intelligent Text and Image Handling (RIAO'91), pages 211-223, Universitat Autonoma Di Barcelona, Barcelona, Spain, April 1991.

[10] Cohen, E., Hull, J. J., and Srihari, S. N., ''Interpretation of handwritten addresses,'' Technical report, State University of New York at Buffalo, Buffalo, 1990.

[11] Cohen, E., Hull, J.J., and Srihari, S.N., "Understanding handwritten text in a structured environment: Determining zip codes from addresses," Int. Journal of PR and AI, 5(1,2):221-264, 1991.

[12] Commike, A.Y. and Hull, J.J., "Rule Learning for Syntactic Pattern Recognition," Proc. 4th U.S. Postal Service Adv. Technol. Conf., November 1990, pp. 621-633.

[13] Dimauro, G., Impedovo, S. and Pirlo, G., "Uncertainty in the Recognition Process: Some Considerations on Human Variable Behaviour, Proc. 2nd International Workshop on Frontiers in Handwriting Recognition," Bonas, France, 1991, pp. 405-411.

[14] Downton, A.C, Tregidgo, R.W.S., Leedham, C.G. and Hendrawan, "Recognition of Handwritten British Postal Addresses, Proc. 2nd International Workshop on Frontiers in Handwriting Recognition," Bonas, France, 1991, pp. 133-147.

[15] Duerr, B., Haettich, W., Tropf, H., and Winkler, G., "A combination of statistical and syntactical pattern recognition applied to classification of unconstrained handwritten numerals," Pattern Recognition, 12:189-199, 1980.

[16] Duvernoy, J. and Charrault, D., "Stability and stationarity of cursive handwriting. Pattern Recognition," 11:145-154, 1979.

[17] Earnest, L. D., "Machine recognition of cursive writing" In C. Cherry, editor, Information Processing. Butterworths, London, 1962.

[18] Edelman, S., Ullman, S., and Flash, T., "Reading cursive handwriting by alignment of letter prototypes," Int. Journal of Computer Vision , 5(3):303-331, 1990.

[19] Frishkopf, L. S. and Harmon, L. D., "Machine reading of cursive script," In Colin Cong, editor, Information Theory . Butterworths, London, 1961.

[20] Fujisawa, H., Nakano, Y., and Kurino, K., "Segmentation Methods for Character Recognition: From Segmentation to Document Structure Analysis," Proceedings of the IEEE," 80(7):1079-1092, July 1992.

[21] Gader, Hepp, D., Forester, B., Peurach, T., and Mitchell, B.T., ''Pipelined systems for recognition of handwritten digits in USPS zip codes,'' Proc. U.S. Postal Service Advanced Technology Conf., pages 539-548, November 1990.

[22] Gaillat, G., ''An on-line recognizer with learning capabilities,'' In Proc. 2nd Int. Joint Conf. on Pattern Recognition, pages 305-306, Aug. 1974.

[23] Groner, G. F., ''Real-time recognition of handprinted text,'' In Proc. FJCC , pages 591-601, 1966.

[24] Guyon, I., Henderson, D., Allbrecht, P., Le Cun, Y. and Denker, J., ''Writer Independent and Writer Adaptive Neural Network for On-line Character Recognition, Proc. 2nd International Workshop on Frontiers in Handwriting Recognition,'' Bonas, France, 1991, pp. 313-326.

[25] Hayes, K. C., ''Reading handwritten words using hierarchical relaxation,'' Computer Graphics, Image process , 14:344-364, 1980.

[26] Hayes-Roth, D.A. Waterman, and D.B. Lenat, editors, ''Building Expert Systems,'' Addison-Wesley, Reading MA, 1983.

[27] Higgins, C. A. and Whitrow, ''On-line cursive script recognition,'' In Proc. Interact'84, 1st IFIP Conf. Human-Computer Interaction , pages 140-144, September 1985.

[28] Huang, J.S. and Chuang, K., ''Heuristic approach to handwritten numeral recognition,'' Pattern Recognition, 19(1):15-19, 1986.

[29] Hull, J.J., Commike, A., and Ho, T.-K., ''Multiple algorithms for handwritten character recognition,'' Proc. Int. Workshop on Frontiers in Handwriting Recognition, pages 117-124, Concordia University, Montreal, April 1990.

[30] Hull, J.J., Ho, T.K., Favata, J., Govindaraju, V. and Srihari, S.N., ''Combination of Segmentation-Based and Holistic Handwritten Word Recognition Algorithms, Proc. 2nd International Workshop on Frontiers in Handwriting Recognition,'' Bonas, France, 1991, pp. 229-240.

[31] Hull, J.J., Srihari, S.N., Cohen, E., Kuan, C.L., Cullen, P., and Palumbo, P., ''A blackboard-based approach to handwritten zip code recognition,'' Proc. U.S. Postal Service Advanced Technology Conf., pages 1018 - 1032, 1988.

[32] Kabir, E., Downton, A. C., and Birch, R., ''Recognition and verification of postcode handwritten and handprinted addresses,'' In Proc. 10th ICPR , pages 469-473, June 1990.

[33] Kimura, F. and Shridhar, M., ''Handwritten Numerical Recognition Based on Multiple Algorithms,'' Pattern Recognition, Vol. 24, No. 10, 1991, pp. 969-983.

[34] Krzyzak, A., Dai, W., and Suen, C.Y., ''Unconstrained handwritten character classification using modified back propagation model,'' Proc. Int. Workshop on Frontiers in Handwriting Recognition, pages 155-166, Concordia University, Montreal, April 1990.

[35] Kuan, C.L. and Srihari, S.N., ''A stroke-based approach to handwritten numeral recognition,'' Proc. U.S. Postal Service Advanced Technology Conf., pages 1033-1041, 1988.

[36] Kurtzberg, J. M. and Tappert, C. C., ''Segmentation procedure for handwritten symbols and words,'' IBM Tech. Disclosure Bull. , 25:3848-3852, December 1982.

[37] Kwan, C.C., Pang, L., and Suen, C.Y., ''A comparative study of some recognition algorithms in character recognition,'' Proc. Int. Conf. on Cybernetics and Society, pages 530-535, Denver, 1979.

[38] Lam, L. and Suen, C.Y., ''Structural classification and relaxation matching of totally unconstrained handwritten zip-code numbers,'' Pattern Recognition, 21(1):19-31, 1988.

[39] Lam, L., Lee, S.-W. & Suen, C. Y., ''Thinning methodologies: A comprehensive survey,'' IEEE Trans. Pattern Anal. Machine Intell., 14(9): 869-885.

[40] Le Cun, Y., Boser, B., Denker, J.S., Henderson, D., Howard, R.E., Hubbard, W., Jackel, L.D., and H.S. Baird, ''Constrained neural network for unconstrained handwritten digit recognition,'' Proc. Int. Workshop on Frontiers in Handwriting Recognition, pages 145-154, Concordia University, Montreal, April 1990.

[41] Legault, R. and Suen, C.Y., ''A Contour-Based Recognition System for Totally Unconstrained Handwritten Numerals. Technical Report, Concordia University, Montreal, 1989.

[42] Legault, R. and Suen, C.Y., '' Review and Comparison of Methods of Extracting Curvature Features,'' submitted for publication.

[43] Mai, T. and Suen, C.Y., ''A generalized knowledge-based system for the recognition of unconstrained handwritten numerals,'' IEEE Trans. Syst. Man and Cybernet., 20(4):835-848, 1990.

[44] Mitchell, B.T. and Gillies, A.M., ''A model-based computer vision system for recognizing handwritten zip codes,'' Machine Vision and Applications, 2:231-243, 1989.

[45] Moreau, J.V., ''A New System for Automatic Reading of Postal Checks, Proc. 2nd International Workshop on Frontiers in Handwriting Recognition,'' Bonas, France, 1991, pp. 121-132.

[46] Mori, S., Suen, C.Y., and Yamamoto, K., ''Historical Review of OCR Research and Development,'' Porceedings of the IEEE, 80(7):1029-1058, July 1992.

[47] Mori, K.-I., Genchi, H., Watanabe, S., and Katsuragi, S., ''Microprogram controlled pattern processing in a handwritten mail reader-sorter,'' Pattern Recognition, 2:175-185, 1970.

[48] Nadal, C., Legault, R., and Suen, C.Y., ''Complementary algorithms for the recognition of totally unconstrained handwritten numerals,'' Proc. 10th Int. Conf. on Pattern Recognition, pages 443-449, Atlantic City, NJ, June 1990.

[49] Nadal, C. and Suen, "Recognition of Totally Unconstrained Handwritten Digit by Decomposition and Vectorisation," Technical Report, Concordia University, Montreal, 1988. Decomposition and Vectorisation. Technical Report, Concordia University, Montreal, 1988.

[50] Nishida, H. and Mori, S., "An Approach to Automatic Construction of Structural Models for Character Recognition," Proc. 1st Int. Conf. on Document Analysis and Recognition, St-Malo, France, September 1991, pp. 231-241.

[51] Pavlidis, T., "A vectorizer and feature extractor for document recognition," Comp. Vision, Graphics, Image Process., vol. 35, pp. 111-127 (1986).

[52] Sayre, K. M., "Machine recognition of handwritten words: A project report," Pattern Recognition, 5:213-228, 1973.

[53] Schürman, J., Bartneck, N., Bayer, T., Franke, J., Mandler, E., and Oberlander, M., "Document Analysis - From Pixels to Contents," Proceedings of the IEEE, 80(7):1101-1119, July 1992.

[54] Shridhar, M. and Badreldin, A., "Recognition of isolated and simply connected handwritten numerals," Pattern Recognition, 19(1):1-12, 1986.

[55] Simon, J.-C., "Off-Line Cursive Word Recognition," Proceedings of the IEEE, 80(7):1150-1161, July 1992.

[56] Srihari, S. N. and Bozinovic, R. M., "A multilevel perception approach to reading cursive script," Artificial Intelligence, 33:217-255, 1987.

[57] Stringa, L., "Efficient classification of totally unconstrained handwritten numerals with a trainable multi layer network," Pattern Recognition Letters, 10:273-280, 1989.

[58] Stringa, L., "A new set of constraint-free character recognition grammars," IEEE Trans. on Pattern Analysis and Machine Intelligence, 12(12):1210-1217, 1990.

[59] Suen, C.Y., "Character recognition by computer and applications," T.Y. Young and K.-S. Fu, editors, Handbook of Pattern Recognition and Image Processing, pages 569-586, Academic Press Inc., Orlando, 1986.

[60] Suen, C.Y., "Distinctive features in the automatic recognition of handprinted characters," Signal Processing, 4:193-207, 1982.

[61] Suen, C. Y., "The role of multi-directional loci and clustering in reliable recognition of characters," Proc. 6th Int. Conf. on Pattern Recognition, pages 1020-1022, 1982.

[62] Suen, C. Y., Berthod, M., and Mori, S., "Automatic recognition of handprinted characters," the state of the art. Proceedings of the IEEE , 68(4):469-483, 1980.

[63] Suen, C.Y., Guo, J. and Li, Z.C., "Computer and Human Recognition of Handprinted Characters by Parts," Proc. 2nd International Workshop on Frontiers in Handwriting Recognition, Bonas, France, 1991, pp. 161-174.

[64] Suen, C.Y., Nadal, C., Legault, R., Mai, T.A. and Lam, L., "Computer Recognition of Unconstrained Handwritten Numerals," Invited paper, Special issue of Proceedings of the IEEE on OCR, 80(7): 1162-1180, 1992.

[65] Suen, C.Y., Nadal, C., Mai, T.A., Legault, R., and Lam, L., "Recognition of handwritten numerals based on the concept of multiple experts," Proc. Int. Workshop on Frontiers in Handwriting Recognition, pages 131-144, CENPARMI, Concordia University, Montreal, April 1990.

[66] Tappert, C. C., Suen, C. Y., and Wakahara, T., "The state of the art in on-line handwriting recognition," IEEE Trans. on Pattern Analysis and Machine Intelligence, 12(8):787-808, 1977.

[67] Wakahara, T., Murase, H., and Okada, K., "On-Line Handwriting Recognition," Proceedings of the IEEE, 80(7):1181-1194, July 1992.

[68] Wang, D. and Srihari, S. N., "Classification of newspaper image blocks using texture analysis," C.V.G.I.P. , 47:327-352, 1989s," Signal Processing, 4:193-207, 1982.

[69] Wang, P.S.P., Nagendraprasad, M.V. and Gupta, A., "A 'Hybrid' Approach to Handwritten Numerical Recognition," Proc. 2nd International Workshop on Frontiers in Handwriting Recognition, Bonas, France, 1991, PP. 101-110.

[70] Ward, J. R., "One view of on-going problems handwriting character recognition," in Proc. Int. Workshop on Frontiers in Handwriting Recognition, pages 101-107, CENPARMI, Concordia University, Montreal, April 1990.

Learning, Representation, Understanding and Recognition of Words - An Intelligent Approach

Patrick Shen-Pei Wang

College of Computer Science
Northeastern University
Boston, MA 02115 U.S.A.

Abstract. This article investigates several line-drawing pattern recognition methods for handwritten character recognition such as picture descriptive language, Berthod and Maroy's method, extended Freeman's chain code, error transformation method, tree grammar, and array grammar. They are compared with a character recognition scheme that uses improved extended octal codes as the primitives, which has the advantages of handling flexible sizes, orientations, and variations, needing fewer learning samples and having lower degree of ambiguity. Also, the concepts of *learning by knowledge with iterations and feedbacks* and *semantic network* are discussed. They have several advantages in easy learning, understanding and recognition versus the traditional *learning by rote* and *meaningful learning.* Finally, examples of learning, representation, understanding, and recognizing two-dimensional Chinese characters and words are illustrated.

Keywords. learning, representation, understanding, pattern/character recognition, degrees of recognizability and ambiguity, artificial intelligence

1 Introduction

How do people learn and recognize things? These amazing capabilities have been taken for granted for years. Until recently, when one tried to use computers or machines to do things like recognizing handwritten characters, it became clear that such seemingly trivial achievements by human beings turn out extremely difficult, if not impossible, by mechanical means such as computers. After decades of rigorous attacks, such research is still as fresh as ever, and the mystery of how human beings can do it remains largely unknown and is just beginning to unfold. In a sense, up to now, "human brain" is still the "smartest" or the "most intelligent" mechanism than any computer can emulate. In a way, the study of *pattern recognition* and *artificial intelligence* techniques has attracted more and more interest and attention. This article is intended to give some inside views of pattern recognition techniques using artificial intelligence methodologies, and their applications to represent, learn, understand and recognize Chinese words, one of the most widely used, complicated and difficult languages in the world.

Recently, there has been growing interest among computer scientists, engineers and researchers in the problems related to the replication of human function and machine emulation of human reading. Intensive research has been done in this area and a large number of technical papers and reports on line-drawing pattern recognition (including character recognition) can be found in the literature [1,3,8,12-15,23,27-32]. This subject has attracted such immense interest and effort not only because it is very interesting and challenging, but also because it provides a strategy for solving many practical problems in the real world, including: automated postal code reading, check verification, office automation, and a large variety of banking, business, medical, industrial, engineering, scientific and military applications [4,25,34,36,39-41].

It is interesting to see that even human beings, who possess the best trained optical reading devices (eyes), make about 5-percent mistakes when reading in the absence of context [24]. These errors are mainly caused by infinite variations of shapes resulting from the writing habit, styles, education, region of origin, social environment, mood, health and other conditions of the writer. For character recognition by computers, the error rate could be even higher because of the reasons described above as well as other factors such as the writing instrument, writing surface, scanning mechanisms, learning techniques and machine recognition algorithms.

We will begin with a brief survey and comparison of several line-drawing pattern recognition methods. These approaches can be basically classified into two categories, namely (1) syntactic approach (such as PDL, tree grammars and array grammars) and (2) structural approach (such as BM method and extended Freeman's chain code (EFCC) method). Their advantages and disadvantages are discussed. The reason we concentrate on syntactic and structural methods rather than conventional statistical methods, is because they are hierarchical in nature, i.e., they divide a large, complicated pattern into smaller subpatterns according to its structure, which in turn can be further divided into smaller subpatterns and so on, till primitives are found which can no longer be divided. Using such structural and syntactic approaches, one can directly take advantages of the powerful data structures using grammatical rules, trees and directed labeled graphs, which are widely used in dealing with linguistic problems [6,7,11, 18,20]. Such approaches are similar to the powerful artificial intelligence problem solving strategies in which a large or complicated problem is reduced to a set of smaller subproblems [17,19,26,37,38]. Further, it has been shown that syntactic and structural approaches can overcome some disadvantages found in classic decision theoretic (statistical) approach, which has difficulty in distinguishing between two very similar patterns (characters) [7,18]. Among the various structural and syntactic approaches, we believe that those with a higher degree of recognizability are normally more natural in that they are more accurate and closer to the intuition of human beings, who possess the best pattern recognition skill in dealing with handwritten symbols.

Another character recognition scheme using improved extended octal code as primitives is re-examined. This scheme provides certain advantages such as flexible size, orientation, variations, fewer learning samples and lower degree of ambiguity and higher degree of recognizability. Then, the concept of *"learning by knowledge"* and *"semantic network"* is discussed. It has several advantages in easy learning, understanding and recognitin versus the traditional *"learning by rote"* and *"meaningful learning"*. Finally, examples of learning, representation, understanding and recognizing two-dimensional Chinese characters and words are illustrated.

2 Notations, Definitions, and Fundamentals

Generally speaking, a *"pattern"* is a class of objects that share some common properties. An example of pattern of handprinted English capital letter "A", in thinned skeletons[16,25,35], is shown in Figure 2.1.

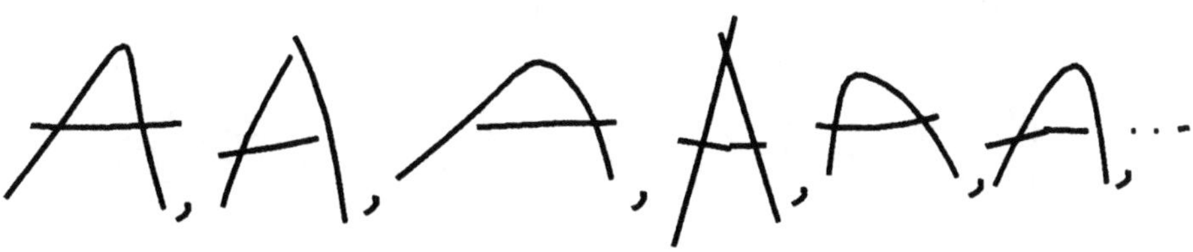

Figure 2.1 A pattern of handprinted English capital letter "A"

A pattern recognition system can be divided into two portions : Learning (Cognition) and Recognition. Figure 2.2 shows a block diagram of a typical character recognition system.

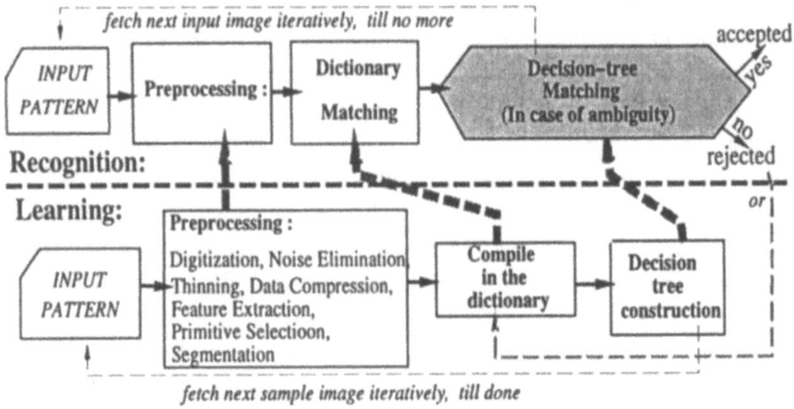

Figure 2.2 A block diagram of a typical character recognition system

We often hear people say, "*Your handwriting is too difficult to recognize.*" But what constitutes a well recognizable or a hardly recognizable handwriting at the level of character, word or sentence? Figure 2.3 shows there exist different categories of recognizability: category 1 is recognizable, category 2 is recognizable with some effort, category 3 is recognizable with great difficulty, and category 4 is beyond recognition.

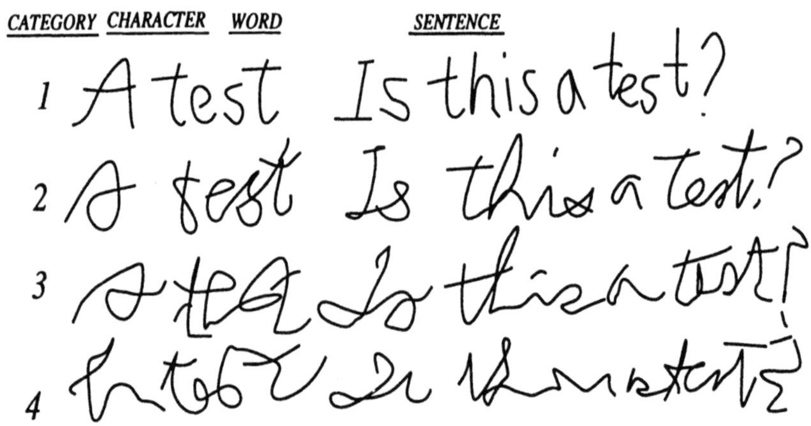

Figure 2.3 Several levels of recognizability

While this is intuitively true, it is necessary to define a more concrete criterion (or criteria) of "recognizable" characters for machine emulation of human reading.

Definition 2.1 The degree of ambiguity of a character B can be defined in terms of the problem domain D and the encoding scheme E as follows :

DegAmb(B,D,E)=max. no. of interpretations of B in D under E.

Definition 2.2 The degree of recognizability of a character B, in the domain of D, under the encoding scheme E can be defined as follows:

$$DegRec(B,D,E) = \begin{cases} 1/DegAmb(B,D,E) & \text{if B is in the dictionary} \\ 0 & \text{otherwise} \end{cases}$$

Conventionally one would conjecture that the easier a character is to learn the easier it is to recognize it and vice versa. However, this is not always true. We can find examples which are easier to learn but harder to recognize and vice versa. Take 'O' and 'Q' for instance. While 'O' is comparatively easy to learn (syntactically) than 'Q', it is harder to recognize (semantically). Notice that Definitions 2.1-2.2 are valid not only for well behaved printed letters, but also for handwriting variations. For instance, in Figure 2.4, DegAmb(C,D,E)$\geq$ 3 and DegAmb(H,D,E)$\geq$ 2. In general, there are 8 possible relations between learning and recognition as shown in Figure 2.5.

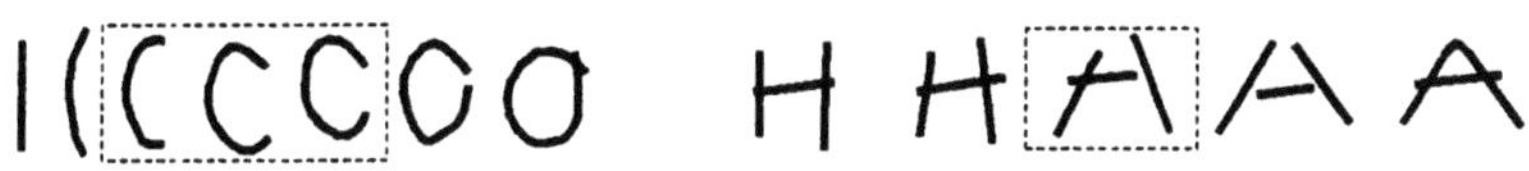

Figure 2.4 Continuous transformation and degrees of ambiguity

Figure 2.5 Relation between 'learning' and 'recognition'

There is also a close relation between *"Pattern Recognition (PR)"* and *"Artificial Intelligence (AI)"*. Historically speaking, PR, among other things, was a part of AI from the beginning around 1960's. Since then, PR has grown steadily to a point, so mature that it became a rather independent discipline itself around 1970's. However, from 1980's till more recently, it has been believed that the two fields have so much in common that in many occasions it is necessary to combine and emerge efforts of both. For instance, the recognition and understanding of sensory data like speech, image or vision, which are major concerns in pattern recognition, have always been considered as important subfields of artificial intelligence. On the other hand, topics like knowledge representation, inference, search or learning, that belong to the center of artificial intelligence, have constantly attracted the attention of resachers working in pattern recognition. Such a close relation between PR and AI is briefly described in Figure 2.6. In this article, we'll explore some AI aspects in application to character and word representation, understanding, perception and recognition.

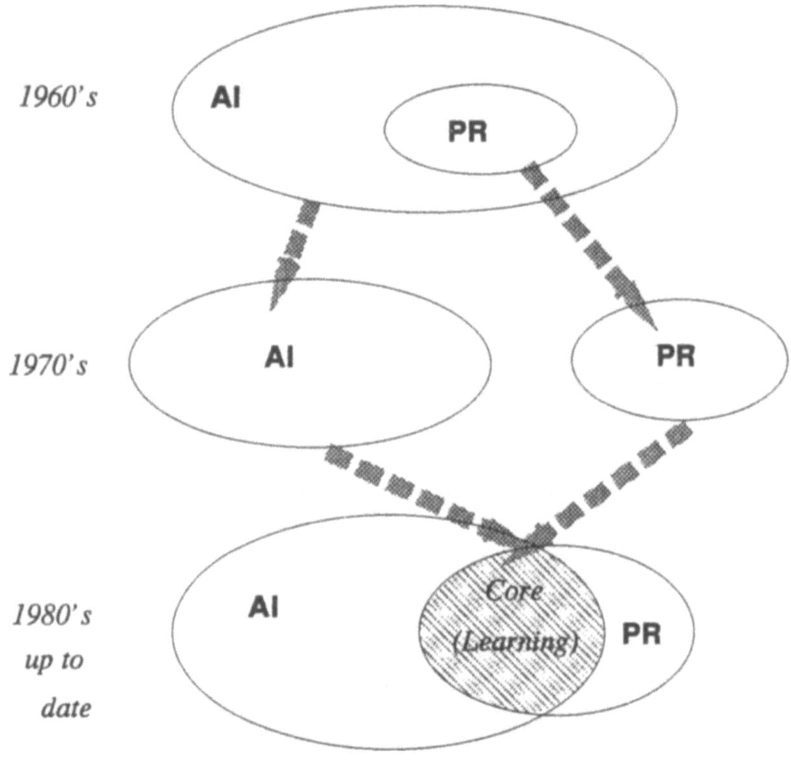

Figure 2.6 Relation between 'PR' and 'AI'

3 Syntactic Methods

This section investigates several syntactic methods for line-drawing pattern recognition, namely, picture descriptive language, tree grammar and array grammar, with an analysis and comparison between them.

3.1 The picture descriptive language PDL [7,20,21]

The picture descriptive language (PDL) was developed by Shaw. Each primitive is labeled at two distinguished points, a tail and a head. A primitive can be linked or concatenated to other primitives only at its tail and/or head.

Primitive Structure Description	Interpretation	Graph
a+b	head(a) CAT tail(b)	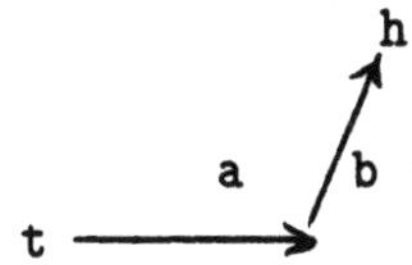
axb	tail(a) CAT tail(b)	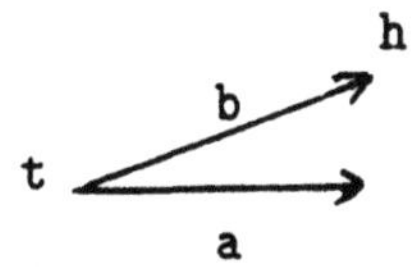
a-b	head(a) CAT head(b)	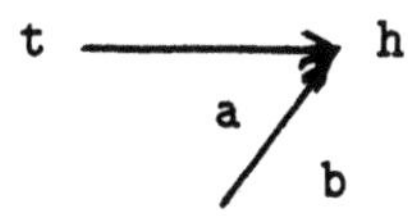
a*b	(tail(a) CAT tail(b)) (head(a) CAT head(b))	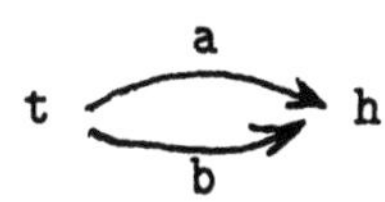

The grammar that generates sentences in PDL is a context-free grammar

G=(Vn, Vt, P, S)
where Vn={S,SL}, Vt={b,+,×,-,*,~,/,(,),l}

b may be any primitive (including the "null point primitive" c, which has identical tail and head) and P:

S ⟶b,	S⟶STS,	S⟶~S,	S⟶SL,
S⟶/SL,	SL⟶S,	SL⟶SLTSL,	SL⟶ ~SL,

SL⟶/SL, T⟶ +, T⟶ ×, T⟶ -,
T⟶ *.

The primitives can be described as follows:

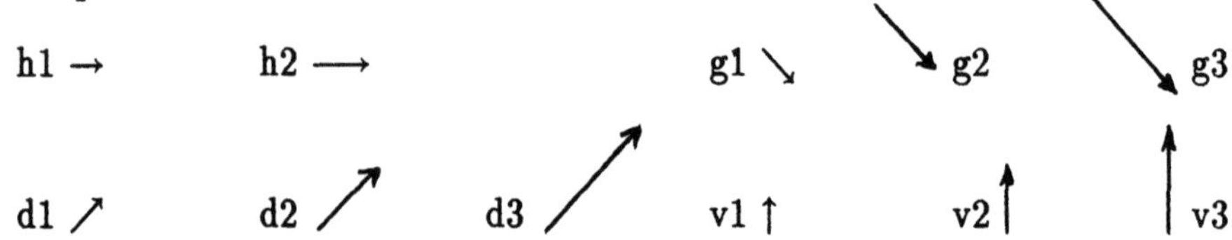

Then, we can express the English characters as follows(in part) [7].

A→ (d2+((d2+g2)*h2)+g2)
X→ (d2+((~g2)×d2×g2))

For example, the character "A" can be described as follows :

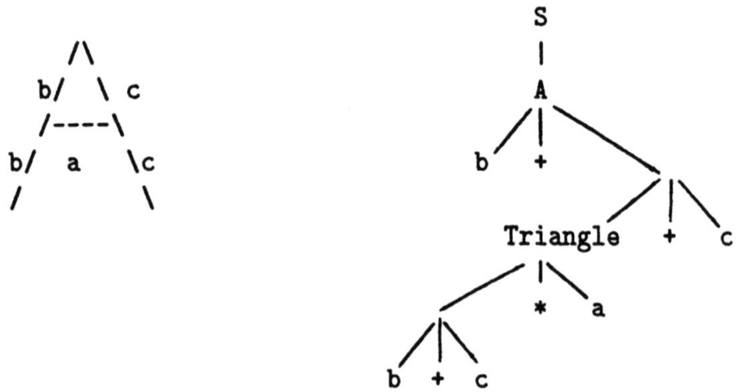

3.2 Tree Grammars [7,11,20]

By extension of one-dimensional concatenation to multidimensional concatenation, strings are generalized to trees. Naturally, if a pattern can be conveniently described by a tree, it can be easily generated by a tree grammar.

Let N^+ be the set of strictly positive integers. Let U be the universal tree domain (the free semigroup with identity element "0" generated by N^+ and a binary operation "."). The depth of a∈ U is denoted by d(a) and defined as : d(0)=0, d(a . i)=d(a)+1, i∈ N^+. a $\leq$ b if and only if there exists x ∈ U such that a . x=b . a and b are incomparable if and only if a $\not\leq$ b, and b $\not\leq$ a. Figure 3.1 represents the universal tree domain U. D is a tree domain if and only if D is a finite subset of U satisfying(1) b ∈ D and $a < b$ implies a ∈ D, and (2)a . j ∈ D and $i < j$ in N^+ implies a . i ∈ D.

A ranked alphabet is a pair $(\sum, r)$ where $\sum$ is a finite set of symbols and

$$r : \sum \longrightarrow N = N^+ \cup \{0\}$$

For a $\in \sum$, r(a) is called the rank of a. Let

$$\sum_n = r^{-1}(n)$$

A tree over $\sum$ (i.e., over $(\sum, r)$) is a function

$$\alpha : D \longrightarrow \sum$$

```
                    0
                  / | \
                1   2   3 ...
              /   \
           1.1      1.2 ...
          /   \      .
      1.1.1  1.1.2 ...
        .      .
        .      .
```

Figure 3.1 Universal tree domain

such that D is a tree domain and

$$r[\alpha(a)] = max\{i \mid a.i \in D\}$$

that is, the rank of a label at "a" must be equal to the number of branches in the tree domain at a. The domain of a tree α is denoted by $D(\alpha)$ or D_α. Let $T_\sum$ be the set of all trees over $\sum$. The depth of α is defined as $d(\alpha)=max\{d(a) | a \in D(\alpha)\}$. Let α be a tree and "a" be a member of $D(\alpha)$. α/a, a subtree of α at "a", is defined as

$$\alpha/a = \{(b, x) \mid (a.b, x) \in \alpha\}$$

For an example, please refer to Fig. 3.2.

$$G_A = (V_A, r_A, P_A, A)$$

where

$$V_A = \{A, A1, A2, N_a, N_d, N_c\}, V_{TA} = \{i, a, c, d\}$$

$$r_A(i) = \{2\}, r_A(a) = \{0, 2\}, \quad r_A(c) = \{0, 1\}, \quad r_A(d) = \{0\}$$

P_A:

```
              i
A   -->      / \
           A1   A2

              a
A1  -->      / \
           Na   Nb

              c
A2  -->       |
              Nc

Na --> a, Nd --> d, Nc --> c
```

```
       $
      / \
   a /   \ c
    /-----\
 a /   d   \ c
  /         \
```

Figure 3.2 A tree grammar for character "A"

3.3 Array Grammar(AG) [6,20,22,29,33]

Definition 3.1

An isometric array grammar is a quintuple

$$G = (V_N, V_T, P, S, \#)$$

where V_N is a finite nonempty set of nonterminal symbols, V_T is a finite nonempty set of terminal symbols, $V_N \cap V_T = 0$ and $\# \notin (V_N \cup V_T)$ is the background or blank symbol. P is a finite nonempty set of rewriting rules of the form $\alpha \longrightarrow \beta$, where array α and array β are geometrically identical over $V_N \cup V_T \cup \{\#\}$: α not all #'s. S$\in V_N$ is the starting symbol.

We say that array x directly generates array y, denoted x$\Longrightarrow$ y, if there is a rewriting rule $\alpha \longrightarrow \beta$, x contains α as a subarray and y is identical to x except that the subarray α is replaced with the corresponding symbols of the array β. Let $\Longrightarrow^*$ be the reflexive transitive closure of $\Longrightarrow$. The language generated by an array grammar G, denoted L(G), is the set of all arrays of terminal symbols and #'s that can be generated from the starting symbol S in a field of #'s.

Definition 3.2

The distance between two arrays X and Y over V_T, denoted as d(X, Y) can be defined as the smallest number of error transformations (insertions, substitutions and deletions) required to derive Y from X.

Example 3.1: Given two arrays over a, b

```
                                        b
          a a a a a                 a   a a a
              a                         a
     X =      a        and     Y =      a
              a                         a
              a                         b
```

we have

```
                    b               b              b
    a a a a a   a a a a a       a   a a a      a   a a a
        a     Ti    a       Td      a      Ts      a
X =     a     |-    a       |-      a      |-      a      = Y
        a           a               a              a
        a           a               a              b
```

where the symbol |- means "becomes".

The minimum number of error transformations required to transform X to Y is 3. Therefore, d(X,Y) = 3.

```
                                 *
                               *   *     *
* * * * * * * * *          *       * * * *        * * * * * *
        *                          *              *
        *                        *                *
        *                        *                *
        *                        *                * * *
        *                          *              *
        *                          *              *
        *                        *                *
        *                      *                  * *
       (a)                    (b)                (c)
```

Figure 3.3 Three arrays over ''*''

Definition 3.2 is not very satisfactory as can be seen from the following example.

Example 3.2 Given the 3 arrays in Fig. 3.3, it can be seen that d[(a), (b)] = 18 and d[(a), (c)] = 6. Therefore one would classify (a) and (c), instead of (a) and (b), into one cluster. Anyone who knows English will easily recognize that (a) is more similar to (b) rather than to (c). In fact, a survey of 18 persons showed that all of them thought that (b) is a T while (c) is probably an F or an E.

The above example shows that the direct distance measure between two arrays is not satisfactory for clustering analysis. This motivates the following method.

Assume that every array $\mathfrak{R}$ is a variation or a noisy counterpart of a pure, noiseless array $\mathfrak{I}$, generated by an array grammar G^c, called 'core grammar'. If additional rules are augmented to G^c, resulting in G^a, called 'augmented grammar', then G^a can also generate $\mathfrak{R}$. For instance, in Fig. 3.3, why does a person recognize (b), instead of (c) as a T? Because the person must have learned this to be a T before, and one can assume that a typical, pure or noiseless T was used as a model when he or she learned it. A description of this model for T could be : "T has a horizontal stroke with a vertical stroke attached below the center of the horizontal ones, and both strokes are of similar length". In other words, when a T is learned, it is learned as if there were an array grammar built into one's brain. This grammar can be considered as a core grammar characterizing T. With a certain kind of flexibility, that is with some extra rules attached to this core grammar resulting in a new augmented grammar, one can also recognize some variations or noisy T's, such as, 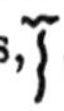,  and .

Definition 3.3

The distance between an array $\mathfrak{R}$ and a group of arrays characterized by an augmented array grammar G^a is d_a (G^a ,$\mathfrak{R}$) = minimum number of $\mathfrak{R}$ symbols not covered by the parsing of G^a.

Definition 3.4

The distance between an array $\mathfrak{R}$ and a group of arrays characterized by a core array grammar G^c is d_c (G^c , $\mathfrak{R}$) = minimum number of $\mathfrak{R}$ parsing steps using non-core rules of G^a + d_a (G^a, $\mathfrak{R}$).

Notice that if there does not exist a parsing sequence for $\Re$, then both its d_a and d_c values are either infinite or undefined. In Fig. 3.2, for instance,

$$d_a[D_3,(a)] = 0, d_c[G_2,(a)] = 0, d_a[G_3,(b)] = 0,$$

$$d_c[G_2,(b)] = 9, d_a[G_3,(c)] = -, d_c(G_2,(c)) = -.$$

The following is an algorithm that will produce an augmented grammar from a core grammar.

Without loss of generality, one can assume that each core grammar is in Chomsky 2-point normal form [6,9,29,33], Notice that because a different definition of connectedness is being used, we have a slightly different Chomsky normal form, in that every rule obeys one of the following:

```
                #     C           #    C          #      C
  A# -> BC,    A   -> B   ,         ->            A ->    B,
                                  A    B

                 A       B          A    B
   #A -> C B,   #      -> C   ,       ->     ,     A     -> B
                                    #    C           #       C
or A ->a
```

where A $\in V_N$, $B, C \in V_N \cup V_T$ and $a \in V_T$.

In general, a rule can be represented by a triple (A, BC,$\overline{d}$), where $0 \le$ d $\le$ 7. For instance, A# $\rightarrow$ BC can be represented by (A, BC,0),

```
     #        C
     A    --> B
```

can be represented by (A, BC, 1), etc., and A $\rightarrow$ a is represented by (A, a, -). Notice that this representation coincides with the Freeman's chain code octal primitives as to be shown in the next section.

Algorithm A_l(Core-to-augmented)
Input. k core grammar

$$G_i = (V_{N_i}, V_{T_i}, P_i, S_i, \#), i = 1...k$$

Output. k augmented grammars

$$G_i^a = (V_{N_i}^a, V_{T_i}^a, P_i^a, S_i^a, \#) i = 1...k$$

Step 1. For i=1 to k do step 2
Step 2.

$$V_{N_i}^a = V_{N_i}, V_{T_i}^a = V_{T_i}, S_i^a = S_i$$

and

$$P_i^a = P_i \cup \{(A, BC, (\overline{d}+1)_{mod8}), (A, BC, (\overline{d}+7)_{mod8}) \mid (A, BC, \overline{d}) \in P_i\}$$

For convenience, if in P_i the jth rule is (A, BC, $\overline{d}$), then add j.$(\overline{d}+1)_{mod8}$ and j. $(\overline{d}+7)_{mod8}$ into P_i^a.
Step 3.

$$G_i^a = (V_{N_i}^a, V_{T_i}^a, P_i^a, S_i^a, \#)$$

Next we present a two-pass clustering procedure.

Cluster Pass I

Input. A set of n digitized patterns X=$\{x_1, x_2, ..., x_n\}$, and a set of k core grammars Z = $\{G_1, G_2, ..., G_k\}$, where L(G_i) $\cap$ $L(G_j) = 0$ for i $\neq$ j, i, j=1,...,k.
Output. The assignment of x_i, i=1,...,n to k clusters characterized by G_i, i= 1, ..., k.

Step 1. Call CORE-TO-AUGMENTED
Step 2. For i = 1 to n do step 3-5
Step 3. For j = 1 to k do step 4-5
Step 4. Compute $d_a(G_j, x_i)$
Step 5. Assign x_i to cluster p with

$$d_a(G_p, x_i) = min_{j=1...k} d_a(G_j, x_i).$$

Notice that if more than one clusters have the same minimum distance with x_i, then x_i should be assigned to all these clusters.

If x_i has been assigned to more than one cluster, then use Cluster Pass II.

Cluster Pass II

For all $x_{i_1}, x_{i_2}, ..., x_{i_m}$ which are assigned to more than one cluster, do the following.

Input. x_{i_j} and its assigned grammars $G_{i_1}, ..., G_{i_h}$ where $1 \leq$ j=m $\leq$ n, $1 \leq$ h $\leq$ k, $1 \leq i_j \leq$ n, and $1 \leq i_h \leq k$.

Output. Assignment of x_{i_j} to a proper cluster.

Step 1. Compute $d_c(G_{i_h}, x_{i_j})$ for all G_{i_k} to which x_{i_j} has been assigned.

Step 2. Assign x_{i_j} to cluster i_q where $d_c(G_{i_q}, x_{i_j}$ = min d_c (G_{i_h}, x_{i_j}) for all G_{i_h} to which x_{i_j} has been assigned.

Recognition of the set of English characters adapted from Fu and Lu[7,11] is illustrated using the above two-pass clustering procedure. There are 51 characters from nine different classes: P, X, D, U, F, Y, K, H, and V characterized by G0, G1, G2, G3, G4, G5, G6, G7, and G8, respectively. Eight of the nine classes are selected from four groups, each with similar structures; that is D and P, H and K, U and V and X and Y. The class of character F is different from the other eight classes. Each character is an array on a 20*20 grid, as shown in Fig. 3.4. Generated in a top down fashion, each pattern is parsed upwards from the bottom. The results of 9 clusters are satisfactory.

In Fu and Lu[7,11], the use of a similarity measure using tree grammar for syntactic patterns in terms of grammar transformations is proposed and a nearest neighborhood rule and a clustering procedure are described. This clustering procedure is quite successful for two-dimensional pattern analysis, especially for English characters. However, in this procedure, every character should be first encoded into a one-dimensional string via Freeman's chain code[5] and Shaw's PDL[21]. Further, pattern 47(Figure 3.4.) is not accurately classified into group 2, D, even when weighted transformations are used with a threshold value as high as 3. In Lu[11], a tree-to-tree distance measurement algorithm is proposed and is applied to clustering analysis for 2-dimensional patterns. Again, in this algorithm, every pattern should be first encoded into a tree representation and, further, there are some confusions between A_5() and E_5() and between E_4() and C_5().

Note that although the purposes of [29] and [7,11] are somewhat similar, in the sense that they all aim at the same target (i.e. they all try to solve the clustering problem for two-dimensional patterns), [29] employs an entirely different approach. For instance, the model used in[29] is "isometric array grammar"—the first time such a model has been tried for two-dimensional pattern clustering analysis. Also, the definition of distance between two patterns introduced in Section 3 of this paper does not use the conventional error transformation method. Instead, we use the concept of parsing and define the distance between an array and a class of arrays characterized by a Context-Free Array Grammar(CFAG)[6]. Even though the same input data

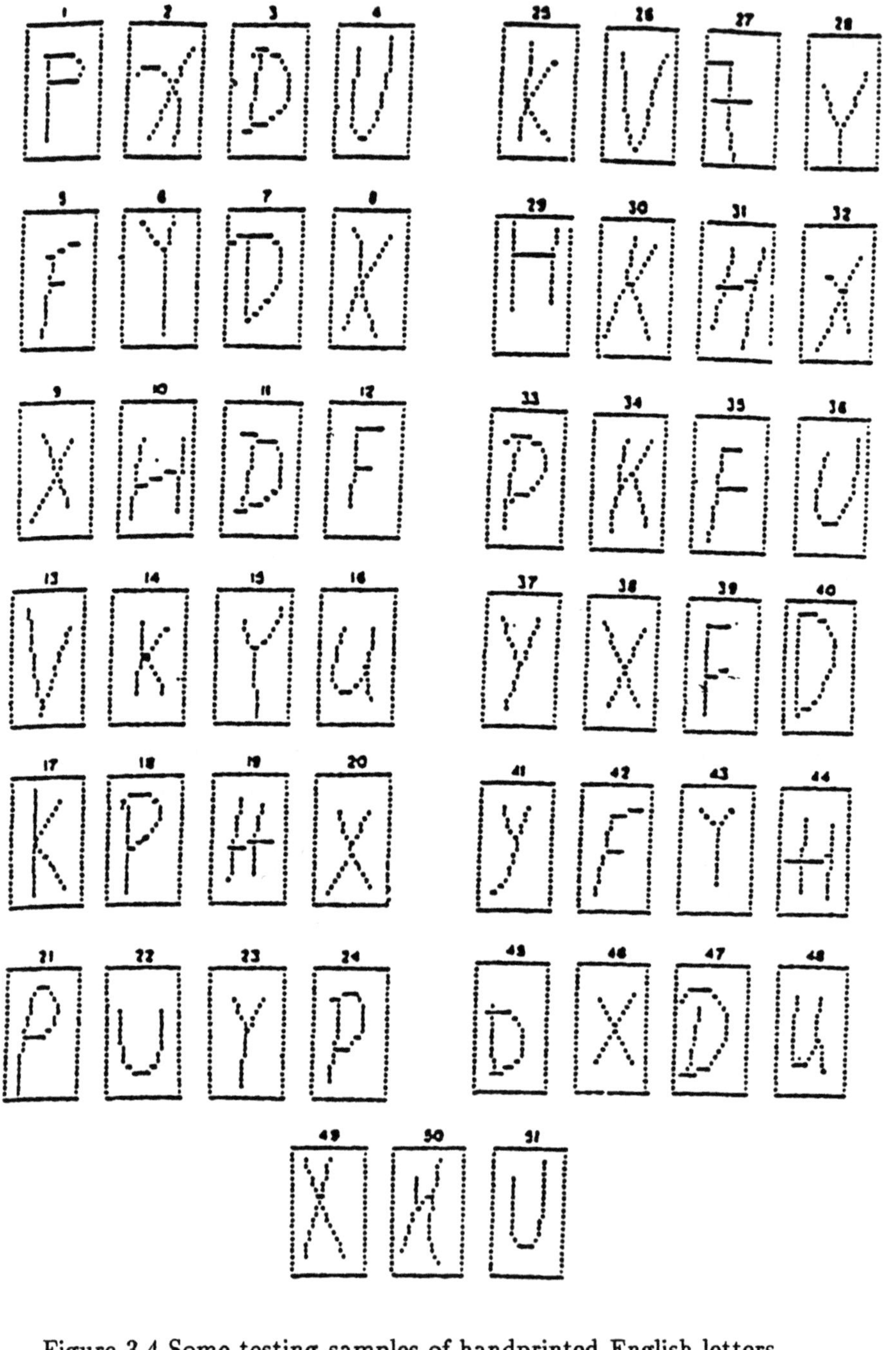

Figure 3.4 Some testing samples of handprinted English letters

adapted from [7,11] is used to test our two-pass clustering algorithm, we obtain a different result. In addition to the differences discussed above, we also notice that pattern 27 of Fig. 3.4 is classified as an X through our algorithm, in contrast to an F through the algorithm of Fu and Lu[7,11]. A survey of 18 persons showed that 7 of them thought of as an X, 8 of them thought it was an F, while 3 of them thought it was neither. Clearly it depends on how one is trained to write.

4 Structural Methods

4.1 Berthod and Maroy's primitives

We denote Berthod and Maroy's method[3] as BM. Every character is encoded into a string of the 5 primitives shown in Figure 4.1.

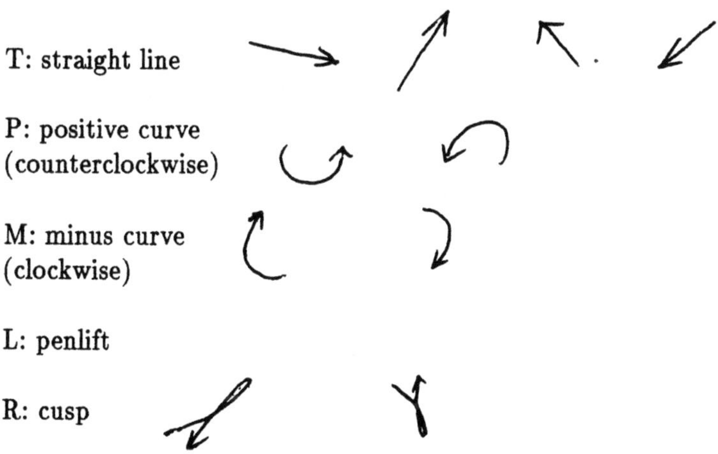

Figure 4.1 The five Berthod and Maroy primitives

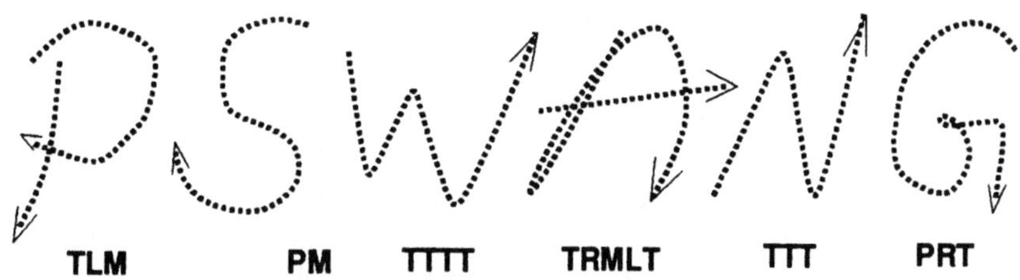

Figure 4.2 Examples of BM codes corresponding to characters

Let the domain D be all English characters. A dictionary consisting of about 26 characters (strings of primitives) resulting from pre-processing of characters drawn on a graphic tablet is compiled.

Code	Symbols	Code	Symbols
M	O	TM	S
MLT	J	TLTTT	M
MM	M	TRM	DP
P	C L U	TRLMLT	AF
PLT	EGQ	TRMLTLT	E
PLTLT	E	TRMM	B
PM	S	TRMRM	BR
PRT	G	TRBT	R
PT	G	TRTTLT	AFK
TLM	DPJ	TRTTLTLT	E
TLMM	BR	TRTTT	N
TLMRM	B	TRTTT	M
TLMT	R	TT	LV
TLT	X Y T	TTLT	J
TLTLT	AFHIKNYZ	TTLTLT	E
TLTLTLT	E	TTT	ZNS
TLTT	N	TTTT	WM
TLTTM	B		

Figure 4.3 A dictionary of 26 English characters using BM

Now, if the domain D is reduced to capital English characters only, the dictionary will contain 13 ambiguous words (Figure 4.3). The most ambiguous word is TLTLT, which has 8 different interpretations. Therefore DegAmb(β,D,BM)=8, where $\beta \in \{A,F,H,I,K,N,Y,Z\}$. The code P has 3 interpretations (C,L,U), TLT has 3 interpretations, and TTT has 3 interpretations (ZNS), etc.

It is seen that characters A,F,H,I,K,N,Y and Z, which are not even syntactically similar, all result in the same encoded word "TLTLT". That makes this word extremely ambiguous and non-informative. A tremendous amount of effort must be spent to disambiguate it. Such a decision tree for disambiguating the encoded word "TLTLT" of characters A,F,H,I,K,N,Y and Z is shown in Figure 4.4.

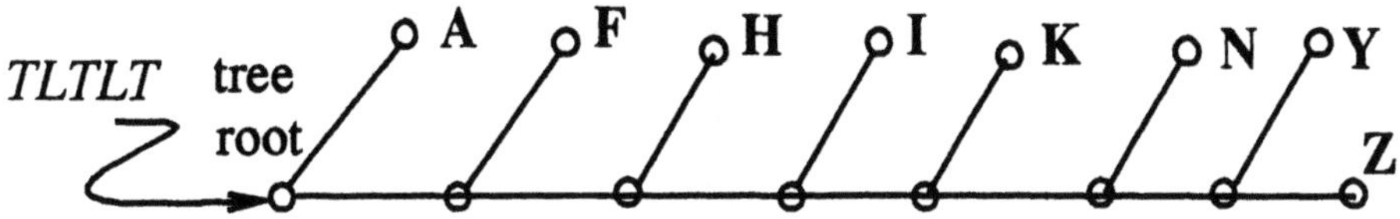

Figure 4.4 A decision tree disambiguating the encoded word "TLTLT"

Besides, obviously unacceptable symbols such as

```
"   |\  "        " \  / \  / "
 \/ | \             \/   \/
 /\ |  \            /\   /\
    |   \          /  \/   \
```

could be mis-recognized as an "E", since both have "TLTLTLT", which is uniquely defined in the dictionary and is unambiguous.

4.2 Extended Primitives

We adapt Freeman's chain code[5] and the 8 direction vectors shown in Figure 4.5 as primitives. Each character is encoded into a string of primitives, but only those local extrema points (points which are tangent to one of the 8 vectors) are extracted. The letter "C" could be encoded as 3456701. To handle penlift, we consider the vector between 'pen-up' and its successive 'pen-down' and choose the closest octal primitive with a bar on it. Therefore the letter "H" could be encoded as $6\bar{1}6\bar{3}\,0$. Some more examples are shown in Figure 4.6.

Let us call the above described encoding scheme EF(for Extended Freeman) and let D= English characters. Using the same sample data , a dictionary consisting of about 48 words is compiled in an ordering $0 > 1 > ... > \bar{6} > \bar{7}$ as shown in Figure 4.7. In this dictionary, only 7 words are ambiguous and DegAmb(B, Dm, EF)=2, B∈{C,O,D,P,X,Y,T}. Further, this method eliminates the possibility of misrecognizing a number of obviously unacceptable symbols. For example,

```
    |\
 \/ | \
 /\ |  \
    |   \
```

will not be interpreted as the valid character "E".

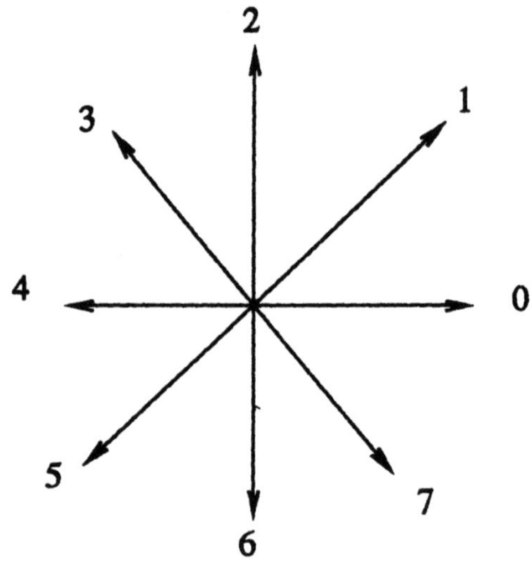

Figure 4.5 Freeman's chain coding

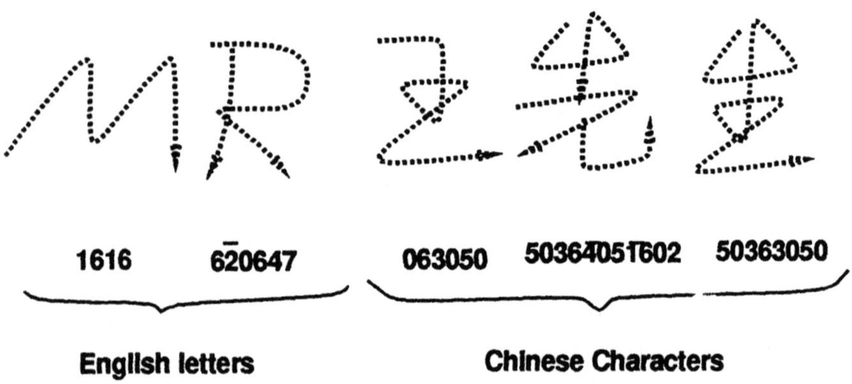

Figure 4.6 Some more examples of Chinese and English characters and their corresponding chain codings

$046\bar{2}0\bar{5}0$	E	$0765\bar{2}6$	P
$0\bar{4}6$	T	$0\bar{4}6\bar{2}0$	F
$046\bar{2}050$	E	$0\bar{4}64$	J
$0\bar{4}6\bar{4}0$	I	161	N
21	V	2121	W
245670123406	G	2716	M
3456701	CO	4560	C
$46\bar{2}0$	F	$46\bar{2}0\bar{5}0$	E
4675	S	560	C
5670123	CO	$567012\bar{3}\bar{6}7$	Q
575	S	$5\bar{1}6\bar{3}0$	A
$5\bar{1}7\bar{1}5$	N	$5\bar{1}7\bar{3}0$	A
$5\bar{2}7$	XY	61	L
602	U	$61\bar{5}7$	K
620657	R	62065765	B
6275	DP	$64\bar{2}0$	J
670	L	67012	U
$6\bar{1}57$	K	$6\bar{1}6\bar{3}0$	H
$6\bar{2}0657$	R	$6\bar{2}065765$	B
$6\bar{2}0765$	DP	$6\bar{2}71$	N
$6\bar{2}716$	M	$6\bar{2}75$	DP
$6\bar{2}7575$	B	$6\bar{3}0$	T
7171	W	72	V
$7\bar{1}5$	Y	$7\bar{2}5$	X

Figure 4.7 An EF Dictionary

4.3 Improved Extended Freeman Approach[IEF]

In the EF approach, the 8 primitives $\bar{0}, \bar{1}, ..., \bar{7}$. can be replaced by 0,1,...,7. Others remain the same and some advantages are gained (Figs 4.8-9).

```
        (3)                           (3)
        ----->                        ----->
              (1)                     |        (1)
    (2)|      -->                 (2)|------>
       |                             |
       |                             |
         (a)                           (b)
```

Figure 4.8 (a) EF($0\bar{4}6\bar{2}0$) versus (b) IEF (04620)

0462050	E	076526	P
046	T	04620	F
0462050	E	0464	J
04640	I	161	N
21	V	2121	W
245670123406	G	2761	M
3456701	CO	4560	C
4620	F	0462050	E
4675	S	560	C
5670123	CO	567012367	Q
575	S	51630	A
51715	N	51730	A
527	XY	61	L
602	U	6157	K
620657	R	62065765	B
6275	DP	6420	J
670	L	67012	U
6157	K	61630	H
620657	R	62065765	B
620765	DP	6271	N
62715	M	6275	DP
627575	B	630	T
7171	W	72	V
715	Y	725	X

Figure 4.9. An IEF dictionary

5 Learning by Pattern and Knowledge

From the above observations and discussions, it is found that a pattern recognition system that has a better performance should not only take care of accuracy rate, speed and memory requirement, but also must satisfy human needs in the sense that it should coincide with human natural habits or conventions. This is true for general pattern recognition. It is certainly true for character and handwriting recognition as well. For such a system would make *learning process* easier, and consequently would make understanding and recognition more effective and efficient.

As mentioned earlier in Section 2, "*learning*" is the core of pattern recognition. It undoubtedly plays an essential role in character and handwriting recognition. Suppose the two systems discussed in the previous sections are called "BM" and "IEF" systems respectively. And suppose all conditions including recognition rate, speed, memory requirement, cost of product are all the same. One probably would like to choose the "IEF" one, because it is more in parallel to our own natural habit. We have already known from accumulated writing and reading habits for years which letters and characters are difficult one (in terms of ambiguity), and will therefore would like to write more carefully on the touch sensitive tablet in order to provide computer more precise data for disambiguation in the secondary decision tree.

On the other hand, however, using the "BM" system, there is no way one could tell which characters are difficult ones (in terms of ambiguity for BM encoded words) and have to force oneself to memorize from a prepared list of such words in order to use the machine in a more effective and efficient way. Further, such a list would vary, depending on the encoding schemes, testing data and many other factors such as penpad hardware structure and software programs. One could classify such a way of learning as "learning by rote" according to Ausubel[2]. In such a learning process, new information is being added to the process's learning structure without establishing any relationship with the concepts already existing in the knowledge of the learner. A slightly better way of learning was proposed later by Millward [13], known as "meaningful learning" by which new information is roughly related to the relevant concepts already existing in the knowledge structure of the learner.

Here we can strengthen this idea to a even more powerful learning methodology, known as *"learning by pattern and knowledge"*, in which old, existing knowledge can be accumulated and iteratively used to enforce and help learn new knowledge via a feedback system, as described in Figure 5.1.

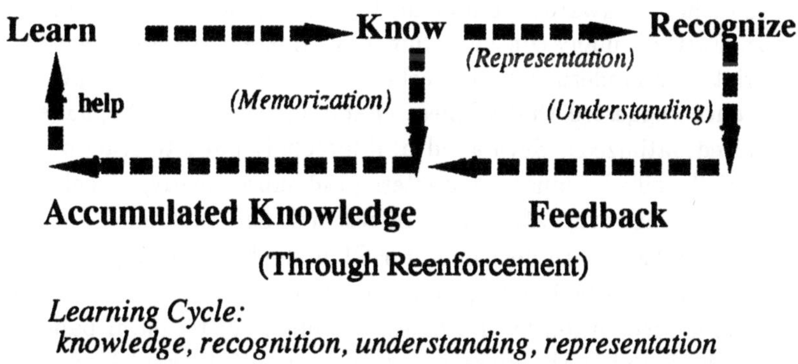

Figure 5.1 Learning by Pattern and Knowledge

In this way, learning, understanding, memorizing and recognizing a complicated object would no longer be a difficult one, as long as this complicated object can be divided into smaller and simpler ones, which can be further divided into even simpler ones and so on. This is pretty much in line with the problem solving strategies in artificial intelligence. Such strategies have been shown particularly effective for problem that have "hierarchical structure". In terms of pattern recognition, it would work particulalrly well for objects or characters that are *"hierarchical"*. Interesting enough, Chinese characters and words - one of the most widely used and difficult languages, believed by many people, posses such a property. We'll explore more details through illustrations in terms of understanding, learning, memorization and recognition in the following section.

6 An Illustration - Chinese Word Recognition

In this section, we will discuss some aspects of advantages of Chinese characters and words, and how "learning by pattern and knowledge" will make it more interesting and easier to learn, understand, memorize and recognize Chinese characters and words - the basic unit of one of the most popular and important languages being used by more than 1.2 billions people around the world.

Unlike alphabetic and one-dimensional western languages such as English, Chinese characters are well known two-dimensional and non-alphabetic. Each Chinese character is confined in a rectangle or square area, henceforth called "square word" 方塊字 . There is essentially no unique linear way of representing a Chinese character and some characters are so complicated that they have more than 30 strokes.[28] Mainly because of this nature, it was widely believed for quite sometime that Chinese characters are rather backward, too difficult to learn, understand, recognize and memorize. Further, many consider Chinese characters are non-scientific and inappropriate for modern use by mechanical means such as computers. It was even once suggested that Chinese characters should be "alphabetized" (or romanized, latinized). Such an idea, if forcefully put into practice, would have essentially killed Chinese characters (and subsequently, its culture).

Fortunately, however, after years of research and experiments many effective methods have been developed for Chinese characters input keyboard design, internal /external codes, and output printout /display techniques, and automatic recognition by machines. Hundreds of technical papers and reports can be found in the literature, and dozens of different kinds of Chinese computers, typewriters and word processors are available in the markets [28]. It turns out that not only Chinese characters avoid the fate of being eliminated but also people began to realize that, after all, may be Chinese characters are not that bad.

From above observations, it can be seen that Chinese characters are indeed not only "not bad" but actually very good from "intelligence", "knowledge" and "pattern recognition" points of view. [28] Using "learning by pattern and knowledge" method will make it more interesting and easier to learn, understand, memorize and recognize Chinese characters and words, in contrast to the conventional "learning by rote" techniques. Note that Chinese characters and words are not just "pictorial", they are also "indicative symbols", "logical aggregates", and "phonetic complexes". They have strong properties in (i)syntax-semantics correlation, (ii)logical relations between characters, (iii)multi-character words hierarchical structures, (iv)induced knowledge, (v)culture continuity, (vi)artistic balance and beauty, and (vii)avoiding ambiguity.

These properties are illustrated in the following figures.

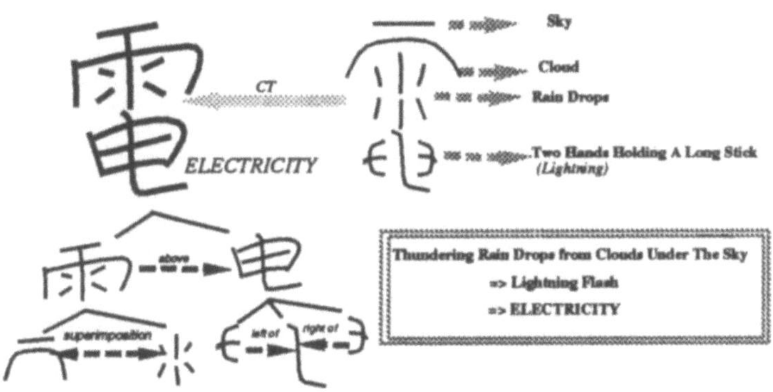

Figure 6.1 Hierarchical structure and semantic network of "electricity"

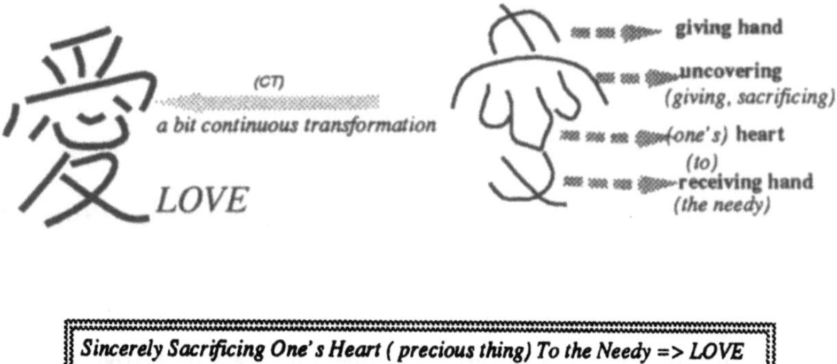

Figure 6.2 Pictorial and indicative symbol of "love"

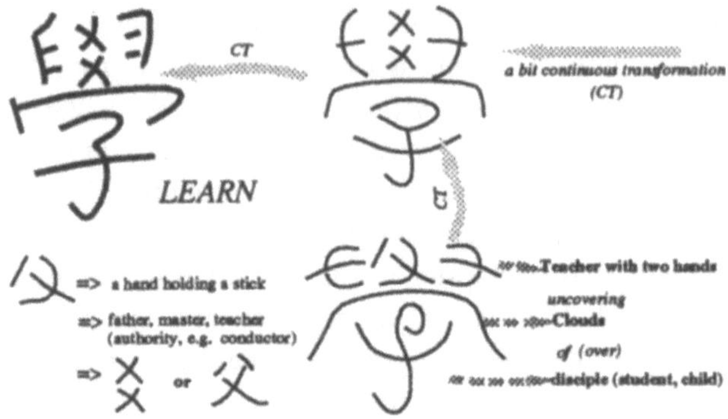

Figure 6.3 Pictorial and indicative symbol of "learn"

Figure 6.4 Some more examples logical aggregates/common properties between characters and multiple character words

For instance, having learned the words "electricity", "ice" and "box", can help one learn, understand and recognize a new word "refrigerator" very easily and immediately, without any further effort. In addition, all words related to "tree" share the common pattern "tree". Such property can help learning, understand and recognition as shown in Figure 6.5. According to the dictionary [10], among 7,000 commonly used Chinese characters, the largest such radical(family) is the "water" (with more than 400 characters), followed by "grass" (350), "hand" (330), "tree" (319) and "heart" (260). Such strong characteristics are also reflected in multi-character words, such as *cow, ox, buffalo, bull. calif, veal, milk, beef, butter, steak, cowhide* and *horn* etc all of which bear the character "牛" in it. Such advantage is rather unique and can not be found in many other western languages such as English.

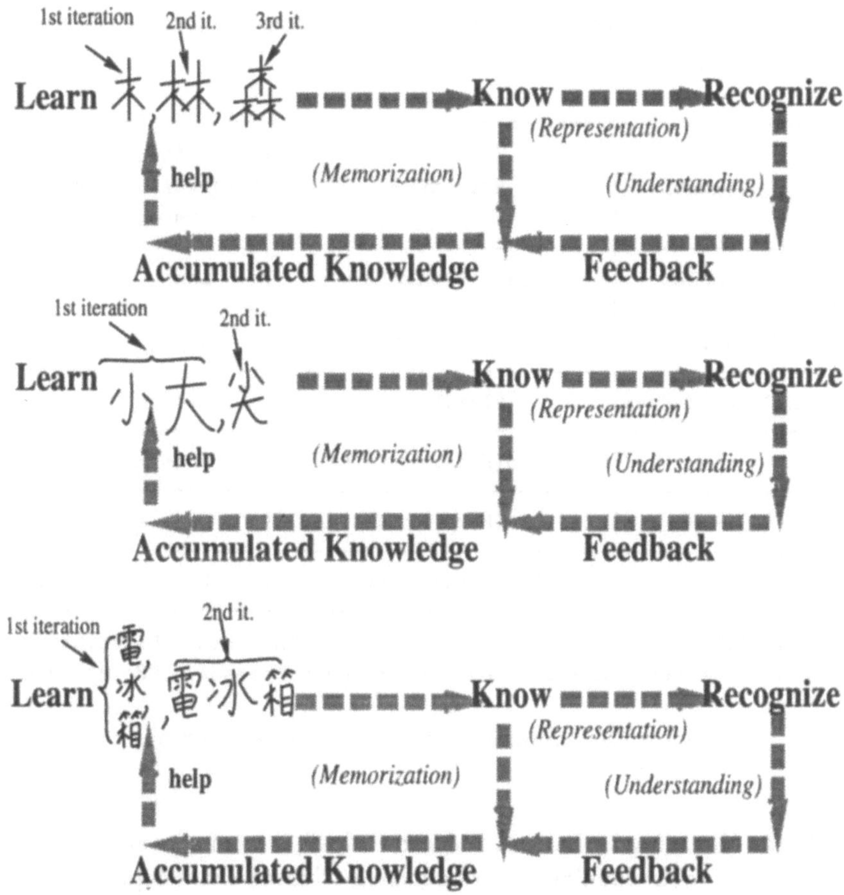

Figure 6.5 Learning, understanding and recognition of Chinese characters/words

7 Discussions and Conclusions

We introduced the basic concept of degrees of recognizability and ambiguity. Their relationship has been discussed. Although there are many other factors such as human factors, social environment, writing instruments, software, hardware, resolution, thresholding and quantization schemes etc, nevertheless, the degree of ambiguity plays an inherent and important role.

Two different methodologies for on-line handwritten symbols were compared. The first used basic structural shapes as primitives while the second used octal chain codes as primitives. The second method provided advantages of flexible sizes, orientations, variations, and fewer learning samples. It also possesses an inherently lower degree of ambiguity. Besides, in this method, it is less likely to mis-recognize an obviously unacceptable symbol as a valid one. A summary is depicted in Figure 7.1.

	Grammar	Structure	Accuracy (degrees of ambiguity and recognizability)
TG	Simpler	Less Flexible	Low
AG	More Complex	More Flexible	High
PDL	Context Free	Flexible	Medium
BM	---	Flexible(Fewer Primitives)	More Ambiguous
EF	---	Flexible(More Primitives)	Less ambiguous
IEF	---	Flexible(Fewer Primitives)	Less ambiguous

where TG:Tree Grammar, AG:Array Grammar, PDL:Picture Descriptive Language, BM:Berthod and Maroy, EF:Extended Freeman, IEF:Improved EF

Figure 7.1 A Summary of qualitative comparisons

As for "Learning by Pattern and knowledge", it is an advantage not only for learning, understanding and recognizing Chinese characters/words, but also for many aspects at Chinese sentence and language levels as well, mainly because of its hierarchical and natural structures. For instance, parsing, searching and pattern matching are very efficient in postal envelops address recognition, name roster list handling and calendar time schedule processing, in comparison with other western langauges such as English. Such a comparison is shown in Figure 7.2.

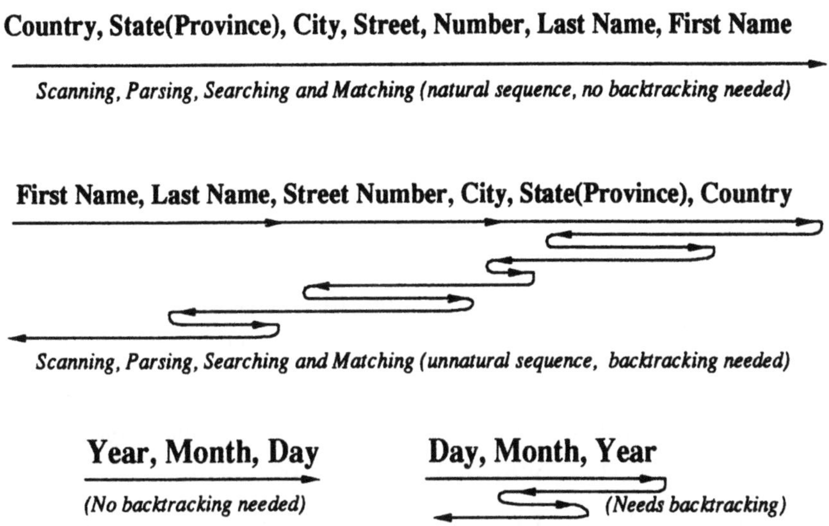

Figure 7.2 Learning, understanding and recognition of Chinese characters/words

A final note: The idea presented here can also be applied to general pattern recognition. The following figures were realistic examples observed from France and USA respectively. They illustrate the importance of clarity, quick grasp of corresponding meanings (semantics) of road traffic sign and fire emergency sign, which must be improved in order to save time and lives.

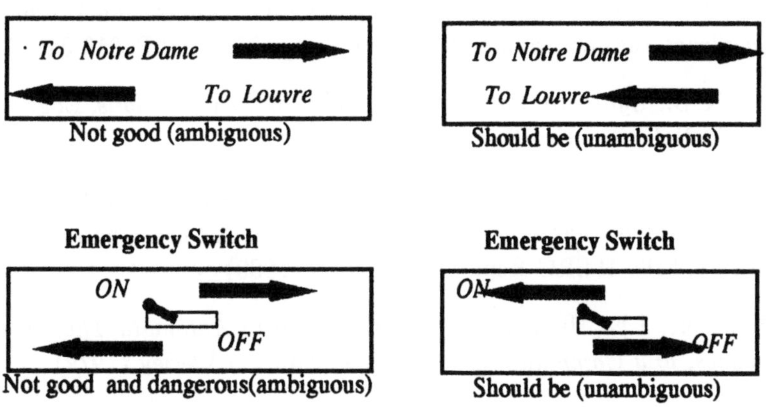

Figure 7.3 Importance of "unambiguity"

Acknowledgement

This project was supported in part by the College of Computer Science, Northeastern University, and NATO ASI. The author would like to thank Dean Larry Finkelstein and Profs. Sebastiano Impedovo and J.C. Simon for providing an excellent environment at the Chateau de Bonas, France, during the NATO ASI Summer Program on *Fundamentals in Handwriting Recognition*, 1993.

References

1. Ahmed, P., Suen, C.Y.: Computer Recognition of Totally Unconstrained Handwritten Zip Codes, *Int. J. of Pattern Recognition and Artificial Intelligence (IJPRAI)*, 1(1), 1-15 (1987)

2. Ausubel, D.P., Novak, J.D., Hanesian, H.: *Educational Psychology: A cognitive view*, New York: HRW Co., 2nd Ed., 1978

3. Berthod, M., Maroy, J.P.: Learning in Syntactic Recognition of Symbols Drawn on a Graphic Tablet. *Comput. Graphics and Image Processing* 9, 166-182, (1979)

4. Chen, C.H., Pau, L., Wang, P.S.P.(eds.) *Handbook of PRCV*, WSP, 1993

5. Freeman, H.: On the Encoding of Arbitrary Geometric Configurations, *IRE Trans. Electronic Comput.* 10, 206-268 (1968)

6. Freund, R.: Syntactic Analysis of Handwritten Characters by Quasi-Regular Programmed Array Grammars, In: H.Bunke (ed.) *Advances in Structural and Syntactic Pattern Recognition*, WSP, 310-319, 1992

7. Fu, K. S.: *Syntactic Pattern Recognition and Applications*, Englewood Cliffs, N.J., Prentice-Hall (1982)

8. Gupta, A., Hazarika, S., Kallel, M., Srivastava, P.: Optical Image Scanners and Character Recognition Devices: A Survey and New Taxonomy, MIT IFSRC Report No. 107-89 (1989)

9. Hopcroft, J.E., Ullman, J.D.: *Introduction to Automata Theory, Languages, and Computation.* New York, Addison Wesley (1979)

10. Liang, S.C.: *A New Chinese/English Dict.*, Far East Book Co., 1971

11. Lu, S. Y.: A Tree-to-Tree Distance and Its Application to Cluster Analysis, *IEEE Trans. Pattern Anal. Mach. Intell.* PAMI-1, 1(2), 219-224 (1979)

12. Mantas, J.: An Overview of Character Recognition Methodologies, *Pattern Recognition*, 19(6), 122-134 (1986)

13. Millward, R.B.: Models of Concept Formation. In: R.E. Snow etal. (eds.) *Aptitude, Learning, and Instruction*, Hillsdale, NJ, L. Erlbaum Assoc., 1980

14. Mori, S. et al.: Research on Machine Recognition of Handprinted Characters, *IEEE-PAMI.* 6(4), 386-405 (1984)

15. Morishita, T., Ooura, M., Ishii, Y.: A Kanji Recognition Method which Detects Writing Errors, *Int. J. of Pattern Recognition and Artificial Intelligence(IJPRAI)*, 2(1) 181-195 (1988)

16. Nage, M.V, Wang, P.S.P., Gupta, A.: Algorithms for Thinning and Thickening, *J. DSP*, 3(2) 97-102 (1993)

17. Nandhakumar, N., Aggarwal, J.: The Artificial Intelligence Approach to Pattern Recognition - A Perspective and Overview, *Pattern Recognition*, 18(6) 383-389 (1985)

18. Pavlidis, T.: *Structural Pattern Recognition*, New York, Springer-Verlag, 1980

19. Rich, E.: *Artificial Intelligence*, McGraw-Hill, 1991

20. Rosenfeld, A,: *Picture Languages: Formal Models for Picture Recognition*, New York, Academic Press 1979

21. Shaw, A.C.: A Formal Picture Description Scheme as A Basis For Picture Processing Systems, *Inf. Control* 14, 9-52 (1969)

22. Siromoney, R.: Array Languages and Lindenmayer Systems, In: Rozenberg, G., Salomaa, A. (eds.) *The Book of L*, Springer Verlag (1985)

23. Suen, C.Y.(ed.), *Frontiers of Handwriting Recognition*, Concordia U. Pub., 1990

24. Suen, C.Y., Berthod, M., Mori, S.: Automatic Recognition of Handprinted Characters - The state-of-the-art, *Proc. IEEE* vol. 68, no. 4, 469-487 (1980)

25. Suen, C.Y., Wang, P.S.P.(eds.): *Advances in Thinning Methodologies*, WSP, 1993

26. Tanimoto, S.: *The Elements of Artificial Intelligence*, CSP, 1991

27. Tappert, C.C., Suen, Wakahara, T.: On-Line Handwriting Recognition - A Survey, *Proc. ICPR'88*, Rome, 1123-1132 (1988)

28. Wang, P.S.P.(ed.): *Intelligent Chinese Langauage, Pattern, and Speech Processing*, WSP, 1988

29. Wang, P.S.P.: An Application of Array Grammars to Clustering Analysis. *Int. J. of Pattern Recognition*, 17, 403-410 (1984)

30. Wang, P.S.P.: *Dual Level Pattern Recognition System - A New OCR Technique*, US Patent PN 4521909 (1985)

31. Wang, P.S.P.: A New Character Recognition Scheme With Lower Ambiguity and Higher Recognizability. *International Journal of Pattern Recognition Letters* 3, 431-436 (1985)

32. Wang, P.S.P.(ed.) *Character and Handwriting Recognition - Expanding Frontiers* (preface by C.Y.Suen), WSP, 1991

33. Wang, P.S.P. (ed.) *Array Patterns, Grammars and Recognizers*, (preface by A. Rosenfeld), WSP, 1989

34. Wang, P.S.P., Gupta, A.: An Improved Structural Approach for Automated Recognition of Handprinted Characters, *IJPRAI*, 5(1,2), 97-121 (1991)

35. Wang, P.S.P., Y.Y. Zhang,: A Fast and Flexible Thinning Algorithm, *IEEE Transactions on Computers*, 38(5), 741-745 (1989)

36. Wang, P.S.P, Nage, M.V., Gupta, A.: A Neural Net Based "Hybrid" Approach to Handwritten Numeral Recognition, In: S. Impedovo and J. Simon (eds.) *From Pixels to Features III : Frontiers in Handwriting Recognition*, Elsevier, 145-154 (1992)

37. Winston, P. H.: Artificial Intelligence, Addison-Wesley, 1992

38. Winston, P.H. (ed.) with Shellard S., *Artificial Intelligence at MIT - Expanding Frontiers*, MIT Press, 1990

39. *Workshop Proceedings of SSPR'90*, Henry Baird (ed.), 1990

Digital Transforms in Handwriting Recognition

Giovanni Dimauro

Dipartimento di Informatica, Università degli Studi di Bari
via Amendola 173, 70126 Bari, Italy

1 Introduction

Digital transforms have been intensively used in the field of pattern recognition with the advance of computers. In the field of handwriting recognition, applications of such mathematical transformations ranges from character and numeral recognition, to word recognition and signature verification. This tutorial presents the fundamentals of digital transforms and their use in handwriting recognition. The tutorial is divided into three parts. The first part deals with the fundamental concepts and an overview of digital transforms. The second part deals with the implementation of digital transforms. Specifically the Discrete Fourier Transform (DFT) is explained in detail. Some computational aspects of the DFT are evaluated and some algorithms for Fast Fourier Transform are presented. In particular the "Radix-2 FFT" algorithms are discussed in detail. In the last part of the tutorial, some applications are presented: the DFT represents one of the most powerful tools for plane curve analysis and recognition. This is useful in handwriting recognition where the major information for the description and the classification of the pattern can be found in its boundary. Furthermore, Fourier Transform allows accurate analysis of plane curves and it was recently used for an experimental observation of human behaviour in recognizing handwritten characters. The results of such experiment pose suggestive questions about human ability in handwriting recognition which are now on the frontiers of the research in this field: How does man recognize handwritten pattern? Which features of a pattern are the most important for its recognition process? What about ambiguous patterns and their properties and about human recognition of ambiguous patterns? How could be automatically treated ambiguous patterns?

2 Fundamental Concepts of Digital Transforms

Frequently the understanding of a signal or image informative contents, or the recover of a part of theirs, is better done if, instead of a temporal or spatial description, a different one is used. It must be underlined that temporal or spatial description is imposed by the phenomena physics. Infact since a signal is generated in time, it is suitable, or even inevitable, to acquire and describe it in the temporal reference; the same can be said for an image that, occuping a physical space, can be naturally described using an Euclidean reference system. The tools used to describe a signal or an image in a different way are offered by mathematics. Even if these tools seem complex, mostly it is a matter of reference system changes and therefore of linear tranformations. The understanding difficulties usually rise from the fact that we deal with many dimensions spaces, even of infinite dimensions and in many cases these last are not sufficient. Really, so that the new signal or image description is efficient, it must be complete at least as the original one, in the sense that from an informative point of view nothing is lost passing from the first description to the second. In maths we talk about completeness of a representation system to say that all elements of a set can be described using that system. Such as we also talk about equipower of two systems to say that the set of all elements which can be described using the first system is equal to the set of all elements which can be described using the second. Two fundamental problems connected to the element description change exist: the first concerns the simple way of characterize the elements for which the different representation is permitted, the second instead concerns the way of identifing the transforms. Generally, the sets of the elements that show the property of being well represented by different systems are characterized through general properties such as continuity, periodicity, the absolute integrability, etc... . Regarding transforms it must be said that they exist of different kinds and they depend on either the nature of the elements that we want to transform or the specific properties of the same elements that we want to point out. In this chapter, after a theoretic description of the best known transforms and of the problems connected to them, the tools for signals and images spectral analysis are shown starting from the orthonormal system of trigonometric functions. Therefore some technics for the fast calculation of the Fourier transform are shown and some applications are suggested.

3 The Orthonormal System of Trigonometric Functions

The problem of the completeness, as presented in the previous section, was faced for the first time by Weierstrass and Stone. They looked at this as a density problem and they defined the conditions under which a lower-algebra is dense in the set of real (and complex), continuous and in a compact space defined functions. One of the most important corollary of this famous theorem that is known as "Weierstrass-Stone Theorem" is the one which shows that the set of trigonometric polynomial with coefficients in a vectorial seminormated space G, i.e. of the kind

$$P(\vartheta) = \sum_{n \in Q} c_n \, e^{j\vartheta n} \quad , \tag{1}$$

is dense in the space of continuous 2π-periodic functions and with values in G [1,c.V. pp 119-200]. Unfortunately the method proposed by Weierstrass and Stone, gives the conditions to verify the density but does not give the method to calculate the coefficients of polynomials that approximate an element of the algebra. Really, the problem of coefficient calculation is much more wide and was solved by Fejer.

We can prove that if we consider the space L_2 of square integrable and defined in $[-\pi,+\pi]$ functions with the ordinary Lebesgue measure, the system of the functions:

$$\frac{1}{\sqrt{2\pi}} \, , \; \frac{\cos nx}{\sqrt{\pi}} \, , \; \frac{\sin nx}{\sqrt{\pi}} \qquad (n = 1, 2, ...) \tag{2}$$

is a complete orthogonal system of L_2. In fact we can verify through direct calculation that the two following relations exist:

$$\int_{-\pi}^{\pi} \cos nx \cos mx \, dx = 0 \qquad \forall \; n \neq m \tag{3}$$

$$\int_{-\pi}^{\pi} \frac{\cos^2 nx}{\pi} \, dx = 1 \; , \; \int_{-\pi}^{\pi} \frac{\sin^2 nx}{\pi} \, dx = 1 \qquad \forall n \in N \tag{4}$$

and then the system in (2) is orthonormal.

Now considering the generic element f of L_2 and calculating the coefficients

$$a_0 = \frac{1}{\pi} \int_{-\pi}^{\pi} f(x) \, dx \tag{5}$$

$$a_n = \frac{1}{\pi}\int_{-\pi}^{\pi} f(x) \cos nx \, dx \quad , \quad \forall n \in N^* \quad , \tag{6}$$

$$b_n = \frac{1}{\pi}\int_{-\pi}^{\pi} f(x) \sin nx \, dx \qquad \forall\, n \in N^* \quad , \tag{7}$$

we can prove that the series:

$$\frac{a_0}{2} + \sum_{n=1}^{+\infty} a_n \cos nx + b_n \sin nx \tag{8}$$

converges in quadratic mean to f [2].
This result can be easily extended to the case that the functions f are defined into the interval $[-l,l]$ instead of being defined in $[-\pi,\pi]$. For this purpose it is enough to set:

$$t = \frac{l}{\pi} x \tag{9}$$

and to consider the coefficients:

$$a_0 = \frac{1}{l}\int_{-l}^{l} f(t) \, dt \quad ; \tag{10}$$

$$a_n = \frac{1}{l}\int_{-l}^{l} f(t) \cos \frac{n\pi t}{l} \, dt \quad , \quad \forall\, n \in N^* \tag{11}$$

$$b_n = \frac{1}{l}\int_{-l}^{l} \sin \frac{n\pi t}{l} \, dt \quad , \quad \forall\, n \in N^* \; . \tag{12}$$

It must be also observed that existing the following equalities:

$$\frac{a_0}{2} + \sum_{n=1}^{+\infty} a_n \cos nx + b_n \sin nx =$$

$$= \frac{a_0}{2} + \sum_{n=1}^{+\infty} (a_n \frac{e^{inx}+e^{-inx}}{2} - ib_n \frac{e^{inx}-e^{-inx}}{2}) =$$

$$= \frac{a_0}{2} + \sum_{n=1}^{+\infty} \frac{a_n - ib_n}{2} e^{inx} + \sum_{n=1}^{+\infty} \frac{a_n + ib_n}{2} e^{-inx} = \tag{13}$$

$$= \sum_{n=-\infty}^{+\infty} c_n e^{inx}$$

$$where \qquad c_0 = \frac{a_0}{2} , \tag{14}$$

$$\forall n \in N^* : \begin{cases} c_n = \dfrac{a_n - ib_n}{2} \\ c_{-n} = \dfrac{a_n + ib_n}{2} \end{cases} \tag{15}$$

it results also that the complex trigonometric Fourier series

$$\sum_{n=-\infty}^{+\infty} c_n e^{inx} \tag{16}$$

converges in quadratic mean to f. Then, through (5),(6),(7) and (16) the formule to calculate directly the coefficients c_n can be extracted. In fact we can observe that multipling f(x) and (16) by e^{-imx} and integrating each of the two expressions we obtain:

$$\int_{-\pi}^{\pi} f(x) e^{-inx} dx = \sum_{n=-\infty}^{+\infty} c_n \int_{-\pi}^{\pi} e^{inx} e^{-imx} dx . \tag{17}$$

Then it is easy to verify that

$$\int_{-x}^{x} e^{inx}\, e^{-imx}\, dx = \begin{cases} 0 & \mathit{for}\ n \neq m \\ 2\pi & \mathit{for}\ n = m \end{cases} \tag{18}$$

and therefore it results:

$$c_m = \frac{1}{2\pi} \int_{-x}^{x} f(x)\, e^{-imx}\, dx \qquad m = 0,\ \pm 1,\ \pm 2,\ \dots . \tag{19}$$

The series development in (16) is still valid for complex and square module integrable defined into the $[-\pi,+\pi]$ interval functions. In other terms the family $(e^{inx})_{n\epsilon Z}$ constitutes a base for the L_2 space of complex, square module integrable defined into the $[-\pi,+\pi]$ interval functions. So the expression in (19) represents the scalar product of f by e^{imx}. If these functions are defined into the interval $[-l,l]$, then the base of L_2 becomes the family $[e^{(in\pi t)/l}]_{n\epsilon Z}$.We can prove that the system

$$(\cos nx)_{n\in N} \tag{20}$$

constitutes a complete orthogonal system for the square integrable functions defined into the $[0,\pi]$ interval. The othogonality between the elements of the sequence in (20) can be proved by a direct calculation. In order to prove the completeness, called f any square integrable on $[0,\pi]$ function, we can consider the function so defined:

$$f^{*}(x) = \begin{cases} f(x) & \mathit{if}\quad 0 \le x \le \pi \\ f(-x) & \mathit{if}\quad -\pi \le x \le 0 \end{cases} ; \tag{21}$$

it is obvious that f^* is square integrable in $[-\pi,+\pi]$ and so can be developed in Fourier series in accordance with the (8). But we must observe that all the b_n coefficients to be calculated using the (7) are identically null due to the effect of the parity of f^*. Therefore it is proved that f^* and, even more f, can be developed in series of only cosines. It can also be proved that the system:

$$(\sin nx)_{n\in N} \tag{22}$$

forms a complete orthogonal system for square integrable defined in $[0,\pi]$

functions. The demonstration can be done as in the previous case but defining f^* in the following way:

$$f^*(x) = \begin{cases} f(x) & if \quad 0 \le x \le \pi \\ -f(-x) & if \quad -\pi \le x \le 0 \end{cases} \quad . \tag{23}$$

The most typical example of a set of functions of those here described is the sine and cosine set as shown in Fig. 1.

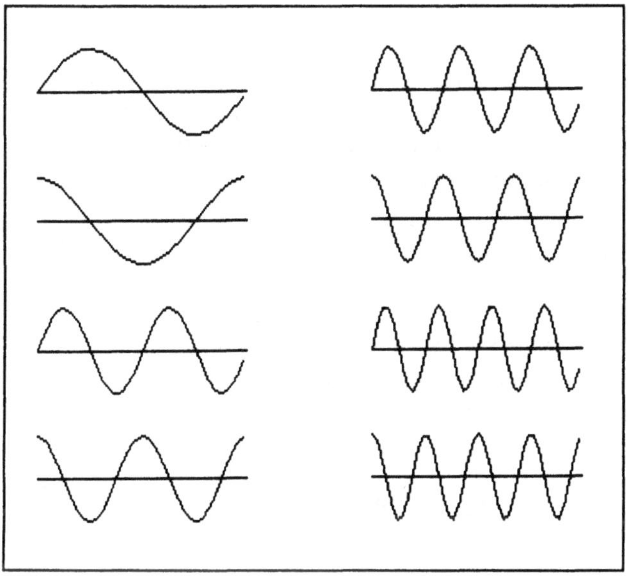

Fig. 1.

4 Other Orthonormal Systems of L_2

It must be underlined that in the L_2 space other orthonormal complete systems exist; for example, remembering that the functions $1, x, x^2, \ldots$. constitute a base for all the polynomials defined in a closed and bounded interval, through the orthonormalization Schmidt's process the following complete orthonormal system can be derived from the above functions:

$$\frac{1}{n!\ 2^n}\sqrt{\frac{2n+1}{2}}\ \frac{d^n}{dx^n}(x^2-1), \qquad n \in N \tag{24}$$

Often, instead of the system in the (24), the following one is used:

$$\frac{1}{n!\ 2^n}\ \frac{d^n}{dx^n}(x^2-1)^n\ , \qquad n \in N \tag{25}$$

which is called "Legendre's polynomial system".
If in particular we consider the L_2 space of square integrable functions defined on the whole numeric line, then a complete orthogonal system of L_2 can be obtained by orthogonalizing the functions of the $x^n e^{-sqr(x)/2}$ sequence. If this is done, we get a complete orthonormal system of the type:

$$¥_n(x) = H_n(x)\ e^{-x^2/2}\ , \qquad n \in N \tag{26}$$

where the $H_n(x)$ are the Hermite's polynomials.
Otherwise, if on the $[0,+\infty[$ half-line we consider the system of the $x^n e^{-x}$ functions, then the orthogonalization process generates the system of the functions:

$$¥_n(x) = L_n e^{-x} \tag{27}$$

called Laguerre's functions. The above mentioned systems have a negligible applicative interest and will be not investigated further on in this chapter.
Among the other orthogonal complete L_2 systems, for their applicative interest, we report Haar's and Rademacher-Walsh's ones. These systems are complete for [0,1] interval defined functions. The Haar's system is defined by the function:

$$¥_0 = 1 \tag{28}$$

and by the series

$$\begin{array}{c} ¥_{01}, \\ ¥_{11}, ¥_{12}, \\ ¥_{21}, ¥_{22}, ¥_{23}, ¥_{24}, \\ \cdot \\ \cdot \\ \cdot \\ ¥_{n1}, ¥_{n2}, \ldots\ldots\ldots\ldots, ¥_{n2^n} \end{array} \tag{29}$$

where the n-th line in the (29) is constituted by 2^n functions and results

$$¥_{ni} = \begin{cases} 2^{n/2} & \frac{i-1}{2^n} < x < \frac{i-1}{2^n} + \frac{1}{2^{n+1}} \\ -2^{n/2} & \frac{i-1}{2^n} + \frac{1}{2^{n+1}} < x < \frac{i}{2^n} \\ 0 & x < \frac{i-1}{2^n} \ o \ x > \frac{i}{2^n} \end{cases} \tag{30}$$

where, fixed $n \in N$, it results $i = 1,2,3,\ldots\ldots,2^n$. Specifically, it can easily be verified that results:

$$¥_{01} = \begin{cases} +1 & \text{if } 0<x<\frac{1}{2} \\ -1 & \text{if } \frac{1}{2}<x<1 \end{cases} \tag{31}$$

$$¥_{11} = \begin{cases} \sqrt{2} & \text{if } 0 < x < \frac{1}{4} \\ -\sqrt{2} & \text{if } \frac{1}{4} < x < \frac{1}{2} \\ 0 & \text{if } \frac{1}{2} < x < 1 \end{cases} \tag{32}$$

$$¥_{12} = \begin{cases} 0 & \text{if } 0 < x < \frac{1}{2} \\ \sqrt{2} & \text{if } \frac{1}{2} < x < \frac{3}{4} \\ -\sqrt{2} & \text{if } \frac{3}{4} < x < 1 \end{cases} \qquad (33)$$

For a demonstration of the completeness of the orthonormal Haar system see [3]. An example of a set of functions of the Haar system is shown in Fig. 2.

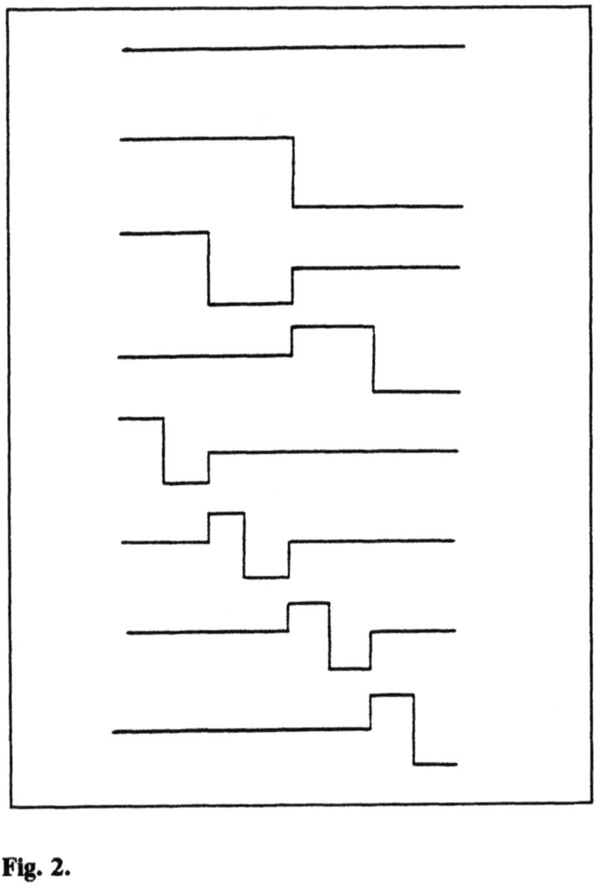

Fig. 2.

On the contrary, dividing, for each n∈N, the [0,1] interval in 2^n equal, $1/2^n$ long sub-intervals, and considering the functions that alternatively assume +1 and -1 values within adiacent sub-intervals, we obtain another orthonormal system of functions called Rademacher's system. An example of the Rademacher functions is shown in Fig. 3.

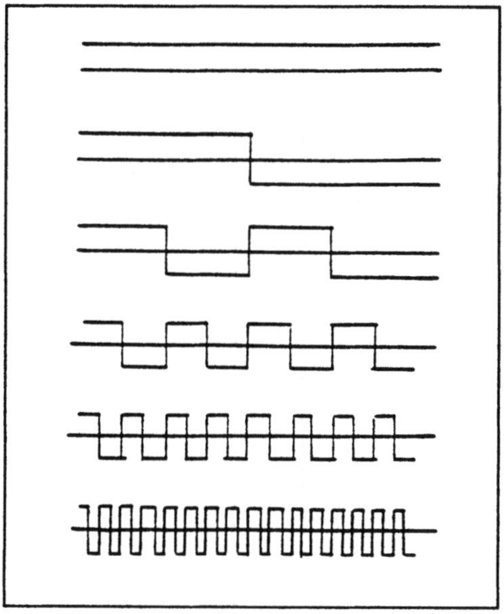

Fig. 3.

However, Rademacher's system is not complete since it is not true that however we take two Rademacher functions ¥ and ¥', with ¥ <> ¥', the product ¥ * ¥' belongs to the space generated by this system, i.e., it is not an algebra. The simple idea proposed by Walsh to extend the system considering as being its parts also the functions that are obtained by multipling among themselves the Rademacher functions, has taken to define an orthonormal, complete system of L_2 called the Rademacher-Walsh system. An example of the Rademacher-Walsh system of functions is reported in [4]. It is well known that sinusoidal functions play an important role in synthesizing smoothly varying plane curves. This is reflected in the effectiveness of the Fourier Transform applied in the synthesis of handwriting. This topic, with particular attention on the application of the Discrete Fourier Transform, will mainly treated in the following sections.

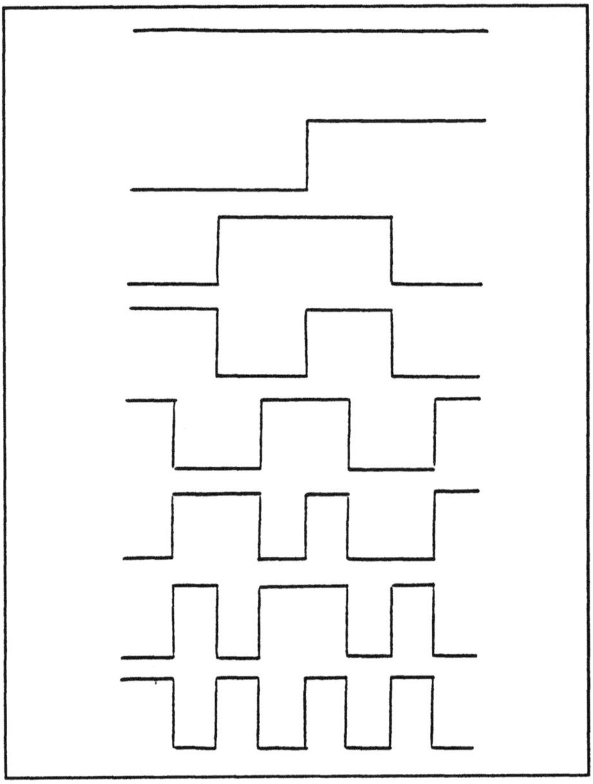

Fig. 4.

5 Introduction to the Discrete Fourier Transform

In section 3 it has been shown that every 2π-periodic function, can be developed in trigonometric polynomial series and that if the function x(t) is continue, periodic of period T_0, that is:

$$x\,(t + mT_0) = x(t) \qquad \forall m \in Z, \tag{34}$$

using the trigonometric system of complex exponentials we obtain:

$$x(t) = \sum_{n=-\infty}^{+\infty} c_n e^{jn\omega_0 t} \tag{35}$$

where $w_0=2\pi/T_0$ is the fundamental harmonic, nw_0 is the harmonic of order n, and further:

$$c_n = \frac{1}{T_0} \int_{-T_0/2}^{T_0/2} x(t) e^{-jn\omega_0 t} dt. \qquad \forall n \in Z. \tag{36}$$

Let now $x_p(t)$ be a periodic function of period T_0, and t_0 a real not null number, let's consider the $x_p(nt_0)$ sequence that represents a sampled version of the $x_p(t)$ function, that is

$$x_p(nt_0) = x_p(t) \Big|_{t = nt_0} \qquad \forall n \in Z . \tag{37}$$

To keep the periodicity we suppose here, more specifically that T_o is multiple of t_o and, for notational simplicity, also that t_o is unitary. So let $x_p(n)$ be the sampled version of the $x_p(t)$ function, that is following the (37) it results:

$$x_p(n) = x_p(t) \Big|_{t = n} \qquad \forall n \in Z . \tag{38}$$

Being $x_p(t)$ periodic, for the (35) it results:

$$x_p(t) = \sum_{m=-\infty}^{+\infty} X_p^1(m) e^{j\frac{2\pi}{T_0} mt} \tag{39}$$

(where now the $X^1_p(m)$ substitute the c_n) and then:

$$\begin{aligned} x_p(n) = x_p(t) \Big|_{t=n} &= \Big(\sum_{m=-\infty}^{+\infty} X_p^1(m) e^{j\frac{2\pi}{T_0} mt} \Big) \Big|_{t=n} = \\ \sum_{m=-\infty}^{+\infty} X_p^1(m) e^{j\frac{2\pi}{N} mn} &\overset{(1)}{=} \sum_{k=-\infty}^{+\infty} \Big(\sum_{m=0}^{N-1} X_p^1(m+kN) e^{j\frac{2\pi}{N}(m+kN)n} \Big) = \\ &= \sum_{m=0}^{N-1} \Big(\sum_{k=-\infty}^{+\infty} X_p^1(m+kN) e^{j\frac{2\pi}{N}(m+kN)n} \Big); \end{aligned} \tag{40}$$

where in the (1) equality it has been considered that

$$e^{j\frac{2\pi}{N}m} = e^{j\frac{2\pi}{N}(m+kN)} \qquad \forall k \in Z\ ; \tag{41}$$

that is, under the enunciated conditions, only N complex exponentials can be discriminated. Still by the observation in (41), from (40) we obtain:

$$x_p(n) = \sum_{m=0}^{N-1} e^{j\frac{2\pi}{N}mn} \sum_{k=-\infty}^{+\infty} X_p^1(m+kN) \tag{42}$$

thus, placed $\sum_{-\infty}^{+\infty} X_p^1(m+kN) = -\frac{X_p(m)}{N}$ *we obtain*

$$x_p(n) = \frac{1}{N} \sum_{m=0}^{N-1} X_p(m)\, e^{j\frac{2\pi}{N}mn} \quad . \tag{43}$$

We call the (43) expression "Inverse Discrete Fourier Transform" (**IDFT**). If now we consider the expression

$$\sum_{n=0}^{N-1} x_p(n)\, e^{-j\frac{2\pi}{N}nm} \tag{44}$$

we can see that its values are exactly the $X_p(m)$ that appears in the (43), that is:

$$X_p(m) = \sum_{n=0}^{N-1} x_p(n)\, e^{-j\frac{2\pi}{N}nm} \tag{45}$$

In fact:

$$\sum_{n=0}^{N-1} x_p(n)\, e^{-j\frac{2\pi}{N}nm} = \sum_{n=0}^{N-1} \left(\frac{1}{N} \sum_{k=0}^{N-1} X_p(k) e^{j\frac{2\pi}{N}kn} \right) e^{-j\frac{2\pi}{N}nm} = \tag{46}$$

$$\sum_{k=0}^{N-1} \frac{X_p(k)}{N} \sum_{n=0}^{N-1} e^{j\frac{2\pi}{N}n(k-m)} = \sum_{k=0}^{N-1} \frac{X_p(k)}{N} N u_0(k-m) = X_p(m)$$

where $u_0(n)$, known in literature as digital impulse, represents a sequence that is anywhere null except for n=0 where it is equal to 1. The expression

$$X_p(m) = \sum_{n=0}^{N-1} x_p(n)\, e^{-j\frac{2\pi}{N}nm} \tag{47}$$

is called "Discrete Fourier Tranform" (**DFT**).
The following couple called Discrete Fourier Transform relations exists:

$$X(k) = \sum_{n=0}^{N-1} x(n)\, e^{-j\frac{2\pi}{N}nk} \qquad (DFT) \tag{48}$$

$$x(n) = \frac{1}{N}\sum_{k=0}^{N-1} X(k)\, e^{j\frac{2\pi}{N}nk} \qquad (IDFT) \tag{49}$$

We can observe that the (48) and (49) relations create a correspondence between N points of the variable with index n and N points of the variable with index k. This can be done either with periodic x(n), X(k) sequences with N points in each period, or with finite sequences with N elements. That is why in the (48) and (49) the sub-index "p" has been omitted.

6 Properties of the DFT

Let N be a natural integer and let's consider the vectorial space C^N on the field C; it must be underlined here that the DFT introduced by the (48) can be considered as an application of C^N on C^N. There are several properties of the DFT that play an important role in practical techniques for signal processing. In the following subsections we will summarize some of these properties.

6.1 Relations between Z-Transform, Fourier Transform and DFT

If x(n) is a sequence, the expression

$$X(z) = \sum_{n=-\infty}^{+\infty} x(n)\, z^{-n} \qquad where\ z \in C\ , \tag{50}$$

if exists, is called "Z-Transform" of x(n). The reader is invited to investigate the properties of the Z-transform of a sequence [4]. Using the Z-Transform, making suitable assumptions on x(n), it can be easily shown that under certain conditions the DFT is nothing but a sampled version of the Fourier Transform of the sequence in object. This gives a method to pass from the Z-transform of a sequence, or from its Fourier Transform, to its Discrete Transform. Now there is the problem to find directly the Z-transform and/or the Fourier Transform of a sequence when the values of its DFT are known. So for this purpose the following interpolating functions can be used:

$$\frac{1-z^{-N}}{1-e^{j\frac{2\pi}{N}k}\, z^{-1}} \tag{51}$$

in fact it is easy to demonstrate that it results:

$$X(z) = \sum_{k=0}^{N-1} \frac{X(k)}{N} \frac{1-z^{-N}}{1-e^{j\frac{2\pi}{N}k}\, z^{-1}}\ . \tag{52}$$

and

$$X(e^{j\omega}) = \sum_{k=0}^{N-1} \frac{X(k)}{N} \frac{1-e^{-j\omega N}}{1-e^{-j\omega} e^{j\frac{2\pi}{N}k}}\ . \tag{53}$$

6.2 How to Increase the Frequency Resolution

The observations made in the previous section allow to develop some very useful considerations. One of these is the way of increase the frequency resolution for a given sequence. In other words, it can be shown that to obtain the values in L harmonics, of an N points sequence, it is sufficient to add L-N zeros to the original sequence and then to calculate the DFT of the new sequence obtained. As we will see in the following sections, the most common algorithms for the computation of the DFT work with sequences constituted by a number of points that is a power of 2; consequently the shown method is also an useful artifice to calculate the DFT of every sequence using these algorithms.

6.3 Linearity property

If x(n) and y(n) are two sequences of C^N and α and β are two elements of the field C, then the DFT of the sequence $\alpha x(n) + \beta y(n)$ is equal to the linear combination, with the same coefficients α and β, of the DFT of x(n) and respectively y(n). Being the DFT a linear application, it can have a matrix representation. In fact, let $W_N=e^{-j(2\pi/N)}$, the writing

$$X(k)=\sum_{n=0}^{N-1} x(n)W_N^{kn} \tag{54}$$

just represents the product rows by coloumns:

$$\begin{bmatrix} X(0) \\ \cdot \\ X(k) \\ \cdot \\ X(N-1) \end{bmatrix}^{transp.} = \begin{bmatrix} W_N^{0,0} & \dots W_N^{n,0} & \dots W_N^{N-1,0} \\ \dots & \dots & \dots \\ W_N^{0,k} & \dots W_N^{n,k} & \dots W_N^{N-1,k} \\ \dots & \dots & \dots \\ W_N^{0,N-1} & \dots W_N^{n,N-1} & \dots W_N^{N-1,N-1} \end{bmatrix} \cdot \begin{bmatrix} x(0) \\ \cdot \\ x(n) \\ \cdot \\ x(N-1) \end{bmatrix} \tag{55}$$

6.4 Translation property

Let x(n) be an N-elements sequence and n_o a natural integer. If X(k) is the DFT of x(n), it can be shown that the DFT of $x(n-n_o)$ is:

$$e^{-j\frac{2\pi}{N}kn_0}X(k). \tag{56}$$

6.5 Symmetry property

Let x(n) be an N real points sequence and X(k) its DFT; if Re[X(k)] is the real part of X(k) and Im[X(k)] its immaginary part, it can be shown that:

a) Re[X(k)] = Re[X(N-k)] and b) Im[X(k)] = -Im[X(N-k)].

6.6 Direct Calculation of the DFT of two Real Sequences

Since one generally deals with real sequences, the symmetry property may be conveniently used to obtain the DFT's of two sequences using a single DFT. Let x(n) and y(n) two N real sequences, and X(k) and Y(k) their respective discrete Fourier transforms. Considered the complex sequence

$$z(n) = x(n) + j\, y(n) \tag{57}$$

and denoted by Z(k) its DFT, from the linearity property we know that results

$$Z(k) = X(k) + j\, Y(k). \tag{58}$$

It can be shown that:

$$Re[X(k)] = \frac{Re[Z(k)] + Re[Z(N-k)]}{2} \tag{59}$$

$$Im[X(k)] = \frac{Im[Z(k)] - Im[Z(N-k)]}{2} \tag{60}$$

$$Im[Y(k)] = \frac{Re[Z(N-k)] - Re[Z(k)]}{2} \tag{61}$$

$$Re[Y(k)] = \frac{Im[Z(N-k) + Im[Z(k)]}{2} \tag{62}$$

Thus, a single N-point DFT can effectively transform two N-point real sequences at the same time.

7 The DFT Calculation Problem

N^2 complex multiplications and N(N-1) additions are required to calculate the (54). Since we can ignore the time necessary to calculate additions in respect to multiplications, we can say that the calculating cost depends almost fully on the N^2 multiplications, then

$$c(N)=N^2 \tag{63}$$

To get an idea about the time required to calculate the (54) it's enough to observe that the resolution of a camera film can reach 500 rows per mm., that means on a 24x36 mm. photogram can exist 36x500=18000 pixels per row, and its DFT would require, to be calculated through the (54), $3.24*10^8$ multiplications; if we consider that the operation must be repeated for all the 12000 rows and for all the 18000 columns, we realize the calculation becomes practically impossible. To reduce the number of operations and consequently the calculation cost of the (54) many algorithms, identified as "FFT" ("Fast Fourier Transform"), were proposed. The first among these was that proposed by Cooley, Lewis and Welch in 1967 and 1968 [5,6]. The most important variations of this algorithm are the "Decimation In Time algorithm (DIT)" and the "Decimation In Frequency algorithm (DIF)". Subsequently, using the polynomial transformations, a systematic approach to the algorithms formulation for the fast DFT calculation was proposed. Other algorithms that we particulary point out are the Winograd-Fourier's and Good's one [7,8].

7.1 Decimation in Time Algorithm

In this section we examine a particular FFT algorithm, known in literature as "Decimation in Time Algorithm". Let us suppose that x(n) has $N=2^\beta$ elements, with ß natural integer. Let

$$x_1(n) = x(2n) \qquad n=0,1,\dots,N/2-1 \tag{64}$$

and

$$x_2(n) = x(2n+1) \qquad n=0,1,\dots,N/2-1 \tag{65}$$

be two sub-sequences of x(n), each one having N/2 elements, the first constituted by all the even index elements of x(n), and the second by the odd index ones. Let us denote with X(k), $X_1(k)$, $X_2(k)$ respectively the DFT of x(n), $x_1(n)$, $x_2(n)$. The following equations allow to find the relationship between X(k) and the couple ($X_1(k)$,$X_2(k)$):

$$X(k)=\sum_{n=0}^{N-1} x(n)W_N^{nk}=\sum_{n=0}^{\frac{1}{2}N-1} x(2n)W_N^{2nk}+\sum_{n=0}^{\frac{1}{2}N-1} x(2n+1)W_N^{(2n+1)k}=$$

$$=\sum_{n=0}^{\frac{1}{2}N-1} x_1(n)W_N^{2nk}+W_N^k\sum_{n=0}^{\frac{1}{2}N-1} x_2(n)W_N^{2nk} = \qquad \textbf{(66)}$$

$$=\sum_{n=0}^{\frac{1}{2}N-1} x_1(n)W_{\frac{1}{2}N}^{nk}+W_N^k\sum_{n=0}^{\frac{1}{2}N-1} x_2(n)W_{\frac{1}{2}N}^{nk} = X_1(k)+W_N^kX_2(k).$$

So the (66) allows to transform the DFT calculation of an N points sequence into the calculation of two N/2 points DFT, reducing so the calculation cost from N^2 to $N^2/2$. It can be calculated dividing itself in two parts: in the first part we calculate the first N/2 values corresponding to k=0,1,...,N/2-1, in the other part the remaining N/2 corresponding to k=N/2,...,N-1; in this way we have:

$$X(k) = \begin{cases} X_1(k)+W_N^kX_2(k) & \text{for } k=0;...;\frac{1}{2}N-1 \\ X_1(k-\frac{1}{2}N)-W_N^{k-\frac{1}{2}N}X_2(k-\frac{1}{2}N) & \text{for } k=\frac{1}{2}N;...;N-1 \end{cases}$$

(67)

The procedure used to formulate the (66) and then the (67) can be repeated first on $X_1(k)$ and $X_2(k)$, and then on the sequences as obtained from these one, till to obtain two elements sub-sequences. Let

$$X_{i_1,\ldots,i_{\beta-1}}(k) \qquad where\ k=0,1 \qquad (68)$$

be a generic sequence among these ones; following the (67) we will be able to individuate the sequences that have been reduced to one element only:

$$X_{i_1,\ldots,i_{\beta-1},1}(k) \qquad where\ \ k=0\ , \qquad (69)$$

$$X_{i_1,\ldots,i_{\beta-1},2}(k) \qquad where\ \ k=0 \qquad (70)$$

so that

$$X_{i_1,\ldots,i_{\beta-1}}(k) = \begin{cases} X_{i_1,\ldots,i_{\beta-1};1}(k) + W_2^0 X_{i_1,\ldots,i_{\beta-1};2}(k) & if\ \ k = 0 \\ X_{i_1,\ldots,i_{\beta-1};1}(k) - W_2^0 X_{i_1,\ldots,i_{\beta-1};2}(k) & if\ \ k = 1 \end{cases} \qquad (71)$$

We can now observe that the (69) and the (70) represents DFT of sequences of one point only. As the DFT of a point is the point itself, the X (upper) in the (71) can be replaced with the x (lower). More generally, if we suppose to denote these points with a and b, then the (71) becomes:

$$X_{i_1,\ldots,i_{\beta-1}}(k) = \begin{cases} a+W_2^0 b & for\ k=0 \\ a-W_2^0 b & for\ k=1 \end{cases} \qquad (72)$$

Looking at the (67) and the (71) we can observe they have the same structure, and it can be shown that the structure in the (72) is constant through the whole decomposition process; this structure can generally be represented by the butterfly of Fig.5. The black points of this figure represent registers, the black arrow represents a multiplier, and the empty circle an adder or a subtracter depending on, as we move along the butterfly branches from left to right, we get up or we get down. So the X(k) calculation algorithm can be represented by a butterflies fall in which each level matches a decompositon step in the iteration shown before. In Fig.6 it is reported the graphic scheme of the DIT algorithm applied to an 8 points sequence. The following two observations will help us in designing an algorithm for the computation of the butterflies in Fig.6.

1) To obtain the output sequence from the pattern of Fig.6 in natural order, it is necessary to change the order of the input sequence. The permuting speed is a very important parameter for the whole method efficacy. An optimal algorithm for the solution of this problem was the "Bit Reversing" algorithm proposed by Rader [1,c.XIII,pp. 484-493].

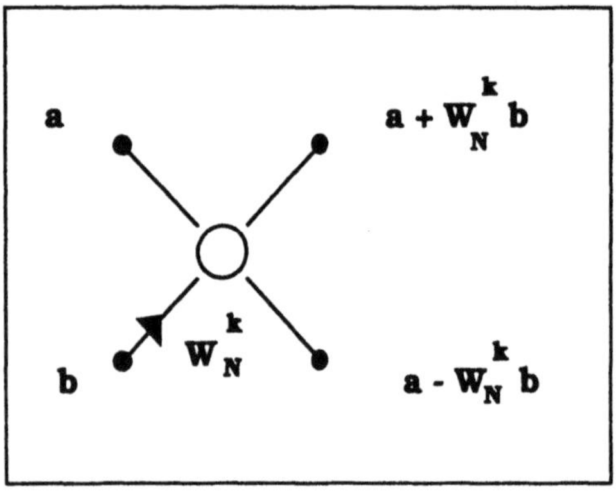

Fig.5. Butterfly representation of the DIT algorithm.

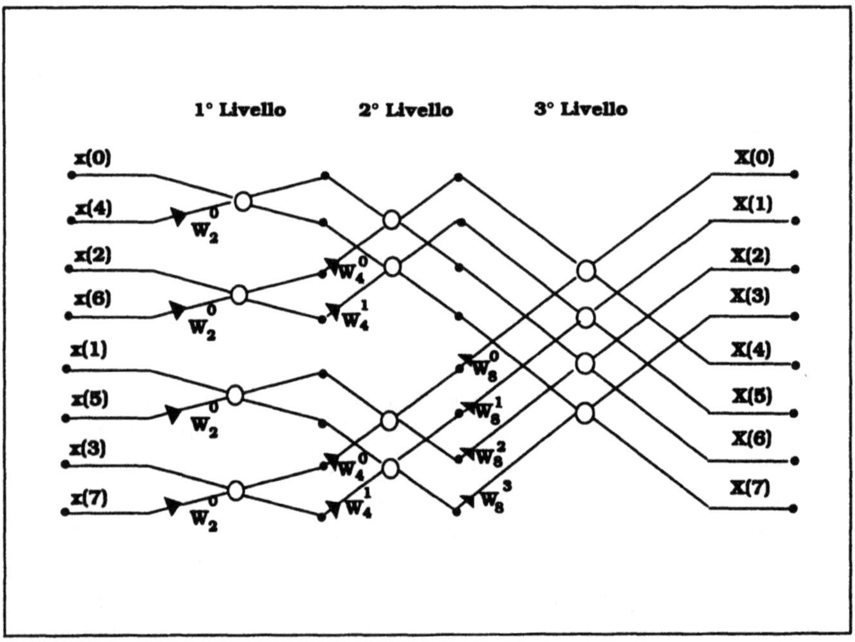

Fig.6. DIT algorithm scheme for an 8 points sequence.

2) Another important problem that raises in the transform calculation according to the pattern of Fig.6 regards the phase factors. Observing that $W_2^0=W_4^0=W_8^0$ and also that $W_4^1=W_8^2$ we can see that the phase factors in Fig.6, can be grouped as $W_2^0=W_4^0=W_8^0$, $W_8^2=W_4^1$, W_8^1 and W_8^3. So a recurrence exists in the value of the phase factors. Further considerations based on the fact that the phase factors are obtainable iteratively with the relation:

$$W_N^k = W_N^{k-1}\ W_N^1 \tag{73}$$

led to the formulation of fast calculation algorithms. In Fig.7 it is reported the flow-chart of an algorithm that provides both for the phase factors generation and the butterflies-fall calculation according to the algorithm derived by the iteration in (67) and exemplified in Fig.6. Particularly we must point out that the strategy used in this algorithm is that of calculating time after time all the butterflies that belong to the same level, and this procedure is repeated a number of times that equals the number of the levels that, as we know, is $M=\log_2 N$. Fixed now a level, we can see that one phase factor can be associated to each butterfly, but, on the contrary, several butterflies are associated to each phase factor: for example, in the first level of figure 2, N/2 butterflies are associated to the phase factor W_2^0. For this reason, all the butterflies of the same level can be grouped so that the butterflies in which the same phase factor appears belong to the same group. Firstly all the same group butterflies, and this group by group in each level, are calculated. For example, in the first level we calculate only the butterflies group in relation with the phase factor $W^0{}_2$, in the second level the two butterflies groups in relation with the phase factors W_4^0 and W_4^1 and so on. In the diagram of figure 7 three nesting loops are evident: the inner performs the calculation of the same group butterflies, the intermediate instead scans the various butterflies groups inside each level. In fact in this loop the instruction U=U*W appears; this instruction, fixed the initial phase factor U and the spacing factor W, allows to generate in iterative manner the phase factor of each group. It is the most external loop that scans the various levels and it provides, from time to time, to determine the initial phase factor and the spacing factor calculated with the sine and cosine standard routines. Fig.6 shows that, for sequences of $N=2^\beta$ elements, the DIT algorithm foresees $\beta=\log_2 N$ levels, and as it is necessary to carry out N/2 multiplications for each level, we can deduce the total number of multiplications equals $1/2N\log_2 N$. Similar observations can be done also for the DIF algorithm. Naturally to determine the effective cost of the DFT calculation by one of these two algorithms, we must consider also other necessary operations as, for example, the bit-reversing one. However we can consider that the cost c(N) is of $1/2N\log_2 N$ order. The reader is invited to confront the two sequences N^2 and $1/2N\log_2 N$, that is respectively the cost of the direct calculation of the DFT and its calculation through the DIT and DIF algorithms.

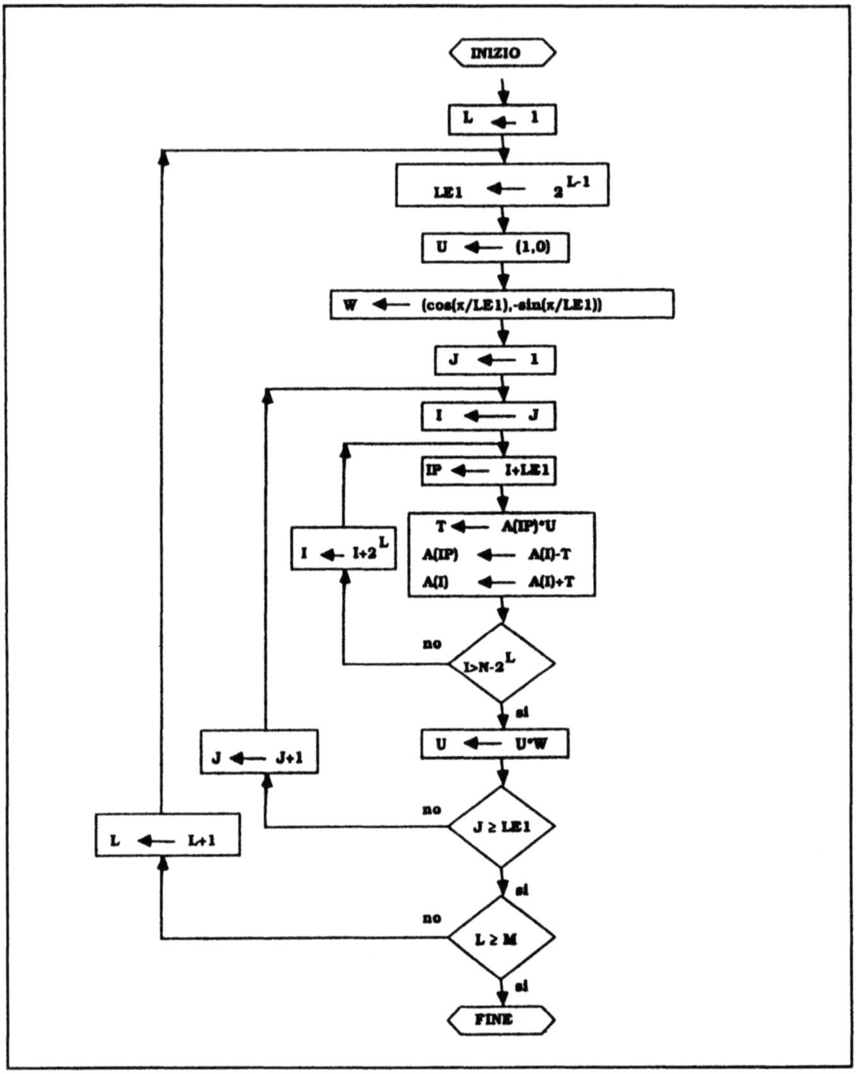

Fig.7. DIT algorithm flow-chart.

The knowledges and the properties of the DFT reported in the preceding sections can be extended to multidimensional sequences. To investigate on this topic the reader is invited to consult specialized publications [9,10].

In conclusion of this chapter the reader's attention is attracted on some applications, here presented as example, about the use of discrete Fourier tranform for signal processing. The following applications refer to the treatment of handwritten characters through the use of unidimensional DFT.

8 Application 1: Description of a Plane Curve through Fourier Coefficents

Let us consider a plane, continue, of finite lenght curve, for example the one that we obtain writing with a pen a one-stroke character on a paper sheet. As the points of the plane (in this case of the paper sheet) can be described by complex numbers considering the abscissa of a point as the real part and its ordinate as the imaginary part of the same complex number, the description of the traced curve can be described by the complex function

$$z = z(t) = x(t) + jy(t)$$

where t could be a time parameter during the writing. Almost in the totality of the cases it is difficult to find a simple analytical expression of z(t). In order to describe z(t) it can be sufficient and useful to discretize it, taking N points distributed on all its lenght, i.e. the sequence of complex numbers

$$z(n) \quad \text{with } n=0,1,.....,N-1$$

that represents the description by points of the curve z(t). The use of any one of the FFT algorithms presented allows to obtain, from the succession that describes the curve, N new complex numbers. Each of this complex number represents the module and the phase of a particular harmonical component of the curve under examination. The reader is invited to do an exercise writing a numeral on a graphic tablet and extracting the z(n) sequence. Then, if necessary he should add as many zeros until he will augment the number of the points that describe the curve up to a power of two. In this way he will be able to apply the DIT algorithm and to calculate the Fourier coefficients. Repeating the exercise for many characters it can be verified that for most of them the value of the modules obtained is low. Only the first ones show a considerable value of the module: consequently we can use only them to rebuild the curve using the inverse transformation process. In Fig.8 it is shown a series of numerals as acquired from a graphic tablet and their reconstruction using only four Fourier Coefficents.

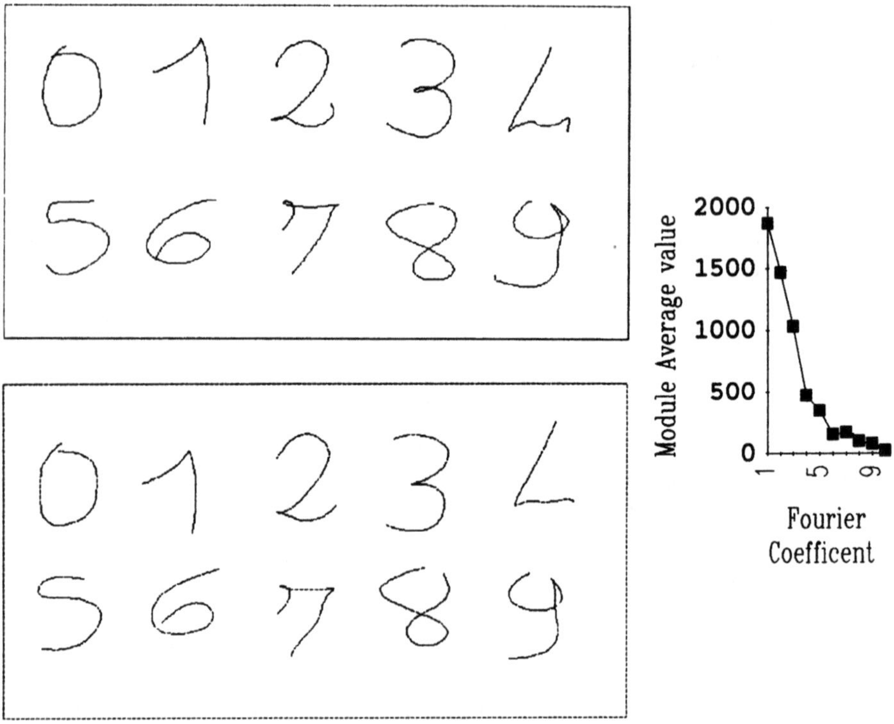

Fig.8. Reconstruction of a plane curve using four Fourier Coefficents

With this exercise, the reader can convince himself that most of the informative contents of an handwritten character stroke is carried by the lowest few order harmonics and then he could think of formulating a recognition algorithm based on the use of these few coefficents. This will be shown in the following section.

12 Application 2: Character Recognition through Fourier Transform

12.1 Introduction

In the character recognition field many efforts were done in order to design reliable machines. In the field of printed characters good results, in terms of high speed and low misrecognition rate, were achieved [11]. Unfortunately in the field of handwritten character recognition the results are not so good, since the machines proposed up to now are slow and show a misrecognition rate which is not negligible. This depends on the fact that different subjects write characters in a different way and even one subject writes the same

character in different ways depending on factors like age, physical and psychological states, the semantic contents of writing as well as environmental conditions [12]. It results that many plane curves represent the same character, i.e. more than one image description of the same pattern can be stored within the same family or class, and different families may be related to the same pattern. Notwithstanding man is not perfect as recognizer, in fact his recognition percentage changes with time and experience, and also he shows some uncertainty [12,13,14], he remains unchallenged in handwritten character recognition. It could be not sufficient but to solve the problem, it is necessary that a totally unconstrained handwritten character recognition machine should be able to extend its knowledge base appreciably [15].
In this section a first prototype of an open machine which can develop in a large way its knowledge base is presented.
A PC based prototype of the system was realized. Problems arised during this first implementation, substantially due to the computation time, suggested to investigate for a parallel architecture oriented machine.
The PC based system and the algorithms which have been implemented are described in the following subsection.

9.2 The PC-Based System

The system consists of a graphic tablet on line with a PC. This peripheral device has been used for data acquisition, monitor and keyboard have been used to transfer human cognition from man to machine i.e. to select the classes of strokes. In this way the machine can develop its knowledge base on a very large scale even when few handwritten samples are taken into consideration for each class of strokes. In fact, the machine, through slight variations of the numerical values of the features taken into consideration, can generate, in the space of the plane curves, all plane curves 'near' to the handwritten one. Man is used to discriminate the plane curves which have the same shape of the handwritten samples from the other, giving suggestion to the machine for selecting the class of the strokes which are similar [16].
Here it has been assumed that a stroke is the writing from pen down to pen up. In the experiments carried on up to now, handwritten numerals have been taken into account and generally no more than two strokes have been registered. In order to classify multi-stroke characters the barycentre and the orientation of each stroke must be recorded in the knowledge base.
More specifically let be $z(t) = x(t) + jy(t)$ (where t belongs to either a bounded and closed real interval) the description of a stroke that is here considered as belonging to a complex plane; then let denote by $\{z(t)\}$ the set of the plane curves, defined in the $[0,T]$ real interval. It has been shown that these plane curves can be represented using Fourier coefficents and, to avoid the effect of position, size and orientation, some suitable Fourier Descriptors have been used [17,18,19,20]. In order to develop the learning phase of the machine it must

be noted that the shape of a plane curve $z_2(t)$ obtained with a slight increment of the Fourier descriptors of the handwritten numeral '$z_1(t)$', is generally recognized by the writer as the same numeral represented by $z_1(t)$. Consequently it can be assumed that $z_1(t)$ and $z_2(t)$ are similar [21]. This procedure can be iterated for $z_2(t)$ and so on, but not indefinetely. The role of man in creating the knowledge base, i.e. in creating the classes of the numerals, is to select all the samples similar to the handwritten one.
It has been shown [17] that to describe the strokes representing handwritten numerals, only the first four Fourier coefficents can be used and experiments to detect class boundaries have been carried out by investigating the tridimensional complex space of the Fourier descriptors d_{12}, d_{13} and d_{14}, where $d_{1j}=c_j/c_1$ for each j=2,3,4, being c_j for j=1,2,3 and 4 the Fourier coefficents. This space can be investigated using the six dimensional real space R^6 and if the polar representation of complex numbers is used, since the phase is periodic, it can be investigated trough a tridimensional array of cubes each one of size $(2\pi)^3$. In this space the boundary of each class is a hypersurface including "the subset of curves recognized similar to the handwritten sample". To detect one of these surfaces the tridimensional finite space of ternaries $(\Phi d_{12},\Phi d_{13},\Phi d_{14})$ must be investigated for each module ternary $(| \Phi d_{12} |, | \Phi d_{13} |, | \Phi d_{14} |)$. The problem of class selection using human knowledge is now met by submitting to the writer the curves obtained and by asking him to discriminate plane curves representing numerals similar to handwritten z(t) from the others. This procedure must be repeated for each sample written on the tablet and rejected by the machine. To accomplish the training of the system many handwritten samples written by different people were employed. During the pre-processing phase, the overlapping points, due to the high sampling rate of the tablet, are eliminated and the remaining are replaced using a B-spline algorithm and their number is normalized to N. N is chosen to be equal to 2^α (α integer) to allow the use of the DIT algorithm to extract the features from the curves. It is important to underline that the set {x(n) n=0,...,N-1} of the points describing the curve is previously duplicated and the new set {x'(n)} = {x(0), x(1),..., x(N-2), x(N-1), x(N-2), ..., x(1)} is taken into consideration: this is a necessary trick to close the curves representing the numerals in order to apply in a better way the DFT theory. Then it must be specified that N is chosen to be $2(N-1)=2^\alpha$ (α integer). Alternatively the DCT (Discrete Cosine Transform) can be used. To create the structure of the knowledge base and fit it in a digital computer a space discretization was realized. In order to do this, a quantum step is taken into consideration for the modules and the phases of the Fourier descriptors. The steps $M_{12} = 0.125$ $M_{13} = 0.08$ $M_{14} = 0.05$ and $F_{12} = 2\pi/16$ $F_{13} = 2\pi/16$ $F_{14} = 2\pi/16$ (where M_{1n} are the modules quanta and F_{1n} the phases quanta) were experimentally determined [22]. A complete description of the structure of the discrete Fourier Descriptors space can be found in the paper of ref.23.

After the numeral acquisition and pre-processing phase the cube of phases including the handwritten strokes, corresponding to one module ternary and including all possible combination of phases was generated and arranged in a group of 16 maps each of 16x16 curves. The class boundaries selected by the writer on the 16 maps were recorded. The value of the first Fourier coefficent of the numeral was also recorded in order to save the orientation of the strokes and used for example to distinguish the curves representing numerals like 6 and 9. An example of map experimentally obtained is reported in Fig.9. It shows the class boundary of a handwritten numeral 'three'.
A good octree method, derived by a quadtree one [24], was utilized to record the boundaries selected. Since the octree is first linearized by reading the tree in an ordered way then packed and finally recorded, the amount of memory required by the knowledge base is very small (about one hundred bytes x octree). In order to classify an unknown sample, its descriptors are computed at first and its "module quantum level" (i.e. the point corresponding to the computed ternary in the module space) of belonging is selected. Subsequently the octree corresponding to the computed ternary of modules and describing the phases boundaries is considered, if it exists, and the inclusion of the unknown point into the class is controlled. If it is included, the sample is recognized otherwise a new class is generated by the interactive process. A rejection occurs both if the quantum level in the module space is not classified yet or the sample is out of the boundaries selected in the phases space.

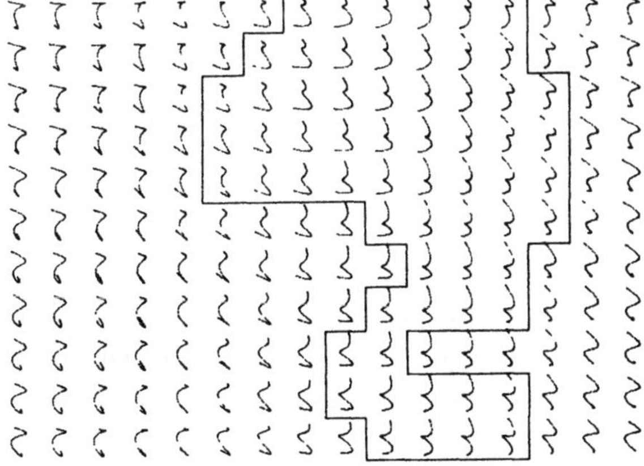

Fig.9.

The real limit of this type of system is the amount of work and time required to select all the boundaries in order to develop the knowledge base. Therefore, to reduce the processing time, the realization of a parallel machine is actually in progress. The HERMIA parallel machine has shown good versatility in solving this problem [25]. A simplified description of a protoype of the working machine is reported now. The on-line input device is a graphic tablet "Summasketch 1201" connected via an RS-232 serial adapter to the PC. A software driver was developed to match the special type of communication of the tablet. The preprocessing module generates the suitable set of points ready to be processed by the FFT. Feature extraction is done still on the PC, since a single FFT is required. Then the generation of the cube of the phases is realized on the parallel machine, since 4096 IFFTs are required. These IFFTs have to process different data derived from the original set in a fixed sequence, giving way to apply parallel algorithms. All the curves generated are visualized on a VGA graphic display and classified by man. At this moment also the octree generation is accomplished on the PC, since this operation requires a short time.

9.3 Experimental Results

The computation time necessary to accomplish the classification phase for each handwritten numeral, i.e. the generation of the 16 maps, was strongly reduced by using the parallel machine. This result, obtained investigating the classes of handwritten numeral 'three', encourage the efforts in the direction of the full Transputer based implementation of the working machine. At this moment the training of the machine with numerals belonging to all classes is in progress in order to evaluate more precisely its performances. However its misclassification rate should be very low, since all the numerals composing the knowledge base are selected by human subjects. Then, personal bias excepted, the system here proposed shows great reliability.

10 Application 3: Use of the Fourier Transform for the Investigation of Human Variable Behaviour in the Handwriting Recognition Process

10.1 Introduction

In this section is reported an excerpt of a work already known in literature [12]. The aim is to show as it is possible to investigate human variable behaviour in the handwriting recognition process through the use of a set of ambiguous curves synthetically generated starting from the Fourier coefficents of a handwritten character. Several research activities concern the design of systems for automatic recognition of handwritten characters which transfer the

human ability in recognizing characters to machine, accomplishing the classification phase basing on human decision. However it has been noticed [13,14] that this classification is strictly related to personal bias. In order to analyze this individual bias, an experiment was done based on a group of human subjects. Specifically, there was also shown that people with different experience, interpret in different manner the same patterns [14]. Few efforts have been made in order to investigate specifically the nature of the patterns on which man shows a high degree of uncertainty. A contribution in the direction to investigate them in a systematic way is the paper of ref.13. In light of the above, it is natural to wonder how much reliable man is in the handwritten recognition process and then how much reliable can be the recognition systems which base their training on human recognition ability. In the paper [12] was shown that the human behaviour in recognizing handwritten characters is not only different from man to man but varies with time and experience in every man. Then it can be stated that in the field of handwritten characters human subjects are not very suitable as source of knowledge in supervised machine learning and that it is necessary to take into account carefully human bias in selecting the 'recognizable' characters.
In the paper [12] an experiment based on the recognition of handwritten numerals was accomplished and the results were reported too.
The aim of the experiment presented was to analyse human behaviour in recognizing handwritten confusing numerals. The peculiarity of this experiment is that only one numeral has been used for the test and some distortions of the numeral itself has been considered. Specifically a handwritten numeral '3' was been used.

10.2 The Synthetic Set of Ambiguous Numerals

In order to grasp human behaviour in recognizing handwritten numerals through this experiment it was individuated a set of curves, derived from a handwritten numeral, which includes numerals similar to the original one and meaningless curves. Moreover, the transition from the subset of recognizable numerals to the subset of the other curves was imperceptible, in order to generate confusion in human recognition process. At this purpose a powerful and well known tool for plane curves description will be used. Specifically, in this experiment we deal with handwritten mono-stroke numerals (where mono-stroke is the writing from pen-down to pen-up), then, as reported in section 12.2, they can be described through Fourier Descriptors (FD) and specifically through a vector of the kind (d_2,d_3,d_4). Consequently, one of the sets of curves can be

$$\{(d_2,\ d_3 \cdot e^{jk\delta\Phi}, d_4), \quad \text{with } \delta\Phi = 2\pi/M \quad \text{and } k=0,1,2,\ldots,M-1\}.$$

In this way through slight variations of the phase of one of the FD describing the original numeral it is possible to obtain a set of curves very similar among them but not always recognizable by man as belonging to the class of the original handwritten numeral. It was shown that man can distinguish curve k and curve k+1 chosing M less than or equal to 16; consequently the variation step $\delta\Phi=2\pi/16$ [21,22] has been considered. The whole set of curves generated by varing Φd_3 is reported in Fig.10 where the original handwritten sample is marked with an asterisk. The curves in Fig.10 are arranged in a circular way to emphasize the 2π-periodicity of the phase (in particular, in this case, the phase of the third Fourier Descriptor).

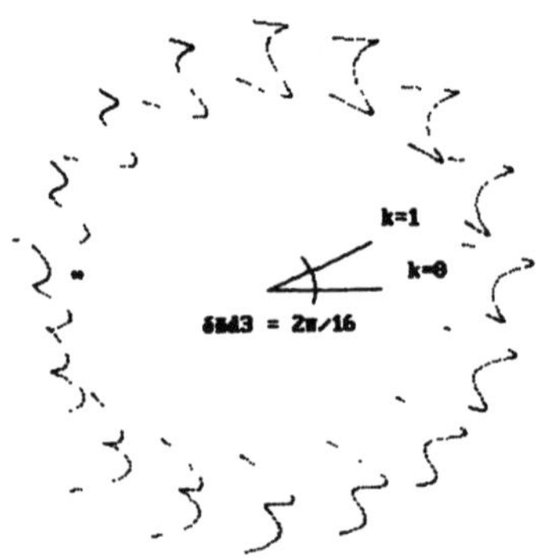

Fig.10.

In order to increment the ambiguity of the curves-numerals considered, a set of M curves (with M>16) could be generated using the variation step $\delta\Phi=2\pi/M$. A combination of variation of more than one FD can also be taken into account. In this sense, in Fig.11 is reported a map of curves derived from a handwritten numeral three combining the variations of the phases of the FDs d_2 and d_3.

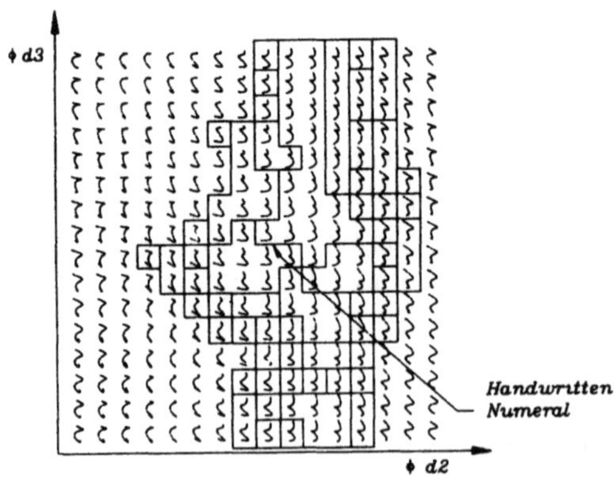

Fig.11.

Seven boundaries enclosing the curves recognized as numeral three by seven different subjects has been traced on this map too. Since a single boundary is composed by one closed broken line, it is evident the great variety of boundaries selected, confirming the ambiguity of the curves generated.

References

1. S. Impedovo, Introduzione all' Analisi Spettrale ed Algoritmi "FFT", Bari. Adriatica Editrice, 1987.

2. I. J. Good, A New Finite Series for Legendre Polynomials, Proc. Camb. Phil. Soc., 51, 385-388, 1958.

3. A. N. Kolmogorov, S. V. Fomin, Elementi di Teoria delle Funzioni e di Analisi Funzionale, Mosca: Edizioni MIR, 1980, pp. 398-399.

4. L. R. Rabiner, B. Gold, Theory and Applications of Digital Signal Processing, Englewood Cliffs, NJ: Prentice-Hall, 1975.

5. J. W. Cooley, P. A. W. Lewis, P. D. Welch, The Fast Fourier Transform, Proc. IEEE, 55, 1675-1677, October 1967.

6. J. W. Cooley, P. A. W. Lewis, P. D. Welch, The Fast Fourier Transform and its Applications, IEEE Transaction and Education, 12 (1), March 1969.

7. S. Winograd, On Computing the Discrete Fourier Transform, Mathematics of computation, 32, 175-199, 1978.

8. H. J. Nussbaumer, Digital Filtering Using Complex Marsenne Transform, IBM Journal of Res. and Dev., 20 (5), 498-504, Sept. 1976.

9. J. H. McClellan, C. M. Rader, Number Theory in Digital Signal Processing, Englewood Cliffs, NJ: Prentice-Hall, 1979.

10. A. V. Oppenheim, R. V. Schafer, Digital Signal Processing, Englewood Cliffs, NJ: Prentice-Hall, 1975.

11. B.A. Blesser, T. Kuklinsky, R.J. Shillman, Empirical tests for feature extraction selection based on a psychological theory of character recognition, Pattern Recognition, 8, 77-85, 1976.

12. S. Impedovo, G. Dimauro, G. Pirlo, Ambiguity in the recognition process: some considerations on human variable behaviour, in From Pixels to Features III - Frontiers in Handwriting Recognition, S. Impedovo and J.-C. Simon (eds.), Elsevier, 1992

13. M. Castellano, G. Dimauro, S. Impedovo, G. Pirlo, Ambiguous Patterns: Investigation on their properties, in Progress in Image Analysis and Processing, Edited by V. Cantoni, World Scientific, 1989.

14. R. Legault, C.Y. Suen, C. Nadal, Classification of Confusing Handwritten Numerals by Human Subjects, First IWFHR, Montreal, Canada, April 1990.

15. C.Y. Suen, P. Ahmed, Computer recognition of totally unconstrained handwritten zip codes, International Journal of Pattern Recognition and Artificial Intelligence, Word Scientific, 1 (1), 1-15, 1987.

16. D. Dutta Majumder et Al., How to quantify shape distance for 2-D regions, Proc. of 7th ICPR, Montreal, Canada, pp. 72-74, 1984.

17. S. Impedovo, B. Marangelli, A.M. Fanelli, A Fourier descriptor set for recognizing nonstylized numerals, IEEE Trans. Syst. Man and Cybern., SMC 8-8, 640-645, Aug. 1978.

18. E. Person, K.S. Fu, Shape discrimination using Fourier descriptors, IEEE Trans. Syst. Man and Cybern., SMC 7-3, 170-179, Mar. 1977.

19. C.T. Zahn et Al., Fourier descriptors for plane closed curve, IEEE Trans. Comp., C21-3, 269-281, Mar. 1972.

20. A. Krzyzak, S.Y. Lueng, C.Y. Suen, Reconstruction of two dimensional patterns by Fourier descriptors, 9-th ICPR, Rome, Italy, pp. 555-558, Nov. 1988.

21. S. Impedovo, N. Abbattista, Hand-written numeral recognition; the organization degree measurement, Proc. 6th ICPR, Munich, Germany, pp. 40-43, Oct. 1982.

22. S. Impedovo, Power pattern-resolution in human vision - some consideration on the handwritten numeral resolution, Proc. SPIE, vol.548 - Appl. of Art. Intell. II, Washington, USA, pp. 263-268, 1985.

23. S. Impedovo, G. Dimauro, An interactive system for the selection of handwritten numeral classes, Proc. of 10th ICPR, Atlantic City, USA, pp. 563-566, 1990.

24. H. Samet, Region representation: quadtrees from binary arrays, Computer Graphics and Image Processing, May 1980, pp. 88-93.

25. "HERMIA: An Heterogeneus and Reconfigurable Machine for Image Analysis, MVA IAPR Workshop on Machine Vision Applications, Tokyo, pp. 397-400, Nov. 28-30, 1990.

Pattern Recognition with Optimal Margin Classifiers

Bernhard E. Boser

Department of Electrical Engineering and Computer Sciences, University of California, Berkeley, CA 94720

Abstract. Pattern classifiers use problem specific knowledge, an example database, or a combination of the two to provide a functional mapping from input patterns to class labels. Several important methods are described, including statistical techniques and neural nets. The tradeoffs between memorization of the training data, and the ability of classifiers to give correct outputs for inputs that are not contained in the example database are described. The notion of capacity of a family of functions is introduced as a means to control this tradeoff. Finally, the optimal margin learning algorithm is described as a means of applying the derived concepts to practical pattern classification problem.

1 Introduction

Classifiers perform the important task of assigning class labels to input patterns. In character recognition, for example, an image of a character may be aquired with a camera, appropriately scaled, and then supplied to a classifier which in turn returns the letter the input most likely corresponds to. More sophisticated classifiers are used for recognition of printed or handwritten text, address blocks on envelopes, amount fields on checks, or in applications such as speech recognition.

Many classification techniques are used today, including statistical methods, artificial intelligence expert sytems, artificial neural networks, or fuzzy logic systems. Of these, methods that learn from examples are particularly important for pattern recognition applications. In Section 2 the various techniques are categorized and some of their properties analyzed. The key objective of classifiers is generalization, i.e. correct classification of examples that are not contained in the training set. The conditions for generalization and their consequences in practice are examined, along with other important considerations such as training speed and sensitivity to initial conditions.

These criteria for learning algorithms form the starting point for deriving a new training method called "maximum margin classification" that is described in Section 3. This algorithm trains a wide variety of important classifiers, including linear discriminant functions, polynomial classifiers, radial basis functions, and neural networks. Examples from the domain of handwritten character classification are presented.

2 Pattern Classification

2.1 Learning from Examples

The "conventional" approach to solving a problem with a computer is to first find a step-by-step "recipe" that describes in exhaustive detail how to arrive at the desired solution for all inputs of interest. This recipe is then programmed and executed on the computer.

The need to specify the recipe with meticulous detail is tedious in practice. At the same time, it has many important consequences. The great detail of information available permits various optimizations, for example maximizing execution speed or minimizing memory requirements. Similarly, the outputs for all possible inputs can be checked exhaustively at least in principle. Illegal states can be detected by the program and corrective actions be taken if necessary. Methodologies have been devised to perform these checks in a consistent manner.

Despite the advantages of conventional programming, an alternative approach is required to solve problems for which no "recipe" solution is known, or which are too complex to specify such an algorithm in sufficient detail. There are three basic techniques for solving such problems: *Deduction, induction,* and *transduction. Deduction methods* derive a particular solution from general knowledge about the problem domain. Expert systems, for example, use a knowledge base of universal concepts to find the answer for a specific case. Conversely, *induction methods* generalize from a particular to the general case. Artificial neural networks, for example, use a set of examples to find a universal mapping from the input to the output domain of the problem at hand. This universal mapping, generally available in the from of a trained neural network, is then used to find the answers to specific inputs. *Transduction techniques,* finally, go directly from the particular to the particular case, without constructing or implying the existence of a general model. Practical implementations of the three techniques, along with their advantages and disadvantages, are summarized below.

Artificial intelligence expert systems are the most prominent deduction technique. Instead of specifying a step-by-step solution approach, the general concepts and knowledge of the problem domain are captured in a knowledge base, and results are derived by logic inference. Expert systems are deployed in many products and perform particularly well in problem domains that are easily described by exact rules. Well known and widely used expert systems include programs for college level calculus, such as Macsyma or Mathematica. Applications to areas of human expertise, such as medical diagnosis systems or factory control applications, face the difficult task of extracting the knowledge base from a human expert.

A serious problem for expert systems are the contradictions that are typical of human knowledge. Ordinary logic cannot deal with contradictions, but alternative methods such as fuzzy logic or non-monotonic reasoning have been developed. In fuzzy logic, the uncertainty of measurements is captured by a *membership function* that assigns data to broad categories. In a particular application, temperature might be coded with the levels "cold", "warm", and "hot". These categories reflect more closely the language and thinking of human experts. This simplifies the formulation of the knowledge base. An arbitration technique is used in cases where more than one rule apply to a set of inputs. Fuzzy logic systems have been applied successfully to many control problems and are used in various consumer products [15, 11].

In many important applications, most prominently many man-machine interface tasks, no or insufficient knowledge is available in the form of rules. Instead, the information of the problem is captured in a set of examples. Learning methods, such as artificial neural networks, various statistical techniques, or genetic algorithms, address this case. The learning process finds a general model from the data by induction. This model, for example a neural network with a particular architecture and weights, is then used to predict the outputs for specific inputs.

Statistics offers an array of techniques for modeling empirical data. While many statistical methods are optimal to fit a small number (less than ten) of variables, some statistical techniques [5] are so closely related to artificial neural networks that a clear separation seems artifical. For example, radial basis functions and nearest neighbor classifiers are also trained from example and often achieve similar performance [8].

In many applications, most of the knowledge is captured in the examples, but some information is more adequately represented by rules. The rules alone may be insufficient to solve the problem, but may capture, for example, essential invariances or constraints that are difficult to enforce in a trained system. A robot arm, for example, should be prevented from crashing into objects, no matter how elegant the trajectory might be otherwise. Similarly, the pitch of a speech signal does not carry much information that is relevant for the recognition process.

Of course, the rules could simply be discarded in this case and a learning method be used. Constraints can sometimes be enforced by appropriate pre- or postprocessing of the data. Better performance is generally achieved, however, if the all available knowledge is used to solve the problem, and the ability of the learning methods to extract fundamental properties of the data is not relied on.

A number of techniques have been developed to explicitly incorporate problem specific knowledge into neural networks, including appropriate encoding of the data before presentation to the network [20], and careful selection of the network architecture [6, 30]. By introducing a similarity function into the training process that enforces the invariance of characters to small rotation, tilt, or pen width, Simard cut the error rate of a recognizer in half [22]. However, these methods rely on the intuition of the designer to find appropriate ways to a priori enforce known rules in neural networks. In many cases they are not applicable at all. Possibly a more satisfactory approach could be found by combining neural networks with fuzzy logic systems.

Induction methods, including artificial neural networks, construct a general input/output mapping from the example database that is then used to find answers for particular inputs. Transduction techniques avoid this detour by finding a specific solution by using the examples directly. This approach is likely important in human thinking. A child does not construct a language model, but finds new sentences that are like ones heard before. A general concept is neither formulated nor implied. Learning theory supports the intuitive feeling that on the average transduction methods will perform better, since finding particular answers is easier than finding a generally valid law. Nearest neighbor or Parzen window classifiers are examples of simple transduction methods.

2.2 Learning Algorithms

The task of a learning algorithm is to find a functional mapping from an input to an output space based on a limited set of examples. The key objective for this mapping is that it predicts the correct output even for inputs that are similar, but not identical to the examples. In other words, a function is sought that generalizes from a usually small number of examples to the general case [31].

Figure 1 illustrates the general concept of training discriminant functions from examples. An artificial neural network architecture or other function is chosen and the parameters set to some initial values. Training examples are presented to the input of the network and the output is compared to the correct labels

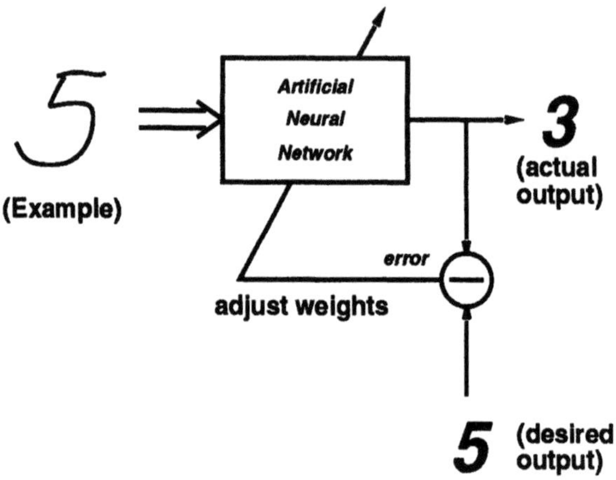

Figure 1. Learning from examples.

for the training patterns. The parameters of the network are then adjusted so as to minimize a suitable difference measure between the actual and the desired output. The objective of the training is to achieve generalization, i.e. to predict correct outputs for inputs that are not contained in the example database. For generalization to be possible, some assumptions about the regularity of the world must be made. For example, in the absence of any assumptions, a child after seeing some objects, all identified as chairs, would be unjustified to reach any opinion whatever about unseen objects.

In [25] Valiant proposes a theory that implies that regularities are not actually imposed by properties of the observed world, but by computational limitations internal to the learner. This approach has the advantage of not making any assumptions about the world, complex as it is. This is important since, in contrast with physics, where many simple laws have been found, at the level of cognition and human concepts no analogous simple regularities have been identified.

A sufficiently sophisticated classifier, e.g. a very large neural network, can in principle learn any possible input/output mapping. Unfortunately, given an equally universal training algorithm, such a network imposes no constraints whatsoever on datapoints not contained in the training sample and will therefore

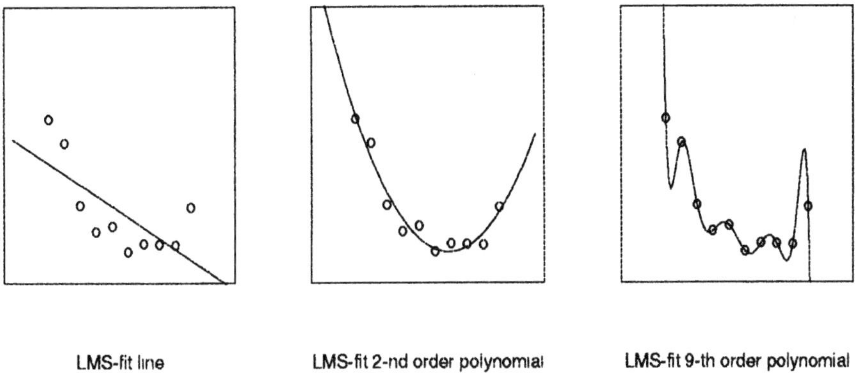

Figure 2. Curve fitting with straight line, and second and ninth order polynomials.

not generalize. Conversely, a network that is too small will not be able to learn the training data with small error. Reasonable generalization can be expected only from a network whose size matches the requirements of the problem at hand.

This situation is illustrated by the polynomial fitting experiment shown in Figure 2. The training data are indicated by circles in the plots, and are fitted to a straight line, and a second and ninth order polynomial by minimizing the mean squared distance between data and fit. A straight line is obviously too simple a model for the given data, which cannot be fitted with small error. The ninth order polynomial passes through all the data points, but does not generalize. Of course, it is still possible to evaluate the fitted polynomial values not contained in the training data, but the result is irrelevant unless the data was perfect and actually generated by a ninth' order polynomial. Valid generalization is achieved only if the solution is constrained by assumptions about the problem, embodied by the limitations of the learner. Of course, the assumptions must be valid themselves; there is for example no point in trying to fit a periodic function with a polynomial.

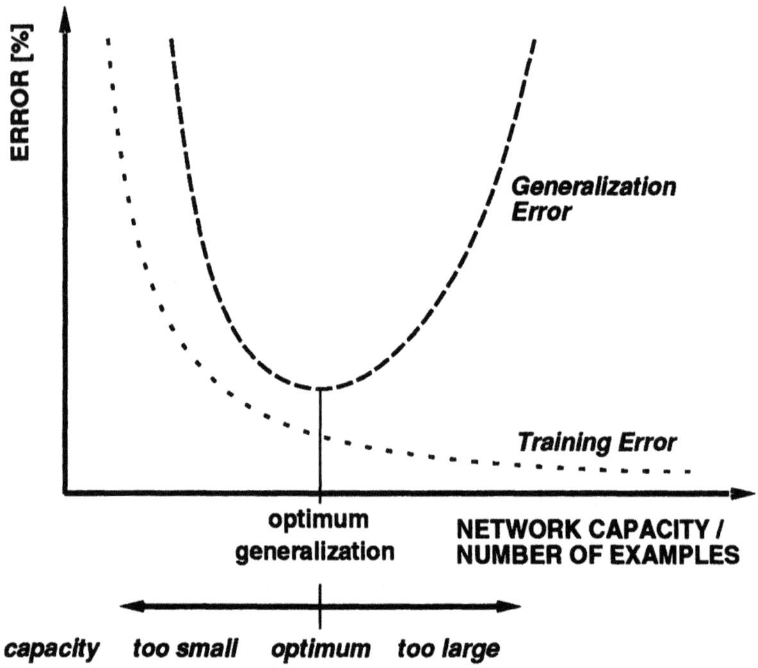

Figure 3. Error rate versus neural network capacity divided by the number of training examples.

The relationship between the relative capacity of a classifier and its ability to generalize is fundamental. The qualitative behavior is expressed in Figure 3. Functions with small capacity cannot learn the training data and therefore exhibit a large error both on the example data and poor generalization. Increasing the capacity first results in a reduction of both the training and the generalization error. However, if the capacity is increased beyond a certain problem dependent value, the generalization performance gets worse despite the fact that the training error continues to decrease. For sufficiently large capacity, the classifier memorizes the training data perfectly, i.e. with zero error, but does not generalize. It resembles a memory which truthfully reproduces whatever data has been stored, but makes no representations whatsoever about data that has not been stored.

The relative capacity of a neural network, for example, is the ratio of its functional complexity, approximated by its size, and the size of the training dataset. Obviously, the more training data is available, the larger a neural network can be trained. Various measures for the capacity of functions are used, such as the Vapnik-Chervonenkis dimension [26], or the minimum description length [18]. Learning theory predicts bounds on the generalization of trained functions based on these bounds, that are however usually too loose to be useful in practice. Instead, the generalization performance is usually estimated with a separate test database that is not used for training.

Rather than maximizing the generalization performance of a neural network, learning algorithms such as back-propagation attempt to minimize the error on the training set. As illustrated by Figure 3, this error is a poor indicator for the true objective of a trained artificial neural network, namely its generalization ability. To optimize the generalization, several networks with varying capacity must be trained and tested and the best one be chosen. A formal approach, called *structural risk minimization*, is developed in [28].

Instead of changing the network architecture directly to change the topology, additional constraints, corresponding to limitations of the learner, can be added to the training algorithm itself. This approach is used widely and known under the name *regularization* [23, 24]. The weight-decay technique employed by some implementations of the back-propagation algorithm, for example, minimizes the sum of the MSE over the training data *plus* the norm of the weight vector. While there may be no simple correspondence between the norm of the weight vector of a neural network and complex assumptions about the workings of the world, this constraint is often observed to improve the generalization.

The fundamental connections between the capacity of a function and its generalization ability has important ramifications for the design of classifiers. It means that classification functions cannot be chosen conservatively large to solve a wide variety of problems, but must be adjusted carefully to each individual problem in order to achieve good performance. Given current practical limitations of trainable functions, learning algorithms, and available training set size, a universal function with large capacity that extracts all information from a database and does not depend on the designer's knowledge to achieve high accuracy is not feasible.

3 Maximum Margin Classifiers

3.1 Introduction

Good generalization performance of pattern classifiers is achieved when the capacity of the classification function is matched to the size of the training set. Classifiers with a large number of adjustable parameters and therefore large capacity likely learn the training set without error, but exhibit poor generalization. Conversely, a classifier with insufficient capacity might not be able to learn the task at all. In between, there is an optimal capacity of the classifier which minimizes the expected generalization error for a given amount of training data (see Figure 3).

In this section we describe a training algorithm that automatically tunes the capacity of the classification function by maximizing the margin between training examples and class boundary [12], optionally after removing some atypical or meaningless examples from the training data. The resulting classification function depends only on so-called supporting patterns [27]. These are those training examples that are closest to the decision boundary and are usually a small subset of the training data.

It will be demonstrated that maximizing the margin amounts to minimizing the maximum loss, as opposed to some average quantity such as the mean squared error. This has several desirable consequences. The resulting classification rule achieves an errorless separation of the training data if possible. Outliers or meaningless patterns are identified by the algorithm and can therefore be eliminated easily with or without supervision. This contrasts classifiers based on minimizing the mean squared error, which quietly ignore atypical patterns. Another advantage of maximum margin classifiers is that the sensitivity of the classifier to limited computational accuracy is minimal compared to other separations with smaller margin.

The proposed algorithm operates with a large class of decision functions that are linear in their parameters but not restricted to linear dependences in the input components. Perceptrons [19], polynomial classifiers, neural networks with one hidden layer, and Radial Basis Function (RBF) or potential function classifiers [1, 2, 14] fall into this class. As pointed out by several authors [1, 5, 17], Perceptrons have a dual kernel representation implementing the same decision function. The optimal margin algorithm exploits this duality both for improved efficiency and flexibility. In the dual space the decision function is expressed as a linear combination of basis functions parametrized by the supporting patterns. The supporting patterns correspond to the class centers of RBF classifiers and are chosen automatically by the maximum margin training procedure. In the case of polynomial classifiers, the Perceptron representation involves an untractable number of parameters. This problem is overcome in the dual space representation, where the classification rule is a weighted sum of a kernel function [16] for each supporting pattern. High order polynomial classifiers with very large training sets can therefore be handled efficiently with the proposed algorithm.

3.2 Maximum Margin Training Algorithm

The maximum margin training algorithm finds a decision function for pattern vectors $\mathbf{x}$ of dimension n belonging to either of two classes A and B. The input to the training algorithm is a set of p examples $\mathbf{x}_i$ with labels y_i:

$$(\mathbf{x}_1, y_1),\ (\mathbf{x}_2, y_2),\ (\mathbf{x}_3, y_3),\ \ldots,\ (\mathbf{x}_p, y_p) \tag{1}$$

$$\text{where} \begin{cases} y_k = 1 & \text{if } \mathbf{x}_k \in \text{class A} \\ y_k = -1 & \text{if } \mathbf{x}_k \in \text{class B.} \end{cases}$$

From these training examples the algorithm finds the parameters of the decision function $D(\mathbf{x})$ during a learning phase. After training, the classification of unknown patterns is predicted according to the following rule:

$$\begin{array}{ll} \mathbf{x} \in \mathrm{A} & \text{if } D(\mathbf{x}) > 0 \\ \mathbf{x} \in \mathrm{B} & \text{otherwise.} \end{array} \tag{2}$$

The decision functions must be linear in their parameters but are not restricted to linear dependences of $\mathbf{x}$. These functions can be expressed either in direct, or in dual space. The direct space notation is identical to the Perceptron decision function [19]:

$$D(\mathbf{x}) = \sum_{i=1}^{N} w_i \varphi_i(\mathbf{x}) + b. \tag{3}$$

In this equation the φ_i are predefined functions of $\mathbf{x}$, and the w_i and b are the adjustable parameters of the decision function. Polynomial classifiers are a special case of Perceptrons for which $\varphi_i(\mathbf{x})$ are products of components of $\mathbf{x}$.

In the dual space, the decision functions are of the form

$$D(\mathbf{x}) = \sum_{k=1}^{p} \alpha_k K(\mathbf{x}_k, \mathbf{x}) + b, \tag{4}$$

The coefficients α_k are the parameters to be adjusted and the $\mathbf{x}_k$ are the training patterns. The function K is a predefined kernel, for example a potential function [1] or any Radial Basis Function [2, 14]. Under certain conditions [3], symmetric kernels possess finite or infinite series expansions of the form

$$K(\mathbf{x}, \mathbf{x}') = \sum_{i} \varphi_i(\mathbf{x})\, \varphi_i(\mathbf{x}'). \tag{5}$$

In particular, the kernel $K(\mathbf{x}, \mathbf{x}') = (\mathbf{x} \cdot \mathbf{x}' + 1)^q$ corresponds to a polynomial expansion $\boldsymbol{\varphi}(\mathbf{x})$ of order q [16].

Provided that the expansion stated in equation (5) exists, equations (3) and (4) are dual representations of the same decision function and

$$w_i = \sum_{k=1}^{p} \alpha_k \varphi_i(\mathbf{x}_k). \tag{6}$$

The parameters w_i are called direct parameters, and the α_k are referred to as dual parameters.

The proposed training algorithm is based on the "generalized portrait" method described in [27] that constructs separating hyperplanes with maximum margin. Here this algorithm is extended to train classifiers linear in their parameters. First, the margin between the class boundary and the training patterns is formulated in the direct space. This problem description is then transformed into the dual space by means of the Lagrangian. The resulting problem is that of maximizing a quadratic form with constraints and is amenable to efficient numeric optimization algorithms.

3.2.1 Maximizing the Margin in the Direct Space

In the direct space the decision function is

$$D(\mathbf{x}) = \mathbf{w} \cdot \varphi(\mathbf{x}) + b, \tag{7}$$

where $\mathbf{w}$ and $\varphi(\mathbf{x})$ are N dimensional vectors and b is a bias. It defines a separating hyperplane in φ-space. The distance between this hyperplane and pattern $\mathbf{x}$ is $D(\mathbf{x})/\|\mathbf{w}\|$ (Figure 4). Assuming that a separation of the training set with margin M between the class boundary and the training patterns exists, all training patterns fulfill the following inequality:

$$\frac{y_k D(\mathbf{x}_k)}{\|\mathbf{w}\|} \geq M. \tag{8}$$

The objective of the training algorithm is to find the parameter vector $\mathbf{w}$ that maximizes M:

$$M^* = \max_{\mathbf{w}, \|\mathbf{w}\|=1} M \tag{9}$$
$$\text{subject to} \quad y_k D(\mathbf{x}_k) \geq M, \qquad k = 1, 2, \ldots, p.$$

The bound M^* is attained for those patterns satisfying

$$\min_k y_k D(\mathbf{x}_k) = M^*. \tag{10}$$

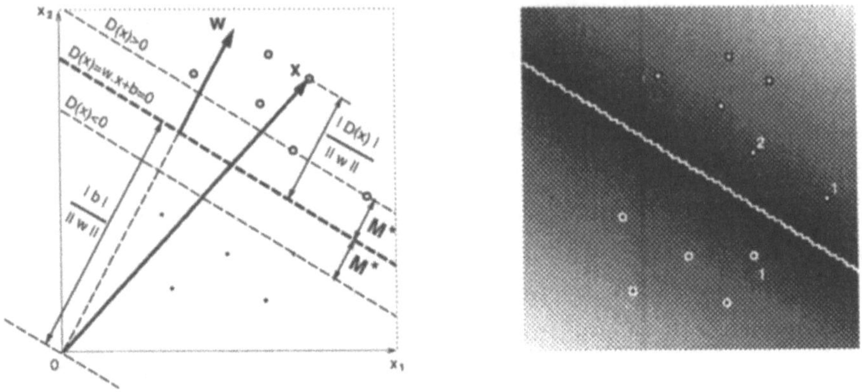

Figure 4. Maximum margin linear decision function $D(\mathbf{x}) = \mathbf{w} \cdot \mathbf{x} + b$ ($\boldsymbol{\varphi} = \mathbf{x}$). The gray levels encode the absolute value of the decision function (solid black corresponds to $D(\mathbf{x}) = 0$). The numbers indicate the supporting patterns.

These patterns are called the supporting patterns of the decision boundary.

A decision function with maximum margin is illustrated in figure 4. The problem of finding a hyperplane in $\boldsymbol{\varphi}$-space with maximum margin is therefore a minimax problem:

$$\max_{\mathbf{w},\|\mathbf{w}\|=1} \min_k y_k D(\mathbf{x}_k). \tag{11}$$

The norm of the parameter vector in equations (9) and (11) is fixed to pick one of an infinite number of possible solutions that differ only in scaling. Instead of fixing the norm of $\mathbf{w}$ to take care of the scaling problem, the product of the margin M and the norm of a weight vector $\mathbf{w}$ can be fixed.

$$M\|\mathbf{w}\| = 1. \tag{12}$$

Thus, maximizing the margin M is equivalent to minimizing the norm $\|\mathbf{w}\|$. Then the problem of finding a maximum margin separating hyperplane $\mathbf{w}^*$ stated in (9) reduces to solving the following quadratic problem:

$$\min_{\mathbf{w}} \|\mathbf{w}\|^2 \tag{13}$$
$$\text{under conditions} \quad y_k D(\mathbf{x}_k) \geq 1, \quad k = 1, 2, \ldots, p.$$

The maximum margin is $M^* = 1/\|\mathbf{w}^*\|$.

In principle the problem stated in (13) can be solved directly with numerical techniques. However, this approach is impractical when the dimensionality of the φ-space is large or infinite. Moreover, no information is gained about the supporting patterns.

3.2.2 Maximizing the Margin in the Dual Space

Problem (13) can be transformed into the dual space by means of the Lagrangian

$$L(\mathbf{w}, b, \boldsymbol{\alpha}) = \frac{1}{2}\|\mathbf{w}\|^2 - \sum_{k=1}^{p} \alpha_k \left[y_k D(\mathbf{x}_k) - 1 \right] \tag{14}$$
$$\text{subject to} \quad \alpha_k \geq 0, \quad k = 1, 2, \ldots, p.$$

The factors α_k are called Lagrange multipliers or Kühn-Tucker coefficients and satisfy the conditions

$$\alpha_k \left(y_k D(\mathbf{x}_k) - 1 \right) = 0, \quad k = 1, 2, \ldots, p. \tag{15}$$

The factor one half has been included for cosmetic reasons; it does not change the solution.

The optimization problem (13) is equivalent to searching a saddle point of the function $L(\mathbf{w}, b, \boldsymbol{\alpha})$. This saddle point is a the minimum of $L(\mathbf{w}, b, \boldsymbol{\alpha})$ with respect to $\mathbf{w}$, and a maximum with respect to $\boldsymbol{\alpha}$ ($\alpha_k \geq 0$). At the solution, the following necessary condition is met:

$$\frac{\partial L}{\partial \mathbf{w}} = \mathbf{w}^* - \sum_{k=1}^{p} \alpha_k^* y_k \boldsymbol{\varphi}_k = 0,$$

hence

$$\mathbf{w}^* = \sum_{k=1}^{P} \alpha_k^* y_k \boldsymbol{\varphi}_k. \tag{16}$$

The patterns which satisfy $y_k D(\mathbf{x}_k) = 1$ are the supporting patterns. According to equation (16), the vector $\mathbf{w}^*$ that specifies the hyperplane with maximum margin is a linear combination of only the supporting patterns, which are those patterns for which $\alpha_k^* \neq 0$. Usually the number of supporting patterns is much smaller than the number p of patterns in the training set.

The dependence of the Lagrangian $L(\mathbf{w}, b, \boldsymbol{\alpha})$ on the weight vector $\mathbf{w}$ is removed by substituting the expansion of $\mathbf{w}^*$ given by equation (16) for $\mathbf{w}$. Further transformations using (3) and (5) result in a Lagrangian which is a function of the parameters $\boldsymbol{\alpha}$ and the bias b only:

$$J(\boldsymbol{\alpha}, b) = \sum_{k=1}^{p} \alpha_k (1 - b y_k) - \frac{1}{2} \boldsymbol{\alpha} \cdot \boldsymbol{H} \cdot \boldsymbol{\alpha}, \tag{17}$$
$$\text{subject to } \ \alpha_k \geq 0, \qquad k = 1, 2, \ldots, p.$$

Here $\boldsymbol{H}$ is a square matrix of size $p \times p$ with elements

$$H_{kl} = y_k y_l K(\mathbf{x}_k, \mathbf{x}_l).$$

In order for a unique solution to exist, $\boldsymbol{H}$ must be positive definite. For fixed bias b, the solution $\boldsymbol{\alpha}^*$ is obtained by maximizing $J(\boldsymbol{\alpha}, b)$ under the conditions $\alpha_k \geq 0$. Based on equations (7) and (16), the resulting decision function is of the form

$$\begin{aligned} D(\mathbf{x}) &= \mathbf{w}^* \cdot \boldsymbol{\varphi}(\mathbf{x}) + b \\ &= \sum_k y_k \alpha_k^* K(\mathbf{x}_k, \mathbf{x}) + b, \qquad \alpha_k^* \geq 0, \end{aligned} \tag{18}$$

where only the supporting patterns appear in the sum with nonzero weight.

The choice of the bias b gives rise to several variants of the algorithm. The two considered here are

1. The bias can be fixed a priori and not subjected to training. This corresponds to the "Generalized Portrait Technique" described in [27].

2. The pattern vectors $\boldsymbol{\varphi}_k$ can be padded with a component φ_0 that is set to a constant and the corresponding additional weight w_0 be trained by solving problem (17) with $b = 0$.

3. The cost function (17) can be optimized with respect to $\mathbf{w}$ and b. This approach gives the largest possible margin M^* in $\boldsymbol{\varphi}$-space [29].

In all cases the solution is found with standard nonlinear optimization algorithms for quadratic forms with linear constraints. The second approach gives the largest possible margin. There is no guarantee, however, that this solution exhibits also the best generalization performance.

The dimension of problem (17) equals the size of the training set, p. To avoid the need to solve a dual problem of exceedingly large dimensionality, the training data is divided into chunks that are processed iteratively [27]. The maximum margin hypersurface is constructed for the first chunk and a new training set is formed consisting of the supporting patterns from the solution and those patterns $\mathbf{x}_k$ in the second chunk of the training set for which $y_k D(\mathbf{x}_k) < 1 - \epsilon$. A new classifier is trained and used to construct a training set consisting of supporting patterns and examples from the first three chunks which satisfy $y_k D(\mathbf{x}_k) < 1 - \epsilon$. This process is repeated until the entire training set is separated.

3.3 Properties of the Algorithm

Since maximizing the margin between the decision boundary and the training patterns is equivalent to maximizing a quadratic form in the positive quadrant, there are no local minima and the solution is always unique if $\boldsymbol{H}$ has full rank. At the optimum

$$J(\boldsymbol{\alpha}^*) = \frac{1}{2}\|\mathbf{w}^*\|^2 = \frac{1}{2\,(M^*)^2} = \frac{1}{2}\sum_{k=1}^{p} \alpha_k^*. \qquad (19)$$

The uniqueness of the solution is a consequence of the maximum margin cost function and represents an important advantage over other algorithms for which the solution depends on the initial conditions or other parameters that are difficult to control.

Another benefit of the maximum margin objective is its insensitivity to small changes of the parameters $\mathbf{w}$ or $\boldsymbol{\alpha}$. Since the decision function $D(\mathbf{x})$ is a linear function of $\mathbf{w}$ in the direct, and of $\boldsymbol{\alpha}$ in the dual space, the probability of misclassifications due to parameter variations of the components of these vectors is minimized for maximum margin. The robustness of the solution—and potentially its generalization performance—can be increased further by omitting some supporting patterns from the solution. Equation (19) indicates that the largest increase in the maximum margin M^* occurs when the supporting patterns with largest α_k are eliminated. The elimination can be performed automatically or with assistance from a supervisor. This feature gives rise to other important uses of the optimum margin algorithm in database cleaning applications [13].

Unlike MSE based decision functions, which simply ignore outliers, optimal margin classifiers are very sensitive to atypical patterns that are close to the decision boundary. These examples are readily identified as those with the largest α_k and can be eliminated either automatically or with supervision. Hence, optimal margin classifiers give complete control over the handling of outliers, as opposed to quietly ignoring them.

3.4 Experimental Results

The maximum margin training algorithm has been tested on two databases with images of handwritten digits. The first database (DB1) consists of 1200 clean images recorded from ten subjects. Half of this data is used for training, and the other half is used to evaluate the generalization performance. A comparative analysis of the performance of various classification methods on DB1 can be found in [10, 9, 7]. The other database (DB2) used in the experiment consists of 7300 images for training and 2000 for testing and has been recorded from actual mail pieces. Results for this

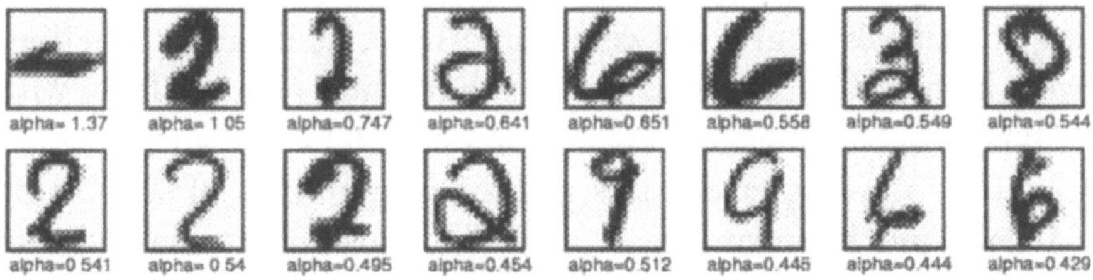

Figure 5. Supporting patterns from database DB2 for class 2 before cleaning. The patterns are ranked according to α_k.

data have been reported in several publications, see e.g. [4]. The resolution of the images in both databases is 16 by 16 pixels.

In all experiments, the margin is maximized with respect to $\mathbf{w}$ and b. Ten hypersurfaces, one per class, are used to separate the digits. Regardless of the difficulty of the problem—measured for example by the number of supporting patterns found by the algorithm—the same similarity function $K(\mathbf{x}, \mathbf{x}')$ and preprocessing is used for all hypersurfaces of one experiment. The results obtained with different choices of K corresponding to linear hyperplanes, polynomial classifiers, and basis functions are summarized below. The effect of smoothing is investigated as a simple form of preprocessing.

For linear hyperplane classifiers, corresponding to the similarity function $K(\mathbf{x}, \mathbf{x}') = \mathbf{x} \cdot \mathbf{x}'$, the algorithm finds an errorless separation for database DB1. The percentage of errors on the test set is 3.2 %. This result compares favorably to hyperplane classifiers which minimize the mean squared error (backpropagation or pseudo-inverse), for which the error on the test set is 12.7 %.

Database DB2 is also linearly separable but contains several meaningless patterns. Figure 5 shows the supporting patterns with large Lagrange multipliers α_k for the hyperplane for class 2. The percentage of misclassifications on the test set of DB2 drops from 15.2 % without cleaning to 10.5 % after removing meaningless and ambiguous patterns.

Better performance has been achieved with both databases using multilayer neural networks or other classification functions with higher capacity than linear subdividing planes. Tests with polynomial classifiers of order q, for which $K(\mathbf{x}, \mathbf{x}') = (\mathbf{x} \cdot \mathbf{x}' + 1)^q$, give the following error rates and average number of supporting patterns per hypersurface, $<m>$. This average is computed as the total number of supporting patterns divided by the number of decision functions. Patterns that support more than one hypersurface are counted only once in the total. For comparison, the dimension N of φ-space is also listed.

	DB1		DB2		
q	error	$<m>$	error	$<m>$	N
1 (linear)	3.2 %	36	10.5 %	97	256
2	1.5 %	44	5.8 %	89	$3 \cdot 10^4$
3	1.7 %	50	5.2 %	79	$8 \cdot 10^7$
4			4.9 %	72	$4 \cdot 10^9$
5			5.2 %	69	$1 \cdot 10^{12}$

The results obtained for DB2 show a strong decrease of the number of supporting patterns from a linear to a third order polynomial classification function and an equivalently significant decrease of the error rate. Further increase of the order of the polynomial has little effect on either the number of supporting patterns or the performance, unlike the dimension of φ-space, N, which increases exponentially. The lowest error rate, 4.9 %, is obtained with a forth order polynomial and is slightly better than the 5.1 % reported for a five layer neural network with a sophisticated architecture [4], which has been trained and tested on the same data.

In the above experiment, the performance changes drastically between first and second order polynomials. This may be a consequence of the fact that maximum VC-dimension of an q-th order polynomial classifier is equal to the dimension n of the patterns to the q-th power and thus much larger than n. A more gradual change of the VC-dimension is possible when the function K is

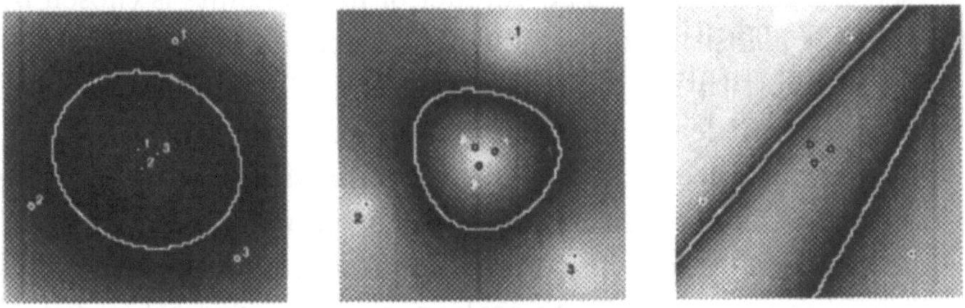

Figure 6. Decision boundaries for maximum margin classifiers with second order polynomial decision rule $K(\mathbf{x}, \mathbf{x}') = (\mathbf{x} \cdot \mathbf{x}' + 1)^2$ (left) and an exponential RBF $K(\mathbf{x}, \mathbf{x}') = \exp(-\|\mathbf{x} - \mathbf{x}'\|/2)$ (middle). The rightmost picture shows the decision boundary of a two layer neural network with two hidden units trained with backpropagation.

chosen to be a power series, for example

$$K(\mathbf{x}, \mathbf{x}') = \exp(\gamma \mathbf{x} \cdot \mathbf{x}') - 1. \tag{20}$$

In this equation the parameter γ is used to vary the VC-dimension gradually. For small values of γ, equation (20) approaches a linear classifier with VC-dimension at most equal to the dimension n of the patterns plus one. Experiments with database DB1 lead to a slightly better performance than the 1.5 % obtained with a second order polynomial classifier:

γ	DB1
0.25	2.3 %
0.50	2.2 %
0.75	1.3 %
1.00	1.5 %

When $K(\mathbf{x}, \mathbf{x}')$ is chosen to be the hyperbolic tangent, the resulting classifier can be interpreted as a neural network with one hidden layer with m hidden units. The supporting patterns are the weights in the first layer, and the coefficients α_k the weights of the second, linear layer. The number of hidden units is chosen by the training algorithm to maximize the margin between the classes A and B. Substituting the hyperbolic tangent for the exponential function did not lead to better results in our experiments.

The importance of a suitable preprocessing to incorporate knowledge about the task at hand has been pointed out by many researchers. In optical character recognition, preprocessings that introduce some invariance to scaling, rotation, and other distortions are particularly important [21]. As in [10], smoothing is used to achieve insensitivity to small distortions. The table below lists the error on the test set for different amounts of smoothing. A second order polynomial classifier was used for database DB1, and a forth order polynomial for DB2. The smoothing kernel is Gaussian with standard deviation σ.

	DB1		DB2	
σ	error	$<m>$	error	$<m>$
no smoothing	1.5 %	44	4.9 %	72
0.5	1.3 %	41	4.6 %	73
0.8	0.8 %	36	5.0 %	79
1.0	0.3 %	31	6.0 %	83
1.2	0.8 %	31		

The performance improved considerably for DB1. For DB2 the improvement is less significant and the optimum was obtained for less smoothing than for DB1. This is expected since the number of training patterns in DB2 is much larger than in DB1 (7000 versus 600).

4 Conclusions

Controlling the capacity of the family of classifiers is the key to achieving good generalization. The maximum margin learning algorithm trains a wide varity of classifiers and performs automatic capacity tuning, in addition to providing means to manually vary the classifier capacity. The algorithm extractions a small number of supporting patterns from the training data that are relevant for the classification and trains efficiently classifiers linear in their parameters with very large capacity, such as high order polynomial or RBF classifiers.

The efficiency and performance of the algorithm have been demonstrated on handwritten digit recognition problems. The achieved performance matches that of sophisticated classifiers, even though no task specific knowledge has been used. The training time in all experiments was less than an hour on a workstation.

Acknowledgements

The research on maximum margin algorithms was started when the author was a member of the technical staff of AT&T Bell Laboratories and is the result of collaboration and suggestions from many collegues. The support from the Semiconductor Research Corporation for the preparation of parts of this paper is gratefully acknowledged.

References

1 M.A. Aizerman, E.M. Braverman, and L.I. Rozonoer. Theoretical foundations of the potential function method in pattern recognition learning. *Automation and Remote Control*, 25:821–837, 1964.

2 D. S. Broomhead and D. Lowe. Multi-variate functional interpolation and adaptive networks. *Complex Systems*, 2:321 – 355, 1988.

3 R. Courant and D. Hilbert. *Methods of mathematical physics*. Interscience, New York, 1953.

4 Yann Le Cun, Bernhard Boser, John S. Denker, Donnie Henderson, Richard E. Howard, Wayne Hubbard, and Larry D. Jackel. Handwritten digit recognition with a back-propagation network. In David S. Touretzky, editor, *Neural Information Processing Systems*, volume 2, pages 396–404. Morgan Kaufmann Publishers, San Mateo, CA, 1990.

5 R. O. Duda and P. E. Hart. *Pattern Classification and Scene Analysis*. Wiley & Sons, 1974.

6 Kunihiko Fukushima and S. Miyake. Neocognitron: A new algorithm for pattern recognition tolerant of deformations and shifts in position. *Pattern Recognition*, Vol. 15:455–469, 1982.

7 S. Geman, E. Bienenstock, and R. Doursat. Neural networks and the bias/variance dilemma. *Neural Computation*, 4 (1):1 – 58, 1992.

8 I. Guyon, I. Poujaud, Personnaz L., G. Dreyfus, J. Denker, and Y. Le Cun. Comparing different neural network architectures for classifying handwritten digits. In *Int. Joint Conference on Neural Networks*, volume II, pages 127–132, Washington DC, 1989. IEEE.

9 I. Guyon, I. Poujaud, L. Personnaz, G. Dreyfus, J. Denker, and Y. Le Cun. Comparing different neural network architectures for classifying handwritten digits. In *Proc. Int. Joint Conf. Neural Networks*. Int. Joint Conference on Neural Networks, 1989.

10 Isabelle Guyon, Vladimir Vapnik, Bernhard Boser, Leon Bottou, and Sara Solla. Structural risk minimization for character recognition. In J. Moody, J. Hanson, and R. Lippmann, editors, *Neural Information Processing Systems*, volume 4, pages 471–479. Morgan Kaufmann Publishers, San Mateo, CA, 1992.

11 B. Kosko. *Neural Networks and Fuzzy Systems*. Prentice Hall, 1992.

12 W. Krauth and M. Mezard. Learning algorithms with optimal stability in neural networks. *J. Phys. A: Math. gen.*, 20:L745, 1987.

13 N. Matic, I. Guyon, L. Bottou, J. Denker, and V. Vapnik. Computer-aided cleaning of large databases for character recognition. In *Digest ICPR*. ICPR, Amsterdam, August 1992.

14 J. Moody and C. Darken. Fast learning in networks of locally tuned processing units. *Neural Computation*, 1 (2):281 – 294, 1989.

15 Y. H. Pao. *Adaptive Pattern Recognition and Neural Networks*. Addison-Wesley, 1989.

16 T. Poggio. On optimal nonlinear associative recall. *Biol. Cybernetics*, Vol. 19:201–209, 1975.

17 T. Poggio and F. Girosi. Regularization algorithms for learning that are equivalent to multilayer networks. *Science*, 247:978 – 982, February 1990.

18 J. Rissanen. *Stochastic Complexity in Statistical Inquiry*. World Scientific, Singapore, 1989.

19 F. Rosenblatt. *Principles of neurodynamics*. Spartan Books, New York, 1962.

20 T. J. Sejnowski and C. R. Rosenberg. Parallel networks that learn to pronounce english text. *Complex Systems*, 1:145–168, 1987.

21 P. Simard, Y. Le Cun, and J. Denker. Tangent prop—a formalism for specifying selected invariances in an adaptive network. In J. Moody, J. Hanson, and R. Lippmann, editors, *Neural Information Processing Systems*, volume 4, pages 895–803. Morgan Kaufmann Publishers, San Mateo, CA, 1992.

22 P. Simard, B. Victorri, Y. Le Cun, and J. Denker. Tangent prop - a formalism for specifying selected invariances in an adaptive network. In J. Moody and et al., editors, *NIPS-91*, pages 895–903, San Mateo CA, 1992. IEEE, Morgan Kaufmann.

23 A. Tikhonov. Solution of incorrectly formulated problems and the regularization method. *Soviet Math.*, pages 1035–1038, 1964.

24 A. Tikhonov and V. Arsenin. *Solutions of ill-posed problems*. Winston, Washington, 1977.

25 L. G. Valiant. A theory of the learnable. *Communications of the ACM*, 27:11:1134–1142, 1984.

26 V. N. Vapnik and A. Ya. Chervonenkis. On the uniform convergence of relative frequencies of events to their probabilities. *Th. Prob. and its Applications*, 17(2):264–280, 1971.

27 Vladimir Vapnik. *Estimation of Dependences Based on Empirical Data*. Springer Verlag, New York, 1982.

28 V.N. Vapnik. *Estimation of dependences based on empirical data*. Springer, New York, 1982.

29 V.N. Vapnik and A.Ya. Chervonenkis. *The theory of pattern recognition*. Nauka, Moscow, 1974.

30 A. Waibel, T. Hanazawa, G. Hinton, K. Shikano, and K. Lang. Phoneme recognition using time-delay neural networks. *IEEE Trans. Acoust., Speech, Signal Processing*, 37(3):328–339, March 1989.

31 H. White. Learning in artificial neural networks: a statistical perspective. *Neural Computation*, 1(4):425–464, 1989.

Part 3

Handwritten word recognition

On the Robustness of Recognition of Degraded Line Images

J.C. Simon

LAFORIA/CNRS & A2IA, ENPC/DIT, 28 rue des Saints Peres 75007 Paris, France. Telefax: +33-14260-5801.

Abstract. Pattern recognition algorithms are not robust compared to human vision. Our recognition systems seem to work like some impaired human cortex, showing agnosia defects. Robustness of human vision is probably the consequence of interaction and feedback of the multiple regions of the vision cortex. Recent results on binary images of handwritten cheques show the interest of approaches based upon multiple operator combinations and soft decisions, recalling the working of a human vision cortex.

Keywords: human versus machine recognition, robustness, degraded line images, vision cortex, agnosia, soft versus hard decisions, multiple operators, interaction, feedback, handwritten cheques.

1. Pattern Recognition Algorithms are not robust, compared to human performances

Considering the problem of printed or handwritten text recognition, several examples may be given of the collapse of algorithmic recognition results, when the quality of the iconic picture is deteriorating, either because the characters are poorly written, degraded, joined, or because background noise or defacing images are added to the text to be read. In most occurences, the collapse is far from the "graceful" degradation of reading performances of a healthy human being on the same images. Compared to some recent algorithmic recognition systems, put in practice in reading handwritten postal adresses or bank checks, human beings show much more robust recognition on degraded images.

We may wonder if there is a basic difference of nature between computer algorithms and human neural processes? Under different but similar input iconic pictures, image processing algorithms usually display "chaotic" properties, in the sense that the result of two similar pictures may be widely apart, even sometime for a change of one pixel. Artificial "neural networks" were advocated as a remedy to this chaotic property of feature detection and structural analysis encountered in OCR. But their implementation to the OCR problems has been up to now rather deceiving. Being somewhat more robust that conventional OCR processes on degraded images, they do not seem to be yet the ultimate answer.

2. What the neurophysiology of mamalian brains may learn to P. R. specialists

Vision neurophysiologists may put us on the way to better solutions. They found that the optical nerves distribute the vision signal in many cortex locations, 20 to 30 for primates. The visual cortex occupies between one third and one half of the total man's cortex, which has of the order of 10 billion neurones, each connected to others through at least one thousand synapses. The striate cortex (area 17 or V1), investigated early, plays probably the role of elementary feature detector. But extrastriate visual cortex, now better known, has at least 20 identified areas, organized in a semihierarchical organization, having feedforward, intermediate and feedback connections. It handles two streams of processes: one for location and motion of objects, the other for identification and recognition. Thus in fact a correct human visual recognition requires a lot of independant parallel processes with interaction and feedback. Robustness of human visual recognition is the probable consequence of these multiplicity and interaction. Accidental destruction of one or several of these cerebral zones leads to defects, i.e. lack of robustness, similar to those encountered in our OCR systems. Agnosia, alexia or dislexia suffered by some human patients, are coming from the destruction or impairment of some specific cortical regions. For instance some patients may recognize letters but are unable to recognize words, some may recognize isolated drawings of familiar objects but are unable to understand a scene made of these objects, or to recognized them if the drawings are superposed. Some patients may be normal at recognition, but unable to locate objects or to orient themselves [1].

From these observations we may conclude that our OCR systems suffer from similar defects, because they are lacking several modules and some basic properties of the extrastriate cortex: simultaneous processing of features by several independant processes, feedback and interaction between these processes.

3. Some algorithmic principles recalling the neurophysiology discoveries

Since several years a research is carried on the recognition of the literal (legal) handwritten cursive amount of cheques, with the support of the S.R.T.P. of the D.G. de la Poste. Though we obtained good results on well written words reported in [2], an important loss of performance was found on the real degraded images of current cheque amounts.

Our group is now developping and applying robust algorithms, adapted to degraded handwritings, using the following main principles:

- Several levels of recognition are established: (i)grapheme (letters or group of letters), (ii)words, (iii)phrases.

- Recognition at each level uses several P.R. operators of different techniques, each giving a probability of occurence (a "soft" instead of a "hard" decision). Bottom up as well as top down processes are utilized.

- Even if the result of each type of operator is not very reliable, the information thus provided may contribute to the overall estimation. We try to use independant sources of information and estimate their joint performances.

- At each level the soft decisions of the previous level are combined using contextual information sources. For example at level (iii) the probabilty of occurence of a word at a position in the phrase, the probability of pairs of words, the syntax of the phrase representing an amount in french francs and centimes.

- Feedback is performed between different levels, when the overall probability is not high enough; in other words decisions may be reversible.

As a proof of the efficiency of such principles, let us give some results:
1) obtained for the recognition of words (lexicon of 25 words) segmented by hand, and of correct phrases of cheque amounts, composed with these words (one million possible phrases). The results are ordered lists obtained on a test set, independant of the learning set.

	1st position	2 first positions	4 first positions	8 first positions
words reco.	79,5 %	88,5 %	94 %	97 %
phrase reco.	74,5 %	85 %	93 %	96,2 %

2) obtained for the recognition of realfull amounts, segmented by program.

	1st position	2 first positions	4 first positions	8 first positions
phrase reco.	57.0%	66,7%	74,3%	80,3%

The decrease in performances comes from the difficult question of segmenting properly the words. Improvements on word recognition may allow to approach the performances of the previous table

3) An example of the recognition of a rather degraded amount shows that the program has similar "hesitations" than a human reader in deciphering the amount of the following Fig. 1.

Fig 1. A defaced legal amount of cheque

A listing given by the programs on the recognition of the amount of Fig. 1:

```
 deux cent soixante francs  (260.00 F)
 ??? soixante francs  ( 0.00 F)
deux cent cinquant francs  (250.00 F)
deux cent trente francs  (230.00 F)
mille soixante francs  (1060.00 F)
deux cent quarante francs  (240.00 F)   <<<<< true phrase
trois cent soixante francs  (360.00 F)
soixante quatorze francs  (74.00 F)
mille cinquant francs  (1050.00 F)
deux mille soixante francs  (2060.00 F)
 trois cent cinquant francs  (350.00 F)
 soixante seize francs  (76.00 F)
 deux cent seize francs  (216.00 F)
 deux cent vingt francs  (220.00 F)
 deux cent treize francs  (213.00 F)
 quatre mille francs  (4000.00 F)
```

Acknowledgement. During his stay at A.2.I.A., N. Gorski of S.P.I.I.A.S. has contributed efficiently to these results through his ideas and his programming.

4. Conclusion

We should be inspired by the recent neurophysiology discoveries on the brain, which seems to show that it may be more important to use several operators and features, i.e. different information sources if possible independant and interactive, rather than a unique "miracle" algorithm. Information interaction at all steps should be implemented under the "soft" form of probabilistic ratings rather than under the "hard" form of a binary decision.

References

1. Cronley-Dillon J. R., general editor, "Vision and Visual Disfunction" a serie of 17 books published by The Macmillan Press Ltd. G.B.
2. Simon J.C. 1992, "Off-line cursive word recognition", Proc. of the IEEE, vol. 80, N° 7, july 1992, pp.1150-1161.

Invariant Handwriting Features Useful in Cursive-Script Recognition

Hans-Leo Teulings

Nijmegen Institute for Cognition and Information (NICI), P.O. Box 9104, 6500 HE Nijmegen, The Netherlands (*).

Abstract. The within-writer variability of handwriting forms one of the problems in the automatic recognition of cursive script. Variability can be handled by choosing handwriting features based upon the process of handwriting generation or upon computational models. Handwriting patterns are represented by a sequence of motor actions, i.e., "strokes", which can be identified by invariant segmentation. Each stroke is characterized by features related to motor memory parameters which can be identified by their high signal-to-noise ratios.

Keywords. Cursive-script recognition, on-line handwriting, movement production models, computational models, movement variability, segmentation, movement features, signal-to-noise ratio, off-line reconstruction from on-line.

1. Introduction

Automatic recognition of cursive handwriting is difficult because handwriting comes in great variety of graphical shapes. Not only do different writing styles exist, but, also within a writer, identical letters vary between instances. In order to make automatic recognition systems robust with respect to these variations it is not only instructive to study human perception and reading, but also the production process of handwriting. This paper provides a guide for finding and verifying handwriting features which are relatively insensitive to spontaneous variations of cursive-script. These features form the corner stone for non-chaotic handwriting recognition systems. A macroscopic handwriting production model will be discussed, and various computational handwriting models will be presented.

---

*) Presently at: Exercise Science and Physical Education, Arizona State University, Tempe, AZ 85287-0404, USA. E-mail: hlt@espe1.la.asu.edu. Fax: +1-602-965-8108.

The macroscopic model of handwriting production proposed, consists of a sequence of modules. The higher-level modules have been hypothesized on the basis of slips of the pen [1], and neurologic disturbances [2]. The lower-level modules have been hypothesized on the basis of delays in movement initiation and movement execution [3, 4]. The handwriting motor system contains in its most simplified form (1) a motor memory, where all letter shapes have been stored [5], (2) movement-unit retrieval, where the appropriate allographs are extracted from that motor memory, and (3) a motor-pattern buffer, the contents of which can be defined as the motor program. Subsequently, this motor program needs to be adapted to each concrete execution condition. The adaptation is done at two levels: (4) At the parameter-setting level, where muscle-independent global scale parameters (e.g., speed, size) are specified, and (5) at the muscular-initiation level, where muscle-dependent parameters (e.g., orientation, slant, limb) are specified [3].

A serial-module model is applicable if feedback loops between modules are not essential. In cursive script, several letters are prepared in advance during writing. Subsequent letters of a writing pattern are prepared while executing the first letters and processing feedback from previous letters [4]. In the multi-module model, feedback loops are included, but, play only a marginal role because handwriting is performed as fast as 200 - 400 ms per letter, which is too fast for processing feedback to monitor letter formation. For example, a sudden increase or decrease of pen-to-paper friction results in an immediate reduction of the letter size and several letters are produced before letter size is restored on the basis of visual or tactile feedback [6]. As biomechanical properties of the wrist and finger joints do not seem to be corrected [7], visual feedback is apparently not used to monitor the performance of straight lines. Only orientation and slant are controlled by visual feedback [8].

A cursive-script recognition system, should operate in the reverse way as the handwriting production system. Firstly, the cursive-script recognition system segments the continuous handwriting movement, into units of movement. Then, lower-level, global features, such as orientation, size, slant, and speed are normalized. Subsequently, features are estimated which are closely related to the movement parameters in motor memory. In order to check the completeness of the features extracted, a legible handwriting pattern should be reconstructible, but not necessarily an exact reproduction.

2. Segmentation of Cursive Script into Strokes

Movement parameters in motor memory are not global parameters but rather local parameters generating small segments of the handwriting pattern. Handwriting patterns need to be separated into discrete segments, each representing a single movement command corresponding to a ballistic "stroke". It consists of an acceleration phase, a velocity peak, and a deceleration phase. Before discussing the features, the invariant segmentation of handwriting will be addressed. Although Guiard [9] questioned whether continuous movement sequences can at all be segmented into discrete aiming movements, segmentation offers a great advantage in reducing the complexity of handwriting patterns. The ideal segmentation procedure should segment similar writing patterns in an invariant way, regardless of the writing speed. In Teulings et al. [10] a highly invariant segmentation procedure has been proposed. Other cursive-script segments have been suggested, e.g., segments of constant parameter settings [11]; partly overlapping segments of constant curvature [12]; pen-down segments [13]; segments of constant curvature versus speed relation [14]; overlapping speed and curvature profiles [15]; segments between absolute velocity minima that are robust under lowpass filtering [16]; segments between top, bottom, or stroke crossing [17]; segments at top and bottom [18-20]; and segments between two tops yielding a pair of ballistic strokes and between two bottoms yielding the overlapping stroke pairs [21-23].

Segmenting at speed minima does not always yield a desirable result [27]. Firstly, at low handwriting rates, a simple, straight stroke is not always ballistic so that several absolute velocity minima appear, suggesting several ballistic "substrokes". Secondly, perfect circles at constant velocities do not yield any segmentation points at all because of the perfectly out-of-phase movement components. In order to make the segmentation more invariant and more intuitively correct (i.e., corresponding to integer up or down strokes), four refinements of the algorithm are necessary [27]. (1) In the estimate of the absolute velocity the horizontal component squared is weighted by 0.1 relative to the vertical component, i.e., v = (0.1 * vx**2 + vy**2) **1/2, which shows low minima between vertical segments, and moderate minima between horizontal segments. (2) Only velocity minima are accepted, which do not have a lower minimum within a time window of -60 and +60 ms. This period corresponds to the time constants in the muscles and the nerves. (3) Segments, shorter than the minimum stroke size of about 0.5 mm, are considered non-significant and are joined with the previous segment. (4) Finally, a segmentation point is removed when the direction changes less then 15 degrees. The change of direction is defined as the angle between the vectors from the current segmentation point to the previous and the following points of speed maxima. This refined segmentation appears to be invariant when handwriting rate is changed across a wide range.

3. Frequency Spectra

When handwriting rate is increased, one may suggest that individual motor commands increasingly overlap [24], or increasingly become smoothed by the hypothetical low-pass filtering of the pen-hand system [25]. In order to check whether this may cause segmentation problems, the frequency spectrum of the handwriting movements was inspected. The frequency amplitude spectrum of the horizontal and the vertical velocity components forms a symmetrical peak around 5 Hz [26]. When the rate of handwriting is increased, it appears that all component frequencies of the spectrum increase proportionally [27]. There is no evidence that the pen-hand system acts as a fixed low-pass filter, nor that the strokes become increasingly overlapping with writing speed. Only topological distortions seem to occur which cause atypical letter shapes.

3.1. Theoretical Minimum Number of Features

A time function of limited frequency bandwidth W and duration T can be reconstructed by 2WT (isochronous) samples (sampling theorem; See [28] for an overview). Handwriting consists of two time functions, one for the horizontal and the other for the vertical component. If both functions are independent, 4WT samples are required to reconstruct a handwriting segment of duration T. The frequency spectrum of handwriting shows a gradual descent to noise level at about W = 10 Hz [26]. Durations of the fastest ballistic strokes are about T = 0.1 s. At least 4 samples, or 2 coordinate pairs, per ballistic stroke are required. Depending upon the speed of writing, the samples will be at different phases of the strokes, and therefore these 4 samples are highly variable and not appropriate as features. Nevertheless, the notion can be upheld that 4 features are sufficient to disambiguate a stroke. In order to compare the invariance of features, a measure for the invariance will be proposed.

4. Defining Invariant Stroke Features by the Signal-to-Noise Ratio (SNR)

When a handwriting pattern is segmented into a sequence of strokes and when each stroke yields a feature, the "pattern" of a stroke feature can be defined. If several replications of a handwriting pattern are available, the random variations of these sequences can be considered as the motor noise of a feature. The signal-to-noise ratio (SNR) is a dimensionless measure, which is useful comparing the extent of invariance of different stroke features. The SNR is the ratio of the standard deviations of the movement amplitude, and that of the movement noise:

$$SNR = (sd(Signal) / sd(Noise))$$

The standard deviations can be derived as follows. Assume Xij describes the pattern of a feature for all strokes i (I strokes) and replications j (J replications). Averages across replications j are denoted as Xi., etc. An analysis of variance schema for the main effect Strokes (I levels) based on J replications yields:

$$sd(Noise)^{**}2 = \Sigma[j=1,J]\ \Sigma[i=1,I]\ (Xij - Xi. - X.j + X..)^{**}2 / (I-1)(J-1)$$

and

$$sd(Signal)^{**}2 = \Sigma[i=1,I]\ (Xi. - X..)^{**}2 / (I-1) - sd(Noise)^{**}2 / J$$

According to Fitts' law, the expected magnitude of the signal-to-noise ratios can be estimated from the speed-accuracy tradeoff. Fitts' law states that the duration T of reciprocal aiming movements of amplitude A (or within a circle of width 2A) towards a target of width W increases linearly with the accuracy measure log2 (2A/W) in "bits" of information. The duration increase with accuracy is less then 50 ms/bit (26 ms/bit and 43 ms/bit for the finger and wrist movements, respectively [29]). This suggests that during short handwriting strokes of 100 ms, the movement amplitude, or stroke sawe, contains about 2 bits of information. Two bits of information implies an "effective quantization" into 4 levels, which corresponds to typical SNR values of 4 [10, 30]. It is possible to estimate the number of discriminable classes of letters under the assumptions that 4 features exist with SNR values of 4 and that the average number of strokes per letter is 4. Then, only 64 different letter shapes can be disambiguated. More than 64 different letter shapes may exist (e.g., 26 lower-case letters and their allographic variations). Some of the features may be dependent, and the SNR values of most features are less than 4. For these reasons it is imperative to employ the features with the highest SNRs and a high extent of independence.

5. Independence of Features

The abstract movement parameters stored in motor memory are the ideal features for the recognizer's database of cursive-script prototypes. One may suppose that these parameters are highly invariant under many different conditions, as they are used to generate all other movement parameters, required to perform the writing pattern in many different conditions. The reverse seems also reasonable. Invariant handwriting features are closely related to the memory representation of the motor program. Therefore, invariant features observed in replications of a handwriting pattern are useful in cursive-script recognition.

In order to evaluate the appropriateness of a set of stroke features, various hierarchical relations can be discerned. A top-down hierarchy can be discerned with high-level features, related to the movement information in memory, and lower-level features, derived from these higher-level features. Furthermore, a random variation occurring in one stroke may, to some extent, occur in neighboring strokes. This constitutes the sequence hierarchy.

5.1. Top-Down Hierarchy

The top-down hierarchy assumes that movement memory contains a parsimonious set of source features which generate the lower-order features. The lower-order features show more and more noise and therefore less and less invariance. Source features can be identified by their high invariance [10, 30]. The following is an example of hierarchical features, which are related through a mechanical rule. The stroke size S is proportional with peak acceleration A and duration T squared, i.e., S = Eff.* A * T**2, where Eff refers to an efficiency constant, characterizing the effect of a particular shape of the acceleration-versus-time curve [30]. It appeared that the pattern of normalized stroke sizes S is more invariant than the pattern of stroke durations T, peak accelerations A, or efficiencies Eff [10, 30] (See Table 1). This suggests that the patterns of duration, peak acceleration, and efficiency are derived from the stroke size according to some rules. In handwriting recognition, normalized stroke size is a more useful feature than the dynamic features such as stroke duration and peak acceleration.

The "between-feature correlation" provides additional evidence in favor of a top-down hierarchy. One may assume that random variations of a higher-order feature are not compensated by variations of lower-order features. If features A, B, and C satisfy a mechanical relation such as A = B + C or A = B * C, and if B and C are independent, then their absolute or relative variances are additive, i.e.: var(A) = var(B) + var(C) or var(A) / mean(A)**2 = var(B) / mean(B)**2 + var(C) / mean(C)**2, respectively. If B and C are negatively correlated, then the (relative) variance of A will be significantly smaller then expected in the uncorrelated case, supporting the conclusion that feature A is a higher-order invariant feature, controlling both B and C. Note that the correlation between B and C can only be caused by noise in the motor system, as opposed to any movement law describing how B changes with varying C, because B and C are based on "identical" strokes in a series of "identical" writing patterns.

Under the assumption that the same memory representation is used to perform a writing pattern under various execution conditions, such as, different sizes, speeds, limbs, orientations, or slants there should be a high similarity between the higher-order patterns of features generated by the same memory representation. If the pattern of a feature changes proportionally or, at least, linearly from one condition to the other, then the "between-condition correlation" will be high. A feature needs to be rescaled or normalized if the transformation of a feature between conditions is proportional.

5.2. Sequence Hierarchy

Sequence hierarchy deals with the variations affecting neighboring strokes. The extreme case of sequence hierarchy is "rescalability", or the proportional change of a feature of all strokes. Depending upon the extent of the sequence hierarchy, two or more consecutive strokes have to be taken into account when representing prototypes in a cursive-script recognizer's database. If the sequence hierarchy would be nonsignificant, only separate strokes would be sufficient to store all prototype letters. This may seem reasonable if one realizes that, within a writer's handwriting, ascenders and descenders of different letters are similar. However, when motor-noise affects each stroke separately, atypical letters would result [22]. In fact, there is evidence that whole letters, counting several strokes, form units in the handwriting motor system [5], so that it is likely that sequential strokes are affected by similar noise sources.

Significantly negative correlations between successive stroke sizes both in x and in y directions were found [10] (See Table 1), indicating that when motor noise causes one stroke-size component to be bigger or smaller than normal, the subsequent stroke will be bigger or smaller in the opposite direction. Noteworthy is that stroke durations do not satisfy any sequence hierarchy, as the correlations between successive stroke durations appear not to be robust. The latter finding confirms that a writing pattern can be split into a strict sequence of movement units. Recognition systems dealing with stroke pairs seem to take the sequence hierarchy of stroke sizes into account to some extent. However, recognition rates of complete letters, counting up to 6 strokes, is not higher than recognition rates of letters on the basis of separate strokes [31] which may indicate that the sequence hierarchy is limited to a few strokes.

Table 1

SNRs and correlations among various stroke features, forming a mechanical relation: vertical strokes size (Sy), vertical peak acceleration (Ay), stroke duration (T), and efficiency (Effy). Results are based on 16 replications of the writing pattern "elementary" in the normal condition and compared to the fast condition in a subject.

	Features			
	Sy =	Effy *	Ay *	T**2
Sequence Hierarchy				
Correlation between Strokes	-0.45	-	-	-0.15
Top-Down Hierarchy				
SNR	5.2	2.5	2.0	3.6
Correlation between Features	+0.24	-0.46	-0.15	
		+0.59	-0.41	
		+0.41		
Correlation between Conditions	0.99	0.95	0.95	0.95

6. Context

Context is a specific case of mutual influencing of letters in handwriting. Yet, the context effects between cursive "e" and "l", are only marginal, especially for spatial features [32]. The major context effects due to size concern the duration of the neighboring strokes. In on-line cursive-script recognition, duration plays a role when characterizing strokes, unless resampling to constant velocity is done [33]. For that reason, it is useful to examine the relation between time and size. Three context levels have been discerned [34]. In each context, specific duration-versus-size relations exist:

o Macro context (i.e., a word in the context of other words of different sizes).

o Meso context (i.e., a single stroke in the context of other strokes of different sizes).

o Micro context (i.e., the local curve radius in the context of a single stroke with varying curvature).

In macro context, complete writing patterns are considered in isolation. As mentioned earlier, in the frictionless case, stroke size S is proportional to the peak acceleration A and the stroke duration T squared: S = Eff * A * T**2, where Eff is an efficiency factor characterizing the effect of a particular shape of the acceleration-versus-time curve. The efficiency Eff plays a minor role in controlling stroke sizes in handwriting [30], which is consistent with the finding that the shapes of the acceleration-versus-time curves are rather constant [35]. The time to produce a writing pattern is virtually independent of size in writing sizes between 0.25 and 1 cm [6, 36, 37]. Apparently, duration is limited by the frequency bandwidth of the pen-hand system so that size is controlled by acceleration level, which is proportional to force level, under the assumption of low friction. Consequently, duration T is constant in the range of writing sizes, so that peak acceleration A is proportional with stroke size S. Force levels will reach a ceiling when the writing sizes are much larger than 1 cm. The height of the ceiling depends on the instructed pace or time pressure [37]. Therefore, when producing large writing sizes or arm movements, force levels remain constant, and size variations are programmed entirely by variation of duration. In macro context, a power relation between T and S, can be proposed:

$$T = k * S^{**}b \qquad (b = 0 \text{ if } S < 1 \text{ cm};\ b = 1/2 \text{ if } S >> 1 \text{ cm})$$

where k is constant per context and instruction.

Meso context refers to the adjacency of strokes of different sizes (such as in "el"). Most observations are compatible with an increase of both time and force. The following power function to describe the relation between duration T and size S in meso context is proposed [34]:

$$T = k * S^{**}b \qquad (b = 0.33)$$

where k is a constant depending upon macro context. The data of "el" or "le" pairs in the literature [32, 34, 11, 38, 39, respectively] yield values for b = 0.22, 0.34, 0.34, 0.38, and 0.41, respectively.

Finally, micro-context describes the time needed per infinitesimal part of the writing trajectory. An estimator of "local size" is curve radius r of the circle, fitting the curve at that point. An estimator of "local duration" is the inverse angular velocity, i.e., r/v = 1/omega. In a large variety of drawing tasks the "2/3-power law" appears to hold [40]:

$$\text{omega} = r/v = k\, r^{**}b \qquad (b = 2/3)$$

where k is a constant gain factor which depends upon meso and macro context. The 2/3-power law can be derived for sinusoidal movements, i.e., two equal-frequency movement components without left-to-right translation, which produces only arbitrary ellipses. In normal handwriting the 2/3-power law holds only marginally [34]. A normal handwriting pattern yields b = 0.41 (instead of 2/3) and correlation 0.83 (instead of approximately 1.0) which are virtually the same values as those of a random-walk. Only continuous ellipses and "llll" patterns yield values which are closer to the ideal value, than to those of a random walk: b = 0.59 and correlations as high as 0.95. The 2/3-power law does not hold for handwriting in general due to the width of the frequency band of handwriting [26], and the left-to-right, which mainly takes place during the upstrokes [41, 42].

7. The choice of features

On-line handwriting can be recorded at a high accuracy [43] without the thinning and sequencing problem known in optical scanning. An appropriate set of features to characterize on-line handwriting can be derived from the movement parameters used in computational models of handwriting production. The set of features contains enough information to reconstruct writing patterns as a legible word. Presenting reconstructed words to subjects, yields indications on the importance of certain features. It is suggested that the downstrokes are more important for recognizing words than the upstrokes, which has been exploited in recognition systems [18].

Stroke features used in cursive-script recognition which show high SNRs [31, 44] are the horizontal and vertical stroke sizes (SNRs = 5.3 and 5.2, respectively), path length (SNR = 4.9), direction of the straight line from begin to end (SNR = 7.8), stroke duration (SNR = 3.6), and the surface of loops (SNR = 5.4). Characterization of stroke shapes can be done by the directions of 5 equal-duration subsegments (SNRs = 6.8, 7.5, 6.5, 4.2, and 2.9, respectively). The SNR values are typical values based on 16 replications of a pattern 'elementary' by one subject. It is interesting to note that the directions of the subsegments at the end of a stroke tend to be unreliable; this is probably due to the programming of the endpoint of the stroke without programming the exact path towards the endpoint [31]. The axial pen pressure is not relevant in on-line handwriting recognition as pen pressure is not related to particular letters or shapes [45].

The following models will be discussed: Orientation-free models, which do not require normalization of orientation of the writing pattern, mass-spring or oscillatory models, movement optimization models, which allow the reconstruction of dynamics from off-line cursive script, and symbolical models.

7.1 Orientation-Free Models

There is a class of models which does not assume any specific x or y axes, nor axes related to biomechanical joints. Movement patterns are unlikely to be specified in the body-oriented horizontal and vertical coordinates [12]. Instead, discrete "circular strokes" are proposed while the inertia of the finger-hand-arm system smooths the movement by acting as a low-pass filter [25]. Circular strokes are described by the following [12]: (1) Circle segments of specific curve radius, arc length, and orientation are fitted to the trace at the point of peak velocity, (2) a half Gaussian velocity function is fitted from the previous absolute-velocity peak to the current peak and the other half phase from the current peak to the following peak, (3) the overlapping functions are averaged sample-by-sample. Therefore, 6 features per ballistic stroke are needed: curve radius, arc length, orientation, peak velocity, duration between previous and following velocity peak, and the asymmetric position of the peak velocity between the previous and following ones. The accuracy of this model does not seem as high as the simpler models, which were based on component movements per axis [35].

A model which allows a more accurate reconstruction of writing patterns has been proposed, but it requires more features per stroke [15]. As in the previous model, absolute velocity is approximated by a piecewise Gaussian function, but, instead of the constant-radius approximation, the angular velocity is also approximated by a piecewise Gaussian function. The piecewise Gaussian functions are generated by a hypothetical neural velocity signal consisting of a sequence of rectangular time functions. The height of each block represents the gain of the muscular speed-generator. In order to simulate sharp movement reversals, discontinuities had to be inserted in the angular velocity. The cursive-script word "bug", containing about 12 ballistic strokes, could be reconstructed accurately using 60 features for the tangential velocity, and, 52 features for the angular velocity, or 9 features per ballistic stroke.

7.2. Mass-Spring Model

The mass-spring model was introduced to model fluent movement trajectories in a parsimonious way [11]. This model inspired several cursive-script recognizers [21, 46]. A horizontal x axis, parallel to the left-to-right translation and a vertical y axis, and fitted piecewise sinusoids as if they resulted from a frictionless mass-spring system. In the vertical movement component, the mass consists of the weights of the pen and the fingers, whereas for the horizontal movement component, the mass consists of the weights of the whole hand and the pen. Various sinusoids can be concatenated to a fluent handwriting trajectory, while the equilibrium points, the stiffness, and some initial conditions of the mass-spring system are changed at specific moments. The major advantage of the model is that it allows the generation of repetitive loops such as "eeee" very parsimoniously as no features need to be changed during this pattern. The model is most easily expressed in terms of the velocity-time functions Vx(t) and Vy(t), respectively:

Vx(t) = Vx_peak * sin (omega_x * t + phi_x) + c

Vy(t) = Vy_peak * sin (omega_y * t + phi_y)

where Vx_peak and Vy_peak are the velocity amplitudes, omega_x and omega_y the angular frequencies, or frequencies multiplied by 2*pi, and phi_x and phi_y the initial phases, respectively. The constant-velocity, horizontal left-to-right movement c, is added to the horizontal component. The position-time functions can be found by integration using zero initial velocity.

Three simplifications can be made. (1) Only the phase difference is relevant, i.e., phi_x - phi_y = phi. (2) Peak velocities can be chosen equal to twice the horizontal left-to-right velocity, i.e., Vx_peak = Vy_peak = 2c. (3) The horizontal and vertical frequencies are equal, i.e., omega_x = omega_y = omega, because unequal frequencies are only needed in rare patterns like "8". Varying the phase difference phi yields various basic patterns: upright loops (phi = 90 degrees), slanted loops (phi = 60 degrees), garlands (phi = 30 degrees), waves (phi = 0 degrees), and arcades (phi = -30 degrees). Another important parameter to influence stroke shape is the horizontal velocity Vx, at the top of a stroke, where Vy changes from upward to downward, i.e., Vx = c -Vx_peak * sin (phi). If a sharp movement reversal has to be programmed, requiring Vx to change sign, the parameters phi, Vx_peak and c need to be adjusted simultaneously.

Ascenders and descenders can be generated by both increasing Vy_peak and decreasing omega. In order to maintain a stable baseline, Vy_peak can only be changed at the top or at the bottom of a stroke, i.e., Vy = 0, yielding a descender or ascender, respectively. If Vy_peak is changed, then the slant would change as well. In terms of model parameters, the slant beta equals:

beta = arctan (Vy_peak / (Vx_peak*cos(phi))),

which again depends upon several parameters. When increasing Vy_peak in order to generate an ascender, either phi or Vx_peak have to be changed in order to maintain slant. Changing two parameters simultaneously does not seem very natural. Ascenders and descenders can be generated, without changing slant, by decreasing angular frequency omega, but this does not seem to be natural either [34].

In summary, it seems not easy to simulate handwriting patterns using these parameters. It is difficult to generate more complex repetitive patterns such as "ellellell...". Furthermore, normal handwriting does not have a predominant sinusoidal movement [26], nor a constant left-to-right trend [41]. An example of a simulation of the letter sequence "elye", counting 11 ballistic strokes, requires 30 parameter changes and time moments apart from the 10 initial parameter settings. This yields only 3.6 parameters per stroke, which is parsimonious indeed, as it is less than 4.

7.3. Movement Optimization Models in Off-line Cursive Script

A general trajectory-formation model minimizes the mean squared rate of force change (i.e., jerk) [24]. In the frictionless case, force can be approximated by the second time derivative of the horizontal and the vertical position time functions. The rate of force change can be approximated by the third time derivative. This model has been used in a cursive-script recognizer [22]. This model allows generation of the "kinematics from shape", so that the recognizer would accept thinned, static images. Scanned images of cursive script can be handled in less flexible stroke models [19]. Pixel maps are analyzed in terms of common strokes having the shapes of half ellipses, thus preventing awkward pixel-quantization effects.

In the "minimum-jerk model" cursive script consists of a sequence of curved segments, e.g., up-down or down-up stroke pairs [24]. In order to simulate curved segments, the minimum-jerk model needed to be extended by a "via point" near the point of maximum curvature [47]. Such a curved segment will be referred to as a "via stroke". A via stroke corresponds to a pair of "ballistic strokes". Minimization of the mean squared jerk with a via-point constraint yields 5th-order spline functions:

$$x(t) = ax0 + ax1*t + ax2*t**2 + \ldots + ax5*t**5 + px*max(0,t-t1)**5,$$

where ax0 ... ax5 and px are the spline parameters and t1 is the optimized time duration to reach the via point. A similar function follows for y(t).

Cursive-script patterns can be simulated using a limited set of basic via strokes:

Hook (like cursive "i" without dot), cup (like cursive "v"), gamma (like cursive "l"), and oval (like cursive "o"). However, the minimum-jerk model with only via-point constraints did not allow simulation of the cup, gamma, and oval [24]. It was unclear where extra via points were needed apart from the natural via point near the point of maximum curvature. In order to generate the latter patterns, the direction (i.e., dy/dx) at the beginning and endpoints of the via stroke was added as a constraint. Under the border condition of zero velocities and accelerations at the endpoints, the directions are undefined. According to the mathematical "de l'Hopital" rule, the next nonzero derivative has to be constrained, which is jerk. When jerk needs to be constrained, mean squared jerk should not be minimized, but the mean squared fourth time derivative (i.e., snap). This yields a 7th-order spline function, analogous to the 5th-order spline function above.

The minimum-snap model employs 18 parameters per via stroke: ax0, ... ax7, px, ay0, ..., t1), however, most parameters, and even duration t1 to reach the via point, are fixed by the boundary conditions. The boundary conditions are that the beginning and end of the via strokes should have a smooth connection to the adjacent via strokes, i.e., equal horizontal and vertical positions, velocities, accelerations, and jerks. The two boundary conditions of the via point, fix 4 parameters per via stroke. The minimization equation for the mean squared snap fixes two more parameters for x and y axes. In total, 6 parameters per via stroke (or only 3 parameters per ballistic stroke) are required: x and y positions at beginning and via points, and direction and amplitude of the jerk at the beginning point.

7.4. Symbolical Models

A symbolic model simulates arbitrary texts of a particular writer's handwriting style [48]. Interesting features of this model are the implementation of visual feedback, and the writer-specific motor memory containing "symbolic letter descriptions". Visual feedback monitors the baseline and the lineation levels. When monitoring a departure from the baseline or the lineation levels, an exponentially decaying lineation memory is used as a reference to adjust vertical sizes of future strokes.

It is interesting to note that the generated handwriting patterns are not based on curve fitting of a particular pattern, but contain departures of the same magnitude as those between individual replications. The correlations of the horizontal and vertical stroke sizes and durations between the original patterns appeared similar as those between the simulated pattern and the original ones. Therefore, the simulation model is sufficiently accurate.

The symbolic letter descriptions of the allographs were trained on the basis of a corpus of a writer's handwriting. Thus, each allograph is represented by a sequence of strokes, where each stroke is represented by 4 stroke parameters: dX (horizontal displacement per stroke), dY (vertical displacement per stroke), T (compound stroke duration), and C (stroke-shape factor). These parameters have been based upon the average of several manually selected replications of the same allograph in various contexts. At the symbolic module, dX/dY was quantized into close, normal, or far, and dY was quantized into descender, descender-plus, base-minus, base, base-plus, body-minus, body, body-plus, ascender-minus, and ascender.

Although there is no evidence that durations are represented in motor memory [10, 30], the "compound stroke duration" T is used as a parameter to conveniently interpret the required "stroke-shape factor" C. Unfortunately, the SNR of the stroke-shape factor appears to be very low. Nevertheless, this model is useful as an example of parsimonious coding of cursive script. The interval between successive zero crossings in the x velocity component (i.e., t1 (vx=0) and t2 (vx=0), respectively) can be defined as the x-stroke duration, and similarly for the y-stroke duration. The compound stroke duration is defined as the average of the x and the y-stroke durations:

$$T = ((t2\ (vx=0) - t1\ (vx=0)) + (t2\ (vy=0) - t1\ (vy=0))) / 2$$

T ranges between about 50 and 150 ms. The stroke-shape factor C is defined as the time interval between two nearby zero crossings of x and y velocities, relative to the compound stroke duration T:

$$C = (t1\ (vx=0) - t1\ (vy=0)) / T.$$

The shape factor is a generalized phase difference between x and y velocity-versus-time functions. If the x velocity component is ahead of the y component, then the stroke shape will form (part of) a counterclockwise loop (i.e., $-1.5 < C < 0$). In the opposite case, the stroke shape will form (part of) a clockwise loop (i.e., $0 < C < 1.5$). In the special case that the x and y zero crossings occur simultaneously ($C = 0$), there will be a sharp stroke ending, followed by a movement reversal.

The procedure to translate the allographic-code into the required movement patterns is as follows: In the symbolic module, specific connecting strokes have to be inserted between pairs of allographs and punctuation signs. The connecting stroke depends upon the final stroke of the preceding allograph and the initial stroke of the subsequent allograph. The parameters of the connecting stroke have been estimated by the average of the replications in a corpus of handwriting. The "cursive connections grammar" contains the generic rules prescribing the connecting strokes; for example, the input "an ad..." is expanded to: "(pendown) (a) (base to midline, clockwise, close progression) (n) (base to base-plus, sharp ending, close progression) (penup) (space) (pendown) (a) (base to midline, sharp ending, normal progression) (d) ...". Note that penup and pendown signals are part of the coding.

At the quantitative level, the strokes per allograph are selected from a letter data base. The "quantitative letter descriptors" describe the strokes in terms of dX, dY, T, and C. The compound stroke duration T, and the form factor C, allow the approximation of the moments in time where x and y velocities change sign. In order to generate the kinematics of a handwriting trajectory, a general form of the velocity pattern is selected. For convenience, a sinusoid velocity time function is selected to fit between successive zero crossings of x and y velocities, which appear to approximate handwriting movement patterns relatively well [35].

8. Summary

1. This paper provides a guide for finding and verifying appropriate handwriting features for on-line cursive-script recognition. Appropriate features for on-line cursive-script recognition systems can be derived from handwriting production models and will be only slightly sensitive to the within-writer motor-noise variations. A macroscopic model of handwriting production, having several modules, was presented. The highest module is a movement memory containing the parsimonious and abstract description of the handwriting letters. In the lower modules, the abstract description is translated into individual motor actions.

2. In order to extract features, handwriting patterns are split into a sequence of motor actions such as ballistic strokes. For that purpose, an invariant segmentation procedure is proposed, using a mixture of motor-based rules (segment at absolute-velocity minima; segmentations at least 60 ms apart) and empirical rules (weigh the horizontal velocity component less than the vertical velocity component when estimating the absolute-velocity; concatenate short strokes and parallel strokes).

3. A spectral analysis shows that the frequency bandwidth increases with writing speed. The bandwidth of 10 Hz and stroke durations of 0.1 s suggests that four sample values are enough to describe both components of an individual stroke. Ideally, four features per stroke are needed in order to disambiguate strokes.

4. Invariant features are the ones showing a high signal-to-noise ratio (SNR). In order to estimate the SNR various replications of a writing pattern are required. SNR values of invariant features are of the order of 4.

5. Invariant features may be closely related to the movement information stored

in motor memory, whereas less invariant features may be derived at the lower levels. The top-down hierarchy describes the causal relations between higher-level and lower-level features. The most invariant features are graphical features, e.g., stroke sizes and directions. Less invariant features are the dynamical parameters, e.g., forces and durations.

Variations in one stroke may affect neighboring strokes. This is described by the sequence hierarchy. Stroke sizes show a sequence hierarchy but stroke duration does not. This supports that the segmentation into strokes yields a sequence of motor actions, but, that strokes do not vary individually. Strokes should be considered in their context. Features which change proportionally or linearly for all strokes are subject to lower-level scale transformations and have to be normalized.

6. Context of stroke size and stroke curvature mainly affects durations and speeds. In normal handwriting, stroke size is varied by both duration and accelerative force. Absolute velocity reaches minima at points of high curvature.

7. The most important features for cursive-script recognition are stroke sizes and stroke directions as they have high SNRs. Computational models suggest complete sets of features which allow legible reconstruction of writing patterns. Movement optimization models allow the reconstruction of the handwriting movement from static images and, therefore, lead to optical recognition of cursive script.

References

1. Ellis, A.W. (1982). Spelling and writing (and reading and speaking). In A.W. Ellis (Ed.), Normality and pathology in cognitive functions (pp. 113-146). London: Academic Press.
2. Margolin, D.I. (1984). The neuropsychology of writing and spelling: Semantic, phonological, motor and perceptual processes. Quarterly Journal of Experimental Psychology: Human Experimental Psychology, 36A, 459-489.
3. Van Galen, G.P. & Teulings, H.L. (1983). The independent monitoring of form and scale parameters in handwriting. Acta Psychologica, 54, 9-22.
4. Van Galen, G.P. (1991). Handwriting: Issues for a psychomotor theory. Human Movement Science, 10, 165-191.
5. Teulings, H.L., Thomassen, A.J.W.M., & Van Galen, G.P. (1983). Preparation of partly precued handwriting movements: The size of movement units in writing. Acta Psychologica, 54, 165-177.
6. Denier van der Gon, J.J. & Thuring, J.Ph. (1965). The guiding of human writing movements. Biological Cybernetics, 2, 145-148.

7. Teulings, H.L., Thomassen, A.J.W.M., & Maarse, F.J. (1989). A description of handwriting in terms of main axes. In R. Plamondon, C.Y. Suen, & M. Simner (Eds.), Computer recognition and human production of handwriting (pp. 193-211). Singapore: World Scientific.

8. Pick, H.L. & Teulings, H.L. (1983). Geometric transformations of handwriting as a function of instruction and feedback. Acta Psychologica, 54, 327-340.

9. Guiard, Y. (1993). On Fitts's and Hooke's laws: Simple harmonic movement in upper-limb cyclical aiming. Acta Psychologica, 82, 139-160.

10. Teulings, H.L. & Schomaker, L.R.B. (1993). Invariant properties between stroke features in handwriting. Acta Psychologica, 82, 69-88.

11. Hollerbach, J.M. (1981). An oscillation theory of handwriting. Biological Cybernetics, 39, 139-156.

12. Morasso, P., Mussa Ivaldi, F.A., & Ruggiero, C. (1983). How a discontinuous mechanism can produce continuous patterns in trajectory formation and handwriting. Acta Psychologica, 54, 83-98.

13. Tappert, C.C. (1986). An adaptive system for handwriting recognition. In H.S.R. Kao, G.P. Van Galen, R. Hoosain (Eds.), Graphonomics: Contemporary research in handwriting (pp. 185-198). Amsterdam: North-Holland.

14. Viviani, P. & Cenzato, M. (1985). Segmentation and coupling in complex movements. Journal of experimental psychology: Human perception and performance, 11, 828-845.

15. Plamondon, R. (1989). Handwriting Control: A functional model. In R.M.J. Cotterill (Ed.), Models of brain function (pp. 563-574). London: Cambridge University Press.

16. Kadirkamanathan, M. & Rayner, P.J.W. (1990). A scale-space filtering approach to stroke segmentation of cursive script. In R. Plamondon & G. Leedham (Eds.), Computer Processing of Handwriting (pp. 133-166). Singapore: World Scientific.

17. Higgins, C.A. & Ford, D.M. (1992). A new segmentation method for cursive script recognition. In S. Impedovo and J.C. Simon (Eds.), From pixels to features III: Frontiers in handwriting recognition (pp. 75-86). Amsterdam: Elsevier.

18. Wright, Ph.T. (1988). Design and implementation of a handwriting recognizer. Plessey New Technology, 2, 1988.

19. Helsper, E., Schomaker, L.R.B., Teulings, H.L., & Abbink, G.H. (1993). Feature description of optically scanned handwritten words. Proceedings of the Sixth International Conference on Handwriting and Drawing (pp. 270-272). Paris: Telecom.

20. Wing, A.M. (1978). Response timing in handwriting. In G.E. Stelmach (Ed.), Information processing in motor control and learning (pp.153-172). New York: Academic Press.

21. Abbink, G.H., Teulings, H.L., & Schomaker, L.R.B. (1993). Description of on-line script using Hollerbach's generation model. Pre-Proceedings of the Third International Workshop on Frontiers in Handwriting Recognition (pp. 217-224). Buffalo, NY: Cedar.

22. Edelman, S., Flash, T., & Ullman, S. (1990). Reading cursive handwriting by alignment of letter prototypes. International Journal of Computer Vision, 5, 303-331.

23. Guberman, Sh.A. & Rozentsveig, V.V. (1976). Algorithm for the recognition of handwritten text. Avtomatika i Telemekhanika, 5, 122-129.

24. Edelman, S. & Flash, T. (1987). A model of handwriting. Biological Cybernetics, 57, 25-36.

25. Van Galen, G.P. & Schomaker, L.R.B. (1992). Fitts' law as a low-pass filter effect of muscle stiffness. Human Movement Science, 11, 11-21.

26. Teulings, H.L. & Maarse, F.J. (1984). Digital recording and processing of handwriting movements. Human Movement Science, 3, 193-217.

27. Teulings, H.L., Schomaker, L.R.B., Abbink, G.H., & Helsper, E. (1993). Invariant segmentation of on-line cursive script. Proceedings of the Sixth International Conference on Handwriting and Drawing (pp. 198-200). Paris: Telecom.

28. Jerri, A.J. (1977). The Shannon sampling theorem -- Its various extensions and applications: A tutorial review. Proceedings of the IEEE, 65, 1565-1596.

29. Langolf, G.D., Chaffin, D.B., & Foulke, J.A. (1976). An investigation of Fitts' law using a wide range of movement amplitudes. Journal of Motor Behavior, 8, 113-128.

30. Teulings, H.L., Thomassen, A.J.W.M., & Van Galen, G.P. (1986). Invariants in handwriting: The information contained in a motor program. In H.S.R. Kao, G.P. Van Galen, & R. Hoosain (Eds.), Graphonomics: Contemporary research in handwriting (pp. 305-315). Amsterdam: North-Holland.

31. Schomaker, L.R.B. & Teulings, H.L. (1992). Stroke- versus character-based recognition of on-line, connected cursive script. In S. Impedovo and J.C. Simon (Eds.), From pixels to features III: Frontiers in handwriting recognition (pp. 313-325). Amsterdam: Elsevier.

32. Thomassen, A.J.W.M. & Schomaker, L.R.B. (1986). Between-letter context effects in handwriting trajectories. In H.S.R. Kao, G.P. Van Galen, R. Hoosain (Eds.), Graphonomics: Contemporary research in handwriting (pp. 273-288). Amsterdam: North- Holland.

33. Seni, G. & Ng, S. (1993). Towards an on-line cursive word recognizer. Pre-Proceedings of the Third International Workshop on Frontiers in Handwriting Recognition (pp. 449-454). Buffalo, NY: Cedar.

34. Thomassen, A.J.W.M. & Teulings, H.L. (1985). Time, size, and shape in handwriting: Exploring spatio-temporal relationships at different levels. In J.A. Michon & J.B. Jackson (Eds.), Time, mind, and behavior (pp. 253-263). Berlin: Springer.
35. Plamondon, R. & Maarse, F.J. (1989). An evaluation of motor models of handwriting. IEEE Transactions on Systems, Man, and Cybernetics, 19, 1060-1072.
36. Michel, F. (1971). Etude experimentale de la vitesse du geste graphique. Neuropsychologia, 9, 1-13.
37. Thomassen, A.J.W.M. & Teulings, H.L. (1983b). The development of handwriting. In M. Martlew (Ed.), The psychology of written language: Developmental and educational perspectives (pp. 179-213). New York: Wiley.
38. Greer, K.L. & Green, D.W. (1983). Context and motor control in handwriting. Acta Psychologica, 54-205-215.
39. Wing, A.M. (1980). The height of handwriting. Acta Psychologica, 46, 141-152.
40. Lacquaniti, F., Terzuolo, C., & Viviani, P. (1983). The law relating the kinematic and figural aspects of drawing movements. Acta Psychologica, 54, 115-130.
41. Thomassen, A.J.W.M. & Teulings, H.L. (1983a). Constancy in stationary and progressive handwriting. Acta Psychologica, 54, 179-196.
42. Maarse, F.J., & Thomassen, A.J.W.M. (1983). Produced and perceived writing slant: difference between up and down strokes. Acta Psychologica, 54, 131-147.
43. Meeks, M.L. & Kuklinski, T.T. (1990). Measurement of dynamic digitizer performance. In R. Plamondon & G. Leedham (Eds.), Computer Processing of Handwriting (pp. 89-110). Singapore: World Scientific.
44. Schomaker, L.R.B. & Teulings, H.L. (1990). A handwriting recognition system based on properties of the human motor system. In C.Y. Suen (Ed.), Frontiers in handwriting recognition (pp. 195-209). Montreal: Cenparmi.
45. Schomaker, L.R.B. & Plamondon, R. (1991). The relation between pen force and pen point kinematics in handwriting. Biological Cybernetics, 63, 277-289.
46. Singer, Y. & Tishby, N. (1993). Cursive handwriting word spotting using a discrete dynamic approach. Pre-Proceedings of the Third International Workshop on Frontiers in Handwriting Recognition (pp. 373-378). Buffalo, NY: Cedar.
47. Flash, T. & Hogan, N. (1985). The coordination of arm movements: An experimentally confirmed mathematical model. Journal of Neuroscience, 5, 1788-1703.
48. Schomaker, L.R.B., Thomassen, A.J.W.M., & Teulings, H.L. (1989). A computational model of cursive handwriting. In R. Plamondon, C.Y. Suen, & M. Simner (Eds.), Computer recognition and human production of handwriting (pp. 153-177). Singapore: World Scientific.

Off-line Recognition of Bad Quality Handwritten Words Using Prototypes

N. D. Gorsky

St. Petersburg Institute for Informatics and Automation,
39, 14th line, 199178 St. Petersburg, Russia
e-mail: gorsky@sial.iias.spb.su.

Abstract. This paper consists of three related parts. First, results of experiments on human perception which demonstrate potentials of text recognition are presented. Second, a representation technique for handwritten words is described which allows to construct word prototypes and apply them for recognition of bad quality words. Third, integration of information from multiple sources in word recognition and sentence recognition tasks is discussed. Results of experiments with cursive words and cheque amounts are also presented.

Keywords. Handwriting recognition, word recognition, learning, image representation, holographs, Bayesian classification, multiple information sources, results integration, perception simulation, document understanding, cheque analysis, cursive amount recognition.

1 Introduction

Despite a long history, the problem of automated text reading becomes more and more actual due to the universal use of computers. Recognition of good quality printed texts or isolated handprinted characters can be considered today as a solved problem [1, 2], and the results achieved are not very far from those of humans. At the same time, computer abilities to recognize bad quality printed documents and handwritings do not compare at all with human ones. To a great extend, this problem comes from the inadequate use of alternative sources of information provided by degraded data of text. In the recognition of good quality texts, the main effort is traditionally put on character recognition. High overall performance of a system is due first of all to reliability of this process. However, character recognition becomes much less reliable and sometimes impossible with bad quality documents and cursive script. Therefore, additional information should be discovered and used to obtain an acceptable recognition quality. A major part of this information is on higher levels of text hierarchy, namely on words and sentences. Many researches in handwriting recognition agree on this [3-5].

In this article, taking the task of cursive amount recognition as an example, I would like to point out different information sources and to show how they can be used to improve recognition results for bad quality handwriting.

Section 2 presents results of experiments on human perception, which demonstrate the potentials of text recognition.

Section 3 describes an approach to construct and apply of word prototypes for recognition of bad quality words.

Section 4 considers integration of information from multiple sources, including sources with minor reliability.

Finally, results and some promising research directions are discussed in Section 5.

2 Experiments on Text Perception and Understanding

Printed or handwritings text contains information from various hierarchical levels. Traditionally, these levels are connected with structural elements of a text: characters, words, sentences, paragraphs, etc. For the perception and understanding of a text, information of each level is used at the others for decision making. Distortion of information of a lower level might provoke fatal errors at subsequent higher levels. This statement is to a great extent true for artificial reading machines, and yet quite inadequate for humans. Physiological and psychological experiments proves the human abilities to recognize and understand a text under various conditions including distortion or the absence of a good part of the total information at various levels of text hierarchy.

Let us consider experiments on word recognition using word elements [6]. Curve 1 of Fig. 1 shows word *legibility*, defined as percentage of correctly perceived words, depending on legibility of phonemes forming these words. (It is easy to see that legibility is proportional to the probability of correct recognition.) Experiments described here are made for speech recognition. Nevertheless, I think of them as very important and demonstrative for printed and handwritten data recognition; also taking into account the correspondence of phonemes, words and phrases of speech to characters, words and sentences of a text.

It is easy to verify that a probability of word recognition equal to 0.8 corresponds to a probability of correct phoneme recognition equalled to 0.6; i.e. word legibility is essentially higher than phoneme legibility. At the same time, if word elements (phonemes or characters) are independent, the probability of correct recognition for 5-elements word is only $(0.6)^5 = 0.078$ (see curve 2 at Fig. 1).

Figure 1 indicates that spoken or textual communication coded by the sequence of sounds or letters has considerable redundancy and noise-immunity. It demonstrates how effectively humans can use additional information existing at the word level, for the level of word elements. Thus, high-performance recognition at the word level can be achieved (at least, in principal) even with a poor efficiency at the lower level of phonemes or characters.

Word legibility increases further with restrictions on the vocabulary volume. The smaller is the lexicon used, the faster and more accurately can words be recognized with incomplete information available at the phoneme level (Fig. 2).

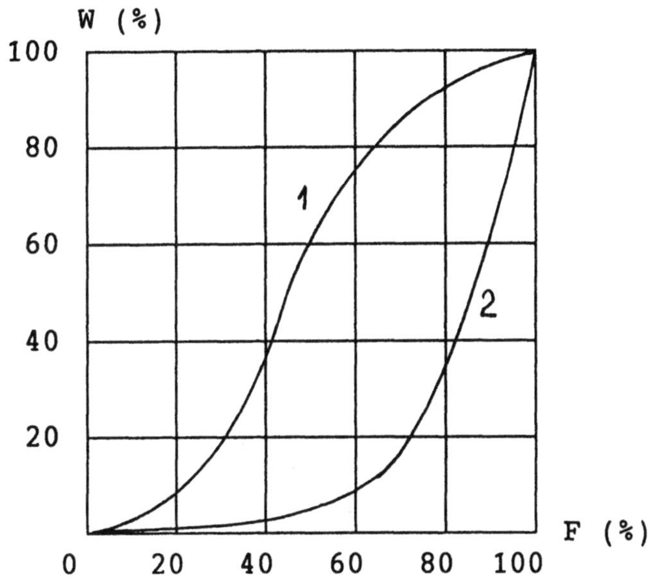

Fig. 1. Word legibility depending on phoneme legibility: 1 - for humans, 2 - probabilistic.

This effect is well known in speech an text recognition. Many researchers point out the necessity of its utilisation, particularly in problem-oriented systems [6-8]. Some of them use for this purpose comparison of various character sequences, produced by the system, with the current vocabulary. It is important that "soft" decisions can be made in this case for characters. Not only one symbol, but a set of them with confidence values is transferred from the character level to the word level. Unquestionably, this approach deserve attention; but it is still based on extraction and recognition of such word elements as characters.

However, another approach to word recognition is possible, namely the analysis and comparison of the whole word pattern. During the process of fluent reading, humans in a large measure rely also upon word patterns instead of separate character patterns. If the reader understands the sense of a text, he normally fixates his attention on words. Fixation points are nonuniformly distributed: often they are at the beginning or/and on the end of the word (Fig. 3), some words are missed completely [9].

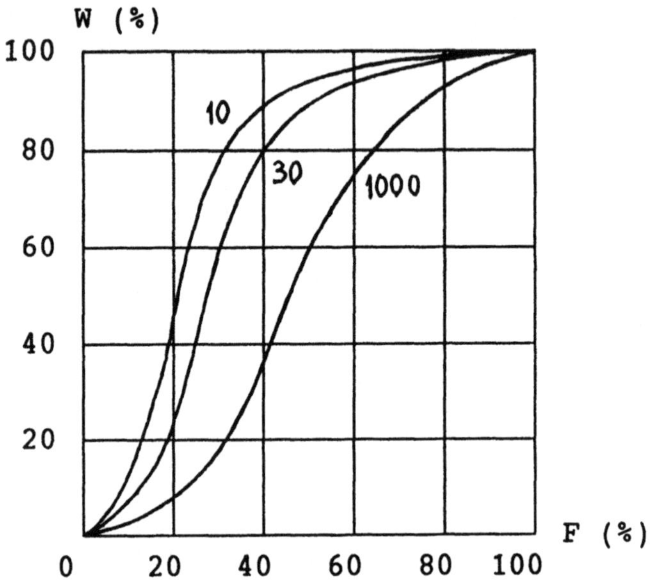

Fig. 2. Word legibility depending on phoneme legibility for various vocabulary volume.

```
    ×          ×    ×          ×     ×
 ПОТОМ   ОХОТНИК  РАССТАВИЛ  СЕТЬ
(than   a hunter   had set   a net)
```

Fig. 3. Sight fixation points while reading a sentence.

It is assumed that in understanding a text, the reader forecasts its continuation, forms current limited lexicon, perhaps, guesses the next word(s) and then just checks his hypothesis by comparing the perceived word image with the expected word(s) or by actively looking for certain words in the text. Character-by-character reading begins only when word comparison/search has failed (in particular, this is true for people with certain damages of visual cortex) [9, 10]. Thus, fluent reading seems to be more word-based than character-based.

There are evidences that human visual perception uses for recognition two main schemes: top-down strategy controlled by the left hemisphere, and bottom-up one controlled by the right hemisphere. The left hemisphere extracts the hierarchy of common classification features and use them for gradual refinement of object recognition, while the right one accumulates individual features or details of an object, and then match them with the known prototypes. It is important that working together these mechanisms reach a decision much faster than if each of them is working alone [9, 11].

In reading, top-down recognition process can be considered as gradual narrowing of the current lexicon at various levels of text meaning, selecting (or searching) for potential words using a hierarchy of appropriate classification features (like, for example, word length or word position in the phrase). Bottom-up process consists in extracting individual, distinctive features from the word image (like configurations of strokes above or below the baseline) and applying them for matching the word with prototypes of words in the vocabulary. One can say that top-down process is controlled by a regular information, and bottom-up process - by a singular one [12]. As this takes place, regular information is extracted not only from words, but comes also from higher levels of text hierarchy (i.e. from sentences, paragraphs,...). Singular data are derived from word images and lower level elements (graphemes, characters, strokes,...). From the above, it might be concluded that:

1. Recognition of entire words plays an important and relatively independent part in text perception and understanding.

2. High performance recognition at the word level can be reached even with an average or a bad quality of character recognition.

3. Recognition process at word level should integrates all available information form other levels both high and low, regular and singular data extracted from the word image itself being of great importance.

These statements are significant to understand how to treat bad quality handwriting, where information from lower levels is unreliable or partially absent.

3 Word Prototypes and Their Use

At present several research groups develop and apply techniques of word recognition based on comparison of word image with prototypes of vocabulary words [13-15]. Prototype can be defined as generalized description of a certain word distinguishing patterns of this word form patterns of other words. This in spite of the changing in style, size and other parameters of the analyzed script. Prototype of a word can be represented as one or several typical word images, or as a structured set of word specific elements, or as a group of features, etc.

Necessary conditions for using prototypes in word recognition are:
(i) a constructive procedure to create prototypes themselves,
(ii) a constructive procedure to compare the image of any word with each prototype.
Usually, prototypes are created at a learning stage. Comparison of the recognized word with all or some prototypes is used for decision making at a recognition stage, i.e. for assigning the word to one of possible classes of the vocabulary words.

Let us consider in more details one of prototype-based technique [16]: the recognition of literal cursive amounts from bank cheques. A distinctive characteristic of this task is the limited lexicon (26 words for French language, with which analyzed cheques were written). Omniscriptor texts are to be recognized, and the quality of handwriting is poor (Fig. 4).

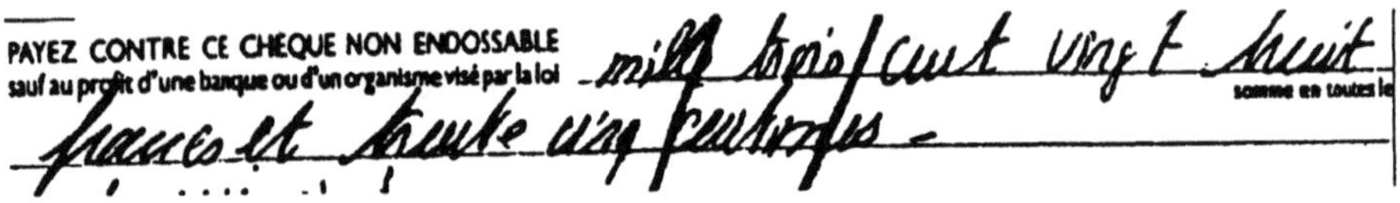

Fig. 4. Typical image of a bank cheque (literal amount field).

3.1 Initial Image Representation

The key question to be solved with the use of prototype-based technique is to find a representation of a word such that it would be invariant to possible modifications and applicable for recognition without any restrictions on the style and quality of handwriting.

Practice shows that there is a lot of variations of the same word, which can be considered as "distortions" of one or several basic types. Most common of them are:

1. Variations of horizontal and vertical sizes of a word or of some characters.
2. Variations of word and/or characters styles.
3. Variations of character positions relatively to the baseline.
4. Linear or nonlinear deformations of some characters or of the word as a whole.
5. Connection or disconnection of characters or of their parts.
6. Variations of the average slant of characters.
7. Variations of line thickness.
8. Noise on the image such as additional or missed strokes, points, etc.

Thus, the class of possible distortions is quite broad and leads naturally to rigourous restrictions on the class of possible representations. It seems reasonable to use several sequential transforms to achieve the desirable invariance to the distortions.

The first question to be solved is to choose the basic element of a word image description. First of all, this element should has such characteristics as *position* (coordinates) and *direction* to describe adequately a line or its parts. Straight line *segment* have been chosen as a basic element for our approach. The technique of extracting segments from a word images described in [13] has been used, which was proved to be efficient for handwriting recognition. The set of segments approximating lines on the binary image is the initial level of word representation (Fig. 5a, b). This allows to eliminate distortions of type 7 and, partially, of type 8.

The strongest argument, proving sufficiency of word representation by such a set of segments, is the fact that the word remains recognizable and readable. Therefore, spatial segment configurations preserves the essential information for further recognition.

To compensate average slant of handwritten words (distortions of type 6), the set of segments is normalized. Normalization can be described as a deformation of the image layout from a parallelogram to a rectangle of the same height (Fig. 5c). The value of the deformation is determined by the average direction of those segments which are "not horizontal" (they are defined as segments the angle of which with the horizontal axis is more than a preset value). Normalization is a very fast operation, as only the coordinates of segments are recalculated.

3.2 Representation of Words by Holographs

After normalization, the set of segments is mapped into a special feature space, to ensure invariance for other types of distortions. This is the next level of word representation. The essential ideas used in this mapping are the following:

1. "Absolute" information (like the coordinates of some pixels or segments) is rather unreliable, because of the variations in character and word sizes (distortions of types 1, 4 and 5). Ordinal characteristics of segments (i.e. relative segment order) are much more robust, and so preferable to use.
2. Spatial position of segments and character-like word basis should be taken into consideration. For this, it is worth to describe a segment as the part of group of neighbouring segments approximately comparable in sizes to characters (though characters themselves can be ignored).
3. Representation should be sequential in some sense to take into account the natural order of characters in a word.

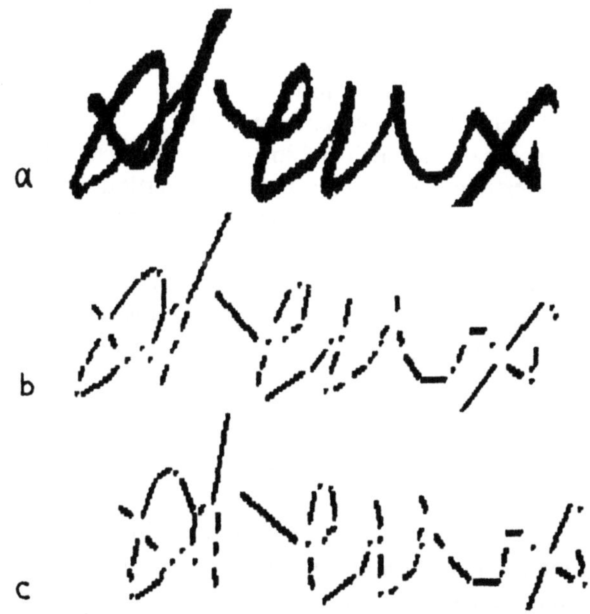

Fig. 5. The first phase of word representation: source image (a), image approximation by the set of segments (b), normalized set of segments (c).

4. The addition or the absence of some segments should not change radically the results, so representation should be additive relatively to its basic element, the segment. This helps to avoid distortions of type 5 and, partially of type 8.

The solution which in general suits the above requirements is the following. Each segment approximating a word is mapped into a parameter space called a *holograph*. In the simplest case, the image of a segment in this space is a pulse-like function, which differs from zero in a single point. Coordinates of this point are determined by the following segment's features:

- *global x-order* (segment's number along the x-axis),
- *local order* of the segment among the neighbouring segments,
- *direction* of the segment.

Value of the function (or *intensity* of the corresponding holograph's point) is proportional to the segment *weight*. The full word is represented as a set of points of different intensities in the holograph.

Let us consider characteristics of the mapping in more details.

Global x-order of a segment is defined by segment's number N in the ordered list of x-coordinates of all segments. In our experiments N has a range from 0 to 15.

Local order of a segment is determined in its *configuration*. A configuration is the set of segments neighbouring to the given one. Two segments are neighbours, if the distance between them less than half of average segment length in the word. (Distance between segments is defined as minimal Euclidean distance between their centres or ends). Two variants of local order (approximately equal in results) have been tested:

- *local orthogonal order* - order in the direction orthogonal to own direction of the segment,
- *local y-order* - order along horizontal axis.

Local order is normalized in the range from 0 to 15.

Direction of a segment is defined as an integer from 0 to 15.

Weight of a segment depends on its length and some other characteristics. Weight is enlarged for segments with extreme values of local order, for vertical segments, and for segments located significantly above or below the main body of the word (i.e. probably belonging to singularities).

Thus the holograph of a particular word is a three-dimensional array with coordinates: global x-order, local order and direction. Resolution for each coordinate equals to 16. Intensity of each holograph element is the sum of weights of those segments which are mapped into this element.

3.3 Comparison of a Word with the Prototypes

A natural way to create the *prototype* of a word with the described technique is to map into a holograph, not the single pattern of a word, but a set of words written with different styles by various people. It is the basis of a learning procedure. In the learning stage, a holograph is filled by numerous points of various intensities. If the learning material is not noise, the spatial distribution of these points appears to be quite nonuniform, with regions of high intensity corresponding to most significant features of the word.

A smoothing operation is then performed by convolution with averaging kernel (in our experiments, of size 3*3*3). This operation is equivalent to taking of a bell-like instead of a pulse-like function, as the image of each segment in the holograph; it can be considered also as blurring the holograph.

After smoothing, a word prototype can be considered as a three-dimensional multiextremal function having non-negative values.

Since each holograph is a three-dimensional matrix, basic matrix operations are formally applicable to it. For example, the sum of N holographs is a new holograph with intensity of each element equalled to the sum of N corresponding intensities. The difference of two holographs is a holograph with intensity equals to the difference of corresponding intensities of two original arrays. Intensities of such a *difference holograph* have both positive and negative value.

It should be natural that difference holographs provide better resolution in distinguishing similar words. Experiments confirm this hypothesis: best results have been obtained for prototypes prepared as difference holographs. Positive part of such prototype is the sum of prototypes for alternate variants of the recognized word (like variants of word "francs": "franc", "Franc", "Frs", "francs", etc.), while negative part was the normalized sum of holographs for all other words. Thus, the prototype of each vocabulary word is constructed as the difference between a word holograph, filled with the set of word's patterns from learning material, and the mean value of holographs of all other words.

Let us consider now the recognition stage. Three basic techniques have been developed and tested for comparing a word represented in holographic form with the set of prototypes. They are the following:

1. Correlation of holographs. The word is compared with each prototype by calculating the cross-correlation of corresponding holographs. With the first variant of this procedure, calculations are made only for nonzero elements of the word holograph (there are typically 20-50 of such elements). The second variant uses the preliminary blurring of the word holograph by convolution with the averaging mask of 3*3*3 size. The first variant is faster, but the second provides more stable results.

2. Identification of segments configurations. Similarity measure of the word and tested prototype is calculated as percentage of word segments "explained" by this prototype. A segment is considered as explained, if the intensities of holograph elements for its configuration (i.e. the set of the neighbour segments) are close in average to the intensities of the corresponding prototype elements. This technique may be thought of as a correlation of groups of segments. It works faster than cross-correlation of total holographs, and give better results when the handwriting is of comparatively good quality.

3. Backward identification of segments. As for the previous case, a similarity measure of a word and of a prototype is computed as the percentage of word segments explained by the prototype. A segment is considered as explained, if the prototype has a local maximum of intensity with coordinates of the same or close values relatively to those of the segment. To do this, local maxima are extracted from each prototype at the stage of learning (a number of maxima for single prototype varies from 10 to 30). This technique is as fast as the previous one, it provides the best results for words with many singularities, however, results are worse than the others for "regular" words with few local maxima in their prototypes.

Comparing all three techniques, one can find out that the first one is the best in average. But the second and the third give better results for some words. Owing to this, a global similarity measure has been defined as the weighted sum of the above three measures. Weight coefficients are estimated at the learning stage for each prototype. Values of the global measure vary approximately from +70 for words typically similar to a prototype, down to 70 for words dissimilar to the prototype.

An investigation of empirical probability density functions of the global measure values for "own" and "alien" words shows that they correlate well with gaussian densities. "Own" words have positive mean value and "alien" words have negative one (Fig. 6). It means that each prototype (or vocabulary word) is represented by a hyper-ellipsoidal cloud of points (the images of its "own" words) in the multidimensional space, where the similarity measure of a word and i-th prototype is plotted on the i-th axis.

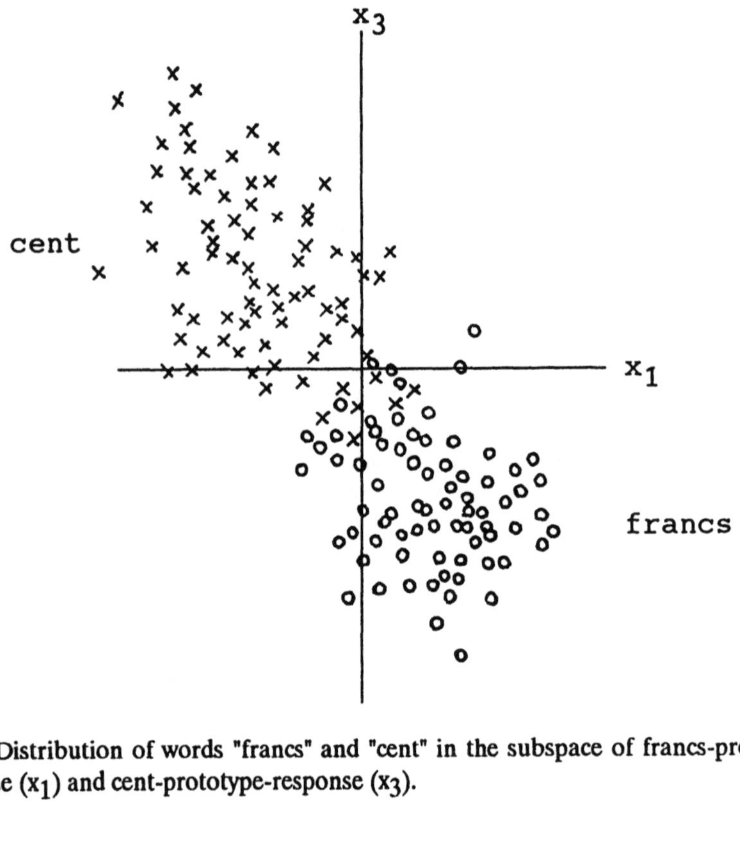

Fig. 6. Distribution of words "francs" and "cent" in the subspace of francs-prototype-response (x_1) and cent-prototype-response (x_3).

Since each cloud may be approximated by gaussian density, it is quite natural to use for word recognition the well known Bayesian Classifier for normally distributed classes, as it guarantees the minimum error rate. Bayes rule enables to find probabilities $P_i(x_1,...,x_n)$ of the recognized word to the i-th class; $x_1,...,x_n$ being the similarity measure between this word and n prototypes.

They are given by (1):

$$P_i(x_1,...,x_n) = P(x_1,...,x_n \mid i)\, P_i / p, \qquad (1)$$

where $P(x_1,...,x_n \mid i)$ is the value of i-th word density function at the point $(x_1,...,x_n)$; P_i is the a priori probability of the appearance the i-th word; and p is a normalizing factor which is equal to the sum of $P(x_1,...,x_n \mid i)\, P_i$ terms on all i values. In the case of normally distributed classes

$$P(x_1,...,x_n \mid i) = N(x_1,...,x_n, M_i, C_i),$$

where N(X, M, C) is the well known expression for multidimensional gaussian density with mean vector M and covariance matrix C (see, for instance, [17]). Then

$$P_i(x_1,...,x_n) = N(x_1,...,x_n, M_i, C_i)\, P_i / p, \quad i = 1,...,n. \qquad (2)$$

To use (2), the mean vector M_i and the covariance matrix C_i have to be estimated for all classes, at the learning stage. At the recognition stage, the simplest Bayesian Classifier assigns to the recognized word the number s of the class for which the probability $P_s(x_1,...,x_n)$ is maximum.

3.4 Experimental Results

Images of words from real bank cheques written in French have been used as learning (2014 words) and testing (1490 words) material. At the learning stage, prototypes for the 26 lexicon words have been prepared using about 100 randomly taken samples of each word (for rear words the volume of learning is smaller). Beside this, weight coefficients of local similarity measures, mean vector M, and covariance matrix C have been estimated for each prototype using the same learning set. At the recognition stage, a word from a position PP of a cheque is compared with all prototypes (to get $x_1,...,x_{26}$ vector) and then 26 probabilities of all vocabulary words at the position PP are computed according to (2). A list of vocabulary words is ordered with the decreasing probabilities $P_i(x_1,...,x_{26})$, $i = 1,...,26$. Such an ordered list of possible answers (decisions) is further called a *candidate list*. Ideally, the correct answer - i.e. the analysed word - should have the maximum probability and should be at the first position in the candidate list. Practically, however, this is not true. In this case, a convenient criterion of recognition quality is the *average position of the correct answer* in the candidate list (averaging is made throughout the results at the recognition stage).

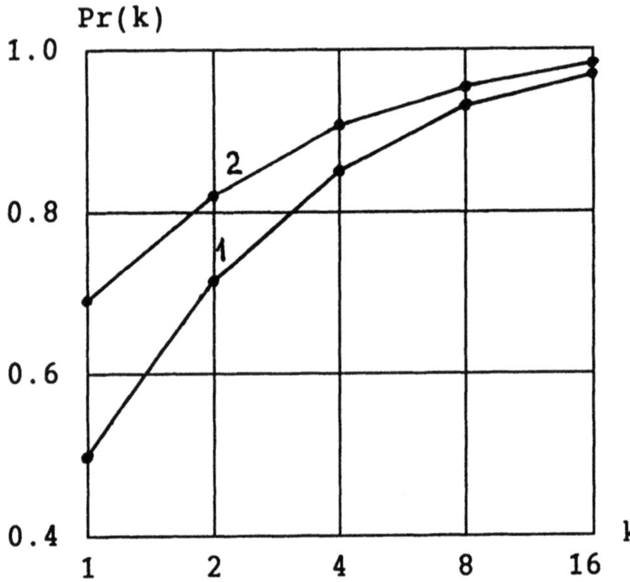

Fig. 7. The probability to find the correct answer among the first k candidates: 1 - using word prototypes; 2 - using prototypes and a priori probabilities of words at different positions in the cheque amount.

In a first experiment, a priori probabilities of vocabulary words (P_i in expression (2)) have not been taken into account to estimate "pure" effect of prototypes. The average position K of the correct answer is then equal to 2.74. A more detailed characteristic of recognition quality is accumulated probability $P_{tr}(k)$, finding the correct answer among the first k words in the candidate list. Figure 7 (curve 1) presents this probability for various k values. It follows from Fig. 7 that the simplest Bayesian Classifier, which use the 1-st candidate only, provides a probability of correct answer $P_{tr}(1)=0.48$.

In a second experiment the a priori probabilities of vocabulary words, appearing at each position in an amount sentence, have been taken into account in the expression (2) as P_i factors. It should be pointed out that these probabilities are more informative than ordinary a priori probabilities of vocabulary words, because they provide some *extra information on the position* of a word in a sentence. Then the probability to find the correct answer at first k positions of the candidate list is shown at Fig. 7, curve 2. The average position of the correct answer K equals to 2.28, and the probability of a correct recognition for the 1-st candidate increases up to 0.68. We shall return to these results in the following sections.

4 Word Recognition with Multiple Information Sources

4.1 Integration of Sources

The Bayes formula (1) already demonstrates how to utilise two independent information sources: conditional probabilities of each class $P(x_1,...,x_n \mid i)$ and a priori probabilities of vocabulary words P_i. Thus, the curve 2 at Fig. 7 is nothing else than a result of integrating (i) the information of word similarity with prototypes and (ii) the information of vocabulary word frequencies at different positions in a cheque amount. Information from other independent sources can be taken into account in quite a similar manner, Bayes formula assuming the form:

$$P_i(X1, X2, ..., XN) = P(X1 \mid i)\, P(X2 \mid i) ... P(XN \mid i) \,/\, p\,, \tag{3}$$

where $P_i(X1, X2, ..., XN)$ is as before the output probability of a recognized word to belong to the i-th class; $P(XL \mid i)$ is the probability this word to belong to the i-th class, obtained by the L-th information source which uses data XL; and p is a normalizing factor which is equal to the sum of $P(X1 \mid i)\, P(X2 \mid i)...P(XN \mid i)$ terms for all i values.

Some peculiarities of expression (3) should be pointed out. Each information source produces its output as probabilities of all vocabulary words, the nature of sources being of no concern. For word recognition, this means that there is a possibility to integrate information coming from all levels of text hierarchy - both high and low. It is very attractive that sources do not have to make decisions by themselves. In questionable or uncertain cases a source might assign equal probabilities to all classes. This will not affect the final result. At the same time, the inclusion of a source producing close probabilities for all classes, uninformative at first sight, increases anyhow the probability of correct recognition, if this source is independent from the other sources.

The requirement of independence is of great importance. If the sources are not independent, output probabilities in (3) may be distorted up to produce incorrect candidate list. However, it is quite difficult to verify are two sources independent or they are not. To do this, joint densities $P(XL,XM \mid i)$ have to be investigated, which is usually rather hard, first of all due to the lack of learning material.

To avoid these difficulties, another approach has been applied for the cheque amount recognition task. At the learning stage, each source (for a moment let us set aside their construction and working algorithms) produces its own set of candidate lists. The average position of the correct answer K_L, $L=1,...,N$ characterizing L-th source is calculated using L-th set of lists, and the sources are ordered according to their K_L values. Then, the recognition of test material is repeated L times with sources accumulation:

first, the probabilities in (3) are computed using the most informative source (N=1);
second, the two best sources are used (N=2);
third, the three best sources are used (N=3), etc.

At each step the global criterion K (average position of the correct answer) is estimated. The inclusion of new sources is continued, as long as K decreases. If K stays constant, then the source is duplicated by others and useless. If K decreases with the inclusion of a new source, an additional useful information is provided by this source (but this do not proves its independence from the other sources!). Thus a pragmatic criterion of recognition quality is found, but at the sacrifice of sources independence. Payment for this is a distortion of probabilities calculated from (3). Typically, large values still increase further, and small ones becomes smaller. Nevertheless, the candidate list quality grows up when the value of K goes down.

4.2 Using Additional Features for Word Recognition

Let us illustrate the foregoing material by considering the additional information sources, useful in the recognition of bad quality handwritten words. Keeping aside for a while informations from the higher levels, let us estimate which information from the word image is overlooked or is not utilized completely.

One available source is the set of word prototypes. However, prototypes actually do not take into account the length of words which obviously is important for word recognition. Therefore, the first additional feature A1 gives the horizontal size of a word. Its value is normalized to the range from 1 to 20.

The second feature A2 describes the combination of word "extending elements". This feature appears to be the most informative among the tested additional sources, so it is worth of consideration. A close inspection of cheque images shows that the best written parts are the first letters of words and the elements which lie off the word's body (like upper parts of "b" and "f" or lower part of "q"; I think, this is purely psychological effect). It is apparent that mutual position of extending elements is of most importance for word recognition. Thus the A2 feature is constructed in the following way: the image of a word is divided into 5 equal parts lengthwise, and the presence or absence of extensions above the upper baseline and below the lower baseline is indicated in each part. So the feature is a 10-dimension binary vector (which by itself can be considered as a word prototype). Certainly, this feature is not completely independent from the holographic word prototype. But a holograph uses only the ordinal segment characteristics, and one can suppose that important information on strong ascenders and descenders is not exhausted by it.

Each of the next features A3 to A6 is a 5-dimension binary vector, which characterize the presence or absence of a certain element in 5 parts of a word image. These elements are:

- for A3, three horizontal segments one above the other in the word body (possible characters "s", "e");
- for A4, closed internal contour in the word body (possible characters "o", "q", "d",...);
- for A5, dot(s) above the upper baseline (possible characters "i", "j");
- for A6, straight vertical segment(s) above the upper baseline (possible character "t");

The last binary feature A7 describes left profile of the first letter in a word.

Methods and programs of extraction the above features from the word image have been developed by V. A. Anisimov of St. Petersburg Institute for Informatics and Automation.

Let us recall that to calculate output probabilities according to (3), it is necessary to estimate not only the features A1-A7 themselves (their values are just XL, L=1,...,7 in (3)), but also conditional probabilities of the classes P(XL | i), i=1,...,26. For this, histograms of all features and for all classes are evaluated at the learning stage. For example, the histogram of the feature A1 has 20x26 dimensions (A1 has 20 possible values), and the histogram of A3 has 5x2x26 dimensions (each of 5 A3 components has 2 possible values). Once learning is finished, histograms are normalized with the volume of learning sets in each class, thus obtaining frequencies of all feature values for all vocabulary words. These frequencies are nothing else than evaluations of all possible variants of required probabilities, and they are used at the recognition stage. Technique is very simple: when computing a feature value, the probability of a certain class is taken from the corresponding histogram cell. (Say, for X1=9, probability P(9 | 2) is found in the cell (9,2) of A1 histogram).

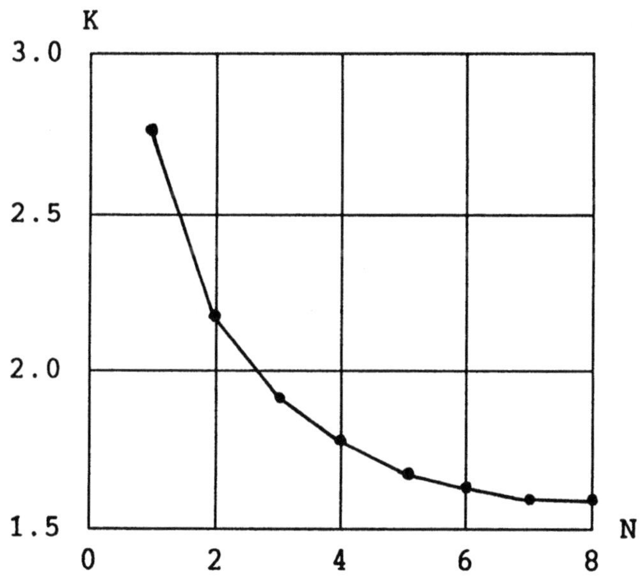

Fig. 8. Average position of the correct answer in the candidate list depending on the number of information sources used for word recognition.

Investigation of features A1-A7 has shown for them the following values of the global recognition quality criterion (enumerated in increasing order): K_2=4.00, K_1=5.42, K_5=5.75, K_4=7.85, K_3=7.95, K_7=8.88, K_6=9.12. Remember, that prototypes provide the best criterion value K_0=2.74. Figure 8 displays the average position of the correct answer depending on the number of features taken into account.

With N=1, only the word prototypes are used, then additional features are included in the increasing order of K_L. As it can be seen from Fig. 8, inclusion of the last feature (A6) did not change the criterion value. Thus this feature is completely duplicated by the others. All other features make their contributions to an increase of performance.

Figure 9 (curve 1) presents the probability to find the correct answer among the first k positions of the candidate list when word prototypes and 6 additional features are used for recognition (compare with Fig. 7). The probability of the correct answer at the 1-st position is equal to 0.76. Curve 2 on the Fig. 9 is analogous to the curve 2 on the Fig. 7: it demonstrates how a result is changed with the inclusion of the information source from the higher level - a priori probabilities of different words at various positions in a cheque. This source is at the sentence level, it is informative and practically independent from the others. Its inclusion increases considerably the recognition quality.

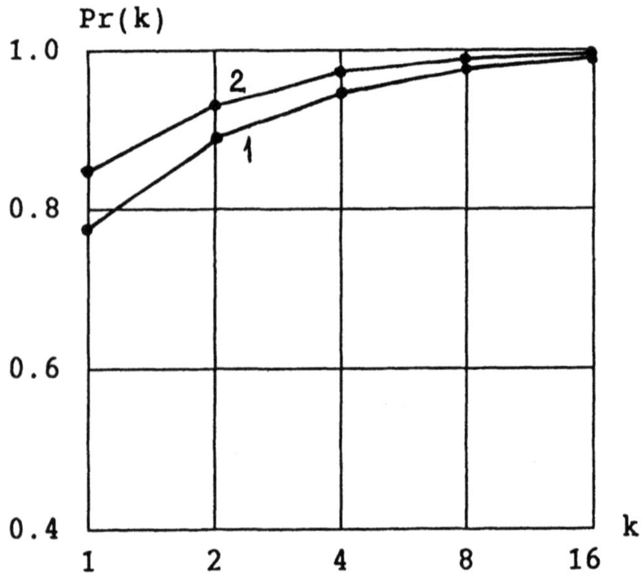

Fig. 9. The probability to find the correct answer among the first k candidates: 1 - using word prototypes and 6 additional features; 2 - the same as 1 with inclusion of a priori probabilities of word appearance at different positions in a cheque amount.

To summarize this section, one can say that described additional features illustrate the search of new sources, which partially duplicate each other (though they have been constructed as much independent as possible). This proves a possibility to integrate statistically dependent sources using the candidate-list-based criterion. Notice that the above feature set (particularly features A3-A7) is assigned arbitrarily to a great extent. Other features or prototypes can be used, those, for instance, which are based on the recognition of characters.

Thus, it seems more essential to extract information from word images with multiple simple algorithms than to develop a single "universal" technique.

5 Conclusion and Perspectives

We have discusses an approach to recognition of bad quality words form a limited lexicon. Particular attention has been given to the use of word prototypes. Different ways of extraction and integration informations from a word image has been shown. Integration of information sources from different text levels (graphemes, words, sentences) has been demonstrated. However, considering word recognition task, we should always remember that neither words nor characters are our final goal in automatic reading. The goal is *text understanding*, and recognition of text elements is, and always will be, only an intermediate stage. Of course, the term "text understanding" is very broad and indefinite, nevertheless for practical application it seems quite enough to reduce it to message understanding (or document understanding [18]). In such a context, understanding means a *mapping of a text* (presented as a command, or a message, or a document) *into the set of possible actions* of a system. For handwritten cheque amount reading, understanding means correct output of the amount in digital form, for address reading it is correct delivering of a letter, etc.

Returning to similarities with speech recognition and understanding, it should be noted that in man the reliability of understanding is extremely high, first of all due to clearly defined increasing of performance at all levels of speech communication hierarchy. The relationship of word and phrase legibility (Fig. 10, curve 1) is quite analogous to the one of characters and words (see Fig. 1), and absolutely inconsistent with "probabilistic" relationship which corresponds to words independent from each other and from elements of other levels (Fig. 10, curve 2).

Many researchers have pointed out the necessity of integrated consideration both of automatic reading and of speech understanding which incorporates available information from different sources of different levels. In this lecture, I have discussed only one of the possible approaches to integrate informations from several sources for recognition of bad quality cursive words. This approach has been demonstrated at the word level, but it is quite applicable also at the sentence level - the level of understanding in the cheque amount recognition task. Some extra information sources at this level are: probabilities of word appearance at various positions in the complete sentence (the use of this source is demonstrated by Fig. 7 and Fig. 9), a priori probabilities of sentences, probabilities of word doublets, triplets, etc. Notice that information from the word level can be transferred to the sentence level in a "soft" form of candidates probabilities, but not as "hard" decisions.

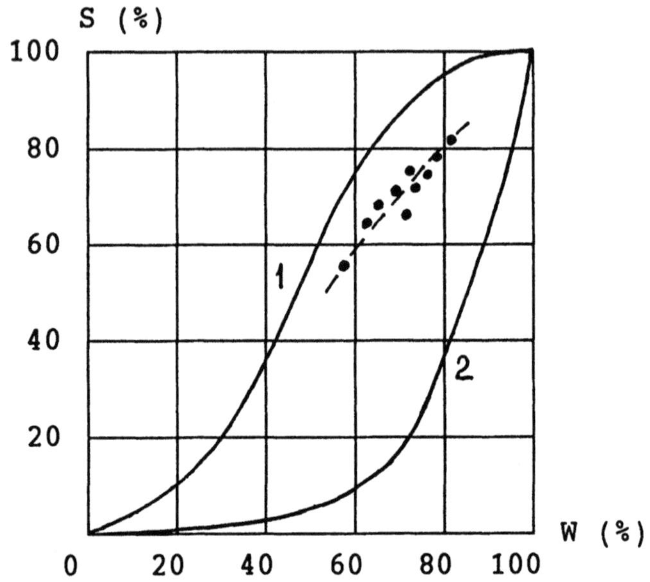

Fig. 10. The phrase legibility depending on the word legibility: 1 - for humans; 2 - "probabilistic" (for 5-word phrase). Points are results of experiments with cursive amounts reading.

Although the topic of sentence recognition is beyond the scope of this lecture, I would like to finish it with experimental results obtained at the sentence level and represented in the same form as the results of phrase recognition for humans. They are shown with points at Fig. 10. As it can be seen, the probability of correct sentence recognition is essentially greater than "probabilistic" level, while is still worse than human abilities. Let us hope that the search and use of new information sources will allow to cut this gap.

Acknowledgements

The bank cheque data have been provided by the french SRTP (Service de Recherche Technique de la Poste), through the A2IA company.

I would like to thank Prof. J.-C. Simon, University Paris-VI and A2IA, for many fruitful discussions and the use his programs of word approximation by segments.

References

1. Mori, S. et al.: Historical review of OCR research and development. *Proc. of the IEEE*, **80**, 7, 1029-1058, 1992
2. Sakai, K., Asami, H., Tanabe, Y.: Advanced application systems for handwritten character recognition. In: S. Impedovo, J.C. Simon, (eds.) *From Pixels to Features III* 201-213, Amsterdam: North-Holland 1992
3. Ho, T.K., Hull, J.J., Srihari, S.N.: Word recognition with multi-level contextual knowledge. *Int. Conf. on Document Analysis and Recognition,* Saint Malo, France, 1991
4. Evett, L.J. et al.: Using linguistic information to aid handwriting recognition. In: S. Impedovo, J.C. Simon, (eds.) *From Pixels to Features III* 339-348, Amsterdam: North-Holland 1992
5. Baret, O., Lecolinet, E.: Cursive word recognition. In the present volume.
6. Pokrovsky, N.B.: *Calculation and Measuring of Speech Legibility.* Moscow: Communication, 1962 (in Russian)
7. Shurmann, J. et al.: Document analysis - from pixels to contents. *Proc. of the IEEE*, **80**, 7, 1101-1119, 1992
8. Downton, A.C. et al.: Recognition of handwritten British postal addresses. In: S. Impedovo, J.C. Simon, (eds.) *From Pixels to Features III* 129-144, Amsterdam: North-Holland 1992
9. Meerson Ya. A.: *High Level Visual Functions*, Nauka, Leningrad, 1986. (in Russian).
10. Zikmunt, V. (ed.): *The Oculomotor System and Brain Functions*, London, 1973.
11. Alexandrov, V.V., Gorsky, N.D.: *From Humans to Computers: Cognition through Visual Perception.* Singapore: World Scientific, 1991
12. Simon, J.-C.: A Complemental Approach to Feature Detection, *From Pixels to Features,* 229-237, Amsterdam: North-Holland 1989
13. Simon, J.-C.: Off-line cursive word recognition. *Proc. of the IEEE*, **80**, 7, 1150-1161, 1992
14. Hull, J.J. et al: Combination of segmentation-based and wholistic handwritten word recognition algorithms. In: S. Impedovo, J.C. Simon, (eds.) *From Pixels to Features III* 261-272, Amsterdam: North-Holland 1992
15. Camillerapp, J. et al: Off-line and on-line methods for cursive handwriting recognition. Ibid, 273-287
16. Gorsky, N.D.: Experiments with handwriting recognition using holographic representation of line images. To be published.
17. Duda, R.O., Hart, P.E.: *Pattern Classification and Scene Analysis.* New York: John Wiley & Sons 1973
18. Srihari, S.: High performance reading machines.*Proc. of the IEEE*, **80**, 7, 1120-1132, 1992

Handwriting Recognition by Statistical Methods

Torsten Caesar, Joachim Gloger, Alfred Kaltenmeier, Eberhard Mandler

Daimler-Benz Research Center Ulm, P.O. Box 2360, 89013 Ulm, Germany

Abstract. In January 1992 a project was started which is focused on the recognition of handwritten words, constraint by a given lexicon. The target application is the recognition of US city names in address reading systems.

An experimental environment was built from scratch. The preprocessing techniques for the normalization of the image are working very efficiently because they are based on the contour description of connected components. The classification is based on the Hidden Markov Model (HMM) approach, using the great experience of our speech recognition group. HMM recognition techniques rely on a sequence of micro features. To consider also the holistic aspects of a pattern a binary associative memory approach will be used. The combination of the HMM approach and the holistic associative memory seems to be very promising.

Keywords: handwriting recognition, Hidden Markov Models, preprocessing

1 Introduction

Handwriting recognition is a challenging task. In contrast to on-line recognition, where the sequence of sampling points along the writing trace is known, the input of an off-line recognition system is a binary image.

For a first approach, it is necessary to restrict the context to well defined and known domains. In our case the domain is defined by a given sample set and a complete lexicon of US city names. In the multicultural American society a very broad range of different writing styles can be found. All difficulties in recognizing handwriting show up: isolated block print mixed up with cursive style letters, overlapping block print letters, partially cursive words and fully cursive words.

Using additional information it is possible to reduce the complete static lexicon of more than 50,000 entries to hundreds. So, for each current recognition task a subset of the complete lexicon is provided keeping the correct meaning of the input pattern.

Using recognition methods which rely on a segmentation first basis seems unable to achieve the desired performance. The segmentation into characters of handwritten words may only be achieved by recognizing in parallel. The research in speech recognition has always been faced with the segmentation problem because there is nothing comparable to single character recognition. So there were always stronger demands for segmentation free techniques. Today, a commonly accepted technique for recognizing continuous speech are Hidden Markov Models (HMM) [1, 2].

As HMM recognition techniques rely on a sequence of micro features, the holistic aspects of a pattern might vanish. Therefore, a combination of this method with holistic ones seems to be plausible and promising. The total approach for recognizing cursive script will end up in a combination of different approaches.

2 Preprocessing

Iconic operations on the level of the binary raster image are performed to reduce noise effects. Subsequent normalization operations are based on the contour code of a connectivity analysis. The result is a normalized skeleton representation of the word image.

To achieve an appropriate input sequence to the HMM classifier a small window is moved over the normalized image representation. Local features detected in different areas of this window build a feature vector. A sequence of such feature vectors are the input for the statistical classifying system.

2.1 Iconic Operations

The first preprocessing step removes the main sources of scanning noise that consists of temporarily breakdown of scanning rows. This is done by applying a special filter on the binary image. The effects observed resemble the skin of a zebra – stripes of black and white rows. Small white inclusions having a height of 1 pixel are closed.

In order to facilitate the later processing of the outer contour, big steps at the outer contour are smoothed into a sequence of smaller steps like a staircase.

2.2 Connected Component Analysis

A binary connected component analysis [3] is performed transforming the binary image into a contour representation. The contour representation is given by an inclusion tree of the connected components describing white and black regions. The algorithm used is very efficient thus further noise reductions can be performed on a symbolic level rather than on an iconic without slowing down the process. Small inclusions in the frame like pepper and on the second level like salt can be removed without disturbing other parts of the image.

2.3 Skeletonization

The central concept for handwritten input patterns is the stroke. In the sample set the stroke width is generally rather small (approx. 3 Pixel). Therefore a skeleton algorithm will have sufficiently good results. The skeleton calculated coincides in most areas with the centerline of the stroke trace [4]. In difficult areas like crossing strokes and attaching strokes a post processing is needed. Therefore, it is important to preserve the local stroke width for each skeleton point [5, 6] .

The skeleton representation will be used in future systems for hypothesizing the writing movement. In the current system, it is taken as the representation of the pen's middle point.

2.4 Shear Angle Normalization

Slant is a common variation in handwritten words. The slant may vary along a word. But it is difficult to detect the slant for a small entity without knowing the letter sequence. Better results are achieved if one constant slant angle is estimated for one word. To reflect the general orientation of the strokes a smoother contour approximation is needed. A very efficient technique is based on a scan along algorithm, introduced by [7]. The slant angle is estimated using a modified Hough transformation of the contour [8].

The normalization is performed on the contour representation in an efficient manner.

2.5 Size Normalization

An important hint for the recognition process is the estimation of the number of characters and the ruler lines such as baseline, x-height and the height of ascenders and descenders.

For the estimation of the ruler lines straight lines are used as a first rough model. The baseline and the x-height line is calculated by a linear regression using the minima and maxima of the convex contour parts of the black regions. Points of descenders and ascenders will not coincide with the baseline and x-height line, respectively. This fact can be determined by the residual variance and the maximum distance of the points from the regression line. Skipping the point under discussion and calculating the regression line again until the fit is well enough solves this problem.

For estimating the number of characters a statistical classifier is adapted. The features are the Fourier descriptors of the black contour on the first level [9]. If the written word consists of several letters or letter groups each is handled separately. The total number of characters in a word is then given by the sum of all estimations.

2.6 Feature Extraction

After estimating global features and normalizing the image with respect to rotation, slant, size, and stroke width the sequence of micro features along the word shape is generated. Therefore, a feature selection window is moved along the shape of the word. This window keeps approximately the third of a character's width. The window itself is subdivided into five regions of interest.

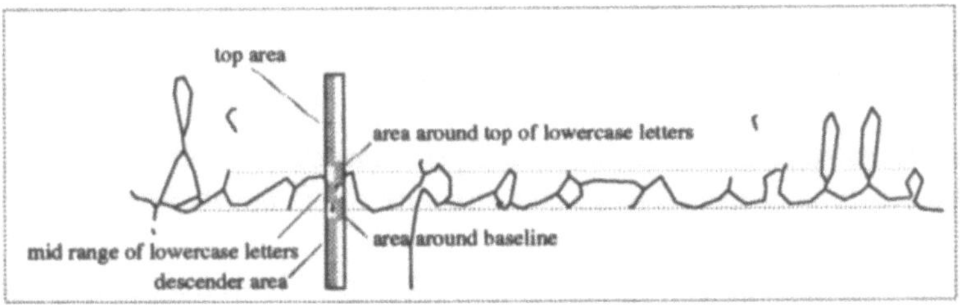

Fig. 1. Generating the feature vectors from the normalized example image

It is desired that the subwindows (see Fig. 1) overlap as well as two succeeding windows along the writing axis.

3 Hidden Markov Models

The enormous variance of handwriting is best handled by a statistical approach where collecting more learning samples will always increase the recognition performance. The sequence of fixed length feature vectors fits very well to the demands of Hidden Markov Models.

It must be distinguished between the learning and application phase of the system. During learning which is time consuming and done before applying the classifier four steps are distinguished:

- Vector Quantization
- Adaptation of HMM parameters
- Linear discriminant analysis
- Adaptation of HMM parameters

In a first step, the vector quantizer is adapted to the statistics of feature vectors with unsupervised learning. Then the HMM parameters are adapted. In the third step the linear discriminant analysis is adapted to clusters directly defined by Hidden Markov Models.

Now the system is ready to adjust the HMM parameters by a semi supervised learning. The word labels must be given to the system but *no segmentation* information. Thus system adaptation is time consuming for the computer but not for the system designer.

A model topology (states and transitions) must be defined. This is done in a systematic way. For each letter the same principal structure is defined. Four different gestalt models for each character class and one overall joker class are chosen according to four different types: uppercase, lowercase, script, and block print characters.

The parameters of the model emission and transition probabilities are estimated from the sample set by the forward/backward adaptation technique [1].

During classification the HMM is evaluated by a modified Viterbi algorithm.

4 First Results and Future Approach

The preprocessing algorithms show good performance in results as well as in the computation time needed. The chosen structure offers the additional property of parallelism in computation.

Several experiments with lexicons of 10, 100 and 1000 words on a test set with handwritten US city name word images from life mail (disjunct to the learning set) show a recognition performance of 95%, 85% and 66% respectively.

Reconstructing the writing trace from the binary image will give more reliable features for the HMM approach. These features offer the additional opportunity to apply recognition techniques known from the on-line field.

Furthermore we expect that a combination of our approach with a single character classifier and associative memories will improve our results.

References

1. Rabiner, L.R.: Tutorial on Hidden Markov Models and Selected Applications in Speech Recognition. Proc. of IEEE, Vol. 77, No. 2, (Feb. 1989)
2. Kaltenmeier, A.: Model Based Word Recognition in Speech Recognizing Systems with Large Vocabulary. VDI Fortschrittsberichte, Vol. 10, No. 174 (in German), (1992)
3. Mandler, E., Oberländer, M.F.: A single pass algorithm for fast contour coding of binary images. Proceedings of the 12th DAGM-Symposium (in German), (1990)
4. Cox, C.H., Coueignoux, P., Blesser B., Eden, M.: Skeletons: A Link Between Theoretical and Physical Letter Descriptions. Pattern Recognition, Vol. 15, No. 1, 11-22, (1982)
5. Zhang, T.Y., Suen, C.Y.: A Fast Parallel Algorithm for Thinning Digital Patterns. Communications of the ACM 27, Vol. 29, No. 3, 236-239, (March 1984)
6. Kwok, P.C.K.: A Thinning Algorithm by Contour Generation. Communications of the ACM, Vol. 31, No. 11, 1314-1324, (November 1988)
7. Wall, K., Danielsson, P.-E.: A New Method for Polygonal Approximations of Digitized Curves. Proceedings of the 3rd Scandinavian Conference on Image Analysis, (1983)
8. Gloger, J.: Use of the Hough Transform to Separate Merged Text/Graphics in Forms. Proc. of 11th IAPR Int. Conf. Pattern Recognition Vol.2, The Hague NL 268-271, (1992)
9. Zahn, C.T., Roskies, R.Z.: Fourier Descriptors for Plane Closed Curves. IEEE Transactions on computers, Vol. C-21, No. 3, 269-281, (March 1972)

Towards a Visual Recognition of Cursive Script

Mohamed Cheriet

Laboratoire d'Imagerie et de Modélisation Tridimensionnelle
Département de génie de la production automatisée
Université du Québec, École de technologie supérieure
4750, avenue Henri-Julien, Montréal (Québec), Canada, H2T 2C8

Abstract. This paper presents a new method for cursive script recognition based on the extraction of key letters which consist of the parts of the handwritten text which are singularities of handwriting. It focuses on the extraction of potentially meaningful shapes, corresponding to visual letters, in the recognition of cursive handwriting. First the key letters of a cursive word are found, such as b, f, p, q, F, t, etc; then a possible word based on these letters is selected. In the testing phase, there are 304 words from 74 cheques in our data base written by 40 writers. 276 words are correctly segmented, which is more than 90% successful segmentation. The problems leading to missegmentation are identified for further improvement.

Keywords: cursive script recognition, automatic reading of cheques, handwriting recognition, symbolic description, structural and syntactic methods.

1 Introduction

Computer based cursive script recognition has numerous applications in the industrial and service sectors and the problem is intrinsically challenging. In reviewing the literature, one can find that two fundamental approaches have been taken to recognize cursive scripts: (i) analytical (recognition of individual characters), and (ii) wholistic (recognition of the entire word). The analytical approach involves the segmentation of a word into the individual characters and recognizing each one separately. Therefore a character must first be extracted from the word before it can recognized. The wholistic approach involves the recognition of the word as a complete entity using global features of the word such as ascenders, descenders, loops, etc. [1]. Individual characters are not recognized as such but features are extracted to indicate which characters may be present in the word. This approach is considered to be nearer to the way humans read and has the advantage to avoid the difficul segmentation process. It is generally believed that none of these two approaches are sufficient to handle the large variety of handwriting styles found in practical application such as cheque processing. Therefore we aim at developing a new system for recognizing legal amounts written on bank cheques. It consists of a combination of both approaches: analytical and wholistic. This is based on key letters extraction. The key letters consist of the parts of the handwritten text which are singularities of handwriting. By processing the raw input data representing the handwritten text, the singular features: loops,ascenders, and descenders are first well defined and determined. Based on the latter, the key letters are then extracted. This paper focuses on this aspect of potentially meaningful shapes to deal with the recognition of cursive handwriting.

2 Processing chain for cursive script recognition

The goal of this research is to recognize the legal amounts in bank cheques. This is a highly complex problem. To cope with this, we have adopted a combined approach using both global and analytic methods. In the case of French and English bank cheques, a small dictionary (around 60 words) is used to reduce the complexity of the problem.

This new approach which uses the raw data of the input image, without any transformation, complements the approach developed by Simon et al. [4]. The latter performs efficient identification of features such as ends of lines, crossings and change of directions from the chain graph image representation. In the present approach, the raw data of the whole text is processed as one entity, and then key letters are extracted, identified, and subsequently used as filters to recognize the different word units of the input text. For instance, the key letters help to reduce the possibilities when comparing the input word symbolic description within the reference descriptions in the dictionary.

2.1 Input image handle, smoothing and connected component finding

The input document is scanned and stored as a binary image of pixel values «0» or «1». By applying the scheme described in Tang et al. [5], different items (the filled data) are extracted. The following discussion deals with the recognition of legal amounts only and any reference to images implies their binary images.

A smoothing filter is first applied to the input image. By following the outer contours, as well as the inner contours of holes related to each connected component, an algorithm is then applied in order to find in one pass the connected components. A set of attributes are computed for both connected components and holes such as: bounding box dimensions and positions, area and perimeter. The computation of these parameters allows for the rejection of small connected components and holes.

2.2 Finding ascenders and descenders

An improved version of the technique described in Cheriet [2], is developed in order to determine more accurately the ascenders and descenders. The latter can be estimated more reliably if they are computed on the whole text rather than on individual words. In fact, the outer contour of the smeared image S is first processed by median filters and analyzed, allowing determination of the body of the input text image. More details of the procedure are presented in Cheriet et al. [1].

2.3 Key letter extraction

From common knowledge of handwriting, the image of a word (a trace) can be formed by discrete characters, broken cursive (group of characters written with a single continuous motion), or a combination of both, or fully cursive. In the cursive tracing portions, letters are linked by ligatures. The purpose of the approach described below is to find a robust algorithm to determine and isolate these ligatures. The remainder of the trace will consist of key letters such as a, b, p, q, t ..., and portions of letters such as m, n, u, w, ... To tackle this problem, the following rule has been developed :

Ligatures are located in the extrema of the cursive tracing of handwritten words.

To do so, we find that the background of the image gives robust knowledge to tackle the variability in styles of handwriting, especially with local shape changes. Therefore, the above rule can be expressed in the following way :

Ligatures are delimited by faceup and/or facedown inter-stroke regions.

The approach described is efficient overall when visual inter-stroke regions or valleys contain several local extrema. Valleys are automatically found by performing two independent filtering steps : top-down filtering and bottom-up filtering, in order to define two types of valleys : faceup valley (FUV) and facedown valley (FDV). These filters are applied at the level of the main body of the handwritten text, in order to well delimit the ligatures within the cursive tracing portions of the text, [1].

For each BUV and FDV a minimal bounding box is computed. Then, the mean coordinates of pixels falling in a region three pixels high at the bottom (top) of the bounding box of the BUV (FDV) are computed. We refer to this pixel as MP. Consequently, the separating path is then generated by removing the stroke pixels from the MP pixel down in case of a FUV valley, and from the MP pixel up in the case of FDV. The result of the above analysis is that for a pair of (BUV, FDV) valleys, the two separating paths delimit well the ligature which is the purpose of this strategy.

After applying the procedure of separating paths, the key letters which are of interest, appear as shapes surrounding ascenders, descenders, or loops; we call their supports from the main body of the text minimum shapes or key letters. For example given the letter «h» written in script, this algorithm will extract the key letter or minimum shape «l». Figure 1 shows the principle step of key letters extraction.

2.4 Preliminary results and data base

In the testing phase, there are 304 words form 74 bank cheques in our data base written by 40 subjects. These testing data cover 39 words form the dictionary of 60 words used for French and English cheques. Since the writing styles differ from one another, the samples vary in size and curviness. Most of the key letters are extracted. 276 words are correctly segmented, that is more than 90% of successful segmentation. Most of the errors were caused by the existence of broken strokes in the input image, the failure of the threshold, empirically computed and used in the smearing process, especially when using thick point pens. Since the segmenter is based on the valleys, their finding can be improved to reduce the errors, especially when a sequence of different depth valleys occur. Another difficulty arises when two adjacent key letters touch each other, e.g. «t» and «h» in a cursive handwritten word «three». The response of the algorithm can only be the key letter «th» as one entity. In this case, the recognizer may involve some linguistic knowledge to deal with such problems.

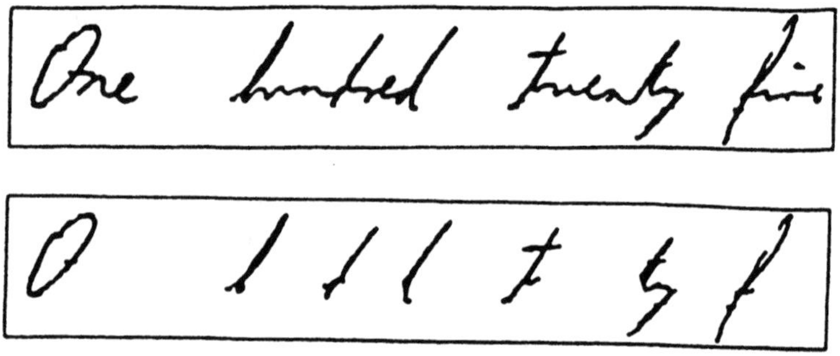

Fig. 1 Key letters of cursive words

2.5 Symbolic description

It is easy at this level to obtain a chain describing each extracted word from the whole text from left to right:

1. Each key letter is given to a specialized operator to be recognized.
2. MP points generated for segmentation in the previous step, may help to estimate the letter number located in the regular part of the word.

Actually we are developing a robust algorithm to tackle the recognition of the extracted key letters. The interesting aspect at this level, is that the operator can profit form certain information already computed in the previous steps of the system. This may help to speed up the recognition process. On the other hand, the symbolic description should contain key letter labels after recognition as well as the number and the nature of MP points, as the following : $(A^*(a \mid b)^*)^+$ where ,

A denotes a set of possible labels of the input key letter, a denotes a top-down segmentation,

b denotes a bottom-up segmentation.

3 Recognition process

From the above analysis related to the generation of symbolic descriptions, the recognition process should be able to benefit from the existence of key letters to be used as filters when comparing the unknown words with prototypes form the dictionary. This may reduce the number of possible candidates. At this level, the program should exploit the number and the nature of MP points to refine the final decision.

An experiment was performed to study the feasibility of this approach. Segmentation results indicate that the global approach might be suitable as a filtering process in its first stage. The objective would be to reduce the size of the dictionary to a small number of candidates that could be further processed by more powerful recognition techniques. This experiment was limited in scope because the investigation of this combined approach is in its preliminary stage. Initial results are encouraging and will lead to further development of this technique. The power of this approach is that it can handle the different styles of handwriting.

4 Concluding remarks

A comprehensive approach for recognition of cursive script was outlined. A study of handwriting styles demonstrated that successful reading of handwritten text requires the recognition of its different components, from discrete writing to fully cursive writing. An application related to the reading of legal amounts on bank cheques is considered.

A combined approach, with analytic and global methods, was presented that is suitable for such a domain. In fact this approach does not rely on lexical module to be used by this system. Thus contextual post-processing with n-grams will be used. Some early results were presented. Future work will include more complete implementation and testing of this promising approach.

References

1. Cheriet, M., Suen, C.Y.: Extraction of key letters for cursive script recognition. In Press. Pattern Recognition Letters, 14:11 (1993).
2. Cheriet, M., Suen, C.Y.: Automated entry system for handwritten documents. Proceedings, Spain 1991. Int. Conf. on Intelligent Text and Image Handling, pp. 211-223. Universitat Autonoma Di Barcelona, Barcelona, Spain: April 1991.
3. Hull J.J., Ho T.K., Favata J.F., Govindaraju V., Srihari S.N.: Combination of segmentaion-based and wholistic handwritten word recognition algorithms. Proceedings, France 1991. IWFHR II, pp. 229-240. Bonas, France: Sept. 1991.
4. Simon, J.C., Baret, O.: Handwriting recognition as an application of regularities and singularities in line pictures. Proceedings, France 1990. IWFHR I, pp. 23-38, CENPARMI, Concordia University, Canada: April 1990.
5. Tang, Y.Y., Yan, C.D., Cheriet, M., Suen, C.Y.: Automatic analysis and inderstanding of documents. In: C.H. Chen, L.F. Pau, and P.S.P. Wang (eds.). Handbook of PR and Computer Vision, World Scientific, Singapore, 1993.

A Hierarchical Handwritten Word Segmentation

Gilles F. Houle

Arthur D. Little Inc., United States Postal Service, 955 L'Enfant Plaza SW
Suite 4200, Washington DC 20024-2119

Abstract. This paper presents a technique to hierarchically segment handwritten words. Handwritten words are broken down into either concave or convex segments called *p-strokes* (partial strokes). P-strokes are recombined to form *Windows of Observation (WO)*, where the number of p-strokes defines the window size. Once a word is segmented into a sequence of p-strokes, window of observation of different sizes are scanned stroke-by-stroke across the word in a fully overlapped manner, producing a stream of potential characters.

Unsupervised clustering of window size 1 to 5 resulted in a codebook of 461 representative windows of observation. Secondly, supervised clustering using 25,000 handwritten alphacharacters resulted in a set of 2,525 prototypes. The segmentation and the clustering techniques are described in this paper.

Keywords. Off-line handwriting recognition, Segmentation-based OCR

1. Introduction

In a previous paper [4] a handwritten word recognition based on collective learning theory [1] was developed to recognize several instantiations of the handwritten word "DETROIT" from a lexicon of 50 words. Good discrimination (99.99% using student-t test) was obtained between words of Detroit from other words. As a result, a powerful technique based on window of observation allowed to overcome the segmentation problem inherent to handwriting. As an extension of that work a segmentation technique to perform word recognition with and without linguistic contextual information is presented.

Section 2. states the problems associated with off-line handwriting recognition. Then Section 3. gives details of an hierarchical handwritten word segmentation. Section 4. describes the unsupervised and supervised clustering techniques. Finally, conclusions and future work are discussed in Section 5.

2. Handwriting Recognition---The Challenge

The challenge in performing handwriting recognition [2-7] comes from the combination of *graphic, dynamic*, and *linguistic* problems. The *graphic* problem consists of recognizing several character topology and shape variations that resulted from evolution of handwriting, the imprecise movement of the arm, and the external (e.g., application) and internal (e.g., feelings, mood) context. The *dynamic* problem is inherent to techniques that require segmentation of a handwritten word into letters. Such segmentation is fraught with ambiguity. It was pointed out that segmentation is more challenging than recognition [3]. Holistic handwritten word-recognition techniques attempt to avoid the dynamic problem.

Because the segmentation and the recognition processes are tightly coupled, high recognition performance of isolated letters and good reject rate are essential. Although the contextual information (*linguistic* problem) is extremely important, its power shouldn't shadow the very high performance achieved by human even without context. For instance, the following word is still readable by human an yet does not follow English syntax.

Fig. 2.1 Word *Bfztpr* with no linguistic context

Lecolinet [5] proposed to recognize *graphemes*, which are character components resulting from a given segmentation process. By training on consistently segmented components the segmentation-based classifier can overcome some of the problems resulting from an ambiguous segmentation.

3. Hierarchical Segmentation

An earlier paper [4] presented an algorithm to extract the curvature of character contours using the contour chain code. A least-mean square fit of the contour (x(t) , y(t)) chain code is computed using parametric quadratic splines. The curvature is then obtained by:

$$\kappa = \frac{\dot{x}(t)\ddot{y}(t) - \ddot{x}(t)\dot{y}(t)}{((\dot{x}(t))^2 + (\dot{y}(t))^2)^{3/2}}$$

Zero-crossing points of the first derivative of the curvature (inflection points) are used to break the contour into segments of similar curvature called *p-strokes* (partial strokes). Creation of p-stroke is in effect a transformation from sub-symbolic to symbolic representation, i.e., a global (rather than point-wise) description is used. The attributes computed for each p-stroke from the spline functions are: the vertical position, the horizontal position relative to the neighbor, the tangent vector of the stroke, the absolute curvature, the first derivative of the curvature estimation along the contour. These are converted into fuzzy values describing characteristics of a p-stroke. To solve the dynamic problem inherent to cursive handwriting we define a *window of observation* to be of a finite number of adjacent p-strokes that form the focus of attention. The size of the window is given by the number of p-strokes regrouped. Windows of observation of different sizes are moved dynamically from left to right one p-stroke at the time. A study of the number of p-strokes for several handwritten letters indicates that 1 to 10 p-strokes is needed to define a letter. On average there are approximately 3.5 p-strokes per character. The same technique is applied to decompose handwritten words into p-strokes as shown.

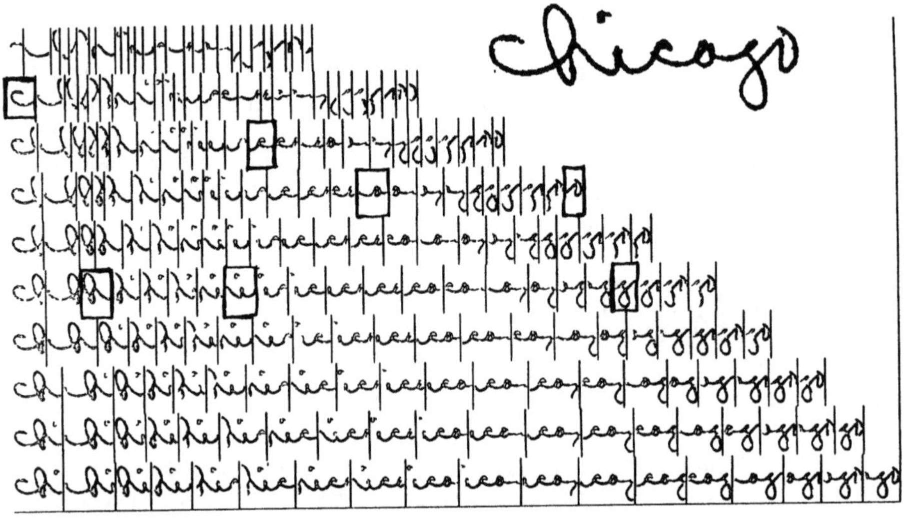

Fig. 3.1 Windows of Observation---Exhaustive Segmentation Map

4. Clustering Techniques

The proposed approach illustrated in fig. 4.1 begins with an unsupervised clustering to generate a representative set (or codebook) of windows of observation. Because larger window size requires huge amount of memory to store several possible shape variations needed for clustering purposes, the window size was

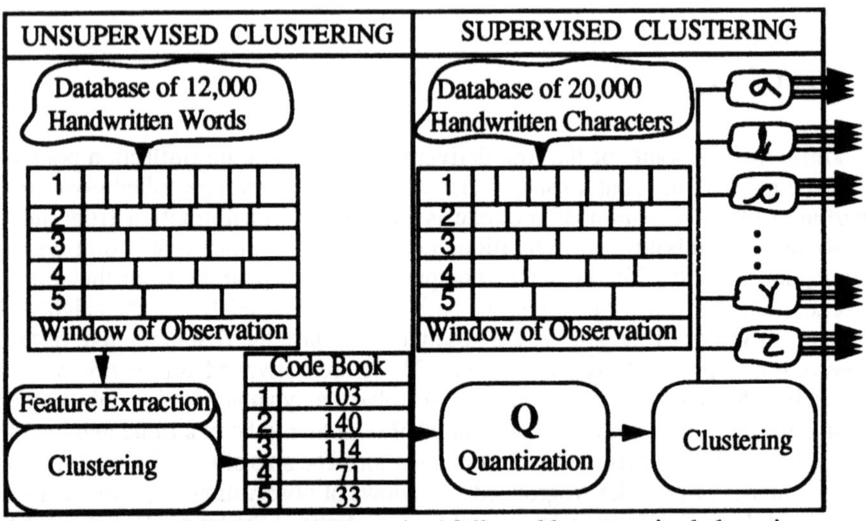

Fig. 4.1 System Overview - Unsupervised followed by supervised clustering

limited to 5 p-strokes. Supervised clustering was then used to create prototypes of isolated handwritten characters represented by the codebook.

4.1 Unsupervised Clustering

The unsupervised clustering process (independent for each window size) is performed by adding a new incoming window to the nearest center according to a linear correlation measure. However if the nearest center is further than 0.95, a new center is created. The following clusters were progressively formed using up to 2 M windows of observation (WOs).

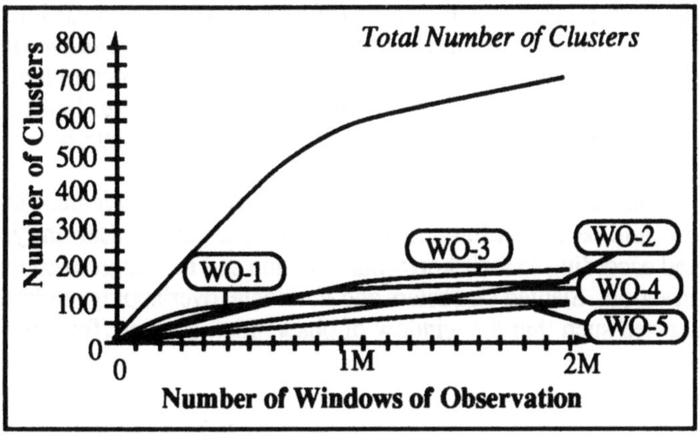

Fig. 4.2 Unsupervised Clustering

Fig. 4.2 indicates that after 2M WOs only the first three window sizes have reached some saturation level. Finally, the overall set of clusters was reduced from 735 to 461 clusters (i.e. 103 one-stroke, 140 two-strokes, 114 three-strokes, 71 four-strokes, and 33 five-strokes) by removing clusters with less than 20 samples.

4.2 Supervised Clustering

During the supervised clustering, handwritten isolated characters are decomposed into p-strokes and then recombined to form overlapping window of observation of size 1 to 5. Once an input WO is quantized by the codebook, the resulting set of vectors must be labelled (a-z , A-Z). To performed that task, a set of labelled isolated handwritten letters were also quantized by the codebook. Then a similarity measure was computed between two sets (input pattern and stored prototype) both expressed as a function of the codebook.

4.3 Matching Process

An input pattern (character or word) is broken into p-strokes and then recombined to form window of observation from size 1 to 5. The information in each window of observation is quantized using the codebook. Then the system attempts to recognize each window of observation using the supervised clusters. The similarity measure between a reference patterns *A* and a window of observation *B* is given by:

$$\Psi(A,B) = \sum_{i=1}^{5} \sum_{j=1}^{N_1(i)} \max_{1 \leq k \leq N_2(i)} [r(a_{ij}, b_{ik})]$$

where *r(a,b)* is a linear correlation measure between *a* and *b*. *N(i)* is the number of window of size *i*.

5. Conclusions and Future Work

A technique to break down a handwritten pattern (of a character or a word) into segments (p-strokes) of similar curvature was described. Then *window of observation* of different size was introduced to overcome the segmentation problem. Clustering of window size ranging from 1 to 5 p-strokes was proposed to build a codebook, and allow matching between an input pattern and a reference pattern.

The analysis of preliminary results indicates that the biggest improvement in the proposed system would be to redefine the window of observation. Currently, the p-strokes are sorted according to their horizontal position and then regrouped to form window of observation. Slanted characters and horizontal overlapping strokes get misplaced when sorted such that the window of observation does not form the best isolated character.

REFERENCES

1. Bock, P.: The Emergence of Artificial Cognition: An Introduction to Collective Learning, World Scientific Publishing Company, 1993

2. Edelman S., Flash, T., Ulmann S.: Reading Cursive Handwriting by Alignment of Letter Prototypes, International Journal of Computer Vision 303-331, 1990.

3. Frishkopf, L.S., and Harmon, L.D., Cherry, C.: Machine Reading of Cursive Script, Information Theory, Butterworth, London, 310-316, 1961

4. Houle, G.F., Radelat, C., Resnick, S., Bock, P.: A Handwritten Word Recognition using Collective Learning Theory, Frontier of Handwriting 1993

5. Lecolinet, E., Cretez, J.: A Grapheme-based Segmentation Technique for Cursive Script Recognition, Proceedings of ICDAR 91, 740-748, 1991.

6. Simon, J.C., Baret, O.: Formes regulières et Singulières; application à la reconnaissance de l'écriture manuscrite, C.R. Académie de Paris, t. 309 (Série II) 1901-1906, 1989.

7. Srihari, S.N., Bozinovic, R.: A Multi-Level Perception Approach to Reading Cursive Script, Artificial Intelligence, 217-255, 1987.

Part 4

Contextual methods in handwriting recognition

Cursive Word Recognition: Methods and Strategies

Eric Lecolinet† and Olivier Baret‡

† E.N.S. Telecom Paris, 46 rue Barrault, 75013 Paris, France.
‡ A.2.I.A., 10 rue de l'Université, 75007 Paris, France.

1. Introduction

Although researchers have been working on the field of cursive script recognition (CSR) for more than thirty years, existing systems are still limited to restricted applications and this field of research remains quite open. This paper aims to present the basic principles of the techniques used so far and to classify them according to the type of strategy they are based on. It will mainly focus on off-line recognition although most of the strategies presented here are also valid for on-line recognition.

1.1. On-line and Off-line Recognition

CSR applications fall into two categories: on-line systems and off-line systems. Cursive script recognition is used in two different kinds of applications: on-line and off-line recognition systems. In the first case, handwriting is produced by using a special device (like an electronic stylus on a notepad) while off-line recognition deals with digitized images (produced by a scanner or a camera). Off-line recognition can be considered as the most general case: no special device is required for writing and "signal" interpretation is independent from signal generation, like in human recognition.

On-line recognition presents several interesting characteristics. First, recognition is performed on one-dimensional data instead of two-dimensional images. On-line data is one-dimensional in nature while off-line recognition deals with two-dimensional images. The writing line is represented by a sequence of dots whose location is function of time. This has several important consequences:

— the writing order is available and can be used by the recognition process,

— temporal information, like velocity can also be taken into account,

— the writing line has no width: input data constitutes a kind of "ordered skeleton".

Additionally, penlifts can also help recognition.

Two main philosophies have been applied to on-line recognition. The first one is *analysis-by-synthesis*, also called recognition by generation. This theory, which was first introduced by Mermelstein & Eden [71] bases recognition on the *modeling* of handwriting generation. This field nowadays constitutes a very important area of research but which is without the scope of the present paper (methods only specific to on-line recognition will not be considered in this survey). Major research in this field has been done by Plamondon & al. [82] [2], Morasso, Schomaker, Teulings & al. [106] [108] etc ...

The second philosophy consists in applying off-line methods to on-line recognition systems. In this case, temporal information is not taken into account except for ordering strokes in some systems. Although feature extraction is performed in a different way and some specificities are introduced in the recognition scheme, such systems follow overall strategies which remain similar to those implemented in off-line recognition. Thus, in addition to off-line methods, similar on-line strategies will also be considered in this paper.

Recently, several methods have been proposed that extract temporal information from static off-line data [19] [38] [8]. In section 1.4, we will discuss those methods.

1.2. The Influence of the Size of the Vocabulary and of the Number of Writers

Machine recognition being obviously far less efficient than human recognition, a tradeoff has to be found between the size of the vocabulary and the number of writers. This tradeoff greatly depends on the field of application:

— as they are mainly designed for personal computers, notepads and other dedicated interacting devices, on-line systems may limit recognition capability to a few users. Recognition is then said to be *mono-* or *multi-scriptor*. In compensation, the size of the vocabulary can be relatively large: up to 20 000 words for certain commercial softwares. An intermediate approach is also proposed by some systems: recognition is basically *omni-scriptor*, but can be more specifically "tuned" to the writing of a few frequent users.

— on the contrary, off-line systems usually require *omni-scriptor* recognition, that is to say the ability to recognize any style of writing without prior word training. This is especially true for postal or banking applications (like mail sorting or check reading) which constitute most of the existing systems or research themes. In this case, constraints are laid on the size of the vocabulary which cannot exceed a few hundred words (up to 1000 words for postal applications, but only a few tens for check reading).

1.3. Categories of Handwriting

Another major constraint is the category of handwriting that recognition systems are able to handle. Constraints can concern the quality of the writing (i.e. careful handwriting versus unconstrained handwriting) but also the style. Tappert proposed five categories to classify handwriting:

— boxed discrete characters

— spaced discrete characters

— run-on discretely written characters

— pure cursive script writing

— mixed cursive and discrete.

Many on-line commercial systems already available only deal with the first two types of writing. But recent systems are now designed for the recognition of mixed cursive writing (i.e. of type 5). This is especially true for off-line systems because of the types of applications which are considered (as in the previous subsection). This also the subject this paper will mainly focus on.

1.4. Pre-Processing and Feature Extraction

For off-line systems, available pre-processings are: binarization, noise filtering, skew correction and slant correction. Skew and slant correction rely on the evaluation of the average slope of horizontal/vertical lines. This slope can be estimated on the vertical parts of a contour-description, after a Hough Transform or directional histograms. For on-line systems, polygonization or resampling are common.

For many systems, line information is required. Some methods only look for a sequence of straight segments, others require a graph representation. Lines can be extracted by means of a global Hough transform, or through skeletonization. New methods have also been proposed on that topic, such as [94], [77].

Some new approaches have been proposed, that extract temporal information from off-line data. All of them define heuristics about handwriting such as smooth continuation of stroke direction and curvature across intersection points. A stroke graph representation is thus necessary.

Doermann and Rosenfeld [19] use a gray scale off-line image and a stroke graph built with an edge cross-section method analog to the one proposed in [102]. Local clues are related to ink deposit variations which may reflect the direction of a stroke. Regional clues involve heuristics about the writing process such as smooth changing of curvature across a junction point. Global clues involve consistency constraints on the whole graph. This "Stroke Recovery Platform" has been used for overlapping lines separation in [20].

Govindaraju and al [38] use a skeletonized binary image, which is equivalent to a stroke graph. Heuristics are applied on the skeleton in order to segment it into ordered strokes. Character templates are proposed, based on a temporal description of strokes.

Boccignone and al [8] also start from a skeleton which has been smoothed with polygonization. Good continuity criterion is combined with width variation of stroke. Variations in length of polygonal segments along a stroke are also taken into account.

1.5. Organization of the Next Sections

The next section contains a discussion about the strategies used for CSR, and their adaptation to different kinds of problems. Section 3 will present the major methods and techniques developed for cursive script recognition. This section is itself divided into three subsections corresponding to the different categories of strategies previously described. Hybrid systems combining different strategies will be considered in section 4. Finally, section 5 will present available results and will then come the conclusion.

2. Strategies

Two main types of strategies have been applied to the CSR problem since the beginning of research in this field: the holistic approach and the analytical approach. In the first case recognition is globally performed on the whole representation of words and there is no attempt to identify characters individually. In the second case, words are not considered as a whole, but as sequences of smaller size units. Recognition is not directly performed at word level but at an intermediate level dealing with these units which are usually more or less closely related to characters. These units can be of different kinds according to the method, like: graphemes, segments, pseudo-letters, etc ...

As they rely on the recognition of intermediate word units, analytical methods are also said to be segmentation based. In this case, "segmentation" refers to "letter" or "word unit" segmentation, that is to say some kind of intermediate unit that is considered as a whole by a recognizing step and which has to be separated from the rest of the word. However, the word "segmentation" can be confusing as all pattern recognition methods basically perform some kind of segmentation. For instance, holistic methods usually perform feature extraction, which can also be considered to be segmentation stage. The main difference lies in the level of abstraction of the segmented elements: features (that is to say low level elements) in the case of holistic methods, versus pseudo-letters in the case of analytical methods. This theoretical difference is also significant from the practical point of view as it can also lead to very different schemes with different properties and performances (as will be seen in further sections).

2.1. Holistic Strategies

Holistic methods follow a two-step scheme:

— the first step performs feature extraction,

— the second step performs global recognition by comparing the representation of the unknown word with those of the references stored in the lexicon.

This scheme leads to two important practical consequences:

- as letter segmentation is avoided and recognition performed in a global way, these methods are usually considered to be tolerant to the dramatic deformations that affect unconstrained cursive scripts.
- as they do not deal directly with letters but only with words, recognition is necessarily constrained to a specific lexicon of words.

The second point is especially critical when training on word samples is required. In this case, the lexicon cannot be automatically updated from letter information. A training stage is thus mandatory to expand or modify the lexicon of possible words. This property makes this kind of method more suitable for applications where the lexicon is statically defined (and not likely to change), like check recognition. They can also be used for on-line recognition on a personal computer (or notepad), the recognition algorithm being then tuned to the writing of a specific user.

More general applications require a dynamic generation stage of holistic descriptions. In this case, a specific stage must be used to convert any word from its ASCII form to the holistic representation required by the considered recognition algorithm. Word representation must then be generated from generic information about letter and ligature representations using a reconstruction model. Word reconstruction is required by all applications dealing with a dynamically defined lexicon, like for instance postal applications where the list of possible city names is derived from zip code recognition. Several studies address this problem and will be considered in the section devoted to the description of holistic methods.

2.2. Analytical Strategies

Analytical strategies deal with several levels of representation corresponding to increasing levels of abstraction. Three levels of representation are usually implicitly considered: the feature level, the word level and an intermediate level dealing with subparts of the words (that we will call "word units"). The way these units are defined and extracted from the whole word is at the very core of analytical recognition. A common rule is that these units must be easily related to characters in order to make recognition independent from a specific vocabulary. Because recognition is then basically letter-based, the vocabulary can be defined dynamically (in a symbolical form which can vary) and no word training is required.

Many kinds of word units (and designations) have been proposed so far. Some methods use letters, others use graphical units called graphemes, segments or pseudo-letters. A major difference between analytical methods lies in the way word unit segmentation is performed. This makes analytical approaches fall into two main categories:

— analytical approaches with *explicit* (or *external*) segmentation,

— analytical approaches with *implicit* (or *internal*) segmentation.

In the first case, words are *explicitly* segmented into letters (or pseudo-letters) which are then recognized individually, while in the second case segmentation and recognition take place at the same time.

2.2.1. Analytical Approaches with Explicit Segmentation

The first step deals directly with pixel (or signal) information in order to detect features. Then these features are compared to class prototypes to recognize the letters contained in the word. Contextual high-level knowledge (that is to say lexical, syntactic or semantic knowledge) is then used at the end of the process to ensure proper word identification.

This category of methods includes the three following steps:

— external segmentation of the word into smaller units (segments, graphemes...),

— individual recognition of these units,

— contextual post-processing (CPP) using lexical, syntactic or semantic knowledge,

The main advantage of the explicit approach is that segmented units can be recognized using a classical OCR technique. Its main drawback is that erroneous segmentation may lead to incorrect recognition. Moreover, as the segmented units are recognized and labeled individually, subtle information about how they differ from the ideal references may be definitively lost instead of being efficiently used by the contextual post-processor to correct possible mistakes.

Contextual post-processing is performed at the end of the process to ensure proper word identification. The techniques used may be of two kinds:

— Orthographic correction techniques using the statistics of the vocabulary (methods mainly based on n-grams frequencies, on Markov Models and the Viterbi algorithm)

— Direct comparison with a lexicon (methods using algorithms based on Dynamic Programming like Edit Distance, DP-matching, etc ..)

In theory, as no lexicon is used in the first case, any word of the considered language can be recognized, while recognition is limited to the words contained in the lexicon in the second case. However, the drawback of statistical methods is that they may possibly produce non existing words. A dictionary lookup is thus necessary and alternative choices have to be considered in case of failure. But still, these techniques can save much computation time for large vocabularies.

A classical remark is that explicit methods lead to the famous paradox according to which "it is necessary to segment to recognize, but it is also necessary to recognize to segment". However these approaches may be justified by visual evidence: objective segmentation marks (like ligatures between letters) really exist in cursive scripts and make the reading process easier, even for humans. According to the principles of perceptual organization and the Gestalt laws, most of the characters should be segmentable without recognition. Thus, these systems usually follow a "double step" segmentation strategy:

— first, the segmentation step explicitly divides the words into smaller units close to characters,

— then, final "segmentation" is performed implicitly at the contextual stage taking simultaneously into account the possible relationships between segments and characters and the lexical constraints of the vocabulary.

2.2.2. Analytical Approaches with Implicit Segmentation

Such methods also segment words into individual units (which are usually letters). But the main difference is that they perform recognition-based segmentation: letter segmentation is then a by-product of letter recognition. The main interest of this category of methods is that they bypass the segmentation problem: no complex segmentation algorithm has to be built and no recognition error may occur because of incorrect segmentation. The basic principle of analytical methods is derived from [14] where a mobile window of variable size is used to provide "tentative segmentations" which are confirmed or not by character recognition.

Word level knowledge can be brought in during the recognition-segmentation stage. This contextual knowledge can either be introduced in a statistical way, by using a lexicon, or even in both ways simultaneously.

Statistical representation has become very popular these last few years with the use of Hidden Markov Models. In these models, contextual information is represented by means of transitional letter probabilities. A specific subsection will be devoted to this important field of research.

2.3. Top-down Versus Bottom-up Strategies

Another point of view is to consider whether these strategies follow a bottom-up or a top-down recognition scheme [92]. Because they perform recognition by a direct comparison with the lexicon of descriptions (without including any intermediate recognition stage) holistic methods have often been considered as following a top-down strategy. Conversely, as they often deal with hierarchical representations (features, letters, words) processed at successive stages, analytical methods are usually seen as bottom-up strategies.

However, holistic methods still incorporate a bottom-up phase as they transform the initial word image (or signal) into a set of features, while some analytic methods deal simultaneously with segmentation, recognition and contextual analysis. So, it can be said that most techniques used today are somewhat hybrid and do not strictly fall into any of these two categories. We will thus consider holistic methods as being "mostly" top-down" and analytical methods as being "mostly" bottom-up.

However, "pure" top-down approaches have also been proposed ([67] [63]) and will be considered in a specific section.

3. Methods and Techniques

3.1. Holistic Methods

3.1.1. Early Studies

Whole word recognition was introduced by Earnest [23] in the beginning of the sixties. Although it was designed for on-line recognition, his method followed an off-line methodology: data was gathered by means of a "photo-style" in a binary matrix (no temporal information was used). The method was based on a comparison of a collection of simple features extracted from the whole word with a lexicon of "codes" representing the "theoretical" shape of the possible words. Feature extraction was based on the determination of the "middle zone" of the words (that is to say the horizontal area that does not contain any vertical extension): ascenders and descenders were found by considering the part of the writing exceeding this zone and internal loops were detected in the included part. This global representation was then compared to those of the lexicon using a transcoding table describing all the usual ways of writing letters.

Another on-line technique proposed by Miller [72] in 1971 was based on a decomposition of the words into macro-feature segments. These segments constituted a set of basic writing units whose combination was assumed to describe the shape of any existing word. They were obtained by shape analysis and were not related to characters (for instance a single feature could be part of several characters). The segments were then encoded to a value representing the successive directions of their contour and angular distance was used for global comparison with the references of the lexicon.

Brown and Ganapathy [11] used features vectors to represent word characteristics in a global way. All the extracted features (which consist in extensions, cups, strokes ...) are related to two sets of overlapping windows which divide the word into equal parts. The number of windows is derived from an estimate of the number of characters contained in the word. Classification is then done on these feature vectors using K-Nearest Neighbors.

3.1.2. Hints, Propositions and Remarks

These three methods are interesting because they introduce several techniques which are still used by current methods (even if calculations are now done in a more sophisticated way). For instance, many techniques still use middle zone determination to detect the ascenders and descenders of the words. The type of features extracted also remains globally the same: ascenders, descenders, directional strokes, cusps, diacritical marks, etc ... Angular differences are also still used for on-line recognition.

On the other hand, the main drawback of these early techniques (and especially the first two ones) lies in the the way they perform comparison between hypotheses and references. The techniques used were not flexible enough and were generally unable to take into account strong deformations of the writing (or segmentation errors in the second case).

More efficient techniques, which were originally introduced for speech recognition are now commonly used. These techniques are based on Dynamic Programming and essentially fall into two categories:

— methods based on distance measurements

— methods based on a probabilistic framework.

The first type of method is based on Edit Distance, DP-matching or similar algorithms while the second one uses Markov or Hidden Markov Chains.

3.1.3. Dynamic Programming and Edit Distance

Dynamic Programming (DP) is a general technique for solving optimization problems. It has been used for many applications in the field of pattern recognition and especially in speech and character recognition. The methods presented in this subsection are based on a specific algorithm called Edit Distance (ED) which was introduced by Wagner and Fischer [109] for speech recognition. Note that other important algorithms, like the Viterbi algorithm [31] which is used to process Markov Chains, are also based on Dynamic Programming.

Edit Distance is a matching algorithm which evaluates similarity (by computing a "distance") between two strings of symbols. Given a set of elementary transformations between the symbols of the two strings (and an associated cost), this algorithm provides the best sequence of elementary transformations necessary to transform the first string into the second one. The cost associated with this optimal transformation gives the "Edit Distance" between the two strings. Moreover, Wagner and Fischer proved that ED defined "real" distance (and was really optimal) under certain assumptions. Many variants (or earlier versions) of this algorithm have been studied like the Levenshtein distance or the DP-matching or "non-linear-elastic-matching" techniques which are suboptimal algorithms.

Given two strings X = X1 X2 ... Xn and Y = Y1 Y2 ... Ym, Edit Distance was originally based on the three elementary transformations:

— substitution of a symbol Xi into Yj with the associated cost d(i,j)
— deletion of a symbol Xi with the associated cost d(i,@) ("@" being the null symbol)
— insertion of a symbol Yj with the associated cost d(@,j)

ED is then computed using the recursive formula (ED(i,j) represents the distance between substrings X1..Xi and Y1...Yj):

$$ED(i,j) = \min \begin{cases} ED(i-1,j-1) + d(i,j) \\ ED(i-1,j) + d(i,@) \\ ED(i,j-1) + d(@,j) \end{cases}$$

$$\text{with } ED(0,0) = 0$$

Such a technique was employed by Moreau & al. for a holistic recognition method which was part of a larger system [74][84]. Words were represented globally by a list of features indicating the presence of ascenders, descenders, directional strokes and closed loops. In order to take into account y-location, the word was divided into three horizontal zones separated by two guidelines which were not mere straight lines, but smooth curves following the central part of the word, even if it was slanted or irregular in size. Relative y-location (to the guidelines) was associated to every feature and uncertainty coefficients were introduced to make this representation more tolerant to distorsion by avoiding binary decisions. Finally, matching was performed globally on the dictionary of encoded references by means of Edit Distance. Variants of this technique have been included in two hybrid systems, one for check recognition and another one for city name identification.

Similar systems were also developed by Paquet & Lecourtier [79] and by Leroux and al. [65] for check recognition. Final decision was based on Dynamic Programming in both methods but the features used were different. In the first case they were based on the notion of "guiding points", which are defined as the intersection of the letters and the median line of the word. In the second case, features were derived from the contours of words.

Camillerapp & al. [13] used graph representation to describe cursive words. Graphs were deduced from a skeleton. Horizontal and vertical locations were also taken into account and two-dimensional tree-to-tree comparison was eventually performed using Dynamic Programming.

Madhvanath and Govindaraju recently designed a holistic method for lexicon filtering [69]. The aim of this method is not to find "the best solution" but to reduce the size of the lexicon (which is then processed using another technique). Representation is based on *wordgraphs*, whose nodes correspond to feature attributes, an associated scalar or positional value and a confidence measurement. Lexicon words (which share the same representation) are "predicted" by using heuristic rules. Constrained bipartite matching is performed using a possible association matrix. Entries of the lexicon are ranked by combining three measures of goodness called: Confidence of Match, Closeness of Match and Degree of Mismatch. The system achieves 50% size reduction with under 2% error.

3.1.4. Markov Models and Probabilistic Methods

One of the first CSR systems using Markov Models was developed by Farag [27] in 1979. In this method (which was designed for on-line recognition), each word is seen as a sequence of oriented strokes obtained by using a graphic tablet. All strokes are of similar length and are represented using the Freeman code. The model of representation is a non stationary Markov Chain of the first or second order. Each word of the lexicon is represented as a list of stochastic transition matrixes. Each matrix corresponds to an interval of time and contains the transition probabilities from the (j)th stroke to the following one. The eight directions constitute the states of the Markov Chain and the initial matrix contains the a priori probabilities of the first stroke of the word. The recognized word is the reference Wi of the lexicon which maximizes the joint probability P(Z,Wi) where Z is the unknown word. Using Bayes formula, this is equivalent to multiplying a priori probability P(Wi) by conditional probability P(Z/Wi) which is also the product of the corresponding elements of the transition matrixes computed for reference word Wi.

More recently, Hidden Markov Models (HMM) became very popular in CSR. Nag, Wong and Fallside [75] used this technique for the recognition of literal digits. This system was also on-line and features were represented using an angular representation. Many other methods are based on HMMs, but are classified (an described) in the section devoted to analytical methods with implicit segmentation.

Gilloux and Leroux [34] use Markov Chains for off-line cheque recognition. Several Markov models are used at different recognition stages (word recognition and cheque amount recognition). Context is taken into account via prior probabilities of words and word trigrams.

Another method for the recognition of noisy images of isolated words such as in cheques was recently proposed by Gorsky in [37]. In the learning stage, lines are extracted from binary images of words and accumulated in prototypes called *holographs*. The technique used for line extraction has been presented in [94]. One prototype is used for each class of words. The vocabulary is fixed and small (less than 30 different words). During the test phase, correlation is used to obtain a distance between an unknown word and each word prototype. Using these distances, each candidate word can be represented in the prototype space. Each class is approximated with a Gaussian density inside this space. For the word under recognition, the probability that it belongs to each class is calculated using those densities. Other simple holistic features (ascenders and descenders, loops, length of the word) are also used and combined with this main method.

Lastly, Houle presented a holistic approach based on Collective Learning Systems (CLS) theory [50]. In this method, a set of fuzzy features is extracted from an observation window which is slided along the word to train a collective learning automaton. This observation window is centered around the successive strokes of the word (which are extracted by analyzing the curvature of the contour) in order to produce a stream of overlapping samples. This method was initially used to discriminate between "Detroit" and "non-Detroit" words taken from real mail.

3.2. Analytical Methods with Explicit Segmentation

Analytical recognition has quite a long history: it was already studied by Frishkopf and Harmon at Bell Laboratories at the very beginning of the sixties for on-line recognition. Their study is probably one of the very first attempts to tackle the difficult problem of character segmentation which is based on "landmark" extraction (like ascenders and descenders) and letter width estimation. Words are then divided into segments of similar width which are centered around the pre-detected landmarks. However, it must be noted that this scheme does not perfectly work with letters "u", "n", "m" ... as they do not contain landmarks.

Letter recognition was done using a decision tree that involved structural features such as: vertical and retrograde strokes, cusps, closures, diacritical marks. The vertical location of these features was also taken into consideration by separating the word into three horizontal zones: the middle, upper and lower zones.

As the authors noticed that many character combinations were not legible, (they report that 42% of all possible bigrams do not appear in any English word, and 50% have a probability which is lower than 0.0003), they eventually added a post-processing phase to the recognition system. This post-processor used bigram statistics to detect errors and trigram statistics to correct them.

In 1973 Sayre published an interesting study which was probably the first off-line system for cursive script recognition. Segmentation was based on the detection of characteristic areas of the drawing and the contextual phase was also based on bigram and trigram analysis. An interesting idea is that the recognized classes of the classifier do not correspond to letters but to the *possible shapes* of letters. Thus, only 17 *non-exclusive* classes were considered, so that several letters can correspond to the same class and vice-versa.

The critical phases of all these methods are obviously segmentation and contextual analysis. Next subsections report a few techniques which have been developed to improve them both. Recognition will not be dealt with as it can be solved by classical OCR or CSR techniques.

3.2.1. Character Segmentation

Techniques for segmenting cursive script are all based on heuristic rules derived from visual observation. Obviously, there is no "magic" rule and it is not possible to segment any handwritten word into perfectly separated characters in the absence of recognition. Thus, word units resulting from segmentation are not only expected to be entire characters, but also parts or combinations of characters. These segmented units are usually called "graphemes" (or "segments" or "pseudo-characters"). It must be noted that the relationship between characters and graphemes must remain simple enough to allow an efficient post-processing stage. In practice, this means that a character must not be divided into more than two graphemes and vice-versa in most cases.

As said before, these methods can be seen as following a double segmentation strategy: first *actual* segmentation points or boundaries are found which are then *implicitly* modified during the contextual (or recognition) stage. Thus, this kind of segmentation is often called "pre-segmentation" or "loose-segmentation", while resulting segmentation points are said to be "possible segmentation points" (PSP).

Most segmentation techniques are based on the fact that most lowercase characters are linked together by *lower ligatures*. So, an easy way to locate ligatures is to detect the minima of the upper outline of words. Unfortunately, this technique has several drawbacks which must be solved in an appropriate way:

— letters "o", "v" and "w" are usually followed by "upper" ligatures,

— letters "u", "w" .. contain "intra-letter ligatures", that is to say that a subpart of these letter cannot be differentiated from a ligature in the absence of context

— artifacts can sometimes cause erroneous segmentation.

Many of these problems can easily be solved at the contextual stage (and especially those of the second type because the drawing is ambiguous in nature without the help of lexical context). However, the quality of segmentation still remains very much dependent on the design of the implemented segmenter.

Segmentation techniques based on the above principle were for instance developed by Ehrich & Koelher [24], Maier [70] and Lecolinet [61] [62]. This last study was based on a dual approach:

— the detection of possible pre-segmentation zones,

— the use of a *pre-recognition* algorithm, whose aim was not to recognize characters but just to evaluate if a piece a drawing was likely to constitute a valid character.

Pre-segmentation zones were detected by analyzing the upper and lower profiles and the opened concavities of the words. Temptative segmentation paths were then created to separate cursive words into isolated graphemes. These paths were required to respect several heuristic rules dealing with continuity and connectivity constraints. Finally, pre-segmentations were only validated if coherent with the decisions of the pre-recognition algorithm. Hierarchical segmentation was also performed in some special cases. An important property of this method was to be mostly independent to character slant, so that no special pre-processing was required.

The same goal was achieved by Holt & al. [49] by analysis of the upper contour and a set of rules based on contour direction, closure detection, and zone location. Upper contour analysis was also used by Kimura, Shridhar & Narasimhamurthi for a pre-segmentation algorithm which was part of the second stage of an hybrid recognition system [59]. Moreover, in the first stage of the same system, they also implemented another segmentation technique based on a "hit and deflect strategy" (HDS). This interesting technique was initially developed for the segmentation of digit strings [93].

Another interesting technique for segmenting handwritten strings was also proposed by Fenrich in [30]. This method, which is able to cope with strings of variable length, proposes a recognition aided approach. It is also based on upper and lower contour analysis and on a splitting technique inspired from HDS.

A few other techniques use different criteria like those of Bozinovic and Srihari where segmentation is based on the detection of minima of the *lower* contour [10]. Presegmentation points (PSP) are found around these locations and emergency segmentation is performed when PSPs are too far from each other. The main drawback of this method is that it requires handwriting to be previously deslanted to ensure proper separation.

In a recent study which aims to locate "key letters" in cursive words Cheriet employed background analysis to perform letter segmentation [18]. In this method, segmentation is based on the detection and the analysis of the faceup and facedown valleys and open loop regions of the word image.

Higgins and Ford designed a two stage algorithm for on-line recognition [46] (all previous techniques being more specially devoted to off-line segmentation). First, possible segmentation points were generated by detecting specific features of the pen-strokes of the script (like cusps, intersections, points of inflection and end points). Then, irrelevant PSPs were eliminated during a second stage based on segment analysis.

Finally, we want to mention that a number of methods for segmenting online cursive script into allographs were reviewed by Teulings and Schomaker [107] (a method of their own based on simulated annealing was also presented in the same paper) and that a recent survey of segmentation techniques was also published by Dunn and Wang [22].

3.2.2. Contextual Post-Processing

In [9], Bozinovic and Srihari presented a string correction algorithm for cursive script recognition which was derived from research on speech recognition [3]. Unlike older techniques such as the Viterbi algorithm [31] this method is not only able to handle substitution errors but also splitting and merging errors (although in an approximate way in the second case). A channel model for CSR is represented by a finite state machine allowing such operations. The best estimate is obtained by using a stack decoding algorithm (a technique derived from the "branch and bound" concept of search) combined with a *trie* structure representation of a dictionary. A trie is a tree representation of a lexicon where nodes represent letters and leaves represent the words which are made of all the encountered (letter) nodes from the root to each considered leaf. This data structure is of great interest for word recognition and has been widely used in that field.

A few years later, the same authors described a whole system based on an adaptation on this previous idea [10]. Their model followed an analytical bottom-up scheme including pre-processing, pre-segmentation, feature extraction and letter and word hypothesization. These words were hypothesized using a modified version of the stack decoding algorithm by storing the most likely prefixes and expanding them until the end of the word was reached. Note that the pre-segmentation stage of this method is described in the previous section.

Lecolinet and coworkers used Extended Edit Distance in a method which was applied to check and city name recognition [61][62]. Grapheme Recognition was either performed using a statistical algorithm (based on linear separation of feature vectors derived from concavity detection) or by using a multi-layered neural network grapheme images. An extended version of the Edit Distance making use of eight elementary transformations (instead of three in classical ED) was implemented to model properly various cases of merging, splitting and contextual substitution of graphemes. In a recent version of the method, automatic learning capability was added.

In [60] Kundu and coworkers propose the use of Hidden Markov Models as a contextual post-processor. In this paper, graphemes were supposed to have been segmented by another technique. More recent papers by the same authors employ implicit HMM systems which will be described in the next section.

Finally, it should be noted that a review of segmentation and contextual analysis techniques for text recognition was published by Elliman and Lancaster in [25].

3.3. Analytical Methods with Implicit Segmentation

Implicit methods have been the subject of great attention during these last few years because they combine most of the advantages of holistic and analytical strategies:

— no complex segmentation algorithm has to be built; this scheme allows one to bypass segmentation problems,

— as they are letter-based, these methods are not limited to a specific lexicon: they can easily be applied to the recognition of any vocabulary,

— the identification of the word is performed globally, segmentation being a consequence of recognition which is itself driven by contextual analysis.

Depending on the type of technique used, recognition can either be performed by following a local or global optimization scheme. In the first case, recognition is done iteratively in a left-to-right scan of words. Conceptually, these methods are derived from a scheme developed by Casey and Nagy [14] for the recognition of handprinted words. The basic principle of their method was to use a mobile window of variable width to provide "tentative segmentations" which were confirmed (or not) by character recognition.

Other methods proceed in a more global way by generating a lattice of all (or many) possible feature-to-letter combinations where final decision is eventually taken by considering the whole graph. Optimization is then performed globally to bypass possible errors occuring on the beginning of the word.

Recent years have seen increasing interest in Hidden Markov Models (HMMs). This technique leads to very interesting and efficient systems, most of which can be considered as following an analytic implicit strategy. The next section will be devoted to their description. However, many other interesting schemes have also been proposed and are the object of the following paragraphs.

3.4. Non-HMM Implicit Methods

Peleg and Hayes [81] [43] used *probabilistic relaxation* to read off-line handwritten words. Hayés model was working on a hierarchical description of words derived from a skeletal representation. Relaxation was performed on the nodes of a stroke graph and of a letter graph where all possible segmentations were kept. Complexity was progressively reduced by keeping only the most likely solutions. N-gram statistics were also introduced to discard unlegible combinations of letters. A major drawback of such techniques is that they require intensive computation.

Tappert employed *Elastic Matching* to match the drawing of the unknown cursive word with the possible sequences of letter prototypes [103]. As it was an on-line method, the unknown word was represented by means of the angles and y-location of the strokes joining digitization points. Matching was considered as a path optimization problem in a lattice where the sum of distance between these word features and the sequences of letter prototypes had to be minimized. Dynamic programming was used with a warping function allowing to skip unnecessary features. Digram statistics and segmentation constraints were also eventually added to improve performance (the purpose of segmentation constraints was both to avoid certain errors and to speed up the process by reducing the number of prototype comparisons).

Berthod and Ahyan developed a structural system involving two complementary notions: the *aspect* and the *structure* of words [6][7]. "Aspect" characterizes the profile of the words and is deduced from ascender and descender detection. "Structure" was defined as a sequence of structural features (like x- and y-extrema, curvature signs, cusps, crossings, penlifts, and closures) collected all along the word. This sequence was used to generate all the legible sequences of letters that would have this "structural" representation. This was done by means of a tree dictionary containing the description of letter scripts (previously learned during the training phase). Linking features (corresponding to ligatures) could be added between letters. "Aspect" was then taken into account to chose the best solution(s) among the list of generated words. Thus, this method was also following a hypothesis testing and verification scheme, an interesting strategy which was first experimented by Hull for handprinted word recognition (see for instance [53]).

A structural approach following a lexicon-based strategy was also proposed by Lorette et Ouladj for on-line recognition [78]. Words and letters were represented by means of two tree dictionaries: a letter tree† in the first case and a feature tree in the second case. These features consisted in 4 directional codes and in ascenders or descender markers. Recognition was done by means of a prediction / verification strategy: letters were predicted by finding in the letter tree the paths compatible with the extracted features and they were verified by checking their compatibility with the word dictionary.

The system of Higgins and Whitrow [45] implemented a hierarchical description where primitive on-line features were progressively grouped into more sophisticated representations. The first level corresponded to the "turning points" of the drawing (and their associated attributes). The second level was dealing with more sophisticated features called "primary shapes". Finally, the third level was a treillis of temptative letters and ligatures. Ambiguities were then resolved by contextual analysis using letter quadgrams to reduce the number of possible words and a dictionary lookup to select the valid solution(s).

A different approach uses the concept of regularities and singularities [95] [96]. In this system, detection of the "singular parts" of the word (which are complementary of the uninformative "regular parts") produces a symbolic description chain. On a stroke graph obtained after skeletonization, the regular part is the sinusoid-like path that joins all cursive ligatures. Singular parts are stroke-trees. The most robust features and characters (the "anchors") are detected first from this description chain. Dynamic matching is then used for analyzing the remaining parts. Segmentation is thus produced implicitly.

An original technique combining dynamic programming and a neural net recognizer has recently been introduced by Burges and coworkers [12]. This technique, called Shortest Path Segmentation (SPS), selects the optimal consistent

† this type of data structure is also called a "trie" and is described in section 3.2.

combination of cuts from a set of candidate cuts generated by using heuristics. Given this set of candidate cuts, all possible "legal" segments (which are expected to correspond to characters) are constructed by combination. A graph whose nodes represent acceptable segments is then created and these nodes are connected when they correspond to compatible neighbors. The paths of this graph represent all the legal segmentations of the word. Each node of the graph is then assigned a cost obtained by the neural net recognizer (which is a Space Displacement Neural Network). The shortest path through the graph thus corresponds to the best recognition and segmentation of the word.

Lastly, Fujizawa proposed an interesting technique called Parallel Dynamic Programming [32], which aims to process all the entries of the lexicon at the same time. The goal of such an approach is to reduce computation time in order to deal with larger lexicons. The method is based on dynamic programming and the A* algorithm.

3.5. Hidden Markov Models

3.5.1. Description

Hidden Markov Models have become a very popular technique for cursive recognition, for on-line as well as off-line systems. The basic idea is to model cursive writing as a hidden underlying structure which is not observable. This underlying structure is a canonical representation of the reference patterns (e.g. a sequence of letters). Deformations in their drawing produce observable symbols. Hence, HMMs are able to model the fact that for example different letters may have similar shapes, and that a given letter may be written in many different ways.

A discrete HMM is entirely defined by a set of states Q, a fixed vocabulary of symbols V, probabilities of initial states "pi", transition probabilities between states A and observation probabilities of symbols within states B [85].

HMMs are probabilistic models, which allows them to integrate easily knowledge coming from different other probabilistic sources. Most of the time, observations are discrete symbols extracted from a fixed vocabulary. Features within segmentation boundaries are quantified using a VQ codebook, or KNN algorithm. In some cases, observations are not discrete symbols, and observation probabilities are continuous probability densities [4]. Most HMM-based word recognition systems use an intermediary level recognition stage, by computing an observation probability at letter-state or letter-subHMM level. Hence they are analytical methods.

Context (word and letter frequencies, syntactic rules) is supported by transitional probabilities between letter states. In most applications, first order Markov models are used: transitional probabilities occur between state t and state t+1 only. [60] is an example of second order HMMs. A path through an HMM is a state sequence. Its evaluation is obtained by multiplying transitional probabilities and observation probabilities along that state sequence, i.e. joint probability of a state sequence and observation sequence, given a model.

In most cases, the evaluation of an observation sequence by a HMM is calculated by finding the best path in the model. This can be done with the Viterbi algorithm, based on a time efficient dynamic programming scheme. HMM transitional and symbol probabilities can be learned using an incremental algorithm: the Baum-Welch algorithm [85]. Starting from an initial evaluation, HMM probabilities are re-estimated using probabilities of observed symbols of the training set. A detailed survey of the learning of HMMs probabilities can be found in [36].

3.5.2. Word HMMs

For word recognition problems, HMM states may be letters or intra-letter states coming from letter-HMM models. They can also correspond to the successive positions of canonical observations.

There are two classes of Hidden Markov Models for word recognition: model discriminant and path discriminant. With model-discriminant HMMs, one model Mk is constructed for each word. Words can be ordered using the probabilistic evaluation of observation sequence O, given the model Mk [33], [17], [89], [5].

With path discriminant HMMs, [60], [15] [16] only one HMM model is constructed. Word recognition is performed by finding the k best paths through this unique model. Each path is equivalent to a sequence of letters. In case of a restricted word lexicon, invalid letter sequences have to be ignored during the search of the k best paths, or eliminated using a lexicon comparison module.

Path discriminant HMMs can handle large vocabularies, but are generally less performing (in terms of recognition rate) than model-discriminant HMMs.

3.5.3. Letter HMMs

In the case of touching discrete or unconstrained writing style, it is impossible to find perfect letter segmentations. HMMs have been used to model the fact that letters do not always fit within segmentation boundaries. Most HMMs dealing with unconstrained cursive script are built from elementary model-discriminant HMMs describing letters, which are then combined into several model discriminant word HMMs [33] [17] or a single path-discriminant model [15]

For a letter HMM model, transition probabilities can be learned by observing the letter segmentation behavior on a training set [17] [89].

Chen and al [17] use compound symbols. Letter HMM states correspond to the different numbers of individual observations (i.e. letter segmentation units) that can be matched to the letter. Thus, letters like 'm' and 'i' can have different HMM state structures. Compound symbol probabilities and time duration probabilities (i.e. the number of segmentation units for a given letter) are learned for each letter during training stage. Virtual observation probabilities and transition probabilities for letter HMM states are defined so that joint probability of observation and intra-states path given a letter HMM are equal to time duration probability multiplied by compound symbol observation probability.

Bellegarda and all [4] propose a model-discriminant HMM for on-line character recognition. Observations are small portions of writing called "frames". Several kinds of feature vectors (each kind belonging to a "chirographic space") are extracted from those frames. For each chirographic space, there is a given set of continuous probability densities within each state of the model. Letter models can be degenerate (using only one state), to provide a time-efficient character pre-recognizer.

4. Hybrid Systems

Many real-world cursive recognition systems have to cope with heterogeneous data. Variability may come from various styles of writing, a great number of scriptors, or writing material (paper or pen). Designing a single module, able to recognize so many different types of input data seems difficult or even impossible, unless identification methods are very approximate and the context very strong. Noisy versus clean data may also require adapted methods.

Such variation of input data can be solved with several specialized modules combined in order to achieve a general system. Module combination can be sequential or parallel. A sequential approach combines pre-classification algorithms, whose output is passed on to specialized recognition modules like top-down word verification procedures or writing-style specific algorithms. A parallel approach will analyze input data through competing points of view and combine them later. The combination output can also be analyzed with specialized or reduced context recognition modules.

4.1. Sequential Approaches: Pre-Classification Methods

Two main approaches have been used to build a sequential system. Some systems analyze the writing style of input data, and apply specialized recognition methods for each writing style. Others use general purpose classifiers whose output consists for example in a reduced word vocabulary.

4.1.1. Writing Style Evaluation

Favata and al [29] first segment the word images into units corresponding to discrete characters. Depending on the confidence levels resulting from a hand-printed recognition module, they classify those units as discrete characters, or not. Non-discrete regions are analyzed with two modules, one designed for touching discrete, the other for cursive script. Each module has its own letter-segmentation rules. Their output consists in character recognition and possible segmentation points. They are combined at word level. Several paths are chosen among the merged possible character identifications and segmentation alternatives. The selected paths are then matched to a word lexicon and a list of possible valid solutions is produced.

Plessis and al [84] directly analyze the writing style. For this task, they estimate the dimensions and shape of connected components. Then, three different recognition modules are used. One is a global method, used only on pure cursive script. The second one is analytical, based on a statistical character recognition module. The third one is also analytical and uses a Neural Network for character recognition.

4.1.2. Reducing Context with Increasingly Detailed Diagnostics

Madhvanath and al [69] present a global handwritten word recognition method for lexicon reduction. This method has been designed to produce a robust word recognition adapted to bad quality data. They use ascenders, descenders and word length.

Kimura and Shridar [59] chain two analytical methods, one with an external segmentation scheme using fuzzy rules and edit distance, the other with an implicit and detailed segmentation algorithm.

Chen and al [17] use a two-stage HMM system for cursive words recognition. An initial large vocabulary is filtered through a path-discriminant HMM, whose output is a middle-sized vocabulary. A set of model-discriminant HMMs then produces a ranking inside this vocabulary subset. Their architecture is based on the fact that model-discriminant HMMs perform better than path-discriminant ones but become prohibitive in terms of speed, memory and learning material when the vocabulary becomes larger.

4.2. Parallel Approaches

For this type of methods, much work has been done to build classifier combination modules. Competing classifiers may provide different levels of information. Different combination shemes must thus be used depending on the type of output which is provided by the individual classifiers to be combined. The three following types of output can be provided by classifiers:

— a list of classes proposed for the candidate description [51].

— a list of classes with their rankings [48].

— a list of classes with a numerical value expressing confidence or diffidence. Most of the time, those values are probabilities.

It should be noted however that some of the methods cited here were not specifically designed for cursive script.

4.3. Methods based on a Verification Strategy

Li and al [67] present a printed word recognizer suitable for reduced vocabulary. Inside this reduced set, they compare words two by two. They have developed a dynamic feature selection algorithm to discriminate between two characters. Hence they construct specialized modules able to discriminate pairs of characters. Given a couple of words, discriminating characters are selected and processed through character discrimination modules. A distance is computed for each pair of differing characters and one of the two words is said to win the competition. Among the reduced vocabulary, words can be ranked according to the number of times they win against the other words.

Lecolinet [63] proposes a top-down directed word verification method called "backward matching". In cursive word recognition, all letters do not have the same discriminating power, and some of them are easier to recognize. So, in this method, recognition is not performed in a left-to-right scan, but follows a meaningful order which depends on the visual and lexical significance of the letters. Moreover, this order also follows an edge-toward-center movement, like in human vision [105]. Matching between symbolic and physical descriptions can be performed at the letter, feature and even sub-feature levels. As the system knows in advance what it is searching for, it can make use of high-level contextual knowledge to improve recognition, even at low-level stages. This system is an attempt to provide a general framework allowing efficient cooperation between low-level and high-level recognition processes.

5. Results

It is very difficult to give comparative results of the methods proposed so far. Most of the methods, and especially the early studies were tested on small databases created from the writing of only a few people. Moreover, all the databases used were different: no common test base was available, this simple fact making comparison quite perilous. This is the reason why we have decided not to include results in the previous sections which are only dedicated to the description of the techniques.

Common databases of cursive script samples have been made available in the recent past with the development of postal research in several countries. For instance, standard databases of checks or mail addresses were respectively created by the research department of the French Postal Service (SRTP) or by CEDAR at Buffalo for the US Postal Service. Furthermore, postal organisms have initiated and funded a large part of research on handwriting recognition. For instance, USPS recently funded a research project on cursive script recognition which involved five major private or academic laboratories. Although work is still under progress, many papers have already been published as well as preliminary results. In our opinion, these research programs constitute the "state of the art" in the field of off-line cursive script recognition and the available results provide a representative idea of the progress in this field. In these projects, recognition was performed on city or state names constituting lexicons of different sizes. Experiments were made on lexicons of three different sizes containing either an average of 10, 100 or 1000 words. Words contained in the databases were belonging to various stylistic categories (handprinted, discrete, cursive and mixed), about two thirds of them being cursive. For instance, the following recognition rates were reported by Kimura and coworkers in [59]:

— 93.5% (and 95.6% if considering the best two choices) for size 10 lexicons,

— 87.6% (93% if considering the best four choices) for size 100 lexicons,

— 80.9% (88.7% if considering the best six choices) for size 1000 lexicons.

On-line recognition constitutes another major field of CSR research. Unfortunately, fewer comparable results are available than in the case of off-line research. A large part of research remains unpublished (especially those concerning commercial products) as well as the corresponding results. Moreover, comparison between the different techniques is difficult because they have not been tested on a common database. The goals are also quite different: the lexicon is usually much larger (up to 20 000 words or even more) but the number of users is also much smaller (learning being often possible if not mandatory) and handwriting is also more constrained. So, recognition rates may vary considerably from one method to another (between 60% and 95%), depending on the size of the lexicon, the number of writers, the quality of the handwriting or whether training was or was not performed.

6. Conclusion

As a conclusion, we would like to make a double statement:

- it can now be said (as Kimura and coworkers write in [59]) that cursive script recognition has now become an achievable goal, provided that strong contextual constraints are available,
- contextual analysis constitutes the future of the field. Most of further improvements in CSR will now probably come from better lexical, syntactical and semantic analysis performed at the word, sentence and text levels.

This is already the direction that several major research teams have decided to follow [58][86][26] and there is no doubt that contextual analysis will be a field of intense research and achievements in the next few years.

References

1. G.H. Abbink, H.L. Teuling & L.R.B. Schomaker, *Description of on-line script using Hollerbach's generation model*, Pre-Procedings IWFHR III, page 217, Buffalo, May 1993.

2. A.M. Alimi & R. Plamondon, *Performance Analysis of Handwritten Strokes Generation Models*, Pre-Procedings IWFHR III, page 272, Buffalo, May 1993.

3. L.R. Bahl and F. Jelinek, *Decoding for Channels with Insertions, Deletions and Substitutions with Applications to Speech Recognition*, IEEE Trans. Inform. Theory, Vol. IT-21, pages 404-410, 1975.

4. E.J. Bellegarda, J. R. Bellegarda, D. Nahamoo and K.S. Nathan *A Probabilistic Framework for On-line Handwriting Recognition*, Pre-Proceedings IWFHR III, page 225, Buffalo, May 1993.

5. S. Bercu, G. Lorette *On-line Handwritten Word Recognition: An Approach Based on Hidden Markov Models*, Pre-Proceedings IWFHR III, page 385, Buffalo, May 1993.

6. M. Berthod and S. Ahyan, *On Line Cursive Script Recognition: A Structural Approach with Learning*, 5th Int. Conf. on Pattern Recognition, page 723, 1980.

7. M. Berthod, *On-line Analysis of Cursive Writing*, in Computer Analysis and perception. Vol. I. Visual Signals. Ch. IV, pages 55-80, CRC Press, 1982.

8. G. Boccignone, A. Chianese, L.P. Cordella and A. Marcelli, *Recovering Dynamic Information From Static Handwriting*, Pattern Recognition, Vol. 26, No. 3, page 409, 1993.

9. R. Bozinovic and S.N. Srihari, *A String Correction Algorithm for Cursive Script Recognition*, IEEE PAMI, Vol.4, No.6, pages 655-663, 1982.

10. R.M. Bozinovic and S.N.Srihari, *Off-Line Cursive Script Recognition*, IEEE Trans. on Pattern Analysis and Machine Intel., Vol. 11, No. 1, page 68, 1989.

11. M.K. Brown and S. Ganapathy, *Cursive Script Recognition*, Proceedings of the Int. Conf. on Cybernetics & Society, 1980.

12. C.J.C. Burges, J.I. Be and C.R. Nohl, *Recognition of Handwritten Cursive Postal Words using Neural Networks*, USPS 5th Advanced Technology Conference, page A-117, Nov. 1992.

13. J. Camillerapp, G. Lorette, G. Menier, H. Ouladj and J-C. Pettier, *On-line and Off-line Methods for Cursive Script Recognition*, From Pixels to Features III, S. Impedovo and J.C. Simon (eds.), Chapter 3, page 273, Elsevier, 1992.

14. R.G. Casey and G. Nagy, *Recursive Segmentation and Classification of Composite Patterns*, 6th Int. Conf. on Pattern Recognition, page 1023, 1982.

15. M.Y. Chen, A. Kundu, J. Zhou and S.N. Srihari, *Off-line Handwritten Word Recognition using Hidden Markov Model*, USPS 5th Advanced Technology Conference, page 563, Nov. 1992.

16. M.Y. Chen, A. Kundu and S.N. Srihari, *Unconstraint Handwritten Word Recognition using Continuous Density Variable Duration Hidden Markov Model*, Proc IEEE Int Conference on Acoustics, Speech and Signal Processing, April 1993.

17. M.Y. Chen and A. Kundu, *An Alternative to Variable Duration HMM in Handwritten Word Recognition*, Pre-Proceedings IWFHR III, page 82, Buffalo, May 1993.

18. M. Cheriet, *Reading Cursive Script by Parts*, Pre-Proceedings IWFHR III, page 403, Buffalo, May 1993.

19. D.S. Doermann and A. Rosenfeld, *Temporal Clues in Handwriting*, 11th IAPR Int. Conf. on Pattern Recognition, Vol. II, page 317, Aug. 1992.

20. D. Doermann and A. Rosenfeld, *The Interpretation and Recognition of Interfering Strokes*, Pre-Proceedings IWFHR III, page 82, Buffalo, May 1993.

21. G. Dimauro, S. Impedovo and G. Pirlo, *From Character to Cursive Script Recognition: Future Trends in Scientific Research*, 11th IAPR Int. Conf. on Pattern Recognition, Vol. II, page 516, Aug. 1992.

22. C.E. Dunn and P.S.P. Wang, *Character Segmenting Techniques for Handwritten Text - A Survey*, 11th IAPR Int. Conf. on Pattern Recognition, Vol. II, page 577, August 1992.

23. L.D. Earnest, *Machine Recognition of Cursive Writing*, C. Cherry editor, Information Processing, pages 462-466, Butterworth, London, 1962.

24. R.W. Ehrich and K.J. Koehler, *Experiments in the Contextual Recognition of Cursive Script*, IEEE Trans. on Computers Vol. 24, No. 2, page 182, 1975.

25. D.G. Elliman and I.T. Lancaster, *A Review of Segmentation and Contextual Analysis Techniques for Text Recognition*, Pattern Recognition, Vol. 23, No. 3/4, pages 337-346, 1990.

26. L.J. Evett, C.J. Wells, F.G. Keenan, T. Rose and R.J. Whitrow, *Using Linguistic Information to Aid Handwriting Recognition*, From Pixels to Features III, S. Impedovo and J.C. Simon (eds.), Chapter 5, page 339, Elsevier, 1992.

27. R.F.H. Farag, *Word-Level Recognition Recognition of Cursive Script*, IEEE Trans. on Computers Vol. C-28, No. 2, pages 172-175, Feb. 1979.

28. C. Faure, *Traitement Automatique de l'Ecrit et du Document*, Congrès biennal de l'AFCET, Versailles, France, June 1993.

29. J.T. Favata and S.N. Srihari, *Recognition of General Handwritten Words using a Hypothesis Generation and Reduction Methodology*, USPS 5th Advanced Technology Conference, page 237, Nov. 1992.

30. R. Fenrich, *Segmenting of Automatically located handwritten numeric strings*, From Pixels to Features III, S. Impedovo and J.C. Simon (eds.), Chapter 1, page 47, Elsevier, 1992.

31. G.D. Forney Jr, *The Viterbi Algorithm*, Proceedings of the IEEE, Vol. 61, No. 3, page 268, March 1973.

32. T. Fujisaki, K. Nathan, W. Cho and H. Beigi, *On-line Unconstrained Handwriting Recognition by a Probabilistic Method*, Pre-Proceedings IWFHR III, page 235, Buffalo, May 1993.

33. A.M. Gillies, *Cursive Word Recognition using Hidden Markov Models*, USPS 5th Advanced Technology Conference, Nov. 1992.

34. M. Gilloux and M. Leroux, *Recognition of Cursive Scripts Amounts on Postal Cheques*, USPS 5th Advanced Technology Conference, page 545, Nov. 1992.

35. M. Gilloux, J.M. Bertille and M. Leroux, *Recognition of Handwritten Words in a Limited Dynamic Vocabulary*, Pre-Proceedings IWFHR III, page 417, Buffalo, 1993.

36. M. Gilloux, *Hidden Markov Models in Handwriting Recognition*, in this volume.

37. N. Gorsky, *Off-line Recognition of Bad Quality Handwritten Words Using Prototypes*, NATO/ASI Fundamentals in Handwriting Recognition, page 155 (working book), Château de Bonas, France, June 1993. Final version in this volume.

38. V. Govindaraju, D. Wang and S.N. Srihari, *Using Temporal Information In Off-Line Word Recognition*, USPS 5th Advanced Technology Conference, Nov. 1992.

39. I. Guyon, D. Henderson, P. Albrecht, Y. LeCun, J. Denker, *Writer Independent and Writer Adaptative Neural Network for On-line Character Recognition*, From Pixels to Features III, S. Impedovo and J.C. Simon (eds.), page 493, Elsevier, 1992.

40. P.A.V. Hall and G.R. Dowling, *Approximate String Matching*, ACM Computings Surveys 12, pages 381-401, Dec. 1980.

41. L.D. Harmon, *Handwriting Reader Recognizes Whole Words*, Electronics, pages 29-31, August 1962.

42. L.D. Harmon, *Automatic Recognition of Print and Script*, Proceedings of the IEEE, Vol. 60, No. 10, pages 1165-1177, Oct. 72.

43. K.C. Hayes, *Reading Handwritten Words Using Hierarchical Relaxation*, Computer Graphics and Image Processing, Vol. 14, pages 344-364, 1980.

44. Y. He , M. Chen and A. Kundu, *Handwritten Word Recognition Using HMM with Adaptative Length Viterbi Algorithm*, ICASSP-92, Vol. 3, page 153, 1992.

45. C.A. Higgins and R. Whitrow, *On-Line Cursive Script Recognition*, Proceedings Int. Conf. on Human-Computer Interaction - INTERACT'84, Elsevier, 1985.

46. C.A. Higgins and D.M. Ford, *On-line Recognition of Connected Handwriting by Segmentation and Template Matching*, 11th IAPR Int. Conf. on Pattern Recognition, Vol. II, page 200, Aug. 1992.

47. T.K. Ho, J.J. Hull and S.N. Srihari, *A Word Shape Analysis Approach to Recognition of Degraded Word Images*, Pattern Recognition Letters, No. 13, page 821, 1992.

48. T.K. Ho, J.J. Hull, S.N. Srihari, *On Multiple Classifier Systems for Pattern Recognition*, 11th IAPR Int. Conf. on Pattern Recognition, Vol. II, page 84, Aug. 1992.

49. M. Holt, M Beglou and S. Datta, *Slant-Independent Letter Segmentation for Off-line Cursive Script Recognition*, From Pixels to Features III, S. Impedovo and J.C. Simon (eds.), page 41, Elsevier, 1992.

50. G.F. Houle, C. Radelat, S. Resnick and P. Bock, *Handwritten Word Recognition Using Collective Learning Systems Theory*, Pre-Proceedings IWFHR III, page 92, Buffalo, May 1993.

51. Y.S. Huang and C.Y. Suen, *An optimal Method of Combining Multiple Classifiers for Unconstrained Handwritten Numeral Recognition*, Pre-Proceedings IWFHR III, page 11, Buffalo, May 1993.

52. J.J. Hull and S.N. Srihari, *Experiments in Text Recognition with Binary n-Gram and Viterbi Algorithm*, IEEE Trans. on Pattern Analysis and Machine Intel., Vol. 4, pages 520-530, Sept 1982.

53. J.J. Hull and S.N. Srihari, *A Computational Approach to Visual Word Recognition: Hypothesis Generation and Testing*, Computer Vision and Pattern Recognition, pages 156-161, June 1986.

54. J. Hull and S. Srihari, *Recognition of Handwritten Words for Address Reading*, USPS Fourth Advanced Technology Conference, page 192, Nov. 1991.

55. J. Hull, T.K. Ho, J. Favata, V. Govindaraju and S. Srihari, *Combination of Segmentation-Based and Wholistic Handwritten Word Recognition algorithms*, From Pixels to Features III, S. Impedovo and J.C. Simon (eds.), Chapter 3, page 261, Elsevier, 1992.

56. J.J. Hull, *A Hidden Markov Model for Language Syntax in Text Recognition*, 11th IAPR Int. Conf. on Pattern Recognition, Vol. II, page 124, The Hague, The Netherlands, Aug./Sept. 1992.

57. J.J. Hull and Y. Li, *Word Recognition Result Interpretation using the Vector Space Model for Information Retrieval*, Proceeding of Symposium on Document Analysis and Information Retrieval, page 147, Las Vegas, 1993.

58. J.J. Hull, *Language-Level Syntactic and Semantic Constraints Applied to Visual Word Recognition*, NATO/ASI Fundamentals in Handwriting Recognition, page 179 (working book), Château de Bonas, France, June 1993. Final version in this volume.

59. F. Kimura, M. Shridhar and N. Narasimhamurthi, *Lexicon Directed Segmentation-Recognition Procedure for Unconstrained Handwritten Words*, Pre-Proceedings IWFHR III, page 122, Buffalo, May 1993.

60. A. Kundu, Yang He and P. Bahl, *Recognition of Handwriten Words: First and Second Order Hidden Markov Model Based Approach*, Pattern Recognition, Vol. 22, No. 3, page 283, 1989.

61. E. Lecolinet and J-V. Moreau, *Off-Line Recognition of Handwritten Cursive Script for the Automatic Reading of City Names on Real Mail*, 10th Int. Conf. on Pattern Recognition, page 674, Atlantic City, June 1990.

62. E. Lecolinet and J-P. Crettez, *A Grapheme-Based Segmentation Technique for Cursive Script Recognition*, Proceeding of the Int. Conf. on Document Analysis and Recognition, page 740, Saint Malo, France, Sept. 1991.

63. E. Lecolinet, *A New Model for Context-Driven Word Recognition*, Proceeding of Symposium on Document Analysis and Information Retrieval, page 135, Las Vegas, April 1993.

64. E. Lecolinet, *Cursive Script Recognition by Backward Matching*, Proceeding of the Int. Conf. On Handwriting and Drawing, page 89, Paris, France, July 1993.

65. M. Leroux, J-C. Salome and J. Badard, *Recognition of Cursive Script Words in a Small Lexicon*, Proceeding of the Int. Conf. on Document Analysis and Recognition, page 774, Saint Malo, France, Sept. 1991.

66. N. Lindgren, *Machine Recognition of Human Language; Part III-Cursive Script Recognition*, IEEE Spectrum, pages 104-116, May 1965.

67. L. Li, T.K. Ho, J.J. Hull and S.N. Srihari, *A Hypothesis Testing Approach to Word Recognition Using Dynamic Feature Selection*, 11th IAPR Int. Conf. on Pattern Recognition, Vol. II, page 586, Aug. 1992.

68. G. Lorette and Y. Lecourtier, *Is Recognition and Interpretation of Handwritten Text a Scene Analysis Problem ?* Pre-Proceedings IWFHR III, page 184, Buffalo, May 1993.

69. S. Madhvanath and V. Govindaraju, *Holisitic Lexicon Reduction*, Pre-Proceedings IWFHR III, page 71, Buffalo, May 1993.

70. M. Maier, *Separating Characters in Scripted Documents*, 8th Int. Conf. on Pattern Recognition, Paris, page 1056, 1986.

71. P. Mermelstein and M. Eden, *A System for Automatic Recognition of Handwritten Words*, IEEE Proceedings-Fall Joint Comp. Conf., 1964.

72. A. Miller, *Real Time Classification of Handwritten Script Words*, Information Processing - Proceedings of IFIP congress 71, Ljubljana, Yugoslavia, Aug. 1971.

73. P. Morasso, A. Pareto and S. Pagliano, *Neural Models for Handwriting Recognition*, From Pixels to Features III, S. Impedovo and J.C. Simon (eds.), Chapter 5, page 423, Elsevier, 1992.

74. J-V. Moreau, B. Plessis, O. Bourgeois and J-L. Plagnaud, *A Postal Check Reading System*, Proceeding of the Int. Conf. on Document Analysis and Recognition, page 758, Saint Malo, France, Sept. 1991.

75. R. Nag, K.H. Wong and F. Fallside, *Script Recognition Using Hidden Markov Models*, IEEE ICASSP, pages 2071-2074, Tokyo, 1986.

76. D.L. Neuhoff, *The Viterbi Algorithm as an Aid in Text Recognition*, IEEE Trans. on Inf. Theory, page 222, March 1975.

77. H. Nishida, T. Suzuki and S. Mori, *Thin Line Representation from Contour Representation of Handprinted Characters*, From Pixels to Features III, S. Impedovo and J.C. Simon (eds.), page 29, Elsevier, 1992.

78. H. Ouladj, G. Lorette, E. Petit, J. Lemoine and M. Gaudaire, *From Primitives to Letters: A Structural Method to Automatic Cursive Hanwritting Recognition*, The 6th Scandinavian Conference on Image Analysis, Finland, page 593, June 1989.

79. T. Paquet and Y. Lecourtier, *Handwriting Recognition: Application on Bank Cheques*, Proceeding of the Int. Conf. on Document Analysis and Recognition, page 749, Saint Malo, France, Sept. 1991.

80. M. Parizeau and R. Plamondon, *A Handwriting Model for Syntactic Recognition of Cursive Script*, Int. Conf. on Pattern Recognition, page 308, The Hague, 1992.

81. S. Peleg, *Ambiguity Reduction in Handwriting with Ambiguous Segmentation and Uncertain Interpretation*, Computer Graphics and Image Processing, Vol. 10, pages 235-245, 1979.

82. R. Plamondon and P. Yergeau, *A System for the Analysis and Synthesis of Handwriting*, Proceedings IWFHR I, page 167, Montreal, May 1990.

83. R. Plamondon, *A Model-Based Segmentation Framework for Computer Processing of Handwriting*, Int. Conf. on Pattern Recognition, page 303, The Hague, 1992.

84. B. Plessis, A. Sicsu, E. Menu and J-V. Moreau, *Isolated Handwritten Word Recognition for Contextual Address Reading*, USPS 5th Advanced Technology Conference, page 579, Nov. 1992.

85. L.R. Rabiner and B.H. Juang *An Introduction to Hidden Markov Models*, ASSP Mag., No. 3, pages 4-16, 1986.

86. R.K. Srihari, S.N. Charlotte, M. Baltus and J. Kud, *The Use of Language Models in On-line Sentence / Phrase Recognition*, Pre-Proceedings IWFHR III, page 284, Buffalo, May 1993.

87. K.M. Sayre, *Machine Recognition of Handwrittten Words: A Project Report*, Pattern Recognition, Vol. 5, pages 213-228, 1973.

88. A.W. Senior, *Off-line Handwriting Recognition: A Review and Experiments*, Technical Report TR 105, Cambridge University Engineering Department, Cambridge, England, Dec. 1992.

89. A.W. Senior and F. Fallside *An Off-line Cursive Script Recognition System using Recurrent Error Propagation Networks*, Pre-Proceedings IWFHR III, page 132, Buffalo, May 1993.

90. B.A. Sheil, *Median Split Trees: A Fast Lookup Technique for Frequently Occurring Keys*, Communications of the ACM, Vol. 221, page 947, Nov. 1978.

91. R. Shinghal and G.T. Toussaint, *Experiments in Text Recognition with the Modified Viterbi Algorithm*, IEEE PAMI Vol.1, No.2, page 184, April 1979.

92. R. Shinghal and G.T. Toussaint, *A Bottom-up and Top-down Approach to using Context in Text Recognition*, Int. J. Man-Machine Studies. Vol. 11, page 201, 1979.

93. M. Shridhar and A. Badreldin, *Recognition of Isolated and Simply Connected Handwritten Numerals*, Pattern Recognition, Vol.19, No.1, page 1, 1986.

94. J.C. Simon and K. Zerhouni, *Robust Description of a Line Image*, International Conference on Document Analysis and Recognition, page 3, 1991.

95. J.C. Simon and O. Baret, *Cursive Words Recognition*, From Pixels to Features III, S. Impedovo and J.C. Simon (eds.), Chapter 3, page 241, Elsevier, 1992.

96. J.C. Simon, *Off-line Cursive Word Recognition*, Proceedings of the IEEE, page 1150, July 1992.

97. J.C. Simon, *On the Robustness of Recognition of Degraded Line Images*, NATO/ASI Fundamentals in Handwriting Recognition, page 177 (working book), Château de Bonas, France, June 1993. Final version in this volume.

98. S.N. Srihari (Editor), *Computer Text Recognition and Error Correction (Tutorial)*, IEEE Computer Society, 1984.

99. S.N. Srihari and C.M. Baltus, *Combining Statistical and Syntactic Methods in Recognizing Handwritten Sentences*, Proceedings AAAI Symposium, page 121, San Jose, USA, 1992.

100. S.N. Srihari, *From Pixels to Paragraphs: the Use of Models in Text Recognition*, Proceeding of Symposium on Document Analysis and Information Retrieval, page 47, Las Vegas, USA, 1993.

101. C.Y. Suen, J. Guo and Z.C. Li, *Computer and Human Recognition of Handprinted Characters by Parts*, From Pixels to Features III, S. Impedovo and J.C. Simon (eds.), page 223, Elsevier, 1992.

102. T. Suzuki and S. Mori, *A Thinning Method Based on Cell Structure*, Proceedings IWFHR I, Montreal, page 39, 1990.

103. C.C. Tappert, *Cursive Script Recognition by Elastic Matching*, IBM J. Res. Develop. 26, pages 765-771, Nov. 1982.

104. C.C. Tappert, C.Y. Suen and T. Wakahara, *The State of the Art in On-line Handwriting Recognition*, IEEE PAMI, Vol. 12, No. 8, page 787, August 1990.

105. I. Taylor and M. Taylor, *The Psychology of Reading*, Academic Press, 1983.

106. H.L. Teulings and L.R.B. Schomaker, *A Handwriting Recognition System Based on the Properties and Architectures of the Human Motor System*, Proceedings IWFHR I, page 195, Montreal, May 1990.

107. H.L. Teulings and L.R.B. Schomaker, *Learning Prototypes in Cursive Handwriting*, From Pixels to Features III, S. Impedovo and J.C. Simon (eds.), page 61, Elsevier, 1992.

108. H.L. Teulings, *Invariant Handwriting Features Useful in Cursive Script Recognition*, in this volume.

109. R.A. Wagner and M.J. Fischer, *The String-to-String Correction Problem*, JACM Vol. 21, No. 1, page 168, Jan. 1974.

110. K.H. Wong and F. Fallside, *Dynamic Programming in the Recognition of Connected Handwritten Script*, 2nd Conf. on Artificial Intelligence Applications, pages 666-670, Dec. 1985.

Hidden Markov Models in Handwriting Recognition

Michel Gilloux

La Poste, Service de Recherche Technique de la Poste, SRTP/RD/RVA, 10, Rue de l'Île Mabon, F-44038 Nantes Cedex, France

Abstract: Hidden Markov Models (HMM) have now became the prevalent paradigm in automatic speech recognition. Only recently, several researchers in off-line handwriting recognition have tried to transpose the HMM technology to their field after realizing that word images could be assimilated to sequences of observations. HMM's form a family of tools for modelling sequential processes in a statistical and generative manner. Their reputation is due to the results attained in speech recognition which derive mostly from the existence of automatic training techniques and the advantages of the probabilistic framework. This article first reviews the basic concepts of HMM's. The second part is devoted to illustrative applications in the field of off- line handwriting recognition. We describe four different applications of HMM's in various contexts and review some of the other approaches.

Keywords: Handwriting recognition, postal code recognition, cheques amounts recognition, cursive script recognition, Hidden Markov Models, automatic learning

1 Introduction

For several years now, Hidden Markov Models (HMM's) [1-3] have been extremely popular in the field of automatic speech recognition, even standing as the prevailing paradigm. HMM's are basically a family of probabilistic tools for dealing with sequences. Besides the significant results achieved in automatic speech recognition, their appeal is mostly explained by the existence of algorithms for automatically tuning the parameters of an HMM in view of a set of training examples. Also, the probabilistic character of HMM's makes them a suitable framework for the sound integration of several knowledge sources. For example, HMM's have been also applied in natural language processing [4-6], in phonology [7], in image restoration [8], in image interpretation, in cryptography, etc. It is only recently that researchers in off-line handwriting recognition have come to consider HMM's as a candidate model in their field.

The introduction of HMM's in handwriting recognition has been first provoked by their use as language models since this knowledge level is shared by speech and handwriting. More importantly, it has been possible to rely on HMM's at the word level since word images have been looked at as sequences of observations. Note that this idea is more natural in on-line recognition where observations are ordered by definition along the time axis [9-10]. HMM's have been applied there too.

The basic notions in HMM theory are the algorithms for computing the probability of an observed sequence given a model and the methods for tuning the parameters of an HMM on a training set. Yet, most of the successes of HMM's rely on their customization to a particular domain. Thus, besides of training and usage, HMM's users should know about ways of incorporating domain knowledge into the architecture of an HMM and also about the different interpretations of the HMM machinery. This paper intends to describe the basic notions needed to start with employing HMM's. This is the aim of part 1. Part 2 is an illustration of HMM's through four ways of applying them in off- line handwriting recognition. We will show how they can be adapted to the recognition of five digits ZIP codes, to the recognition of cursive script words in a small or large vocabulary and for modelling language knowledge.

2 An introduction to Hidden Markov Models

2.1 Definition

Hidden Markov Models have been designed to account generatively for sequences of observations for which we can assume that these observations are conditioned by an underlying Markov chain. The Markov chain is not directly observed thus the term hidden. The following toy example in the spirit of Polya's urns and which is inspired from [2] is useful to understand what is basically an HMM. Assume we have two urns each containing white and black balls in a specific proportion. The urns are marked respectively with a 1 and a 2. We also have two mugs (see Fig. 2.1) filled with balls which are labelled with a 1 or a 2. Each mug has a different proportion of 1's and 2's. Given this apparatus we can build an HMM by the following process. A first ball is selected randomly from say mug 1. Depending on what is read on this ball, we then select randomly another ball from the urn corresponding to the number on the first ball. We then go on by repeating this procedure starting with the mug associated to the last urn used. The sequence of white and black balls is the observation. The mugs used at each step constitute the Markov chain since the next mug chosen depends only on the current one. The formal theory of Hidden Markov Models gives us a set of algorithms for recovering the hidden Markov chain of mugs, for computing the probability of a given sequence of black and white balls, for estimating the proportions of white and black balls in each urn and of 1 and 2 balls in each mug, etc. More formally now, a Hidden Markov Model is a structure $M = \langle S, s_f, O, A, B, C \rangle$ where S is a finite set of states, $s_f \in S$ is the final state, O is a set of symbols, $a_{r,s} = p(s \text{ at } t | r \text{ at } t-1), r \in S - \{s_f\}, s \in S$ are the transition probabilities between states, the $b_s(o) = p(o \text{ at } t | s \text{ at } t)$ are the emission probabilities of symbols in each state and $c_s = p(s_1 = s), s \in S$ are the initial probabilities of states. The observations may be the elements of a finite alphabet (e.g. a vector-quantized codebook, a set of letters, etc.), or the elements of a countably infinite set (e.g. integers), or of a continuum (e.g.; real numbers, real vectors, etc.) Accordingly, the distributions b may be matrices or probability functions or probability

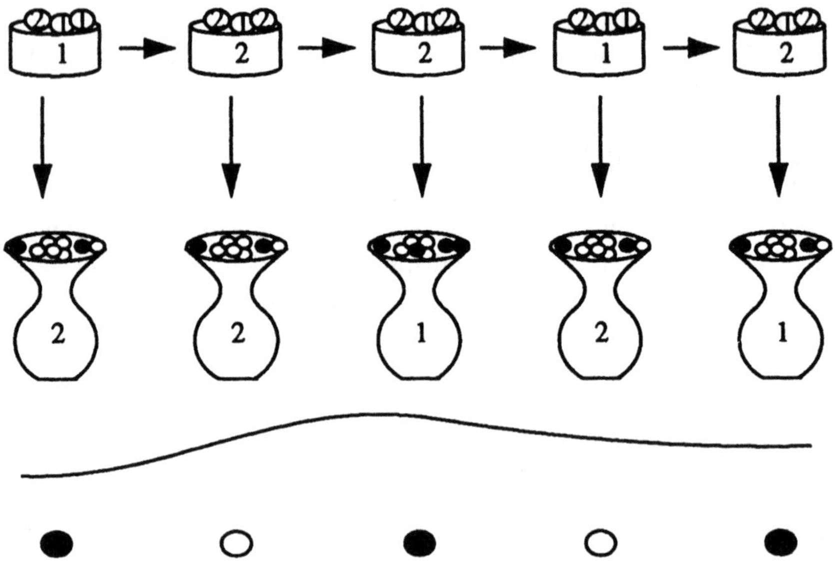

Fig 2.1. A simple Hidden Markov Model.

densities (e.g. normal laws). An alternative definition of HMM's allows the observations to be emitted along the transitions instead of the states. In some applications where this representation is more natural it may be used exactly the same. In particular it is possible to demonstrate the equivalence between transition emission and state emission by associating a virtual state to each transition.

This formal definition may receive an open set of interpretations and may also serve in different ways. In pattern recognition we generally have to classify an observed sequence in a set of categories. We may also wish to estimate the parameters of a given model (not only an HMM) in view of a set of examples. In this context, the typical interpretations of Hidden Markov Models are the following:

- Given several HMM's, classify the observation according to the model that generates the sequence with the highest probability. This is referred to as *model discriminant* HMM's.
- Given one model, classify the observation in the class denoted by the hidden state sequence. This is referred to as *path discriminant* models.
- Given a set of examples, estimate the model that accounts the best for the examples. We will see later on what the term *best* means.

It is important to understand that these typical interpretations are not the only ones. In particular, HMM's are now being used in image interpretation to assign labels to pixels or simply to remove noise from an image [8]. Here the interpretation schema is the following:

- Given only one model, interpret the hidden state sequence as a noiseless version of the observation.

To be able to use HMM's we have to answer the following questions: How can we compute the probability $p(O)$ of an observation O? How can we estimate the parameters of the model that generated O? How can we estimate the hidden state sequence given the observation? The next sections are the answers to these questions which have also been described in a number of introductory papers [1-3,11].

2.2 Computing the probability of observations

The probability $p(O)$ on an observation O of length T may be decomposed into the sum on all possible sequences of states (or paths) of the product of the probability of the path (given by the Markov chain) by the probability of the observations given the path (defined by the emission probabilities):

$$p(O) = \sum_{pth \in S^{T-1} \times \{s_f\}} p(O, pth) = \sum_{pth \in S^{T-1} \times \{s_f\}} p(O|pth) \times p(pth)$$

Whenever possible, we shall abuse notation by replacing $p(X = x)$ by $p(x)$ in case there is no ambiguity created. The probability of each path is easily computed from the initial and transitions probabilities of the Markov chain:

$$p(pth) = p(s_1) \times \prod_{t=2}^{T} p(s_t | s_{t-1}) = c_{s_1} \times \prod_{t=2}^{T} a_{s_{t-1}, s_t}$$

Given the path, it is also straightforward to compute the probability of observations:

$$p(O|pth) = \prod_{t=1}^{T} b_{s_t}(o_t)$$

Note that when the symbols belong to a continuum, this term, like the emission probabilities, is a probability density.

Finally *p(O)* is given by

$$p(O) = \sum_{pth \in S^{T-1} \times \{s_f\}} b_s^t(o_1) \times c_{s_1} \times \prod_{t=2}^{T} a_{s_{t-1}, s_t} b_s^t(o_t)$$

This formula exhibits the apparent complexity of the computation of *p(O)*. This complexity is a consequence of the independent computation of the probabilities of paths. Note that the number of paths grows exponentially with the number of states. It is possible to simplify the computation of *p(O)* by remarking that we can share between all paths with a common initial part the probability of this part. This is due to the properties of Markov chains. We thus define two auxiliary quantities:

$$\alpha_t(s) = p(o_1 \ldots o_t, s_t = s)$$
$$\beta_t(s) = p(o_{t+1} \ldots o_T | s_t = s)$$

α and β at time t may be computed iteratively through the following algorithm:

$$\alpha_1(s) = c_s b_s(o_1) \qquad \beta_T(s) = \delta(s, s_f)$$

$$\alpha_t(s) = \sum_{r \in S} \alpha_{t-1}(r) a_{r,s} b_s(o_t) \qquad \beta_t(s) = \sum_{r \in S} \beta_{t+1}(r) a_{s,r} b_r(o_{t+1})$$

Finally, the probability *p(O)* is given by:

$$p(O) = p(o_1 \ldots o_t, s_T = s_f) = \alpha_T(s_f)$$

This algorithm makes it possible to compute *p(O)* in a linear time with respect to the length of the observation and in a quadratic time with respect to the number of states. The forward computation with alpha and the backward computation with beta are equivalent here. We will see below that both are needed to estimate the parameters of an HMM. Despite the reduction of complexity, the Baum-Welch algorithm is still plagued in practice by numerical problems affecting the computation of the probabilities of paths. These probabilities may become so small that underflows are possible. Also, the summation of probabilities coming from different paths may cause scaling troubles. In light of these difficulties, we may remark that it is desirable for *p(O)* to be explained mostly by only one path in the model. This is particularly reasonable in some applications where the path itself matters. In this cases the model is said to be *unifilar*. Assuming the model to be unifilar, $p(O)$ may be computed through dynamic programming using the following algorithm:

$$v(o_1, s) = c_1(s) \times b_s(o_1)$$
$$v(o_1 \ldots o_t, s) = max_{r \in S} a_{r,s} \times b_s(o_t) \times v(o_1 \ldots o_{t-1}, r)$$
$$p(O) = v(o_1 \ldots o_T, s_f)$$

The Viterbi algorithm refers to this computation where back pointers are used to recall the path that led to the highest value for $p(O)$. The Viterbi algorithm is particularly interesting from a computational point of view since the disappearance of sums makes it possible to replace probabilities by their log and products by sums.

2.3 Estimating the parameters of an HMM with the Baum-Welch algorithm

In pattern recognition, if we assume that a set of examples has been generated by an HMM, the structure and the parameters of this HMM are usually not known. In practice, the structure (number and connectivity of states) is always postulated from application specific knowledge. Given that structure it is possible to estimate the parameters of the model from the set of examples. It is intuitively tempting to estimate the probabilities involved in the model by observing the a posteriori frequencies of transitions and emissions in a model whose parameters have been randomly chosen. Given this approach, the reestimates of the probabilities are the following

$$\hat{a}_{r,s} = \left(\sum_{t=1}^{T-1} p(s_t = r, s_{t+1} = s | O) \right) / \left(\sum_{s' \in S} \sum_{t=1}^{T-1} p(s_t = r, s_{t+1} = s' | O) \right)$$

$$\hat{a}_{r,s} = \frac{\sum_{t=1}^{T-1} \alpha_t(r) a_{r,s} b_s(o_{t+1}) \beta_{t+1}(s)}{\sum_{s' \in S} \sum_{t=1}^{T-1} \alpha_t(r) a_{r,s'} b_{s'}(o_{t+1}) \beta_{t+1}(s')}$$

$$\hat{b}_s(o) = \sum_{t \text{ such that } o_t = o} p(s_t = s | O) / \sum_{t=1}^{T} p(s_t = s | O)$$

$$\hat{b}_s(o) = \sum_{t \text{ such that } o_t = o} \alpha_t(s)\,\beta_t(s) \Big/ \sum_{t=1}^{T} \alpha_t(s)\,\beta_t(s)$$

$$\hat{c}_s = p(s_1 = s | O) = \frac{p(s_1 = s, O)}{p(O)} = \frac{\alpha_1(s)\,\beta_1(s)}{\alpha_T(s_f)}$$

Note that this is valid only when the observations belong to a finite alphabet. This intuitive approach is confirmed by theory and is has been proven that this iterative way of performing the estimation of parameters does converge to a stationary configuration of the parameters which is a local maximum for the likelihood of the examples [12]. At each iteration, the likelihood of the examples given the model improves (see Fig. 2.2). Moreover, the estimation loop is greatly simplified by the use

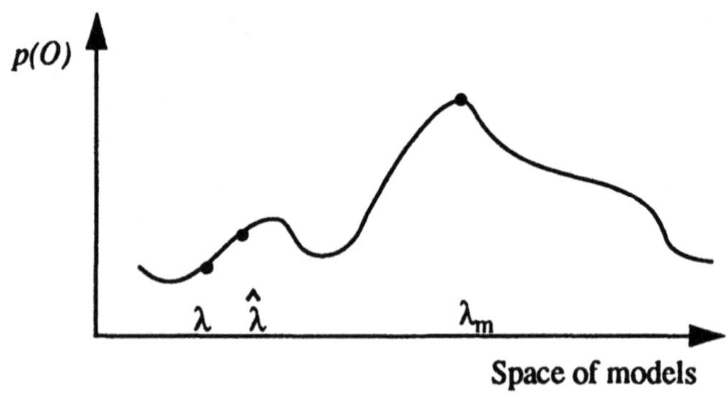

Fig 2.2. Parameter estimation with the Baum-Welch algorithm.

of the forward and backward probabilities alpha and beta. This procedure is referred to as the Forward-Backward or Baum-Welch algorithm [1-3,11-12]. The first name derives from the combined use of forward and backward probabilities which is apparent in the formulas. The stationary values of the probabilities are only guaranteed to be a local optimum for the maximum likelihood estimation criterion (MLE). This optimum is conditioned by the initial random values for the probabilities (see Fig. 2.2). It is thus useful in practice to perform several trials and to finally keep the one that resulted in the best likelihood. Yet, nothing guarantees that this is the global optimum. A variant in the spirit of simulated annealing [13] has been used by several researchers [14]. It consists in adding some noise to the reestimates and to make this noise decrease along time according to some cooling scheme. Better estimates have been rapidly found using this strategy. It has also been proven that the same type of estimation applied only to the most likely path converges to a local optimum of the MLE criterion [2]. The Viterbi algorithm [15] may thus be applied instead of the forward-backward computations with a significant improvement in computational complexity. Yet, we have no theory to compare the quality of Viterbi estimates vs. Baum-Welch estimates and only practice may indicate the best choice. The above algorithms are appropriate when the symbols in the observations belong to a finite alphabet. It has been shown that they can be soundly extended to several families of continuous emission probability densities [2] including multi dimensional Gaussian densities and finite mixture distributions. In the case of finite mixtures of Gaussian densities of form $\sum_i \omega_{s,i} N(\mu_{s,i}, \Sigma_{s,i})$, the Baum-Welch reestimates are the following:

$$\hat{\mu}_{s,i} = \sum_t p(s_t = s, i_t = i | O) \times o_t / \sum_t p(s_t = s, i_t = i | O)$$

$$\hat{\Sigma}_{s,i} = \frac{\sum_t p(s_t = s, i_t = i | O) \times (o_t - \hat{\mu}_{s,i}) \otimes (o_t - \hat{\mu}_{s,i})}{\sum_t p(s_t = s, i_t = i | O)}$$

$$\hat{\omega}_{s,i} = \sum_t p(s_t = s, i_t = i | O) / \sum_{t,i} p(s_t = s, i_t = i | O)$$

where

$$p(s_t = s, i_t = i | O) = p(i_t = i | s_t = s, O) \times p(s_t = s | O)$$

$$p(s_t = s, i_t = i | O) = \frac{\omega_i N(\mu_{s,i}, \Sigma_{s,i})(o_t)}{\sum_i \omega_i N(\mu_{s,i}, \Sigma_{s,i})(o_t)} \times \frac{\alpha_t(s) \beta_t(s)}{p(O)}$$

Gaussian density mixtures are often used as a means for approximating the unknown emission probability distributions.

Another way of approximating these distributions relies on the use of neural networks. In this case a global training of the neural nets and the Markov chain based on gradient ascent is possible [16].

2.4 Advanced Issues With HMM

In addition to the basics of HMM's there are a number of extensions, tools, algorithms, and recipes for drawing the best possible results from their application despite of their known flaws. These aspects are concerned with different kinds of training, typical interpretations, extensions to other types of representation, etc.

2.4.1. Nesting a hierarchy of HMM's

In a given application domain, several types of knowledge may be represented through the use of HMM's. In some cases these knowledge sources are organized into a hierarchy. For example, in automatic speech recognition syntactic knowledge resides at a higher level than phonetic knowledge. When both are amenable to HMM modelling, their combination may still be viewed has a global HMM with transitions corresponding either to one model or the other. This constitutes a very useful technique for integrating different sources of knowledge.

2.4.2. Discriminant Training

With model discriminant HMM's, each HMM is trained separately on a different training set while they are *all* used jointly during recognition. It is thus possible that while these models are optimal with respect to the Maximum Likelihood criterion, they are not optimal in the sense of discriminative power. Maximum Likelihood training has been proved able to find the optimal model only under certain conditions which are not met in pattern recognition applications. In particular, the training examples have to be generated by a HMM the structure of which is identical to that of the trained model, and the training set must be «sufficiently» large. Discriminant Training [17] is a technique which is adequate to improve the discriminative power of a set of HMM's. The training is done jointly for all the HMM's and the training criterion is the Maximum A Posteriori probability (MAP) $p(model|O)$. With such a criterion, it is no longer possible to use the Baum-Welch algorithm. The parameters for all models have to be optimized by gradient ascent, and some heuristics are necessary to avoid numerical problems [17]. It may also be proved that Discriminant Training is equivalent to Maximum Mutual Information training where the criterion is

$$I(O, model) = \frac{p(O, model)}{p(O) \times p(model)}$$

Discriminant training has also been related to the quadratic error minimization criterion used in multilayer perceptrons [18].

In practice, Discriminant Training has improved the performances of HMM's recognition systems compared to Maximum Likelihood Training. Note that these criteria require the training to be done jointly for all the word classes and not as before class after class. However, for each class it is possible to consider only the other word classes that may lead to errors since the other classes do not contribute much to the denominator in the MAP criterion.

2.4.3. Corrective Training

Although showing significant improvements over Maximum Likelihood Training, Discriminant Training is optimal only under the same conditions concerning the adequacy of models and the representativity of the training set. Corrective training

[19] is an empirical method which is designed to achieve the best discrimination power possible by focusing on the near-misses of the models trained with the Maximum Likelihood criterion. It is probably not reasonable to expect a correct recognition for examples whose bayesian probability as estimated by the HMM is significantly low. Yet, in discriminant training these examples affect the gradient ascent. In corrective training, they are not taken into account as long as they do not become near-misses. At the other end of the spectrum, correctly recognized examples are still considered to prevent them from becoming errors. The learning rule of corrective training assumes that the models have been trained with another method as a first approximation. The remainder of the training is done as if the Baum-Welch algorithm was used on a virtual training set where each example would appear with a frequency which is a function of the a posteriori probability.

2.4.4. Training with Sparse Data

Like any other estimation technique, the Baum-Welch and Viterbi algorithms require the training set to be large enough with respect to the number of parameters which are estimated. When the training set is sparse, the estimation may well be too much specialized for the training examples and perform poorly on a different test set. The theoretical work of Vapnik [20] provides estimates of the number of examples needed. However its practical value is questionable since these estimates are usually large. In practice, it is possible to use two different training sets. The first (*training set*) is used for the estimation of the parameters. The second (*validation set*) is used to test the generalization capabilities of the estimated parameters. The training is stopped when the likelihood of the validation set decreases over a certain number of iterations, that is before the likelihood of the training set becomes optimal. It is also possible to force the transition probabilities to rest above some small minimal value in order to cope with transitions not encountered on the training set. The *deleted interpolation* method described in [11] is another solution which performs an interpolation between two HMM's with «compatible» structures. The two HMM's are trained on the same set in a first pass. One is assumed to be defined with less parameters than required by the application so that it generalizes well but its accuracy is low. The second is suspected to use more parameters than necessary so that it is accurate but specialized to the training set. The deleted interpolation has to find the best compromise between accuracy and generalization, that is between the two HMM's. The HMM's have to be compatible in the sense that the state of the first one correspond to equivalence classes of the states in the second (see Fig. 2.3). The choice of the equivalence classes is problem dependent. The interpolation parameters are interpreted as transition probabilities in a third HMM. Finally, the interpolation parameters are estimated on a different validation set. This method may also be viewed as sharing values between different states. The technical concept for sharing values is the notion of tied states [11]. Two states s_1 and s_2 are tied whenever

$$\begin{cases} \forall r, a_{s_1,r} = a_{s_2,r} \\ c_{s_1} = c_{s_2} \end{cases}$$

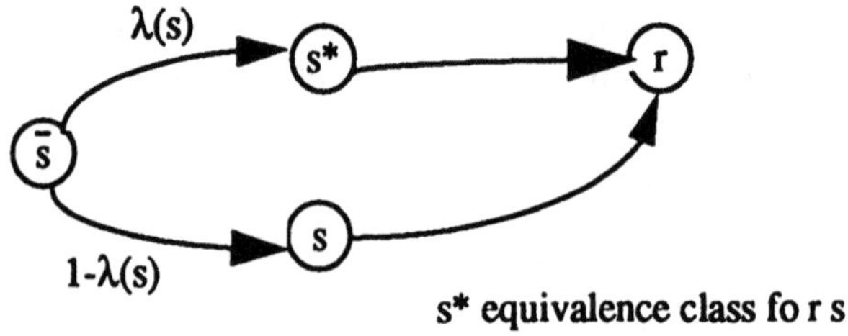

Fig. 2.3. The deleted interpolation model.

Tying states clearly reduces the number of free parameters. Sets of mutually tied states form the equivalence classes of the deleted interpolation algorithm. This approach is related to that of shared weights in Time Delay Neural Networks [21].

2.4.5. HMM for Speech Recognition

HMM's have been widely used in speech recognition and have become almost a standard in this field [11,22-25]. The adequacy of HMM's to speech recognition is mostly due to their ability to model the time variations of the speech signal. These variations are such that a given sound may last for a time which is partly independent from the duration of other sounds in the same word or phrase. The structure of HMM's for speech recognition models the duration of sounds in the manner depicted on Fig. 2.4. This structure is known under the name of Bakis machine [11] or

Fig. 2.4. The structure of Bakis models.

left- to-right model. The loops on each state and the jumps over states correspond respectively to shorter and longer sounds by modelling the repetition or the deletion of a given signal frame. Analog structures have been used in handwriting recognition.

2.4.6. HMM's for Natural Language Processing

HMM's have also been used for modelling languages [4-6], especially at the syntactic level. In this cases observations are strings of words or syntactic categories. The best compromise between the long distance dependencies in natural languages and the tractability of training sets has often resulted on the use of tri-grams composed of word or categories triples. The states of the models are pairs of categories so that each state <*a, b*> may only emit the symbol *b* and is only reachable from states of form <*x,a*>. Since language modelling is often relevant in handwriting recognition, this technique has found several applications in that field including cases in which the tri-grams are triples of letters used to model letter statistics.

2.4.7. Computing N best paths-The modified Viterbi Algorithm

In many applications of HMM's, it is useful to be able to search not only for the most probable path but also for paths of higher rank in the order of decreasing probabilities. This is the case for example when the relative probability of the two most probable ones is an argument for deciding upon rejection. Also, it is often the case that there exist several knowledge sources of various level, including the HMM, which are used in combination to assign a score to each hypothesis. The N-Best paradigm [26] is a method which achieves a significant reduction of the search space by relying on a single knowledge source to focus on a small set of likely hypotheses and then computing the final score for each using the remainder of the knowledge sources. When the distinguished knowledge source is an HMM, a technique is sought to be able to compute the N-best hypotheses at minimum computational cost. The Modified Viterbi Algorithm [27] is an efficient solution for the computation of the N-best paths in an HMM. The core idea in the Modified Viterbi Algorithm is that the path of rank n+1 is likely to share subpaths with paths of rank 1 to n. For each time t and each state s, a stack is kept to describe all the paths already computed which go through state s at time t. Pointers are also used to record the predecessors for s at time t-1 (see Fig. 2.5). It can be proved that the n+1th best path to state s at time t comes necessarily from one of the paths to each state at time t-1 which are pointed by the pointers. Thus only N hypotheses where N is the number of states in the HMM have to be considered. Only the stacks and the pointers on the n+1th path have then to be respectively extended and readjusted before the next step. The Modified Viterbi Algorithm is tractable since its complexity is linear with respect to the number of hypotheses sought (each step in this algorithm is equivalent to a simple Viterbi algorithm). It may also be remarked that the N-best hypotheses are computed incrementally, that is in the order of decreasing probability. This property may be employed e.g. when the other knowledge source is a lexicon that tells to stop the search when a path corresponding to a word in the vocabulary has been found [27].

2.4.8. Higher order HMM's

One of the shortcomings of Bakis type HMM's is that they do not take into account the history of the path under consideration since at a given state if is not possible to recover the preceding ones. The history may be encoded in a more complex structure by forcing the connectivity of states to represent this history. Usually, this results in large state sets with complicated structures. Another way of encoding history is the use of higher order HMM's where the underlying Markov chain is of order more than unity since the next state is conditioned by more than one preceding state. For example, in a second order HMM, the transitions probabilities will be

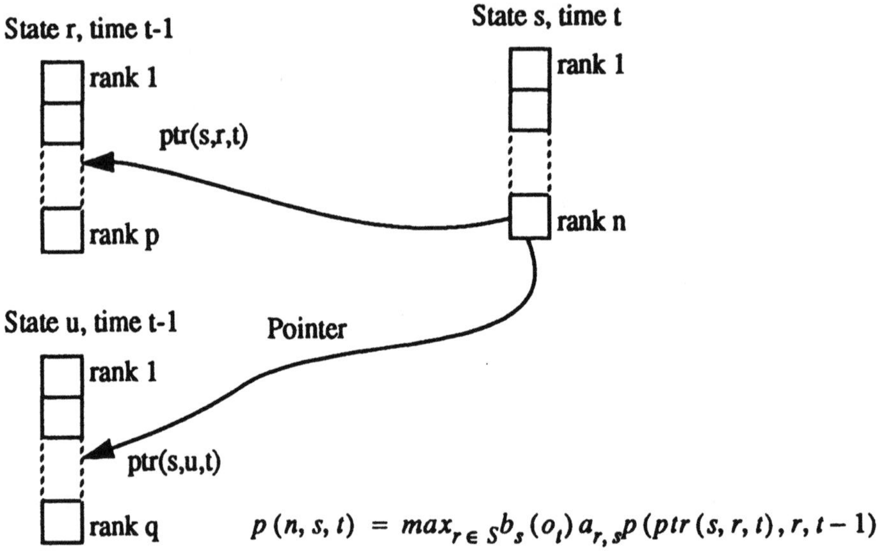

Fig. 2.5. The Modified Viterbi Algorithm.

$p(s_t | s_{t-1}, s_{t-2})$ In some sense, tri-grams models used for modelling natural languages are second-order HMM's since their states may be interpreted as pairs of elementary states. Models with variable order have also been defined to account for non constant depth of dependency [28]. The concept of probabilistic grammars and the inside-outside algorithm for estimating production probabilities is also useful for accounting for varying distance dependencies [29].

2.4.9. Representing Duration

Bakis machines used in automatic speech recognition and sometimes in handwriting recognition fail to represent correctly the duration of segments since the probability of staying in one particular state decreases exponentially with the length of repeated visits to that state. Several solutions to that problem have been proposed. One consists in modelling the duration of visits to one state independently from the base HMM through a duration distribution [30]. The transition probabilities between one state and itself are now replaced by the duration distribution. The Baum-Welch algorithm may be soundly extended to estimate the parameters of the distribution. Another approach relies on the use of two level HMM's, one for modelling contextual duration and one for modelling the signal itself with a finer grain [31].

2.5 Discussion

The adequacy of HMM's to pattern recognition and especially off-line handwriting recognition is first and foremost a consequence of the choice of the representation and of the markovian nature of the problem given this representation. Many different HMM's may be defined in a given context. To guide their selection, one has to keep in mind that hidden Markov modelling is characterized by the assumption that the observations are independent given the hidden states and that states only depend on their immediate predecessors. This assumption may often be false and real world problems are certainly not markovian. Nevertheless, HMM's can be highly successful provided that the representation chosen is a suitable one. In such cases, the numerous theorems and algorithms concerning HMM's can prove really useful. In particular, the capacity to estimate bayesian probabilities and to nest hierarchical knowledge sources is a positive fact.

3 Application of HMM's to Handwriting Recognition

HMM's have been recently applied extensively to handwriting recognition mostly in the domain of cursive word recognition. [27,32-42]. Applying HMM's to handwriting recognition requires mainly to answer two different questions:

- What are the relevant features (symbols) for encoding word images as sequences?
- What is the structure of the HMM which accounts best for handwriting variability?

The features proposed in the literature have been mainly distributed between explicit segmentation types of representation [27,32,33,35,36,39] and implicit ones [44,38,40,42]. In explicit segmentation, a non markovian algorithm is first used to segment the word image into letters or letter parts which are totally ordered. In implicit segmentation, it is the HMM which is in charge of discovering the correct letter segments and the symbols in the sequence correspond to the pixel columns or overlapping sliding windows. In both cases, several techniques have been used to transform segments, pixel columns or sliding windows into discrete or continuous values: unsupervised clustering [27], vector quantization [34], continuous densities [38], structural features [40], etc.

We shall describe below four different illustrative approaches to the application of HMM to handwriting recognition. The first approach is concerned with postal codes and belongs to the implicit segmentation family. The second is an explicit segmentation method for recognizing cursive words in a small vocabulary. The third is a model for representing contextual knowledge at the language level. The last approach is an extension of cursive word recognition with HMM's to open vocabularies.

3.1 5-digits postal code recognition

A large proportion of french 5-digits postal codes features touching characters (see Fig. 3.1). This makes difficult the recognition since digits have to be segmented in the first place. Usually, this segmentation is done in a bottom up fashion, that is without relying on the knowledge of digit shapes. it is desirable to be able to use that knowledge as soon as possible to improve segmentation. An HMM has been used in this respect [42].

The feature extraction process is based on the contour of the postal code image (Fig. 3.1). The upper and lower contour are sampled and each sample is transformed into the corresponding Freeman code. By combining the 8 Freeman codes in both contours through their cartesian product, we are left with a 64 symbols alphabet which is used by the HMM.

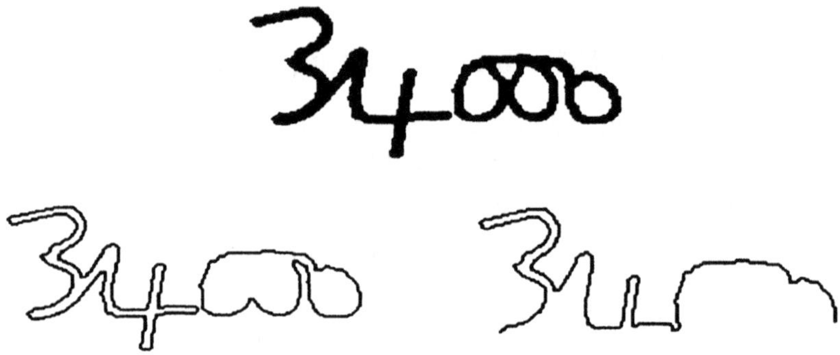

Fig. 3.1. Feature extraction on postal code images.

Variability in postal code images may be viewed in a first approximation has the consequence of variations in the width of digits or of digit parts. We thus used a Bakis topology. Since all combinations of 5 digit are potential postal codes, we used the notion of tied states to share digit models between postal code models (Fig. 3.2).

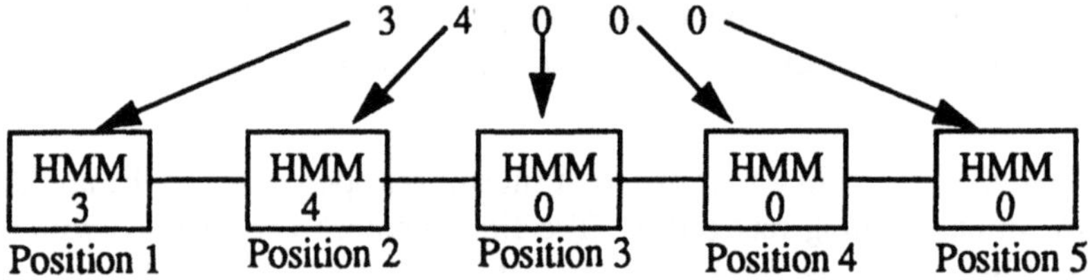

Fig. 3.2. HMM for postal codes.

Our approach is thus model discriminant. The global HMM representing all possible postal codes if formed by combining all digit models into 5 element sequences (Fig. 3.3).

This model has been trained with the Viterbi algorithm on a set of 3251 postal codes. Examples were not explicitly segmented so that the learning phase had also

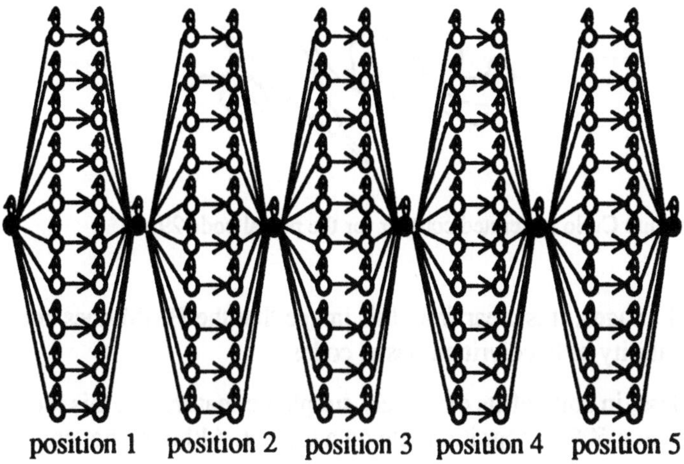

Fig. 3.3. The HMM for all postal codes.

to infer the best segmentation points. The recognition of test images may be assessed by looking at the segmentation points proposed by the HMM. Fig. 3.4 shows that

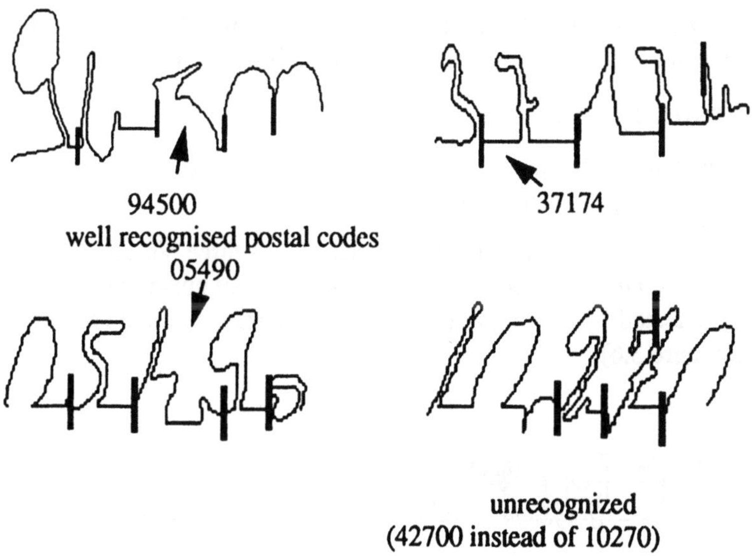

Fig. 3.4. Recognition of postal codes.

recognition errors are mainly explained by an inadequate modelling of digit width.

The particular set of features that we used makes it possible to generate virtual postal code contours using Monte Carlo simulations. Fig. 3.5 gives an example of

Fig. 3.5. A Monte Carlo generated contour for the postal code 29110.

these virtual images. It is clear from this image that the HMM does not model well the true variability of handwritten postal codes.

Nevertheless, in spite of its extremely simplistic feature set, this model has been able to achieve a 60% recognition rate on a test set. Although not comparable with figures achieved using classical methods, this result is significant if we consider that no a priori knowledge of character segmentation has been given to the system.

3.2 Recognition of cursive script words in a small vocabulary

The vocabulary of french postal cheques legal amounts is composed of thirty different words. This size makes is reasonable to envision the recognition of cursive handwritten amounts. We have used an HMM modelling of these words which employs coarse but robust features and a model discriminant strategy.

3.2.1. Feature extraction

This section is an overview of the feature extraction method. The interested reader is referred to [43] for a detailed description.

In a first step, the image is segmented vertically in three horizontal regions. The middle region is intended to correspond to letters without upper or lower extensions. It is easily detected by looking at the vertical histogram of pixel horizontal transitions (see Figure 3.6).

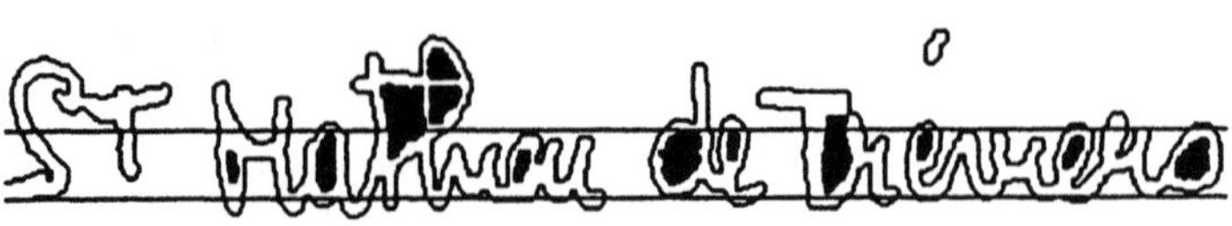

Feature description: HdhOL--o--#Kok-o---o--O

Fig. 3.6. Vertical segmentation and detection of loops on word images.

The image is also segmented horizontally into pseudo-letter segments. The detected segments may span other several letters or even cut letters into pieces, like it is often the case with letters *m*, *n* and *w* This is why we prefer to live with an imperfect segmentation process. We will see below how the Markov model is robust to segmentation errors. Then, in each letter segment, we look for loops and upper or lower extensions. The sizes of loops and extensions are quantified over a small number of levels.

Finally, a different symbol is assigned to each possible configuration of loops, extensions and sizes. Together with the symbol for representing spaces, this constitutes a 27 symbols set. For each image, the final feature description is a string of symbols.

When recognizing words in a small and constant vocabulary, it is possible to learn one HMM for each word in the vocabulary. Thus the HMM technique is suited to this context is a wholistic one.

3.2.2. Automatic learning of word references

An analysis of real examples shows that word patterns seldom contain as many segments as letters. Rather, they exhibit many variations among which some are caused by character interactions. For example, Fig 3.7 shows that a loop may appear at the juncture between the letters *f* and *r* in the word *franc*. We have used several Markov

Fig. 3.7. Several examples of the word "francs".

models to infer the real references for each word class. These models describe the probability that a given observation o is observed for a word of class w as: $p(O = o|\, W = w) \;\; = p_w(O = o)$.

By analogy with speech recognition, we have chosen to represent each word class by a left-to-right model respecting the Bakis-like topology of Fig 3.8. This architecture takes into account deletions, insertions and substitutions and uses the transition emission variant of HMM's. The jumps other 4 states represent deletions, while the odd states encode insertions. For each word category *w*, the corresponding model has been defined with a number of states n depending on the most probable length of examples of this category.

Since we are interested in the a posteriori probability $p(W = w|O = o)$ rather than the a priori one given by the Markov model, we have to deduce the former from the latter. This is done through the application of the bayes theorem:

$$p(W = w|O = o) = p(O = o|W = w) \times p(W = w) / p(O = o)$$

The a priori probability $p(W = w)$ is easily evaluated by computing the frequency of each word class in the training set. Since $p(O = o)$ does not depend on the word hypothesis, the recognition scores used are $p_w(O = o) \times p(W = w)$.

3.2.3. Results

The word recognition method described above has been trained on a set of 2492 word examples written by unknown writers on real postal cheques. We used the Viterbi Algorithm in this phase. The method has been tested on a different test set of 2492 words using the Viterbi algorithm. There are 27 word classes in the french vocabulary for expressing amounts. The results are reported on Table 5.1.

Table 3.1. Word recognition results on the test set for the global description method. R(n) is the percentage of presence of the correct word hypothesis among the n best rated.

n	1	2	3	4
R(n)	79%	87%	95%	98%

3.3 Modelling language knowledge using HMM's

Since we have been able to establish a model that outputs evaluations of the Bayes probability of word classes, we would like to benefit from this by using contextual knowledge at the sentence level. This knowledge is twofold. First we know the syntax of well formed sentences. This knowledge is used by filtering all word hypotheses combinations that do not respect the syntax. Second, we know that all amounts are not equally likely. In particular amounts around 100 FFr and amounts with no cents are more likely than others. Thus we would like to be able to evaluate the fre-

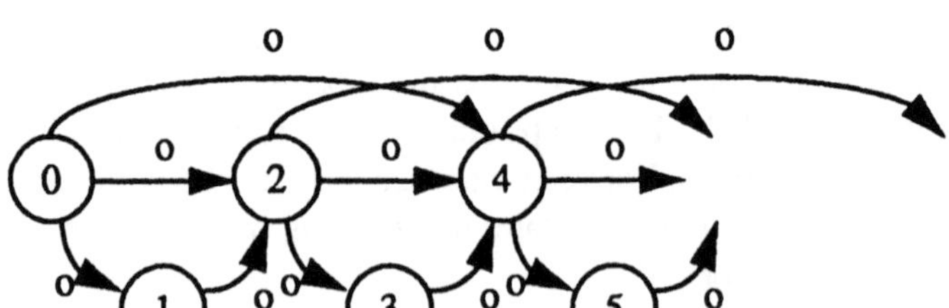

Fig. 3.8. A word Markov model.

quency of each amount and to combine it with the confidence scores provided by the word recognition level.

The combination of scores is made by the application of the Bayes theorem. The probability of an amount a expressed as $w_1...w_n$ given the observation o is:

$$p(a|o) = \frac{p(o|a) \times p(a)}{p(o)}$$

By assuming that the probability of the word descriptions o_i only depends on the corresponding word, this becomes:

$$p(a|o) \cong \frac{p(o_1|w_1) \times \ldots \times p(o_n|w_n) \times p(a)}{p(o)}$$

The probabilities of individual observations $p(o_i|w_i)$ are evaluated by the Markov models while *p(o)* does not depend on the hypothesis. Thus, only *p(a)*, the a priori probability of the amount remains to be evaluated.

Since there are 10 000 000 different possible amounts in the applications dealt with, it is impractical to evaluate the probability *p(a)* by mere counting. We need to induce *p(a)* for amounts not present in a tractable training set. Markov models have been used in computational linguistics to address this type of problem. The probability *p(a)* may be decomposed into:

$$p(a) = p(w_n|w_{n-1}...w_1) \times p(w_{n-1}|w_{n-2}...w_1) \times \ldots \times p(w_1)$$

where $p(w_i|w_{i-1}...w_1)$ is the probability that word w appears in position i given the words appearing in positions 1 to i – 1.

We may assume with no great loss in accuracy that the presence of some word in some position is only conditioned by a little number of its predecessors. In practice, we have chosen to assume that this presence only depends on the two preceding words. This choice leads to tractable training sets while giving a sufficient precision in practice. Thus the probability *p(a)* may be approximated by:

$$p(a) = p(w_n|w_{n-1}w_{n-2}) \times p(w_{n-1}|w_{n-2}w_{n-3}) \times \ldots \times p(w_1)$$

Now, it is possible to estimate the values $p(w_i|w_{i-1}w_{i-2})$ by just counting the relative frequency of tri-grams $(w_iw_{i-1}w_{i-2})$ and di-grams on a training set.

An interesting thing with this method is that it not only evaluates the probability of amounts but it also estimates the frequency of the different expressions of one particular amount. The French language allows to express certain numbers in different ways, e.g. 1500 may be written "*mille cinq cent*" or "*quinze cent*".

3.3.1. Results

The amount recognition method has been trained on 100 000 amounts and tested on 250 images of amounts written by unknown writers on real postal cheques. Note that the reason for the difference in size between the training set and the test set is that, for training, only the list of words is needed but not their image. The results are reported on Table 3.2. They show a significant improvement in the recognition rates when the a priori probability of amounts is used.

Table 3.2. Amount recognition rates using the a priori probability of amounts.

n		1	8	16
R(n)	Not using $p(a)$	53%	82%	86%
	Using $p(a)$	60%	91%	91%

3.4 Recognition of handwritten words in a dynamic vocabulary

In some contexts, the vocabulary is open but context may be used to reduce it dynamically to a limited subset of tractable size. For example, in the case of mail addresses, the image of the postal code may be used to focus on certain city names.

We will describe below a set of HMM's for recognizing cursive handwritten words in dynamic vocabularies [40]. When dealing with a small but dynamic vocabulary it is no longer possible to learn one HMM for each word. Rather, we use HMM's at the letter level. The HMM for one word is just obtained by concatenating the HMM of its letters. The global strategy thus remains model discriminant.

3.4.1. Learning letter models

The notion of tied states in HMM [11] provides the solution for sharing letter models. Wherever a letter appears in some word, we tie the sets of states in each copy of the letter model. In order to obtain a structure similar to that of Fig 3.8 for whole word HMM, we use 3 states letter models. For example, the name *laval* induces the model depicted on Fig 3.9.

3.4.2. Application to word recognition

Like with wholistic HMM, we are interested in $p(W = w | O = o)$. However, it is difficult to estimate the a priori probability of words $p(W = w)$ since the vocabulary is open. Also, it is not possible to rely simply on the form of names (*Paris* is much more likely than *Palis*). We thus only used statistics on word lengths, first and last letter to estimate $p(W = w)$.

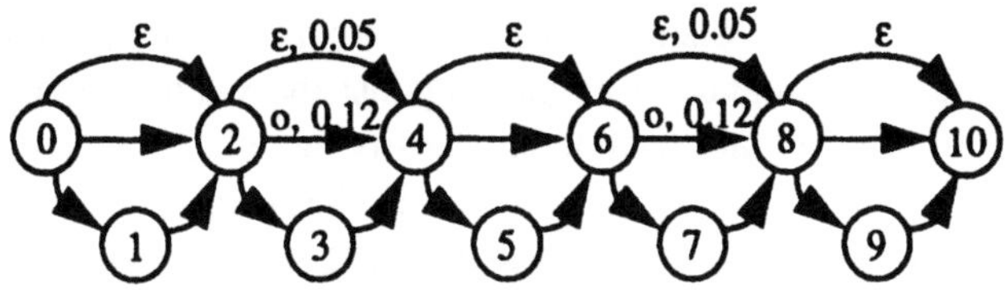

Fig. 3.9. Outline of the model for the word "*laval*".

3.4.3. Results

The word recognition technique for dynamic vocabularies was trained on a set of 904 city name images localized manually on ordinary mail and was tested on a different set of 226 images. The training was based on the Viterbi algorithm. Given that the training set items were labelled with the correct city name without distinguishing capital and small letters, we used different models for the first letter in each name and the other letters. In order to simulate the address recognition task, we assumed that city names in competition in this task are independent given the corresponding postal codes hypotheses. In other words, confusable postal codes do not lead to resembling city names. Under this assumption, we chose randomly 9 city names in a 3628 entries lexicon to compete with the correct one. The parameter 10(9+1) was chosen because when a digit is not well recognized, 10 postal codes are in competition. The results of this test are reported on table 5.2.

Table 5.2. Recognition of names in a 10 elements dynamic vocabulary.

n	1	2	3	4	5	10
R(n)	91.2%	97.3%	99.1%	99.6%	100%	100%

3.5 Discussion

We have shown how several HMM's may be applied with profit to the recognition of cursive script words. These methods present several advantages. They are compatible with different types of vocabulary. They allow to automatically optimize the parameters of the system instead of tuning them manually. They also provide recognition scores which may be interpreted as probabilities. As a consequence, it is possible to integrate soundly the pattern recognition level with more abstract knowledge sources at a higher level.

3.6 Other approaches

HMM's have been applied to off-line handwriting recognition by a number of other researchers. Chen [27] has used an automatically segmented image as input to a left-to-right HMM to recognise handwritten words. The segments are described as features vectors made of the concatenation of various features classically used in character recognition. Emission distributions are approximated by the k-NN rule. The training examples were manually aligned against the word references. Later on, Chen used a path discriminant continuous density model [36] and a variable duration model discriminant strategy [39]. Caesar [38] has proposed a path discriminant model with observations corresponding to a sliding window. This method was applied to handwritten words. Gillies [34] employs a pixel column description together with the k-means algorithm to cluster pixel columns. Here too the application is word recognition. Kundu [33] uses a higher order model to account for letter statistics in a word recognition system.

4 Conclusion

Recent applications of HMM's to off-line handwriting recognition are strongly encouraging and explicate most of the progress in cursive word recognition research. A majority of approaches consisted in straightforward transpositions of methods developed in the automatic speech recognition world. However, many problems remain unsolved and important issues have to be addressed before the handwriting recognition community could experience the same type of success that the speech recognition world has enjoyed. A crucial aspect of HMM application in handwriting recognition is the availability of relevant features. Explicit segmentation methods have circumvented most of the feature extraction problem by trying to use letters as features. Classical character recognition features can then be imported in HMM's without any amendment. Obviously, the price to pay for this is the painful design of heuristic segmentation methods which are unlikely to be completely reliable. On the contrary, implicit segmentation approaches have often relied on pixel columns or sliding windows feature extraction. Both are clearly arbitrary since the first does not address the problem of overlapping characters and the second is faced with the hazardous choice of a relevant window width. The deep cause behind those defects is that HMM's take for granted the sequential nature of off-line handwriting. In fact, handwritten word images are only approximately sequential. This way of looking at words has been successful for some time and probably will remain successful in the near future until all benefits will have been drawn out from HMM's. Then, the 2-dimensional nature of word images could be the clue to further progress. The Markov Random Field model [44] may well be the concept that will enlarge the present frontiers of handwriting recognition without throwing away the basic intuition behind markovian modelling.

References

1. Rabiner, L.R., Juang, B.H.: An introduction to hidden Markov models, *IEEE ASSP Magazine* 3(1) (1986).
2. Poritz, A.B.: hidden Markov models: a guided tour, Proc. of the IEEE Int. Conf. on Acoustics, Speech, and Signal Processing (ICASSP'88), 7-13 (1988).

3. Rabiner, L.R.: A tutorial on hidden Markov models and selected applications in speech recognition, *Proc. of the IEEE* 77(2), 257-286 (1989).
4. Church, K.W.: A stochastic parts program and noun phrase parser for unrestricted text, Proc. of the Second Conf. on Applied Natural Language Processing, 136-143 (1988).
5. Derouault, M., Mérialdo, B.: Natural language modelling for phoneme-to-text transcription, *IEEE Trans. on Pattern Analysis and Machine Intelligence*, vol. 8, 742-749 (1986).
6. Kuhn, R., De Mori, R.: A cache-based natural-language model for speech recognition, *IEEE Trans. on Pattern Analysis and Machine Intelligence*, vol. PAMI-12(6), 570-583 (1990).
7. Gilloux, M.: Automatic learning of word transducers from examples, Proc. of the 5th Conf. of the European Chapter of the Association for Computation Linguistics (EACL'91), 107-112 (1991).
8. Vstovsky, G.V., Vstovskaya, A.V.: A class of hidden Markov models for images processing, *Pattern Recognition Letters* 14, 391-396 (1993).
9. Bellegarda, E.J., Bellegarda, J.R., Nahamoo, D., Nathan, K.S: On-line handwriting recognition based upon continuous parameter mixture densities, Proc. of the Third International Workshop on Frontiers in Handwriting Recognition (IWFHR-3), 225-234 (1993).
10. Bercu, S., Lorette, G.: On-line handwritten word recognition: an approach based on hidden Markov models, Proc. of the Third International Workshop on Frontiers in Handwriting Recognition (IWF-HR-3), 385-390 (1993).
11. Bahl, L. R., F. Jelinek, and R. L. Mercer: A maximum likelihood approach to speech recognition, *IEEE Trans. on Pattern Analysis and Machine Intelligence* 5(2), 179-190 (1983).
12. Baum, L. E.: An inequality and associated maximization technique in statistical estimation of probabilistic functions of Markov processes, *Inequalities* 3, 1-8 (1972).
13. Kirkpatrick, S., Gelatt, C.D., Vecchi, M.P.: Optimization by simulated annealing, *Science* 220, 671-680 (1983).
14. Jouvet, D., Monné, J., Dubois, D.: A new network-based speaker independent connected-word speech recognition system, Proc. of the Int. Conf. on Acoustics, Speech, and Signal Processing (ICASSP'86), 1109-1112 (1986).
15. Forney, G.D.: The Viterbi Algorithm, Proc. of the IEEE 61(3) (1973).
16. Bengio, Y., De Mori, R., Flammia, G., Kompe, R.: Global optimization of a neural network- hidden Markov model hybrid, *IEEE Trans. on Neural Networks*3(2), 252-259 (1992).
17. Mérialdo, B.,: Phonetic recognition using hidden Markov models and maximum mutual information training, Proc. of the Int. Conf. on Acoustics, Speech, and Signal Processing (ICASSP'88), 111-114 (1988).
18. Bourlard, H. Wellekens, C.J.: Links between Markov models and multilayer perceptrons, *IEEE Trans. on Pattern Analysis and Machine Intelligence* 12(12), 1167-1178 (1990).
19. Bahl, L.R., Brown, P.F., de Souza, P.V., Mercer, R.L.: A new algorithm for the estimation of hidden Markov model parameters, Proc. of the Int. Conf. on Acoustics, Speech, and Signal Processing (ICASSP'88), 493-496 (1988).
20. Vapnik, V.N.: Estimation of dependencies based on empirical data, Springer-Verlag (1982).
21. Lang, K.J., Waibel, A.H., Hinton, G.E.: A Time delay Neural network architecture for isolated word recognition, *Neural networks* 3(1), 23-44 (1990).
22. Lee, K.F. Hon, H., Hwang, M., Mahajan, S., Reddy, R.: The SPHINX speech recognition system, Proc. of the IEEE Int. Conf. ASSP, 445-448 (1989).
23. Picone, J.: Continuous speech recognition using hidden Markov models, *IEEE ASSP Magazine*, 26-41 (1990).
24. Waibel, A., Lee, K.-F. (eds): Readings in speech recognition, Morgan Kaufmann (1990).
25. Levinson, E.S, Rabiner, L.R., Sondhi, M.M.: An introduction to the application of the theory of probabilistic functions of a Markov process to automatic speech recognition, *The Bell System Technical Journal* 62(4), 1035-1074 (1983).
26. Schwartz, R., Austin, S.: A comparison of several approximate algorithms for finding multiple (N-best) sentence hypotheses, Proc. of the Int. Conf. on Acoustics, Speech, and Signal Processing (ICASSP'91), 701-704 (1991).

27. Chen, M.-Y. et al.: Off-line handwritten word recognition using hidden Markov model, Proc. of the 5th USPS Advanced Technology Conf., 563-577 (1992).
28. Tao, C.: A generalization of discrete hidden Markov model and of Viterbi algorithm, *Pattern Recognition* 25(11), 1381-1387 (1992).
29. Lari, K., Young, S.J.: The estimation of stochastic context-free grammars using the Inside-Outside algorithm, *Computer Speech and Language* 4, 35-36, 1990.
30. Levinson, S. E., Continuously variable duration hidden Markov models for automatic speech recognition, *Computer Speech and Language* 1, 29-45 (1986).
31. Brugnara, F., et al.: A family of parallel hidden Markov models, Proc. of the Int. Conf. on Acoustics, Speech, and Signal Processing (ICASSP'92), 377-380 (1992).
32. Kundu, A., Bahl, P.: Recognition of handwritten script: a hidden Markov model based approach, Proc. of the Int. Conf. on Acoustics, Speech, and Signal Processing (ICASSP'88), 928-931 (1988).
33. Kundu, A., He Y., Bahl, P.: Recognition of handwritten word: first and second order hidden Markov model based approach, *Pattern Recognition* 22(3), 283-297 (1989).
34. Gillies, A. M.: Cursive word recognition using hidden Markov models, Proc. of the 5th USPS Advanced Technology Conf., 557-562 (1992).
35. Gilloux, M., Leroux, M.: Recognition of cursive script amounts on postal cheques, Proc. of the 5th USPS Advanced Technology Conf., 545-556 (1992).
36. Chen, M.-Y., Kundu, A., Srihari, S.N.: Unconstrained handwritten word recognition using continuous density variable duration hidden Markov model, Proc. of the IEEE Int. Conf. on Acoustics, Speech, and Signal Processing (ICASSP'93) (1993).
37. Park, H.S., Lee, S.-W.: Off-line recognition of large-set handwritten Hangul (Korean script) with hidden Markov models, Proc. of the Third International Workshop on Frontiers in Handwriting Recognition (IWFHR-3), 51-61 (1993).
38. Caesar, T., et al.: Recognition of handwritten word images by statistical methods, Proc. of the Third International Workshop on Frontiers in Handwriting Recognition (IWFHR-3), 409-416 (1993).
39. Chen, M.-Y., Kundu, A.: An alternative to variable duration HMM in handwritten word recognition, Proc. of the Third International Workshop on Frontiers in Handwriting Recognition (IWFHR-3), 82-91 (1993).
40. Gilloux, M., Bertille, J.-M., Leroux, M.: Recognition of handwritten words in a limited dynamic vocabulary, Proc. of the Third International Workshop on Frontiers in Handwriting Recognition (IWFHR-3), 417-422 (1993).
41. Ha, J.-Y., et al.: Unconstrained handwritten word recognition with interconnected hidden Markov models, Proc. of the Third International Workshop on Frontiers in Handwriting Recognition (IWFHR-3), 455-460 (1993).
42. Bertille, J.-M., El Yacoubi, M.: Global cursive postal code recognition using hidden Markov models, Proc. of the 1st European Conf. on Postal Technologies (JetPoste'93), 129-138 (1993).
43. Leroux, M., Salomé, J.-C., Badard, J.: Recognition of cursive script words in a small lexicon, Proc. of the 1st International Conf. on Document Analysis and Recognition (ICDAR'91), 774-782 (1991).
44. Geman, S., Geman, D.: Stochastic relaxation, Gibbs distributions, and the bayesian restoration of images, *IEEE Trans. on Pattern Analysis and Machine Intelligence* 6, 721-741 (1984).

Language-Level Syntactic and Semantic Constraints Applied to Visual Word Recognition

Jonathan J. Hull

Center of Excellence for Document Analysis and Recognition
Department of Computer Science
State University of New York at Buffalo
Buffalo, New York, 14260
hull@cs.buffalo.edu

Abstract. Various aspects of using language-level syntactic and semantic constraints to improve the performance of word recognition algorithms are discussed. Following a brief presentation of a hypothesis generation model for handwritten word recognition, various types of language-level constraints are reviewed. Methods that exploit these characteristics are discussed including intra-document word correlation, common vocabularies, part-of-speech tag co-occurrence, structural parsing with a chart data structure, and semantic biasing with a thesaurus.

1. Introduction

Information above the level of individual words can significantly improve the performance of algorithms that transform images of text into their ASCII equivalent. This area of research uses algorithms and techniques from graphical text layout, information retrieval, and natural language processing, to modify recognition decisions so that they are consistent with the contextual information provided by a coherent passage of text.

The paradigm for handwriting recognition assumed by the techniques presented in this paper is shown in Figure 1. Word images segmented from a passage of text are passed to a word recognition algorithm that computes a ranked set of n hypotheses or potential word decisions that are chosen from a dictionary. Referred to as the *neighborhood* of the word, this hypothesis set should rank the correct decision at the top position as often as possible. In cases where the most highly ranked choice is not the correct decision, it should appear somewhere in the neighborhood. The word recognition algorithm can use a combination of isolated character recognition, postprocessing of the character decisions versus the dictionary, and wholistic word recognition [12]. The methods for language-level analysis discussed in this paper utilize global contextual information extracted from the entire document to improve the performance of the word recognition technique.

The definition of *improved performance* in word recognition has many aspects. The most basic is an overall improvement in correct rate, i.e., rearranging the neighborhood so that the top decision is correct more often. Also, a reduction in the size of the neighborhood improves performance as long as an error is not introduced. This happens when the correct word is removed. Another important aspect of improving performance is determining a subset of words from the input document that have a higher probability of correctness than that provided by the recognition algorithm. Such a subset of high confidence decisions can be used as "islands" to drive further processing of the other neighborhoods.

Many techniques have been used to improve the performance of text recognition algorithms. Baird used the semantics of chess to select a sequence of character decisions that produced a legal series of chess moves [1]. The simultaneous use of character transitional probabilities and word collocation statistics has also been addressed [16]. Natural language information, including orthographic constraints, syntactic and semantic knowledge have been discussed [5]. Language-level syntactic knowledge is also an important part of many approaches to speech recognition [27]. Several methods have been used that incorporate syntactic information including probabilities [25], and chart parsing [3,26].

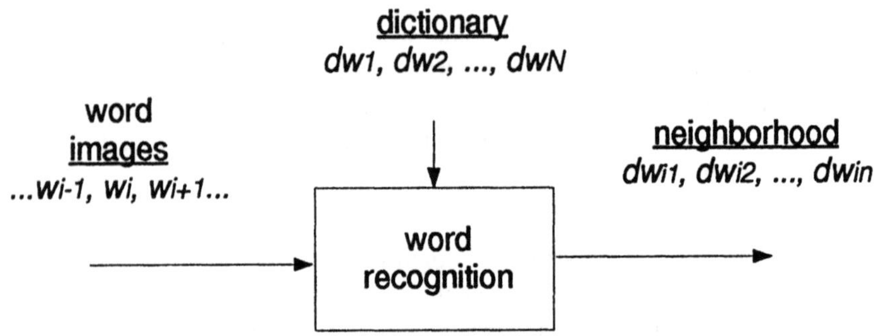

Figure 1. Paradigm for text recognition.

Five contextual constraints that are useful for improving the performance of a text recognition algorithm are discussed in this paper. *Graphical* constraints refer to the context between words within a document prepared by a single writer. The consistency of physical writing style within a document allows for the determination of clusters of equivalent word images. The clusters are then mapped onto language statistics and function words (short, frequently occurring words such as *the, of, and, a,* and *to.*) are recognized. Also, clusters are located that contain potential keywords or *content words* that indicate the topic of the passage of text. This method improves performance by recognizing function words with high confidence. Also, clusters of potential content words are used to generate feature representations that improve their recognition performance.

Vocabulary constraints are the commonality between the words used by authors when writing a passage of text about a specific topic. These constraints narrow the gap between the large dictionary that is needed for general purpose word recognition (on the order of 100,000 or more words) and the limited vocabulary that may be used in a given document (maybe as few as 200 to 500). Techniques from information retrieval are used to match the neighborhoods of word decisions calculated from an image to ASCII documents in a free-text database. The vocabularies from the most similar documents are used to locate a subset of word decisions that are correct with high confidence.

Statistical constraints quantify the predictive ability of words or other grammatical characteristics in a text passage. The most common of these are word collocation data. Another technique is to use the information given by the part-of-speech tag (e.g., noun, verb, etc.) for a word to constrain adjacent part-of-speech tags. Only word decisions with those tags are "legal" in the given context. This technique improves the overall performance of a word recognition algorithm by removing words from neighborhoods that do not have the estimated grammatical characteristic.

Structural-syntactic constraints refer to the information provided by a full parse for a sentence. Typically calculated by a structural method such as a chart parser, the parse for a sentence expresses syntactic information from several contiguous words. A modified chart parser that operates directly on the neighborhoods provided by a word recognition algorithm can choose decisions from the neighborhoods that are consistent with the entire sentence. This technique improves text recognition performance by choosing the single best decision for each word. Modifications that use multiple parses to increase the number of choices for each word are also possible.

Structural-semantic constraints refer to the "glue" that binds together words within a document. Because of the commonality of theme within a coherent passage, it has been observed that groups of words can be identified that are about the same subject. For example, a passage of text about a river is likely to contain the words *water, boat, dock, bank,* and so on. The semantic relationship between words can be calculated from a data structure such as a thesaurus. This information is used to improve the performance of a text recognition algorithm by constraining decisions for selected words to be similar in topic.

The rest of this paper discusses each of the categories mentioned above in more detail. Example algorithms are given and the ability of those techniques to improve text recognition is discussed.

2. Graphical Constraints

The consistency of writing style within a handwritten document is a valuable source of information that can improve recognition performance. Given a document written by a single person, the commonality of appearance between images of the same word can allow for the determination that two images are equivalent. That is, they represent the same word.

Statistics about the frequency of word occurrence within documents are a valuable constraint on the repetition of distinct words. This has been used for solving substitution ciphers and OCR processes [20]. Two especially useful word occurrence characteristics are the frequency of *function* words and the internal frequency of *content* words within a document.

Function words are short determiners or prepositions that supply syntactic information about nearby words. For example, over 75 percent of the words that follow a determiner are either common nouns or adjectives. Examples of function words include *the, of, and, a,* and *to*. In fact, these five words as well as the other five most common function words account for about 23 percent of the word tokens in the over one million words of running text known as the Brown Corpus [18].

Content words are usually nouns that convey information about the topic of an article. Often, the same content words recur several times within an article. This effect is utilized in document classification and information retrieval techniques that select keywords based on their frequency. Often the first step in locating a keyword (index term) is to discard the most frequent words, which tend to be function words, and choose the words from the remaining set that have high internal frequency within the document [24]. These methods have also been extended to phrasal indexing that uses repeated groups of words to improve the effectiveness of document classification.

The accurate recognition of both function and content words is essential in a text recognition system. The syntactic information provided by function words can be used to constrain the choices for nearby words. Because of their importance for document classification and subsequent information retrieval processes, content words must also be correctly recognized.

An algorithm has been proposed that uses information about the repetition of words within a document to improve the recognition of both function and content words [17]. Clusters of *equivalent* word images are determined by *matching* images to one another and improved prototypes are generated for the words in a cluster by using inter-image redundancy to eliminate noise. Function words are then recognized by a combination of intra-cluster and inter-cluster statistical characteristics as well as matching to stored prototypes.

Advantages of the technique include its limited use of an explicit recognition algorithm. The basic operation of word image matching implies that relatively high noise levels can be tolerated. Touching, broken, or degraded characters that would render typical recognition algorithms useless are easily compensated for by inter-word redundancy.

Figure 2 outlines the steps of the word image matching algorithm. Word images from an entire sample of text are segmented, and sent to a clustering algorithm sequentially. The algorithm iteratively groups the images into clusters of equivalent words. The ideal result is a number of clusters, each containing all the occurrences of a specific word in the document.

Several operations are then performed on the resulting word image clusters. *Cluster identification* refers to the process of identifying the word contained in a given cluster, possibly without direct recognition of the word images. This is done by using both language statistics and cluster properties. This method of identifying the content of clusters is more effective with clusters containing the function words because their frequency of occurrence in the language is more likely to match their frequency of occurrence in a document.

The clusters containing potential content words are located by inspecting the number of words in each cluster and the lengths of those words. Using the redundancy between images in these clusters, improved (less noisy) prototypes for the content words are generated. A word recognition algorithm (not described here) could then be applied to the improved prototypes to yield better performance than would be possible on the individual images.

This technique has been successfully applied to machine-printed documents. Over 95 percent of the function words in a set of documents were recognized and 93 percent of the important keywords were located [17]. These experiments were conducted on documents that exhibited moderate to extreme noise.

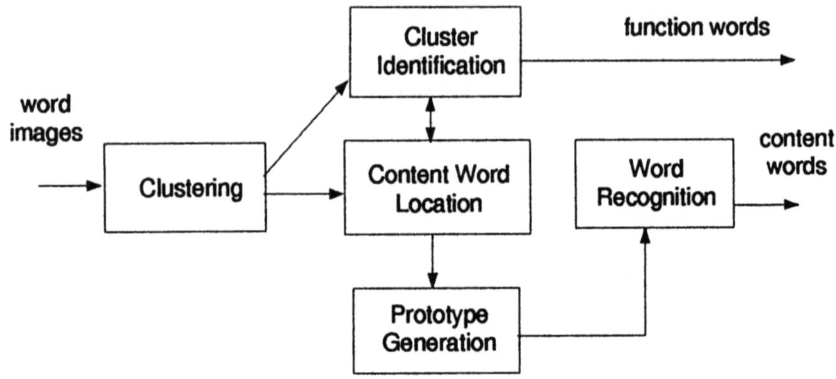

Figure 2. Word image matching algorithm.

The extension of this and other techniques that use graphical context to handwritten documents would depend on the success of the algorithm that determines whether two words are equivalent. This poses an interesting problem for future research. An important consideration would be whether on-line or off-line samples would be used.

3. Vocabulary Similarity

Word recognition algorithms utilize the dictionary directly in the recognition process, effectively employing word-level context in processing image data. Representations for words from a dictionary are matched to word images in documents. The result is a ranking of the dictionary for each word image where words that are ranked closer to the top have a higher probability of being correct. A consideration in using word recognition is that a large dictionary (on the order of 100,000 or more words) may be needed to guarantee that almost any word that could be encountered in an input document would exist in the dictionary.

Errors in the output of a word recognition system can be caused by several sources. When a noisy document image is input, the top choice of a word recognition system may only be correct a relatively small proportion of the time.

However, the ranking of the dictionary may include the correct choice among its top N guesses (N=10, for example) in nearly 100 percent of the cases.

An observation about context beyond the individual word level that is used here concerns the vocabulary of a document. Even though the vocabulary over which word recognition is computed may contain 100,000 or more words, a typical document may actually use fewer than 500 different words. Thus, higher accuracy in word recognition is bound to result if the vocabulary of a document could be predicted and the decisions of a word recognition algorithm were selected only from that limited set.

A technique has recently been proposed in which the N best recognition choices for each word are used in a probabilistic model for information retrieval to locate a set of similar documents in a database [15]. The vocabulary of those documents is then used to select the recognition decisions from the word recognition system that have a high probability of correctness. A useful side effect of matching word recognition results to documents from a database is that the topic of the input document is indicated by the titles of the matching documents from the database.

3.1. Algorithm Description

The algorithmic framework discussed in this paper is presented in Figure 3. Word images from a document are input. Those images are passed to a word recognition algorithm that matches them to entries in a large dictionary. *Neighborhoods* or groups of words from the dictionary are computed for each input image. The neighborhoods contain words that are *visually* similar to the input word images.

A matching algorithm is then executed on the word recognition neighborhoods. A subset of the documents in a pre-classified database of ASCII text samples are located that have similar topics to the input document. The hypothesis is that those documents should also share a significant portion of their vocabulary with the input document.

Entries in the neighborhoods are selected based on their appearance in the matching documents. The output of the algorithm are words that have an improved probability of being correct based on their joint appearance in both the word recognition neighborhoods as well as the matching documents. These are words that are both visually similar to the input and are in the vocabulary of the documents with similar topics.

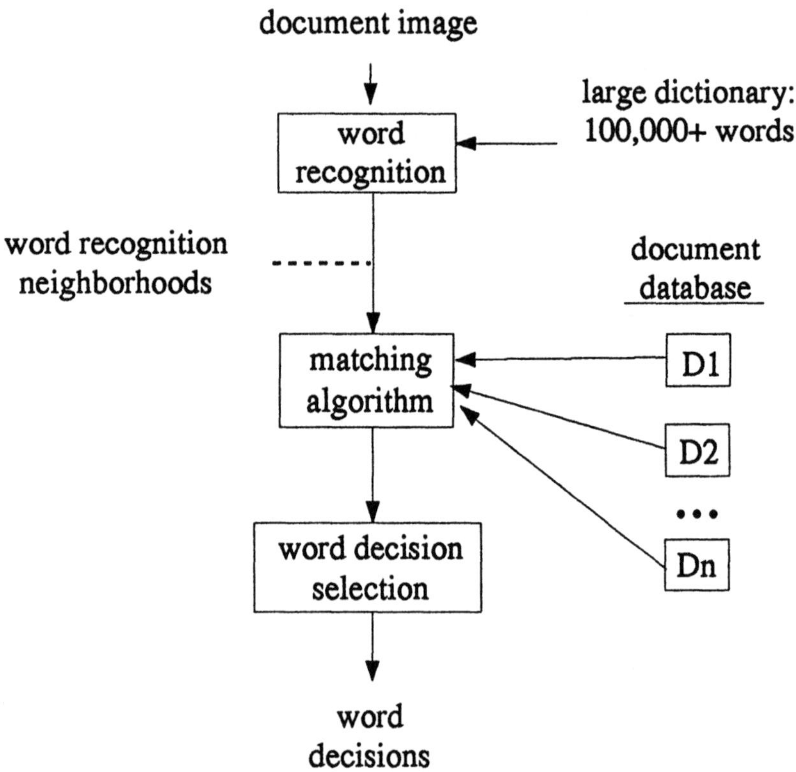

Figure 3. Vocabulary matching algorithm.

3.2. Document Matching Algorithm

The matching algorithm that determines the documents in the database that are most similar to the input is based on the *vector space model* for information retrieval [23]. In this approach, a document is represented by a vector of index terms or keywords. The similarity between a query and a document or between two documents is calculated by the inner product of the term vectors where each entry in the vectors is equal to one if the corresponding term is present and zero otherwise.

An alternate formulation is to replace the binary values by weights that represent the importance of the corresponding word or phrase in representing the content of the document. One method for calculating the weight assigned to word k in document i is:

$$w_{ik} = \frac{tf_{ik} \log\left(\frac{N}{n_k}\right)}{\sqrt{\sum_{k=1}^{t} (tf_{ik})^2 [\log\left(\frac{N}{n_k}\right)]^2}} \qquad (1)$$

where, tf_{ik} is the frequency of term k in document i, n_k is the number of documents in the database that contain term k, and N is the total number of documents in the database.

This formulation assigns higher weights to terms that occur frequently inside a document but less frequently in other documents. This is based on the assumption that those terms should be more important for representing the content of the document. Thus, the co-occurrence of terms with high weights in two documents should indicate that their topics are similar.

The direct use of the weight calculation expressed in equation (1) would assume the presence of a word recognition system with 100 percent accuracy. A modification is proposed in calculating the term frequency for a word in an input document that accounts for the imprecision in the recognition results. Instead of accumulating a unit weight for each occurrence of a word, the term frequency for a word is taken as the sum of the probabilities assigned to that word by the recognition algorithm.

The calculation of the external frequency of words in other documents in the database is unchanged since their true ASCII representation exists.

3.3. Similarity Calculation

The similarity between two documents i and j, as mentioned above, can be calculated as the inner product between their weight vectors:

$$sim(D_i, D_j) = \sum_{k=1}^{t} w_{ik} \cdot w_{jk}$$

for the t index terms that occur in either one or both of the documents.

In the application discussed here, the index terms in an ASCII document are calculated from the non-stop words and non-proper nouns. Stop words occur frequently in a normal text passage and convey little meaning. Proper nouns are names of specific persons, places, or things. Every other word is assumed to be an "index term" for the purpose of matching.

3.4. Experimental Results

The word decision selection algorithm discussed above was demonstrated on the Brown corpus [18]. The Brown corpus is a collection of over one million words of running text that is divided into 500 samples of approximately 2000 words each. The samples were selected from 15 subject categories or genres and the number of samples in each genre was set to be representative of the amount of text in that subject area at the time the corpus was compiled.

One of the samples in the Brown corpus was selected as a test document to demonstrate the algorithm discussed above. This sample is denoted G02 (the second sample from genre G: *Belles Lettres*) and is an article entitled *Toward a Concept of National Responsibility,* by Arthur S. Miller that appeared in the December, 1961 edition of the Yale Review.

There are 2047 words in the running text of G02. After removing stop words and proper nouns, there were 885 words left. Neighborhoods were generated for those words by a simulation of a word recognition algorithm that used the 53,000 unique words from the entire Brown corpus as its dictionary.

The ten most visually similar dictionary words were calculated for each input word. This provided 8850 neighbors overall. The word shape calculation had performance of 87 percent correct in the top choice and 99 percent correct in the top ten choices.

The training data for the matching process and the word decision selection algorithm was the other 499 samples in the Brown corpus besides G02. The document matching algorithm described earlier was used to rank the other 499 samples for their similarity to G02.

The ten most similar samples in the Brown corpus, as determined by the matching algorithm, are listed in Table 1. It is interesting to observe how similar their titles are to that of G02. For example, the most similar sample is J42 whose title is *The Political Foundation of International Law.* This group of similar articles illustrates the side-effect of the matching algorithm since it essentially classifies the content of a document by indicating the samples that it is most similar to. The effectiveness of the document classification task could be improved by applying further preprocessing to the text samples in the database. More detailed representations of the database documents could be used in a more complex classification algorithm.

Table 1. Ten most similar samples to G02

rank	sample	title
1	J42	The Political Foundation of International Law
2	J22	The Emerging Nations
3	G25	The Restoration of Tradition
4	H02	An Act for International Development
5	H20	Development Program for the National Forests
6	G72	For a Concert of Free Nations
7	G35	Peace with Justice
8	H22	U.S. Treaties and Other International Agreements
9	H19	Peace Corps Fact Book
10	G10	How the Civil War Kept you Sovereign

3.5. Word Decision Selection Results

The ability of the most similar samples determined by the matching procedure to select the correct word decisions from the neighborhoods was tested. The top choices of the recognition algorithm were filtered by comparing them to the most similar samples and retaining the words that occurred in those samples. The three selection criteria that were tested included *overall* performance in which all the top recognition choices in G02 that occurred anywhere in the similar samples were retained.

The *G02-nouns* condition refers to the case where only the top choices for the nouns in G02 that matched any of the nouns in the similar samples were retained. The application of this selection criteria in a working system would assume the presence of a part-of-speech (POS) tagging algorithm that would assign POS tags to word images.

In the *matching-nouns* condition, only the nouns in the similar samples were used to filter the top recognition choices. This case was explored because the nouns may be considered to carry more information about the content of a text passage than verbs or words with other parts of speech. Thus, the co-occurrence of nouns in two documents about similar topics should be due less to chance than other word types.

The results of word decision selection when applied to the original word recognition output (with 13% error at the top choice) are summarized in Table 2. When all the words in the most similar sample (J42) were matched to the top recognition decisions for G02 (top left entry in Table 2), it was discovered that 251 of those top decisions also occurred in J42. Of those, only nine words were erroneous matches. This corresponds to an error rate of about four percent. In other words, the correct rate for 28 percent of the input words was raised to 96 percent from the 87 percent provided by the word recognition algorithm alone.

The other results show that as more of the similar samples are used to filter the word recognition output, a progressively higher percentage of the eligible neighborhoods are included and the correct rate remains stable. For example, in the *overall* condition using the four most similar samples, 441 of the 885 (50%) input words were effectively recognized with a correct rate of 97.2 percent. The results for the *G02-nouns* matching condition show that up to 26 percent of the input can be recognized with a 99.16 percent correct rate. In the *nouns-matching* condition, 29 percent of the input words can be recognized with a 97 percent correct rate.

Table 2. Word selection performance on the 885 neighborhoods.

samples used	decision selection criteria								
	overall			*G02-nouns*			*nouns-matching*		
	matches	errs	corr.%	matches	errs	corr.%	matches	errs	corr.%
1	251	9	96	130	2	98	187	6	97
2	345	11	97	177	2	99	206	6	97
3	393	12	97	199	2	99	241	6	98
4	441	12	97	229	2	99	257	8	97
5	451	12	98	234	2	99	258	9	97
6	459	13	97	248	2	99	272	9	96
7	474	16	97	254	3	99	280	11	96
8	483	16	97	254	3	99	284	11	96
9	498	16	97	261	3	99	288	11	96
10	526	22	96	300	4	99	296	12	96

4. Statistical Constraints

The statistical transitions between pairs of words are one source of syntactic information that have been used to improve word recognition [10]. Alternatives for the identification of a word were removed from consideration if they never followed the previous word in a large training sample of text. Even though this technique improved performance, it was computationally unacceptable as the transitions were difficult to estimate with even very large samples of text.

An improvement on word-to-word transitions was to model language syntax with binary constraints between a group of words with the same shape and the syntactic classes that could follow them [11]. The constraints were compiled from a training text and applied to restrict the decisions for the syntactic class of a word to be consistent with the shape of the previous word. Even this limited binary information was shown to be effective at reducing the average number of words that could match any image by about 16 percent on average with an error rate of about one percent. An error occurred when a word was erroneously removed from consideration.

This section discusses an algorithm that models English grammar as a Markov process where the probability of observing any syntactic category is dependent on the syntactic category of the previous word or words [14]. This model is applied to text recognition by first using a word recognition algorithm to supply a number of alternatives for the identity of each word. The syntactic categories of the alternatives for the words in a sentence are then input to a modified Viterbi algorithm that determines the sequences of syntactic categories that best match the input. An alternative for a word decision is output only if its syntactic category is included in at least one of these sequences. The Markov model improves word recognition performance if the number of alternatives for a word are reduced without removing the correct choice.

4.1. Syntax Model

The syntax of a sentence is summarized as the sequence of grammatical categories for each of its words. There are several ways to define the grammatical categories. The part-of-speech (POS) tags assigned to each word are one definition. For example, in the sentence "He was at work.", *He* is a pronoun, *was* is a verb, *at* is a preposition, and *work* is a noun.

Since the appearance of a grammatical category probabilistically constrains the categories that can follow it, a Markov model is a natural representation for syntax [19]. An example of such a constraint are the probabilities that certain

POS tags follow an article in a large sample of text. The word following an article is a singular or mass noun in 51 percent of all cases and is an adjective 20 percent of the time. The other 29 percent of occurrences are scattered over 82 other syntactic classes [7].

A hidden Markov model (HMM) can be specified that links the recognition process described earlier and a Markov model for language syntax [21]. The grammatical categories in the English language are assumed to be the N *states* of a discrete r^{th} order Markov process. The states are defined to be POS tags. Many words can be assigned one POS tag and a relatively small number (typically 25 to 100) of POS tags have been used for English.

In the word recognition algorithm, the states are "hidden" because they are not observable at run-time. Rather, the feature vector that describes a word image is the observable event. The number of such feature vectors is finite and provides a fixed number of *observation symbols.*

The transition from one state to another is described by a *state transition probability distribution.* If the Markov process is assumed to be first order, this distribution can be given by an $N \ x \ N$ matrix. A second order assumption would imply the use of an $N \ x \ N \ x \ N$ probability distribution matrix.

There is also a probabilistic mapping function from the set of observations onto the set of states. Each observation is first mapped onto a set of words by the neighborhood generation or word recognition algorithm. Each word is assigned a probability of correctness by this process. Those words are then mapped onto the set of POS tags by a many-to-one function. The probability of an observation given that the process is in a specific state is provided by a combination of the recognition and word-to-state mapping probabilities. This is sometimes referred to as the *confusion probability.*

There are also *initial and final state distributions* that specify the probability that the model is in each state for the first and last words in a sentence. These constraints can be powerful. For example, it has been observed in a sample of newspaper reportage that the first word in a sentence is an article or a proper noun with probability 0.31 and 0.14, respectively. The other 55 percent is divided among 24 other classes.

The HMM is completely specified by the five elements just described (states, observation symbols, state transition probabilities, observation symbol probabilities, and initial probabilities). The HMM is applied to word recognition by estimating the sequence of states with the maximum a-posterior probability of occurrence for a given sequence of observations (feature vectors). The performance of the word recognition algorithm is improved by reducing neighborhoods so that they contain only words that map onto states in the estimated sequence.

The estimation of the sequence of states with the maximum a-posterior probability of occurrence is efficiently performed by the Viterbi algorithm [6]. The adaptation of the Viterbi algorithm to this problem is similar to its use in post-processing character decisions [9]. The Viterbi algorithm has also been successfully used for speech recognition [2].

4.2. Example

An example of applying the HMM for syntactic constraints is shown in Figure 4. The original input sentence is shown along the the top of the figure (HE WAS AT WORK.). The complete neighborhoods for each word are shown below the input words. Each word is shown along with an indication of its syntactic class and the confusion probability for that neighborhood given the syntactic class. The first and third words in the sentence have only one word in their neighborhoods. The second neighborhood contains eight different words, two of which have different syntactic classes. The fourth neighborhood contains six different words, one of which has three different syntactic tags.

The transition probabilities are shown along the arcs. It is seen that some transitions, such as PPS-NNS (third person nominative pronoun followed by a plural noun) never occurred in the training text and hence have a probability of zero. Other transitions are much more likely, such as PPS-VBD (third person nominative pronoun followed by a verb in the past tense, e.g., *he ran*) which has a probability of 0.3621.

In this case, the top choice of the Viterbi algorithm was PPS-BEDZ-IN-NP and the second choice was PPS-BEDZ-IN-NN. In the top choice, three of the four classes included the correct identification for each word. The correct answer for the fourth word (NN) was only contained in the second choice of the Viterbi.

4.3. Experimental Investigation

Experimental tests were conducted to determine the ability of the HMM to reduce the number of word candidates that match any image. Given sentences from test samples of running text, a neighborhood was calculated for each word by a simulation of the word recognition process. These data were then processed by the HMM.

Performance was measured by calculating the average neighborhood size per text word before and after the application of syntax. This statistic is defined as:

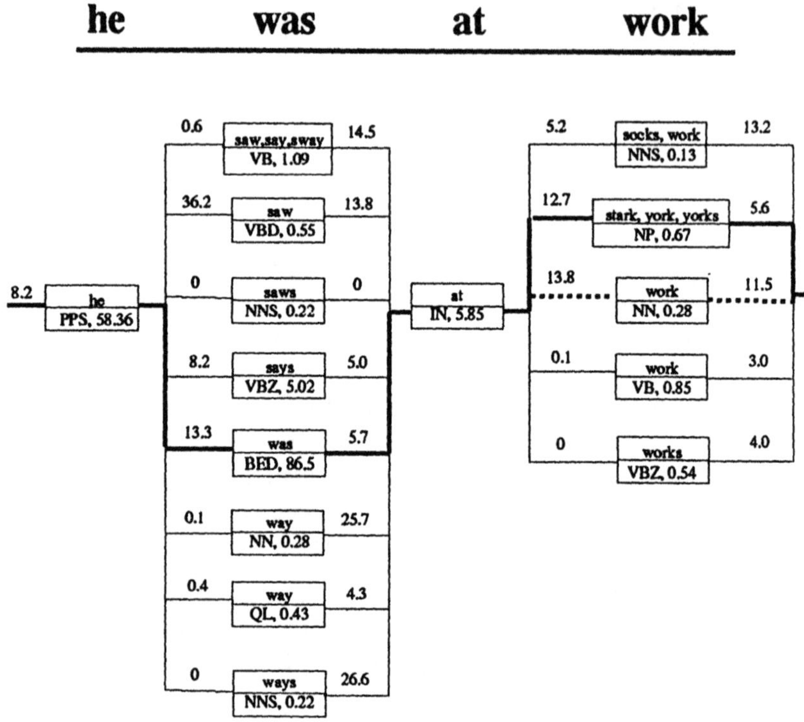

Figure 4. Example of applying the Viterbi algorithm .

$$ANS_t = \frac{1}{N_w} \sum_{i=1}^{N_w} ns_i$$

where N_w is the number of words in the test sample and ns_i is the number of words in the neighborhood for the ith word in the text. The improvement in performance is measured by the percentage reduction in ANS_t. The *error rate* was also measured. This is the percentage of words with neighborhoods that do not contain the correct choice after the application of syntax.

In the example presented in Figure 4, N_w is 4, $ns_1 = 1$, $ns_2 = 8$, $ns_3 = 1$, and $ns_4 = 6$. $ANS_t = \frac{1}{4}$ (1+8+1+6) = 4.0. After the application of both parses,

ANS_t was reduced to 1.75. This is an overall reduction of about 44 percent in ANS_t with a zero percent error rate.

4.4. Experimental Results

The HMM was applied to correct the text recognition results for the neighborhoods generated from sample A06. A06 is a sample of newspaper reportage that contains excerpts from the *Newark Evening News* of March 22, 1961.

Five state-sequences were output for each sentence by the HMM and used to filter the neighborhoods. Both first and second-order syntactic class transition probabilities were estimated from the remainder of the corpus.

Results showed that the neighborhoods could be reduced by between 70 and 80 percent with an error rate that ranged from one to five percent. The best performance was achieved with five state sequences and first order transition probabilities. Interestingly enough, using second order transitions had little effect on performance. This might be attributed to a lack of training data.

5. Structural Syntactic Constraints

Structural techniques that produce a complete parse (or a number of parses) for a sentence have been used to improve the performance of speech recognition devices. Typically, such methods require that a grammar and lexicon be supplied that summarize the syntax of the sentences of the language that will be encountered. An input sentence is then parsed and word decisions are output that appear as terminal nodes in the parse tree(s).

Difficulties with such techniques include the need to specify a grammar that will cover all the instances of a language that will be encountered in practice. Recently, statistical and structural approaches have been combined to overcome some of the difficulties in extending parsing techniques to unrestricted text. Automatic acquisition of lexical knowledge also has become a promising approach for building the large-scale dictionaries needed by such techniques.

Recently, parsing techniques have been applied to correct the output of a word-based text recognition system [8]. A probabilistic lattice was described that used syntactic and semantic constraints to find the best candidate for each word image.

Two types of linguistic constraint were used. One is local word collocation in which the identity of a word is used to predict the identity of other nearby words [4]. Global structural constraints are exploited with a chart parsing model. A lattice parser was used that allows for several word candidates at the same position, and therefore can be directly applied to correcting the neighborhoods output by a word recognition algorithm. The parser chooses the words on a path through the lattice that correspond to a legal sentence with the highest probability of being correct, given the sentences represented in the lattice.

Given the word images from an English sentence, a word recognition algorithm generates a neighborhood for each word image; next, a relaxation procedure reduces the top-n candidates for each image to the two best candidates by applying word collocation information; the top-2 lists for a sentence form the word lattice processed by the probabilistic lattice chart parser. All possible parse trees are built from the reduced word lattice; finally, the word candidates involved in the most preferred parse tree are selected as the correct word candidates and the most preferred parse tree is output.

5.1. Word Collocation Data

A relaxation algorithm based on word collocation statistics is used as a filter to reduce the top-n word candidates at each location to the into top-m, where $m < n$. The basic idea of the relaxation algorithm is to use local word collocation constraints to select the word candidates that have stronger word collocation with their neighbor words.

Let W_i denote the word image at position i and w_{ij} denote the jth word candidate for the word image W_i, where $1 \le j \le n$. The word collocation score of w_{ij}, where $1 \le j \le n$, is

$$\max_{k=1}^{n} WordCollocationScoreOf\ (w_{i-1,k}\ ,\ w_{ij})$$

$$+ \max_{k=1}^{n} WordCollocationScoreOf\ (w_{ij}\ ,\ w_{i+1,k})$$

where $WordCollocationScoreOf\ (word_1\ ,\ word_2)$ is the measurement of the strength of word collocation of the word pair $(word_1, word_2)$. After sorting the word collocation scores of w_{ij}, for $j=1, \cdots ,n$, the first m word candidates with the highest word collocation scores are output.

5.2. Probabilistic Lattice Chart Parser

There are 668 rules in the CFG used in this system. For example, the following rules are typical.

```
S       <- S-BODY .
S       <- WH-S-BODY ?
S       <- YN-S-BODY ?
S-BODY  <- NP VP
S-BODY  <- S-BODY CC S-BODY
NP      <- NN
NP      <- NP PP
NP      <- NP CC NP
VP      <- VB NP
VP      <- VB
```

Each of the rules in the grammar is associated with a confidence score which indicates the priority of the rule in comparison to other rules. A rule with a high score means that it is more likely to be used.

The parser is a bottom-up chart parser. A chart is a graph, that is a set of nodes and a set of edges linking them. As a data structure, the chart provides a general, flexible, efficient and economic framework for parsing. Every constituent or structure derived during parsing is recorded as an edge.

There are five steps in the parser. They are:

1. loading a word sequence or word lattice;
2. loading word tags;
3. noun phrase parsing;
4. sentence parsing;
5. checking the chart to find the most preferred parse tree if it exists.

When parsing is finished, the parser decides whether it failed by checking whether there exists any edges with label "S". If parsing succeeds, it will print out the parse tree represented by the "S" edge with the highest confidence score. If parsing fails, parse trees for fragments of the input word sequence are output.

5.3. Experimental Results

The chart parsing model was applied to sentences from sample G02 of the Brown corpus. A model for word recognition was used to generate neighborhoods for the words in the sample. Each neighborhood contained ten words on average and no information about the confidence value for the recognition decisions was used. The overall correct rate for relaxation was 86.4% and the parser correctly selected 76.2% of the words. This is a significant improvement over the ten percent correct rate that would be obtained from the neighborhoods.

6. Structural Semantic Constraints

The underlying meaning of text has been utilized in an innovative way to improve performance in a restricted domain by allowing only alternatives that were sensible in context [1]. The use of definitional overlap in machine-readable dictionaries and word collocations as semantic representations to improve the performance of a handwriting recognition system has also been discussed [5,22]

This section discusses a technique that models the semantic relationships between words by the network of connections in a thesaurus [13]. The thesaurus is represented by a directed graph in which root nodes point to related words. These words can also be root words that in turn point to other words, and so on. This structural representation is applied to text recognition by first using a word recognition algorithm to supply a number of alternatives for the identity of each word. The alternatives for the words in a passage of text are then recursively looked up in the thesaurus. Counters associated with each thesaurus word are incremented when the words are encountered in the lookup process. Semantically related alternatives in the neighborhoods from a passage of text are thus reinforced and unrelated words are suppressed. A threshold is applied to the scores to remove unrelated words from neighborhoods.

6.1. Semantic Model: The Thesaurus

The thesaurus used in this work was a directed graph of words that was commercially available. The thesaurus contained entries for 25,072 words. Each entry provides a root word and a list of related words. A minimum of two, a maximum of 257, and an average of 49.2 related words are in each entry. There are 50,357 different non-root words in the thesaurus.

The potential usefulness of the thesaurus in text recognition is illustrated by looking up all the words in a sample of text, accumulating the counts, and observing their distribution of values. The result of applying this process with two levels of lookup to 2000 words of a story about golfing[1] is illustrated in Table 3. The top 40 scores and the associated words are shown. It should be noted that no scores were accumulated for the true words. Thus any natural bias is eliminated and the pure effect of the thesaurus is given.

---

[1] Alfred Wright, "A duel golfers will never forget," Sports Illustrated, 64, pp. 18-21, April 17, 1961.

Table 3. Thesaurus activation values after two levels of lookup

COURSE	3423	ROUND	3187	CUT	2445	LINE	2427
RANGE	2360	HOLE	2330	POINT	2121	SET	1990
TURN	1985	CRACK	1885	PLACE	1862	CHECK	1794
SPACE	1790	MEASURE	1708	MARK	1687	PERIOD	1625
SCALE	1608	STEP	1607	ORDER	1571	FIELD	1561
STAGE	1548	RANK	1526	BEAT	1493	LEVEL	1393
OPENING	1383	NOTCH	1374	CYCLE	1350	PIT	1348
SHADOW	1334	RACE	1318	BANK	1304	GROUND	1304
DESCENT	1292	STRING	1290	PASSAGE	1274	CIRCUIT	1260
INTERVAL	1239	GALLERY	1237	COVER	1227	WAY	1224

It is very interesting to observe that key terms about golf are very frequent. For example, *golf* COURSE, ROUND *of golf*, *make the* CUT, *driving* RANGE, HOLE *in one*, are all near the top of the ranking. Numerous other similarities are also observed.

6.2. Algorithm

A statement of the algorithm for applying the thesaurus constraint to filtering neighborhoods output by the word recognition process is below:

1. Initialize counters for every thesaurus word (50,357)
2. For every word in every neighborhood:
   Recursively increment activation counters for lookup(word).
3. Rank the neighborhoods of content words (nouns) by:
   Confidence(word) = counter(word) / sum of counters in neighborhood
4. Reduce neighborhoods by thresholding the confidence value.

The function lookup(word) returns the list of related words from the thesaurus.

6.3. Experimental Results

The thesaurus algorithm was applied to correct simulated text recognition results from subset A38 of the Brown corpus. Two levels of thesaurus lookup were performed and the lexicon for the entire corpus was used. Using one level of lookup in the thesaurus, a neighborhood size reduction of about ten percent was achieved with an error rate of less than half a percent. Using a simulation in which the input neighborhoods contained approximately 15 words, a reduction of 14.82 percent was achieved with an error rate of 1.54 percent. When two levels of lookup were used, this was improved to a 19.59 percent reduction with a 0.77 percent error rate.

7. Discussion and Conclusions

This paper discussed several classes of technique that utilize language level syntactic and semantic constraints to improve the performance of a word recognition algorithm. The information used by such methods can generally be classified as graphical, vocabulary, statistical, structural-syntactic, and structural-semantic. Each area was discussed and algorithms that use each type of information were presented.

Acknowledgments. Siamak Khoubyari, Yanhong Li, and Tao Hong contributed to the preparation of this paper.

References

1. Baird, H. S. and Thompson, K., "Reading Chess," *IEEE Transactions on Pattern Analysis and Machine Intelligence 12* (1990), 552-559.

2. Cherkassky, V., Rao, M., Weschler, H., Bahl, L. R., Jelinek, F. and Mercer, R. L., "A maximum likelihood approach to continuous speech recognition," *IEEE Transactions on Pattern Analysis and Machine Intelligence PAMI-5*, 2 (March, 1983), 179-190.

3. Chien, L. F., Chen, K. J. and Lee, L. S., "An augmented chart data structure with efficient word lattice parsing scheme in speech recognition applications," *13th International Conference on Computational Linguistics 2* (1990), 60-65.

4. Church, K., Gale, W., Hanks, P. and Hindle, D., "Parsing, word associations, and typical predicate-argument relations," *International Workshop on Parsing Technologies*, Pittsburgh, Pennsylvania, August 28-31, 1989, 389-398.

5. Evett, L. J., Wells, C. J., Keenan, F. G., Rose, T. and Whitrow, R. J., "Using linguistic information to aid handwriting recognition," in *From Pixels to Features III: Frontiers in Handwriting Recognition*, S. Impedovo and J. C. Simon (editor), Elsevier Science Publishers B.V., 1992.

6. Forney, G. D., "The Viterbi algorithm," *Proceedings of the IEEE 61*, 3 (March, 1973), 268-278.

7. Francis, W. N. and Kucera, H., *Frequency Analysis of English Usage: Lexicon and Grammar*, Houghton Mifflin, Co., Boston, Massachusetts, 1982.

8. Hong, T. and Hull, J. J., "A Probabilistic Lattice Chart Parser for Text Recognition," *ICDAR-93: Second IAPR Conference on Document Analysis and Recognition*, Tsukuba Science City, Japan, October 20-22, 1993. submitted.

9. Hull, J. J., Srihari, S. N. and Choudhari, R., "An integrated algorithm for text recognition: comparison with a cascaded algorithm," *IEEE Transactions on Pattern Analysis and Machine Intelligence PAMI-5*, 4 (July, 1983), 384-395.

10. Hull, J. J., "Inter-word constraints in visual word recognition," *Proceedings of the Conference of the Canadian Society for Computational Studies of Intelligence*, Montreal, Canada, May 21-23, 1986, 134-138.

11. Hull, J. J., "Feature selection and language syntax in text recognition," in *From Pixels to Features*, J. C. Simon (editor), North Holland, 1989, 249-260.

12. Hull, J. J., Ho, T. K., Favata, J., Govindaraju, V. and Srihari, S. N., "Combination of segmentation-based and wholistic handwritten word recognition algorithms," *From Pixels to Features III: International Workshop on Frontiers in Handwriting Recognition*, Bonas, France, September 23-27, 1991, 229-240.

13. Hull, J. J. and Chin, A. T., "Semantic information extraction with a thesaurus for visual word recognition," in *Advances in Structual and Syntactic Pattern Recognition*, H. Bunke (editor), World Scientific, 1992, 342-351.

14. Hull, J. J., "A hidden Markov model for language syntax in text reconition," *11th IAPR International Conference on Pattern Recognition*, The Hague, The Netherlands, August 30 - September 3, 1992, 124-127.

15. Hull, J. J. and Li, Y., "Word recognition result interpretation using the vector space model for information retrieval," *Second Annual Symposium on Document Analysis and Information Retrieval*, Las Vegas, Nevada, April 26-28, 1993.

16. Jones, M. A., Story, G. A. and Ballard, B. W., "Integrating multiple knowledge sources in a Bayesian OCR post-processor," *First International Conference on Document Analysis and Recognition*, Saint-Malo, France, September 30 - October 2, 1991, 925-933.

17. Khoubyari, S. and Hull, J. J., "Keyword location in noisy document images," *Second Annual Symposium on Document Analysis and Information Retrieval*, Las Vegas, Nevada, April 26-28, 1993.

18. Kucera, H. and Francis, W. N., *Computational analysis of present-day American English*, Brown University Press, Providence, Rhode Island, 1967.

19. Kuhn, R., ''Speech recognition and the frequency of recently used words: A modified Markov model for natural language,'' *Proceedings of the 12th International Conference on Computational Linguistics*, Budapest, Hungary, August 22-27, 1988, 348-350.

20. Nagy, G., Seth, S. and Einspahr, K., ''Decoding substitution ciphers by means of word matching with application to OCR,'' *IEEE Transactions on Pattern Analysis and Machine Intelligence PAMI-9*, 5 (September, 1987), 710-715.

21. Rabiner, L. R. and Huang, B. H., ''An introduction to hidden Markov model,'' *ASSP Magazine 3*, 1 (1986), 4-16.

22. Rose, T. G., Evett, L. J. and Whitrow, R. J., ''The use of semantic information as an aid to handwriting recognition,'' *First International Conference on Document Analysis and Recognition*, Saint-Malo, France, September 30 - October 2, 1991, 629-637.

23. Salton, G., *Automatic text processing*, Addison Wesley, 1988.

24. Salton, G., ''Developments in automatic information retrieval,'' *Science 253* (1991), 974-980.

25. Seneff, S., ''Probabilistic parsing for spoken language applications,'' *International Workshop on Parsing Technologies*, Pittsburgh, Pennsylvania, August 28-31, 1989, 209-218.

26. Tomita, M., ''An efficient word lattice parsing algorithm for continuous speech recognition,'' *Proceedings of the International Conference on Acoustics, Speech, and Signal Processing*, 1986, 1569-1572.

27. White, G. M., ''Natural language understanding and speech recognition,'' *Communications of the ACM 33*, 8 (August, 1990), 74-82.

Verification of Handwritten British Postcodes Using Address Features

Hendrawan and A.C. Downton

Department of Electronic Systems Engineering, Univeristy of Essex, Wivenhoe Park, Colchester CO4 3SQ, UK

1 Introduction

The British postcode system consists of between five and seven alphanumeric characters which can specify any geographical postal location in the United Kingdom down to the resolution of a single office block or a group of several residential houses in a street. It is therefore possible to attempt to automatically sort handwritten letter mail by locating and recognising the handwritten characters of the postcode. However, OCR of handwritten characters is not perfect and misrecognitions will occur resulting in an unacceptable error rate in the sorting performance.

A verification process based upon correlating the postcode against the remainder of the handwritten or hand-printed address can reduce the error rate. In practical applications of automatic mail sorting, a low error rate is essential, although a higher rejection rate can be tolerated.

In this paper a verification method based on the concept of fuzzy sets is proposed. The verification is carried out by first defining a fuzzy membership function to measure the word similarities between an address image and the reference address corresponding to the recognised postcode. Degree of word matches are derived by measuring positional and structural feature similarities. The degree of similarity of the whole handwritten address is then obtained by finding the aggregation value of optimal word matches derived using the assignment problem in linear programming.

Postcode recognition and generation of the reference address corresponding to the recognised postcode are described in [1,2].

2 Preliminary Processing

In this work the handwritten addresses are partially constrained in that boxes are provided to write the postcode and horizontal guidelines are provided for guiding the position of the rest of the address. Therefore, whilst location and separation of the individual postcode characters can be achieved using a fairly simple algorithm, segmentation of the rest of the address is not trivial. The address images were scanned using the front end of an AEG postal sorter producing binary images of 512 x 2048 pixels at a resolution of a little better than 200 pixels per inch.

2.1 Address Words Segmentation

The first stage to verify a recognised postcode is to extract words from the address image to enable matching with words from the reference address. The process of segmenting the address into words is accomplished by applying rules which exploit positional information, estimated centre lines and basic blocks derived using a shading technique [3].

Some special cases, such as hyphen removal and street number detection are processed independently of the general word segmentation algorithm.

2.2 Slant Correction

Since some features to be extracted in the next stage are variant relative to slant, slant correction is applied to the original word image. Slanted word is corrected based on the slant angle of the word which is derived by averaging the slope of its main strokes.

2.3 Word Case Classification

Word case classification is needed since some features to be extracted from lower case and upper case words are different. The word case estimation is determined by identifying the body of the word and the first character of the word. Since in the postal domain, the first letter of each word in the address is generally a capital letter, the word is consider as a lower case if the distance between the top of the first letter and start of the main body is greater than some threshold value, otherwise it is an upper case word.

3 Feature Extraction

A set of features are extracted from each word of the address image: these are matched against words from the reference address(es) derived from the postcode database. The features which have been chosen for use in the verification stage are as follows:

- Line and word position.
  The positional information of each word in an address (line position and word position in the line) defines a fixed hierarchy of address field.
- Number of characters.
  The method of estimating the number of characters is based on counting the number of line crossings through the central point of the word divided by the average number of line crossings through one character.
- First character (and last character for uppercase words).
  These characters (always written as upper case letters in addresses) are seg-

mented from the remaining address within a predefined window. The segmentation in each window is then performed using three techniques in cascade: a simple gap search in the vertical pixel density histogram, component labelling analysis, and character splitting. The isolated character images from both windows are then recognised using a character recognition algorithm [5], where the results are a ranked list of the most probable character first.

- Number of ascenders, number of descenders and ascender/descender sequences. These features are extracted in the case of lower case words. Ascender and descender thresholds are determined heuristically based on the height of the body of the word and the height of the word.
- Number of loops.
  The number of loops is counted using analysis of concavities. The method is to start from the top and bottom of each column of a word and try to penetrate vertically until the first black pixel is encountered [6]. Each concavity that is not reached is analysed to determine whether it is a loop or not. Some adjustments are employed to cope with breaks or unconnected loops.

4 Address Verification

In address verification we deal with imprecise data derived from global feature extraction of the address image which will be compared against a reference address. Imprecise data arises because of the enormous variety of handwriting styles, variable address formats and inexact results of segmentation and feature extraction. Accordingly, a fuzzy approach for this problem is being developed. The method of this approach is to produce a membership function associated with a word from the address image describing its similarity to the words from the reference address. The membership function for each word from the address image is calculated as follows:

Let A_1, A_2, ..., A_j, ... A_n be the words from the address image. Consider a word A_j from the address image as a vector: where its element a_i measures the ith feature, and let R_1, R_2, ..., R_k, ... R_m be the words from the reference addresses, which constitute references/prototypes to be compared with each word from the address image. The word A_j can then be assigned a degree of similarity with a word R_k from the reference address as measured by the following algorithm:
Define a membership function $X_{j,k}$ associated with the similarity of the word A_j to the word R_k from reference address.

$$X_{j,k} = \left[1 + \left(\frac{d(A_j, R_k)}{E}\right)^F\right]^{-1.0}$$

where E is an arbitrary positive constant, F is any integer, and both have the effect of altering the fuzziness of a set [7], $d(A_j, R_k)$ is the distance between A_j and R_k, and

$$d(A_j, R_k) = \left[\sum_i (W_i(a_{ji} - r_{ki}))^2\right]^{0.5}$$

where a_{ji} corresponds to the ith feature of the word A_j from the address image, r_{ki} corresponds to the ith feature of the word R_k from the reference address, and W_i denotes the magnitude of the weighting coefficient corresponding to the ith feature, where the optimum weighting coefficient is derived using simulated annealing, see for example [9,10].

The distances or disparities for most of the features are obvious, that is the differences between values extracted from the address image and ideal values for particular words derived from a reference address. The distance for an initial character is the position of the actual character (derived from the reference address) in the recognised character ranked list of the address image.

Finally, the distance for an ascender/descender sequence is derived based on the similarity measure between two strings. Let u and v be two ascender/descender sequences of m and n ordered elements, respectively, where the element can be either 'a' (ascender) or 'd' (descender). Let $p(s{:}z)$ denote the number of times sub-ascender/descender sequence z occurs in ascender/descender sequence s, including partial overlaps, and let $|z|$ be the length of sub-ascender/descender sequence z [8]. The distance $D(u, v)$ is then measured as follows:

$$D(u,v) = [\ \textstyle\sum_{(z)}\ p(u{:}z) - p(v{:}z)\ |\ .\ |\ z\ |]$$

All the degrees of similarity are then recorded in the matching matrix. The problem now is to find the optimal combination of matches between the words from the address image and the reference address. This problem can be considered as an assignment problem in linear programming which can be solved using the Hungarian method [9]. However, some modification must be made since the Hungarian method deals with the problem of minimum criterion, and in this case we deal with a maximum criterion. Another constraint in the Hungarian method is that it deals with a square matrix, but in our case the number of words in the address image and reference address might not be equal. The total matching score for the whole address image which will be in the interval [0,1] is then determined as the normalised sum of the optimal word matches.

5 Overall Result

The verification method as described above was tested using a Colchester database This database contains a total of 516 address images of tagged random addresses, each written by a different writer on a card. The verification performance varied with chosen threshold. The results show that 72.4% correct sorting of outward postcodes can be achieved with an error rate of 1.9% and 43.2% correct sorting of full postcodes can be achieved with an error rate of 1.5%. These results are based upon a limited optimisation of parameters achieved at the time the paper went to press, and would benefit from further optimisation.

6 Conclusions

This paper has described a verification method for handwritten British Postal addresses. A set of features which is relatively easy to extract was chosen in the verification process where the fuzziness of features were taken into account. The main benefit of the fuzzy matching process compared to previous algorithm [3] that ignored any information concerning the degree of matching of the features, has been to reduce the instances of falsely verified postcodes to around 1.5%. Further analysis is being carried out to determine the exact causes of correctly recognised postcodes being rejected and the wrongly recognised postcodes being verified.

Acknowledgement

The authors gratefully acknowledge financial support from Royal Mail Research and Development.

References

1. Downton,A.C., Tregidgo,R.W.S., Kabir,E.: Recognition and Verification of Handwritten and Hand-printed British Postal Addresses. International Journal of Pattern Recognition and Artificial Intelligence, vol.5(1-2), 265-291 (1991)
2. Downton,A.C., Tregidgo,R.W.S., Leedham,C.G., Hendrawan: Recognition of Handwritten British Postal Addresses, In Impedovo,S., Simon,J.C., (eds.) From Pixels to Feature III - Frontiers in Handwriting Recognition, Elsevier 1992.
3. Srihari,S.N., Cohen,E., Hull,J.J., Kuan,L.: A System to Locate and Recognize Zip Codes in Handwritten Addresses. International Journal of Research and Engineering - Postal Applications, vol.1, 37-45 (1989)
4. Bozinovic,R.M., Srihari,S.N.: Off-line Cursive Script Word Recognition. IEEE Trans. On PAMI, PAMI-11(1), 68-83 (1989)
5. Tregidgo,R.W.S., Downton,A.C.: High Performance Character Recognition for Off-line Handwritten British Postcodes. In: Binary Image Processing - Techniques and Applications. IEE Colloquium, London 1991, Digest No: 1991/059.
6. Lecolinet,E., Moreau,J.: Off-line Recognition oh Handwritten Cursive Script for The Automatic Reading of City Names on Real Mail. Proc. of the 10th. Int. Conf. on Pattern Recognition, Atlantic City 1990, USA, 674-676
7. Pal,S.K., Majumder,D.D.: Fuzzy Sets and Decision Making Approaches in Vowel and Speaker Recognition. IEEE T. On SMC., SMC-7(8), 625-629 (1977)
8. Findler,N.V., Leeuwen,J.V.: A Family of Similarity Measures Between Two Strings. IEEE Trans. On PAMI, PAMI-1(1), 116-118 (1979)
9. Wilkes,F.M.: Elements of Operational Research. McGraw-Hill: 1980
10. Kirkpatric,S., Gelatt,C.D., Vecchi,M.P.: Optimisation by Simulated Annealing. Science (220) 671-680 (1983)
11. Selim,S.M., Alsultan,K.: A Simulated Annealing Algorithm for the Clustering Problem. Pattern Recognition, vol.24(10), 1003-1008 (1991)

Improvement of OCR by Language Model

I.G. Koh[1], J.D. Kim[1], J.W. Lee[1], M.R. Han[1],
M.G. Koh[2], H.B. Jeon[2], H.J. Min[2], S.Y. Kim[2]

[1]Physics Dept., Korea Advanced Institute of Science and Technology, 343-1 Kusong-Dong, Yusong-Gu, Taejeon, 305-701 Korea (South)
[2]Research Division, KoTech Co., Ltd., Renaissance Officetel Rm.702, 1598-3 Seocho-Dong, Seocho-Gu, Seoul, 137-070 Korea (South)

1. Why does OCR make errors?

Optical character recognition (OCR) suffers from less than 100% recognition rate for handwritten documents. Main sources of the imperfections are

1. the poor quality of images
2. flaws in recognition algorithms. Some of these can be indeed improved.

Images of broken lines or missing pixels can be improved by applying convolutions with directional and stroke-thickness dependent kernels. The flaws in statistical recognizers (hidden Markov model, neural network, nearest neighbor,....) are that the unimportant variations of strokes make for errors in recognition. The flaws of syntactic recognizers are that some of the results are lost in the top stage of the decision-tree. There are rigorous efforts to improve these flaws by inventing better distance measures in statistical recognizers, and delaying the final decision right to the end in the syntactic recognizer.

However, there is a point where additional efforts to improve either the quality of images or the algorithms do not result in significantly better recognition rates by the law of diminishing returns. Here, we discuss alternative methods to correct the misrecognized characters by postprocessing based on the language redundancies.

2. Improvement of OCR by Language Model

Language redundancies are exploited in hierarchical levels of increasing long-distance correlation moving upward from the bottom as

- generalized phrase structure grammar (GPSG)
- word n-gram + adjacency table with frequency
- letter n-gram

Fig. 1 Language redundancies are exploited to improve the OCR results

shown in **Fig.** 1.

The letter n-gram $P(S_{1,\ldots\ldots}S_n)$ of written texts is measured by counting $C(S_{1,\ldots\ldots}S_n)$ string "$S_{1\ldots\ldots}S_n$" and normalized as

$$P(S_{1\ldots\ldots}S_n) = \frac{C(S_{1,\ldots\ldots}S_n)}{\sum_{S_{1,\ldots}S_n} C(S_{1,\ldots\ldots}S_n)} \tag{1}$$

The inclusion of space in the character set has the effect of distinguishing the letter "o" whether in the beginning ("optical") or in the middle of word ("phonetic").

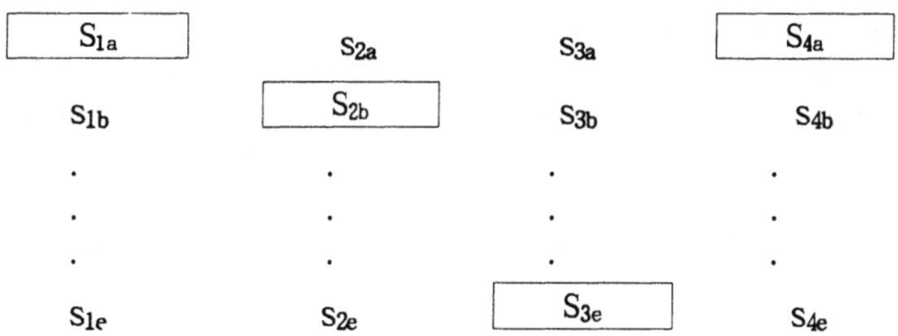

Fig. 2 Among five S_{ia}- S_{ie} candidates, string S_{1a} S_{2b} S_{3e} S_{4a} of 4 letter length giving maximum in equation (2) is selected as the best choice

2.1 Letter n-gram

Best recognition is achieved for the given features of documents by preferring string of letter

$$\max_{\text{string}} P(\text{string} \mid \text{features}) = \max_{\text{string}} \frac{P(\text{features} \mid \text{string})P(\text{string})}{P(\text{features})} \tag{2}$$

The results of OCR and the language redundancy should be combined in the right mixture to select the best string for given features. We give the results for string of 4 letter length using 3-gram.

$$P(s_1\ s_2\ s_3\ s_4 | \text{features } f_1\ f_2\ f_3\ f_4) \simeq$$
$$P(f_1|s_1)P(s_1\ s_2\ s_3)P(f_2|s_2)P(f_3|s_3)\frac{P(s_2\ s_3\ s_4)}{P(s_2)P(s_3)}P(f_4|s_4) \tag{3}$$

where $P(f_1|s_1)$ is the probability that the letter s_1 may be represented as feature f_1, and $P(s_1\ s_2\ s_3)$ and $P(s_1)$ and the letter 3-gram and 1-gram defined in equation(1).

Note that (features) in the denominator of (2) is fixed, and not relevant in choosing the best ($s_1\ s_2\ s_3\ s_4$) sequence. In the hidden Markov or neural network, $P(f_1|s_1)$ is the output probability for letter s_1. In the nearest neighbor model, it is approximated as

$$P(f \mid s) \approx \frac{1}{\sqrt{\pi}\sigma} e^{-\frac{(f-\bar{f}_s)^2}{\sigma^2}} \tag{4}$$

where $\overline{f_s}$ is the average of feature for the letter in the training data s, and σ is its standard deviation.

We have experimented with various values of n-gram in the OCR. With higher n, the result improves, but it also depends strongly on the domain of text. Empirically the best value n = 3 in unit of syllables for Korean syllables (n = 7.5 in terms of letter) and n = 6 for English letters. (Korean syllable is either consonant + vowel or consonant + vowel + consonant).

Entropy per letter

$$H = -\sum_{s_1 \dots s_n} P(s_1 \dots s_n) \operatorname{Log}_2 P(s_1 \dots s_n) \tag{5}$$

decreases rather rapidly when higher n-gram is used.

In Korean, the entropy per letter is

H = 4.0 for 1-gram,
H = 3.4 for 3-gram,
H = 1.8 for 5-gram.

For example, we obtained 6-gram $P(s_1\ s_2\ s_3\ s_4\ s_5\ s_6)$ from Korean corpus (150 M characters long) and 3-gram $P(s_1\ s_2\ s_3)$ from Brown and LOB corpus. In the case of English, the domain has been selected to cover the diverse fields simulating the frequencies of discourse. In actual implementation, not all of $P(s_1 \dots s_n)$ are stored, but a small fraction of them is stored

- to reduced the storage requirement,
- to stabilize against dependancy of domain.

For example,

$$P(s_1 s_2 s_3) = (1-q_2-q_3)P(s_1\ s_2\ s_3) \qquad \text{if } s_1\ s_2\ s_3 \in \text{3-gram table}$$

$$+\ q_2 \frac{P(s_1\ s_2)\ P(s_2\ s_3)}{P(s_2)} \qquad \text{if } s_1 s_2 s_3 \notin \text{3-gram table but } (s_1\ s_2) \in \text{2-gram},\ (s_2\ s_3) \in \text{2-gram}$$

$$+\ q_1\ P(s_1)P(s_2)P(s_3) \qquad \text{if } s_1 s_2 s_3 \notin \text{3-gram table},\ (s_1 s_2) \text{ or } (s_2 s_3) \notin \text{2-gram table} \tag{6}$$

The smoothing factors are calculated as

$$q_2 = 1 - \sum_{\substack{s_1\ s_2\ s_3 \\ \text{in 3-gram table}}} P(s_1\ s_2\ s_3)$$

$$q_1 = 1 - \sum_{\substack{s_1\ s_2 \\ \text{in 2-gram table}}} P(s_1\ s_2) \tag{7}$$

In the limiting case where all the $s_1\ s_2\ s_3$ are stored in 3-gram table, $q_2 = 0$. In Korean language implementation, we have $q_2 \simeq 0.06$, and $q_1 \simeq 0.005$.

2.2 Word n-gram

To cover the longer n-gram ($n \geq 7$ or 20), one can use the n-gram for words. Even the modest 2-grams for words become quite wasteful of memory. Instead, the part of speech (POS) (for example,"noun","verb".....) n-gram is utilized to select the best sequences of words. One selects the sequence of words by

$$\mathbf{max} P(\text{words}|\ \text{features}) = \mathop{\mathbf{max}}_{\text{words}} \frac{P(\text{features}|\text{words})\ P(\text{words})}{P(\text{features})} \tag{8}$$

We give detailed formula for 2-gram words as

$$P(w_1 w_2) = \sum_{c_1\ c_2} P(w_1|c_1)\ P(w_2|c_2)\ P(c_1 c_2) \tag{9}$$

where c_1 and c_2 are the POS of words w_1 and w_2.

The $P(w_1|c_1)$ is the probability of word w_1 in POS c_1, and $P(c_1c_2)$ is the probability of "POS c_1 followed by POS c_2." The number of POS in our implementation is 30. A rather large number of POS compared to the standard grammar is to enhance the selectivity by increasing the size of POS.

2.3 Probabilistic GPSG (generalized phrase structure grammar)

To disambiguate a certain word in the process of applying formulas (2) and (8), the GPSG is applied to the level of phrase of approximately 5-10 words length.

The implementation of the system "READEX" includes some of these features, and tested for several months over 150 M character sets. Two-thirds of errors in the original recognitions have been corrected. Remaining errors are traced to the different domain of subjects, very short word, the POS containing large number of words.

Acknowledgements

The work was carried out by KAIST-KoTech collaboration. We acknowledge the staff of KAIST and KoTech for their contributions.

Citations

1. Shannon, C. E.: Prediction and entropy of printed English. Bell Syst. Tech. J. 30, 50-64 (1951)
2. Bahl, L. R., Jelinek, F., and Mercer, R. L.: Maximum likelihood approach to continous speech recognition. IEEE Transactions on pattern analysis and machine intelligence (1983)
3. Konhein, A. G.: Cryptography, a primer. John Wiley & Sons 1981
4. Hull, J. J. and Srihari, S. N.: Text recognition with binary n-gram and Viterbi algorithms. IEEE Transactions on pattern analysis and machine intelligence, PAMI-4 520-530 (1982)

An Approximate String Matching Method for Handwriting Recognition Post-Processing Using a Dictionary

Dimo T. Dimov

Central Lab of Bioinstrumentation and Automation, Bulgarian Academy of Sciences
P.O.Box 132, Sofia 1113, BULGARIA

Abstract. A brief analysis of existing methods for performance improvement of handwriting recognition (HR) that are based on text-to-lexicon matching post-processing is provided in the paper. A method for search in a dictionary is proposed, based on knowledge about error statistics at the output of a HR-classifier. The method is developed for the most probable misspellings, namely a character substitution, omission, insertion and neighboring character reversal. Method applicability to HR is assessed in terms of "Damerau-Levenstein" metrics that is frequently used for similarity definition of HR strings. The error modelling proposed is distributed between the dictionary structure and the processing algorithm. Character deletion is the only operation utilized. Thus, a substantial amount of errors are implicitly represented, resulting in a comparatively low processing time and space complexity. The method is implemented in a software subsystem for fault-tolerant keyboard input processing of natural language names. The experimental results are briefly reported.

Keywords. Handwritten text recognition, handwriting post-processing, approximate string matching, misspelling errors correction, fault-tolerant key access to files by dictionary.

1 Introduction

Although substantial progress has been recently achieved, handwriting recognition (HR) is still assumed to be an open area for research and novel ideas [8]. Two major aspects of the topic can be identified: Off-Line HR meaning that the input text is taken as a complete 2-dimensional image, and the On-Line HR meaning that data about the text under recognition is gathered during writing. In general, HR deals with identification of entire words from the text, while OCR, which is another aspect of HR, is usually concerned with recognition of isolated characters (printed or handwritten). But in all cases, the expected output is a string of characters that should correspond to the input handwritten text [8,10,11].

Although vast diversity of existing HR methods is observed, analogies between them can be derived in terms of correspondence between both types of the input text representation - raster/grid vs. vector/polygonal. After the appropriate pre-processing and normalization, the recognition process follows one of the two basic strategies - "bottom-up" vs. "top-down" (or their combination) [7]. Reference to a lexicon (dictionary, thesaurus) is a common procedure in most of the well-known methods, no matter what recognition strategy is applied [1,2,7,9,10].

The reference procedure, in general, consists of the following: The HR classifier output is assumed a set of strings of a given alphabet. Matches between these strings and the a priori stored in a lexicon, is sought for according to a given criterion. Different constraints on this description are possible:

• The alphabet is specified for the particular recognition method implemented in the classifier, and usually consists of mono-type elements - basic elements [13], strokes [7,11], graphemes [8], isolated characters and/or digits [4,10,12], shapes [2], etc. A common practice is that alphabet elements are coded for convenience [2,9,13].

• Strings are defined as finite sequences of the alphabet elements. Their length is usually equalized by insertion of the "empty" element. Strings can represent separate characters, words (or part of words) or even whole phrases, corresponding to the input text under recognition [2,4,10,12].

• Complementary structures that reflect statistical information, syntactic and semantic constraints etc., can be additionally introduced and mapped onto the set of strings [1,5,9,12]. Structures of the kind are generated by the classifier or by another source, and can be stored on-line, or ad hoc for example, in the lexicon, but all these aspects are concerned with issues about optimal performance as well as the recognition method itself.

• The lexicon search implementation is also a matter of structural organization. The process can be performed sequentially or directly by key, as a tree, or by indexing over the whole lexicon or part of it, and this is of primary concern with processing time and space complexity, especially when more extended lexicon is needed [10,11,12].

• The similarity criterion is usually defined in terms of a metrics over the set of strings. Several modifications [7,12,13] of the generalized *"Damerau-Levenstein"* (DL) metrics [2,4], are often utilized where the distance between two strings is defined as dependent on the minimum number of deletions, insertions and substitutions of symbols, necessary for transformation of the first string into the second and vice versa. As a result, a dynamic programming task of second order complexity is formulated in most of the cases [2,4].

In practice, the HR classifier output verification task by a lexicon is reduced to the classical task [4] of *approximate string matching* between strings of two sets - the first one generated from the classifier output, and the second one stored in the lexicon. These sets are often enriched with a structure of probabilistic nature, for example: a posterior probability [5,10]; value rates for the hypotheses about characters, words or parts of them [1]; clustering of graphemes from the basic alphabet (for example in 7 groups in [9]) to guide the string generation process; string hypotheses description as trees of possible sub-strings [12], etc.

In general, it is relied upon the limited volume of the lexicon [1,7,9,11]. As a result, the complete reproduction of the items (candidates, hypotheses, etc.) to be compared does not substantially slow down the processing even in the cases of sequential search in the lexicon. For example, the "edit distance calculation of 92ms per word" of such a powerful computer as the "Sun Spare Station 2" is reported in [9]. An expected near-future method for DL-distance calculation of linear complexity is evident from [2]. The realistic possibility for sharp reduction of the number of accesses to the lexicon is illustrated in, for example, [10] ("simultaneous binary search"). The strategies for lexicon access along a tree-like structure induced by the solely input structure of string-hypotheses [1,10] does not account in full range for the problem of processing speed and physical storage space, especially in cases when richer lexicon is necessary. The classical approaches such as index-sequential access, direct key access (e.g. Hash procedure) etc. [6], are not sufficient. New types of lexicon access methods that are comparatively simple and of closer correspondence to HR specificity, are necessary to be developed.

An approach to the problem concerned has been proposed in the paper. It was initially developed for the purposes of automatic correction of the most probable mistyping errors [4] that occur during keyboard input of natural language names. The term "*dictionary*" is used instead of "lexicon". The reasons for the expected applicability of this approach to a great number of HR cases are the following:

- Existence of a metrics of the DL type for the set of strings is assumed, although not explicated;
- A topological clusterization of the closest strings for a given string is used, i.e. wide range of possibilities for adaptation of the string probability space for the purposes of HR post-processing can be considered;
- The proposed technique can be directly applied to recognition of handwritten lists of natural language names.

Description of the method especially with respect to isolated word recognition is provided further in the paper as well as the results from an experiment on text recognition. Finally, advantages and shortcomings of method applicability are discussed. The presentation style is rather descriptive than formal in the strict sense of the word because of the limited space provided for the text.

2 Method Description

Input texts are assumed word segmented. The set of words for recognition are denoted by $\mathbb{W}$ and the set of their input versions - by $\mathbb{V}$. The words $W \in \mathbb{V} \cup \mathbb{W}$ are considered strings of length k, $k=S(W)$, $k_{min} \le k \le k_{max}$, over a finite alphabet A of nonwhite and nonterminal symbols (characters, digits and punctuation marks). The constraints of k_{min} and k_{max}, $0 < k_{min} \le k_{max}$, derive only from requirements imposed by practice.

2.1 Input Error Distribution

The most probable errors of characters in a word W, $W \in \mathbb{V} \cup \mathbb{W}$, are assumed independent events, of m number. Their probabilities P_i , $i=0 \div m$, are assumed known and constrained as follows:

$$\sum_1^m P_i < P_0 \ , \qquad | 1 - P_0 - \sum_1^m P_i | \approx 0 \ ; \qquad 0 < P_i < i \ , \quad i = 0,1,2,...m \qquad (1)$$

For example, the most probable mistyping errors - substitution, omission and insertion of a character and neighboring character reversal, have a total probability of ≈10% in accordance with the statistics referred to in [4], (cf. also Table 1), and for the particular case here,

$$m=8\,,\ P_0 \approx 89\%\,,\ P_1+P_2+P_3+P_4 \approx 10\%\,,\ P_5+P_6+P_7+P_8 \approx 1\% \qquad \text{(1a)}$$

2.2 Word Recognition: General Assumptions

Each word W, $W \in \mathbb{V} \cup \mathbb{W}$ is mapped onto a modelling set $\mathbb{G}(W)$ of word derivations called "*lexemes*", extracted from the word by the *only operation of symbol deletion*, and performed by a generation procedure $\mathbb{G}$. Input words are considered as trivial lexemes, i.e. $W \in \mathbb{G}(W)$.

Dictionary $\mathbb{D}$ contains a priori generated lexemes of the modelling sets for all of the words to be recognized, $W \in \mathbb{W}$, while for the input words $V \in \mathbb{V}$, the generation processing is on-line.

The fact of coincidence (*match*) between the input lexeme and the lexeme from the dictionary models a given error belonging to the pre-defined topology of errors (cf. Table 2). The absence of the input lexeme in the dictionary means that: first - the lexeme is quite distant from the words represented in $\mathbb{D}$ (in terms of some metrics (!)), i.e. it would model an error of low probability; or second - the lexeme corresponds to an unknown word for the dictionary $\mathbb{D}$.

Each lexeme match in $\mathbb{D}$ adds a contribution to the probability value estimate of the corresponding input word similarity to some limited set of words in the dictionary that are candidates for recognition. All the contributions gathered for a given candidate are summed up and the totals are arranged in rank order. The candidate word with the highest total estimate is the most probable correct value for the input word. The following interpretation is suggested:

• If the highest estimate is rather low, then the input word should be classified as unknown to the dictionary because it is relied upon the model adequacy to the input error distribution (1).

• Any concentration of a great number of estimates that are very close to the highest value, points out to recognition collision, i.e. the input word is not informative enough with respect to the content of the dictionary.

2.3 Representation Models. Generating Procedure

Most probable error representation is designed in accordance with the input error distribution (1), and is based on the concept of modelling sets $\mathbb{G}(W)$, $W \in \mathbb{V} \cup \mathbb{W}$. Four models of practical interest are proposed following the rules:

•Ø_model (m=0) ::= <the word W itself>; i.e. the only lexeme which is identical with W.

• A_model (m=3) ::= <Ø_model> & <a character substitution, omission and insertion into W>; i.e. along with Ø_model, A_ includes all the lexemes of length $S(W)-1$, which can be derived by omission of a character from W.

• B_model (m=4) ::= <A_model> & <a neighboring character reversal into W>; i.e. along with A_model, B_ additionally represents all the lexemes of length $S(W)$-2, which can be derived by omission of two neighboring characters from W.

• C_model (m=8) ::= <B_model> & <all remaining lexemes derived by omission of two characters from W>. C_model corresponds to the situation (1a).

Models of error depth higher than 2 are not under consideration here. Separate procedures $\mathfrak{G}$ is provided for each of the models for lexeme generation from the input words $V \in \mathbb{V}$ as well as from the words $W \in \mathbb{W}$, before their representation in dictionary $\mathbb{D}$. The procedure $\mathfrak{G}_{\varnothing}$ is trivial. $\mathfrak{G}_A$, $\mathfrak{G}_B$ and $\mathfrak{G}_C$ are performed only by the operation of character deletion !

2.4 Dictionary Structure

Dictionary $\mathbb{D}$ consists of records for each lexeme L, $L \in \mathfrak{G}(W)$, $W \in \mathbb{W}$. The record logical format is as follows:

(2)

LEXKEY	N_L	PTD_1, E_1	…	PTD_i, E_i	…	PTD_{NP}, E_{NP}	*free*

LEXKEY: - primary access key containing the lexeme L;
N_L: - number of all records for lexeme L;
[PTD_i, E_i]: - a compound field (data for the word W_i generating L);
where:

PTD_i: - a pointer to the word W_i into the file of words;

E_i: - error depth, i.e. number of characters deleted in W_i, during lexeme L generation, $1 \le i \le NP \le NP_{max}$, where NP_{max} is a dictionary parameter determining the maximum number of words that can be represented per record.

In brief, the NP_{max} optimum choice is of primary relation to the physical structure of $\mathbb{D}$ and will not be considered now. It is more appropriate for the dictionary to be built using some direct key access, although an indexed one is also appropriate, considering the system software available [6].

2.5 Most Probable Error Modeling

The lexemes $L \in \mathfrak{G}(V)$, generated by $\mathfrak{G}$ from the current input word $V \in \mathbb{V}$, are searched for match in the dictionary $\mathbb{D}$. Each match success (*hit*) represents an error of (E_G,E_D)-kind, occurring somewhere in the word. According to the 4 models considered, E_G is the number of character deletions in V, $0 \le E_G \le 2$, and the similar E_D is retrieved from $\mathbb{D}$, $0 \le E_D \le 2$. The error position in V is also known, but it is not processed now.

Each hit adds its contribution $\omega(E_G,E_D)$ to form the probability of the errors modeled. The lack of hit does not contribute anything, i.e. zero probability contribution. In this way, all the hits for the input word V compose its most probable errors, cf. Table 1. Each model (namely ∅_, A_, B_ and C_) is an extension of its predecessors and is characterized by the following:

- The set of the most probable errors it represents;
- The $\mathbb{D}$-accesses number per input word $V\in\mathbb{V}$, that is equal to the number $|\mathfrak{G}(V)|$ of the lexemes, currently generated for V, i.e. $\sim k$ for A_ and B_, a nd $\sim k^2$ for C_ models, where k is the length of V.
- The average number $\alpha(V)$ of hits into $\mathbb{D}$ per input word $V\in\mathbb{V}$: Most frequently $\alpha(V)\leq|\mathfrak{G}(V)|$, but in cases of very close words stored in $\mathbb{D}$, we usually obtain $\alpha(V)\geq|\mathfrak{G}(V)|$;
- The dictionary $\mathbb{D}$ size, which is of linear dependence on the average value of $|\mathfrak{G}(W)|$, $W\in\mathbb{W}$, and on the number $|\mathbb{W}|$ of words represented in $\mathbb{D}$.

2.6 Illustrative Examples

The set $\mathfrak{G}(W)$ of modelling lexemes which are written in $\mathbb{D}$ for each of the models mentioned, is illustrated on Table 2 by means of the word $W\equiv$"*think*". The hits in the dictionary are indicated for the same word $V\equiv W$ and for 5 more illustrative versions of it. The formulae are shown for hit number $\alpha(V)$ separately for each error type.

Table 1. Errors representation models of the method

Model	Maximal accesses number $\lvert\mathfrak{G}(V)\rvert$	Errors for $V\in\mathbb{V}$: Kind $E_G E_D$	Most probable input error description	Other errors	# i	Total hits number (vs. the model) $\alpha(V)$: C_	B_	A_	Ø_
Ø_	1	0 0	No errors	-	0	$1+k+k(k-1)/2$	$2k$	$1+k$	1
A_	$1+k$	1 1	Substitution <1S>	<1O + 1I>	1	k	3	1	
		0 1	Omission <1O>	-	2	$k+1$	3	1	
		1 0	Insertion <1I>	-	3	k	3	1	
B_	$2k$	2 2	Neighbour reversal <1N>	<2S> <1S+1O+1I>	4	$2k-1$	3		
C_ *	$1+k+k(k-1)/2$	2 2	<2S>	<2O+2I>	*4	1			
		2 2	<1S + 1O>	<2O+1I>	5				
		2 2	<1S + 1O>	<2I + 1O>	6				
		2 2	<2O>	-	7				
		2 2	<2I>	-	8				

(*) The <1N>-kind error is more probable than the <2S>-one in case of B_ and C_ models, and the table separation only represents the different access number into $\mathbb{D}$.

Table 2. How the models work on the example of the word "think"

Hits' kind in D			Model sets G(V) of the input words examples (V) ...					
Model set G(W)			Ø_	A_			B_	C_
W = "think"	L ε D	S(L)	think	th*a*nk	thik	thi*i*nk *	*h*tink	t*n*i*h*k *
Ø_	think	5	(0,0)	-	-	(1,0) AA	-	-
A_	_hink	4	(1,1)	-	-	(2,1) CC	(1,1)	-
	t_ink	4	(1,1)	-	-	(2,1) CB	(1,1)	-
	th_nk	4	(1,1)	(1,1)	-	(2,1) B	-	-
	thi_k	4	(1,1)	-	(0,1)	(2,1) BC	-	-
	thin_	4	(1,1)	-	-	(2,1) CC	-	-
B_	__ink	3	(2,2)	-	-	-	(2,2)	-
	t__nk	3	(2,2)	(2,2)	-	-	(2,2) C	(2,1) *
	th__k	3	(2,2)	(2,2)	(1,2)	-	-	(2,1) *
	thi__	3	(2,2)	-	(1,2)	-	-	-
C_	_h_nk	3	(2,2)	(2,2)	-	-	(2,2)	
	_hi_k	3	(2,2)	-	(1,2)	-	(2,2)	-
	hin	3	(2,2)	-	-	-	(2,2)	-
	t_i_k	3	(2,2)	-	(1,2)	-	(2,2)	(2,2)
	t_in_	3	(2,2)	-	-	-	(2,2)	-
	th_n_	3	(2,2)	(2,2)	-	-	-	-
Err.	Input kind		no err	<1S>	<1O>	<1I>	<1N>	<2S>
	(E_G+o, E_D+o)		(0,0)	(1,1)	(0,1)	(1,0)	(1,1)	(2,2)
Length $k=S(V)$			5	5	4	6	5	5
Number of hits by their kind	Mod	ω(E,E)						
	Ø_	(E_G+o, E_D+o)	1					
		α(W)	1					
	A_	(E_G+o, E_D+o)	1	1	1	1 (2)		
		(E_G+1, E_D+1)	k	-	-	0		
		α(W)	k+1	1	1	1		
	B_	(E_G+o, E_D+o)	1	1	1	1 (2)	2	
		(E_G+1, E_D+1)	k	2	2	2 (3)	1	
		(E_G+2, E_D+2)	k-1	-	-	0	-	
		α(W)	2k	3	3	3	3	
	C_	(E_G+o, E_D+o)	1	1	1	1 (2)	2	1 (3)
		(E_G+1, E_D+1)	k	k-1	k	k-1 (2k-3)	2k-3	-
		(E_G+2, E_D+2)	k(k-1)/2	-	-	0	-	-
		α(W)	1+k+ +k(k-1)/2	k	k+1	k	2k-1	1

(*) An input error specificity is chosen in the case

2.7 Model Set-up

The set-up can be performed by ad hoc calculation of the contributions $\omega(E_G,E_D)$, $E_G, E_D \in \{0,1,2\}$, with respect to the average word length k, and for the given probability distribution (P_i, $i=0 \div m$) of the input errors expected (1). Thus, for C_model chosen ($m=8$), having in mind Table 2, the following system of contributions is obtained:

$$\left\| \begin{array}{l} \omega(0,0) = (P_0 - 2P_1 + P_4) + (-P_1 + \frac{3}{2} P_4)\,k + (P_1 - \frac{1}{2} P_4)\,k^2 \\ \omega(1,1) = P_4 + (2P_1 - P_4)\,k \\ \omega(0,1) = P_2 - P_5\,k \\ \omega(1,0) = (P_3 + P_6) - P_6\,k \\ \omega(2,2) = -2P_1 + P_4 \\ \omega(1,2) = P_5, \quad \omega(2,1) = P_6, \quad \omega(0,2) = P_7, \quad \omega(2,0) = P_8 \end{array} \right. \tag{3}$$

where $k = k_{mean}$, $k_{min} \leq k_{mean} \leq k_{max}$.

The contributions in the case of Ø_, A_ and B_ models, have to be also assessed by analogy of (3).

2.8 Word Similarity Function and Decision Rule

The similarity function $\mathbb{F}: \mathbb{W} \rightarrow [0,1]$, is defined heuristically as the proximity probability of the words represented in $\mathbb{D}$ to the input word $V \in \mathbb{V}$:

$$\left\| \begin{array}{lll} \mathbb{F}(W) = P(W) \sum\limits_{L \in \mathbb{G}(V)} \dfrac{\omega(E_G,E_D)}{N_L} \,, & \text{for} & W \in \mathbb{W}_V \\ \mathbb{F}(W) = 0 \,, & \text{for} & W \in (\mathbb{W} \setminus \mathbb{W}_V) \end{array} \right. \tag{4}$$

$\mathbb{W}_V \subset \mathbb{W}$ - subset of candidate words, i.e which lexemes stored in $\mathbb{D}$ match with the currently generated from V;

$\omega(E_G,E_D)$ - hit contribution of an input lexeme $L \in \mathbb{G}(V)$, where E_G is given by $\mathbb{G}$, and E_D is retrieved from $\mathbb{D}$, cf. (2);

N_L - an informational measure of L, cf. (2);

$P(W)$ - probability of word W occurrence, $W \in \mathbb{W}$.

The decision rule for recognition of $V \in \mathbb{V}$ is defined by the maximum over $\mathbb{F}(W)$, $W \in \mathbb{W}_V$. The subset $\mathbb{W}_V$ should always be non-empty so long as the input error representation model is properly chosen. The distribution $P(W)$, $W \in \mathbb{W}$, can be evaluated on-line and stored in the file that is pointed out by $\mathbb{D}$, see (2). Besides:

$$|\mathbb{W}_V| \leq |\mathbb{G}(V)| \sum_{L \in \mathbb{G}(V)} N_L << |\mathbb{W}| \,, \quad V \in \mathbb{V} \tag{5}$$

that defines the operational search speed in $\mathbb{D}$ as well as the sorting of $\mathbb{W}_V$ on $\mathbb{F}$.

2.9 Text Recognition

The proposed approach is developed up to a method for fault-tolerant access-by-key to file records, where keys are natural language names, i.e. character strings of significant length that usually occur as a common error source of input misspellings.

Other type of errors are also possible at the text level such as unexpected abbreviations, whole words or ends-only omissions, word permutations in the name, etc. For this reason, names are assumed subsets of the $\mathbb{V} \cup \mathbb{W}$ set and this is the main constraint concerning grammar rules. Similarity between names is derived from similarities among their component words. The relevant dictionary $\mathbb{D}$ and the similarity function $\mathbb{F}$ are formulated by analogy with the above described, using additional statistic assumptions.

3 Experimental Results

The proposed method was implemented in a geographic database system for the capital city of Sofia's street network [3]. The texts for recognition were street names, each composed of 1 to 5 words. 5696 words were extracted from 3576 names for representation in the dictionary. C_model was utilized and the word length k was restricted in the range of $k_{min}=3$, $k_{max}=9$. Thus, the total number of generated lexemes was equal to 54668, 28618 of them being different. The physical storage of the dictionary was ≈2,5MB. Using an IBM-XT/6MHx compatible PC with disk access time ≈40ms, the averaged system response time was ≈1,7s per name.

4 Conclusions

The general characterization of the proposed method can be summarized as follows:

- Good adaptability to different applications: Four models (∅_, A_, B_ and C_) of successive extension have been formulated for correction of the most probable mistyping errors. The perspectives for model advancement are still not exhausted.
- Possibilities for model set-up and current training: Calculations of the proximity contributions, cf. (4), can be performed for input error variations. This also holds for the statistics of the input words, cf. (2,4), when actualization of the dictionary content takes place.
- Comparatively low requirements for additional memory needed by the dictionary: Storage space primary depends on the number of lexemes for the words represented, and the dependency is linear (for model A_ and B_) or second order (for model C_) on the average word length because of the character deletion operation only utilized.
- Relatively short average recognition time: It depends on the model choice

(Ø_, A_, B_ and C_) and on the entered text length (number of words), but at the same time it is practically independent of the total number of words and texts represented in the dictionary.

The method has been developed as a technique for reliable direct access by key to file records in a database, but it is also applicable for the purposes of text processing as well as of HR, as it is stated in the introduction. The method is compatible with more complex structures of statistical characteristics, syntactic and/or semantic rules. Method utilization is not constrained in principle by the available computer and software appliances.

Acknowledgements

I would like to thank Prof. H. Bunke (Univ. of Bern, Switzerland) and Prof. E. Lecolinet (E.N.S.T., Paris) for sending me copies of their recent publications and Prof. S. Impedovo (Univ. of Bari, Italy) for the fruitful discussion of this paper.

References

1. Bozinovic, R.M., Srihari, S.N.: Off-Line Cursive Script Word Recognition. IEEE Trans. on PAMI, Vol.11, No.1, 68-83 (1989)
2. Bunke, H.: Recent Advances in String Matching. In: H. Bunke (ed.) Advances in Structural and Syntactic Pattern Recognition. Proceedings, Bern, 1992. Series in MP&AI, Vol.5, 3- 21, London: World Scientific 1993
3. Dimov, D.T., Radev, Ch.: A Distributed Graphic Visualization System in a Computer Network. In: D.I. Mladenov (ed.) Distributed Intelligence Systems - Methods and Applications. IFAC Proceedings Series, No.4, 1989, 273-278, Pergamon Press 1989
4. Hall, P.A.V., Dowling, G.R.: Approximate String Matching. ACM Computing Surveys J., Vol.12, No.4, 381-402 (1980)
5. Jones, M.A., Story, G.A., Ballard, B.W.: Integrating Multiple Knowledge Sources in a Bayesian OCR Post-Processor. First Int. Conf. on Document Analysis and Recognition, Saint-Malo, France, Sep.30 - Oct.02, 1991. Proceedings, Vol.2, 925-933
6. Knuth, D.E.: Sorting and Searching. The Art of Computer Programming, Vol.3, Reading, MA: Addison-Wesley, 1973
7. Lecolinet, E.: Top-Down and Bottom-Up Strategies for Cursive Script Recognition. Sixth Int. Conf. on Handwriting and Drawing, Paris, France, July 04-07, 1993, 117-119
8. Optical Character Recognition. In: T. Pavlidis and S. Mori (eds.) Special Issue of Proceedings of the IEEE, Vol.80, No.7 (1992)
9. Paquet, T., Lecourtier, Y.: Recognition of Handwritten Sentences Using a Restricted Lexicon. Pattern Recognition J., Vol.26, No.3, 391-407 (1993)
10. Schurmann, J. and others.: Document Analysis - From Pixels to Contents. Proceedings of the IEEE, Vol.80, No.7, 1101-1119 (1992)
11. Tappet, C.C., Suen, C.Y., Wakahara, T.: The State of the Art in On-Line Handwriting Recognition. IEEE Trans. on PAMI, Vol.12, No.8, 787-808 (1990)
12. Weigel, A.: Using Approximate String Matching for Handwriting Recognition. Eight Scandinavian Conf. on Image Analysis, May 1993. Proceedings, Vol.1, 397-404
13. Xia, Y., Sun, C.: Recognizing restricted handwritten Chinese characters by structure similarity method. Pattern Recognition Letters, Vol.11, 67-73 (1990)

Part 5

Neural networks in handwriting recognition

Neural-Net Computing for Machine Recognition of Handwritten English Language text

Yoh-Han Pao and Gwang-Hoon Park

Electrical Engineering and Applied Physics, Case Western Reserve University, Cleveland, Ohio 44106, U. S. A.

Abstract

The task of recognizing handwritten English language text in off-line manner is described in terms of four interacting steps: from pixels to features, from features to letters, from letters to words and acceptance of words in terms of context. We report on investigations of the second and third steps, especially the use of multiple neural-nets to go from nonsegmented sequences of features to letters. Indications are that our procedure is robust and promising.

Introduction

It is expected that neural-net computing will play a significant role in computer-based systems for automatic recognizing of cursive script. This is because neural-net can be trained quite readily to recognize several distances of a written letter or word, and can then generalized to recognize yet other different distances of that same letter or word. This capability is vital to the realization of robust automatic recognizing of cursive script, where handwritten letters are rarely, if ever, written twice in a exactly same form.

There have been reports of successful use of neural-nets for the recognition of handwritten characters [Kunihiko, F. and Nobuaki, W., 1991; Blackwell, K.T., Vogl, T.P. and Hyman, S.D., Barbour, G.S., and Alkon, D.L., 1992], under carefully controlled circumstances, but we are not aware of any general investigation which might shed light on the systematics of (say) a complete neural-net system for the automatic recognizon of cursive script.

In this paper we report on progress made in a continuing research effort aimed at discovering such system-level knowledge.

This paper is made up of four sections. In the remainder of this section we state our view of what is involved in the design and implementation of a system for machine learning and automatic recognition of cursive script. One of the subsystems deals with the task of interpreting groups of features in terms of letters. This paper reports in some detail on the performance of that subsystem and the relationship of that performance with other subsystems.

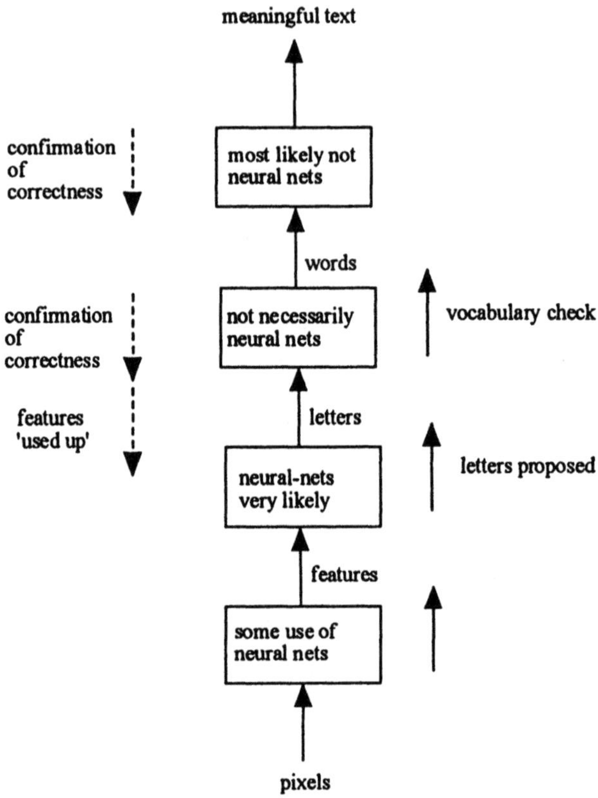

Figure 1. Overview of System for Automatic Recognition of Cursive Script

Before going on to the matter of recognizing letters, we digress from the main theme to describe a special form of neural-net called the Functional-link net and the learning algorithm used with that type of net. The Functional-link net can be trained in times which are orders-of-magnitude less than that required for the more conventional Backpropagation-of-error net. All that is briefly described in section 2.

An experiment in the recognition of handwritten words is described in section 3 and the results are reported and discussed in section 4.

Our view of a complete subsystem for the automatic recognition of cursive script, even though it might be for a severely curtailed vocabulary, is illustrated schematically in Figure 1. There are four subsystems for

1. the formation of features from pixels,
2. the interpretation of features in terms of letters,
3. the interpretation of letters in terms of words, and
4. the confirmation of the words in terms of semantic correctness.

We believe that Professor Simon and his colleagues [Simon J. C., Zerhouni K., 1991; Simon J. C., 1989] have made significant headway in the matter of going from pixels to features and this paper is primarily concerned with subsystems 2 and 3.

As shown in Figure 1, the computing paradigm consists of a neural-net proposing a letter and having that proposal accepted or rejected. The resulting effects of that acceptance or rejection propagate backward as well as forward. If a proposed letter does not make sense in the forward direction, that is, if it does not fit in a word, it might not be accepted. If accepted, that action 'consumes' several features and these are no longer available for the support of any subsequent proposal. Our interest at this point has focused on the formation of neural nets which can take one, two or more features and prepare an interpretation of them in terms of letters.

2. The Functional Link Net

The work of Hornik, Stinchcombe and White [Hornik, K., Stinchcombe, M., and White, H., 1989], Funahashi [Funahashi, 1989] and others assure us that a multilayer feedforward neural net with only single hidden layer of nodes can nevertheless serve as a universal approximator of a (well-behaved) function f(.) which maps $R^N \longrightarrow R$. In other words $\hat{f}(\mathbf{x}) = \sum_j \beta_j g(\mathbf{a}_j \mathbf{x} + b_j)$ is a universal approximator for the function f(.).

Pao and his collaborators [Pao, Y. H. and Takefuji, Y., 1991; Pao, Y. H., Phillips, S. M. and Sobajic, D. J., 1992] have found experimentally that this simple result can be further simplified. They found that the parameter learning task can be separated into two, one being the learning of the external parameters $\{\beta_j\}$ and the other being the learning of the 'internal' parameters, the vector $\mathbf{a}_j$. and the biases b_j. And in addition they found that in practice the internal parameters need not be learned but can be prescribed.

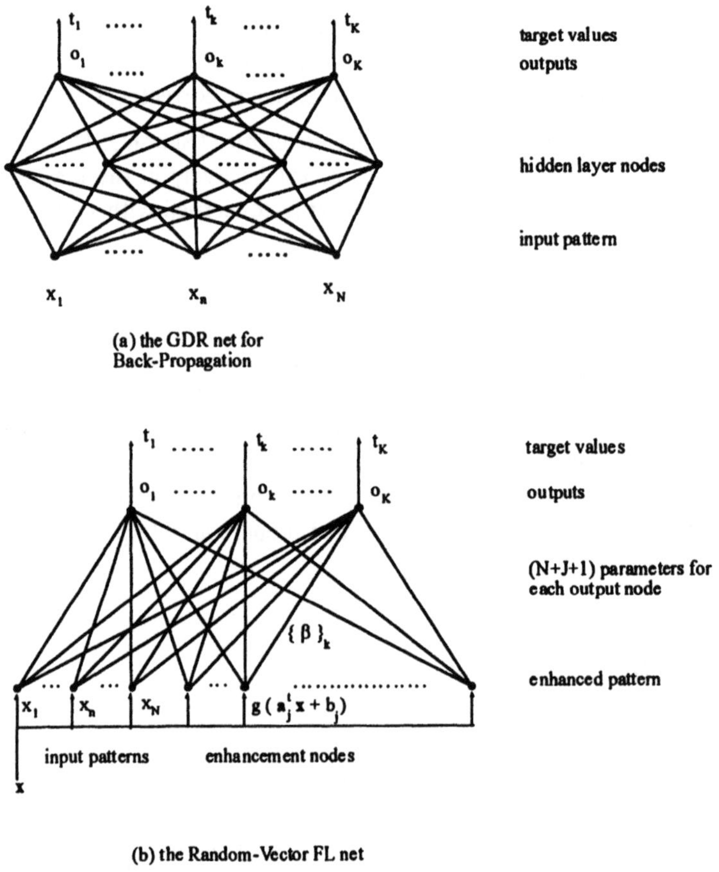

Figure 2. Back-Propagation net and Functional Link Architectures.

In retrospect, this result can be rationalized. From a geometric point of view, in a three layered net such as that shown in Figure 2, the transition from the input layer to the hidden layer may be viewed as a nonlinear transform of coordinates, so that the input vector in described in a new coordinate system. Nothing needs to be learned because in the next stage, the coefficients $\{\beta_j\}$ will be vanishingly small for all those coordinates which are not relevant. There has been substantial experience to provide pragmatic evidence that there is indeed no need to learn the internal parameters. More recently we have proved mathematically that there is a sound theoretical basis for the adequacy of Functional Link nets [Igelnik, B. and Pao, Y. H., 1993]. The parameters $\{\beta_j\}$ are learned in a quadratic optimization procedure; the outer two layers of nodes form a linear net. Because of these circumstances, a conjugate-gradient search for the single global minimum can be carried out with dispatch and with guaranteed success. In the interest of completeness, the conjugate gradient optimization process is described and illustrated in Appendix 1.

3. Description of the Experiment

We describe our work in terms of an experiment. The objective is to determine if it is possible to train neural-nets to 'recognize' a train of features in the sense that these features are collected and interpreted correctly in terms of English language letters. Currently only a limited vocabulary of words (100 words) is involved and some of examples are shown in Figure 3 but the experiment is realistic and of interest because a wide collection of samples is used and very different feature sequences may be obtained for different writings of the same letter and word.

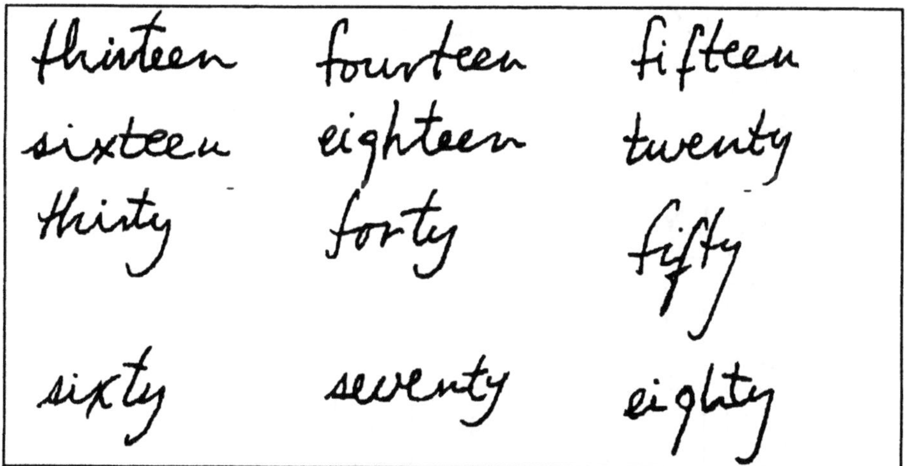

Figure 3. Example of Handwritten Words

There are various ways for going from pixel to features. We divide the image into characteristic regions consisting of the ascenders (upper region), the descenders (lower region) and the on-line main body. In each region, there are predefined feature sets which can be compared with the input images. Some of the features are more distinctive, more easily detected and identified. Examples of these might be the crossed tie, the dot on "i" and "j", the long upper and lower strokes of "t", "h", "f", "z", "y", "q" and "p", the ovals of "o", "a" or "s", and so on, corresponding perhaps to the singularities in the approach of Simon or Bozinovic and his collaborators [Bozinovic, R. M. and Sargur, N. S., 1989]. The remaining parts then perhaps would be recognized in terms of none regular features such as upward-facing curves and downwards facing curves. At that juncture a line of cursive handwriting would have been perceived and interpreted in terms of a sequence of features. But these features would be concepts rather than precise arrays of pixels. The next step is then to attempt to unsegmented sequences of features in terms of letters. Any specific line of handwriting might give to several candidate interpretations. The feature set used in our investigation is shown in Figure 4. We assume that these representations refer to image after slant modification have been made. The feature set is accordingly quite small. Some examples of feature-representation-of sample words are shown in Figure 5.

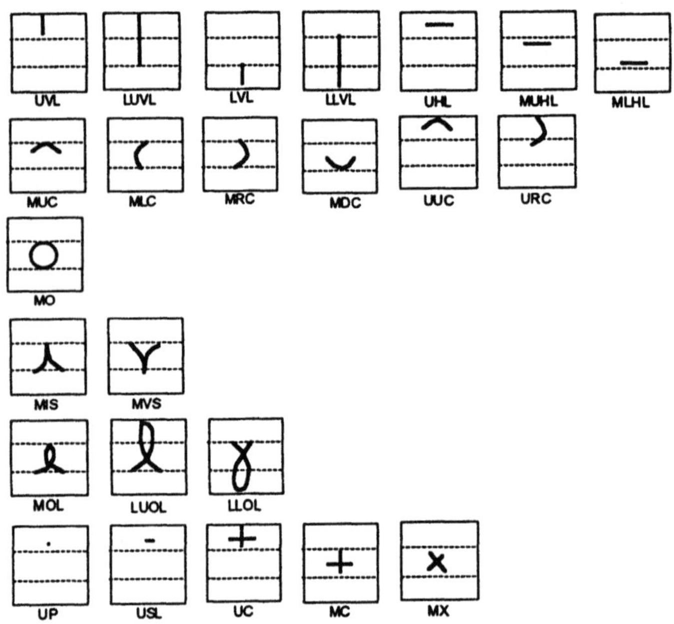

Figure 4. Set of Features used in Investigation

one	mo muhl mvs mis mlhl mol mlhl
three	luvl muhl mc mdc luvl mdc mis mdc mis mol mol
four	luvl urc muhl mdc mo muhl mdc mis mdc mis mvs muhl
seven	mdc mis mo mol mlhl mis mdc mis mo mdc mis mis mlhl
eight	mo mdc mis usl mdc mo llvl luvl muc mdc luvl muhl mc mlhl
nine	mvs muc mdc mis usl mdc mis mis mol
eleven	mo mdc luol mol mis mdc mis mo mdc muc mdc muc mlhl
seventeen	mlhl mo mlhl mo mis mdc muc mdc muhl mo mdc muc mus muc mdc luvl uhl uc mis mdc mo mdc mol mdc muc mvs muc
eighteen	mo mis mdc mis up mdc mo llol luol luvl mvs muc mdc luvl uhl uc mis mol mo mdc muc mis muc

Figure 5. Examples of Unsegmented Feature Representation of Words

There are two known ways of going from the feature representation to the recognition of entire words. One way consists of having predefined models of words in the vocabulary [Amlan K., Yang H., and Paramvir B., 1989]. This way is perhaps rather human-like because a human probably learns the vocabulary and the methods of recognition year after year, improving on the process with time. This method seems to be capable of coping with scribbled writing but many models are needed for each word. If we increase the vocabulary size, very large number of models are required. The other approach for recognizing words is the analytical method based on recognition of separated letters [Maier, M., 1986; Bozinovic, R. M. and Sargur, N. S., 1989]. This method does not require large numbers of models for each word, but if the handwriting word is bad, improper segmentation of word can lead to erroneous recognition of words.

In this work, we develop the segmentation based recognition method using neural networks. The recognition process would start with the partitioning of a number of contiguous features and accepting a set as a reasonable representation of a letter of the alphabet. Acceptance of one set would certainly affect what remains available for formulation of other letters. Accordingly any sequence of features might give recognition process to get a number of different possible interpretations in terms of letters. The letter interpretations are accepted with a growing degree of confidence if collections of contiguous letters do indeed form recognizable words and a further acknowledgment of the correctness is attained if the sentences so formed make sense semantically. In practice there is a constant interplay of acceptance or rejection throughout the entire multilayered perception and acceptance process. And underlying it all is the role of interpolation, namely there is no precise or unique set of features which corresponds to any specific letter, and words can be slightly misspelled and still be accepted. Accordingly any technology proposed for recognizing handwriting need to be able to interpolate, to accommodate many alternate descriptions of any specific conceptual object. When handled well, neural-nets indeed learn descriptions of objects in a manner tolerant of distortions and variations in the description. It seems therefore that neural-net might indeed play a critical role in the realization of machine reading of cursive handwriting.

In this section, we report on a continuing effort aimed both at exploring the roles which neural-net computing can play in the handwriting recognition process and also the details of possible implementations of such roles. We use the neural network to segment the feature sequences and to propose interpretation in terms of letters and words, simultaneously.

As we can see in the Figure 5, each letter actually can have a variable number of features depends on the preprocessing and how it was (poorly) written. For example, the letter 't' can be divided into 4 features such as '*UVL UHL UC MIS*', 'g' as '*MO LLOL*' and 'n' as '*MVS MUC MDC*', and so on. Each letter can be composed with different feature streams depending on the style of the writer. The feature streams, '*MUC MVS MUC MLHL*', '*MVS MUC MDC*' or '*MIS MDC MIS*', can be found in the letter 'n'. To handle such various lengths of letters embedded in the word, we use five neural nets which have different input feature streams from one to five.

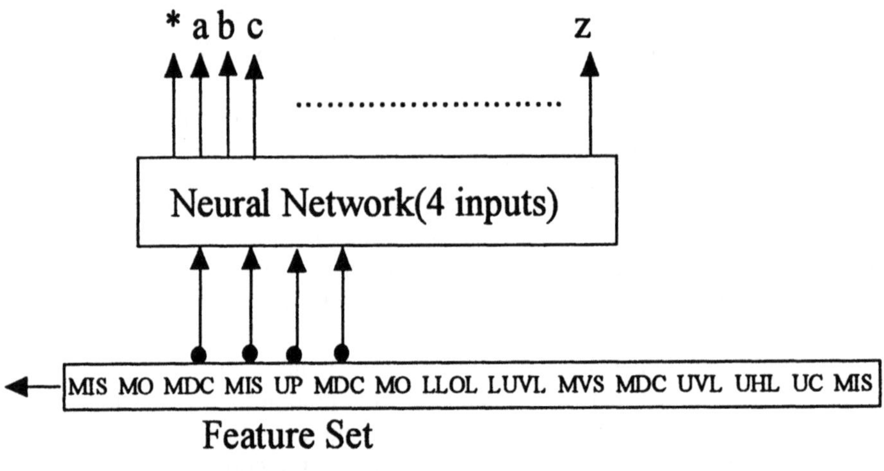

Figure 6 Schematic Description of Neural Net Processing from Feature to Letter

The schematic description of neural net processing from feature to letter is shown in Figure 6. The net shown in the figure accepts four features at a time. We combine the five neural nets which have 1-5 input features in the process, respectively and they are executed in parallel to get possible letter candidates. In the process, the queue containing the feature stream shifts left, and all the neural nets have the outputs corresponding to their own input feature streams. Each net has now 27 outputs (from a to z and an additional meaningless connection between letters denoted as *) but it can be easily expanded to accommodate the capital letters (A, B,.., Z) and special characters ($. &, or %) if we needed to do so.

A schematic illustration of the training of the neural net is shown in Figure 7. In training the neural net, the desired target values are decided on the basis of 'which features are actually belong to which letter'. For example,. in Figure 7, the current neural net has the inputs such as '*MO LLOL LUVL MVS*'. Among them, '*MO LLOL*' are actually belong to 'g' and '*LUVL MVS*' are components of letter 't', so the neural net is trained to believe this combination of features can be g or h with 50% probabilities, respectively. In this way, if all N inputs belong to the same letter, the neural net is trained with ascribe 100% belief to that letter. Assigning the desired output for each set of features is currently carried out 'by hand'.

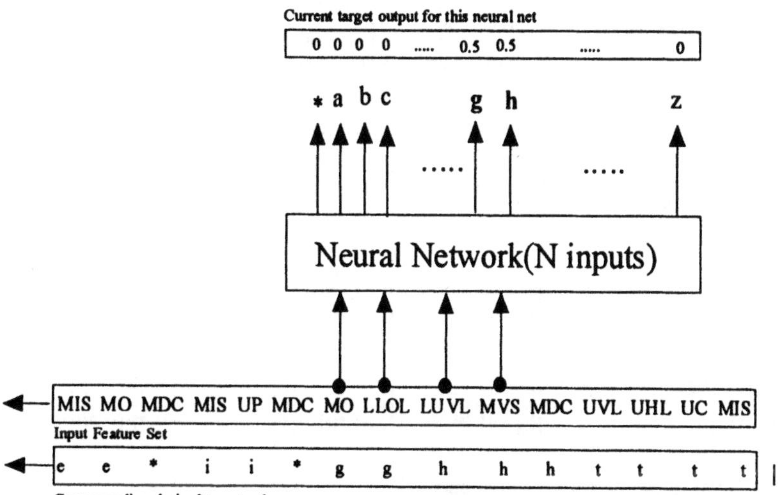

Figure 7. Schematic Description of Neural Net Training

Even though 5 neural nets have estimated outputs at each step, threshold values are used to suppress insignificant neural net outputs, i.e., if the neural net output is less than predefined threshold, that output is disregarded.

In the experiment, we currently use a small number of words such as 50 words (278 letters are involved) in the training and a remaining 50 words are used in testing to see whether they can be recognized correctly.

'eight'

```
o9.... ...... ...... ...... ...... o9.... ...... ...... ...... ...... ...... ...... ...... ......
e9.... ...... i9t6.. t9i3.. ...... g9.... ...... f8.... n3.... t5.... t9.... t9.... t9....
e8.... i6.... i9*2.. t2.... g9.... g9.... ...... h9.... n3t2.. t5.... t9.... t9....
i6e4.. i5.... i5.... g6.... g3.... h5g4.. h5.... h7.... t3.... t7.... t9....
e5i5.. i3.... g3i2.. g6.... h7g5.. g2.... h5.... h3t2.. t5.... t7....
```

'nine'

```
...... ...... ...... ...... ...... ...... ...... ...... e9....
n5.... n3.... ...... i9t6.. t9i3.. ...... n2.... n3....
n6.... ...... i6.... i9*2.. *2t2.. ...... n8....
n6.... i5n4.. i5.... i4.... ...... n6....
n7.... i2*2.. n5*2.. i3.... n3....
```

'ten'

```
...... ...... ...... ...... o9.... ...... ...... ...... ...... ...... ......
t9.... t9.... t9.... ...... e9.... ...... n4.... n5.... n9....
t9.... t9.... e5.... e9.... e8.... ...... n7x2.. n9....
t9.... t8.... e9t6.. e5.... e5.... n6.... n9....
t8e3.. e8t3.. e7.... e6.... n5e3.. n9....
```

'eleven'

```
o9.... ...... i9.... e9.... ...... ...... ...... o9.... ...... ...... ...... ...... ......
e9.... ...... ...... n4.... ...... ...... ...... e9.... n3.... n3.... n3.... n9....
e7.... e6.... ...... e2.... ...... ...... e8.... e9.... n7.... n9.... n9....
e9.... ...... ...... ...... n5.... e6.... e5.... e3.... n8.... n9....
e7.... ...... t4e2.. ...... v7e7.. e5v2.. n5e2.. e3n2.. n7....
```

'twelve'

```
...... ...... ...... ...... ...... ...... ...... o9.... ...... i9.... ...... ...... ...... ...... e9....
t9.... t9.... t9i3.. ...... n3.... n3.... ...... e9.... ...... ...... ...... ...... ...... n3.... ......
t9.... t9.... t7.... w4.... n7.... ...... e9.... e7.... ...... ...... ...... ...... e3.... e3....
t9.... t8.... t6.... w3.... w4.... e6w3.. ...... e9.... ...... ...... ...... ...... ......
t9e2.. t7.... t5.... w6e2.. e5.... ...... ...... e3.... ...... ...... ...... ......
```

'thirteen'

```
...... ...... ...... i9.... ...... ...... ...... ...... ...... ...... ...... ...... ...... o9.... ...... e9.... ...... ......
t9.... t9.... t9.... t5.... n3.... ...... i9t6.. i7.... n3.... t5.... t9.... t9.... t6.... e9.... n3.... n4.... ...... n3....
t9.... t7.... t5.... ...... ...... i6.... i9.... i2.... n3t2.. t5.... t9.... t9.... e8.... e9.... n8.... e2.... n3....
t6.... t6.... ...... h4.... i5n4.. i5.... i4.... i3t2.. t3n2.. t7.... t9.... t4e2.. e8.... n6.... n5.... n6....
t8h2.. ...... t5h5.. h2.... ...... i2.... t2.... t3.... t5.... t7.... t8e5.. t5.... e5u2.. n5.... n5....
```

'fourteen'

```
...... ...... ...... o9.... ...... ...... ...... ...... ...... ...... ...... ...... o9.... ...... o9.... ...... ...... ......
f9.... f9.... ...... e9.... ...... ...... r8.... r4.... ...... t9.... t9.... t6.... e9.... ...... e9.... ...... ...... n3....
f9.... f5.... e7.... e8.... ...... ...... r9.... n3t3r2 t5.... t9.... t9.... e9.... e9.... e9.... e8.... ...... n3....
f5.... e3u3.. e3.... e4.... ...... r9.... r5x2.. r4t3n2 t7.... t7.... e8t5.. e9.... e9.... e6.... e4.... n7....
f4.... e2.... ...... ...... ...... r3.... t3n2.. t5.... t7.... t9e2.. e6t4.. e9t4.. e9e2.. e5.... e4n2..
```

Figure 8. Examples of Neural Net Outputs
(the five outputs for five different networks running in parallel ; the first process has one feature input at a time, the second two features , the third three features and so on)

Figure 8 shows the examples of neural net outputs in the consulting mode. The neural net output of each feature stream indicates the candidate letter [a..z] with variable probabilities [0% - 90%]. For example, the output "o9...." indicates that the possible letter is strongly "o" with 90% probability, and "r4t3n2" means there are three candidate characters for that feature stream such as "r" with 40% possibility, "t" with 30% and "n" with "20%", respectively.

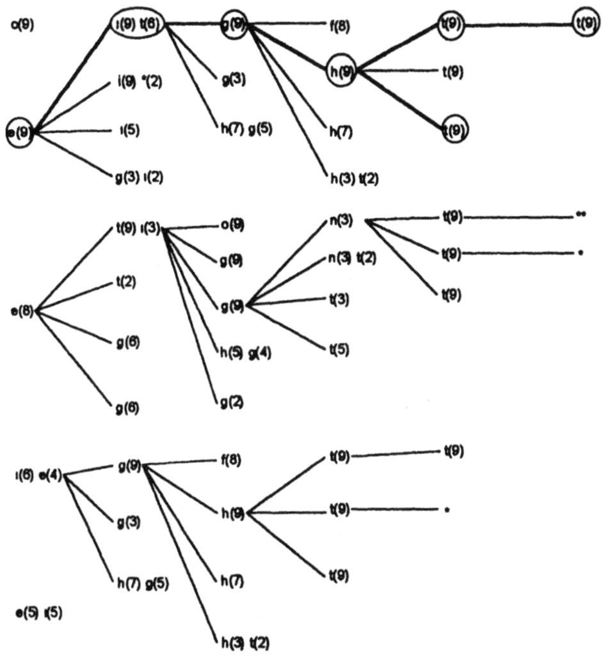

Figure 9. Going from Letters to Possible Words : Finding the most Plausible Candidate (Schematic Illustration in the Form of A Tree Search)

The next processing step consists of going from sequences of letters to words, the letters having been formed from segmented sequences of features by neural nets as described. At that point, various different ways might be used for determining the plausibility of any particular sequence of letters actually constituting one of the words in the vocabulary. Tree search, possibly with a Hidden Markov implementation, would be an example of such method. For the present we illustrate an exhaustive tree search procedure as shown in Figure 9. Actually the so-called exhaustive search is not terribly costly in most cases because we can use a heuristic to prune the paths. The heuristic consists of giving higher emphasis to findings where the number of features in the recognized letter matches or nearly matches the number of required inputs of the net. For the trees in Figure 9, the finding of e(9) should be further increased in significance because the letter 'e' is made up of two features and is recognized as such by a net which takes two input features at a time. In the Figure 9, the children such as i(9) t(6); i(9) *(2); i(5); g(3) i(2) can be selected to form the next segmented letter. For the path where the tree generates children from i(9) t(6), letters such as g(9), g(3), h(7) g(5) are candidates for the next letter, and so on. Finally the strongest plausible candidate words such as "e(9)i(9)g(9)h(9)t(9)t(9) or e(9)i(9)g(9)h(9)t(9)" can be generated along 'thick lines' in the Figure 9, because those words all have 90% probabilities. This kind of search can generate several possible word candidates even if the paths are weighted. It may happen that none of the 'words' really correspond exactly to one of the words in the vocabulary. For example, an actual input of "three" can be recognized such as "threee" or "tthn" and "six" as "eix", "seven" as "eeven", "thirteen" as "thinteen" after transformed to features. This is due to ambiguities in human handwriting. Even a human cannot always distinguish among "r", "n", "m", "u", "v", "w" "a", "s" or "o" in the handwritten words, if one does not know the vocabulary or sometimes, the context of the material. So, to recognize word from these candidates, we need to depend on the dictionary and perhaps the context to reject implausible word candidates.

4 Summarizing Remarks

The purpose of this paper is primarily to comb out conceptually the interrelations between the various interacting processes which together comprise the handwriting recognition act. At present we use a vocabulary of 30 words and a sample size consisting of 100 words samples. The recognition accuracy is higher than 90%. Further quantitative results will be reported subsequently.

References

Hornik, K., Stinchcombe, M., and White, H., 1989: Multilayer feedforward networks are universal approximations, *Neural Networks*, 2, 359-366

Funahashi, 1989: On the approximate realization of continuous mappings by neural networks, *Neural Networks*, 2, 183-192

Pao, Y. H. and Takefuji, Y., 1991: Functional-link net computing: theory, system architecture, and functionalities, Special issue of *Computer* on Computer Architectures for Intelligent Machines, IEEE Computer Society Press, 3, 76-79, also published in Readings in *Computer Architectures for Intelligent Systems* (expanded version), J. Herath (ed.), in press

Pao, Y.H., Phillips, S.M. and Sobajic, D.J., 1992: Neural-net computing and the intelligent control of systems, Special Intelligent Control Issue of *International Journal of Control*, 56(2), 263-289, Taylor and Francis, London.

Igelnik, B. and Pao, Y.H., 1993: Additional prespectives of feedforward neural-nets and the functional-link, IJCNN-93, Nagoya, Japan, Oct. 25-29.

Simon, J.C., Zerhouni, K., 1991: Robust description of a line image, *ICDAR-91*, 3-14, Sept. 30 to Oct.2, Saint Malo, France.

Simon, J.C. (ed.), 1989: *From pixels to features*, North-Holland, The Netherlands.

Kunihiko, F. and Nobuaki, W., 1991: Handwritten alphanumeric character recognition by the neurocognitron, IEEE Trans. on Neural Networks, 2(3), 355-365.

Blackwell, K.T., Vogl, T.P. and Hyman, S.D. Barbour, G.S., and Alkon, D.L., 1992: A new approach to handwritten character recognition, *Pattern Recognition*, 25(6), 655-666.

Bozinovic, R. M. and Sargur, N.S., 1989: Off-line cursive script word recognition, *IEEE Trans. on Pattern Analysis and Machine Intelligence*, 11(1), 68-83.

Amlan K., Yang H., and Paramvir B., 1989: Recognition of handwritten word: first and second order hidden Markov model based approach, *Pattern recognition*, 22(3), 283-297.

Maier, M., 1986: Separating characters in script documents, *8th Int. Conf. on Pattern Recognition*, Paris, 1056-58.

Appendix Observations on Rapid Convergence Attainable with the Random Vector FL Net

A typical RV Functional-link net is depicted in Figure 2-(b) of text. It is useful and important to note that the output of an augmentation node is a scalar, but that scalar is a function of the entire input pattern vector. In a functional mapping

$R^N \longrightarrow R$, the output is $o = \sum \beta_j g(\mathbf{a}_j\mathbf{x} + b_j)$.

In practice, we have the original vector components as well as the augmentation nodes. In the interest of simplicity in representation we do not distinguish between the two different types of input nodes in the following formalism. That is, all the weights are denoted β_j, each one of which weights the output of corresponding node j and all of the weighted values are summed to yield the output.

The scalar output o is computed as $o = \mathbf{B}^t\mathbf{d}$

where $\mathbf{B} = [\beta_1 \quad \beta_2 \quad \ldots \quad \beta_{N+J}]^t$

$\mathbf{d} = [\delta_1 \quad \delta_2 \quad \ldots \quad \delta_{N+J}]^t$

The symbol J denotes the total number of augmentation nodes and N denotes the number of components of the original input vector.

For the augmentation nodes, $\delta_m = g(net_m)$ for $m = N, N+1, \ldots, N+J$

where $net_m = a_{m1}x_1 + \ldots + a_{mN}x_N + b_m = \mathbf{a}_m^t\mathbf{x} + b_m$

$\mathbf{a}_m^t = [a_{m1}, \ a_{m2}, \ \ldots, \ a_{mN}]^t$

$\mathbf{x} = [x_1, \ x_2, \ x_3, \ \ldots, \ x_N]^t$

The $\mathbf{a}_m, b_m$ parameters are selected at random but are scaled to avoid saturation of $g(\cdot)$. For pattern $\mathbf{x}^{(p)}$, we get $net_m^{(p)} = \mathbf{a}_m^t\mathbf{x}^{(p)} + b_m$, $\delta_m^{(p)} = g(net_m^{(p)})$ and $o^{(p)} = \mathbf{B}^t\mathbf{d}^{(p)}$.

For a given set of input and target data pairs $\{\mathbf{x}^{(p)}, \ t^{(p)}\}$, p = 1,2,...,P, the task is to determine (learn) unknown β parameters. The learning process can be posed as an optimization problem, where the criterion function E defined as

$$E = \frac{1}{2P}\sum_{p=1}^{P}(t^{(p)} - \mathbf{B}'\mathbf{d}^{(p)})^2$$

is to minimized.

We observe that equations $t^{(1)} = \mathbf{B}'\mathbf{d}^{(1)} = (\mathbf{d}^{(1)})'\mathbf{B}$, $t^{(2)} = \mathbf{B}'\mathbf{d}^{(2)} = (\mathbf{d}^{(2)})'\mathbf{B}$,..., $t^{(P)} = \mathbf{B}'\mathbf{d}^{(P)} = (\mathbf{d}^{(P)})'\mathbf{B}$ can be written in a compact form as $\mathbf{t} = \mathbf{VB}$ where $\mathbf{t} = [t^{(1)},\ t^{(2)},\ \ldots,\ t^{(P)}]'$ and $\mathbf{V} = [(\delta^{(1)})',\ (\delta^{(2)})',\ \ldots,\ (\delta^{(P)})']'$ so that criterion E can be expressed as $E = \frac{1}{2P}(\mathbf{t} - \mathbf{VB})'(\mathbf{t} - \mathbf{VB})$. The gradient is accordingly $\mathbf{r} = \frac{\partial \mathrm{E}}{\partial \mathbf{B}} = -\frac{1}{P}\mathbf{V}'(\mathbf{t} - \mathbf{VB})$ and the learning process can be written as

$$\mathbf{B}^{new} = \mathbf{B}^{old} + \frac{\eta}{P}\mathbf{V}'(\mathbf{t} - \mathbf{VB}^{old}).$$

Search for an optimal $\mathbf{B}^*$ in the negative direction of the gradient of E (denoted as $\mathbf{r}$) is usually efficient for a quadratic E function but there is some waste motion due to the zig-zagging nature of the search process.

The waste motion can be eliminated with use of the Conjugate Gradient (CG) method, a first-order indirect optimization process. That method uses gradient information for finding better directions for search. In all cases of quadratic optimization, the system optimum can be reached in a *finite number of iterations* but the CG method guarantees convergence in a specific predetermined number of operations.

According to CG methodology, parameter update is defined by

$$\mathbf{B}^{new} = \mathbf{B}^{old} + \eta\mathbf{s}$$

Directions of search $\mathbf{s}$ are computed at every point $\mathbf{b}^{(\cdot)}$ as

At $\mathbf{B}^{(0)}$: $\mathbf{s}^{(0)} = -\mathbf{r}^{(0)}$

$\mathbf{B}^{(1)}$: $\mathbf{s}^{(1)} = -\mathbf{r}^{(1)} + \gamma_1\mathbf{s}^{(0)}$

$\mathbf{B}^{(2)}$: $\mathbf{s}^{(2)} = -\mathbf{r}^{(2)} + \gamma_2\mathbf{s}^{(1)}$

$\mathbf{B}^{(N+J-1)}$: $\mathbf{s}^{(N+J-1)} = -\mathbf{r}^{(N+J-1)} + \gamma_{N+J-1}\mathbf{s}^{(N+J-2)}$

$\mathbf{B}^{(N+J)}$: **True Optimum**

where M=N+J is the dimension of the parameter vector **B**, and $\gamma_1 = \frac{\|\mathbf{r}^{(1)}\|^2}{\|\mathbf{r}^{(0)}\|^2}$,

$\gamma_2 = \frac{\|\mathbf{r}^{(2)}\|^2}{\|\mathbf{r}^{(1)}\|^2}$ and so on.

In general

$$\mathbf{B}^{(\lambda+1)} = \mathbf{B}^{(\lambda)} + \eta \mathbf{s}^{(\lambda)}$$

$$\mathbf{s}^{(\lambda)} = -\mathbf{r}^{(\lambda)} + \frac{\|\mathbf{r}^{(\lambda)}\|^2}{\|\mathbf{r}^{(\lambda-1)}\|^2} \mathbf{s}^{(\lambda-1)}$$

for $\lambda = 0, \quad \mathbf{s}^{(0)} = -\mathbf{r}^{(0)}$

and $\lambda = K, \quad \mathbf{B}^{(K)}$ is optimum

In figure A.1, we demonstrate graphically the difference which occurs during the minimization of a quadratic function of two variables (M=2) using the directions of search

(a) along the negative gradient of criterion function E or

(b) along in the direction computed according to the CG methodology.

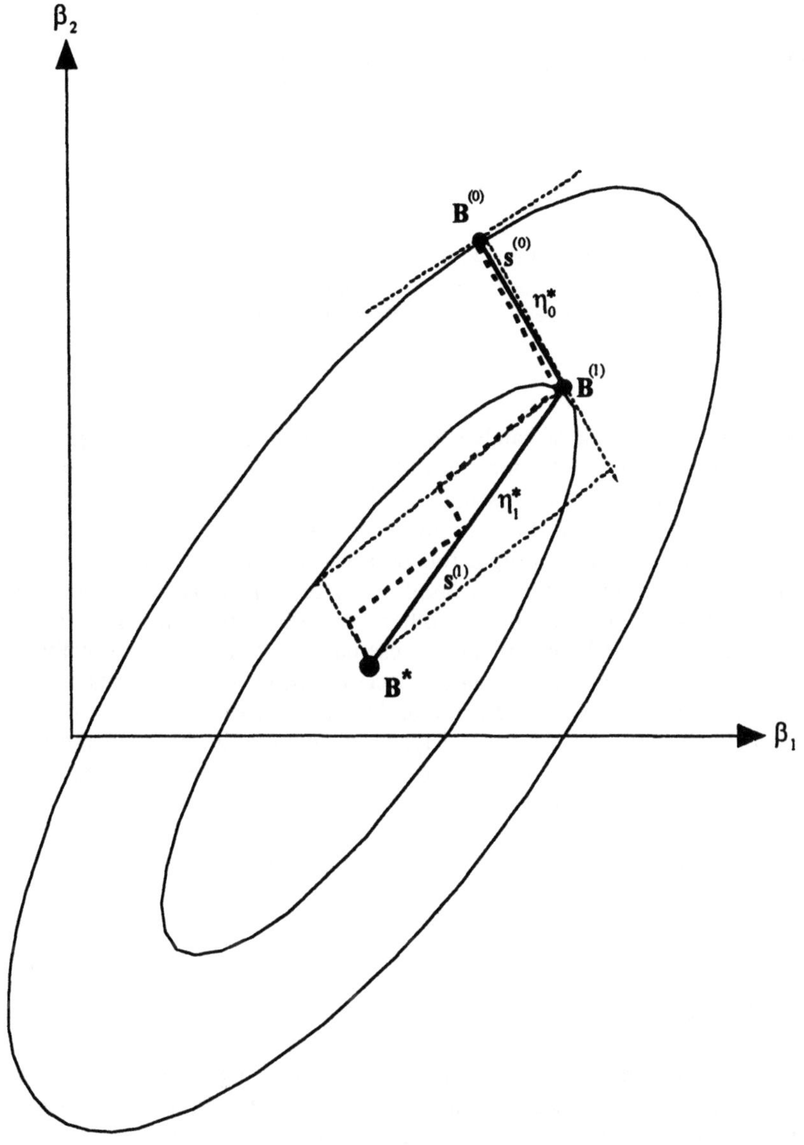

A Comparison of Two Search Strategies:
- - - quadratic descent minimization
—— conjugate gradient method
- - - lines used to establish direction for conjugate gradient method

Cooperation of Feedforward Neural Networks for Handwritten Digit Recognition

David Price[1] and Stefan Knerr[2]

[1] A2IA and Ecole Superieure de Physique et de Chimie Industrielle, 75005 Paris, France
[2] Ecole Superieure de Physique et de Chimie Industrielle, 75005 Paris, France
and International Computer Science Institute, Berkeley CA 94704, USA

Abstract. In the framework of handwritten digit recognition, we investigate the cooperation of two feedforward neural networks which are identical in structure but which use two different data representations. Edge detection is performed as a preprocessing for the first network, whereas a more elaborate image description in terms of line strokes is used as input for the second network. It turns out that many of the examples which are misclassified by one of the two networks are correctly classified or rejected by the other network. This demonstrates the complementary character of the two data representations, which can be effectively used to increase the recognition rates and/or decrease the error rates by making the two networks cooperate. We present the architecture of the networks and the training algorithm used, discuss several types of cooperation between the two networks, and report results obtained on a U.S. Postal Service data base comprising 9,002 segmented digits.

Keywords. Neural networks, handwritten digit recognition, cooperation of classifiers, committee-machine, voting.

1 Introduction

Recent developments in the field of handwritten digit recognition using neural networks and related approaches show a convergence in recognition rate towards human performance: raw recognition rates up to 97.5% were reported on unconstrained, real-world, isolated digits, such as the data used in this paper, which originates from the address blocks of letters going through a U.S. post office [1-5]. For comparison: humans achieve approximatively a 98% recognition rate on comparable data. However, for many real world applications, including zip code recognition and bank cheque reading, it is more important to reject ambiguous data and thereby to minimize the error rate of the classifier rather than to maximize the raw recognition rate: it is cheaper to sort a letter "by hand" than to send it to the wrong address. While many classification algorithms yield excellent raw recognition rates, they often have the problem that their recognition rate drops dramatically when low error rates are enforced by a rejection rule (see figure 5).

There are mainly two reasons which can lead to poorly positioned decision boundaries in pattern space and therefore to erroneous classification or rejection: (i) in regions of the pattern space with no or not many examples, the decision boundary defined by a given classifier after training will be somewhat arbitrary and therefore the classifier will not generalize well in these regions; (ii) in regions of the pattern space where different classes are close to each other and the exact positioning of the decision boundary is important, ambiguous patterns (with respect to a given data representation) may be misclassified with a high probability.

The first problem can be effectively addressed by local control of the capacity of the classification algorithm, as shown by [4]. In the regions of the pattern space which are well described by the data, the decision boundary can be made complex and a high capacity classifier (large number of hidden units in a Multilayer Perceptron; no or small weight decay; etc.) can make its decision with high confidence. In the poorly sampled regions of the pattern space, a low capacity classifier defines a simple decision boundary and makes its decision with low confidence. Such a classifier system results in higher rejection rates in regions with no or not many examples, but reduces the number of errors. For the control of the capacity of a classifier, see also [6].

Another possibility to solve the first problem is to use several classifiers which differ only in the random initialization of their parameters before training. Training of these classifiers will result in different decision boundaries in the poorly sampled regions, and a vote of these classifiers on an example from such a region will hopefully not lead to an unanimous vote, in which case the example can be easily rejected.

The second problem is more difficult since it relies essentially on the distribution (not the number) of the examples in the pattern space and thus on the data representation. To solve this problem, we propose a cooperation of two neural network classifiers, henceforth termed committee-machine (CM), using a different data representation each. Some of the patterns which are ambiguous with respect to one of the data representations may be easy to recognize or to reject with respect to the other data representation. By making the two neural network classifiers vote, this fact can be used to reject some of the ambiguous patterns which would have been misclassified by a single classifier.

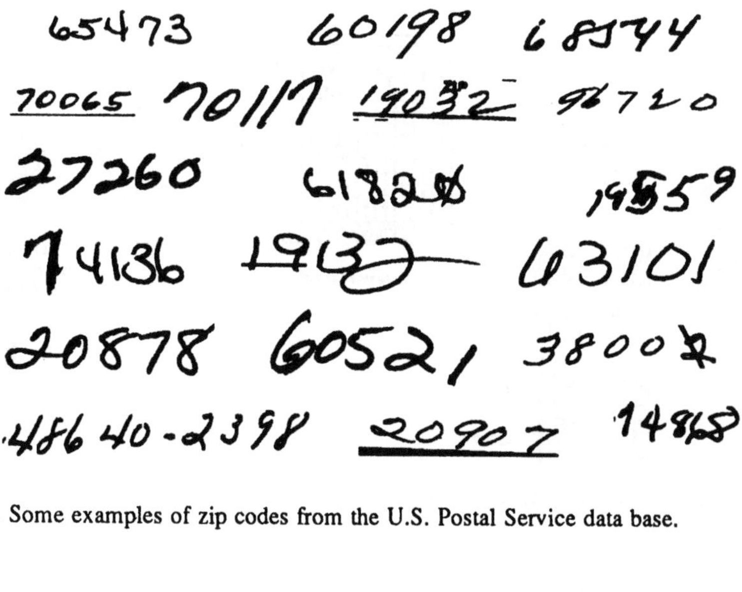

Fig. 1. Some examples of zip codes from the U.S. Postal Service data base.

2 Data Base

For our experiments we used 9002 hand-segmented digits from the U.S. Postal Service OAT Handwritten Zip Code Data Base (1987). In addition to strong variations in writing style, some of the digits are cut in part, include extraneous marks or parts from other digits. Figure 1 shows some examples of zip codes.

The data base was randomly divided into training sets of 7287 examples and test sets of 1715 examples: both contain highly ambiguous examples which are hardly recognizable by humans as well as mis-labeled examples. The performance results reported later are averaged over five different random partitions.

3 Preprocessing

3.1 Digits are Line Drawings

Digits can be conveniently interpreted as line drawings, i.e. essentially one-dimensional structured objects in a two-dimensional world. Therefore, the detection of line segments seems to be an adequate preprocessing. For each location in the image, information about the presence of a line segment of a given orientation is stored in a feature map. We used four feature maps, representing horizontal, vertical, and diagonal (±45°) line segments respectively. These feature maps are normalized in size, resulting in a 256 dimensional feature vector for each pattern, which is the input to the network classifier. The data representations for the two networks differ in the way the line segments are localy detected.

3.2 Preprocessing for the First Network

The data representation for the first network is obtained by performing edge detection (see figure 2). The original pixel image is convoluted with 4 pairs of Kirsch`s edge operators (3x3 pixels), resulting in 4 graded feature maps, coding for the presence of horizontal, vertical, and diagonal edges. Note that a pair of "anti-parallel" edges forms a line segment which is represented in a single map.

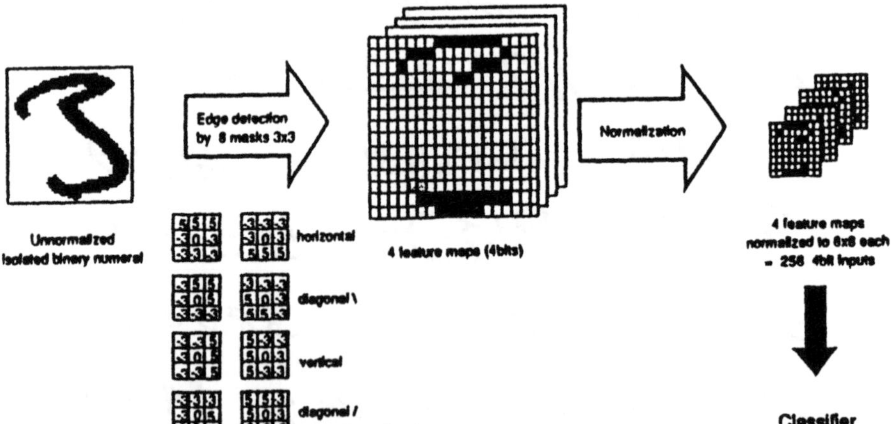

Fig. 2. Preprocessing steps for the first network.

However, the Kirsch operators do not result in a unique orientation for a given edge: mostly, there is one orientation which is most prominent and therefore yielding the highest value in the corresponding map, but the other maps may have non zero values too. This is due to the fact that only four orientations are taken into account; we believe that, while some redundancy in the coding is useful, it would be more appropriate to consider at least eight orientations. The feature maps are normalized in size to an 8x8 format using a linear transformation which preserves the aspect ratio of the pattern. The four maps are finally concatenated, thereby loosing the two-dimensional topology of the image, and result in a 256 dimensional feature. Each element of the vector is coded by 4 bits.

3.3 Preprocessing for the Second Network

While no higher level concepts are used in the preprocessing steps for the first network, here the concept of a stroke is explicitly used to remove ambiguities in the orientations of the local coding of the line segments. The processing is somewhat elaborate and we will not describe the details here; we refer the interested reader to [7].

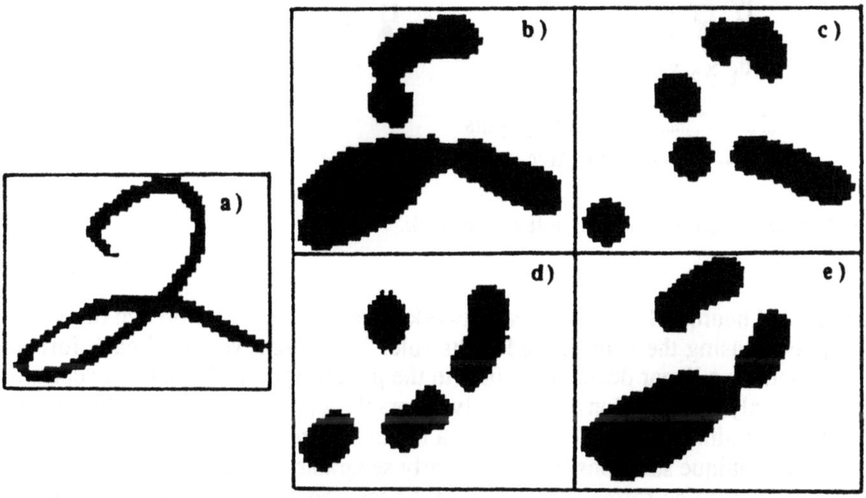

Fig. 3. Description of a digit resulting from the preprocessing used for the second network: original binary image (a), and the strokes found for the four orientations (b-e).

First, the binary pixel image is scanned for supports of at least 3x3 ink-pixels of a given orientation, called quanta. The same orientations as in the first preprocessing are used. All the pixels of a quantum have the same orientation, whereas all ink-pixels which can not be unanimously interpreted as a quantum are considered singular and are not taken into account any further. The pixels of the quanta are stored in the corresponding map according to their orientation. Figure 3 shows an example of the representation of a digit. Again, the four maps are normalized in size as for the first preprocessing, also resulting in a 256 dimensional feature vector.

4 Network Architecture and Cooperation of Networks

Both neural networks used in the CM consist of a single layer of 45 formal neurons, fully connected to the 256 inputs (figure 4); the final decision is taken by ten AND gates and is explained later in more detail together with the rejection rule. Each formal neuron in the first layer is specialized in discriminating two classes and is therefore intended to operate in a localized part of the pattern space only; all 45 pairs of classes turned out to be linearly separable.

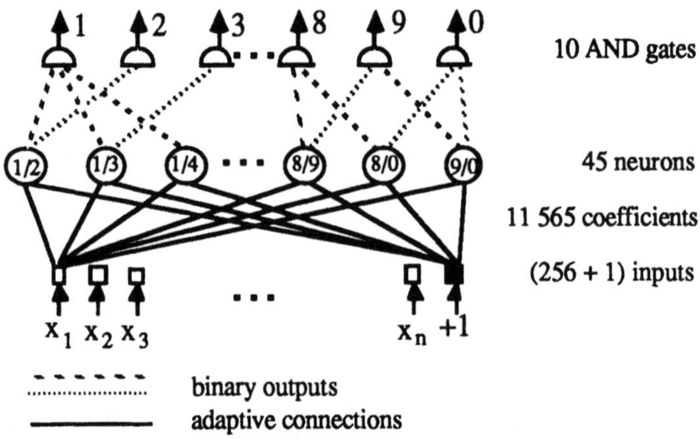

Fig. 4. Architecture of one single-layer network.

Each formal neuron of the discussed network is trained separately on two of the ten digit classes using the Generalized Delta rule. The weight vector of each formal neuron defines a linear decision surface in the pattern space. Whereas Perceptron-type rules only find solutions for linearly separable sets of examples, the Delta rule and the Generalized Delta rule minimize a Mean Square Error criterion (MSE) and converge to unique solutions for non-linearly separable sets as well [8]. However, the Delta rule trains formal neurons with linear transfer functions and does not necessarily converge to a separating solution, even if such a solution exists. The Generalized Delta rule trains formal neurons using sigmoidal transfer functions and is guaranteed to find a separating hyperplane, if such a hyperplane exists. There are no local minima in the MSE landscape and, by initializing the weights to zero and controlling the learning rate carefully, a gradient method always finds the minimum, i.e. the best hyperplane with respect to the MSE criterion. In the case of the Generalized Delta rule, this hyperplane is positioned so as to maximize the distance to the marginal examples of the classes. Once the single-layer network is trained, the sigmoidal transfer functions of the formal neurons are replaced by simple threshold functions which provide binary inputs to the ten subsequent boolean operations.

In order to implement a rejection rule for this network, the values of the *linear* outputs are taken into account for the final decision made by the AND gates: a small magnitude of a linear output indicates an ambiguous situation. A formal neuron, separating class i from class j, compares its linear output $v_{(i/j)}$ to a common rejection threshold θ; the two binary outputs $s_{(i/j)j}$ and $s_{(i/j)i}$ are then:

- if $v_{(i/j)}<-\theta$, then $s_{(i/j)j}=1$ and $s_{(i/j)i}=0$;
- if $v_{(i/j)}>\theta$, then $s_{(i/j)j}=0$ and $s_{(i/j)i}=1$;
- otherwise $s_{(i/j)j}=s_{(i/j)i}=0$, indicating an ambiguous input pattern.

The final decision of the network is as follows:

- if $s_{(i/j)i}=1$ for all j, the output of the AND gate "i" is one, and the input pattern is assigned to class i ;
- if all AND gates have zero outputs, the input pattern is rejected.

A low rejection threshold results in a high percentage of well classified examples, whereas a high threshold yields a low error rate. Note that this rejection rule uses a single parameter in order to set the error rate to a prescribed percentage.

A hardware implementation of the single-layer network classifier, performing a classification of a 256 dimensional input vector in approximatively 130 µs is discussed elsewhere [9].

For a cooperation of two such single-layer networks, we investigated several types of voting. The first, and simplest, requires that both networks agree on the class label in order to classify a given pattern. A pattern which is (i) rejected by at least one of the networks or (ii) attributed different class labels by the two networks is rejected by the CM.

The second voting mechanism differs from the first insofar as a pattern which is rejected by only one network is classified by the CM according to the class label suggested by the other network.

The third type of voting we have implemented consists of a second layer of 10 formal neurons, one for each class, being fully connected to the first layer of 2x45=90 formal neurons (using sigmoids) of *both* networks. The second layer is trained, again using the generalized Delta Rule, while the weights of the first layer are fixed.

It turned out that the first type of voting is the most efficient one for low error rates, whereas the second and third type yield higher recognition rates for error rates above 1.5%. Since we are chiefly interested in low error rates, we focus in the following on the first voting mechanism.

5 Results and Discussion

When we applied the CM on the test data, it turned out that many of the examples which are misclassified by one of the two networks are correctly classified or rejected by the other network. This demonstrates the complementary character of the two data representations: while both result in pairwise linear separable training sets, they yield different sets of marginal examples (examples which are close to other classes in pattern space). By making the two neural network classifiers vote, the CM rejects some marginal patterns which would have been misclassified by a single classifier.

Figure 5 shows the recognition rate as a function of the error rate for one of the five partitions of the data base into training set and test set: the recognition rate of the CM stays considerably above the recognition rates of the single-layer networks for low error rates. In order to achieve a 1% error rate, the single-layer network using the quanta has to reject 9% of the test data, the single-layer network using the edges needs a 7.5% rejection rate, whereas the CM only rejects 6%. At a 10% rejection rate, the CM misclassifies three patterns, one of which is mislabeled, the other two being unrecognizable also for humans.

Figure 5 reflects the general behavior of the single-layer networks and the CM with respect to rejection. However, when the average over the five different partitions is computed, the rejection rates are somewhat higher: the single-layer networks using the quanta have to reject 12.5% of the test data in average, the single-layer networks using the edges need an average rejection rate of 10.5%, whereas the CMs only reject 8.2% in order to obtain a 1% error rate. To achieve a 0.5% error rate, the CMs reject an average of 12% of the test data.

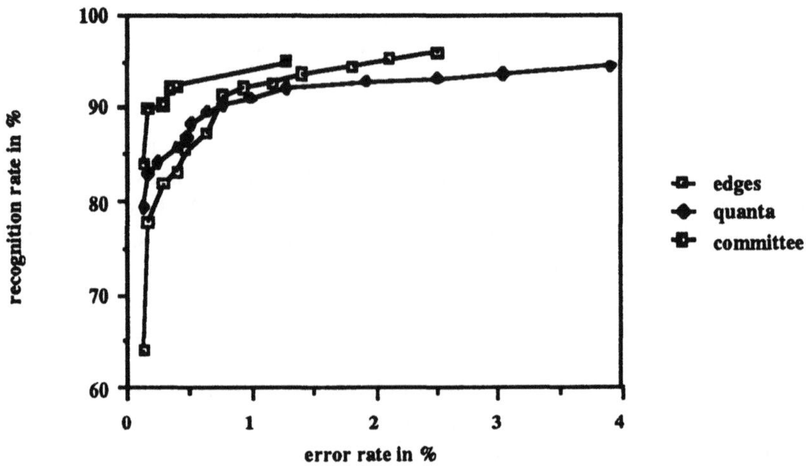

Fig. 5. Relationship between recognition rate and error rate for a single partition of the data base.

These results show, how much the performance of a network depends on the marginal examples in the data base (training set and test set), and demonstrates that it is necessary to test a classification algorithm on several partitions into training set and test set in order to get a reliable estimate of its performance.

Despite the fact that our data originates from the same zip codes as the data used by [1, 4, 5], a direct comparison of the results is not easy since the procedures of extracting the digits from the zip codes were not the same and resulted in different pixel images and a different number of examples.

6 Conclusion

For many real world applications, such as zip code recognition or bank cheque reading, it is more important to minimize the error rate of the classifier rather than to maximize the recognition rate. The problem is that usually the recognition rate of a classification algorithm drops dramatically when low error rates are enforced by a rejection mechanism. We have shown that a cooperation of two neural network classifiers using *different* data representations effectively decreases the error rates compared to a single network while maintaining high recognition rates. Many of the examples which are misclassified by one of the two networks are correctly classified or rejected by the other network. By making the two networks vote, these examples can be easily rejected. On a real-world data base of isolated digits we obtained an average rejection rate of 8.2% at a 1% error rate. This is more than 2% better than our best result with a single network. To achieve a 0.5% error rate, 12% of the test data had to be rejected.

Acknowledgements. We thank the U.S. Postal Service for providing us with the U.S. Postal Service OAT Handwritten Zip Code Data Base (1987). It is a pleasure to thank Jean-Claude Simon, Olivier Barret, Léon Personnaz, and Gérard Dreyfus for many useful discussions.

References

1. LeCun, Y., Boser, B., Denker, J.S., Henderson, D., Howard, R.E., Hubbard, W., Jackel, L.D.: Backpropagation Applied to Handwritten Zip Code Recognition. Neural Computation 1, 541-551, 1989.
   LeCun, Y., Boser, B., Denker, J.S., Henderson, D., Howard, R.E., Hubbard, W., Jackel, L.D.: Handwritten Digit Recognition with a Backpropagation Network. In: D.S. Touretzky, (ed.), Advances in Neural Information Processing Systems. Vol. 2, Morgan Kaufmann, 1990.
2. Knerr, S., Personnaz, L., Dreyfus, G.: Handwritten Digit Recognition by Neural Networks with Single-Layer Training. IEEE Transactions on Neural Networks, Vol. 3, No. 6, 1992.
3. Martin, G.L., Pittman, J.A.: Recognizing Hand-Printed Letters and Digits Using Backpropagation Learning. Neural Computation 3, 258-267, 1991.
4. Bottou, L., Vapnik, V.: Local Learning Algorithms. Neural Computation 4, 888-900, 1992.
5. Simard, P., LeCun, Y., Denker, J.S.: Efficient Pattern Recognition Using a New Transformation Distance. In: L. Giles, S. Hanson, J. Cowan (eds.), Advances in Neural Information Processing Systems. Vol. 5, Morgan Kaufmann, 1993.
6. Guyon, I., Vapnik, V., Boser, B., Bottou, L., Solla, S.A.: Structural Risk Minimization for Character Recognition. In: R.P. Lippmann, J.E. Moody, S.J. Hanson (eds.), Advances in Neural Information Processing Systems. Vol. 4, Morgan Kaufmann, 1992.
7. Simon, J.C.: Off-Line Cursive Word Recognition. Proceedings of the IEEE, Vol. 80, No. 7, 1992.
8. Knerr, S., Personnaz, L., Dreyfus, G.: Single-Layer Learning Revisited : A Stepwise Procedure for Building and Training a Neural Network. In: Neurocomputing : Algorithms, Architectures and Applications, F. Fogelman-Soulie, J. Hérault (eds.), NATO ASI Series, Springer, 1990.
9. Alla, P.-Y., Saucier, G., Knerr, S., Personnaz, L., Dreyfus, G.: Design and Implementation of a Dedicated Neural Network for Handwritten Digit Recognition. In: Silicon Architectures for Neural Nets, M.G. Sami (ed.), Elsevier, 1991.

Normalisation and Preprocessing for a Recurrent Network Off-line Handwriting Recognition System

A.W.Senior

Cambridge University Engineering Department, Trumpington Street, Cambridge, CB2 1PZ. England. E-mail: aws@eng.cam.ac.uk

Abstract This paper describes the normalisation and preprocessing operations which have been implemented as the preprocessing stages of a complete off-line handwriting recognition system based on recurrent networks. These operations remove shears, rotations and scaling from words, and estimate the position of the important base-lines. The paper also describes the methods used to encode the data and to determine the presence of writing features which are of benefit in the recognition processes.

Keywords Off-line, cursive script, normalisation, preprocessing, recurrent networks.

1 Introduction

The greatest problem with off-line handwriting recognition, as for on-line or speech recognition, is the tremendous variety in handwriting which is readily accepted and correctly read by human readers. This variation can be ascribed to many causes: from mood, the type of writing implement and the document type which can affect the form of an individuals writing from occasion to occasion; to factors like education, anatomy and personality of the author which contribute to that author's idioscript. While these variations may be of interest to the forensic scientist or graphologist, it is these factors that must be eliminated to carry out effective handwriting recognition. All these unwanted variations would ideally be removed by a preprocessor so that characters as close as possible to the archetypes are presented to the recogniser, simplifying the discrimination that it must make.

This paper describes the procedures that are carried out to take a handwritten text and normalise each word so that rotations, shears and scaling transformations are removed ready for parametrisation. The encoding procedure is described, together with a novel approach to feature spotting which identifies characteristic features of handwritten letters and highlights them to aid recognition. The actual recognition method used is a recurrent error-propagation network whose implementation is described elsewhere [5].

2 Preprocessing

Lower case, cursive script words were written on a plain A4 sheet, each surrounded by white space to facilitate word extraction. These sheets were then scanned at 300 dpi resolution, in 8 bits to produce one file per page. These files are automatically segmented into separate words which are processed individually. Figure 2a shows one such word, binarised for printing clarity.

The first concern is to remove shear and rotation transformations from words which have been written slanted or on a sloping baseline, or which have been scanned slightly skew. Slant and slope are both removed by shears — parallel to the x- and y-axes respectively — but in each case require a reliable estimate of the angle of shear. The following paragraphs describe the procedure for estimating the slope and then the shear.

Figure 1: Histograms and half, centre and base lines.

The heuristic used to determine the angle of the base line is as follows:

1 Calculate the vertical density histogram by counting the number of black pixels in each horizontal line. (Vertical and horizontal density histograms are shown on the right and bottom edges of figure 1.)

2 The peak value of the histogram is found, and the histogram is searched downwards for a large slope through the value 40% of the maximum. This slope roughly corresponds to the position of the baseline, so the areas below the bottom of this slope are discarded as consisting only of descenders.

3 Find the lowest remaining pixel in each vertical scan line, retaining only the lowest portion of each continuous curve. (So as to work with only the lowest part of each stroke.)

4 Find the line of best fit through these points.

5 Remove the outliers and calculate the new line of best fit. This is now considered to be the base line of the word.

Given this estimate, the grey-level image is sheared parallel to the y-axis (see figure 2b) and the slant can be determined using a technique based on that described by Božinović & Srihari [1]. This involves isolating areas of the text which are near-vertical strokes and estimating the slant of each of these. This procedure has been found to be very sensitive to the thickness of the writing and is unreliable when the writing is thinner than expected. However, by making an estimate of the writing thickness from the distance transform (see section 4) and using an iterative technique, a much more stable version of this algorithm has been developed.

Božinović & Srihari's algorithm commences by eliminating all horizontal strips in a word which contain horizontal strokes. These are found by finding any rows which contain long runs of black pixels. The maximum number of consecutive black pixels which can be permitted before a line is eliminated is a parameter which need to be specified. After each row with such a long black run is eliminated, the remaining image is in horizontal strips, some of which are too narrow to use and are eliminated. (A second, less critical, parameter is the smallest height of horizontal strip which can be used to

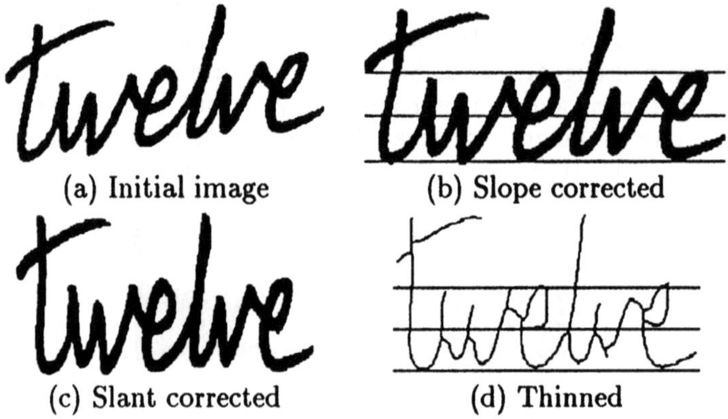

(a) Initial image (b) Slope corrected

(c) Slant corrected (d) Thinned

Figure 2: Successive stages in the preprocessing.

estimate the slope.) The remaining strips are divided into boxes containing separate, near-vertical strokes in each of which the centroids of the upper and lower halves are determined, and the slant of the line between the two is calculated. Averaging the slants across all such strokes gives an estimate of the average overall slant of the word.

The modification which has been found to stabilise this algorithm is to split the word into strokes for a range of values of the run-length parameter and to use the value which gives the largest number of boxes. It is under these conditions that the best slant estimates are obtained. A further refinement is to discard boxes in which the stroke fragments in the top and bottom sections are not connected and cannot be sensibly used to estimate the stroke slant. The best slant estimate is corrected with shear parallel to the x-axis. Figure 2d shows a slant-corrected word.

Finally, a more accurate estimate of the baseline (now assumed to be horizontal) is made. Here a more complex method is used which finds the maximum likelihood position of the baseline given a variety of criteria. The various criteria (our initial estimate of the position of the baseline before it was sheared; the fact that the baseline will generate a steep slope in the histogram and at about the 40% value in the histogram) are assigned Gaussian probabilities which are multiplied together and the scanline with the maximum probability is considered to be the baseline.

The same techniques are used to estimate the half-line (which runs along the tops of the bodies of lower case letters), and the distance between the half- and base-lines is used as an estimate of the character height to provide scale invariance. This divides the word into bodies, ascenders and descenders. (As used by Gilloux this volume, for instance.)

Smoothing and thinning

To remove noise from the image, either from scanning defects or from applying transforms to discrete images, it is useful to smooth the image. This is carried out by convolution with a 2-dimensional Gaussian filter. It has been found that there is negligible noise on a scanned image when using a black fibre-tip pen on plain white paper, but degradation from this ideal situation is possible from a large number of sources (such as paper quality, age and condition; whether there is any printing on the paper; and the pen or pencil type.)

Having normalised and smoothed the image, it is thresholded to leave every pixel black or white. An iterative thinning algorithm is applied to reduce the lines in the writing to one-pixel width so that the strokes can be followed later. (See figure 2d.) The algorithm used is that due to Davies' [2] p153 which is guaranteed to leave a connected skeleton and was found to be the best of the three investigated.

3 Parametrisation

Now that the image has been normalised to a standard form, which highlights invariants of the words and suppresses spurious variations, the preprocessed image needs to be parametrised in an appropriate manner for input to the network which is to carry out the recognition process. Since the recognition system chosen is a special sort of back-propagation network, it was decided to code the word in a largely binary form, so that each unit of the input would correspond to the presence or absence of a feature. Also, the network must be able to recognise words of variable length, so the recurrent network architecture was chosen because of its ability to process sequences of arbitrary length. Although originally developed as a temporal recognition system (for instance Robinson and Fallside have used it for speech recognition [4]), like the TDNN described by Guyon in this volume, by treating the x-axis as a time dimension, off-line writing can be processed. The TDNN was also tried on this application, but its large number of architecture parameters, and its fixed window size meant that the results obtained were poorer than with the recurrent network which can deal with variable context lengths and processes time-dilated signals better. The network is trained with a full train/validation/test procedure to avoid overtraining. One of the great advantages of the system is that, like that of Houle in this volume, it avoids the complex problem of segmenting the word. The scheme chosen to parametrise the data for this network is described below.

The area covered by the word is first divided into rectangles. There are sixteen horizontal rows and a variable number of vertical frames of a width proportional to the estimated character width. Long words thus have more frames than short words, but a given character will always occupy approximately the same number. For each of these rectangles, four bins are allocated to represent different line angles (vertical, horizontal, and the lines 45 degrees from these). Given this framework, the lines of the skeleton image are coarse coded:

Working from left to right in the thinned image, each stroke (a one-pixel wide line in the skeleton between junctions or end points) is divided into equal length segments (the length being determined by the character size) for which the centroid position and angle are calculated. The box associated with this segment's (x, y, θ) values is now 'filled'. Segments which are not perfectly aligned with the angles of the bins are coarse coded — that is they contribute to the two bins representing the closest orientations.

4 Feature identification

Given the importance of features demonstrated by studies of reading, further improvements are to be expected if this parametrisation approach is combined with that of feature spotting (Pao and Cheriet describe methods based on features in this volume). In this work, two methods have been used to determine the presence of features. The first of these is a rule-based approach which uses simple, reliable rules to spot local features. Thus, in addition to the skeleton the network is given explicit information about the presence of '*i*' dots as well as turning points, junctions and endpoints in the skeleton.

The second approach uses constrained snakes to determine the presence of larger scale features. This builds on the technique of point distribution models used by Lanitis [3] for postcode reading. Constrained snakes allow B-spline models to be trained to capture the shape and variability of features (such as the strokes '*n*','*u*','*i*','*o*') of be measured, and then permits these models to be matched against a character image. A match metric is used and good matches are found where the feature is present in the word image. In this case, the B-splines are moved to energy minima on the distance transform of the snake. The distance transform of a pixel in a binary image is the shortest distance to the nearest edge, and can be found by a simple two-pass algorithm. More details of this feature identification technique are given in [5]. Figure 3 shows some of the features found in a set of word images.

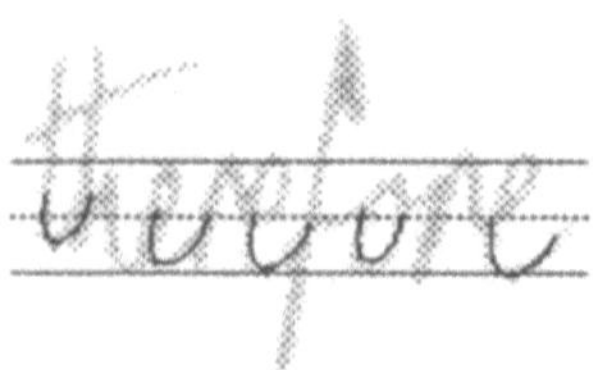

(a) *u* feature

(b) *o* feature

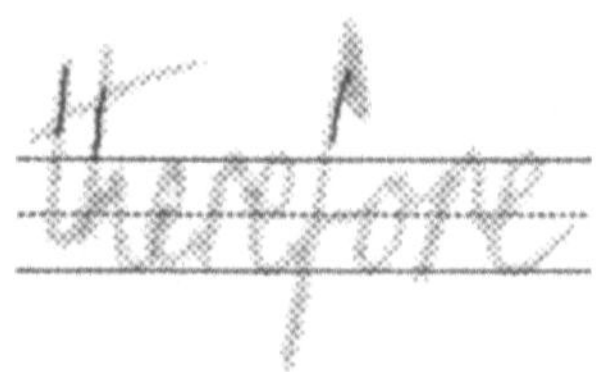

(c) ascender

Figure 3: Different features found automatically in several words.

5 Conclusions

The above techniques have been used in a complete system which uses real handwritten documents, achieving 78.7% accuracy on a single-author database with an 825 word vocabulary. New methods have been used to correctly determine the word baselines and the Božinović and Srihari method for slant correction has been stabilised. Both the feature identification methods have been shown to improve the recognition performance. Development of the feature-spotting methods is expected to result in greater writer independence by abstraction away from the low-level and more variable skeleton level, to a representation of the features which are more common between different styles of handwriting.

Acknowledgements

The author would like to acknowledge the assistance of Tony Robinson and Professor Frank Fallside in the work described here.

References

[1] R.M. Božinović and S.N. Srihari. Off-line cursive word recognition. *IEEE PAMI*, 11(1):68–83, January 1989.

[2] E.R. Davies. *Machine Vision: Theory, algorithms, practicalities*. Microelectrics and signal processing Number 9. London Academic, 1990.

[3] Andreas Lanitis. Applications of point distribution models in handwritten optical character recognition and face recognition. Transfer report, Dept. of Medical Biophysics, University of Manchester, 1992.

[4] Tony Robinson and Frank Fallside. A recurrent error propagation network speech recognition system. *Computer Speech and Language*, 5:259–274, 1991.

[5] A.W. Senior and F. Fallside. Using constrained snakes for feature spotting in off-line cursive script. In *International Conference on Document Analysis and Recognition 93*, 1993.

Part 6

Architectures for handwriting

Architectures for Handwriting Recognition

A. C. Downton

Department of Electronic Systems Engineering, University of Essex,
Wivenhoe Park, Colchester, Essex CO4 3SQ, UK.
Email: acd@essex.ac.uk

Abstract. This paper presents a review of computer architectures for image analysis, pattern recognition, and in particular, handwriting recognition. Emphasis is placed upon parallel architectures used in the development system environment and in embedded systems. A design philosophy and generalised parallel applications architecture for handwriting recognition are presented, based upon the characteristics of embedded real-time systems. The architecture is based upon a pipeline of tree processor farms of MIMD distributed memory processors and is fully scalable to meet throughput and latency requirements.

Keywords. Image analysis, pattern recognition, parallel processing, embedded systems, real-time systems, processor farm, distributed memory multiprocessors, tree topologies, pipeline topology, transputers.

1 Introduction

This paper is concerned with hardware architectures for image processing, image analysis and pattern recognition. Computer programs written to implement algorithms within these fields are computationally intensive; real applications have to meet demanding real-time performance constraints; and so it is natural that research and development effort is applied not just to algorithms, but also to the design of supporting hardware architectures.

In particular, our interest is in architectures which support algorithm and application development within the field of computer recognition of handwriting. In practice, however, this application area has much in common with the broader fields identified above, and therefore the material within this paper is also generally applicable to this broader field.

Although it does not make sense to differentiate handwriting recognition architectures from architectures for other applications in image processing and pattern recognition, some other characteristics provide a better taxonomy of the subject. In this paper the following criteria are used to subdivide the review presented:

- Type of processing - low, intermediate or high-level
- Existing classification schemes for parallelism
- Parallel processing elements
- Architectures for the development system environment
- Architectures for the target system environment

Parallel processing, which provides the most obvious way to increase execution speed, naturally forms the major theme of the paper, but this is not a general purpose review of parallel architectures. Instead, the characteristics of image analysis and pattern recognition applications are analysed; these characteristics are then used to identify a subset of parallel processing techniques which are useful both in the engineer's development environment and in target embedded system applications.

1.1 Requirements

Image analysis and pattern recognition attempt to parallel the processes of human vision and human visual interpretation. Computer vision can be viewed as a bottom-up hierarchy of operations which attempt to extract features and interpret objects from the initial physical (pixel-based) image. In addition, in human visual interpretation, this process is assisted by top-down domain knowledge which is applied subconsciously to restrict the possible interpretations of the image. Figure 1 illustrates this process and identifies some of the typical image analysis operations which are performed at different levels in the hierarchy. A classical example of this approach can be found in the Acronym vision system developed by Brooks [1].

Within the field of document analysis, the objective of computer vision is to convert an initial pixel image of a document (equivalent to the bit image manipulated by typical PC Paint software) into a structured symbolic document representation containing lines, characters, arcs, and their relationships (as for example found in PC Drawing software). Handwriting recognition is a special case of document analysis, in which the hierarchy of image analysis processes uses features, objects and domain knowledge related to characters, words, and handwriting.

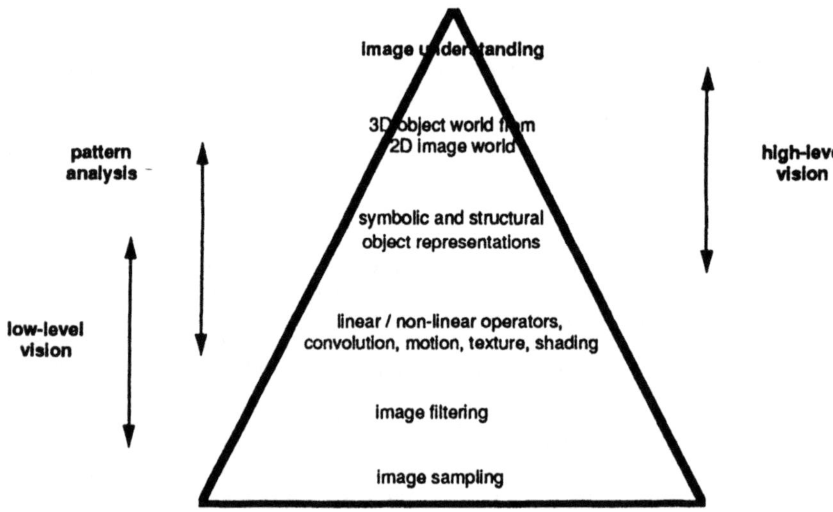

Figure 1. Hierarchy of image analysis and pattern recognition operations

1.1.1 Low-level image processing

Low-level image processing is concerned with sampling, filtering, convolution and other pixel-level operations on the image. In handwriting recognition, low-level processing may also include character thinning, segmentation and normalisation. The operations required are typically quite straightforward, but the sheer volume of data to be processed generates a requirement for enormous processing power. For example, a real-time image coding system which works with common intermediate format (CIF) images must process a frame of data of 352 x 288 pixels x 24 bits/pixel (total 304 kbytes) every 1/25th or 1/30th of a second - a total data transfer rate of about 8

Mbytes/s. This requires not only substantial parallel processing to meet computational needs, but also enormous data input/output bandwidth to shift the images between source and display at the requisite rate. The terms *geometric parallelism* and *data parallelism* are often used interchangably to indicate this type of situation; a simple approach to scaling performance is to subdivide the data set onto an array of processors (see Section 3).

1.1.2 Intermediate level image analysis

Here, the low-level pixel image is analysed to extract intermediate level features such as edges, lines, and corners. In document analysis, specific features which reflect the structural properties of handwriting may be extracted, for example hooks, loops, cusps, etc.

The algorithms applied for intermediate level processing are more complex than those used at low-level, but the amount of data processed is typically reduced by at least an order of magnitude, for two reasons. First, the input data typically represents a subset of the total image, for example normalised arrays representing a set of character images, rather than the (much larger) array representing the complete document page. Second, the process of feature extraction results in a further reduction of data, since its output is typically a set of symbolic parameters defining the features identified and their positions with respect to each other.

The introduction of more complex algorithms at this level also has another implication: algorithm execution time often becomes context dependent, whereas in low-level processing it is typically context independent. Thus, while it is possible to implement low-level algorithms using synchronised arrays of processors, this is not normally feasible with intermediate (and high) level processing.

1.1.3 High-level image analysis and pattern recognition

High-level image analysis and pattern recognition are exclusively concerned with operations on symbolic data objects. For example, in character recognition it would represent the classification process which determines the appropriate class for a character to be assigned to, based upon the features extracted from the character by the intermediate level analysis. High level algorithms are typically quite computationally complex, with data parallelism at the level of symbolic data structures rather than pixel data, and some potential also for *algorithmic parallelism* (in which different parts of the algorithm are partitioned onto separate processors).

High-level processing also covers processing beyond the level of character recognition, for example contextual processing at the level of complete words, using dictionaries or Markov models.

1.2 Classification schemes

Several alternative classification schemes for parallelism can be defined according to whether the point of view chosen is processor-centred, production-line (embedded system) centred, or development system centred. These are discussed individually below.

1.2.1 Processor-centred classification

Flynn's 1972 [2] taxonomy of computer architectures is still the most generally used method of classifying parallelism. Flynn divided computers according to whether they used single or multiple streams of data, and single or multiple streams of instructions, as shown in Table 1.

	Single Instruction	Multiple Instruction
Single Data	SISD	MISD
Multiple Data	SIMD	MIMD

Table 1. Flynn's taxonomy of computers

An SISD computer carries out one instruction on one datum at a time. This is the conventional 'von Neumann' sequential architecture as used in almost all current commercial computers[1].

There is some debate as to whether MISD (multiple instruction, single data) computers exist. One interpretation is to classify pipelining as a form of MISD, and this is the approach used here. As will be shown, pipelining has an important role to play in performance scaling for embedded applications.

In an SIMD computer, many processors simultaneously execute the same instruction, but on different data. This was the first form of parallelism to be commercially exploited, and remains an important approach towards achieving parallelism for applications with massive data sets. Many scientific and engineering problems (for example fluid dynamics, quantum chromodynamics, finite element analysis, etc.) conform to this model.

MIMD computers contain a number of independent processors, each of which is capable of executing its own program on its own independent data set. Within the MIMD designation there are many subsidiary degrees of freedom, such as the method of processor interconnection, the processor topology and the number of processors. This has tended to lead to an 'anarchist philosophy' of system design (see section 6.1) in which different designs are proposed for almost every different problem. In the long term, the anarchist approach is unlikely to bring the economies of scale needed for MIMD machines to move into the mainstream of computing, and so in this paper, an alternative generalist approach for embedded systems design developed in the author's own research group is presented for comparison.

1.2.2 Production line-centred classification

The production line-centred taxonomy of parallelism is due to Waltz [3], and classifies parallelism according to how multiple processors process a continuous stream of input data, such as might come from a camera observing a production line as part of an industrial vision system, or in the context of handwriting recognition, a continuous stream of characters or document images. Such scenarios are typical of real-time embedded systems. Four possible ways of parallelising a continuous stream of data can be identified; these are discussed below and illustrated in Figure 2.

Spatial multiplexing is the equivalent of data parallelism as identified earlier. Each full image is broken down into a number of subcomponents, with each subcomponent being processed simultaneously by a separate processor.

Temporal multiplexing exploits the continuous stream of images by assigning each image to a separate processor. This has the effect of scaling up the throughput of the system *pro rata* to the number of processors, but does not reduce the processing time for each individual image.

Spatial/Temporal multiplexing combines the two methods outlined above; some data parallelism in the image is exploited, and this is augmented by temporal multiplexing.

---

[1] In fact, most current conventional computers employ some pipelining to increase performance and so could be classified as MISD machines; however this is hidden from the user.

Pipelining involves breaking the sequential application algorithm down into components and assigning each component to a processor or set of processors. Pipelining is effectively a form of algorithmic parallelism.

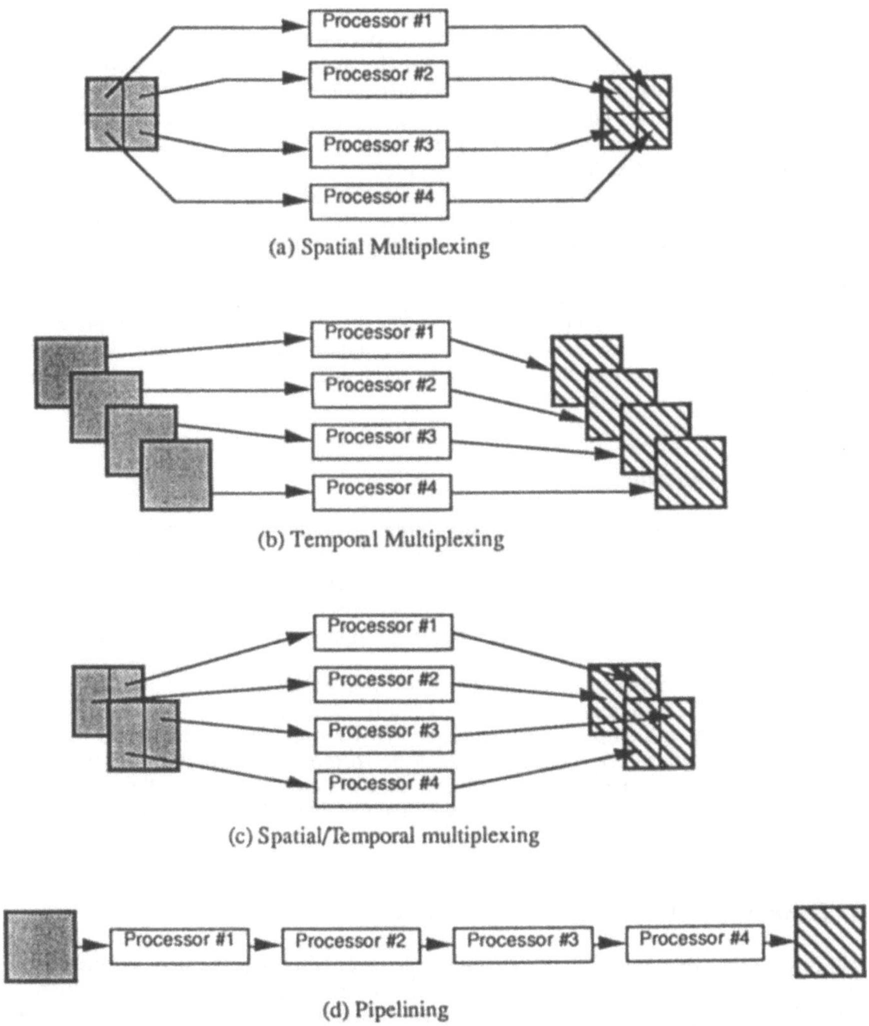

Figure 2. Symbolic representation of Waltz's production line-centred taxonomy of parallelism

1.2.3 Development vs. target system classification

The development vs. target system classification is based upon the premise that the typical engineering research and development life-cycle involves initial algorithm research undertaken on a workstation, usually leading to a non-real-time implementation. Subsequent development then refines the initial implementation to improve performance and increase execution speed until the required target system specification is met. This process is expedited if there is a simple mapping from the development environment to the target system environment.

In the development system, an interactive, interpretive development facility is required, which will efficiently support experimentation and optimisation of algorithms for the target system. Enough performance is required that experimental algorithms can be executed in a few seconds, otherwise the design environment ceases to be interactive; strict real-time operation is not normally required however. Experiments will normally be carried out with off-line data, so substantial test database storage facilities (disks) will be required.

Ideally, the target system should be realisable as a direct mapping from the development system. In this environment however, real-time operation is required, leading to a direct specification for throughput scaling from the development environment. The target system does not support development interactions, but must be capable of handling real-time input and output devices. It will be based upon compiled rather than interpreted software and/or dedicated hardware. Nevertheless to maximise generality, it is desirable to have a standard scalable system level design model, since bespoke architectures are only justified in very high volume applications.

1.3 Other architectures

The discussion above has only considered 'conventional' parallel computer architectures. The reason for this is that only these architectures support a straightforward mapping from a typical procedural language such as C or Fortran to a parallel implementation. In practice, most researchers in handwriting recognition tend to use such languages, either from the start, or as soon as implementation issues begin to be addressed.

In contrast, a number of other more radical approaches to parallelism exist which are not considered in this paper, for example Dataflow machines and Neural Networks. While both these approaches have many attractions, each requires that the image analysis/pattern recognition problem be formulated from the start with the relevant implementation model in mind. It is thus not easy to separate the process of researching a problem solution from the architecture that solution requires.

2 Development System Architectures

Although there are many special purpose image processing development systems now available linked to conventional Unix workstations and PCs, the use of highly specialised hardware to accelerate image processing performance forces the researcher to program to fit the hardware model, and presents problems in porting software to any other system. Such systems are also often quite expensive and only support low-level image processing operations, and are thus of limited value for research.

Most researchers have therefore found that more conventional workstations and PCs provide a cheaper and more flexible development environment. Amongst such products, the main issue of concern (apart from basic processor performance) is the performance of the imaging system, and the support it provides for typical display operations required in interactive image analysis and pattern recognition research. Imaging systems are therefore briefly reviewed below.

2.1 Raster-scan frame buffer architecture

Figure 3 shows a general architecture of a frame buffer display system. The video display generator reads data from the frame-buffer memory according to the raster scan format. In the simplest case, a monochrome single bit per pixel display, words within the frame buffer generally represent consecutively displayed pixels and so are serialised and then converted directly into an analogue signal which switches on or off the scanning electron beam. In the more general case, where the display provides grey-scale or colour capabilities, p bits are used to specify the grey-scale or colour value of the pixel within the frame buffer. Each pixel value fetched is then used to index a video lookup table (VLT) which typically maps the 2^p possible grey or colour values specified in the frame buffer into a larger set of 2^d possible grey or colour display values. For example, if p=8 and d=15 (5 bits for each primary colour), a set of 256 displayable colours can be selected out of a colour palette of 32,768 possible colours. The VLT is itself normally connected to the processor address and data busses so that colour palette selection can be accomplished under software control (for clarity, this connection is omitted in Figure 3). In the case of grey-scale or colour displays, Digital to Analogue converter(s) are also required to convert the d bits of the specified grey level or colour into the corresponding analogue signals which control the intensity of the electron beam(s).

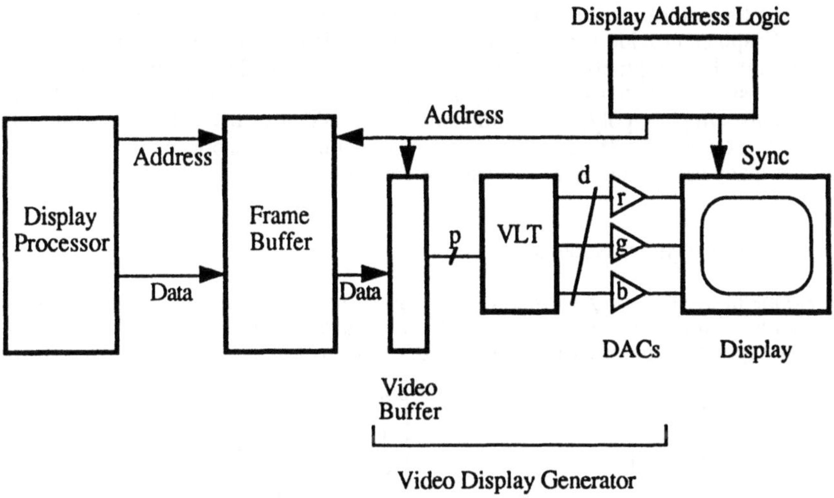

Figure 3. Raster-scan frame buffer architecture

2.2 Display processor architecture

Figure 4 shows a number of possible display processor architectures. The simplest option (Figure 4(a)), often used in PCs, is for the system's general-purpose processor to access the frame buffer directly. A common alternative in workstations and personal computers is for the general-purpose processor to be augmented by a graphics co-processor or RasterOp processor (Figure 4(b)). This device typically provides support for rapid execution of simple Boolean operations between specified source and destination pixel regions, allowing independent components of the display to be rapidly and flexibly combined, moved, cleared or overlaid [4]. At the same time, the general-purpose processor retains full access to the frame buffer so that functions not supported on the co-processor can be implemented directly.

If a full range of display processing capabilities can be provided independently of the general purpose processor, the architecture of Figure 4(c) may be used, where the host processor communicates exclusively with the display processor, which in turn has exclusive access to the frame buffer. This architecture is commonly used in network-based windowing systems such as X, where network communication overheads preclude the repeated transmission of low-level graphics primitives. A more complete review of raster scan image display architectures can be found in [5].

2.3 Attached image processors

Most current workstations include (at least as an option) an attached image display processor, which extends the basic framestore architecture by providing specialised high performance image display support for the host processor (or client in an X terminal). Although the coprocessor may logically be viewed as a single processor system, in practice it is commonly implemented using several special purpose processing modules with the general architecture of Figure 5. Each processor provides dedicated high speed performance for a few limited image display functions, for example integer arithmetic, floating point arithmetic, barrel shifter, and look-up tables. The image bus is actually a group of busses allowing several of these primitive operations to be performed simultaneously - a form of MISD parallelism.

At the top end of the workstation range, workstations such as those provided by Silicon Graphics provide far more complex image display processor systems, which are structured as a pipeline of SIMD processor arrays. These systems provide hardware support for texture mapping, 2D and 3D transformations, lighting calculations, clipping, polygon decomposition and hidden surface removal. Although originally intended for 3D graphics and CAD applications, these facilities are also useful in many aspects of image analysis for computer vision.

2.4 Software support systems

Development system software support for handwriting recognition applications can be subdivided into two aspects: support for the basic algorithm design process, and software support for parallelism. These are discussed below.

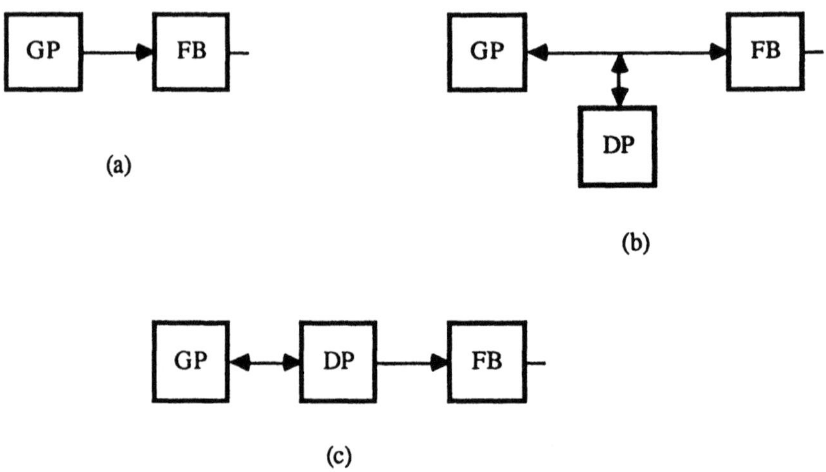

Figure 4. Alternative display processor architectures

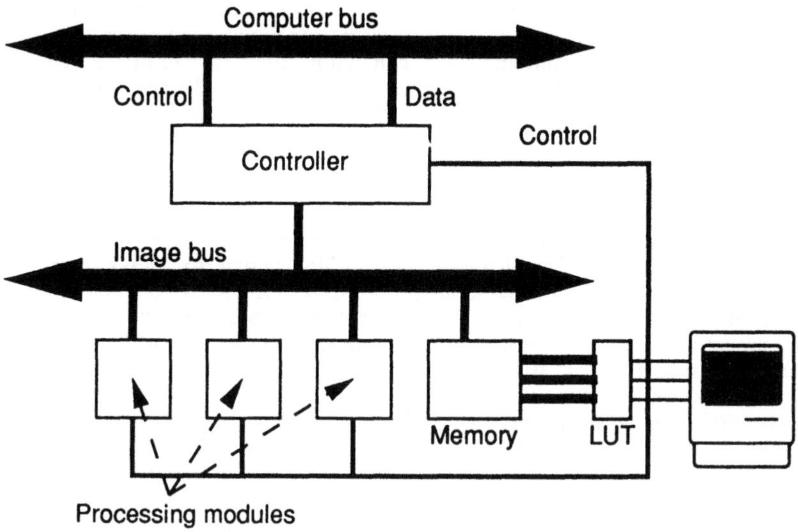

Figure 5. Typical attached image display processor architecture

2.4.1 Software system design support

Many of the software tools required to support research into handwriting recognition are the standard tools provided in the Unix environment: compilers, program maintenance tools (make, SCCS, etc.), data analysis and report generation tools such as awk, and commercial CASE tools. It is notable however, that although graphically oriented CAD tools have been available for nearly a decade, graphical environments for signal processing applications are only now beginning to become widespread, and still do not provide proper support for 2D signals. The SPW DSP Framework[2] provides an example of a possible graphical paradigm for image analysis which may become established in the future, as workstation performance and display capabilities increase to permit reasonable interaction.

SPW is a graphically-oriented development environment developed for DSP applications and implemented using the Motif X-windows interface. It provides the following key features:

- *Block diagram description of the system.*
  The complete DSP system is implemented as a hierarchy of block diagrams. Each block within a block diagram is either a library block (supplied with the system) or a custom-coded block (defined by the user).
- *Signal generation and manipulation facilities through a graphical signal calculator.*
  The signal calculator allows many standard signals (sine, square, triangular and ramp waveforms, phasors, noise, etc.) to be generated with user-defined parameters, and then combined together in various ways (mathematical functions, filters, sampling etc.). User defined signals (such as speech segments) can be manipulated as well as synthetic signals.
- *Simulation and code generation.*
  SPW provides the capability rapidly to simulate the performance of systems defined as block diagrams and also to generate code (in C) which can be directly executed on the host processor.

---

[2]'SPW' and 'DSP Framework' are trademarks of Comdisco Systems , Inc.

Although the system is easy to use it does not yet provide the tools required for image and pattern analysis: a library of image processing functions, support for 2D signal manipulation and display within the signal calculator, filters to read image files in a variety of standard formats, etc. Such facilities are reportedly under development, but will need to be integrated with accelerated graphics display hardware of the type described above if reasonable interactive performance is to be achieved.

2.4.2 Parallel processing support

Parallel processing software tools have the more restricted objective of providing support for parallelisation of application codes. In SIMD processor arrays and vector processors, extensions are provided to a standard C or FORTRAN compiler to allow loops and arrays to be parallelised over the available hardware. In distributed memory MIMD processors (for example transputer-based systems) a much wider variety of programming models are available, reflecting the wider range of ways in which parallelism can be exploited in such machines.

In general, the most successful approach has been to augment the normal programming language (such as C) or operating system (Unix) with a higher level component description language which provides the specification for the topology and interconnection of the parallel network of processors, and the mapping of code to each processor. The component description language may be provided as an extension to a standard compiler (e.g. 3L Parallel C) or a special purpose parallel processing language (e.g. Occam, Strand88), as part of a parallel operating system (e.g. Helios), or as a set of additional software tools integrated with an existing operating system such as Unix (e.g. Tiny, Express, Meiko CSTools).

A key requirement of any parallel processing tool is software support for *virtual channels*, preferably linked to an ability to reconfigure the network of processors under software control (see Section 4.2.1). Virtual channel routing provides support for communication between arbitrary processors, whether or not they are directly connected, by means of packet network techniques. Without this capability, significant programming effort will be expended on re-inventing through-routing communications software, once the network of processors expands beyond the point where each processor can be fully connected to every other.

It should be emphasised that the provision of virtual channels does not in any way solve the problem of partitioning an algorithm onto multiple processors: it simply ensures that whatever partitioning is chosen, the overhead of programming inter-processor communications is minimised. The choice of topologies and methods of partitioning algorithms for handwriting recognition are discussed in detail in Section 6.

3 Low-Level Image Processing - SIMD Processor Arrays

SIMD processor arrays were originally developed in the 1970s, with the objective of addressing 'massive data set' scientific and engineering problems at low cost using the fairly limited VLSI technologies available at that time. It was recognised at an early stage that their potential for parallelising low-level image processing operations was excellent, and this lead to the development of architectures and devices specifically targeted towards image processing.

The key characteristic of SIMD arrays is their use of 2D arrays of simple processing elements (originally 1-bit processors) with very limited memory, which are mapped directly onto the data elements of the problem. Processors are normally connected to some or all of their 8 nearest neighbours, but all processors operate in synchrony from the same instruction stream, so there are no problems of bus contention or memory access to resolve. If sufficient processors are available, a complete image can be processed in parallel, leading to very fast pixel-level operations. The architecture is well-suited to low-level image processing, where communications are normally only required with neighbouring processors, and all pixels have the same operations performed on them.

SIMD arrays have some very obvious disadvantages however. First, the limited processing power of individual processing elements means that they are poorly suited to intermediate or high-level image analysis. Second, mapping from the image to the processor array can be a problem if there is not one processing element per pixel. Finally, input/output direct to each pixel is prohibitive, so it is usually provided to each row, with data being serially shifted to each bit; this incurs a significant processing time overhead.

3.1 Example 1 - Cellular Logic Image Processor (CLIP)

The CLIP series of image processing chips was developed at University College London [6,7] in the 1970s and 1980s. Figure 6 shows the architecture of a CLIP4 system and individual CLIP processor. The CLIP4 system contains an array of up to 128 x 128 1 bit processors, each of which has 32 bits of memory and is connected to its 8 nearest neighbours. Each processor element has a control bus connection to the host processor (a Sun workstation), and two arithmetic and logic units (ALUs), one of which operates on the local RAM, while the other propagates data to the neighbouring processors.

Other CLIP architectures have included the CLIP4S, a 512 x 1 array in which large images are processed a row at a time, and the CLIP7, a 256 x 1 array with a larger 16 bit processing element, 64 kbytes storage and 8 bit external datapaths.

To support the hardware, an augmented version of C was produced (image processing C - IPC), which allowed the CLIP7 to be programmed as if it were a square array.

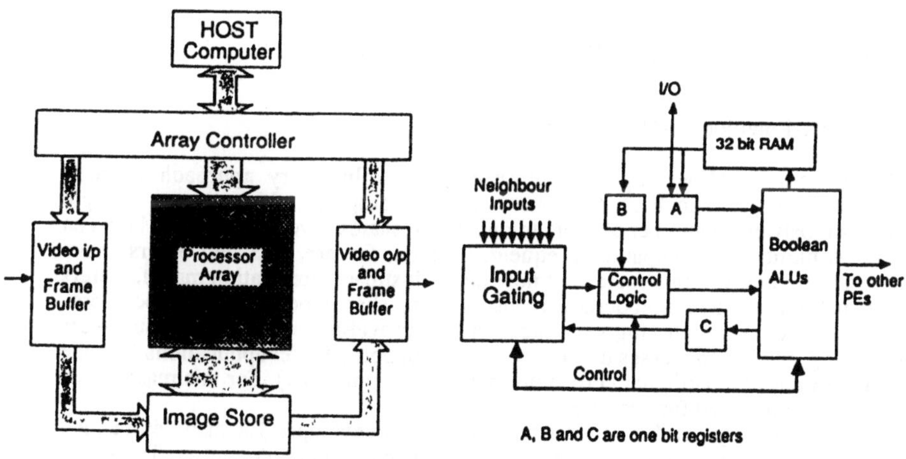

Figure 6. A CLIP4 system and individual processing element

3.2 Example 2 - AMT Distributed Array Processor (DAP)

The DAP was originally developed by ICL as an attached mainframe processor. In the mid-1980s, the development was spun off as a separate company, Active Memory Technology (AMT) [8,9]. The DAP was targeted at more numerically intensive applications than CLIP, for example FFTs and Karhunen-Loeve transforms. A DAP consists of a 2D array of 1024-4096 1-bit processing elements, each with up to 1 Mbit of memory, running on a 10 MHz clock, and hosted by a Sun workstation or Vax minicomputer. It is programmed using DAP-Fortran, a parallel extension of Fortran.

3.3 Example 3 - TMC Connection Machine

The Connection Machine was developed by Thinking Machines Corporation (TMC), based originally on Danny Hillis's seminal PhD work at MIT [10]. It is a more ambitious machine than AMT's, and is aimed squarely at supercomputer markets. Although the original machines (CM1 and CM2) are similar to the DAP in using 1 bit processing elements, the communications structure is more sophisticated (a hypercube of order up to 16 with routing chips allowing software control of the topology), the system can be augmented with floating point processors (one per 32 processing elements), and high performance disk farms can be configured into the system. It does not directly compete with the AMT machine, since processor configurations supported range from a minimum of 4096 processors to a maximum of 65536. Even though the machine is much larger than a DAP however, it is still hosted by a workstation.

Most recently TMC have announced that the next generation of Connection machines will use a proprietary microprocessor (Sparc) as the processing element. This will obviously increase the versatility of the machine, but indicates an intention to continue to address the supercomputer market.

4 Multi-Instruction Multi-Data (MIMD) systems

4.1 Shared memory MIMD systems

Shared memory MIMD systems represent an evolutionary approach towards parallelism: it is a small step to move from a computer which shares a single processor between a number of users to one which shares several processors between users. A number of companies (Sequent, Convex, Encore, FPS and others) have successfully followed this route, and now the mainstream workstation manufacturers (HP/Apollo, DEC, Sun, Solbourne) are also offering shared memory multiprocessors.

Such systems are proving very successful in providing cost-effective multi-user computing, but in most cases do not attempt to support parallel applications (i.e. the parallelisation of a particular code onto more than 1 processor). For this reason they will not be considered further here.

Shared memory MIMD systems have also been developed for many embedded applications, including some within the field of handwriting recognition. Typically, such systems have utilised a limited number of processors interconnected via standard bus systems such as VMEbus. The main advantage such systems have over distributed memory MIMD systems is the availability of shared memory for common data areas. Bus-based shared memory systems have however proved to be significantly more complex and expensive to build than distributed memory systems based around transputers, which include most of the communication components on the processor chip. Furthermore, bus-based systems have an inherent von Neumann bottleneck in the available bandwidth to the shared memory, which restricts the degree of parallelism which can be achieved with this topology. As a result, there is now a strong trend towards distributed memory embedded systems, based upon processing elements with inbuilt communications, such as transputers (T800 and T9000) and the Texas Instruments TMS 320C40 DSP chip.

4.2 Distributed memory MIMD systems

4.2.1 Transputers - T800 and T9000

The transputer has been both an innovatory and a successful product, achieving a large market share through its use in many embedded applications, as well as in a variety of commercial parallel computers. It is a 32 bit microprocessor which has been specifically designed for use in concurrent message-passing systems, through the inclusion of 4 point-to-point serial communication links on the CPU chip (Figure 7). A key feature is that the links and the processor all operate concurrently, allowing processing to continue while data are being transferred. In addition, the T800 includes a 64 bit floating point unit and 4 kbytes of static RAM on chip (the T400 family of integer transputers omits this floating point unit).

The transputer was originally launched complete with its own parallel programming language, Occam, based on Hoare's Communicating Sequential Process (CSP) model [12]. In spite of its theoretical advantages, Occam proved unattractive to users with large investments in existing programming languages, and this restricted the commercial success of the transputer initially. Although Inmos continue to extol the virtues of Occam, they now also provide full support for other languages such as C and Fortran.

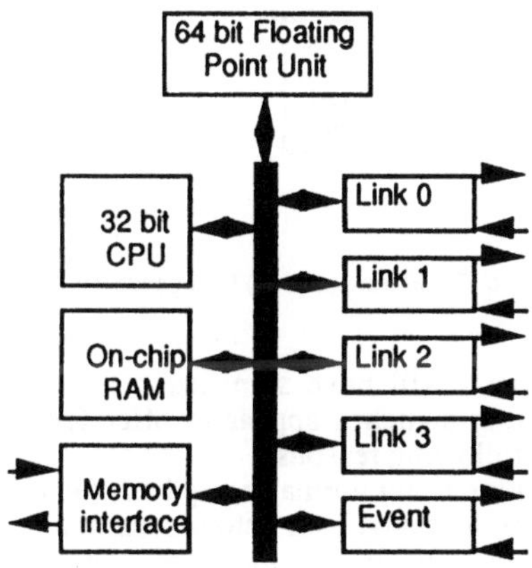

Figure 7. Architecture of the T800 transputer.

The basic architecture of the next generation transputer, the T9000 (Figure 8a) is very similar to that of the T800, and includes an on-chip floating point unit, four communication links and a memory cache. As might be expected, both processor and communication link performance are substantially increased to 20 MFLOPS and 80 Mbytes/s total respectively. The major innovation in the T9000 architecture however is the inclusion on-chip of hardware support for virtual channel routing through packetised communication, as described in Section 2.5.2. Although T9000s can be configured as point-to-point processor networks like the T800, the intention is that systems will often be built using a composite node comprising a T9000 processor and a crossbar message routing chip (the C104) as shown in Figure 8b. This will effectively allow all processors to be directly connected to each other (though not necessarily simultaneously), thus reducing the parallel design procedure to one of deciding which processes and data are local to each processor and which are global (on another processor). The communication bandwidth limitation between processors will however still remain, and thus there will continue to be a need for formalised parallel design procedures which minimise communication requirements between processors.

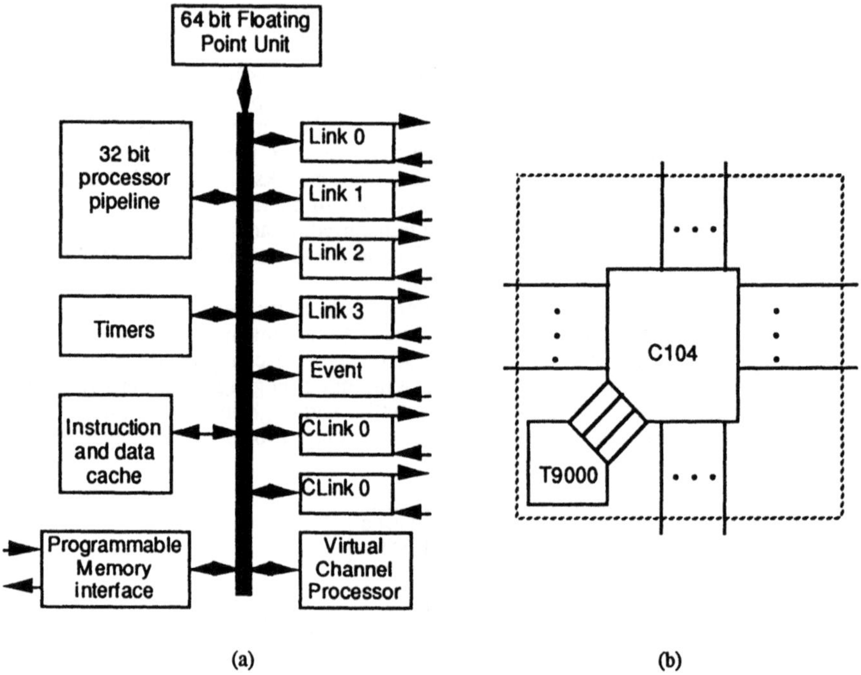

Figure 8. (a) Architecture of the T9000 tranputer (b) Composite T9000/C104 node.

Although this approach will have significant advantages in general purpose parallel computers, routing switches appear to offer fewer benefits for embedded parallel systems, for the following reasons:

- Dynamic reconfiguration is not normally required, since the design process results in a static decomposition of processes onto processors.
- Processes are not usually independent of one another, since they form subcomponents of a complete application.
- The use of routing chips increases implementation costs in embedded applications.

4.2.2 Texas Instruments TMS 320C40

The delay in the introduction of the T9000 has opened up opportunities for other chips in the parallel processing market. Most significant among these has been Texas Instrument's introduction of the TMS 320C40, a floating point DSP device with six byte-wide concurrent communication links. TI's entry to the parallel processing market has been a bottom-up evolution, based upon the observation that many users of their earlier TMS 320C30 floating point DSP processor were already building embedded systems which used more than one device. As a result, although the C40 has state of the art processor and communication link performance, there is as yet little experience of using the device in large scale parallel applications, and no routing chips to enable software reconfigurable systems to be built.

5 Architectures for High-Level Vision

5.1 Problem characteristics

In high-level image analysis and pattern recognition, symbolic rather than geometric data structures are normally used and algorithmic as well as data parallelism needs to be exploited. Furthermore, in real-time applications, numerous data sets must be presented to the processors every second, resulting in large global input/output requirements, in addition to the predominantly neighbourhood communication inherent in most low-level image processing operations. Thus, current generalised techniques for real-time image analysis are largely confined to low-level processing. The purpose of the following sections is to show that by fixing the multi-processor topology, a generalised, scalable parallel architecture for real-time vision can be achieved, and that the performance penalties in doing this are much less than might intuitively be imagined.

5.2 Amdahl's law

An insight into the fundamental problem to be overcome in parallelising vision applications is provided by Amdahl's law [11], which states in its simplest form that the performance of a parallel algorithm is limited by the number of inherently sequential operations in that algorithm. Consider a problem where a fraction f of the work must be performed sequentially. The speed-up, S, possible from a machine with N processors is:

$$S \leq \frac{1}{f + \frac{1 - f}{N}}$$

Clearly if $f = 0.2$ (i.e 20% of the algorithm is sequential) then the maximum speedup however many processors are added is 5. It is thus clear from Amdahl's law that no matter how successful parallelisation of the low-level components of a vision system may be, unless similar speed-up can be obtained for the high-level components, the performance improvement for the system as a whole will be quite limited.

Many current systems require speed-ups of several orders of magnitude to achieve real-time performance. This implies that not only must substantial parallelism be achieved for each component of the vision hierarchy in isolation, but also that the performance of the different components must be balanced and matched together to meet the overall system real-time performance specification. These constraints can only be met by choosing a topology for which performance measures are well understood, and which is incrementally scalable.

5.3 Technology trends

It is a mistake to base the design of parallel systems around current hardware standards, since processor performance and bus standards are evolving very fast. The key to achieving generality is scalability: if the abstract design model can be rescaled to cater for changes in processor and communication link performance, the existing application can be readily ported to the next generation environment.

We must nevertheless impose some fundamental constraints. First, we constrain ourselves to work with MIMD processors, because of their capability of being applied to both high and low-level aspects of image analysis. SIMD architectures such as the DAP and CLIP described earlier have achieved success in low-level image processing operations, but are too inflexible for high-level vision where significant processing power is required within each element. Second, we assume a distributed CSP processing model with point-to-point communication [12], rather than a bus or other more restrictive communication model.

With these constraints, performance analysis to define upper bound solutions to maximum performance and critical processor numbers becomes practicable for a variety of possible topologies [13]. Although the analysis does not solve the very practical problems of mapping algorithms onto a multi-processor network, it shows the feasibility (or not) of doing so. If the design is feasible with current technology, it will invariably become progressively easier to rescale it as future processor and communication link performance improves.

5.4 Performance criteria

There are two major classes of parallel performance index. The first class indicates how successfully a problem has been parallelised over N processors. The second class is used to decide whether the system has the processing power to satisfy certain specified time constraints (irrespective of how effectively the processors are being utilised). Possibly the most popular index in the first class is Efficiency, which can be defined as:

$$\eta = \frac{T_1}{NT_N}$$

where T_1 and T_N are the times taken for one processor and N processors to perform the same task, respectively. From this another index, Speedup, can be defined as:

$$S = N\eta$$

There are also other indices in the first class that have been suggested as conveying useful information, such as Effective Processing Power [14], and Serial Fraction [15].

In engineering problems the point of parallelism is usually to decrease the processing time (typically to enable some task to be performed in real time). If speed-up or efficiency are plotted against N and the grain size decreases as N increases (which would for example be the case if successively larger grids of processors were applied to a video image) then the scaling is not linear, but flattens out as communication overheads begin to dominate. This means that Efficiency and Speedup are not particularly good measures of system performance for embedded real-time applications.

In the second class, the *rate* that results are produced by the system is the most commonly used performance index. For embedded system designs, the rate of results required is usually explicitly defined in the system specification. Rate is therefore the performance index used in this paper. Another useful index in this class is *responsiveness* or *response time* [16,17] of the parallel system, which can be equated to *latency* in a real-time system.

5.5 Paradigms for parallelism

There are three basic and well understood methods or paradigms [18] for the parallelisation of problems:

- *Geometric (or Data) Parallelism* - in this paradigm the topology of the processors reflects the physical structure of the data. For example the pixels that make up a video image, or the elements in a matrix can easily be decomposed onto a mesh of processors [19,20].
- *Algorithmic Parallelism* - here the topology of the processors reflects the structure of the algorithm to be parallelised. For example the butterfly topology reflects the algorithmic structure of some sorting algorithms and FFT's [21].
- *The Processor Farm Paradigm* - in this case the topology does not necessarily reflect that of either the data or the algorithm. However, the programmer has observed that the algorithm and data can be split into a number of independent parts with no need for communication between them. The 'master' processor distributes data packets to 'worker' processors, and the fact that there is no synchronisation between these 'worker' processors allows automatic load balancing [22,23].

5.6 Generality of parallel systems

Generality in the context of parallel processing can be defined as applicability to a large class of problems. The idea of a parallel embedded system exhibiting generality may appear to be contradictory since most embedded systems are designed to solve one particular problem. However, the general purpose embedded system is one which exhibits a design and design methodology that reflect the broad similarities between many applications, rather than application specific customisation. The same hardware structure should be reusable in many applications, and the system performance should be incrementally scalable to meet the desired system specification, as defined by the Rate performance index. In addition, embedded parallel systems should support modification or expansion (as is often required) with the performance changing in a predictable manner.

Currently embedded parallel systems are notable for their lack of any systematic general purpose design methodology. The reasons for this are discussed in section 6.1.

6 Embedded System Architectures

6.1 The anarchist philosophy

Much of the success of the modern day sequential microprocessor can be attributed to its generality. This allows different problems to be compiled and executed in different languages on the same or different processors. Currently parallel processing does not possess the generality of sequential processing. This is because several new degrees of freedom have been introduced into the design process:

- *Programming paradigm.* When tackling a parallel processing problem, the programmer's objective is to identify and exploit the form of parallelism that will maximise performance.
- *Topology.* The interconnection between processors, which can be heavily dependent on the programming paradigm.
- *Number of processors used.*
- *Reconfiguration.* In a general purpose parallel computer system one might wish to

be able rapidly to reconfigure the topology to suit a particular programming paradigm or application data structure; this is unlikely to be required in embedded applications.

Currently all these new degrees of freedom have been left to the programmer to tackle. The complex inter-relationship between them means that performance estimation is a difficult task. It appears that the potential offered by parallel processing has led to an insistence by designers on obtaining maximum performance, with a consequent loss of generality. This is not surprising, because parallel solutions are typically investigated for the very reason that conventional sequential systems do not provide sufficient performance, but it ignores the benefits of generality which are accepted in the sequential processing field.

6.2 The generalist philosophy - generality by constraint

A possible solution to this problem is to fix one or more degrees of freedom. The decision of which degree of freedom to fix cannot be made on the basis of performance alone, but must also take into account generality. The parameter or degree to fix is the Topology, since the Programming Paradigm, Number of Processors and the Reconfigurability all largely depend on the Topology.

We have proposed that tree topologies programmed using the processor farm paradigm represent a good compromise in embedded systems applications. These choices have several advantages. First, the use of tree topologies means that a single design methodology can be developed and that one basic system design can be mapped to a large variety of applications, substantially reducing prototyping costs. Equally, it has been shown [13] that a wide range of embedded applications can be effectively mapped onto tree topologies with little reduction in performance, compared with optimised topologies. Because the inter-processor communication model is simple and identical for each processor, the performance of trees is scalable according to the number of processors used: this variable can therefore be chosen exactly to meet the throughput requirements of the application.

The processor farm paradigm is more general than data parallelism, algorithmic parallelism or pipelining. This does not mean that alternative forms of parallelism are never used. In practice the approach is to use processor farming where possible to avoid explicitly rewriting sequential algorithms in parallel. However, the overall input/output latency of the application may impose limits on the degree of farming which is allowed.

A key advantage of tree processor farms (hereafter abbreviated to TPFs) is that static performance estimation models have been developed and can be applied to determine maximum performance, critical processor numbers, and safe design regions [13]. Therefore the design procedure is one in which processor and communication link performance constraints are inherently inbuilt.

It is important to realise that there will always be some problems that cannot be performed efficiently enough on a fixed topology system. This is equivalent to the case in sequential processing where a special purpose co-processor such as a DSP chip is added to the conventional processor, but with an associated loss of generality.

6.3 Applying the general philosophy

6.3.1 Alternative models for embedded parallelism

Performance scaling for embedded applications with continuous data input/output can be achieved in a number of ways:

1. Each data set can be subdivided over multiple processors (data parallelism or spatial multiplexing);

2. The algorithm can be partitioned in parallel over multiple processors (algorithmic parallelism);
3. Multiple processors can each process one complete data set in parallel (processor farming or temporal multiplexing).
4. The algorithm can be partitioned serially over multiple processors (pipelining);
5. The four basic approaches outlined above can be combined as appropriate.

We use the term *temporal multiplexing* to distinguish the pure form of task farming identified in (3) above (in which the complete application task is performed by each processor, and a number of complete data sets will be within the TPF simultaneously) from the generic form of processor farming in which other forms of parallelism are recast to fit the processor farm paradigm.

6.3.2 Farming data and algorithmic parallelism

A typical example of data parallelism is where a frame of image data is decomposed onto a grid of processors. Typical low-level image processing operations such as convolution and filtering can then be carried out independently on each sub-image requiring reference only to the four nearest neighbour processors for boundary information.

To adapt such operations to a processor farm, the required boundary information for each processor must be included in the original data packet sent to the processor. This communication overhead is however offset by the fact that the average input/output path length to the master processor is shorter for a tree than for a grid. We have shown that this performance difference between tree structures and grids can be quantified theoretically, and that the performance of trees can exceed that of grids in input/output intensive applications [13]. Sousa et al. [24] and Lotufo et al. [19] report some experiments on the performance and scalability of image processing algorithms mapped onto unbalanced farms of transputers which confirm the practical advantages of trees.

In the case of algorithmic parallelism, different parts of an algorithm which are capable of concurrent execution can be farmed to different processors, for example in the case of a Sobel edge detector, the two convolutions with horizontal and vertical masks could be executed on separate processors concurrently. The advantage of a processor farm in this context is that no explicit synchronisation of processors is required; however, the algorithm itself normally defines explicitly the possible degree of parallelism (i.e. incremental scaling is not possible).

6.3.3 Temporal multiplexing

Applying each data set to a separate processor does not speed up the time to process an individual data set, but enables the average system throughput to be scaled up in direct proportion to the number of processors used (ignoring communication overheads). This can be an effective and straightforward parallelisation technique, since the complete sequential algorithm is run on each individual processor, and no explicit parallelisation of data or algorithm is required. However, the approach is limited by the allowable latency between the input and output of the system: in a control or signal processing system, this will be defined by stability constraints; in an industrial inspection system it would be defined by the allowable delay between image sampling and the resulting action on the object.

Kalberg [25] reports an effective application of task farming for recognising Dutch postcodes on envelopes at a rate of 10 envelopes a second. A serial algorithm written in C for the complete application was developed to run on a single transputer; this took 3-4 seconds to process each envelope. A processor farm of 40 worker transputers (organised as 3 linear chains connected to the master processor) was then used to achieve the specified throughput; the processing latency of 3-4 seconds on each image was accommodated by a suitable length of mechanical pipeline.

6.3.4 Pure pipelining

Pure pipelining has the same effect as temporal multiplexing in speeding up overall application throughput without reducing the latency for any particular data set, but it is achieved by sequentially subdividing the complete application algorithm and placing each component onto a separate processor. In this basic form, the throughput increase is constrained by the maximum processing time for any one stage within the pipeline. Thus the pipeline of four processors shown in Figure 9(a) increases the task throughput from 0.09 tasks/second for a single sequential processor to 0.2 tasks/second.

Pure pipelining has no practical purpose within our design philosophy, since the same performance scaling can be achieved by temporal multiplexing with less design effort, but pipelining can be used to reduce overall application latency when combined with the other methods described earlier, as illustrated in the next section.

6.4 Integrating the different parallelisation techniques

If the allowable latency in the application is greater than the total sequential application execution time on one processor, then performance scaling by temporal multiplexing of the complete application over the required number of processors is a straightforward parallelisation technique. The static performance analysis equations derived in [13] can then be used to determine whether sufficient performance can be achieved or if a communication bottleneck will restrict the performance.

If the latency constraint on the application cannot be met purely by temporal multiplexing, latency can be reduced by combining the techniques of data/algorithmic parallelism, temporal multiplexing and pipelining discussed in sections 6.3.2, 6.3.3 and 6.3.4 above (see Figure 9(b) and 9(c)). In this case, the objective is firstly to scale the throughput of each pipeline stage to the same value, so that each processor is utilised effectively, and then to exploit data or algorithmic parallelism within each individual pipeline stage to reduce the overall latency.

This design procedure is based upon the restriction that any TPF will handle only homogeneous work packets (i.e. all processors in a TPF execute the same algorithm on data packets of the same size). There are three reasons for applying this restriction. First, the static and dynamic analysis which underpin the design methodology [13] are based upon the assumption that all work packets run on a TPF have the same mean and probability distribution of processing times. Second, although it is possible to pipeline work packets within a single TPF to reduce latency, this requires increased communication bandwidth compared with the case where the same pipeline is distributed over a TPF-pipeline. Third, if heterogeneous work packets were allowed within a TPF, the placement of processes on processors would be dynamic rather than static. This would reduce the overall system efficiency, as either process code as well as data would have to be distributed by the master processor, or additional code (and thus memory) would be needed at each node.

The approach outlined above exhibits a number of important design characteristics:

- Each stage of the pipeline is constructed from a separate TPF, leading to a generic TPF-pipeline architecture for the complete system.
- If the pipeline is to be balanced (i.e. the output rate of each stage matches the input rate of the next consecutive stage in the pipeline), incrementally scalable throughput is required at each stage. This is inherent in the TPF model.

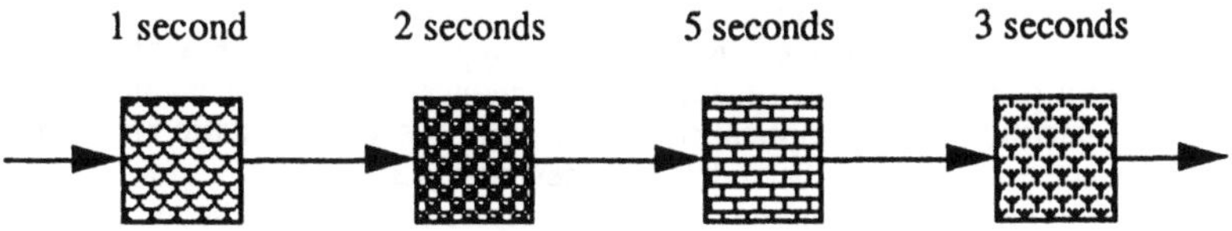

(a) Simple pipeline of processors:
Throughput = 0.2 tasks/second; Latency = 11 seconds

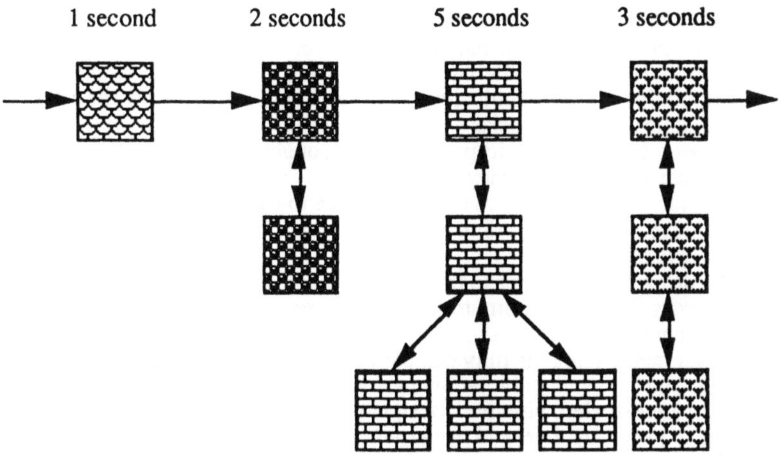

(b) TPF-pipeline with temporal multiplexing:
Throughput = 1 task/second; Latency = 11 seconds

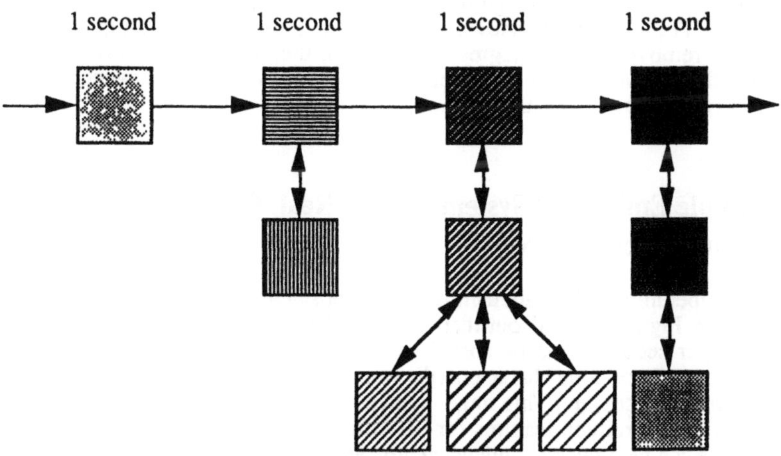

(c) TPF-pipeline with farmed data/algorithmic parallelism:
Throughput = 1 task/second; Latency = 4 seconds

Figure 9. Alternative pipeline structures

- The purpose in using a TPF-pipeline rather than a single TPF is to identify sequential subcomponents of the complete application within which data or algorithmic parallelism can be exploited to reduce application latency. Design rules for partitioning the application sequentially based upon static and dynamic performance analysis have been defined elsewhere [13].
- Different stages of the pipeline can, in principle, use heterogeneous processors optimised for different types of processing task, as long as a consistent communication model is maintained. For example in an embedded computer vision system, the initial stages might be most efficiently implemented using DSP processors to process pixel-level data, whereas later pipeline stages would utilise conventional processing elements optimised for handling symbolic data such as features and characters.
- The design philosophy is inherently conservative:
  - the granularity of parallelism is maximised, ensuring the largest possible computation to communication ratio, and thus minimising the chance of communication bottlenecks;
  - no more data/algorithmic parallelism is sought than is needed to meet the specified application latency;
  - temporal multiplexing is used in preference to data or algorithmic parallelism to achieve throughput scaling;
  - scaling is incremental.

  Thus the design process aims to produce a solution utilising the minimum number of processors with the maximum possible processor efficiency, ensured through load balancing.
- The design methodology is fully compatible with the use of sequential procedural languages and conventional top-down software engineering development.

The 'performance-scaled pipeline' design philosophy outlined above was first proposed in a paper by Lee and Aggarwal [26]. Within our design philosophy however, Lee and Aggarwal's method is extended by the introduction of temporal multiplexing (which was not considered in their paper) and because the use of a TPF allows true incremental performance scaling to balance the throughput of different components of the pipeline.

The complete iterative design procedure for embedded applications based upon the generic TPF-pipeline is shown in outline in Figure 10. Although the design philosophy removes several degrees of freedom, the design process is still under-constrained and may require significant trade-offs to be made between algorithm design and system parallelisation.

7 Example Embedded System Design: Real-Time Postcode Recognition

The basic pipelining and parallelism within the postal address recognition problem is as shown in Figure 11 and outlined below. The system specification is that 10 envelopes per second must be sorted by the machine, and it is assumed that all envelopes have 7 postcode characters (the worst case).

- *Low Level Processing*. This stage involves processing binary images of postcode characters to produce features for classification. Each of the characters in the postcode can be processed independently, and thus in parallel.
- *Classification of Postcode Characters*. In this stage the data structure has moved to the symbolic level, where a feature array is presented to classifiers and a ranked list of options is produced.

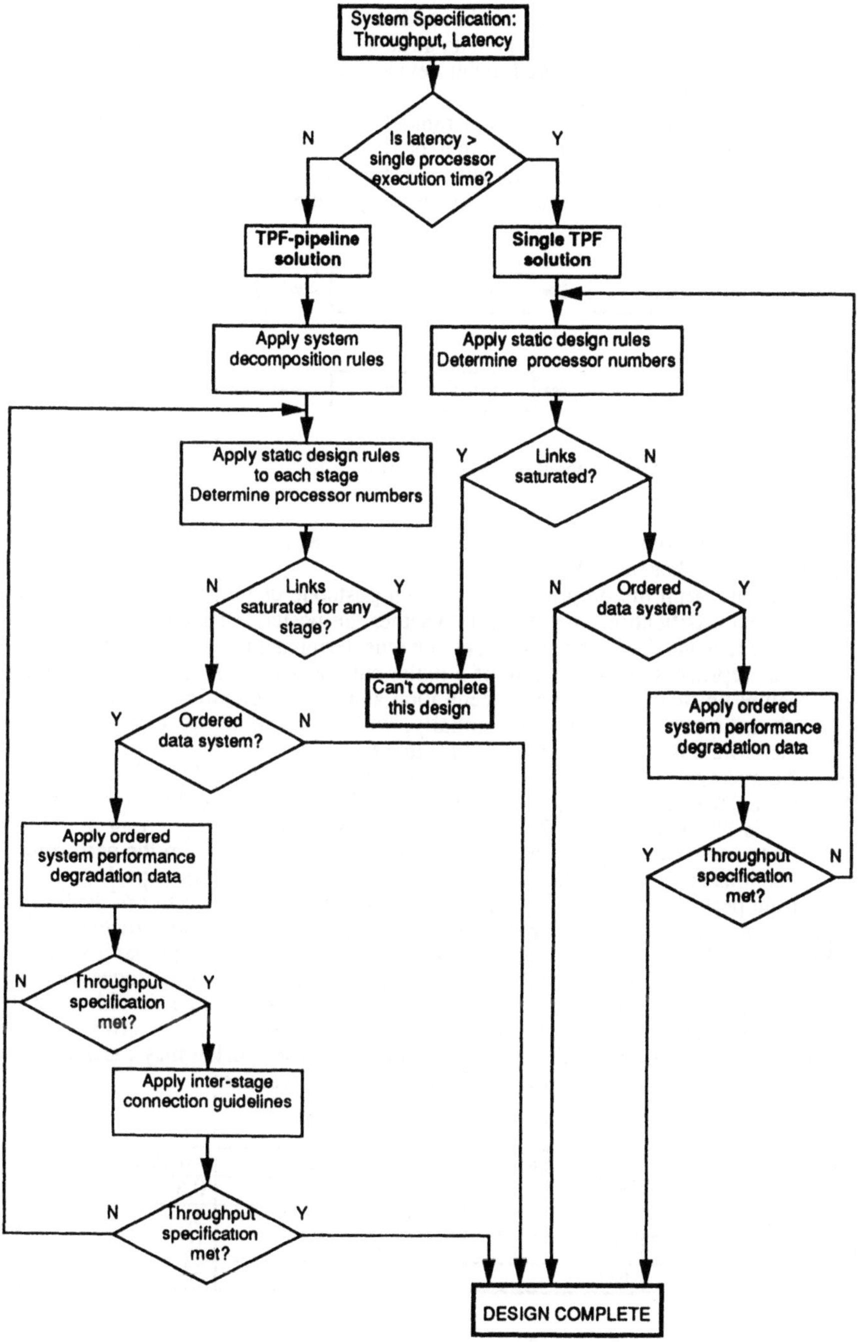

Figure 10. The complete system design procedure.

- *Verification.* This is carried out in parallel with the character preprocessing, and involves converting array-type data structures to feature vectors (Algorithms to implement this stage are still under development and so performance figures are not included in this paper).
- *Dictionary Search.* In this stage ranked postcode options are presented to a postcode dictionary until a match is found. The address produced by the dictionary is then compared with the features produced by the town name processing, to decide whether to accept or reject the envelope.

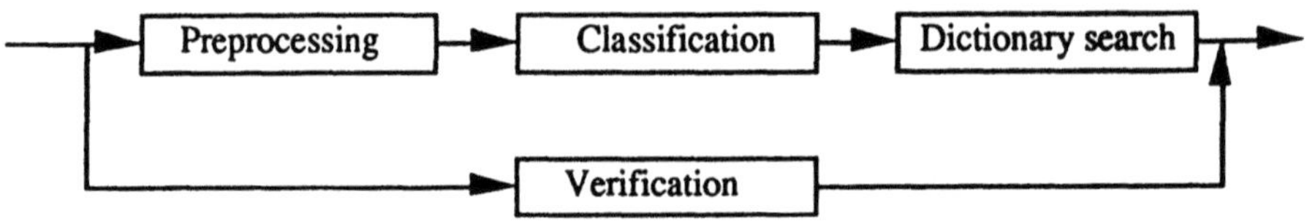

Figure 11. Components of the postal address OCR system

The design procedure for the preprocessing stage is as follows (a similar approach is applied to the other stages):

- The data from the preprocessing of each postcode character must be combined before classification, to determine whether the postcode should be submitted to the next stage. Therefore preprocessing must terminate at the top of a tree.
- The preprocessing is made up of 5 major sub-tasks (filtering, feature extraction, feature unification, feature concentration and feature counting). However, these sub-tasks can take place sequentially, without reference to other characters. Therefore only one tree is required for this stage.
- The average calculation time for preprocessing a character is .503 seconds on a single T800 transputer, the data packet size is 2105 bytes and the results packet size is 355 bytes. Table 2 shows the performance of corresponding 2, 3 and 4 level tertiary trees for the postcode preprocessing, derived from the performance equations [13], and verified using a transputer network simulation package [27].

What the performance equations do is to demonstrate the feasibility of scaling the application component to a particular size of tree. They do not however define exactly how the algorithm should be partitioned into the tree, except that it should be done as a processor farm. Clearly a 4 layer tertiary tree (40 processors) can theoretically satisfy the specification that the preprocessing stage should attain the required throughput of 10 envelopes per second. However, the effects of the probability distribution for the completion time of a work packet may mean that this upper bound performance estimate is not obtainable in practice.

No. of levels	*No. of processors*	*Chars./sec.*	*Postcodes/sec.*
2	4	5.9	0.8
3	13	23.6	3.4
4	40	76.4	10.9
5	121	233.9	33.4

Table 2. Preprocessing performance from a tertiary tree

A similar partitioning procedure can be applied to the other components of the system based on corresponding performance figures for each of these stages. Table 3 below shows simulated performance figures for a complete three-stage system in which the preprocessing and classification stages act on complete postcodes rather than single characters.

The drop in performance for the dictionary search stage is because this stage exhibits a large standard deviation in search execution times for different postcodes. This is an example of how radically the *dynamic* performance can differ from that predicted using the static performance equations.

Stage	*Exec. time (1 T800)*	*Required procs.*	*Postcodes/sec.*
preprocessing	3.176	36	10.80
classification	5.056	57	10.18
dictionary search	2.685	31	5.61

Table 3. Performance scaling for the complete OCR system

8 Conclusions

The conclusions of this paper can be divided into two categories, general conclusions and specific conclusions. The general conclusions are based simply upon reviewing current developments in computer architectures and vision systems. They show that distributed memory MIMD with point-to-point communication offers the best prospect for generalising parallelism within real-time embedded vision systems.

More specific conclusions can also be drawn from the analyses of performance and generality which we have carried out. These show that one possible route towards achieving generality for MIMD parallelism is based upon fixing the topology as a tree and the programming paradigm as processor farming. This results in analysable, scalable parallel processing systems which are capable of addressing a large proportion of parallel embedded system needs.

Acknowledgement. The research reviewed in Sections 5-7 of this paper was carried out in collaboration with Robert Tregidgo, and is fully reported in his PhD thesis [28]. The author gratefully acknowledges financial support for this work from UK Royal Mail Research and Development, and from the Science and Engineering Research Council.

References

1. Brooks, R.A. : Model-based three-dimensional interpretations of two-dimensional images, IEEE Trans. PAMI 5(2), 140-149, (1983). Also in: Readings in Computer Vision: issues, problems, principles and paradigms (eds. M.A. Fischler and O. Firschein), Morgan-Kaufmann, 1987.
2. Flynn, J.: Some computer organisations and their effectiveness, IEEE Trans. Computers, C-21, 948-960, (1972).
3. Waltz, F.M.: Hardware-based image processing (tutorial notes) IEEE Int. Conf. Image Processing, Singapore, September 1989.
4. Bennett, J.: Raster Operations, Byte 10(12), 187-203, (1985).

5. Sproull, R. F.: Frame buffer display architectures' Ann. Rev. Comp. Sci. 1, 19-46, (1986). Also in Readings in Human-Computer Interaction: a multidisciplinary approach, (eds. R. M. Baecker and W. A. S. Buxton), Morgan-Kaufmann, 1987.
6. Duff, M.J.B.: A cellular logic array for image processing, Pattern Recognition, 5, 229-247, (1973)
7. Fountain, T.J., Matthews, K.N. and Duff, M.J.B.: The CLIP7 image processor, IEEE Trans. PAMI-10(3), 311-319, (1988).
8. Hunt, D.J.: The AMT DAP - a processor array in a workstation environment, submitted to Computer Systems Science and Engineering, (1988).
9. Parkinson, D., Hunt, D.J. and MacQueen K.S.: The AMT DAP 500, Proc. 33rd IEEE Comp. Soc. Int. Conf., 196-199, (1988).
10. Hillis, W.D.: The Connection Machine, ACM distinguished dissertation series, MIT Press, Cambridge, Ma, 1985.
11. Amdahl, G.M., Limits of Expectation, Int. Journal Supercomput. Appl. (USA), .2, 88-94, (1988).
12. Hoare, C. A. R.: Communicating Sequential Processes, CACM, 21, 8, 666-677, (1978).
13. Downton, A. C. and Tregidgo, R.W.S.: Parallel architectures for image analysis and pattern recognition, in From pixels to features III: Frontiers in handwriting recognition, (eds. S. Impedovo and J.C. Simon), 395-408, North-Holland 1992.
14. Vrsalovic, D. F., Siewiorek, D. P. , Segall, Z. Z. and Gehringer, E. F. : Performance prediction and calibration for a class of multiprocessors, IEEE Trans. Comp., 1353-1364, November 1988.
15. Karp, A. H. and Flatt, H. P.: Measuring parallel processor performance, Comm. ACM, 33(5), May 1990.
16. May, D.: Towards general purpose parallel computers, in: Natural and artificial parallel computation, 91-121, MIT Press, 1990.
17. Allworth, S. T. and Zobel, R. N.: Introduction to real-time software design (2nd ed.), Macmillan, 1987.
18. Pritchard, D.: Mathematical Models of Distributed Computation, Proceedings of the 7th Occam User Group Technical Meeting, IOS, 1987.
19. Lotufo, R.A., Dagless, E.L., Milford, D.J., Morgan, A.D., Morrissey, J.F., and Thomas, B.T.: Hough transform for transputer arrays, Proc. 3rd IEE Int. Conf. on Image Processing and its Applications, (Conf. Pub. 307), 122-130, 1989.
20. Shea, D. G., Giampapa, M. E., Huisman, L., Irwin, G. R., Johnson, T. A., Ma, E., Murakami, T.T., Pattnaik, P.C., Varker, P. R., Wilcke, W. W., and Zukowski, D. J.: IBM victor 256 applications, in: Applications of Transputers 2, 1-12, IOS Press, 1990.
21. Valiant, L. G.: General purpose parallel architectures, Technical report TR-07-89, Aiken Computation Laboratory, Harvard University, Cambridge, Ma. 02138, April 1989.
22. Stavenuiter, T. and Roebbers, H.: Control of a servo loop for a vision system, in: Proc. 12th Occam User Group technical meeting, IOS, 1990.
23. Walden, M. and Sere, K.: Free text retrieval on transputer networks, Microprocessors and Microsystems, 13(3), April 1989.
24. Sousa, L., Barrios, J., Costa, A. and Piedade, M.: Parallel image processing for transputer based systems, Proc. 4th IEE Int. Conf. on Image Processing and its Applications, (Conf. Pub. 354), 33-36, (1992).
25. Kalberg, R. J. N.: ptt research, P.O. Box 421, Leidschendam, The Netherlands, personal communication, 8 April 1992.
26. Lee, S.-Y. and Aggarwal, J. K.: A system design/scheduling strategy for parallel image processing, IEEE Trans. PAMI-12, 2, 194-204, 1990.
27. Hart, E.: Transim user manual, Polytechnic of Central London, 1989.
28. Tregidgo, R. W. S.: Parallel processing and automatic address recognition, PhD thesis, Department of Electronic Systems Engineering, University of Essex, 1992.

Part 7

Databases for handwriting recognition

Large Database Organization for Document Images

Jonathan J. Hull and Richard K. Fenrich

Center of Excellence for Document Analysis and Recognition
Department of Computer Science
State University of New York at Buffalo
Buffalo, New York, 14260
hull@cs.buffalo.edu

Abstract.

Methodologies and techniques for constructing document image databases are discussed. Specific experience and considerations in creating a database for handwriting recognition research are presented. Practical considerations, including the choice of an image digitizer for such a database are presented. Examples of existing databases for handwriting recognition research are discussed. Also, various issues in testing pattern recognition algorithms and how they apply to database design are presented.

1. Introduction

The creation of an image database for experimental pattern recognition research is an important aspect of algorithm development [2]. A database must include samples that represent different problems that can occur in practice so that developers can create solutions for them. Often the desire to create a truly representative database has to be balanced versus the costs that are incurred to collect the database. Not only monetary expenses but also time constraints must be taken into account so that related research tasks can be executed on schedule and within budget.

The definition of the objectives of a database is the most important step in its design. Precisely what is being sampled should be made clear and the similarity of the sample to the final application should be defined. Ideally the database is gathered from exactly the same environment that will be used when the techniques are finally deployed. For example, a database developed for handwritten word recognition from postal addresses should be captured from envelopes in a working post office if possible. In this way the performance of algorithms developed on that database should easily project onto the use of those techniques in a system for handwritten address recognition.

The sampling strategies used are a critical aspect of database design. A simple random sample should give a good general overview of a problem domain. However, because such a sample is necessarily small, it may not sufficiently represent problems that are significant for system design. In such a case, a stratified or enhanced sample may be called for. For example, it is known that ZIP Codes that contain touching digits cause many failures (on the order of five percent) in handwritten ZIP Code recognition. A random sample of 10,000 ZIP Codes will thus only contain about 500 examples of such images. If this is insufficient for the development of robust recognition algorithms, an enhanced sample of as many ZIP Codes as needed that only contain touching digits can be collected.

The data collection procedures that are followed in the field should be clearly defined and precisely carried out to insure the success of the database. The imaging device should be as equivalent as possible to the one that will be used when the system is deployed. This is important to help insure that the results achieved with the database reflect those that will be achieved when the algorithms are placed in field use.

The truthing of a database is often the most expensive aspect in its collection. The desired type of truthing should be clearly defined and the most cost-effective way of achieving that level of truthing should be used. For example, in truthing mailpiece addresses, it is sometimes desired that every character be individually segmented. While this can be done manually at a significant cost, a semi-automatic process in which the results of an segmentation algorithm are confirmed by an operator can be much more efficient.

The remainder of the paper discusses aspects of the above points in more detail. Examples of various databases available to the handwriting recognition research community are presented. Also, several aspects of algorithm testing and how they impact on database design are discussed.

2. Sampling Strategies

There are several basic sampling strategies that are often considered in database collection. In a simple random sample, the population is numbered from one to N and a random number generator is used to select a subset of the population. This subset is the sample on which various measurements are computed. Often sample statistics such as the mean and variance of those measurements are used to summarize the knowledge gained from the sample. An objective usually is to construct confidence intervals around the sample mean that measure how well it represents the true population mean. The size of the confidence interval is measured by the value of the standard error of the mean. A small standard error corresponds to a small confidence interval which represents a precise estimate of the population mean.

There are several problems with a direct implementation of simple random sampling. One is that it is often difficult to physically carry out the sampling. For example, in sampling the population of pieces entering the U.S. mailstream each day, it would be necessary to travel to some subset of the 473 facilities that process incoming mail and find the identified piece(s) from among the 160 billion pieces processed each year. Another problem is that a simple random sample may obscure significant aspects of a problem because of the relatively small numbers of pieces in the sample. An example of this is the incidence of touching digits in ZIP Codes mentioned earlier. A simple random sample would probably not contain enough examples of ZIP Codes with touching digits to allow for the development of a robust segmentation algorithm. Thus it would be impossible to recognize many of those ZIP Codes.

A solution to many of these problems is to construct a *stratified* sample [5]. In this procedure, some a-priori measurements are used to sub-divide the sample space. The sample statistics are then calculated within the sub-spaces. This results in smaller values for the standard error of the mean and hence more precise estimates of the population statistics because the variance caused by sampling indiscriminantly is eliminated.

An example of a stratified sample of the U.S. mailstream illustrates these points [4]. The objective was to gather about 100 measurements significant to automation (such as height, weight, color, etc.) from mailpieces at the point in the postal system where they are first processed. The proportion of acceptance versus collection mail processed at each site as well as the volume of mail that passes through the site were used to characterize the 473 postal sorting centers. Acceptance mail refers to large numbers of pieces from a few companies while collection mail is large numbers of pieces from many individuals. Five strata were drawn along each variable so that about 20 percent of the total volume of 160 billion pieces were included in each stratum. Each postal facility was assigned to one of the 25 cells and a single facility was randomly selected to represent each cell. Then 4000 pieces were selected at each facility by selecting 500 pieces each day over a period of eight days. A systematic sampling procedure was used in which the estimated daily volume was divided into 500 equal-sized sequences and one piece was chosen at the end of each sequence. The statistics gathered from each piece were summarized with a statistical weighting scheme that provided for projections from the sample to the overall U.S. mailstream.

3. Data Collection Procedures

This section discusses several important considerations in implementing a collection.

3.1. Selection of image lift

The image lift or digitizing device that is used to collect the data can have a profound effect on the quality and long term usefulness of the database. Ideally, the image lift is equivalent to the device that will be used when the research phase is complete and the algorithms are used in practice. Even though implementing this may be difficult in practice because of cost or convenience, it may be a requirement so that results achieved on the database can project to an implementation in the field.

An example of correctly carrying out this strategy is given by the CEDAR CDROM. This data was collected at 300 pixels per inch with eight bits of gray scale resolution. This was done to maximize the usefulness of the data over a long period of time.

An example of an ill-advised choice of an image lift device is given by one of the early databases of mailpiece images gathered for USPS. This collection was performed by taking positive photographic transparencies in a post office and digitizing the transparencies in a laboratory. While this was convenient at the time the data was collected, it resulted in many image defects and grain noise caused by the film. This necessitated the development of algorithms for noise removal that would have been unnecessary if the original mailpieces had been digitized in the post office.

3.2. Sampling in lab vs. in the field

An important consideration in the development of a database is whether the samples will be gathered in a laboratory setting or whether they will be gathered in the field under realistic conditions. Often, it is much less expensive to set up a laboratory collection. However, caution must be observed because an unintentional bias can be introduced by the subjects. For example, abnormally good samples may be produced because of the similarity of the laboratory collection to a testing environment and the desire of many people to perform well in such a situation. Also, abnormally poor samples might be submitted by subjects that wish to "fool the computer."

An interesting example of the subject bias problem is given by the NIST databases of handwriting samples that are discussed later in this paper. The original set of data used as a training base were sampled from employees of the U.S. Census Bureau that filled out forms on a regular basis as part of their job. Their handwriting was significantly neater, in many cases, than the samples used to construct a test data set that were produced by a group of high school students. This experience emphasizes the importance of ensuring the consistency between the population of individuals that are sampled in the laboratory and the target population for the eventual deployment of an algorithm.

3.3. Truthing

Truthing refers to the assignment of the ''correct'' truth value to an image. The truthing process is often the most expensive part of the database collection process and one which has a significant impact on the use of a database for performance comparison.

It has been found after much experience that a semi-automatic truthing process in which a recognition algorithm assigns a decision or perhaps several possible decisions to an image that are subsequently confirmed by a human operator produces the most reliable results [2]. This process typically requires those decisions to be double-checked by another operator for increased accuracy. While this approach needs an up-front investment in truthing software, the benefits are manifest in the long-term production of larger volumes of data with higher accuracy truth information than would be possible with a completely manual truthing process.

4. Handwriting Databases

Several databases available to the handwriting recognition researcher are discussed in this section. Specific contact points for further information about acquiring the databases are listed in the appendix.

4.1. CEDAR CDROM

The CEDAR CDROM contains handwritten words (city names, state names, and ZIP Codes), mixed alphabetic and numeric characters, as well as digits that were extracted from the digital images of handwritten addresses [3]. On two occasions (once in 1987 and again in 1988), data gathering operations were conducted at the main post office in Buffalo, New York. Mailpieces with handwritten addresses were selected and scanned on a state-of-the-art image digitizer at 300 pixels per inch in 8-bit grayscale. Truth values were assigned by drawing bounding boxes around the city, state, and ZIP Code words and typing in their identities.

Because they were scanned from "live" mail, the data were unconstrained for writer, style and method of preparation. These characteristics help overcome the limitations of databases that contain only isolated characters or were prepared in a laboratory setting under prescribed circumstances.

The images were divided into subsets, indicated by a two-letter abbreviation, by the sampling procedure that was used for that subset. The BB, BD, BS, BR, and BU data sets were gathered with procedures that basically balanced on the first two digits of the ZIP Code. Each image in the BC set was selected because it contained the ZIP Code 14222. The BL images were chosen because they contained the city name "Buffalo". Each subset of the database is also divided into explicit training and testing sets to facilitate the sharing of results among researchers as well as performance comparisons.

4.1.1. Handwritten words

The handwritten words (cities, states, and ZIP Codes) are provided on the CDROM in full 8-bit grayscale. These data were divided into training and testing sets by randomly choosing approximately ten percent of the ZIP Code images and placing those images as well as the city and state name from the corresponding address in the test data. The remainder of the data were retained for training purposes.

Because of the sampling procedures that were used, the BB, BD, and BS city and state names should be distributed randomly across the United States. Almost all of the city and state names in the BS and BL data sets should be "Buffalo", and "NY". The breakdown into training and testing data is shown in Table 1. Multiple-word city or state names are split into separate files but not split across the training and test sets.

Each city or state word in the test data is provided with three dictionaries that simulate the results of recognition of the corresponding ZIP Code. The dictionaries contain lists of all the city or state words that could match the ZIP Code that corresponds to those words when one, two, or three of the digits (randomly chosen) are allowed to vary. The data from the USPS database of cities, states, and ZIP Codes were used to determine the dictionaries. This file is also included in the database.

Table 1. Numbers of handwritten word images in the training and test sets

Numbers of training and testing data						
	training set			testing set		
subset	cities	states	ZIPs	cities	states	ZIPs
BB	363	277	269	37	31	30
BC	190	217	190	21	23	21
BD	3106	2490	2201	317	252	238
BL	877	1017	875	97	114	97
BS	564	467	450	60	50	49
BR	n.a.	n.a.	3962	n.a.	n.a.	n.a.
BU	n.a.	n.a.	1072	n.a.	n.a.	n.a.
totals	5100	4468	9019	532	470	435

An illustration of the use of the dictionaries is presented in Figure 1. It is assumed that the ZIP Code from the address is first recognized. The result is then looked up in the USPS directory of ZIP Codes and associated city and state names. These lexicons are then passed to a word recognition algorithm that is applied to the city or state name from the corresponding image.

By providing dictionaries for the city and state names in an address based on partial recognition results of the corresponding ZIP Code, it is possible to develop word recognition algorithms independent of ZIP Code recognition. Also, a composite decision maker can be developed that determines the city, state, and ZIP Code to which the address should be routed.

4.1.2. Mixed alphabetics and digits

The database contains a quantity of segmented, binary alphabetic characters and digits. These characters and digits were extracted from address blocks and should be suitable for general algorithm development.

The data in this portion of the collection were segmented from the BD and BL address blocks. This was done to satisfy a need for training data for

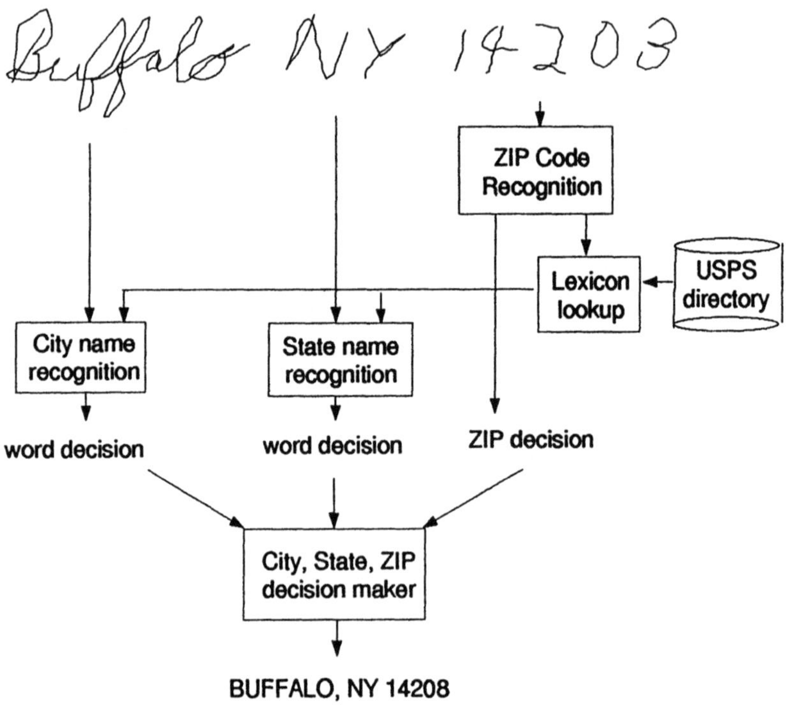

Figure 1. Simulated recognition system.

character and digit recognition algorithm development. The extraction and truthing of this data was performed by a program that displayed single connected components in isolation to an operator. A truth value was assigned to the component if the truth was obvious in isolation. If the truth was not obvious, the operator used the coordinates of the component to locate it in the original address block. The surrounding context of the component was then used to assign the truth value. It should be noted that this procedure caused each of the alphabetic and numeric characters in this portion of the database to be composed of just one component. A test set was chosen from the alphanumerics by randomly choosing ten percent of the available images. Altogether, there are 24,947 characters in the training set and 2890 in the testing set. There are 5802 digits and 19,145 examples of the characters A-Z and a-z in the training data. The test data contain 707 digits and 2183 alphabetic characters.

4.1.3. Digits only

Another portion of the database is composed of binary digits that were extracted from ZIP Codes. The binary digits in the training set were extracted from the BR ZIP Codes after they were truthed. This was done by segmenting the BR ZIP Codes into isolated digits and mapping the truth value for each position in the ZIP Code onto the isolated digit that was output by the segmentation algorithm at the corresponding position. Each digit image was then manually inspected. Any images that resulted from poor segmentations or had been assigned incorrect truth values were removed. The 18468 images that remained after this process are included on the CDROM.

The binary digits in the test set were generated from the BS ZIP Codes. A segmentation algorithm was applied to these images and every single digit that was output by this technique were saved to separate files. This resulted in a test data set of 2711 digit images. Each of these digits is provided with its associated truth value by corresponding the position of the segmented digit to the truth value at that position in the ZIP Code. The objective of this test set is to provide as realistic as possible a simulation of the data that would be encountered by an isolated digit recognition algorithm when it is applied to the results of segmenting handwritten ZIP Codes.

A carefully chosen subset of the BS digits are also provided. This set contains 2213 digits chosen from the 2711. Each of the 2213 were judged to be well-segmented by three USPS contractors. Thus, any obvious segmentation artifacts should have been removed. Table 2. provides a histogram of the number of images in each digit class in both the training and test sets.

Table 2. Bi-tonal digit images on the CEDAR CDROM

	class										
data set	0	1	2	3	4	5	6	7	8	9	total
training - BR	2866	2544	2047	1731	1676	1459	1722	1616	1453	1354	18468
test - all BS	434	345	296	260	234	193	281	241	216	211	2711
test - good BS	355	289	224	208	183	117	245	221	191	180	2213

4.2. NIST databases

The United States National Institute of Standards and Technology (NIST) has made available three databases on separate CDROMs that are of significant interest to the handwriting recognition research community. These database were developed as part of an effort, sponsored by the US Census Bureau, to determine the feasibility of automating the recognition of Census forms.

NIST Special Database 1 contains binary images of 2100 pages scanned at 300 pixels per inch. Each 8.5" by 11" page contains handprinted numerals and text prepared by a single person. The form contains numeral strings with 2, 3, 4, 5, and 6 digits, the full upper case and lower case English alphabet, and the preamble to the U.S. Constitution. The characters in all fields were supposed to have been discretely printed. However, there is no guarantee of this. In total, the database contains 273,000 numerals and 707,700 alphabetic characters.

The forms were completed by sending them to Census Bureau field offices throughout the United States and having each form filled out by a unique Census Bureau employee. The completed forms were then returned to NIST where they were scanned. The database, furnished on CDROM, contains images of the entire forms and truth data that specifies the location and content of each string of characters on the form. The exception is the ''Constitution box'' for which specific truth data is not supplied.

NIST Special Database 3 contains all the images in the first database, plus individual characters segmented from each form. The characters were assigned individual truth values by a laborious manual process that was designed to insure the integrity of the data. Reportedly, more than six person-months were needed for truthing.

Overall, 313,389 isolated character images are supplied in this data set. This includes 223,125 digits, 44,951 upper case, and 45,313 lower case characters. Each character image is centered on a 128 by 128 pixel region. The error rate in truthing is less than 0.1 percent.

NIST Special Database 7, also known as NIST Test Data 1, contains 83,000 binary images of handprinted segmented characters. These include approximately 59,000 digits and 24,000 upper case and lower case alphabetic characters. This database was gathered specifically to test algorithms developed on Special Database 3.

The images in the test data set were captured by a process that is similar to the one used for special database 3. The same forms were used and students at a High School nearby Washington, D.C. filled out the forms. Overall, 500 images of forms were captured and the characters from each form were segmented and truthed. However, because these data were to be used for blind tests, the truth values are supplied on a separate 5.25 inch floppy disk.

The data were used to test over 40 systems for isolated handprint recognition and the results were reported at a workshop sponsored by NIST in May, 1992. The results of this test are discussed in a technical report available from NIST [7].

4.3. CENPARMI Databases

Several databases of handwritten ZIP Codes and isolated digits are available from the Center for Pattern Recognition and Machine Intelligence (CENPARMI) at Concordia University in Montreal, Canada. These databases have been used for recognition experiments presented elsewhere [6]. Some of the details of these databases are presented here.

One of the CENPARMI databases were extracted from 3400 ZIP Codes that occurred on dead letter mail. Each ZIP Code was prepared by a different writer and the writers did not know that their ZIP Codes were being entered in a database. Each ZIP Code was digitized at 166 pixels per inch (ppi) with four bits of grayscale.

Approximately 17,000 binary digits were extracted from the ZIP Codes. To provide a fixed number of examples in each class, three standard sets containing 2000 digits each were created from the ZIP Codes. Each set had 200 examples of each class zero through nine. Those sets are denoted A and B for training and set T for testing.

An additional set of 20,000 unconstrained handwritten numerals were also collected from 500 students at Concordia University. Each person prepared 40 examples of each digit zero through nine. These are known as the *Quebec data* and are unique in that they contain a mixture of North American and European writing styles. These data were digitized at 200 ppi with one bit of resolution.

4.4. Essex Databases

A database of handwritten postal addresses and characters extracted from post codes is available from the University of Essex in the United Kingdom This database was created by choosing addresses from the U.K. standard address file and having subjects hand-write those addresses on standard envelopes. Those envelopes were then digitized on a working postal OCR at 212 ppi with one bit of resolution.

Three data sets were created for training and testing address recognition algorithms. The standard training set contains 1680 address images. Each address was prepared by a different writer and the addresses were chosen so that the number of different characters in the post codes were equalized. Overall, 10693 characters were segmented from the postcodes of which approximately 5700 were chosen because they were of "good" quality.

The first test set contains 753 addresses that were randomly chosen from the U.K. address file. 4801 characters were segmented from these addresses. The second test set contains 1040 randomly chosen addresses from Colchester and Milton Keynes. From this set, 3392 characters were segmented from the Colchester addresses and 3491 from the Milton Keynes addresses.

4.5. ETL Databases

Overall nine separate databases have been produced by the Electrotechnical Laboratory in Japan during the period from 1973 until about 1989. These data sets are denoted ETL1 to ETL9 and contain a mixture of alphanumeric, Hiragana, Katakana, and Kanji characters. ETL2 is composed of machine-printed characters and the other data sets are made up of handwritten characters.

The ETL1 and ETL6 databases are most useful for the development of alphanumeric recognition techniques. ETL1 was produced by 1445 writers, each of whom wrote 36 different alpha-numeric characters, 12 special characters, and 51 Katakana characters for a total of 141,319 images. ETL6 was produced by 1383 writers each of whom wrote 36 alpha-numerics, 32 special, and 46 Katakana characters for a total of 157,662 images.

The most recent of the databases (ETL9) provides some indication of the variability of the data and its potential for use in handwriting recognition research. ETL9 was prepared by 4000 subjects each of whom wrote 2965 Kanji and 71 Hiragana characters. This resulted in 607,200 character images in the database.

4.6. SCRIPSIT Database

The SCRIPSIT project is an on-going effort to collect and distribute a standard database of on-line handwriting samples. Contributions of data from various corporations, Universities, and Government research labs are being solicited. The objective is to produce a CDROM with a large amount of various data such as signatures, gestures, phrases, in various alphabets.

Various characteristics of the data will be recorded including the purpose for which the data was collected, the conditions under which it was recorded, and who collected the data. Also, various measures on the writers themselves will be gathered, if possible, including their age, sex, handedness, native language, country in which they were educated about handwriting, and their motivation for providing data (paid or volunteer).

A part of this effort will be the development of a standard interchange format for the data that will include tools to convert between the file formats used by different digitizers. This will help improve the usefulness of the data.

5. Issues in Testing

The testing of algorithms for text recognition as well as digit and character recognition is often performed under many different conditions. The results expressed in papers are often misleading and do little more than demonstrate that a program has been run on some data and some results have been produced. Comparison of performance between methods based on their published results is impossible since strict experimental conditions were not adhered to. This state of affairs is typified by reports that some technique achieved a 99.99 percent correct rate. If this were true in general, then the problem under consideration would be solved and research emphasis could shift to another area. However, this is often not the case and this is only apparent to experts in the field. Others sometimes have difficulty in interpreting results because they do not possess the necessary in-depth familiarity.

This section of the paper discusses some of the experimental conditions that should be followed in recognition algorithm testing. An example of how the CEDAR CDROM helps to address some of these concerns is also presented.

5.1. Definitions

Any test set is parameterized by one important value; that is, N, or the number of samples in the test set. Good research practice suggests that the total number of samples submitted for testing should not be adjusted by a researcher. Often, outliers will be removed because they were deemed inappropriate or too difficult. However, this is a dangerous procedure as even removing a single sample can lead to results that are completely incomparable. This is because a test procedure may require that the correct rate be reported with a given error rate, say one percent. Since such normalization is often performed by thresholding on a confidence measure, if that *bad* sample occurred near the top of the ranking, it could cause the reported performance to be skewed.

Holding the sample size constant is an especially important consideration when comparing the performance of two algorithms. Unless the sample size is *exactly* the same, even down to just one sample, then a comparison may be impossible for the reason stated above.

A definition for *correct rate* is:

$$100 * \frac{\textit{number of correct decisions}}{N}$$

where a decision is considered correct if it matches the truth value of the image. A useful alternative is sometimes to measure the correct rate in the top m choices. In this case, a decision is considered correct if any of the first m choices of a classifier match the truth value of the image.

A definition for *error rate* is:

$$100 * \frac{\textit{number of erroneous decisions}}{N}$$

where a decision is erroneous if its class does not match the truth value of the image. An analogous interpretation applies for error rate in the top m choices.

An alternate definition for error rate preferred by some researchers is:

$$100 * \frac{\textit{number of erroneous decisions}}{\textit{number of images assigned a decision}}$$

This measures the expectation that a given decision is incorrect, versus other decisions (not including rejects). The previous definition for error rate measures the expectation that, for any given image, the classifier will produce an incorrect decision.

The tradeoff between reject rate and error rate is also valuable in comparing performance. A technique that is only able to produce a decision for 50 percent of its inputs but when it makes such a decision is better than 99 percent correct, may be preferred to one that accepts a higher percentage but makes more errors. This information is often presented in the form of a reject versus error rate curve where the points on the curve are derived by thresholding a confidence measure output by the recognition algorithm.

5.2. Environments for applications and tests

In considering the use of any particular technique, the environment in which the method will be applied should be equivalent to the environment in which the test is conducted. So if a method for isolated handwritten digit recognition is to be applied to data extracted from bank checks and a projection is needed of how well such a method would perform in practice, then the relevant test results would be for exactly that type of data.

An ideal test would be provided every digit output by a segmentation routine when it is applied to a fixed database. Even digits that were mis-segmented would need to be considered because these digits would be input to the recognition algorithm at run-time. Knowledge of how well the method performs on such data is needed. A poor segmentation output that contains, for example, two digits instead of one, should be recognized as such or rejected. A technique that can correctly recognize such cases may be preferred over a method that would reject them. This characteristic could be missed unless the test is conducted properly.

5.3. Training and testing data

It is a basic procedure that the data used for training an algorithm should be disjoint from the data used to test the technique. The training data should be used to develop all the parameters and thresholds that might be needed. The testing data should not even be looked at until the test is conducted. At this time, the testing data should be run only once and the performance to be reported should be tabulated from this run. After that, the test set should either be folded into the training data or it should be thrown away.

When these procedures are not followed, performance figures can be distorted. When results are reported only on training data, they are bound to be abnormally high. Also, testing data sets are often used more than once. This can lead to "tainting" of the testing data caused by patches being made to the algorithm based on the contents of the test set.

A further consideration is the equivalence of training data between techniques. It is sometimes believed that this is a requirement for a "fair" test. However, this may only be true in an academic sense. In an application environment, the training a method has been subjected to is an advantage that is difficult to quantify. For example, in a recent structured test of handwritten digit recognition algorithms, the method with the best performance had the benefit of many years of development on different training sets [7]. The test set used for evaluation contained a large number of images (crossed sevens) that had not occurred in the fixed training data supplied to the other participants. However, this writing style had been seen in the other training sets used to develop the method with the best performance.

5.4. Evaluator and relevance of technique

In comparing performance, the individual or organization that conducted a test should be considered. When the group that developed a particular technique is the same one that performs the evaluation, there is bound to be some element of favoritism involved. Since the degree to which this occurs is often difficult to detect, the only solution is for performance comparison to be carried out by an independent organization. While this may be difficult to organize, it is a requirement for an impartial evaluation.

The topic of performance comparison must include mention of the relevance of the particular technique used in any system. The notion that some method is better than another because it is based on a particular methodology is unfounded. After all, the bottom line is how well a method performs in an application environment.

5.5. Example of performance analysis

An example of reporting performance on a portion of the database presented earlier using the considerations discussed above is given in this section. A multiple classifier digit recognition algorithm was tested on every one of the 2,711 images in the BS test set [1]. Overall, 2,590 correct decisions were achieved, with 54 errors and 67 rejects. This is a correct rate of 95.54 percent, an error rate of 1.99 percent and a reject rate of 2.47 percent. A breakdown of performance by class is shown in Table 3. This shows that the system performed best in classifying

Table 3. Digit recognition performance on the 2,711 images in the BS test set

criterion	class by class performance									
	0		1		2		3		4	
	N	%	N	%	N	%	N	%	N	%
correct	421	97.0	331	95.9	270	91.2	260	96.2	222	94.9
error	8	1.9	7	2.0	6	2.0	6	2.3	3	1.3
reject	5	1.2	7	2.0	20	6.8	4	1.5	9	3.9

criterion	class by class performance									
	5		6		7		8		9	
	N	%	N	%	N	%	N	%	N	%
correct	181	93.8	270	96.1	229	95.0	212	98.2	204	96.7
error	3	1.6	2	2.1	9	3.7	1	0.5	5	2.4
reject	9	4.7	5	1.8	3	1.2	3	1.4	2	1.0

zeroes and eights. The poorest performance was achieved for twos and fives, probably the most difficult digits to recognize in isolation.

The environment for this test was precisely the intended application. That is, every digit output by the segmentation algorithm was input to the digit recognition algorithm. The testing data were disjoint from the training data. The algorithm used here has been compared to other methods on precisely the same data. Several techniques have produced similar performance but none has clearly surpassed the multiple classifier algorithm.

6. Discussion and Conclusions

Several practical considerations in the design and collection of large image databases were discussed. These included a precise definition of the objectives of the database as well as the sampling techniques and procedures that are used for collecting and truthing the data.

A brief review of the various databases that are available to the handwriting recognition researcher was also conducted. This included the CEDAR CDROM, NIST, CENPARMI, Essex, ETL, and SCRIPSIT data. Also, a discussion of important procedures in algorithm testing was presented.

References

1. Cohen, E., Hull, J. J. and Srihari, S. N., "Understanding handwritten text in a structured environment: Determining ZIP Codes from addresses," *International Journal of Pattern Recognition and Artificial Intelligence 5*, 1&2 (1991), 221-264.

2. Fenrich, R. K. and Hull, J. J., "Concerns in creation of image databases," *Pre-proceedings, IWFHR-III, Third International Workshop on Frontiers in Handwriting Recognition*, Buffalo, New York, May 25-27, 1993, 112-121.

3. Hull, J. J., "A database for handwriting recognition research," *IEEE Transactions on Pattern Analysis and Machine Intelligence*, 1993. accepted to appear.

4. *Mail characteristics study findings: Volume 1 - summary report*, Kenan Systems Corporation, March, 1991. available from USPS Library.

5. Kish, L., *Survey Sampling*, Wiley, New York, 1965.

6. Suen, C. Y., Nadal, C., Legault, R., Mai, T. A. and Lam, L., "Computer recognition of unconstrained handwritten numerals," *Proceedings of the IEEE 80*, 7 (July, 1992), 1162-1180.

7. Wilkinson, R. A., Geist, J., Janet, S., Grother, P. J., Burgess, C. J. C., Creecy, R., Hammond, R., Hull, J. J., Larsen, N. J., Vogl, T. P. and Wilson, C. L., "The first census optical character recognition systems conference," NISTIR 4912, National Institute of Standards and Technology, Gaithersburg, Maryland, August, 1992.

Appendix

Specific individuals to contact for further information about each of the databases discussed earlier are presented below.

CEDAR CDROM: Dr. Jonathan J. Hull, Center of Excellence for Document Analysis and Recognition, State University of New York at Buffalo, Buffalo, NY, 14260 USA; email: hull@cs.buffalo.edu.

NIST Databases: Ms. Joan Sauerwein, National Institute of Standards and Technology, Gaithersburg, Maryland, 20899; email: srddata@enh.nist.gov, fax: 301-975-2183.

CENPARMI Databases: Prof. C.Y. Suen, Center for Pattern Recognition and Machine Intelligence (CENPARMI), Concordia University, Montreal, Quebec, Canada; fax: 514-848-2830.

Essex Databases: Prof. Andy Downton, Department of Electronic Systems Engineering, University of Essex, Wivenhoe Park, Colchester, Essex, C04 3SQ, UK; email: acd@essex.ac.uk.

ETL Databases: Dr. K. Yamamoto, Electro-Image Understanding Section, Machine Understanding Division, Electrotechnical Laboratory, 1-1-4, Umezono, Tsukuba Science City, Ibaraki 305 Japan; email: yamamoto@etl.go.jp.

SCRIPSIT Database: Dr. Isabel Guyon, AT&T Bell Laboratories, Holmdel, New Jersey; email: isabelle@neural.att.com. Prof. Lambert Schomaker, Nijmegen Institute for Cognition and Information (NICI), University of Nijmegen, The Netherlands; email: schomaker@nici.kun.nl.

Part 8

Signature recognition and verification

A Model-Based Dynamic Signature Verification System

Réjean Plamondon
Laboratoire Scribens, École Polytechnique de Montréal
Département de génie électrique & génie informatique
C.P.6079, Succ. "A", Montréal, QC, H3C 3A7

Abstract. This paper reports on some of the questions raised by designers of automatic signature verification systems. It shows how knowledge about signature control and generation, in terms of a realistic mathematical and psychophysical model, can be helpful in guiding and orienting design choices and related research activities.

Keywords: dynamic signature verification, handwriting generation model, input space representation, signal comparison algorithm, segmentation theory

1 Introduction

Dynamic signature verification has been a challenge for researchers in the field of pattern recognition for more than twenty years [1,2,3] and many solutions have been proposed to cope with the major difficulties related to this problem [4,5]. Among the approaches that have been used to design prototypes, model-based methods have recently been shown to be very promising [6,7,8,9].

This paper describes the development of a model-based approach, showing how its philosophy has been integrated at the various stages in the design of an automatic signature verification system [10,11]. Specifically, the focus here is on some of the major decisions that have to be made throughout the design process, and an attempt is made to highlight how a good understanding of the neuromuscular processes involved in the production of a signature might be helpful in guiding and orienting the design choices and related research activities.

The first step in the model-based approach is to select a representation space for the input data. Then, a general signature generation model has to be proposed. One of the key problems after this, is the selection of the appropriate system functions for describing the generators. We report below on various comparative studies that have been carried out to propose solutions to these problems. We then show how the selected model can be used to segment a signature. A few studies dealing with the selection of the type of script to be used as an identifier and the choice of a comparison algorithm are then presented. Finally, the complete model-based system for automatic signature verification is briefly described. Problems dealing with system testing and database validation are discussed in the conclusion.

2 Selecting a Signal Representation Space

A fundamental question that must be answered prior to becoming too deeply immersed in process modeling and system design is what types of signals will be most appropriate for representing a signature. It is well-known that automatic verification systems using functions to represent a signature perform better than systems based on parameters [1,2]. However, various types of signals have been used in the past and it is not clear which is the most representative.

To provide a partial answer to this question, two different studies were conducted. The first explored the stability of pressure signals in handwriting [12]. Investigation of the spectral coherence and time domain correlation between pen pressure and several kinematic variables in drawing simple patterns and in writing cursive script suggests that there are three types of subjects in terms of pressure control. In the first group of subjects, reliable pressure patterns were observed, suggesting a high level of control of this variable by the central nervous system. The second group showed partial pressure control, while the third group, representing about one-half of the subjects tested, manifested no control at all over pressure. Although this study was not conducted using signatures specifically, its results suggest that a large number of individuals might not really control pressure while writing. We therefore decided not to use the analogic information from this signal for signature verification, but to keep only the on-off signal provided by a digitizer as pen-paper contact information.

The second study [13] deals with the choice of displacement, velocity or acceleration signals as a representation space. Variance analysis on signature comparisons based on three different algorithms shows that significant differences do exist between the three signal representations and that the best representation space for a 2D signature verification system is the velocity domain. Moreover, in an independent and very different study dealing with the dependence of peripheral and central parameters describing handwriting generation on movement direction [14], the reduction of the complex phenomenon of handwriting to the product of two simple movement generators acting in some principal motor axes linked to wrist and finger activity is seriously questioned, providing support for a representation space based on differential geometry [15]. Indirect support for this approach is also provided by the study reported previously on pressure analysis. It was in fact found that pen pressure, when controlled, appears to be a separate control variable with respect to coherence with tangential and angular velocities.

Based on this direct and indirect evidence, a decision was made to work in the velocity domain, using curvilinear and angular velocities. This decision was also supported by numerous studies reporting that velocity profiles in rapid-aimed movements are approximately bell-shaped and that the shape of the curve is approximately invariant in form for movements that vary in duration, distance, peak velocity and inertial load [16,17,18,19,20,21,22,23,24,25].

3 Signature Generation Model

All these observations and results suggest that velocity is the controlled output of the signature generation system and that movement planning and control are independent of the reference axis and thus rely on differential geometry [15,26]. On this basis, a continuous handwritten specimen can be considered as a plane curve described by its curvature as a function of its curvilinear abscissa. Similarly, the process of signing can be defined by the generation of this equation as a function of time. This view immediately leads to a description of the signature generation process in terms of curvilinear and angular velocity generators that control the magnitude and orientation of the pentip velocity vector, each of these generators being characterized by an appropriate impulse response.

In other words, a general way to look at a velocity generator is to consider the overall sets of neural and muscle networks involved in the production of a single curvilinear or angular movement as a linear system producing a velocity profile from an impulse command $U_0(t-t_0)$ of amplitude D occuring at t_o [27]. In this case, we can write:

$$V(t) = \int_0^t D U_0(t-t_0-\tau) H(\tau) d\tau \tag{1}$$

$$V(t) = DH(t-t_0) \quad \text{with} \quad t \geq t_0 \tag{2}$$

Equation (2) shows that the velocity profile directly reflects the impulse response $H(t-t_0)$ of the global system. Since the generation of different rapid movements involves the activation of the same neuromuscular systems under different experimental conditions, the similarity of the velocity profiles and their invariance for different experimental conditions therefore follows directly.

4 Selection of the Impulse Response

The key idea behind the use of a handwriting generation model for describing the signing process is that the knowledge provided by the model can be useful in understanding the basic control processes involved in the production of a signature and that this information can be used, in one way or another, to discriminate between authentic specimens and forgeries. The more realistic the model, in terms of how well it represents the psychophysical data on human movement, the more reliable the information extracted from a signature in the context of that model. It should be clear that a great deal of effort will have to be put into selecting of the appropriate impulse response of the velocity generators to ensure that this requirement is met.

The processes involved in handwriting are rather complex and have been analyzed during recent decades from many perspectives by various groups of researchers: physicists, engineers, computer scientists, experimental psychologists, neurologists, cognitive scientists, educators, forensic experts, graphoanalysts, paleontologists. Several conceptual, physical and empirical models have been developed by these scientists, and they generally differ greatly in their description of the phenomena, depending on the context and purposes for which they have been developed. Of interest to us here is the group of models that have been referred to as bottom-up models [28]. These models deal with the description of the movement generation system from the central nervous system down to the hand, and generally focus on the reproduction of a movement trajectory using different sets of equations and parameters. A survey [29] carried out on previously published models of the movement generation system reveals that the authors had two main two interests:

1. The physical aspects of the system (muscle geometry, mechanical properties, etc.);
2. The control processes of the system involved in trajectory formation.

In the first category of models (which will be called *dynamic-oriented* below) are included those for which the mechanism of trajectory formation is directly related to the geometry of the muscles and to their mechanical properties [30]. These models consider the movement generation system to comprise two levels: a cognitive/symbolic level and a joint/muscular level. The high level is assumed to be for coding and planning. The low level contains a geometrical and mechanical transformation mechanism and a high-level decision execution mechanism [31]. In this group, three subclasses can be distinguished: models considering the muscles as force generators [32,33,34,35,36], models considering the muscles as oscillation generators [37,38] and models considering the muscles as speed generators [39].

The second category of models (which will be called *kinematic-oriented models* below) are those for which the trajectory formation mechanism is independent of the actual joint and muscle patterns, and are based on the capability of expressing and controlling the trajectory of the hand in space. These models also rely on the fact that the kinematic patterns of the hand are invariant with respect to variations of starting point, of inclination and of size [40,41]. To represent the mechanisms of movement generation, kinematic-oriented models consider a three-level system in which an intermediate level for information processing is added to the two previous levels of the dynamic-oriented models. This intermediate level is used to generate spatio-temporal patterns for a given planned movement and to transform spatial sequences into angular/muscular sequences. In our survey, nine previously published models were found to belong in this category [21,27,30,36,42,43,44,45,46]. To expand our comparative study, nine other potential kinematic-oriented models were also added [29,47], which led us to compare the performances of twenty-six models under the same experimental protocol based on analysis-by-synthesis experiments and using the same database [48,49].

Statistical analysis of the results obtained from these studies clearly confirms the superiority of a double log-normal model [50,51] and of a support-bounded log-normal model [27,52]. The former predicts a huge body of psychophysical data [50,51,53,54] and is very well supported theoretically in the context of applying the central-limit theorem to predict the asymptotic behavior of a large number of dependent linear systems [27,50,51]. The latter performs less well in terms of theoretical predictions, but offers the advantage of being based on five parameters instead of seven, which simplifies trajectory reconstruction.

To be more specific, a signature can be considered as the output of two velocity generators. The first controls the curvilinear velocity, and the second the angular velocity. Both of these generators are made up of a sequence of neuromuscular processes that can be grouped under two synergies representing the set of neural and muscular networks involved in the generation of the agonist and antagonist activities that result in a specific curvilinear or angular stroke.

Each of these channels constitutes a linear time-invariant system producing a velocity output from an impulse command of amplitude D_1 or D_2, Θ_1 or Θ_2 occurring at specific moment $t_{\sigma 0}$ or $t_{\theta 0}$. Due to the opposite action of the agonist and antagonist synergies, the global output of a velocity generator is obtained by substracting these two outputs:

$$v_\sigma(t) = v_{\sigma 1}(t) - v_{\sigma 2}(t) \tag{3}$$

$$= D_1 H_{\sigma 1}(t - t_{\sigma o}) - D_2 H_{\sigma 2}(t - t_{\sigma o}) \tag{4}$$

and $$v_\theta(t) = v_{\theta 1}(t) - v_{\theta 2}(t) \tag{5}$$

$$= \Theta_1 H_{\theta 1}(t - t_{\theta o}) - \Theta_2 H_{\theta 2}(t - t_{\theta o}) \tag{6}$$

Under very general conditions dealing mainly with subprocess interdependency [50,51,55], it is predicted that the impulse responses $H_{ij}(t\text{-}t_{jO})$ of each synergy can be described by a log-normal curve and, in this context, each velocity generator is governed by a $\Delta\Lambda$ law. Moreover, computer simulations show that under certain conditions [47,50,51], the $\Delta\Lambda$ law can be approximately fitted by a support-bounded log-normal. So, depending on the goal of a particular design step, the double log-normal model will be preferred if correspondence of model parameters with real psychophysical processes is important, while the support-bounded log-normal model might be a better choice when the number of parameters is more critical than their basic significance.

5 Signature Segmentation

This model-based approach results in a general framework that can be used to segment a signature [8]. In this context, a signature can be considered as made up of components, that is, pentip traces, produced during a continuous pen-down signal, starting and ending at null velocity. Each of these components is made up of strings that are portions of the trace between two angular discontinuities or between the beginning (or the end) of a component and the next (or previous) angular discontinuity. These concepts of component and string take on a specific meaning in this model. On the one hand, a component represents the longest path that can be traced by the pentip from a particular origin (between components, subjects tend to move their arms). On the other, a string represents the longest sequence of stimuli that can be fed into the system, starting from a particular rest point. Strings are generally limited by zero speed conditions at both ends. In terms of motor programming, a string can be viewed as the longest sequence of strokes with which the system can be pipelined. It represents the longest ballistic trajectory that can be produced by the system at a particular point in the execution of the movement.

Each string is made up of a combination of curvilinear and angular strokes, that is, curvilinear and angular displacements resulting from the activation of the corresponding generators. Practically, strokes can be described in terms of five or seven different parameters, depending on the impulse response chosen for the generators. In this general context, a curvilinear (or angular) stroke is thus defined as a portion of the pentip trajectory that corresponds to the curvilinear (or angular) displacement resulting from the production of a double or a support-bounded log-normal velocity profile, produced by a specific generator in response to a specific impulse command applied to it. These strokes are assumed to be the fundamental units of human handwriting movement and serve as the coding elements of motor programs used in trajectory planning.

This segmentation framework is very general in the sense that it provides a broad view of signature trace partitioning, using a model-based hierarchical representation of segments and focusing on a dual description of the pentip trajectory, in terms of both curvilinear and angular strokes.

6 Selection of a Comparison Algorithm

Another major issue in designing a dynamic signature verification system is how to compare the various segments of a test signature to those of a reference signature. To help us resolve this issue, we conducted a comparative study [55] on the performance of three well-known algorithms: regional correlation [57,58,59], dynamic time warping [60,61,62] and skeletal tree matching [63,64]. To simplify and standardize the test, this experiment was performed on a database consisting of unsegmented signatures, handwritten passwords and initials.

We concluded [55], among other things, that where significant differences were observed among the averages error rates regional correlation performed best in five cases. Skeletal tree matching was a close second to regional correlation in one case and came first in another (dynamic time warping being a close second in this case). Regional correlation was the fastest, followed by dynamic time warping. Skeletal tree matching was found to be very time-consuming. It was also observed at regional correlation was more parameter-sensitive than dynamic time warping. In other words, the general feeling was that none of these algorithms could be considered the best one to use. Moreover, a comparison of the different types of input clearly confirmed that signatures outperform handwritten passwords and initials [65,66].

A follow-up to this study extended the comparison of regional correlation and dynamic time warping to a parallel environment [67]. A parallel processor system, using four TMS320C30 digital signal processors was designed for this purpose. The study showed that the performance of regional correlation in terms of execution time could be greatly improved. That of dynamic programming was also improved, but to a lesser extent due to the communication overload between the processors for this algorithm.

7 Signature Verification System

Although these various studies were done in an evolving research context, involving many different collaborators and sometimes with other important goals, they were conclusive enough to give us some basic starting design principles that would be useful in developing and building a system. In addition, major survey of previous work in the domain [1,2] provided us with some specific guidelines.

It was decided that the new signature verification system should meet the following requirements:

1. The system should use more than one input representation space for the signatures.
2. The processing steps should be based on the signature generation model and its resulting segmentation theory.
3. A multi-step comparison should be performed between reference and test signatures using a new signal comparison approach.
4. All the processing steps should be driven by personalized thresholds.

Based on these guidelines, a multi-level signature verification system was developed [11,68], which works as follows.

The signature coordinates, $D_x(t)$, $D_y(t)$, is acquired in real-time from a digitizer. The coordinates can be stored on a disk unit for system tuning or preprocessed immediately for filtering and derivation. The filtering is done with a third-order linear low-pass filter with a bandwidth of about 10 Hz. The time-derivation of the coordinates generates two new signals, $V_x(t)$ and $V_y(t)$, representing respectively the velocity of the pentip according to the X and Y axes of a cartesian reference system. The system then calculates the curvilinear $V_\sigma(t)$ and the angular $V_\theta(t)$ velocity signals from $V_x(t)$ and $V_y(t)$ and segments them into components and strings. The next step involves the calculation of some simple dynamic parameters. These parameters are selected to allow the rapid pre-classification of a signature. The choice of these parameters is also model-driven. The system then normalizes the signature image, rotating the coordinates $D_x(t)$, $D_y(t)$ according to the signature base line and scaling its dimensions.

Globally, a signature is verified at three distinct levels [11]. At the first level, a weighted distance is computed between the simple dynamic parameters of the test and reference signatures. At the second level, the intrinsic local correlation is computed between portions of the test signature velocity signal with corresponding portions of the reference signature velocity. The third level of verification consists in calculating the distances between the test and reference signature trajectory images by local elastic pattern matching. These levels of verification rely on a set of cost functions based on exponentials, growth factors and some shifting constants.

Decisions are made from threshold values that are personalized and calculated automatically from several reference signatures. Generally three references are sufficient.

The three verification steps can be combined in different ways to build one specific system. A global classification function can be obtained, for example, by a linear combination of weighted costs associated with the levels of verification. Preferably, decisions can be based on personalized threshold values as determined from several reference signatures. The automatic determination of these personalized threshold values is based on the worst verification results obtained by comparing the reference signatures among themselves, taken two by two. This allows an adaptation of the discriminating functions with respect to the stability of the reference signatures that are provided.

8 Conclusion

One major problem with such a system when it becomes functional is tuning and validating it. This is even more critical when there is no application context to direct decisions concerning the fixing of thresholds. Indeed, one application might require minimizing type II errors (false acceptation) at the expense of type I errors (false rejection), while another might call for the reverse. Ideally, a system should also be tested with a large non homogeneous population over a long period time. This generally necessitates large financial and technical resources to run the experiment and to maintain the motivation of the subjects. Moreover, the quality of the signature database, in terms of number of specimens, their intrinsic variability the type of forgery used, etc., constitutes a key question that must be addressed in designing a validation protocol [69].

To avoid some of these difficulties, we have designed a powerful testing benchmark that minimizes time and effort while providing robust cues for tuning and validating an automatic signature verification system. The experiment took the form of an exam in which some subjects were required to imitate some target signatures, both geometrically and dynamically, each within a specified and controlled time limit [68]. Information was provided to the subjects on the dynamics of these signatures in the form of modulated sound, since this enabled the imitator to use this information at the same time as he or she was viewing the trajectory image information of the signature to be imitated. Eight people (one European, one Asian and six North Americans) provided us with three target reference signatures. Eight North American imitators were then asked to produce the imitations.

To make sure that the thresholds that were fixed based on this first experiment were not too restrictive in terms of type I error, a second experiment was performed using only true specimens. This second group comprised six right-handed signers (one European and five North Americans). Each signer provided nine signatures. The first three were used as reference signatures. The reference specimens in each small database were also analyzed in terms of how difficulty they were to imitate. This was done with the collaboration of forensic scientists [70] and with the help of a complexity measure specifically derived for this purpose [71].

These tests enabled us to tune the various decision parameters of the system and, since then, to use it in successful demonstrations for numerous visitors and potential customers (male and female, of different ages, North Americans, Europeans, Asians and Arabs). We are now in the process of planning complete experimental beta tests for some specific applications.

Acknowledgements

This work was supported by grants CRP-2097 from FCAR and OGP-000915 from CRSNG to Réjean Plamondon.

References

1. Plamondon, R., Lorette, G.: Automatic signature verification and writer identification: The state of the art. Pattern Recognition 22/2, 107-131 (1989).

2. Lorette, G., Plamondon, R.: Dynamic approaches to handwritten signature verification. In: R. Plamondon, C.G. Leedham (eds.) Computer Processing of Handwriting, pp. 20-47, World Scientific, Singapore: 1990.
3. Plamondon, R. Lorette, G.: On-line signature verification: How many countries are in the race? Proc. Int. Carnahan Conf. on Security Technology. Zurich 3-5, 183-191 (1989).
4. Plamondon, R., Lorette, G., Poulin G.: On the intrinsic, theoretical and technical difficulties of designing an automatic signature verification system. Proc. Third International Symposium on Handwriting and Computer Applications. Montréal, pp. 154-156 (1987).
5. Plamondon, R., Lorette G.: Designing and automatic signature verification system: Problem definition and system description. In: R. Plamondon, C.G. Leedham (eds.) Computer Processing of Handwriting, pp. 3-20, World Scientific, Singapore: 1990.
6. Plamondon, R., Yergeau, P.: A system for the analysis and synthesis of handwriting. Proc. Int. Workshop on Frontiers in Handwriting Recognition, pp. 167-179 (1990).
7. Leclerc, F., Plamondon, R.: Validation d'un modèle de la fonction de transfert du bras sur des signatures manuscrites. Proc. Vision Interface '90, 105-111 (1990).
8. Plamondon, R.: A model-based segmentation framework for computer processing of handwriting. Proc. 11th Int. Conf. on Pattern Recognition. The Hague, pp. 303-307 (1992).
9. Leclerc, F., Plamondon, R., Lorette, G.: Des gaussiennes pour la modélisation des signatures des tracés manuscrits. Traitement du signal, 347-358 (1992).
10. Plamondon, R., Yergeau, P., Brault, J.J.: A multi-level signature verification system. In: S. Impedovo, J.C. Simon (eds.) From Pixels to Features III, pp. 363-370, Elsevier, Amsterdam: 1992.
11. Plamondon, R.: Method and apparatus for comparing a test handwritten signature with a reference signature by using information relative to curvilinear and angular velocities of the signature. US Patent 5 101 437 (1992).
12. Schomaker, L.R.B., Plamondon, R.: The relation between axial pen force and pen-point kinematics in handwriting. Biol. Cybernetics 63, 277-289 (1990).

13. Plamondon, R., Parizeau, M.: Signature verification from position, velocity and acceleration signals: A comparative study. Proc. 9th Int. Conf. on Pattern Recognition, Rome, pp. 260-265 (1988).
14. Plamondon, R., Clément, B.: Dependence of peripheral and central parameters describing handwriting generation on movement direction. Human Movement Science, Thematic Issue on Handwriting 10, 193-221 (1991).
15. Plamondon, R.: What does differential geometry tell us about handwriting generation? Proc. Third Int. Symp. on Handwriting and Computer Applications, Montréal, pp. 11-13 (1987).
16. Hollerbach, J.M., Flash, T.: Dynamic interactions between limb segments during planar arm movements. Biol. Cybernetics 44, 67-77 (1982).
17. Evinger, D., Shaw, M.D., Peck, C.K., Manning, K.A., Baker, R.: Blinking and associated eye movements in humans, guinea pigs and rabbits. J. Neurophysiology 52, 323-339 (1984).
18. Ruitenbeek, J.C.: Invariants in loaded goal-directed movements. Biol. Cybernetics 51, 11-20 (1984).
19. Soechting, J.F.: Effect of target size on spatial and temporal characteristics of a pointing movement. Experimental Brain Research 54, 121-132 (1984).
20. Atkeson, C.G., Hollerbach, J.M.: Kinematic features of unrestrained vertical arm movements. Journal of Neuroscience 5/9, 2318-2330 (1985).
21. Flash, T., Hogan, N.: The coordination of arm movements: An experimentally confirmed mathematical model. J. Neuroscience 5, 1688-1703 (1985).
22. Gielen, C.C.A.M., van den Oosten, K., Pulltergunne, F.: Relation between EMG activation patterns and kinematic properties of aimed arm movements. J. Motor Behavior 17/4, 421-442 (1985).
23. Munhall, K.G., Ostry, D.J., Parush, A.: Characteristics of velocity profiles of speech movements. J. Exp. Psychology (Human Perception) 11, 454-474 (1985).
24. Ostry, D.J., Cooke, J.D., Munhall, K.G.: Velocity curves of human arm and speech movements. Exp. Brain Research 68, 37-46 (1987).

25. Kaminski, T.R., Gentille, A.M.: A kinematic comparison of single and multi-joint pointing movements. Exp. Brain Research 78, 547-556 (1989).
26. Plamondon, R.: A handwriting model based on differential geometry. In: R. Plamondon, C.Y. Suen, M. Simner (eds.) Computer Recognition and Human Production of Handwriting, pp. 179-192, World Scientific, Singapore: 1989.
27. Plamondon, R.: A theory of rapid movements. In: G.E. Stelmach and J. Requin (eds.) Tutorials in Motor Behavior II, pp. 55-69, Elsevier, The Netherlands: 1992.
28. Plamondon, R., Maarse, F.J.: An evaluation of motor models of handwriting. IEEE Trans. on Syst. Man Cybernetics 19/5, 1060-1072 (1989).
29. Plamondon, R., Alimi, A., Yergeau, P., Leclerc, F.: Modelling velocity profiles of rapid movements: A comparative study. In press, Biological Cybernetics.
30. Morasso, P., Mussa-Ivaldi, F.A.: Trajectory formation and handwriting: A computational model. Biological Cybernetics 45, 131-142 (1982).
31. Van Galen, G.P.: Handwriting and drawing: A two-stage model of motor behavior. In: G.E. Stelmach and J. Requin (eds.) Tutorial in Motor Behavior, pp. 567-578, North-Holland, Amsterdam: 1980.
32. Denier van der Gon, J.J., Thuring J.P., Strackee, J.: A handwriting simulator. Physics in Medecine and Biology 6, 407-414 (1962).
33. Dooijes, E.H.: Analysis of handwriting movements. Acta Psychologica 54, 99-114 (1983).
34. MacDonald, J.S.: Experimental studies of handwriting signals. Ph.D. Dissertation, MIT, Cambridge, MA (1964).
35. Yasuhara, M.: Experimental studies of handwriting process. Rep. Univ. Electro. Comm. 25, 233-254 (1975).
36. Maarse, F.: The study of handwriting movement. Ph.D. Dissertation, University of Nijmegen, The Netherlands (1987).
37. Mermelstein, P., Eden, M.: Experiments on Computer Recognition of Connected Handwritten Words. Inform. Contr. 7, 225-270 (1964).

38. Hollerbach, J.M.: An oscillation theory of handwriting. Biological Cybernetics 39, 139-156 (1981).
39. Plamondon, R., Lamarche, F.: Modelization of handwriting: A system approach. In: H.S.R. Kao, G.P. van Galen, R. Hoosain (eds.) Graphonomics: Contemporary Research in Handwriting, pp. 169-183, Elsevier, Amsterdam: 1986.
40. Abend, W., Bizzi, E., Morasso, P.: Human arm trajectory formation. Brain 105, 331-348 (1982).
41. Morasso, P.: Spatial control of arm movements. Exp. Brain Res. 42, 223-227 (1981).
42. Flash, T.: Organizing principles underlying the formation of arm trajectories. Ph.D. Dissertation, MIT, Cambridge, MA (1983).
43. Edelman, S., Flash, T.: A model of handwriting. Biological Cybernetics 57, 25-36 (1987).
44. Plamondon, R.: Handwriting control: A functional model. In: M.J.R. Cotterill (ed.) Models of Brain Function, pp. 563-574, Cambridge University Press, U.K.: 1989.
45. Gutman, S.R., Gottlieb, G.L.: Exponential model with non-linear time of reaching movement: Trajectory time profile, strategies, variability. Third IBRO World Congress of Neuroscience, Montréal, Canada, August 4-9, Paper P39.23, 262 (1991).
46. Plamondon, R.: On the origin of asymmetric bell-shaped velocity profiles in rapid-aimed movements. In: G.E. Stelmach and J. Requin (eds.) Tutorials in Motor Neuroscience, pp. 283-295, Kluwer: 1991.
47. Alimi, A., Plamondon, R.: Performance analysis of handwritten stroke generation models. Proc. 3rd International Workshop on Frontiers in Handwriting Recognition, Buffalo (1993).
48. Plamondon, R., Li-de Yu, Stelmach, G.E., Clément, B.: On the automatic extraction of biomechanical information from handwriting signals. IEEE Trans. on Systems, Man, and Cybernetics, SMC-21, 90-101 (1991).
49. Plamondon, R., Stelmach, G.E., Teasdale, N.: Motor program coding representation from a handwriting generator: The production of line responses. Biological Cybernetics 63, 443-451 (1990).

50. Plamondon, R.: The generation of rapid human movements. Part I: A Δlog-normal law. Technical Report EPM/RT-93/4, École Polytechnique de Montréal (1993).
51. Plamondon, R.: A kinematic theory of rapid human movements. Part I: Movement representation and generation. Submitted to Biological Cybernetics (1993).
52. Plamondon, R.: Looking through handwriting generation from a velocity control perspective. In: G.E. Stelmach and G.P. van Galen (eds.) Acta Psychologica Special Issue on Motor Control of Handwriting: 1993.
53. Plamondon, R.: A kinematic theory of rapid human movements. Part II: Movement time and control. Submitted to Biological Cybernetics (1993).
54. Plamondon, R.: The generation of rapid human movements. Part II: Quadratic and power laws. Technical Report EPM/RT-93/5, École Polytechnique de Montréal (1993).
55. Plamondon, R.: Understanding stroke generation: A global neuromuscular approach. Proc. 6th Int. Conf. on Handwriting and Drawing, Paris (1993).
56. Parizeau, M., Plamondon, R.: A comparative analysis of regional correlation, dynamic time warping and skeletal tree matching for signatures. IEEE Trans. on Pattern Analysis and Machine Intelligence 12/7, 710-717 (1990).
57. Herbst, N.M., Morrisey, H.: Signature verification method and apparatus. U.S. Patent 3 983 535 (1976).
58. Herbst, N.M., Liu C.N.: Signature verification method and apparatus utilizing both acceleration and pressure characteristics. U.S. Patent 4 128 829 (1978).
59. Worthington, T.K., Chainer, T.J., Williford, J.D., Gundersen, S.C.: IBM dynamic signature verification. In: J.B. Grimson and H.J. Kugler (eds.) Computer Security, pp. 129-154, Amsterdam: 1985.
60. Sakoe, H., Chiba, S.: Dynamic programming algorithm optimization for spoken word recognition. IEEE Trans. Acoust., Speech, Signal Processing ASSSP-26/1, 43-49 (1978).
61. Sato, Y., Kogure, K.: On-line signature verification based on shape, motion, and writing pressure. Proc. 6th Int. Conf. Pattern Recognition, Munich, pp. 823-826 (1982).

62. Yasuhara, M., Oka, M.: Signature verification experiment based on non-linear time alignment: A feasibility study. IEEE Trans. Syst., Man, Cybern. SMC-17, 212-216 (1977).
63. Cheng, Y.C., Lu, S.Y.: Waveform correlation by tree matching. IEEE Trans. Pattern Anal. Machine Intell. PAMI-7/3, 299-305 (1985).
64. Lu, S.Y.: A tree matching algorithm based on node splitting and merging. IEEE Trans. Pattern Anal. Machine Intell. PAMI-6/2, 249-256 (1984).
65. Parizeau, M., Plamondon, R.: Relative performances of signature, handwritten password and initials for personal identification. Proc. Third International Symposium on Handwriting and Computer Applications, Montréal, pp. 164-166 (1987).
66. Parizeau, M., Plamondon, R.: What types of scripts can be used for personal identity verification? In: R. Plamondon, C.Y. Suen, M. Simner (eds.) Computer Recognition and Human Production of Handwriting, pp. 77-90, World Scientific, Singapore: 1989.
67. Fréchette, P., Plamondon, R.: Architecture parallèle basée sur des TMS 320C30 pour la comparaison de signaux. Proc. Vision Interface '91, Calgary, pp. 128-134 (1991).
68. Plamondon, R., Yergeau, P., Brault, J.J.: A multi-level signature verification system. In: S. Impedevo, J.C. Simon (eds.) From Pixels to Features III, pp. 363-370, Elsevier, Amsterdam: 1992.
69. Brault, J.J., Plamondon, R.: How to detect problematic signers for automatic signature verification? Proc. 1989 Int. Carnahan Conf. on Security Technology, Zurich, pp. 127-132 (1989).
70. Brault, J.J., Plamondon, R.: Can we measure the intrinsic complexity of a signature to be imitated? Proc. 5th Handwriting Conference, Tempe, Arizona, pp. 169-171 (1991).
71. Brault, J.J., Plamondon, R.: A complexity measure of handwritten curves: Modelling dynamic signature forgery. In press. IEEE Trans. on System, Man and Cybernetics (1993).

Algorithms for Signature Verification

Giuseppe Pirlo

Dipartimento di Informatica, Università degli Studi di Bari
via Amendola 173, 70126 Bari, Italy

1. Introduction

The need to assure that only the right people are authorized to high-security accesses has led to develop systems for automatic personal verification.

In general, personal verification can be established using [1]:

1. Physical mechanism belonging to the individual (i.e., key or badge)

2. Information (i.e., numeric combination or password)

3. Personal identifying characteristics (i.e., fingerprint or signature).

Traditional systems for high security accesses, which are based on physical mechanisms or information, did not involve personal characteristics of the individual. They can be used by anyone which is suitably trained and therefore they do not allow to perform secure verification of the declared identity of an individual. In this sense, systems based on personal characteristics of identification are much more significant. Personal characteristics can be divided into two classes: physical and behavioural.

- The physical characteristics of the individual are almost unchangeable and stable during the life of the individual. Physics characteristics useful for personal verification are fingerprints, face profile, retina, palmprint and 3D geometry of the hand, DNA factor.

- The behavioural characteristics of the individual can change depending on environmental and personal conditions. Behavioural characteristics used for personal verification are speech, signature, keystroke dynamics and rhythm of pulsations.

In order to evaluate the effectiveness of the characteristics used for personal verification, several factors must be considered. Among the most significant ones there are the accuracy of the system, the verification speed, the simplicity of the enrolment process, the capability to work on distribuited systems in remote access mode and the consensus of the users in utilise specific devices for personal verification. For istance, techniques based on retina analysis are very effective in terms of error rates, but they are generally not accepted by the users which fear for their health. Conversely, techniques based on fingerprint analysis are usually not accepted because they inspire the idea of criminality. Among the others, the signature has the fundamental advantage that it is the customary way of identifying an individual in daily operations such as automated banking transactions and electronic fund transfers. Moreover the signature is the most common form in legal attestation and it is frequently used in our daily life as materials for certification of an individual. Furthermore, the signature is written for identification purposes rather than legibility and people continuously try to personalize it, therefore it contains a lot of information about the writer.

In this field, the most significant attempts to develop high performance Signature Verification Systems (SVS) for signature verification are based on the common knowledge that the process of signature apposition originated from ballistic bodily motions, i.e. rapid, practiced motions which do not involve sensory feedback but are predetermined by the brain. Thus, signing is very different from other handwriting processes. In fact unlike controlled motions, which are generally slow and precise, ballistic motions are rapid, practiced motions whose accuracy increases with speed [2]. Furthermore, although the signature always contains informations about the signer, it is an extremely individual entity which depends on many physical and cultural factors. Additional factors, which range from the state of mind of the writer to the posture adopted during signing, can produce other variations on a day-to-day basis. The conclusive result is that no two genuine signatures of the same writer are ever precisely the same [3]. The consequence is that signature verification is a very difficult task. User's applications of secure personal verification require a very high accuracy and therefore the major efforts are rightly devoted to develop systems with very low error rates. Specifically, in this field two types of error rates must be considered: the false-rejection error rate (called type I error rate) caused by the rejection of genuine signatures, and the false-acceptation error rate (called type II error) caused by the acceptance of forgeries [3].

2. Signature Verification Systems

The diagram of Figure 1 shows the fundamental steps in the signature verification process.

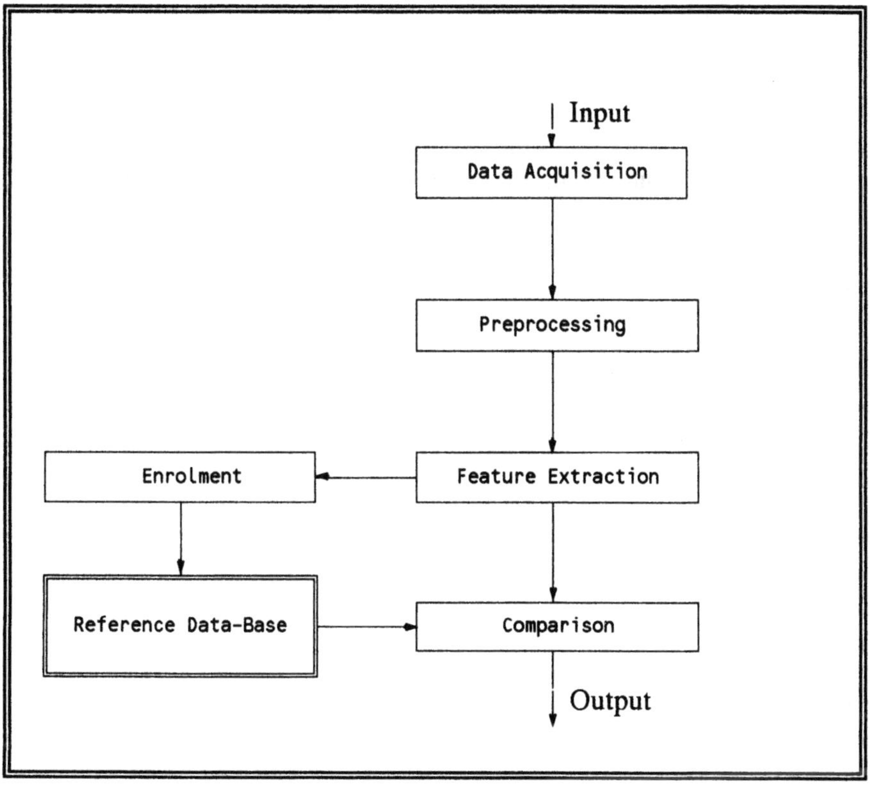

Figure 1. The Signature Verification Process

After data acquisition, the preprocessing step removes spurious noise on the input signature to get significant informations from raw data. In the feature extraction step, some discriminant features, which will be used to discriminate genuine signatures from forgeries, are extracted. These features are stored into a personal data-base by an enrolment step of the training phase. In the test phase the comparison step allows to match features of the input signature with those in the reference data-base. The result is used to judge the authenticity of the input signature.

2.1. Data Acquisition

The kind of data acquisition device strongly differentiates the systems for signature verification. An acquisition device can be for on-line signature acquisition or for off-line signature acquisition.

On-line (or dynamical) acquisition devices generate electronic signals representative of the traced signature during the writing process. The signals generated can be coordinate signals, pressure and force signals but also pen-down and pen-up signals (a pen-down movement is the operation of pulling down the tip of the pen toward the writing plane, while a pen-up movement is the operation of lifting the tip of the pen from the writing plane). Figure 2 shows two examples of on-line signatures. Pen-down (*) and pen-up (•) signals are also reported. Conversely, off-line (or static) acquisition devices perform data acquisition after the writing process has been completed. In Figure 3, two off-line signatures acquired by real noisy images are shown.

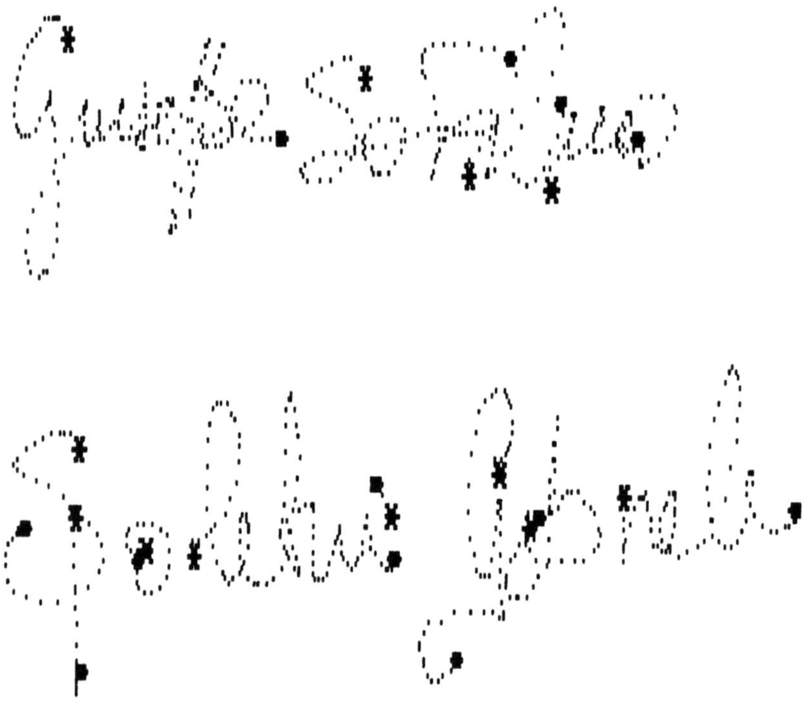

Figure 2. Example of on-line signatures

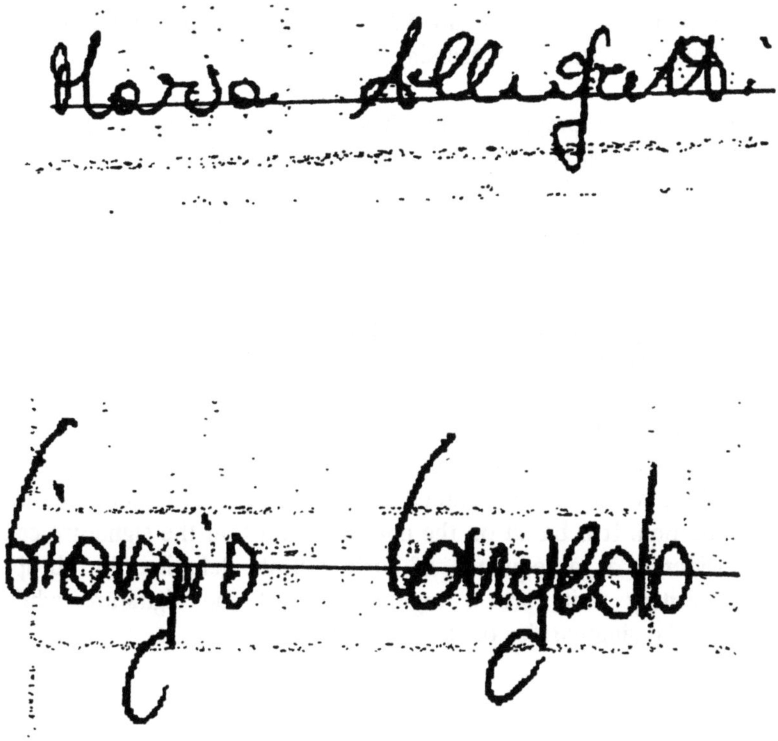

Figure 3. Example of off-line signatures

The acquisition technology of handwritten data is also a field of relevant interest. Nowadays graphic tablets or integrated tablet-display devices are generally used for on-line signature acquisition [4], while cameras or scanners are used for off-line data acquisition [5]. Two significant papers concerning with on-line and off-line acquisition technologies and devices are those of refs. [4] and [5] respectively.

Depending on the input device two classes of systems have been designed for signature verification: on-line or dynamic SVSs and off-line or static SVSs. On-line SVSs offer some advantages such as the high man-computer interactivity and the possibility for the user to adapt himself to the machine and vice-versa. They are generally more efficient than off-line systems and real systems for dynamical signature verification have already been commercialized.

2.2. Preprocessing

The aim of this phase is to process raw data, signals or images, to emphasize information relevant for further processing.

In an on-line SVS, the preprocessing phase reduces noise on signature, normalize signature length and performs signature segmentation.

Noise reduction and length normalization is accomplished by traditional techniques. Noise reduction is usually carried out by Fourier analysis. Length normalization can easily be performed by several different approaches, among the others a simple approach is based on a b-spline interpolation procedure and on a fast resampling process [6].

A more complex task is the segmentation of the signature into basic strokes. The approach proposed by Dimauro, Impedovo and Pirlo consider a segment as each piece of the written trace included between a pen-down and a pen-up movement of the pen. It is based on the consideration that the signature can rightly be considered as a sequence of writing units delimited by abrupt interruptions. Writing units are a regular part of the signature while interruptions are the singularities of the signature [7].

Figure 4. A signature with its components

From the demonstration that singularities occur in definite positions in the signature of an individual, it follows that only a finite set of writing units, called *components or fundamental strokes*, can be generated by each signer [8]. Figure 4 shows a signature and its components.
Moreover, the ballistic motion underlying the generation of writing units of the signature is the product of several antagonist muscle pairs. The biomechanical characteristic of each muscle pair is strictly personal, such as the synchronization of the motions due to several muscle pairs. Therefore, the identification of the writing units of complex handwriting signals provides certain informations for personal verification. Thus, although signatures of the same writer may be composed by a different number of strokes, and also signatures with the same number of components may result very different each other because of the different pen-lift distribution, the strokes that each writer uses to affix his signature are well defined and belong to a finite set of components.

Another approach has been proposed by Plamondon, Yergeau and Brault [9]. It is based on the curvilinear and angular velocity signals of the pen movements during signing. In this approach the basic elements of the handwritten signature are the *components* and the *strings*. To locate these segments, four threshold values must be set: the upper bound for the angular velocity value, the lower bound for the curvilinear velocity value, the minimal period of time for a handwritten string and the minimal period of time for lifting of the pen tip. Each handwritten component is delimited by two successive significant liftings of the pen along the trajectory of the signature, and each handwritten string is delimited by two successive portions of the trajectory verifying specific characteristics in terms of time-duration and angular/curvilinear velocity.

Another interesting approach has been proposed by Brault and Plamondon [10]. In this approach the segmentation points are found with the help of a two steps procedure. The first step weights the perceptual importance of every signature coordinate. The second step identifies the segmentation points as the points which are locally more significant from a perceptual point of view.

A more recent segmentation technique is based on a dynamical splitting procedure. The basic idea is to perform the splitting by using the informations about both the reference signatures and the input signature, in fact the reference signature are segmented into basic components taking into consideration the characteristics of the input signature. This technique firstly detects the Candidate Splitting Points, which are the maximum points and minimum points in the vertical direction on each reference signature and on the input signature. Then, by an elastic matching procedure, the best coupling between the Candidate Splitting Points of the input signature and of the reference signatures allow to identify the set of coupled strokes [11].

An off-line system for signature verification must be able process a signature apposed on specific paper forms (like checkes). In this kind of systems the preprocessing phase deals with the localization of the signature in the picture, the extraction of the signature from the background, the thresholding and filtering. While noise reduction can be performed by Fourier analysis, the extraction of a signature image from the background can be solved with the help of a simple window operator [6]. A more complex task is the segmentation, in fact no dynamical information is available. Ammar, Yoshida and Fukumura [12] propose the segmentation of a signature by a tree structure identifying fundamental segments of the static image.

2.3. Feature Extraction

System proposed for signature verification can be classified according to the type of features used for verification: functions or parameters. When functions are used as features, the signature is characterized in terms of a mathematical time-function whose values constitute the feature set. Thus, function features are oriented to on-line signature verification. When parameters are used as features, the signature is characterized in terms of a set of values which are computed directly from the measured signals.

The performance of those systems based on function features are generally better than those which use specific parameters, but they are less efficient in term of computation speed.

In the past, a lot of parameters have been considered for signature verification [3]. In dynamic signature verification, parameters like total duration of the signing process, number of pen lifts and specific coefficients of the Walsh or Haar or Fourier Transform can be considered [13,14,15]. In static signature verification, the number of local extrema, the signature slant and also some coefficients derived from the Hadamard Transform can be used [16,17]. In both cases, the selection of the optimal set of parameters is a very difficult task due to the difficulty in obtaining useful statistical models of true and forgeries signatures [18].

For that to concern the main signals considered as feature functions, they are the position of the tip of the pen during the writing process [19], its velocity [20] (which can be computed from the first time derivative of position signals or by special devices), its acceleration [21] (which can be computed from the first time derivative of velocity signals or by special devices), and also the pressure or force of the tip of the pen on the writing tablet [22].

Furthermore, in the case of both parameters and functions, there are two approaches to the problem of feature selection: global and local. Global approaches analyse the signature as a whole, local approaches obtain features concerning with each segment of the signature. Local approaches are usually more time-consuming than global ones but they allow more accurate verification.

2.4. Comparison Process

The comparison process in a signature verification system tries to evaluate the authenticity of the test specimen by matching its features against those stored in the reference data-base. Several matching strategies can be adopted as Figure 5 shows:

- The simplest strategy is based on a *wholistic approach* and it consists in matching the test signature S^t with each one of the N^r reference signatures S^r, $r=1,2,...,N_r$, considered as a whole. This approach does not allow any regional evaluation of the signature.

- Another strategy is based on a *regional matching* approach. In this case the test signature S^t is splitted into segments $(S^t_1,S^t_2,...,S^t_k,...,S^t_n)$ as well as each reference signatures S^r into segments $(S^r_1,S^r_2,...,S^r_k,...,S^r_n)$. The matching between the test signature and each one of the reference signatures is performed by matching the corresponding segments. This approach allows a regional analysis of the signature but it is carried out in a one-by-one comparison process. Therefore a test signature is judged to be a genuine specimen if and only if a reference signature exists which is similar to the test signature in each one of its splitted regions. Then, this matching approach requires a very large set of reference signatures.

- The most powerful matching approach is the *multiple regional matching.* In this case each segment S_s^t, $s=1,2,...,N^s$, of the test signature is matched against the entire set of the corresponding segments $(S_s^1,S_s^2,...,S_s^h,...,S_s^{Nr})$ in the set of reference signatures. Therefore for each segment of the test signature a verification response R_s can be obtained. Then the test signature is judged to be a genuine specimen if each segment is judged to be genuine. This approach allows a regional evaluation of the signature without requiring a large set of reference signatures.

WHOLISTIC MATCHING

$$S^t \longleftrightarrow S^r \quad for \quad r = 1,2,\ldots,N^r$$

REGIONAL MATCHING

$$\left\{ \begin{array}{c} S_1^t \leftrightarrow S_1^r \\ S_2^t \leftrightarrow S_2^r \\ \ldots \\ S_k^t \leftrightarrow S_k^r \\ \ldots \\ S_n^t \leftrightarrow S_n^r \end{array} \right\} \; for \quad r = 1,2,\ldots,N^r$$

MULTIPLE REGIONAL MATCHING

$$for \;\; s = 1,2,\ldots,N^s \quad do \; \left\{ \begin{array}{c} S_s^t \leftrightarrow S_s^1 \\ S_s^t \leftrightarrow S_s^2 \\ \ldots \\ S_s^t \leftrightarrow S_s^h \\ \ldots \\ S_s^t \leftrightarrow S_s^{N^r} \end{array} \right\} \; obtaining \;\; R_s$$

Figure 5. Basic matching strategies

Furthermore, each comparison technique is based on a suitable similarity (or dissimilarity) measure. According to the type of features that are used, two kind of comparison techniques can be distinguished:

- When parameters are considered as features, the signatures are often described by vectors of parameters in a multidimensional feature metric space. The authenticity of a test specimen with respect to a set of training samples is then evaluated accordingly with traditional clustering criteria [23].

- When functions are considered as features, the matching techniques must also take into account the variations of signal duration from one signature to another (even if the specimens are produced by the same writer). Furthermore, random variations, due to pauses or hesitations of the writer, can create portions of signals, deletions, additions and gaps and complicate the problem of matching. To this purpose, several approaches have been proposed. The more interesting are those based on regional correlation and on dynamical non-linear time warping functions. Regional correlation tries to cut the signals into regions and to correlate corresponding regions over different time lags to find the best possible match for each pair of regions [24,25]. Dynamical non-linear time warping functions, which have been firstly used for speech recognition [26], allow to compress or expand the time axis of two specimens producing a minimum distance value [27].

In both cases, two of the most important problems which strongly affect the effectiveness of the comparison process are the selection of the optimal set of reference signatures and the selection of the optimal set of personal thresholds. In some cases the procedure for the selection of reference signatures considers both genuine specimens and forgeries. This approach is weak since in many practical cases fraudulent specimens are not available or they are of poor quality. Then it is much more significant to select the reference signatures directly from the set of genuine specimens and without any information about forgeries. In this direction, Yoshimura, Kato, Matsuda and Yoshimura [28] verified that three specimens are enough as representative, then they proposed a system which selects three signatures out of the reference writings. The selection is realized by clustering the reference writings into three clusters and selecting one specimen with minimax property from each cluster.

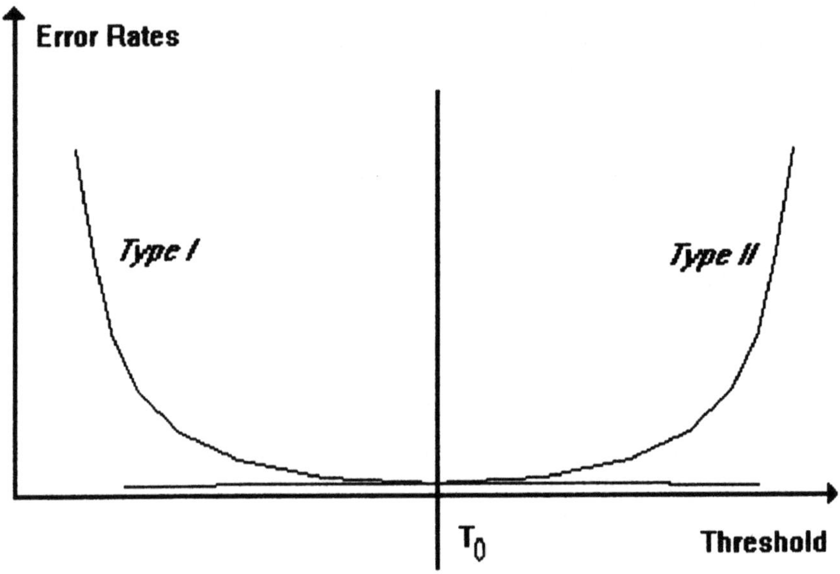

Figure 6. Threshold selection

Personal thresholds are generally obtained by comparing the reference signatures among themselves, taken two-by-two and storing the worst result of verification [9]. The proper selection of the threshold value for the acceptation / rejection rule strongly effects the performance of the system and specialize it for working in practical environement which generally requires different system characteristics. In Figure 6 the typical trend of Type I and Type II error rates versus the threshold value is displayed for a system with a classification rule of the kind:

if Similarity Measure $\geqslant T_0$ then reject the signature

if Similarity Measure $< T_0$ then accept the signature.

It is easy to observe how the selection of the threshold value T_0 allows to obtain different Type I and Type II error rates on average.

3. Systems Implementation

A lot of systems for signature verification have been developed in scientific laboratories and some of them have also been commercially distributed already. Them all have been designed by choosing suitable solutions in terms of devices and algorithms for each processing step. In the following some of the most recent systems for on-line and off-line signature verification which allow to focuse the major trends in current scientific research are introduced.

3.1. Systems for On-line Signature Verification

At present, in the field of on-line systems for signature verification, research is mainly dedicated to the detection of original features to be used for high-performance signature verification and to suitable matching techniques also with respect to local analysis of signatures.

A significant attempt in the first direction of the research has been accomplished by Yoshimura and Yoshimura [28]. In their work, they acquire the signature as coordinate signals and pressure signals and perform the comparison process by an elastic pattern matching technique. In fact, the dissimilarity measure between two signatures is obtained by following a procedure of six successive steps:

Step 1. Deletion of meaningless points (motionless or pressureless points).
Step 2. Adjustment of sampling points (by linear interpolation).
Step 3. Standardization of the location (he shifts the location of each signature in such a way as the centroid is located on the origin).
Step 4. Standardization of the size (he changes the size of each signature so that the variance of the coordinates and the variance of the pressure is uniform).
Step 5. Comparison by elastic matching of two signatures (he searches for and gets the warping function which minimizes a dissimilarity function).
Step 6. Determination of the dissimilarity measure (i.e. the minimal value of the dissimilarity function).

The novelty of this approach is in the formulation of the dissimilarity function which is different from the others proposed in the past. In fact it incorporates neither the velocity of pen movements nor the acceleration of it, but instead it uses the direction of pen movement [27]. The experimental test shows the effectiveness of this measure.

The second direction of research has been recently investigated by Plamondon, Yergeau and Brault which tries to combine both a parameter and a function approach [9]. They developed a multilevel signature verification system that uses one representation of the signature based on global parameters and two representations based on functions. The verification is performed by the step-wise process reported in the following:

Step 1. Calculation of curvilinear and angular velocity signals.
Step 2. Segmentation of signature in components and strokes.
Step 3. Calculation of dynamic parameters: total time of the trajectory during which the tip of the pen is contacting the digitizer, the percentage of time during which the tip is lifted, the percentage of time during which the pen is stopped etc.
Step 4. Normalization of the signature image (rotation and scaling).
Step 5. Signature verification by three distinct levels. The first level computes a weighted distance between the dynamic parameters of the test and the reference signatures. The second level computes intrinsic local correlation between portions of the test signature velocity signal with corresponding portions of the reference signature velocity. The third level of verification consists in calculating distances between the test and the reference signature trajectory images by local elastic matching. The three verification responces are combined in a global classification function, for example by a linear combination.

In order to emphasize the role of local characteristics for signature verification two new systems have been proposed by Dimauro, Impedovo and Pirlo [8,11].

The first system performs signature verification by a local verification strategy based on the spectral analysis of *components* (also called *fundamental strokes*). It is based on a segmentation of signatures in component. In the learning phase the components of the training specimens are classified by an improved k-means clustering technique using the following topological features:

- the index of the start point of the component
- the index of the end point of the component
- the component length (the number of samples)
- the number of local maxima in the vertical direction in the component
- the number of local minima in the vertical direction in the component.

For each cluster, some statistical parameters are calculated from the set of Fourier descriptors derived from each component, then a structured knowledge-base for each individual was obtained. It consists in the *Component Reference Table* and the *Structural Description Graph*. The Component Reference Table contains the features representative of the components of the signer. The

Structural Description Graph reports the acceptable sequences of components in the genuine signatures. Figure 7 illustrates the structure of the Structural Description Graph and of the Component Reference Table for the signatures of the signer of the specimen in Figure 4.

A COMPONENT DESCRIPTION GRAPH

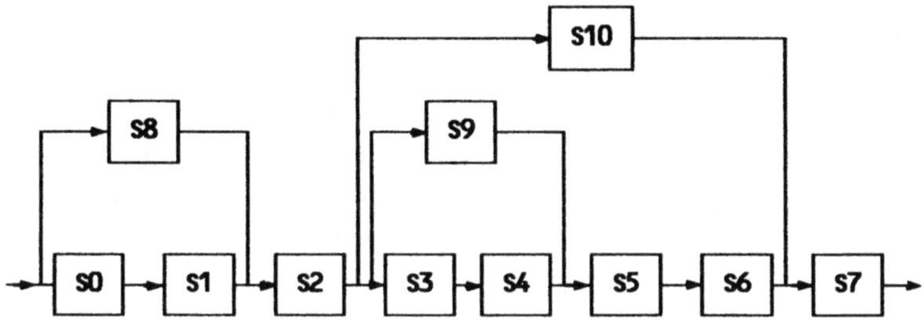

A COMPONENT REFERENCE TABLE

Signer Code : i	Class : S0 Set of Components of the Class S0	Class : S0 Feature Vectors
	Class : S1 Set of Components of the Class S1	Class : S1 Feature Vectors
	...	...
	Class : Sk Set of Components of the Class Sk	Class : Sk Feature Vectors
	...	...
	Class : S10 Set of Components of the Class S10	Class : S10 Feature Vectors

Figure 7. Example of knowledge-base

The verification process is then accomplished in two successive steps. In the first step the structural organization of the unknown signature is verified. In the second step each fundamental component of the signature is verified to obtain the conclusive verification response [8].

The second system uses a stroke-oriented verification strategy based on a new dynamical segmentation procedure. From the sets of Candidate Splitting Points, detected on each reference signature and on the test signature, a suitable set of coupled strokes is obtained. After the segmentation, regional thresholds are automatically computed for each set of coupled strokes of the reference signatures. The verification process follows a two-level strategy. At the first level, the segmentation results are used to perform a fast rejection of poor forgeries. At the second level, each stroke of the test signature is matched against each corresponding stroke of the reference signatures and the overall result is used to judge the whole signature [11].

3.2. Systems for Off-line Signature Verification

Static signature verification is rightly considered more difficult than the verification of dynamical signatures. In this field, the definition of methodologies for the description of the signature is of great relevance. In the approach proposed by Ammar, Yoshida and Fukumura [12], the signature is segmented horizontally into zones and vertically into elements. Information about the signature and its parts are organized in features and relations which are extracted quantitatively:

- In the *global description*, the signature is represented by a character string formed by concatenating the symbols corresponding to the value of the following five Global Constituents (features): the dominant slant in the signature, the presence of the lower zone parts, the number of elements in the signature, the comparison relation between signature length and its width, the ratio between the middle zone width and the signature width.

- In the *local description*, the signature is represented by a tree structure and is considered as composed by a set of ordered elements which are its vertically separable parts. Each element is described by two groups of constituents:

  - *Permanent Constituents*: global slant of the element, high density factor, comparison relation between the length of each element and its precedent, the position relation between the Element Baseline and the Global Baseline.

- *Nonpermanent Constituents*: the presence of upper, lower zone parts, the ratio between the middle zone width and the vertical extension of the element upper zone parts, the ratio between middle zone width and the element width, the ratio between the middle zone width and the vertical extension of the element lower zone parts.

A more recent attempt has been proposed by Sabourin and Drouhard [29] which uses the Directional Probability Density Function as a global feature vector. The comparison step is based on a completely connected feed-forward neural network classifier with a back-propagation learning algorithm.

4. Discussion and Conclusion

Signature verification is one of the most promising approaches for personal verification. Many algorithms have been proposed in order to develop high-performance systems for automatic signature verification. Obviously, as the experimental tests shown, these systems strongly differ in terms of accuracy even if it is not possible to compare their performances [30]. This is mainly due to the lacking of widely accepted protocol for experimental tests as well as of public signature data-bases. In fact, the experimental protocols can be very different from one research laboratory to another. All laboratory tests are certainly completely different from field-tests in which no control on the signer is generally required. Furthermore, genuine signatures are not easy to forge and laboratory tests generally take into consideration poor forgeries obtaining, of course, better experimental results. In order to face this problem a suitable set of classes of forgeries is commonly considered: the class of "random" forgeries, in which the forger uses his own signature instead of the signature to be tested; the class of "simple" forgeries, in which the forger makes no attempt to simulate or trace a genuine signature, and the class of "freehand" or "skilled" forgeries, in which the forger tries and practices imitating as closely as possible the static and dynamic informations of a genuine signature.

Then, for the development of the future SVSs, additional reasearch is necessary both in the theoretical field of handwriting generation processes for a complete understanding about the signing process and in the practical field for the development of ergonomic I/O devices and advanced algorithms able to face with the high variability of humans in signing.

References

1 Proc. of SECURTECH, Washington D.C., April 7-9, 1992.

2 R.Plamondon and F.J.Maarse, "An Evaluation of Motor Models of Handwriting", *IEEE Trans. on SMC*, vol. 19, n. 5, pp. 1060-1072, 1989.

3 R.Plamondon and G.Lorette, "Automatic signature verification and writer identification - the state of the art", *Pattern Recognition*, vol. 22, no. 2, pp. 107-131, 1989.

4 C.A.Higgins and D.M.Ford, "Stylus driven interfaces - The electronic paper concept", in Proc. of ICDAR '91, Sept.30-Oct.2, 1991, pp. 853-862.

5 S.Impedovo, L.Ottaviano and S.Occhinegro, "Optical character recognition - A survey", International Journal of Pattern Recognition and Artificial Intelligence, vol.5, n. 1-2, June 1991.

6 T.Pavlidis, "Algorithms for Graphics and Image Processing", Berlin Heidelberg, Springer Verlag 1982.

7 M.Castellano, G.Dimauro, S.Impedovo and G.Pirlo, "On-line signature verification system through stroke analysis", in Proc. AFCET Int. Conf. on New Concepts in Computer Science, 1990, pp. 47-53.

8 G.Dimauro, S.Impedovo, G.Pirlo, "A stroke-oriented approach to signature verification", in *From Pixels to Features III - Frontiers in Handwriting Recognition*, S. Impedovo and J.C.Simon eds., Elsevier Publ., pp. 371-384, 1992.

9 R.Plamondon, P.Yergeau and J.J.Brault, "A multi-level signature verification system", in *From Pixels to Features III - Frontiers in Handwriting Recognition*, S.Impedovo and J.C.Simon eds., Elsevier Publ., pp. 363-370, 1992.

10 J.J.Brault and R.Plamondon, "Segmentation des Signatures Manuscrites", Proc. of Vision Interface '89, London, Ontario, pp. 110-116, 1989.

11 G.Dimauro, S.Impedovo and G.Pirlo, "On-line Signature Verification by a Dynamical Segmentation Technique", Proc. of IWFHR-3, Buffalo, NY, pp. 262-271, May 1993.

12 M.Ammar, Y.Yoshida and T.Fukumura, "Structural Description and Classification of Signature Images", *Pattern Recognition*, vol. 23, n. 7, pp. 697-710, 1990.

13 M.Castellano, S.Impedovo, A.Mingolla and G.Pirlo, "A spectral analysis based signature verification system", in Lecture Notes in Computer Science, vol. 399, *Recent Issues in Pattern Analysis and Recognition*, G. Goos and J.Hartmanis Eds., Berlin-Heidelberg: Springer Verlag, 1988, pp. 316-323.

14 C.F.Lam and D.Kamins, "Signature recognition through spectral analysis", *Pattern Recognition*, vol. 22, n. 1, pp. 39-44, 1989.

15 K.P.Zimmermann and M.J.Varady, "Handwriter identification from one-bit quantized, pressure patterns", *Pattern Recognition*, vol. 18, pp. 63-72, 1985.

16 M.Ammar, Y.Yoshida and T.Fukumura, "Feature extraction and selection for simulated signature verification", Proc. of 3rd Int. Symp. on Handwriting and Comput. Applicat., pp. 167-169, Montreal 1987.

17 W.F.Nemcek and W.C.Lin, "Experimental investigation of automatic signature verification", *IEEE Trans. on Sys. Man and Cybern.*, vol. 4, pp. 121-126.

18 M.Castellano, G.Dimauro, S.Impedovo and G.Pirlo, "Decision making process in a signature verification system", in *Progress in Image Analysis and Processing*, V. Cantoni Ed., Singapore: World Scientific, 1989, pp. 610-614.

19 Y.Sato and K.Kogure, "On-line signature verification based on shape, motion and handwriting pressure", Proc. of 6th ICPR, vol. 2, pp. 823-826, Munich, 1982.

20 G.Lorette and R.Plamondon, "On-line handwritten signature recognition based on data analysis and clustering", Proc. of 7th ICPR, vol. 2, pp. 1284-1287, Montreal, 1984.

21 N.M.Herbst and C.N.Liu, "Automatic signature verification based on accelerometry", in *IBM Journal Res. and Develop.* pp.245-253, 1977.

22 H.D.Crane and J.S.Ostrem, "Automatic Signature Verification Using a Three-Axis Force-Sensitive Pen", *IEEE Trans. on Sys. Man and Cybern.*, vol.13, n. 3, 1983.

23 D.J.Hand, *Discrimination and Classification*, John Wiley and Sons Publ., 1981.

24 J.S.Lew, "Optimal accelerometer layouts for Data Recovery in Signature Verification", *IBM J. Res. Dev.*, vol. 24, pp. 496-511, 1980.

25 J.S.Lew, "An Improved Regional Correlation Algorithm for Signature Verification which permits small Speed Changes between handwriting Segments", *IBM J. Res. Dev.*, vol. 27, pp. 181-185, 1983.

26 L.R.Rabiner and S.E.Levinson, "Isolated and Connected Word recognition - Theory and Selected Applications", *IEEE Trans. on Communications*, vol. 29, n. 5, pp. 621-659, May 1981.

27 I.Yoshimura and M.Yoshimura, "On-line signature verification incorporating the direction of pen movement - An experimental examination of the effectiveness", in *From Pixels to Features III - Frontiers in Handwriting Recognition*, S.Impedovo and J.C.Simon eds., Elsevier Publ., pp. 353-362, 1992.

28 M.Yoshimura, Y.Kato, S.Matsuda and I.Yoshimura, "On-line Signature Verification Incorporating the Direction of Pen Movement", IEICE Transactions, vol. 74, n. 7, July 1991.

29 R.Sabourin and J.P.Drouhard, "Off-line Signature verification Using Directional PDF and Neural networks", Proc. of 11th IAPR, The Hague, The Netherlands, pp. 321-325, 1992.

30 M.Perizeau and R.Plamondon, "A Comparative Analysis of Regional Correlation, Dynamic Time Warping, and Skeletal Tree Matching for Signature Verification", *IEEE Trans. on PAMI*, vol. 12. n. 7, pp. 710-717, July 1990.

Handwritten Signature Verification: A Global Approach

Fathallah Nouboud

Département Math-Info, Université du Québec à Trois-Rivières, C.P. 500, Trois-Rivières, Québec, Canada G9A 5H7, Fax: (int)-1-819-376-5012. E-mail: fathallah_nouboud@uqtr.uquebec.ca

Abstract. This paper presents an off-line handwritten signature verification system based on a global approach. The signature is represented by characteristic curves extracted from its image. These curves describe the general shape of the signature and ignore the slight details that vary from a genuine signature to another. The verification is based on the comparison of characteristic curves by dynamic programming, which is a very powerful method for curves comparison. The experimental results are very promising. Some improvements of the comparison method are under way. A large database is under construction and other methods are being explored (neural networks, geometric parameters,..).

Keywords: handwritten signature verification, off-line identification, images, dynamic programming.

1. Introduction

The verification of handwritten signatures is a very difficult problem [1]. It is even more difficult when we deal with off-line aquisition, since all the dynamic feature are lost (duration, velocity, acceleration, pressure,..). The difficulty is increased by the variations between genuine signatures, since the same person can write quite different signatures.

An automatic system for signature verification can be very helpful in the processing of bankchecks, since it will allow the verification of all checks and the reduction of fraud. But, the procedure should be fast, use inexpensive hardware and have a good recognition rate. Particularly, the acceptance rate of genuine signatures must be very high, even at the expense of a moderately high acceptance rate of forgeries. The rejected checks will be verified by human operators [2,3].

2. Data acquisition and preprocessing

The signatures are written on plain white paper (we used pens of different types and colors). We will use bank checks later, and implement methods for extracting the signature from the background.

The acquisition of the signature image can be performed either by a camera or a scanner. When the camera is used, binarization and filtering must be performed before further processing. But with the scanner, the image is automatically thresholded and the output is of high quality.

The size of the signature must be normalized since we use a cumulative distance (dynamic programming) during the comparison step. Thus we realized a software zoom to perform the size normalization. The system also corrects the orientation of the signature to the horizontal position. Figure 1 shows the data-flow diagram of the system.

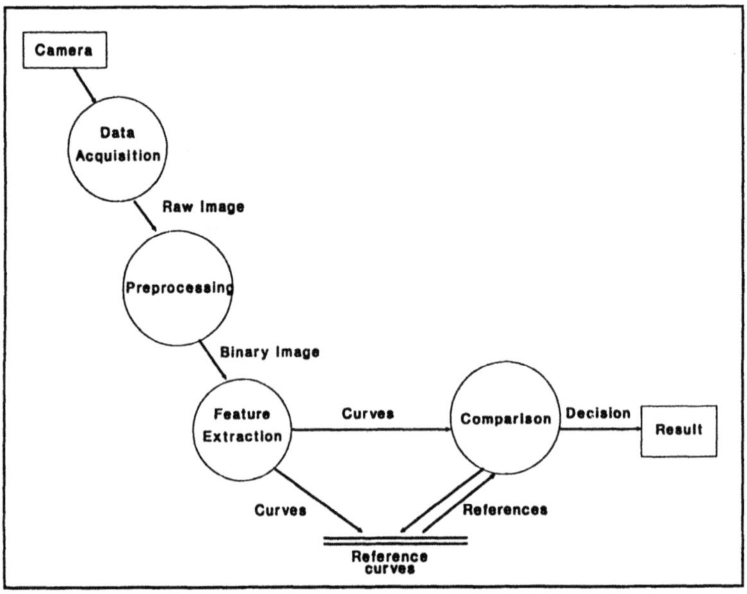

Fig. 1. The data-flow diagram of the system

3. Characteristic curves extraction

Characteristic curves are extracted by scanning the image. Figure 2 shows an example of such a curve. This curve describes the general shape of the signature. Other similar curves can be used too.

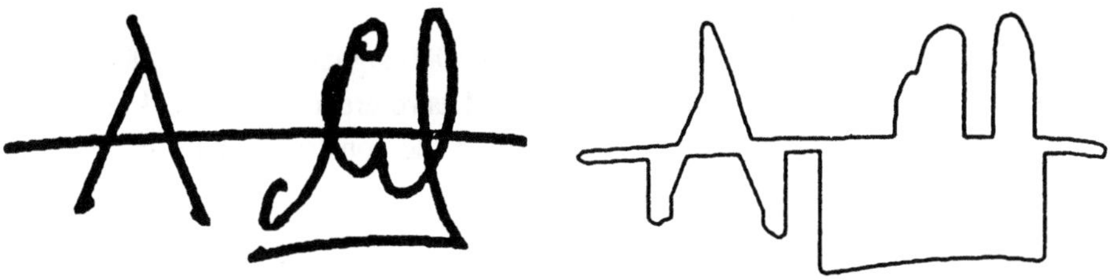

signature outlines of the signature

Fig. 2. External lines of the signature

4. Comparison

The curves representing the input signature are compared to those of the references. This comparison is carried out by dynamic programming. We use the method of [4] where the distance is computed in a strip around the line (0,0) to (I,J), rather than around the diagonal line (I and J being the lengths of the curves being compared).

The cumulative distance g(i,j) is recursively computed by

$$g(i,j) = \min \left| \begin{array}{l} d(i,j) + g(i,j-1) \\ d(i,j) + g(i-1,j) \\ 2*d(i,j) + g(i-1,j-1) \end{array} \right|$$

This algorithm is very efficient but it can be improved [5]. When the comparison is performed uniformly on the entire curves, the cumulative nature of the distance can sometimes affect the result. There are parts of the curves that are more invariant and contain more information. We are working on a method to detect automatically these parts and compute a weighted distance between the two curves. This method should increase the effectiveness of the comparison process and improve the recognition results.

5. Experimentation

Three experimental studies have been carried out on the system. The fourth one is under way.

5.1. Characteristic curves only

In this experience the database contained 1000 signatures from 100 persons [3]. For each signer 6 signatures were retained as references and the 4 remainder for test. The recognition result is 92.5%. With the constraint of keeping the FRR(1) under 2%, the FAR(2) is of about 8%.

5.2. Curves and parameters

This experience was carried out on a set of 1000 bank checks (48 signers). In addition the module based on characteristic curves (described above), another module based on geometric parameters was used too [6]. In this module 39 parameters are computed: inertia moments, slopes of the signature outlines, density of the lines, perimeter, surface..

The most stable and discriminating parameters are selected to represent the signature. The recognition result was significantly improved: FRR=2.1% and FAR=1.8%.

5.3. Curves, parameters and Neural Networks

This experience used the same database as the previous one. Three representations of the signature were used: image, curves and geometric parameters [7]. The system contains two layers involving 4 networks. The recognition result was: FRR=3.3% and FAR=0.6%.

5.4. Experience under way

The previous experiences were carried out on european signatures witch can be very different from north-american ones. We are constructing a large database of north-american signatures. We are building a database involving different categories of the population (based on age, occupation, sexe, writing hand, etc..).

We are working on an improved version of the comparison method described above. We will also use some geometric parameters in order to complete the representation of the signatures.

Neural networks can be of great interest for signature verification. Several systems are based on this technology. For example Sabourin et al [8,9] use a directional probability density function, derived from directional values of gradient vectors located on the signatures's line. They use a connected feed-forward neural network classifier. The recognition rate they obtained is almost 96%.

We believe that neural networks constitute a very promising way for this field and we are working on a new method based on the previous works and using neural networks.

---

(1) FRR: False Rejection Rate (i.e. rejection of genuine signatures).
(2) FAR: False Acceptance Rate (i.e. acceptance of forgeries).

Conclusion

The various experiences carried out on this system show that it is a good approach for signature verification. However it must be improved (by improving the dynamic programming method) and completed with other methods such as geometric parameters and neural networks.

We are working on these improvements and we will carry out the experimental tests on the new database under construction.

Acknowledgements. This work was supported by grants from SEPT (Service d'Études communes de la Poste et de France Télécom), and by FIR grant from Université du Québec à Trois-Rivières. We thank Stephane Turcotte and Marc Nolette for their collaboration.

References

1. Plamondon R. and Lorette G.: "Automatic signature verification and writer identification. State of the art". Pattern Recognition vol.22 no.2 p. 107-131 1989

2. Nouboud F., Cuozzo F., Collot R. and Achemlal M.: "Authentification de signatures manuscrites par programmation dynamique" Congrès PIXIM, Paris, p. 345-360, 1988

3. Nouboud F.: "Contribution à l'étude et à la mise au point d'un système d'authentification de signatures manuscrites". Doctorate thesis from université de Caen. 1988

4. Paliwal K.K., Agarwal A. and Sinha S.S.: "Modification over Sakoe and Chiba's dynamic warping algorithm for isolated word recognition" IEEE International conference on Acoustics Speech and Signal Processing, vol. 2-3 p. 1259-1261. 1982

5. Brault J.J. and Plamondon R.: "Global and local time warping function for handwritten curves comparison". Proc. 3rd Int. Symp. on Handwriting and Comut. Applic., p. 56-58. Montréal 1987.

6. Revillet M.J. "Vérification de signatures sur chèques postaux" International Workshop on Frontiers in Handwriting recognition, p. 767-773 1991

7. Cardot H., Revenu M., Victorri B. et Revillet M.J.: "Des réseaux neuronnaux pour l'authentification des signatures manuscrites". Colloque National sur l'Écrit et le Document, Nancy. p. 250-255 1992

8. Sabourin R. et Drouhard J.P.: "Off-Line Signature Verification Using Directional PDF and Neural Networks". Proc. 11th Int. Conf. on Pattern Recognition. The Hague, The Netherlands, 1992.

9. Sabourin R. Drouhard J.P., Gagné L. and Paquet N.: "Automatic Handwritten Signature Verification Using Directional PDF and Neural Networks: a Feasibility Study". Conférence et Exposition sur l'automatisation Industrielle, Montréal. 1992

Part 9

Application of handwriting recognition

Total Approach for Practical Character Recognition System Development

Kunio Sakai, Yoshiaki Kurosawa, and Takeshi Mishima
Toshiba Corporation

Abstract

This paper gives an overview of OCR and its applications. We focus on character recognition technology rather than other technologies such as layout understanding, post-processing, and other topics, because the character recognition is more important for OCRs. The other technologies are briefly explained. An overview of application is given in the last sections, with some actual examples. The purpose of this paper is to look at both sides of the OCR field - technology and applications - because it is the combination of both which has been a critical factor for character recognition development in the past. This is also likely to be the case in the future.

1. Introduction

The development of the OCR field has two major thrusts: technology improvement and expansion of applications field. This is one of the distinguishing features of the OCR field when compared with other fields such as speech recognition and image understanding. The difference is that OCR has had a certain market size in the past even when its capabilities were limited. This reason is that limited specifications for a sheet of paper, format, and especially for the quality of handprinted and printed characters was possible in the OCR field.

In that sense, it is important to look at both sides of OCR at the same time; they are closely related to each other. That is the purpose of this paper.

On-line Character Recognition is an important part of the character recognition field and it is best to consider it in terms of OCR technology and applications. However, it is too large to cover in this paper, so it has been left out.

The overall structure of an OCR is shown in Figure 1. A scanned image is analyzed in the pre-processing section and the characters contained in it are detected there. The process comprises image processing - such as skew detection -, document analysis, layout understanding, and character segmentation. The characters detected are identified in the character recognition unit. After that, the recognition results are examined and modified in the post-processing section.

This paper focuses mainly on character recognition technology, but the other processes are briefly described in Section 2 before the overview of character recognition in Sections 3, 4, and 5. System implementation and OCR applications are described after that in Sections 6 and 7.

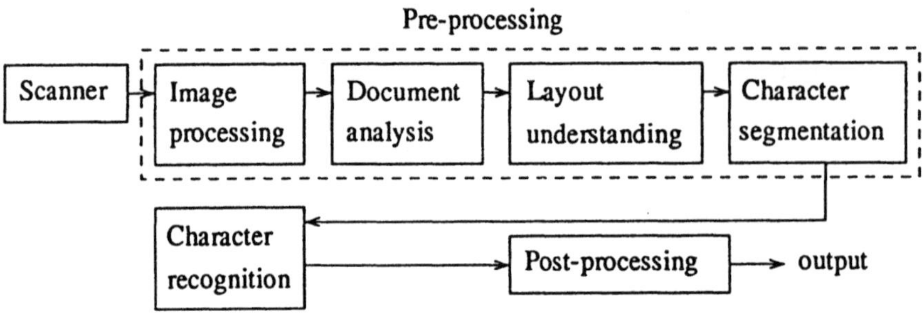

Fig. 1. Example of an OCR

2. Pre-Processing and Post-Processing

An OCR should be seen as a total system comprising several sub-systems: image processing, document analysis, layout understanding, character segmentation, character recognition, post-processing, plus the units needed for its actual use such as a user interface. Together, these technologies are called "Document Image Understanding" and they use overall information about a document to read or obtain its contents.

2.1 Document Skew Detection

Documents which are not carefully handled or which are of poor quality may be skewed. Document skew detection and correction are essential reqwirements for that kind of input. These processes are achieved by image processing based on Fourier transform, Hough transform, or other techniques. The following is one of interesting example of this type of processing.

Skew can be detected using the value $V(\theta)$ below, which is based on the complexity of the document. Its value is calculated on parallel scanning lines which cover part of the document image and have an angle of θ to the horizontal line [7].

$$V(\theta) = (1/n) \times \sum_{i=1}^{i=n} (N_i - M)^2, \tag{1}$$

where N_i is the total number of transition points from white to black pixels in each scanning line i on a document. The number n is the total number of scanning lines and M is the mean value, as follows.

$$M = (\sum_{i=1}^{i=n} N_i)/n. \tag{2}$$

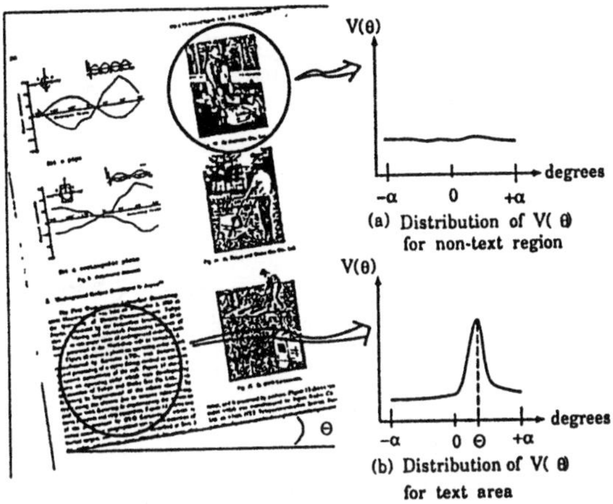

Fig. 2. Distribution of complexity $V(\theta)$ for skew detection

A sharp peak is found in $V(\theta)$ if the region contains only text lines, as shown in Figure 2(b). In contrast, if the region contains non-text elements, there is no peak in $V(\theta)$, as shown in Fig. 2(a). This sharp peak indicates an angle of skew because a scanning line parallel to text lines has the largest number of transitions.

2.2 Layout Understanding

The layout understanding of a text reader makes a good example of this problem [8].

Figure 3 (a) shows a page which contains blocks with many lines, headers which contain one or two lines, and ruled lines. These elements are extracted by the document analysis section of a text reader. The geometrical relationship between each block and the others are expressed in the form of a tree, as shown in Fig. 3 (b), in which each node represents a block, a header, or a ruled line. A branch means the geometrical relationship between them.

On the other hand, Fig. 3 (c) expresses the relationships between blocks and other elements in a logical sense. The nodes represent blocks and other elements as before, but here a branch defines a master and slave relationship; that is, one node belongs to a superior one.

The geometrical tree can be converted into the logical one using knowledge about document layout. This transformation is called "layout understanding" in this paper. It is one approach to an understanding of what "layout understanding" means.

2.3 Character Segmentation

Earlier OCRs had fewer problems with character segmentation compared with current models because the recent demands of users are for higher performance and the ability to read heavily distorted characters in low quality documents. The problems

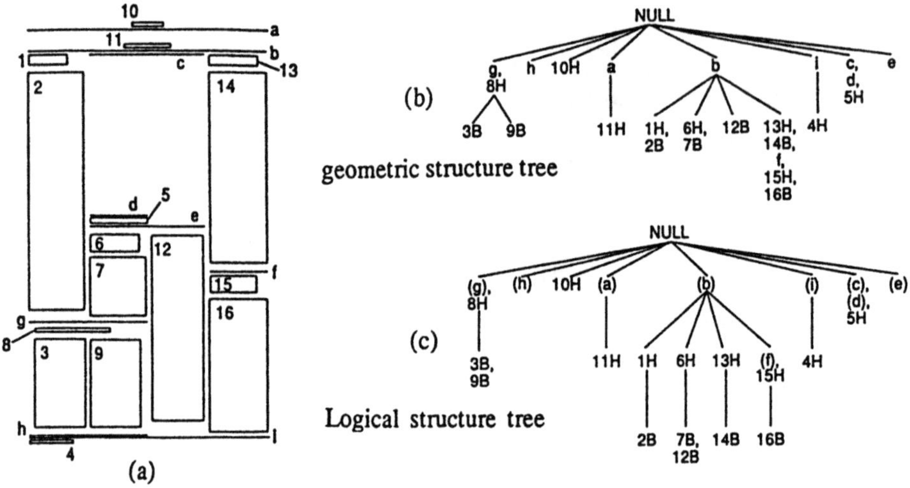

Fig. 3. A geometric expression of the document shown in (a) is a tree, and it is converted into a logical tree expression. The letter "H" means header and "B" means block. Lower case letters indicate ruled lines in a document.

encountered in analyzing such documents are simply expressed by the terms touching characters and broken characters. Recognition results are useful for this kind of problem as a feedback whatever segmentation method is used.

The following is one solution to this problem based on a feed-forward architecture [8].

Figure 4 (a) shows the touching characters "r" and "m" and some candidate cut positions. There are many possible combinations of these cut. The segmentation possibilities are expressed by the tree shown in Fig. 4 (b), in which each possibility is represented by one path. Each branch has a cost, which is defined by the recognition result, and the cost of a path is a sum of its branchs' costs. A depth-first strategy is used to search for the lowest cost path, and the best one is the resulting segmentation.

2.4 Post-processing

The basic concepts of a post-processing can be explained as follows. Let a_i be the i-th character in an input word A. The value $P(A|R)$, obtained using equation (3), is the probability that the input word is A when the recognition result is R; r_i represents the recognition result of a_i. In the equation, n is the number of characters in word A.

$$P(A|R) = (P(R|A)P(A))/P(R) = ((\prod_{i=1}^{i=n} P(r_i|a_i)) \cdot P(A))/P(R) \qquad (3)$$

Here, it is assumed that the character recognition process is independent for each character. This equation can be re-written into the equation below.

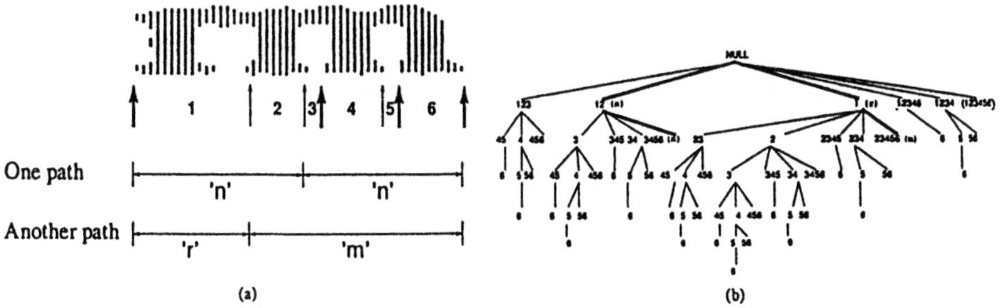

Fig. 4. (a) Touching characters "r" and "m" offer several candidates for cut locations. (b) A tree shows the search paths for correct cut positions. Character recognition results are used in this search.

$$\log P(A|R) = \sum_{i=1}^{i=n} \log P(r_i|a_i) + \log P(A) - \log P(R) \quad (4)$$

The probability $P(R)$ is a constant obtained through the recognition process of word A. Therefore, if $P(A)$ is constant for all words, the following value $S(A|R)$ can be used to compare the probabilities $P(A|R)$ for all A in the dictionary.

$$S(A|R) = \sum_{i=1}^{i=n} logP(r_i|a_i) \quad (5)$$

If it is assumed that $logP(r_i|a_i)$ is represented by the position of character candidate a_i in the recognition results, equation (5) can be written as below.

$$S(A|R) = \sum_{i=1}^{i=n} Q(position(a_i)) \quad (6)$$

where $position(a_i)$ means the position of a_i in r_i, and $Q(k)$ corresponds to $logP(r_i|a_i)$ on the assumption that $logP(r_i|a_i)$ depends only on position in the recognition result.

The maximum value of $S(A|R)$ gives the best candidate for word A in the word dictionary [10]. This basic idea is used in almost all the techniques of post-processing.

3. Character Recognition

3.1 Two Types of Character Recognition Methods

Character recognition technology has developed over many years and many techniques have been proposed [9]. There are too many to cover in detail, so some examples of the techniques are given in here.

All techniques can be classified into two categories. One is a pattern matching method and the other is a structure analysis method. Put simply, "pattern matching" means that an input pattern and a reference pattern are put together for comparison.

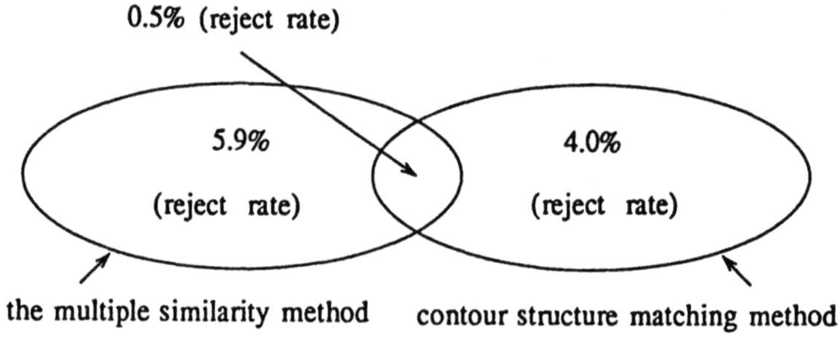

Fig. 5. A combination of two methods offers the capability to avoid rejects.

However, it also implies another approach in which a feature vector is extracted from a pattern and its vector space is separated into several subsets. Pattern classification then takes place according to these subsets. This kind of technique is often called "pattern matching" because it makes use of a distance or a similarity, which are analogies to the difference between two patterns side by side.

The following is a general description of the pattern matching method. A feature vector, which is considered a point in feature space – generally a linear space – is extracted from the pattern, and distance or similarity is calculated within this feature space.

On the other hand, the structure analysis method operates as follows. It also comprises two parts: one is matching as before, but the other is the extraction of primitives, representing small parts of the pattern, and their relations. The difference between matching techniques in two methods is that matching in the pattern matching method is very simple – simply a calculation of distance or similarity for example – but matching in structure analysis is usually complex, involving techniques such as automaton, syntactic approach, dynamic programming, and relaxation.

3.2 Combination of two or more methods

To achieve a highly accurate character recognition system, the critical factor is adopting a combination of complementary methods. Figure 5 shows an example of such a combination of the multiple similarity method and the contour structure matching method, both of which are detailed later. In this case, a combination can reduce the reject rate to one tenth that of each single method. The reject rate that a character is rejected by both method is only 0.5%, where as the individual reject rates are 5.9% or 4.8%. Of course, this rate is not a real reject rate by an actual combining method, but it demonstrates the potential of such a combination.

4. Pattern Matching Methods

4.1 Basic Techniques of Pattern Matching Methods

The simplest means of pattern matching methods consists of an input pattern and a reference pattern represented by "0" and "1" in an $n \times m$ array which are matched together to obtain Hamming distance. This distance is calculated by counting up the number of pixels for which the exclusive-or has a value of one. The patterns are identically same if this distance is zero.

Next is a slightly modified Hamming distance method. With this method, pixels have values "-1" and "1" instead of "0" and "1". The pattern similarity, S, is given as follows where N is the total number of pixels.

$$S = \sum_{x,y} f(x,y) \cdot g(x,y)/N, \tag{7}$$

In this case, a similarity value of -1 means that negative image patterns are matched and a similarity of one means that the patterns are identical. On the other hand, a similarity of zero means that half the areas match and half do not. This means that the patterns have no correlation.

This idea can be extended to a system in which each pixel can have one of three values, black, white or gray which means that the pixel is not determined as either black nor white. The similarity is then also given by equation (7), where a white pixel has a value "-1", a gray one is "0", and a black is "1". This basic idea is described in one of the Japanese textbooks on character recognition [1].

If the three values in the previously mentioned technique are extended to the real number, it becomes one of techniques similar to productive methods. Similarity in this system is again defined by equation (7), where each pixel has a real number as its value. In this equation, N is considered to be $N = \|f\| \cdot \|g\|$. The absolute value of this similarity – that is $|S|$ – is called the simple similarity. It becomes one if f and g are completely the same or completely opposite, while it is zero if they have no correlation.

Figure 6 shows the difference between this and the Euclidian distance, which is one of the standard distance measures.

4.2 The Multiple Similarity Method

The multiple similarity method [1] [2] is now introduced as an actual example of a productive method. This is an extension of the simple similarity.

The multiple similarity method was developed in the early 1970s as a Japanese national project resulting in systems named ASPET'70 and ASPET'71. The target of these systems was recognition of single font printed characters; now, however, the method is used for handprinted character recognition, Kanji character recognition, and speech recognition.

The features evaluated in this method are patterns obtained by blurring the original image. The Gaussian function is used to do this.

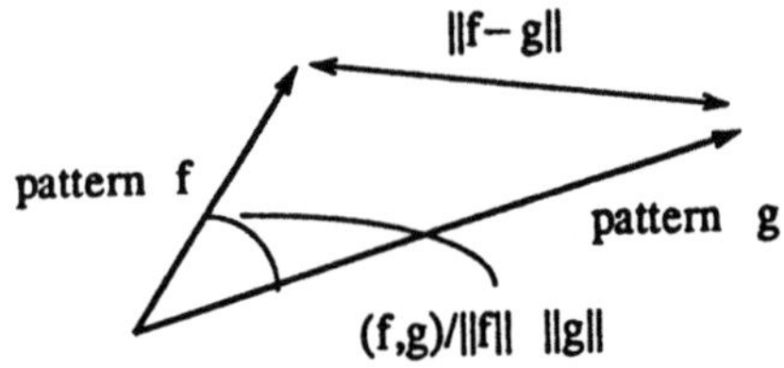

Fig. 6. Difference between the simple similarity $(f, g)/\|f\| \cdot \|g\|$ and Euclidian distance $\|f - g\|$

Pixel sampling is applied at the same time to reduce the amount of data. The importance of blurring has been recognized recently, but a reduction in vector dimension is also a very important role of the blurring technique.

The next step is principal component analysis in the feature vector space, where the collected patterns are distributed. The N principal components with the largest eigen-values extracted as a reference. When φ_i denotes an eigen-vector and λ_i an eigen-value, the multiple similarity is defined by the following equation:

$$S = \sqrt{\sum_{i=0}^{i<N} (\lambda_i/\lambda_0) \cdot ((\varphi_i, f)^2/\|\varphi_i\|^2 \cdot \|f\|^2)}, \quad (8)$$

where f is the input. This equation is generally called the multiple similarity, but in fact the complete system – including blurring techniques and other pre-processing techniques – may also be called the multiple similarity method. The subspace method is a special case of equation (8).

4.3 Neural Network System for Character Recognition

Let us consider a neural network system with a layer structure. Such a system can be described by a function which converts a point to a point in linear space. One of its features is that the conversion is non-linear. But this is less important if we recall that there are several methods which have non-linear classifiers in a linear space, such as the multiple similarity method. The important feature is that it is able to give the best-fitting transformation for a corrected pattern set. It has been proven that the net has the ability to approximate any function without any limit [3]. The most desired feature of a neural network system is just this point.

Unfortunately, this advantage often turns into a bad feature when excessive fitting has occurred through learning. In this case, the performance as measured on a learning sample is extremly high, while it is quite low for other samples. In addition, a neural net is useless if the feature extraction process attached to it is poor. This is true even if the net itself offers high performance. Thus it is of great importance how

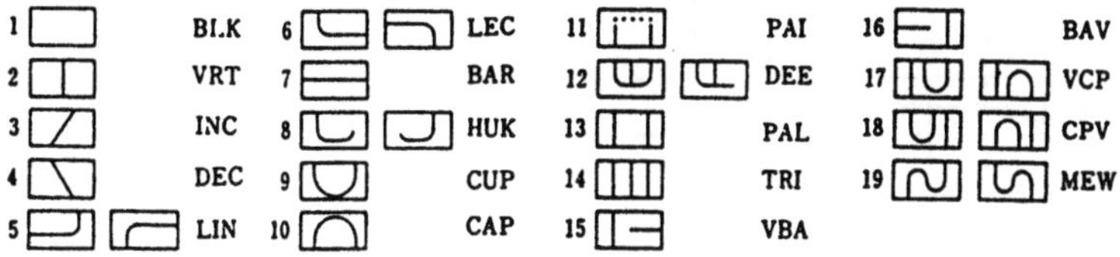

Fig. 7. Nineteen partial features observed when a numeral character pattern is sliced horizontally.

the feature extraction and neural net systems suit each other.

Generally speaking, any single technique for character recognition offers little power considering the difficult problems which exist in this field. The critical factor is how to combine these different techniques. It may be better to take the approach that each technique is a single part of a complete system rather than to look for one powerful technique that solves everything. In this sense, a neural net is expected to be a good unit in a complete character recognition system.

4.4 General Description of Pattern Matching Methods

A general description of the pattern matching method defines it as "feature vector extraction + pattern classification in feature vector space". There are two principal issues. One is how the feature vector is designed and the other is the pattern classification method; that is, how similarity is designed. The combination of features and similarities is as significant as performance itself.

The feature vector design is just as important as the similarity. For example, the blurring technique is used in the multiple similarity method while the Freeman code chain is often used in Kanji character recognition, as in the neighbor similarity method [4]. These techniques are simple, but are a key factor in realizing good performance.

One merit of pattern matching method is that the reference can be made automatically and mathematical analysis is possible. Generally speaking, the reference can only be produced by analyzing the pattern space mathematically.

5. Structure Analysis Methods

5.1 Some Examples of Structure Analysis Methods

Some simple examples of structure analysis are explained here. One of methods is a combination of subpattern extraction and automaton.

Figure 7 shows 19 partial features extracted by slicing a pattern of numeral horizontally. The features extracted from the actual pattern image are described as a one-dimensional sequence. This is input to the automatons, each of which is designed for each character category, and the character category is output as a result if the corresponding automaton accepts it. This is a simple and rather standard approach to the structure analysis method.

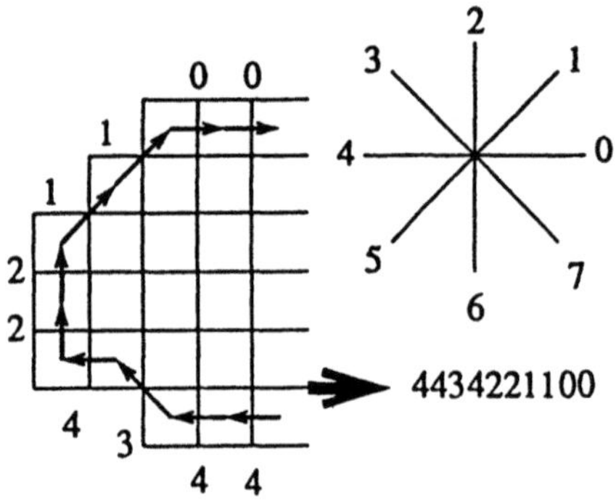

Fig. 8. An example of contour tracking.

Thinning and contour tracking are two major approaches adopted in many feature extraction techniques. They are often combined with an automaton for recognizing characters. In that sense, contour tracking is convenient because it is basically one-dimensional, whereas thinning requires some process to convert two-dimensional data to one-dimension. Generally, the thinning technique suffers from the problem of creating useless small, thin lines and an inability to describe junction areas precisely. These defects can be avoided by use of contour tracking.

Figure 8 shows an example of contour tracking with eight direction codes, called the Freeman code.

Figure 9 shows how thinning creates a useless thin line where contour tracking simply forms a convex section. As for processing speed, contour tracking is generally faster than thinning.

On the other hand, the problem with contour tracking is that it sometimes identifies a stroke and a loop as the same thing, since it does not fundamentally include the concept of strokes (Figure 10).

Many different techniques have been proposed, and it is impossible to describe all of them. One example of a method for recognizing unrestricted handprinted characters is introduced below.

5.2 Contour Structure Matching Method

The contour structure matching method was developed in 1986 for the purpose of reading unrestricted handprinted characters [5]. This method has the following three major features:

(1) Segmented contours with attributes

This method obtains a Freeman code as the primary feature extracted from the original image. This is smoothed and segmented based on the curvature of the contours [6]. Each segmented part of a contour is called a segment in this method, and is classified as convex, line, or concave. These segments are given attributes, including length, curvature, position, and orientation.

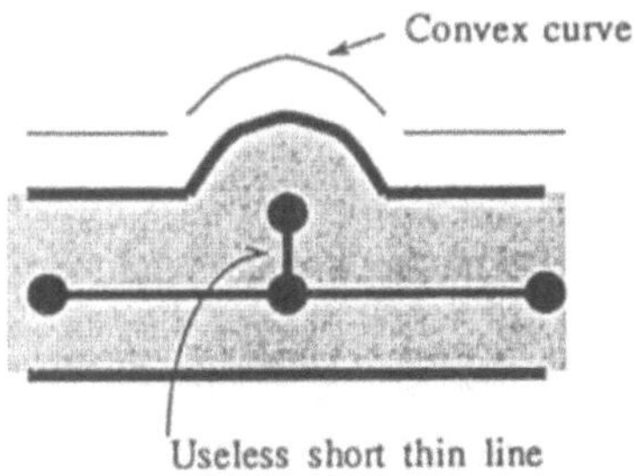

Fig. 9. If part of a pattern has a convex or concave curve, the thinning technique creates a useless thin line; the contour tracking technique, however, is able to simply extract this as a convex or concave shape.

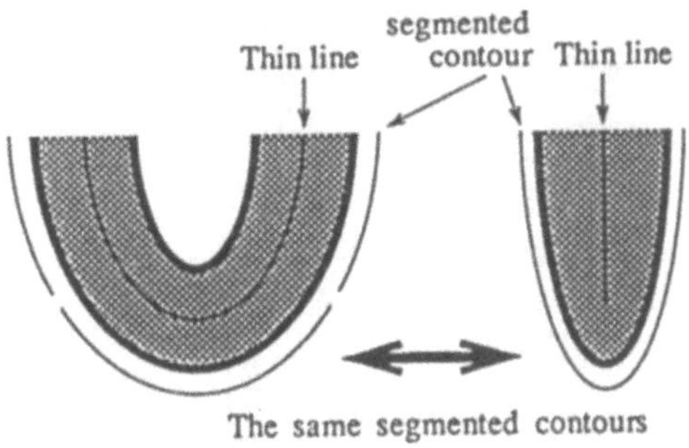

Fig. 10. A stroke and a loop are both recognized as the same by the contour tracking technique.

(2) SIUW matching

A reference is described as a sequence of segments with an upper limit and a lower limit for the value of each attribute. If each attribute's value satisfies these limits, the input and reference segment are considered matched.

The reference segments are classified into four types: S,I,U, and W. "S" means a stable segment which corresponds to only one input segment. "I" means an ignorable segment which can be ignored or corresponds to only one input segment. "U" means a unifiable segment which may correspond to plural input segments. "W" is a combination of "I" and "U"; that is, it may be ignorable or may correspond to plural input segments.

This classification contributes to reduced processing time. For example, it is faster than a method based on relaxation [11]. Also, it effectively describes heavily distorted characters easily.

(3) Discrimination based on partial structure in a pattern

An input pattern sometimes matches two or three references if it is ambiguous. In this case, a further discrimination process is carried out by using the attribute values of certain segments. Because input and reference matching has already been successful, the segment's correspondence is already known. As a result, it is easy to define a certain part of a pattern and it's attributes by marking certain reference segments. In another words, discriminating features are easily extracted from the input pattern.

Figure 12 shows an example of extracting the discriminating features of an ambiguous pair of characters "1" and "7". In this example, the angle between the segments [1] and [2], the length of segment [1], and the orientation of segment [1] are extracted. Then, the following if-then rules are checked to determine the input category.

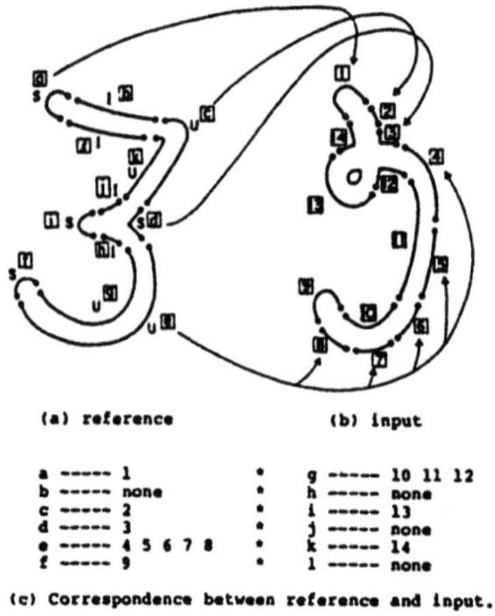

Fig. 11. An example of matching by the contour structure matching method.

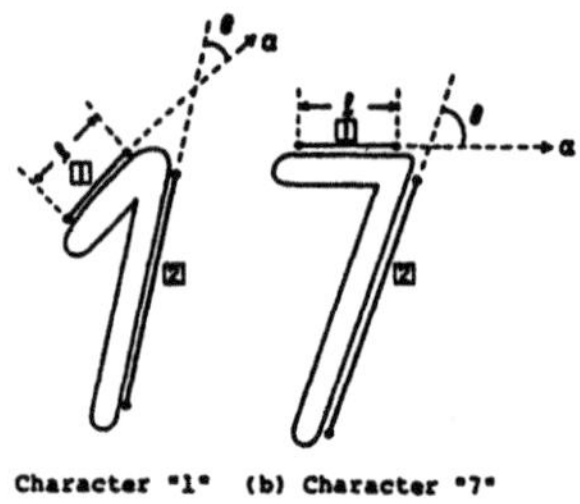

Fig. 12. An example of discrimination for an ambiguous pair of patterns.

If $\theta < T1$, then input is "1"
else if $\ell < T2$, then input is "1"
else if $\alpha > T3$, then input is "7"
else input is rejected.

Here, T1, T2, and T3 are predetermined thresholds obtained by statistical analysis. This feature extraction and discrimination process are carried out by a procedure designed for each set of ambiguous pairs, one by one. The importance of this stage is that each pair of characters is checked at different portions by a different procedure.

5.3 General Description of Structure Analysis Methods

A general definition of the structure analysis method is "primitives each of which represents small part of a pattern and their relationship + matching". The matching process is based on the structure or the relationship of the primitives. Many techniques, such as automatons, DP, the rubber matching method, and relaxization, are based on this kind of matching.

Note that there are also intermediate matching techniques which make use of the concept of similarity or distance as well as the concept of primitive comparison. As with the pattern matching method, importance is attached not only to the matching method or primitive extraction, but also to combinations of these.

The advantages and disadvantages are just the reverse of the pattern matching method. Generally, making reference for the structure analysis method takes a long time – it is usually a manual task. Also mathematical analysis is difficult with this

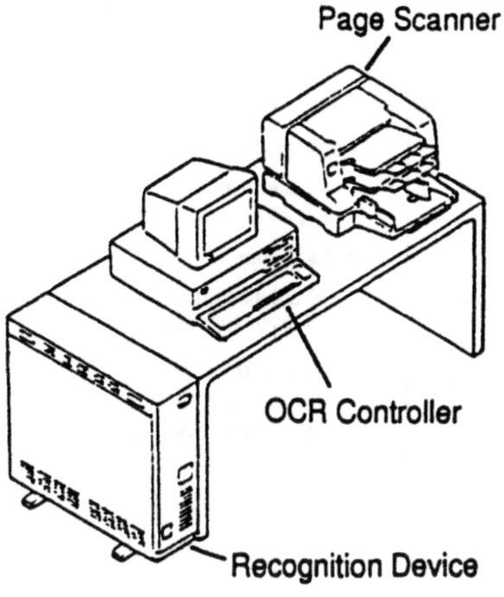

Fig. 13. OCR outline.

method.

One merit is that it allows reference designer to change any detail of a reference pattern without influencing the rest of it. Another advantage is that it may be easy to introduce human character recognition methods.

6. OCR Implementation

6.1 OCRs

6.1.1 System Configuration

An outline of a standard page OCR is given in Figure 13. It consists of a page scanner, a recognition device, and an OCR controller (such as a PC-AT). The page scanner takes in sheets of paper one by one and captures the images. The recognition device recognizes characters in the image taken from the page scanner and outputs character codes to the OCR controller. The OCR controller completes the data processing and controls the whole system.

The OCR controller is connected to the recognition device through a GP-IB or SCSI interface. The recognition device is connected to the page scanner through a GP-IB, SCSI, or other special interface. In most cases, the OCR controller is connected to a host computer through a local area network.

6.1.2 System Performance

Table 1 shows the average recognition accuracy and processing speed of Toshiba's page OCRs.

6.2 Scanner Hardware

The scanner hardware consists of a paper handling mechanism and an optical system. A typical page scanner is shown in Figure 14.

Table 1. Recognition accuracy and processing speed of Toshiba's OCRs.

	Numerals	Alphabets and Symbols
Under Heavy Constraints	99.99 %	——
Under JIS Guidelines	99.5 %	97 %
Free Style (Not Cursive)	99 %	93 %

OCR-V3070
70 sheets/min.
A4, 300 chars./sheet

OCR-V3050
30 sheets/min.
A4, 300 chars./sheet

OCR-V3010
6 sheets/min.
A4, 300 chars./sheet

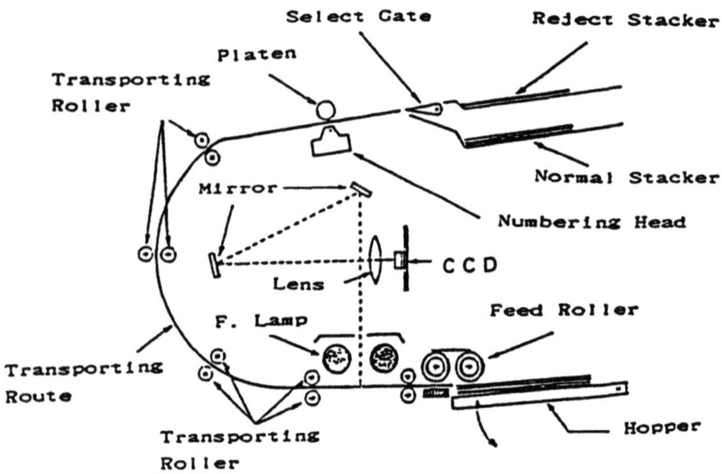

Fig. 14. Scanner scheme.

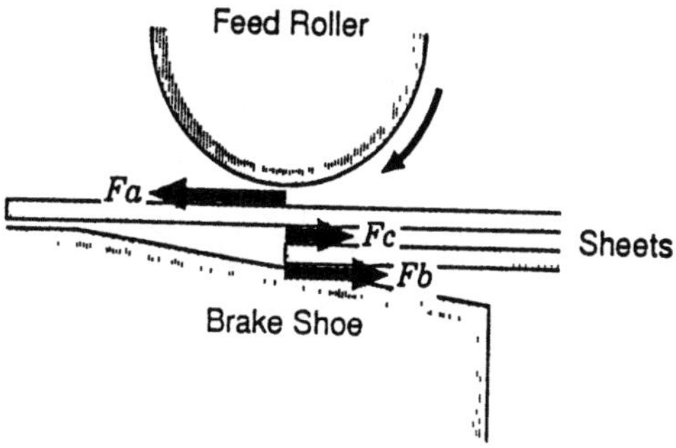

Fig. 15. Friction feed.

6.2.1. Paper Handling Mechanism

The paper handling mechanism in a page scanner is required to handle a wide range of paper sheet sizes and thicknesses. For example, the specifications of Toshiba's OCR-V3070 allow paper sizes in the range 74mm x 52mm to 364mm x 364mm, and thicknesses (weights) ranging from $65\mu m$(45kg) to $195\mu m$ (135kg).

The paper handling mechanism consists of a feed mechanism, a transport mechanism, a stacking mechanism, and a number of sensors.

6.2.1.1. Feed Mechanism

The feed mechanism transfers sheets of paper into the scanner one by one. It consists of a hopper and a feeder.

A stack of sheets to be read is placed on the hopper table, which is then raised to the sheet feed position. When the top sheet on the hopper table reaches the feed position, a sensor detects it and feeding begins. Hopper capacity ranges from 50mm to 250mm in height.

Several types of feed mechanism are in use, including friction and vacuum types. In general, a friction feed is used in small page scanners. The principle of the friction feeder is shown in Figure 15. A feed roller takes up a sheet as a result of the frictional force between the sheet and the roller. A separator (like a brake shoe) holds the lower sheets to prevent the feed roller taking up two sheets at a time. The condition which ensures that the feeder takes up only one sheet at a time is expressed as follows.

$Fa > Fb > Fc$

where Fa is the frictional force between the sheet and the roller, Fb is the frictional force between the sheet and the separator, and Fc is the frictional force between the two sheets. However the frictional force is affected by the environment (temperature, humidity) and paper (quality, thickness, size). Thus it is difficult to design a roller and separator with optimum coefficients of friction.

6.2.1.2. Transport Mechanism

The sheets taken up by the feeder are fed through transport rollers driven by a stepper

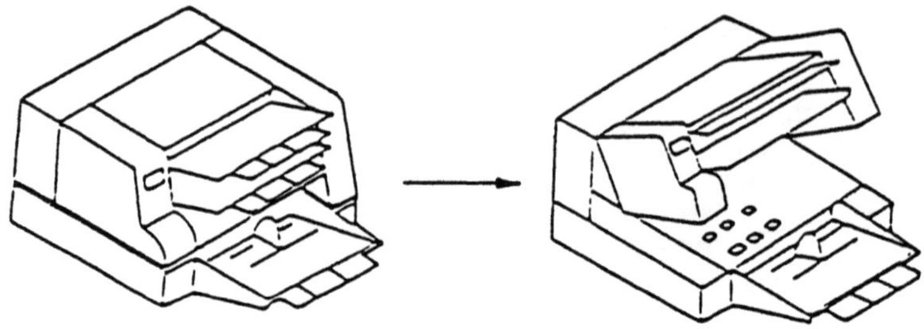

Fig. 16. Shell structure of an OCR

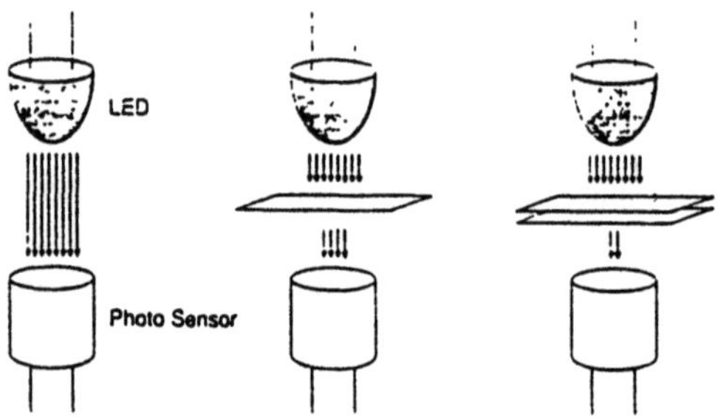

Fig. 17. Double feed sensor

motor and a timing belt. The transport mechanism is required to transport the sheets in a straight line at constant speed. Slight skewing of a sheet may be corrected by the image processing module in the recognition device, however.

Usually, the body of the scanner has a shell structure as shown in Figure 16 so that it can be easily opened to remove a jammed paper.

6.2.1.3. Stacking Mechanism

Each sheet which has been scanned passes through a select gate and it is ejected to a normal stacker or a reject stacker. Sheets which have been successfully read go to the normal stacker while rejected sheets (containing unreadable characters) or the misfed sheets are output to the reject stacker.

6.2.1.4. Sensors

The scanner contains a number of photoelectric or mechanical sensors such as a hopper empty sensor, a stacker full sensor, a double feed sensor, a sheet jam sensor, etc.. Figure 17 shows the double feed sensor, which checks for double feeding sheets by checking transmittance of light.

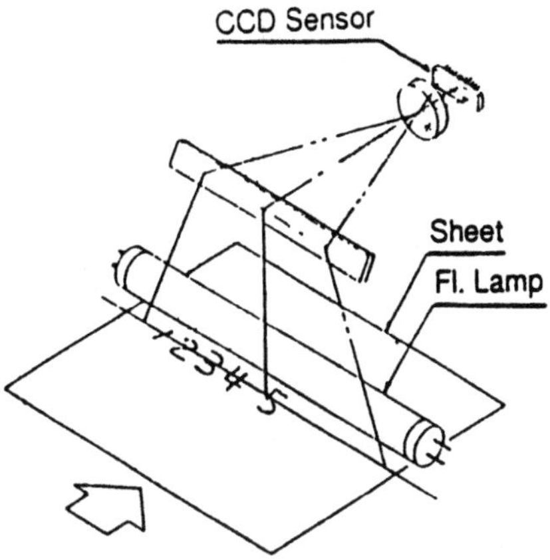

Fig. 18. Optical system

6.2.2. Optical system

The optical system of a page scanner consists of a light source and an image sensor. To achieve a two-dimensional scan of each sheet, the line image sensor usually scans the sheet in the x-direction (main scan) electronically, while the y-direction scan (sub scan) is obtained by moving the sheet mechanically as shown in Figure 18.

In a typical reduction-type optical system which is commonly used, a fluorescent lamp and a CCD (Charge Coupled Device) line image sensor are adopted. On the other hand, a contact-type optical system, which is effective for small scanners, consists of an LED array and a contact image sensor.

The resolution of OCR scanners ranges from 200 dpi (dots per inch) to 400 dpi. On the basis of experience, 200 dpi is enough to recognize handprinted characters, but 400 dpi is necessary to recognize printed Kanji characters.

Such an optical system suffers from defects in shading due to a non-uniformities in the brightness of the light source, in the sensitivity of the image sensor, and in the transmittance of the lens. This shading is corrected mechanically or electronically by the system.

The optical system has spectral characteristics that depends on both the source of light and the image sensor as shown in Figure 19. An ink can be used, that has high reflectivity in the sensitive range of the optical system. Such an ink has the same reflectivity as the white background in the OCR, yet on the other hand it has enough contrast to be seen by human eyes. Such an ink is called dropout (undetectable) color ink. It is used to print writing boxes and preprinted characters on forms to be scanned.

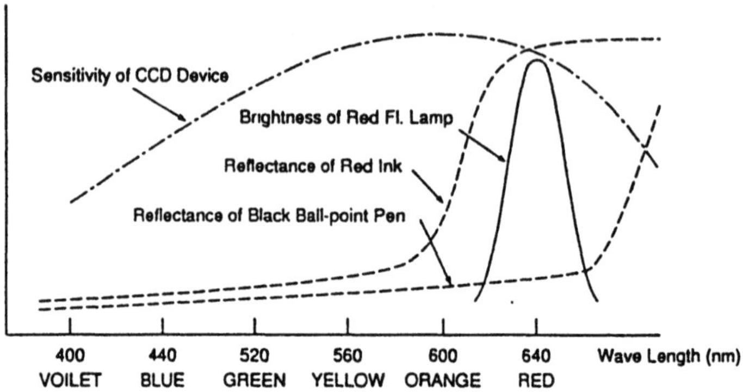

Fig. 19. Dropout color

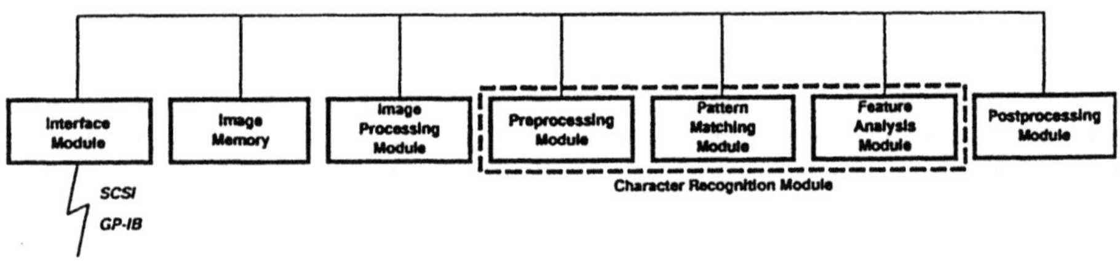

Fig. 20. Block diagram of recognition device

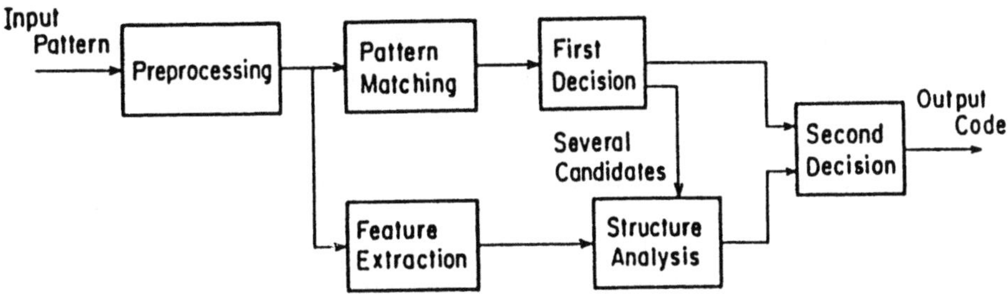

Fig. 21. Combination of pattern matching and structure analysis

6.3. Recognition Device

The recognition device consists of an image memory, an image processing module, a character recognition module, and a post-processing module. Figure 20 shows a block diagram of Toshiba's OCR.

6.3.1. Image Memory

In conventional OCR, the image memory was only able to store the image of a line of characters. Currently, however, systems are able to store a full page image. In the case of a 400 dpi scan, around 2M bytes are necessary to store a binary image of an A4 sheet. A full-page image memory is useful for realizing a flexible OCRs which can read complex forms. In addition, it allows the OCR to scan sheets in both the horizontal and vertical directions. To accelerate processing speed, an OCR has two image memories; one for executing the scan process and one for the recognition process in the pipeline.

6.3.2. Image Processing Module

The image processing module implements for noise suppression, sheet edge detection, skew correction, form analysis, character line detection, and character segmentation. Generally, these processes are carried out by a high-performance CPU such as a 32-bit RISC processor. A programmable module enables complex character segmentation from various scripts which have free format, free pitch, cursive characters, characters protruding out of writing boxes, characters in non-dropout color writing boxes and other items.

6.3.3. Character Recognition Module

Many techniques are used for character recognition, as described previously. In current OCR, these methods are effectively combined to reduce substitution errors, as shown in Figure 21.

For example, in Toshiba's OCR, the following processes are carried out to recognize handprinted alphabetic or numeric characters. A segmented pattern is normalized in size and then blurred. The blurred pattern is matched against reference patterns to calculate similarities. Several character categories are then selected as candidates based on their similarities. This was described as the multiple similarity method in the previous section. After this, contour features are extracted from the segmented pattern for comparison with the candidate reference categories, which also consist of contour features. This is also described in previous section as the contour structure matching method. Through these processes, the final result is generated. In general, the character recognition processes are carried out on parallel dedicated hardware.

6.3.4. Post-processing Module

An OCR used to read a limited vocabulary such as people's names or mailing addresses uses linguistic post-processing to reduce substitution errors. Generally, such linguistic post-processing is executed on special hardware. The word database stored in the post-processing module needs to contain more than 150,000 words for Japanese mailing address, more than 15,000 words for Japanese family names, and more than 25,000 words for Japanese first names.

In the case of Toshiba's OCR-V3050, post-processing improves the recognition accuracy of a mailing address (each letter in a separate writing box) from 93.0% to 96.5%.

6.4. OCR Software

The OCR software consists of an OCR execution program and a format control data generator. This OCR software is available for use under various operating systems, including DOS, OS/2, and UNIX.

6.4.1. OCR Execution Program

The OCR execution program controls the OCR hardware, displays the recognized data, checks for substitution errors, helps with verification, helps in the correction of reject or substitution error data, and outputs recognized data to the host computer.

This includes a large number of checking functions, such as character length checking, character type checking, all-blank checks, inner-blank checks, and check-digit checks.

There are several verification/correction modes, such as a real-time correction mode and a batch mode. In the real-time correction mode, the machine reads a sheet line by line and allows the operator to correct characters if a reject is found or if a checking error occurs. When a reject character is found, the segmented pattern for it is displayed on the screen together with candidate characters, each of which is associated with a number; correction can then be done by selecting only this number. In the batch mode, recognized data and segmented patterns are stored temporarily on hard disk as an intermediate file format. An operator can then correct them later.

6.4.2. Format Control Data Generator

The format control data generator is a tool which defines OCR control data based on the sheet form (such as sheet size, line position, field position, character size, character font, number of columns, and others), error checking function, verification/correction mode, screen format, output format, and other information.

7. OCR Applications

7.1 Actual Applications

Table 2. Relationship between OCR and other devices

Factor / *Devices*	*Centra-lized input*	*Distri-buted input*	*Remote input*	*Recoded on sheets*	*Elimina-tion of labor*	*Accu-racy*	*Ease of use*	*System cost*
Key to disk (special machine)	E	P	F	G	F	E	G	F
PC/WS (standard machine)	G	E	G	G	E	G	F	E
Pointing devices	P	G	F	P	G	G	G	G
Push button telephone	P	G	E	P	G	F	E	F system
Bar code	G	F	P	G	E	E	G	G
OCR	E	E	G with FAX	E	G	G	F	F
OLCR	P	G	P	P	G	G	F	G
Speech recog-nition	P	G	E	P	F	P	G	F system

E...Excellent, G....Good, F....Fair, P...Poor

Table 2 shows the relationship between OCR and other input devices. OCR has merits in the batch processing of large amounts of data, and in the case of real-time input of medium or a small amounts of data. In addition, the fact that OCR can read from paper is another advantage. Usually, sheets of paper are easy to handle and the media is generally suited to human use. In the case of a system crash and all data is lost, it is possible to retrieve the lost data from the original paper after input by OCR.

One of the demerits of OCR is the cost of paper, including the printing and/or writing costs. The OCR device itself is expensive when compared with other more inexpensive input devices. Therefore, a large throughput of data is needed to achieve low running cost, with OCR. Costs may then be lower than by using the other inexpensive input systems where the input process itself is expensive. The basic problem with OCR is its accuracy and its limited functional ability. The quality of the input characters and the input document's characteristics must be carefully examined to determine whether it can be adequately interpreted by OCR before introducing a system. Usually, systematic method of recovery from OCR errors is needed.

Nevertheless, the most important feature of OCR is that characters readable by OCR are easy for humans to understand. Future improvements of OCR are looked for and its applications will expand greatly.

Table 3. Applications of OCR

OCR type / *Field*	*Page OCR*	*Text reader*
Government, Public service	Application forms, Survey sheets, Money exchange documents	Documents for law, Judicial precedent database, Tables of statistics
Retailers, Distributors, Service industry	Purchase order forms, Forms for shipments	Customer database, Name lists
Financial markets, Insurance	Forms for sending money, Contract application forms	Balance sheets, Documents of regulations
Manufacturers	General financial forms, Management of working time	Manuals, Patent documents, Technical reports
Education	Application forms for classes	Text books, Lists of students
Journalism, Publications,	TV program tables, Tags for books	Manuscripts, Input for reprints and CD
Information services	Creating dadabases of job offers and worker lists	Customer databases, Product databases, Translations

Table 3 shows the major application areas for page OCR and text readers. Some actual applications of OCR are described below.

(1) OCR Systems are used for billing and receipts in the electronic power companies. This reduces peak load for collecting the data of used electric power.

(2) The order form system used by Coop comprises an OCR to reduce data input costs and to avoid duplicate orders.

(3) An OCR input system has been effective as a gift ordering system in a department store. This is connected to the shipment system. The merits of introducing such a system are reduced shipping errors, elimination of labor in writing addresses, and easy maintenance of customer information.
(4) OCR is used in the mail-order business for effectively reducing shipment times.
(5) Application forms for non-life insurance are another examples where the time taken to issue documentation related to a contract is reduced.
(6) The credit card business is also a good example of OCR usage. The time to taken to transfer funds and the cost of inputting data can both be reduced.

The important fact is that expectations of OCR have changed from a simple idea - that is reduction of labor - to the realization of high-level management systems such as those used by sales departments, labor management, and market management.

7.2 OCR Evaluation

The major factors which can be used to measure the cost performance of an OCR are recognition accuracy and processing speed.

The costs of adopting OCR are the machine costs, labor costs, maintenance fees, cost of paper, electricity rates, costs of space, and expense of making OCR forms. In addition, there are same examples of hidden costs: stress on the operators.

The performance of an OCR is defined as the number of sheets or characters recognized and corrected by operators within a fixed time. The overall processing time includes the recognition time and error correcting time plus any waisted time.

This demonstrates that a system's performance is low if there are many errors in the recognition results, since these devices require a large amount of time to be spent on error correction, which results in slow processing. In this sense, the user interface used to correct errors and for other operations is a critical part of the overall system. A poor user interface in an OCR always results in poor overall performance of the system.

Table 4. Typical OCR user interfaces

Purpose	*Actual example*
Reduction of labor	Error correction mechanism , Help messages, Ease of removing jammed paper, Machine size and weight
Automatic processing	Error checking by check-digit, Spell checking by context knowledge, Numbering, Sorting, Auto coding
Cooperation between human and machine	No synchronised processes of reading and error correction, Mixed forms identified by ID field, CAD for form design

Table 4 describes typical user interfaces used in OCRs.

When evaluating an OCR, a key point is to define the test data set and operators in a fair manner and to measure processing time in terms of recognition time, error correction time, and waisted time. It is better to prepare data sets with as much variety as possible for such tests. The other important point is the difference between

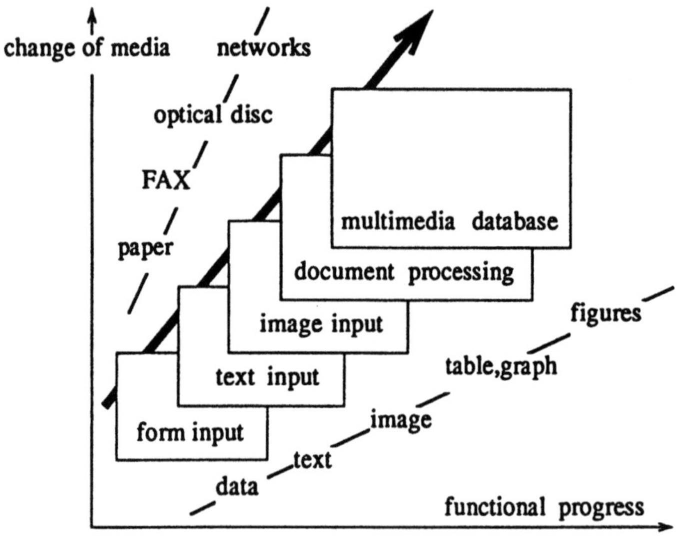

Fig. 22. Functional progress and progress with input media

rejected characters and substituted error characters. Generally, a reject is better than an error; for example, an error may cost ten times more than a rejected characters. Actually, this rate depends on the system and its actual application.

8. Conclusion

8.1 Future needs in OCR

The history of character recognition has now reached almost 30 years. The final target of this technology is to realize a machine which has the same ability as one part of our human intelligence. Current progress is dependent on new research and development based on the technology available now, and it is moving toward this final goal. Recent improvements in devices such as CPU and memory have encouraged workers in the field to develop new theories and methods for character recognition. This has allowed the technology to support the stricter demands of users. Thus, recent developments in OCR have tended to be more market driven.

Figure 22 shows the expected applications of OCR on the axes of functional progress and progress with input media. The thick arrow towards the upper right corner in the figure indicates the time scale.

Progress with OCR opens up a new possibility for users: system integration incorporating OCR. Conventionally, only one angle has been considered – recognition accuracy. Nevertheless, recent developments such as reading unrestricted handprinted characters, layout understanding in a text reader, and other functions allow users to consider integrating OCR into their systems. This may include network systems incorporating image processing, databasing with full text search technology, and multimedia systems with other information sources. Generally, future OCR applications will tend to accept data from devices other than scanners.

Progress in the following OCR areas is anticipated in the 21st century:

(1) A wide range of functions supported by a high-performance machine intelligence technology
(2) Intelligent input devices which accept any data, text and images in documents and carry out the required processes on them
(3) Large and complicated applications such as systems integrated into workstations, media converters for use as servers, recognition engines for special purpose processors, and other systems

8.2 Future OCR technology

The features of OCR based on pattern recognition technology are as follows.
(1) A lot of technical fields including a human factor, are related to OCR technology.
(2) There is no end to the development of OCR technology, so products must be created along the way.
(3) There has always been an ambiguity in the performance of OCR, especially in the specification of recognition accuracy and functions.
(4) On the other hand, users always demand completeness.
(5) The evaluation of OCR is a multi-dimensional process and it varies according to the kind of task and the environment.
(6) Relaxation of restrictions on OCR use expands the market.

The need in future OCR which has the above characteristics, is the following:
(1) A long range plan for the development of OCR leading to step-by-step improvement
(2) A greater emphasis on a technology particular to document image understanding rather than other areas
(3) Standardization of peripheral sub-systems forming part of OCRs
(4) Selection of targets for OCR development from an actual applications
(5) A mechanism for recovering from errors originating in the character recognition unit
(6) A control mechanism which makes the system adaptive to any kind of applications

The following are the actual requirements of OCR development:
(1) A control architecture in which a variety of techniques, items of knowledge, processes, and data types are integrated and controlled. This kind of approach will be needed for recognition of low-quality documents such as the output from facsimile machines and roughly written characters.
(2) The ability to read colored characters on colored backgrounds or on backgrounds with a texture or picture
(3) The ability to use color or gray level information in the recognition mechanism

(4) An automatic learning system which is easy to use for operators is essential. Learning should not only be a feature of the character recognition unit but also of the image processing unit, the pre-processing unit, the character segmentation unit, the post-processing unit, and the user interface.
(5) A scanner which can handle very thin sheets or an unusual materials is needed. Recovery techniques for images taken from such materials are also sought, in addition to improvements to scanner technology to cope with them.

There is much research and development to be done in the OCR field before the final goals are reached and there are an almost unlimited number of problems to solve. These will be resolved step by step, and the ultimately a truly intelligent OCR machine with the ability to read any characters just like a human will be developed.

References

[1] Iijima, T. : *Pattern Recognition.* Korona-sha, 1973 (in Japanese)

[2] Iijima, T. et al. : *A Theory of Character Recognition by Pattern Matching Method.* Proc. 1st. IJCPR, pp.50-56, 1973

[3] Irie, B. et al. : *Capabilities of Three-layered Perceptrons.* Proc. ICNN88, 1, pp.641-648, 1988

[4] Irie, B. et al. : *Handprinted KANJI Character Recognition Using the 2 × 2 Neighbor Pattern Distribution.* Proc. Annual Conf. IECE Japan, D-453, p.1-196, 1988 (in Japanese)

[5] Kurosawa, Y. et al. : *Attributed String Matching with Statistical Constraints for Character Recognition.* Proc. 8th. ICPR, pp.1063-1067, 1986

[6] Asada, H. et al. : *The Curvature Primal Sketch.* IEEE Trans. PAMI, Vol.8, No.1, pp.2-14, 1986

[7] Ishitani, Y. : *Document Skew Detection Based on Local Region Complexity.* ICDAR93 (Submitted), 1993

[8] Tsujimoto, S. et al. : *Major Components of a Complete Text Reading System.* Proc. of IEEE, Vol.80, No.7, pp.1133-1149, 1992

[9] Mori, S. et al. : *Historical Review of OCR Research and Development.* Proc. of IEEE, Vol.80, No.7, pp.1029-1058, 1992

[10] Abe, K. et al. : *Performance Evaluation of Character Recognition System with Dictionary.* Trans. of IECE Japan, Vol.52C, No.6, pp.305-312, 1969 (in Japanese)

[11] Yamamoto, K. : *Recognition of Handprinted Hiragana Characters by Concave and Convex Features and Automatically Merging the Dictionary.* Trans. of IECE Japan, Vol.65D, No.6, pp.774-781, 1982 (in Japanese)

A Pen-Based Music Editor

Annick Leroy

IRISA, Campus de Beaulieu, 35042 Rennes Cedex, France
aleroy@irisa.fr

Abstract: Graphic tablets bring a more natural way of entering information, especially for languages for which no alphanumeric keyboard exists. Music is a perfect example of such a language. The editor realized here allows on-line recognition and proof-reading of musical symbols with a possible adaptation to the writer. The recognition is done by a neural network but relies both on music syntax and on a graphic syntax of the musical symbols. The editing commands are fixed, but the gestures are totally left to the user's choice.

1 Overview

The tedious entry of music on a computer, even when shared between a synthesizer, for pitch and rhythm, and a computer, for correcting and entering various other symbols belonging to the musical language, distracts the composer's attention from his first preoccupation. Paper and pen remain the favorite tools and only the necessity for printing a music score or the use of sound manipulation tools might justify such a burden. The growing technical progress in digitizing tablets opens the door to new applications. These are particularly well suited for languages for which there is no keyboard. Music is a perfect example of it.

Unlike a natural language, music has the advantage of possessing a syntax which, although voluminous and complex, is nevertheless precise and non-ambiguous. Graphically the shapes are distinctive and the ambiguity comes from the writer's distortions, from the varying distance between the strokes for a particuliar symbol or from the numerous ways of splitting a symbol into strokes. For example, when the distance between a dotted E and a bar-line is very small, it might be confused with 2 consecutive E's. One can also find without too much effort a dozen ways of composing an duplet, see Figure 1. Compared to cursive handwriting, the segmentation is a lot easier, but the graphic syntax is far more complex and must describe all the possible ways of splitting a symbol into strokes. The training phase must adjust the relative acceptable position of the strokes for a symbol.

Figure 1: Different ways of writing a duplet.

Figure 2: Possible interpretations of a group of strokes.

2 Ergonomy

Wishing not to disturb the composer in his conception and writing work, the recognition phase should start only at his will and be displayed in a separate window. It seems that, when the recognition occurs in parallel with the writing process, our attention is permanently deviated by the need to control the output solution and therefore troubles our concentration. On the other hand strokes are not entered in a left to right order, see for example the writing process for a group of notes in which noteheads might be written before the note stems and also before or after the writing of the beam. This order will be worse for an instrument requiring two staves or for an orchestration. All these are good reasons for letting the user choose the right moment for starting the recognition phase. At the same time, the very precise syntax of music and the finite set of symbols suggest that we use it to improve the recognition. It is in our interest to wait for the end of a bar to check the time signature and eliminate the inappropriate solutions. From an ergonomic point of view, the writer might prefer correcting the script version to the translated version. The representation choice leaves the composer totally free in that matter.

3 Recognition

If music symbols form a finite set, the composition into note groups is infinite and it is impossible to conceive a one exit per element classifier. In order to limit the number of possibilities, one can only try different strokes combinations after having identified the nature of those strokes we are trying to combine. Another difficulty comes from the numerous ways of drawing an object. The figure 1 shows an example of a few possibilities for writing a duplet. The figure 2 shows a few possible interpretations one can generate for a set of strokes.

The recognition takes place in two phases :

- First we try to classify the strokes, either into elementary patterns (vertical or horizontal bar, circle, point,...), or into more elaborate patterns corresponding to one-stroke symbols (quarter-notes, G clef, quarter rest,..). The entry is the list of the stroke coordinates. Two classification methods are competing : a Time Delay Neural Network (TDNN), [5], which is particularly suited for complex shapes (like a G clef) and a 'manual' primitive extraction. Since the manual extraction is not sophisticated enough in some cases and since the neural network might be confused between symbols that are close in form but not in size for example (i.e. a G clef and a quarter-note made of a spiral), we introduce a set of rules, based on the size or the position on the staff, in order to eliminate some hypothesis or to reinforce others. This phase produces a hypothesis list with the associated probabilities.

- The second phase starts at the user's request and translates the script symbols into typographic symbols. It is done through a bottom-up analysis according to a graphic grammar of the music symbols. The algorithm is as follows :

  1. When the user asks for the recognition to start, the strokes are first ordered from left to right, then split into sublists according to a distance criterion between the strokes.

  2. We gather the strokes into elementary music symbols (notes, accidentals, keys,...) based on their graphic syntax and calculate their probability according to the distance and position of the strokes. Here is a rule example for describing a quarter-note formed of one or two strokes (non-terminals are in capital letters) :

QUARTER-NOTE → *quarter-note*
QUARTER-NOTE → *FULL-NOTEHEAD STEM*
  condition : *lower-right-connection(FULL-NOTEHEAD, STEM)*
  or *upper-left-connection(FULL-NOTEHEAD, STEM)*
FULL-NOTEHEAD → *spiral | point*
STEM → *vertical-bar*
  condition : *min-height(STEM, hmin)*

3. We gather the elementary symbols into more complex symbols like groups of notes.

   Example :

   GROUP → *BEAM NOTE-LIST*
   condition : connection(BEAM,NOTE-LIST)
   GROUP → *BEAM GROUP*
   condition connection(BEAM, GROUP)
   GROUP → *BEAM NOTE-LIST GROUP*
   condition : connection(BEAM,NOTE-LIST)
   and connection(BEAM, GROUP)
   GROUP → *BEAM GROUP NOTE-LIST*
   NOTE-LIST → *NOTE* | $NOTE\ NOTE - LIST$
   NOTE → *ACCIDENTAL NOTE* | $NOTE\ DOT$ |
   WHOLE-NOTE | $HALF - NOTE$ |
   QUARTER-NOTE | $EIGHT - NOTE$ | ...

4. We choose the possible symbols in such a way that a stroke is used only once and that all strokes are used. We produce a list of possible solutions and rank them according to their probability. See Figure 2.
5. Syntactically incorrect solutions are eliminated.
6. The winning solution is displayed on the screen.

4 User Adaptation

The recognition is for a large part based on a TDNN . The adaptation to the user is based on a algorithm presented by Isabelle Guyon in [4]. It allows the writer to choose his way for drawing symbols on-line and use them right away. Actually this works only for one stroke symbols.

5 Internal Representation

The bottom-up analysis allows us to create a hierarchy of objects, the structure of which is identical for the script and the typographic form. Figure 3 shows the hierarchy for a duplet. This identical representation will give us the possibility of proof-reading the music sheet in either form (or window). For example, the selection of a duplet in the script window will cause the note to be displayed in red in that window and in the typographic window. In this case a call to a 'display-typo' function will redisplay ellipses and bars in red in one window and a call to a 'display-script' function will redisplay the set of points drawn by the user. The functions access to the complex object and propagates the call to the objects down the hierarchy.

6 Layout

Music layout is very complex and the realization of a whole editor does not fit in this study. Currently the page layout simply follows the composer's, but in the future a rule-based system will help following the graphic constraints between the objects for time synchronization and spacing...

7 Editing Gestures

The editing commands are predefined, there are the classics : 'cut', 'paste', 'copy', 'change', 'undo',... As for musical symbols, the editing gestures can be chosen by the user and associated with predefined commands. These gesture are composed of one or more strokes. In this case the recognizer is called after a timeout. It is important to choose simple and non-ambiguous gestures in order to get a good recognition. This editor will be a platform for studying new kinds of gesture adapted to the music language.

8 Conclusion

This first prototype is very encouraging. We are going to collect musical data in collaboration with CNMAT in Berkeley and IRCAM in Paris. This will allow us to train a music dedicated recognizer. The development of the 'real' editor is under way using an object-oriented lisp. It allows us to change rules or parameters dynamically and is also a very fast developing tool. This choice has been made to be compatible with a common composer's tool, the Macintosh, but the development is done on a Sun Sparc station.

References

[1] Roger Dannenberg. Music representation issues : a position paper. In *ICMC*, pages 73–75, Columbus, Ohio, 1989.

[2] Glendon Ross Diener. *Modelling music notation : a three-dimensional approach*. PhD thesis, Stanford University, 1990.

[3] H. Fahmy and D. Blostein. A graph grammar for high-level recognition of music notation. In *ICDAR / International Conference on document analysis and recognition*, pages 70–78, Saint-Malo, 30-09-1991.

[4] I. Guyon, Henderson D., Albrecht P., LeCun Y., and Denker J. Writer independent and writer adaptive neural network for on-line character recognition. In *From pixels to features.*, pages 493–506, 1992.

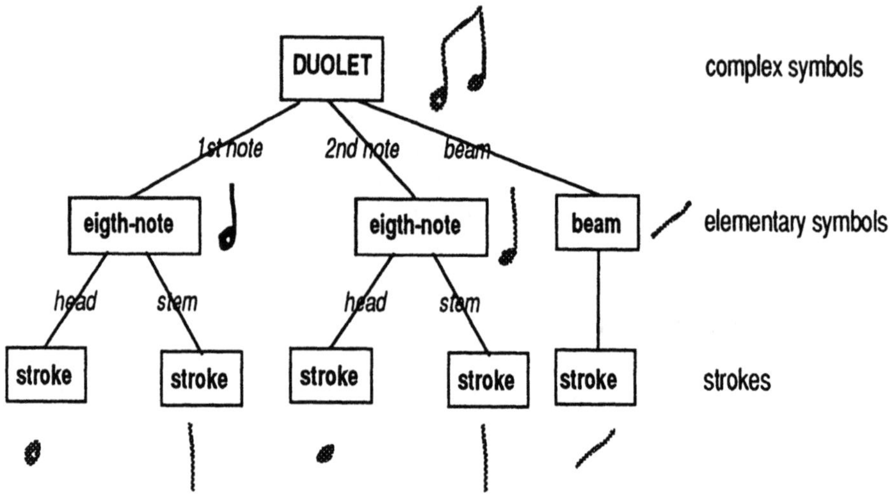

Figure 3: Duplet representation.

[5] I. Guyon, Albrecht P., Le Cun Y., Denker J., and Hubbard W. Design of a neural network character recognizer for a touch terminal. *Pattern Recognition*, February 1991.

[6] Annick Leroy and Isabelle Guyon. *A Pen Editor Prototype*. Technical Report, ATT, 1993.

[7] Philippe Martin. *Reseaux de neurones artificiels : Application a la reconnaissance optique de partitions musicales*. PhD thesis, IMAG, Grenoble, 1992.

[8] John Roeder and Keith Hamel. A general-purpose object-oriented system for musical graphics. In *ICMC*, page 260 263, Columbus, Ohio, 1989.

[9] Dean Harris Rubine. *The automatic recognition of gestures*. PhD thesis, Carnegie Mellon, 12-1991.

Subject Index

NATO ASI Series F

Including Special Programmes on Sensory Systems for Robotic Control (ROB) and on Advanced Educational Technology (AET)

Vol. 1: Issues in Acoustic Signal - Image Processing and Recognition. Edited by C. H. Chen. VIII, 333 pages 1983. *(out of print)*

Vol. 2: Image Sequence Processing and Dynamic Scene Analysis. Edited by T. S. Huang. IX, 749 pages. 1983.

Vol. 3: Electronic Systems Effectiveness and Life Cycle Costing. Edited by J. K. Skwirzynski. XVII, 732 pages. 1983. *(out of print)*

Vol. 4: Pictorial Data Analysis. Edited by R. M. Haralick. VIII, 468 pages. 1983.

Vol. 5: International Calibration Study of Traffic Conflict Techniques Edited by E. Asmussen. VII, 229 pages. 1984.

Vol. 6: Information Technology and the Computer Network. Edited by K. G. Beauchamp. VIII, 271 pages. 1984.

Vol 7 High-Speed Computation. Edited by J. S. Kowalik. IX, 441 pages. 1984.

Vol. 8: Program Transformation and Programming Environments. Report on a Workshop directed by F. L Bauer and H Remus. Edited by P. Pepper. XIV, 378 pages. 1984.

Vol. 9: Computer Aided Analysis and Optimization of Mechanical System Dynamics. Edited by E. J. Haug. XXII, 700 pages. 1984. *(out of print)*

Vol. 10: Simulation and Model-Based Methodologies: An Integrative View. Edited by T. I. Ören, B. P. Zeigler, M. S. Elzas. XIII, 651 pages. 1984.

Vol. 11: Robotics and Artificial Intelligence. Edited by M. Brady, L. A. Gerhardt, H. F. Davidson. XVII, 693 pages. 1984.

Vol. 12: Combinatorial Algorithms on Words. Edited by A. Apostolico, Z. Galil VIII, 361 pages. 1985.

Vol. 13: Logics and Models of Concurrent Systems Edited by K. R. Apt VIII, 498 pages 1985

Vol. 14: Control Flow and Data Flow Concepts of Distributed Programming. Edited by M. Broy VIII, 525 pages. 1985 *Reprinted as Springer Study Edition 1986.*

Vol 15 Computational Mathematical Programming Edited by K Schittkowski. VIII, 451 pages. 1985.

Vol. 16: New Systems and Architectures for Automatic Speech Recognition and Synthesis. Edited by R. De Mori, C.Y. Suen. XIII, 630 pages. 1985 *(out of print)*

Vol 17: Fundamental Algorithms for Computer Graphics. Edited by R. A. Earnshaw. XVI, 1042 pages. 1985. *Reprinted as Springer Study Edition 1991.*

Vol 18: Computer Architectures for Spatially Distributed Data Edited by H Freeman and G. G. Pieroni. VIII, 391 pages 1985. *(out of print)*

Vol. 19: Pictorial Information Systems in Medicine Edited by K. H Höhne. XII, 525 pages 1986

Vol 20. Disordered Systems and Biological Organization. Edited by E. Bienenstock, F. Fogelman Soulié, G. Weisbuch. XXI, 405 pages. 1986

Vol 21 Intelligent Decision Support in Process Environments. Edited by E. Hollnagel, G. Mancini, D D Woods. XV, 524 pages 1986

Vol. 22: Software System Design Methods. The Challenge of Advanced Computing Technology. Edited by J. K. Skwirzynski. XIII, 747 pages. 1986. *(out of print)*

Vol. 23: Designing Computer-Based Learning Materials. Edited by H. Weinstock and A Bork. IX, 285 pages. 1986 *(out of print)*

Vol. 24: Database Machines Modern Trends and Applications. Edited by A. K Sood and A H. Qureshi. VIII, 570 pages. 1986.

NATO ASI Series F

Including Special Programmes on Sensory Systems for Robotic Control (ROB) and on Advanced Educational Technology (AET)

Vol. 25: Pyramidal Systems for Computer Vision. Edited by V. Cantoni and S. Levialdi. VIII, 392 pages. 1986. *(ROB)*

Vol. 26: Modelling and Analysis in Arms Control. Edited by R. Avenhaus, R. K. Huber and J. D. Kettelle. VIII, 488 pages. 1986. *(out of print)*

Vol. 27: Computer Aided Optimal Design: Structural and Mechanical Systems. Edited by C. A. Mota Soares. XIII, 1029 pages. 1987.

Vol. 28: Distributed Operating Systems. Theory und Practice. Edited by Y. Paker, J.-P. Banatre and M. Bozyiğit. X, 379 pages. 1987.

Vol. 29: Languages for Sensor-Based Control in Robotics. Edited by U. Rembold and K. Hörmann. IX, 625 pages. 1987. *(ROB)*

Vol. 30: Pattern Recognition Theory and Applications. Edited by P. A. Devijver and J. Kittler. XI, 543 pages. 1987.

Vol. 31: Decision Support Systems: Theory and Application. Edited by C. W. Holsapple and A. B. Whinston. X, 500 pages. 1987.

Vol. 32: Information Systems: Failure Analysis. Edited by J. A. Wise and A. Debons. XV, 338 pages. 1987.

Vol. 33: Machine Intelligence and Knowledge Engineering for Robotic Applications. Edited by A. K. C. Wong and A. Pugh. XIV, 486 pages. 1987. *(ROB)*

Vol. 34: Modelling, Robustness and Sensitivity Reduction in Control Systems. Edited by R.F. Curtain. IX, 492 pages. 1987.

Vol. 35: Expert Judgment and Expert Systems. Edited by J. L. Mumpower, L. D. Phillips, O. Renn and V. R. R. Uppuluri. VIII, 361 pages. 1987.

Vol. 36: Logic of Programming and Calculi of Discrete Design. Edited by M. Broy. VII, 415 pages. 1987.

Vol. 37: Dynamics of Infinite Dimensional Systems. Edited by S.-N. Chow and J. K. Hale. IX. 514 pages. 1987.

Vol. 38: Flow Control of Congested Networks. Edited by A. R. Odoni, L. Bianco and G. Szegö. XII, 355 pages. 1987.

Vol. 39: Mathematics and Computer Science in Medical Imaging. Edited by M. A. Viergever and A. Todd-Pokropek. VIII, 546 pages. 1988.

Vol. 40: Theoretical Foundations of Computer Graphics and CAD. Edited by R. A. Earnshaw. XX, 1246 pages. 1988. *(out of print)*

Vol. 41: Neural Computers. Edited by R. Eckmiller and Ch. v. d. Malsburg. XIII, 566 pages. 1988. *Reprinted as Springer Study Edition 1989, 1990.*

Vol. 42: Real-Time Object Measurement and Classification. Edited by A. K. Jain. VIII, 407 pages. 1988. *(ROB)*

Vol. 43: Sensors and Sensory Systems for Advanced Robots. Edited by P. Dario. XI, 597 pages. 1988. *(ROB)*

Vol. 44: Signal Processing and Pattern Recognition in Nondestructive Evaluation of Materials. Edited by C. H. Chen. VIII, 344 pages. 1988. *(ROB)*

Vol. 45: Syntactic and Structural Pattern Recognition. Edited by G. Ferraté, T. Pavlidis, A. Sanfeliu and H. Bunke. XVI, 467 pages. 1988. *(ROB)*

Vol. 46: Recent Advances in Speech Understanding and Dialog Systems. Edited by H. Niemann, M. Lang and G. Sagerer. X, 521 pages. 1988.

NATO ASI Series F

Including Special Programmes on Sensory Systems for Robotic Control (ROB) and on Advanced Educational Technology (AET)

Vol. 47: Advanced Computing Concepts and Techniques in Control Engineering. Edited by M. J. Denham and A. J Laub. XI, 518 pages. 1988. *(out of print)*

Vol. 48: Mathematical Models for Decision Support. Edited by G. Mitra. IX, 762 pages. 1988.

Vol. 49: Computer Integrated Manufacturing. Edited by I. B. Turksen. VIII, 568 pages. 1988.

Vol. 50: CAD Based Programming for Sensory Robots. Edited by B. Ravani. IX, 565 pages. 1988. *(ROB)*

Vol. 51: Algorithms and Model Formulations in Mathematical Programming. Edited by S. W. Wallace. IX, 190 pages. 1989.

Vol. 52: Sensor Devices and Systems for Robotics. Edited by A. Casals. IX, 362 pages. 1989. *(ROB)*

Vol. 53: Advanced Information Technologies for Industrial Material Flow Systems. Edited by S. Y. Nof and C. L. Moodie. IX, 710 pages. 1989.

Vol. 54: A Reappraisal of the Efficiency of Financial Markets. Edited by R M. C Guimarães, B. G. Kingsman and S. J. Taylor. X, 804 pages. 1989.

Vol. 55: Constructive Methods in Computing Science. Edited by M. Broy. VII, 478 pages. 1989.

Vol. 56: Multiple Criteria Decision Making and Risk Analysis Using Microcomputers. Edited by B. Karpak and S. Zionts. VII, 399 pages. 1989.

Vol. 57: Kinematics and Dynamic Issues in Sensor Based Control. Edited by G. E. Taylor. XI, 456 pages. 1990. *(ROB)*

Vol. 58: Highly Redundant Sensing in Robotic Systems. Edited by J. T. Tou and J. G. Balchen. X, 322 pages. 1990. *(ROB)*

Vol. 59: Superconducting Electronics. Edited by H. Weinstock and M. Nisenoff. X, 441 pages. 1989.

Vol. 60: 3D Imaging in Medicine. Algorithms, Systems, Applications. Edited by K. H. Höhne, H. Fuchs and S. M. Pizer. IX, 460 pages. 1990. *(out of print)*

Vol. 61: Knowledge, Data and Computer-Assisted Decisions. Edited by M. Schader and W. Gaul. VIII, 421 pages. 1990.

Vol. 62. Supercomputing Edited by J S. Kowalik. X, 425 pages. 1990.

Vol. 63: Traditional and Non-Traditional Robotic Sensors. Edited by T. C. Henderson. VIII, 468 pages. 1990. *(ROB)*

Vol. 64: Sensory Robotics for the Handling of Limp Materials. Edited by P. M Taylor. IX, 343 pages. 1990. *(ROB)*

Vol. 65: Mapping and Spatial Modelling for Navigation. Edited by L. F. Pau. VIII, 357 pages. 1990. *(ROB)*

Vol. 66: Sensor-Based Robots: Algorithms and Architectures. Edited by C. S. G Lee. X, 285 pages. 1991. *(ROB)*

Vol. 67: Designing Hypermedia for Learning. Edited by D. H. Jonassen and H Mandl XXV, 457 pages. 1990. *(AET)*

Vol. 68: Neurocomputing Algorithms, Architectures and Applications. Edited by F. Fogelman Soulié and J. Hérault. XI, 455 pages. 1990.

Vol. 69: Real-Time Integration Methods for Mechanical System Simulation. Edited by E. J. Haug and R. C. Deyo. VIII, 352 pages. 1991.

Vol. 70: Numerical Linear Algebra, Digital Signal Processing and Parallel Algorithms. Edited by G. H. Golub and P Van Dooren XIII, 729 pages. 1991.

NATO ASI Series F

Including Special Programmes on Sensory Systems for Robotic Control (ROB) and on Advanced Educational Technology (AET)

Vol. 71: Expert Systems and Robotics. Edited by T. Jordanides and B.Torby. XII, 744 pages. 1991.

Vol. 72: High-Capacity Local and Metropolitan Area Networks. Architecture and Performance Issues. Edited by G. Pujolle. X, 536 pages. 1991.

Vol. 73: Automation and Systems Issues in Air Traffic Control. Edited by J. A. Wise, V. D. Hopkin and M. L. Smith. XIX, 594 pages. 1991.

Vol. 74: Picture Archiving and Communication Systems (PACS) in Medicine. Edited by H. K. Huang, O. Ratib, A. R. Bakker and G. Witte. XI, 438 pages. 1991.

Vol. 75: Speech Recognition and Understanding. Recent Advances, Trends and Applications. Edited by P. Laface and Renato De Mori. XI, 559 pages. 1991.

Vol. 76: Multimedia Interface Design in Education. Edited by A. D. N. Edwards and S. Holland. XIV, 216 pages. 1992. *(AET)*

Vol. 77: Computer Algorithms for Solving Linear Algebraic Equations. The State of the Art. Edited by E. Spedicato. VIII, 352 pages. 1991.

Vol. 78: Integrating Advanced Technology into Technology Education. Edited by M. Hacker, A. Gordon and M. de Vries. VIII, 185 pages. 1991. *(AET)*

Vol. 79: Logic, Algebra, and Computation. Edited by F. L. Bauer. VII, 485 pages. 1991.

Vol. 80: Intelligent Tutoring Systems for Foreign Language Learning. Edited by M. L. Swartz and M. Yazdani. IX, 347 pages. 1992. *(AET)*

Vol. 81: Cognitive Tools for Learning. Edited by P. A. M. Kommers, D. H. Jonassen, and J. T. Mayes. X, 278 pages. 1992. *(AET)*

Vol. 82: Combinatorial Optimization. New Frontiers in Theory and Practice. Edited by M. Akgül, H. W. Hamacher, and S. Tüfekçi. XI, 334 pages. 1992.

Vol. 83: Active Perception and Robot Vision. Edited by A. K. Sood and H. Wechsler. IX, 756 pages. 1992.

Vol. 84: Computer-Based Learning Environments and Problem Solving. Edited by E. De Corte, M C. Linn, H. Mandl, and L. Verschaffel. XVI, 488 pages. 1992. *(AET)*

Vol. 85: Adaptive Learning Environments. Foundations and Frontiers. Edited by M. Jones and P. H. Winne. VIII, 408 pages. 1992. *(AET)*

Vol. 86: Intelligent Learning Environments and Knowledge Acquisition in Physics. Edited by A. Tiberghien and H. Mandl. VIII, 285 pages. 1992. *(AET)*

Vol. 87: Cognitive Modelling and Interactive Environments. With demo diskettes (Apple and IBM compatible). Edited by F. L. Engel, D. G. Bouwhuis, T. Bösser, and G. d'Ydewalle. IX, 311 pages. 1992. *(AET)*

Vol. 88: Programming and Mathematical Method. Edited by M. Broy. VIII, 428 pages. 1992.

Vol. 89: Mathematical Problem Solving and New Information Technologies. Edited by J. P. Ponte, J. F. Matos, J. M. Matos, and D. Fernandes. XV, 346 pages. 1992. *(AET)*

Vol. 90: Collaborative Learning Through Computer Conferencing. Edited by A. R. Kaye. X, 260 pages. 1992. *(AET)*

Vol. 91: New Directions for Intelligent Tutoring Systems. Edited by E Costa X, 296 pages. 1992. *(AET)*

Vol. 92: Hypermedia Courseware: Structures of Communication and Intelligent Help. Edited by A. Oliveira. X, 241 pages. 1992. *(AET)*

Vol. 93: Interactive Multimedia Learning Environments. Human Factors and Technical Considerations on Design Issues. Edited by M. Giardina. VIII, 254 pages. 1992. *(AET)*

NATO ASI Series F

Including Special Programmes on Sensory Systems for Robotic Control (ROB) and on Advanced Educational Technology (AET)

Vol. 94: Logic and Algebra of Specification. Edited by F. L. Bauer, W. Brauer, and H. Schwichtenberg. VII, 442 pages. 1993.

Vol. 95. Comprehensive Systems Design: A New Educational Technology. Edited by C M. Reigeluth, B. H. Banathy, and J R. Olson. IX, 437 pages. 1993. *(AET)*

Vol. 96: New Directions in Educational Technology Edited by E. Scanlon and T. O'Shea. VIII, 251 pages. 1992 *(AET)*

Vol. 97: Advanced Models of Cognition for Medical Training and Practice. Edited by D. A. Evans and V. L. Patel. XI, 372 pages 1992. *(AET)*

Vol. 98: Medical Images: Formation, Handling and Evaluation. Edited by A. E Todd-Pokropek and M. A. Viergever. IX, 700 pages. 1992.

Vol. 99: Multisensor Fusion for Computer Vision. Edited by J K Aggarwal XI, 456 pages 1993 *(ROB)*

Vol. 100: Communication from an Artificial Intelligence Perspective. Theoretical and Applied Issues. Edited by A. Ortony, J. Slack and O. Stock. XII, 260 pages. 1992.

Vol. 101: Recent Developments in Decision Support Systems Edited by C. W. Holsapple and A. B. Whinston. XI, 618 pages. 1993.

Vol. 102: Robots and Biological Systems: Towards a New Bionics? Edited by P Dario, G Sandini and P Aebischer. XII, 786 pages. 1993.

Vol. 103: Parallel Computing on Distributed Memory Multiprocessors. Edited by F. Özgüner and F. Erçal. VIII, 332 pages. 1993

Vol 104: Instructional Models in Computer-Based Learning Environments Edited by S. Dijkstra, H. P. M. Krammer and J J G van Merriënboer. X, 510 pages. 1993 *(AET)*

Vol. 105. Designing Environments for Constructive Learning. Edited by T. M. Duffy, J. Lowyck and D. H. Jonassen. VIII, 374 pages. 1993. *(AET)*

Vol. 106: Software for Parallel Computation. Edited by J. S Kowalik and L. Grandinetti IX, 363 pages. 1993.

Vol. 107: Advanced Educational Technologies for Mathematics and Science. Edited by D. L Ferguson. XII, 749 pages. 1993. *(AET)*

Vol. 108: Concurrent Engineering: Tools and Technologies for Mechanical System Design. Edited by E. J. Haug. XIII, 998 pages. 1993.

Vol. 109: Advanced Educational Technology in Technology Education. Edited by A Gordon, M Hacker and M de Vries. VIII, 253 pages. 1993 *(AET)*

Vol. 110. Verification and Validation of Complex Systems: Human Factors Issues. Edited by J A. Wise, V D Hopkin and P Stager. XIII, 704 pages. 1993.

Vol. 111: Cognitive Models and Intelligent Environments for Learning Programming. Edited by E. Lemut, B. du Boulay and G Dettori. VIII, 305 pages 1993. *(AET)*

Vol. 112: Item Banking: Interactive Testing and Self-Assessment. Edited by D A Leclercq and J E. Bruno. VIII, 261 pages. 1993. *(AET)*

Vol. 113: Interactive Learning Technology for the Deaf Edited by B. A G. Elsendoorn and F. Coninx. XIII, 285 pages. 1993. *(AET)*

Vol. 114: Intelligent Systems: Safety, Reliability and Maintainability Issues. Edited by O Kaynak, G. Honderd and E. Grant XI, 340 pages. 1993.

Vol. 115: Learning Electricity and Electronics with Advanced Educational Technology Edited by M. Caillot VII, 329 pages 1993 *(AET)*

NATO ASI Series F

Including Special Programmes on Sensory Systems for Robotic Control (ROB) and on Advanced Educational Technology (AET)

Vol. 116: Control Technology in Elementary Education. Edited by B. Denis. IX, 311 pages. 1993 *(AET)*

Vol. 118: Program Design Calculi. Edited by M. Broy. VIII, 409 pages. 1993.

Vol. 119: Automating Instructional Design, Development, and Delivery. Edited by. R. D. Tennyson. VIII, 266 pages. 1994 *(AET)*

Vol. 120: Reliability and Safety Assessment of Dynamic Process Systems. Edited by T. Aldemir, N. O. Siu, A. Mosleh, P. C. Cacciabue and B. G. Göktepe. X, 242 pages. 1994.

Vol. 121: Learning from Computers: Mathematics Education and Technology. Edited by C. Keitel and K. Ruthven. XIII, 332 pages. 1993. *(AET)*

Vol. 122: Simulation-Based Experiential Learning. Edited by D. M. Towne, T. de Jong and H. Spada. XIV, 274 pages. 1993. *(AET)*

Vol. 123: User-Centred Requirements for Software Engineering Environments. Edited by D. J. Gilmore, R. L. Winder, F. Détienne. VII, 377 pages. 1994.

Vol. 124: Fundamentals in Handwriting Recognition. Edited by S. Impedovo. IX, 496 pages. 1994.

Vol. 125: Student Modelling: The Key to Individualized Knowledge-Based Instruction. Edited by J. E. Greer and G. I. McCalla. X, 383 pages. 1994. *(AET)*

Vol. 126: Shape in Picture. Mathematical Description of Shape in Grey-level Images. Edited by Y.-L. O, A. Toet, D. Foster, H. J. A. M. Heijmans and P. Meer. XI, 676 pages. 1994.

Vol. 127: Real Time Computing. Edited by W. A. Halang and A. D. Stoyenko. XXII, 762 pages. 1994.

MIX
Papier aus verantwortungsvollen Quellen
Paper from responsible sources
FSC® C105338

If you have any concerns about our products,
you can contact us on
ProductSafety@springernature.com

In case Publisher is established outside the EU,
the EU authorized representative is:
Springer Nature Customer Service Center GmbH
Europaplatz 3, 69115 Heidelberg, Germany

Printed by Libri Plureos GmbH
in Hamburg, Germany